Tony Rossi
311

USING LATIN

Annabel Horn, Wesleyan College

John Flagg Gummere, William Penn Charter School

Margaret M. Forbes, University of Minnesota

SCOTT, FORESMAN AND COMPANY
Chicago   Atlanta   Dallas   Palo Alto   Fair Lawn, N. J.

BOOK TWO

The meeting place of the Roman Senate, called the Curia, was built, destroyed, and rebuilt many times. The first building was burned in 52 B.C. This brick building, ornamented with stucco and marble, was the last. Its original bronze doors were removed for use in the Church of St. John Lateran in Rome. The cover design of the Using Latin series is derived from the ornamentation of those doors.

CONTENTS

4

REVIEW OF LATIN 1

Four-wheeled carriages like the one pictured here were used for fast transportation on long journeys. The two boys and their father, whose travels are described in the stories of this unit, may have been passengers in such a vehicle when they set out from Capua. This relief, found at Vaison-la-Romaine in southern France, is in the Calvet Museum at Avignon.

Many Latin words have English derivatives that show little or no difference in spelling or meaning. For each Latin word below give the corresponding English word. Where changes are necessary, explain the principle involved in forming the English word. Example: **agricultūra**/agriculture (Latin final -**a** replaced by English -e).

ascendō	**prōvincia**	**contrōversia**	**vēstīgium**	**respondeō**
dēnsus	**epistula**	**legiōnārius**	**admittō**	**tribūnal**
index	**maximum**	**impedīmentum**	**pauper**	**comparō**
frīgidus	**rūmor**	**audītōrium**	**fugitīvus**	**jūstitia**

Other Latin words have English derivatives that are spelled the same, but their meanings are different. What is the meaning of each of these words as used in English? Example: **posse** (to be able); "posse" (English) = a body or force armed with legal authority.

ante	(before)	**biceps**	(two-headed)	**tandem**	(at length)
bonus	(good)	**nostrum**	(our/ours)	**videō**	(I see)

Latin nouns with the suffix -**tūdō** or -**tās** are often formed from Latin adjectives. Corresponding English words end in -tude or -ty. Using -**tūdō**/-tude or -**tās**/-ty as a suffix, form Latin/English nouns from these adjectives.[1] Example: **multus** + -**tūdō** = **multitūdō** multitude.

sōlus	**brevis**	**necesse**	**celer**	**similis**
liber	**fēlix**	**antīquus**	**fortis**	**vīcīnus**

The suffix -**or**, when added to the base of some Latin verbs, forms nouns, most of which name the act or condition expressed by the verb. Many of these nouns have come into English without change. Form Latin/English nouns from the bases of these verbs. Example: **ārdeō** (ārd- + -**or**) = **ārdor**/ardor.

clāmō	**errō**	**faveō**	**tremō**	**terreō**

More numerous are Latin/English nouns ending in -**tor** or -**sor**, based on the Latin perfect participle. Most of these

---

[1]Note that in Declension III the base can be determined from the genitive singular.

nouns name the agent of the action expressed by the Latin verb. Form Latin/English nouns from the perfect participle of each of the following verbs, and give the present meaning in English. Example: **vincō/victum (vic- + -tor) = victor/** victor (one who conquers/winner).

audiō	**dīvidō**	**cūrō**	**instruō**	**moveō**	**prōtegō**
crēdō	**dēpōnō**	**faciō**	**inveniō**	**doceō**	**opprimō**

Action nouns in Latin (with meaning often transferred to the result of the action) are formed from Latin verbs by means of the suffixes **-iō/-tiō/-siō** and correspond to English words ending in -ion/-tion/-sion.

legiō/legion from **legō** (gather together/pick)
āctiō/action from **āctum/agō** (drive/do)
vīsiō/vision from **vīsum/videō** (see)

Find in your reading of books, magazines, and newspapers at least six more -ion/-tion/-sion nouns and give the related Latin nouns.

L O O K   A N D   T H I N K Why do so many Latin nouns end in **-tor/-sor** and **-tiō/-siō?**

U S E   Y O U R   E Y E S What connecting vowel is used to join the base of a Latin adjective to the suffix **-tūdō** or **-tās?**

J O U R N E Y   T O   P O M P E I I

The words printed in italics pertain to late first-year grammar, which is retaught on pages 47-57. Also see the Summary of Grammar at the back of this book. The symbol (°) in the reading refers to help with translation in a note below.

Duo puerī Rōmānī, Mārcus et Sextus, in oppidō Capuā° habitābant. Cum Lūciō patre itinera ad variās Ītaliae partēs faciēbant.

°Capuā (abl. sing. in apposition with **oppidō**) Capua, a town in Campania

The best-preserved relic of Roman Capua is the amphitheater, which must have been a familiar sight to Marcus and Sextus.

(p. 54)

Ōlim puerōs Lūcius rogāvit, *"Vultisne°* mēcum iter ad oppidum Pompeiōs° facere?"

5

"Maximē," puerī respondērunt.

Proximō diē prīmā lūce, sub caelō serēnō et sōle clārō, trēs viātōrēs in raedīs ab equīs validīs tractīs ex oppidō exiērunt. Pater in raedā suā sedēns tabulīs° studēbat; puerī in raedā suā sedentēs viātōrēs spectābant quī itinera aut 10 pedibus aut in lectīcīs° faciēbant.

Post paucās hōrās raedāriī dē viā dēclīnāvērunt et in caupōnam° minimam intrāvērunt. Lūcius dīxit, "Hīc pānem petēmus et vīnum."

Dum edunt Lūcius dīxit, "Memoriāne tenētis, puerī, 15 amīcum meum Cassium? Vīllam magnificam Viae Appiae propinquam habet. Mox viam vidēbimus quae ad vīllam Cassiī dūcit."

Mārcus statim quaesīvit, "Dormiēmusne hāc nocte in vīllā Cassiī?"

20

"Minimē," respondit pater. "Vīlla Cassiī quīnque mīlibus° passuum ā Viā Appiā abest. Dormiēmus hāc nocte in parvā caupōnā. Crās iter nostrum renovābimus."

(p. 50)
Post complūrēs hōrās viātōrēs ad vīcum parvum advēnē- runt, ubi erat caupōna. Caupō, *bonā cēnā parātā*, eīs as- 25 paragum,° ōva, pernās,° fabās,° carōtās,° ūvās apposuit.

Dum viātōrēs edunt caupō saepe in hortum parvum cur- rēbat et caelum spectābat. Dēnique puerīs dīxit, "Vesuvius iterum murmurat. Mox terra sub pedibus nostrīs tremet."

Puerī rīdēbant, sed pater in cōgitātiōne dēfīxus est. In- 30

°**vultisne** do you wish? • **Pompeiōs** (acc. pl. in apposition with **oppidum**) Pompeii, a town in south Campania • **tabulīs** writing tablets • **lectīcīs** litters • **caupōnam** inn, tavern, hostel **mīlibus passuum** (abl. of degree) miles • **asparagum** aspar- agus • **pernās** hams • **fabās** beans • **carōtās** carrots

The Appian Way outside Rome with the remains of tombs which lined it over a distance of many miles

terim duo aliī viātōrēs in caupōnam vēnerant. Prope puerōs
sedentēs inter sē dīcēbant. Fābulam dē Vesuviō nārrābant,
sed mediā in fābulā fessī puerī cubicula sua petīvērunt.

raeda, -ae	F., carriage
ūva, -ae	F., grape
raedārius, -ī	M., driver
***cubiculum, -ī**	N., sleeping room
***ōvum, -ī**	N., egg
caupō, -ōnis	M., innkeeper
***cōgitātiō, -ōnis**	F., meditation, thinking
pānis, -is	M., bread
viātor, -ōris	M., traveler
magnificus, -a, -um	magnificent
***serēnus, -a, -um**	clear
***varius, -a, -um**	various
complūrēs, -a	very many; several
***murmurō, -āre, -āvī, -ātum**	roar, rumble
***renovō, -āre, -āvī, -ātum**	renew
***studeō, -ēre, -uī, —**	be busy with
***appōnō, -ere, -posuī, -positum**	serve, put on the table
dēfigō, -ere, -fīxī, -fīxum	fasten, fix firmly
***adveniō, -īre, -vēnī, -ventum**	come to

REVIEW EXERCISES I

I Change all singular verbs to plural and all plural verbs to
singular. Translate all forms.

1	docēbō	5	facite	9	poterit	13	erunt
2	nōlī	6	aperiunt	10	dormiō	14	dīc
3	dēbēmus	7	jacēbāmus	11	pōnam	15	ferte
4	juvās	8	appāret	12	mittit	16	audiēbās

II Supply forms of each verb to complete the present system
active in the same person and number.

nūntiās   dēlēbat   vincētis   fugimus   sentiō   sunt   potestis

*Words with (*) contain clues to their meaning through related English words.

Mosaic of a Roman inn where a party is going on. A table and an amphora symbolize the food and drink served there.

III Arrange nouns below to form Declension I (feminine) and II (masculine and neuter) singular and plural. Any word may be used more than once.

1 agrōrum   5 equum   9 initium   13 nymphā   17 scūtī
2 bēstia   6 folia   10 jūdiciō   14 ōrārum   18 tyrannō
3 corōnae   7 gladiī   11 liber   15 perīculīs   19 ursīs
4 dīvitiās   8 hortōs   12 mūrīs   16 rēgnōrum   20 vītam

IV Translate the following sentences; then use one of the forms at the right to change each Latin sentence into a question. Translate the questions.

1 Sociī in magnā cavernā latent.   **nōnne**
2 Incolās malōs pūniēmus.   **cūr**
3 Servus puerōrum fēminās terrēbat.   **ubi**
4 Dīs grātiās agere dēbētis quod nunc vīvitis. **-ne**

V Change these verbs from singular to plural or from plural to singular in the same tense and person.

1 aperīs   4 facite   7 lateō   10 occīdam
2 datis   5 fer   8 mūniēmus   11 poterunt
3 erant   6 jaciēbāmus   9 nōlīte   12 sentit

VI Change the underlined words from singular to plural or plural to singular and make other necessary changes.

1 Agricolae miserī in īnsulīs propinquīs habitābant.
2 Vēlum nāviculae in saxō altō jacet.
3 Aliī fluviī per oppida parva ad prōvinciās proximās fluunt.
4 Puerī arma in laurīs dēnsīs cēlābunt.

13

VII Match each superlative form of the adjective in B to its positive in A.

A

1 altus	5 parvus		
2 bonus	6 magnus		
3 multī	7 sacer		
4 malus			

B

a) optimus	e) plūrimī
b) pessimus	f) minimus
c) maximus	g) altissimus
d) sacerrimus	

VIII Choose an appropriate adjective for each noun and apply the proper ending. Translate each phrase.

1 casārum	6 mendīcō	a) angustissimus	g) miser
2 deae	7 equī	b) benignus	h) optimus
3 dōna	8 hastās	c) clārissimus	i) pessimus
4 in viā	9 pīrātae	d) ēgregius	j) pretiōsus
5 līberīs	10 templum	e) ferus	k) sacerrimus
		f) minimus	l) validissimus

IX Translate the sentences; then explain the case, number, and use of each underlined word.
1 In silvā saepe ambulābāmus.
2 Interdum pīrātae incolās oppidī necant.
3 Vāstābitisne, nautae, casās agricolārum?

The proud owner of a villa in Pompeii had the picture of his seaside villa painted on the wall. The fresco is now in the Naples Museum.

14

4 Fīlius avunculī tuī erat magister meus.
5 Ad rēgiam scholae propinquam līberī currunt.
6 Discipulō fābulās deōrum nārrābō.

X For each noun in the numbered list select from the lettered
list a verb of appropriate meaning and form so that the noun
may be its subject/object.

1	agricolae	6	dōnum	a) agam	f) fluit
2	auxilia	7	fluvius	b) audīsne	g) gerent
3	aquam	8	grātiās	c) bibent	h) juvant
4	arma	9	fīliī	d) date	i) labōrābant
5	cibum	10	sonōs	e) edite	j) vidēbunt

VISIT TO A POMPEIAN HOME

Postrīdiē viātōrēs iter renovāvērunt; nūllam Vesuviī mentiōnem fēcērunt. Post paucās hōrās ad oppidum Pompeiōs
(p. 50) pervēnērunt. *Raedīs et raedāriīs* prope caupōnam *relictīs*,
pater et fīliī ad vīllam Rūfī properāvērunt per viās angustās.

Vīlla Rūfī erat maxima atque magnifica. Mūrus autem 5
exterior erat sine ōrnāmentō. In pavīmentō vestibulī erat
figūra canis sub quā haec verba scrīpta erant, "Cavē canem."
Ā vestibulō viātōrēs in ātrium intrāvērunt. Ibi impluvium
in quod aqua per compluvium fluit puerī vīdērunt. In ātriō
Rūfus cum Fulviā uxōre trēs amīcōs salūtāvit. 10

"Salvēte,° amīcī," dīxit Rūfus, cujus uxor eandem salūtem
dīxit.

"Salvē,° Rūfe; salvē, Fulvia," respondit Lūcius. "Dīcite
salūtem, puerī."

"Salvēte," dīxērunt duo puerī cum dignitāte. 15

Dum Lūcius Rūfusque multa inter sē dīcunt, puerī plūra
dē Vesuviō cognōscere dēsīderābant. Ubi facultās data est,
(p. 47) Mārcus igitur quaesīvit, "Putāsne *hunc montem* umquam
(p. 50) proximās urbēs *dēlētūrum esse?*"
(p. 55) "Hanc *rem* ego nōn timeō," respondit Rūfus. "Multōs 20
annōs ēruptiōnēs accidērunt; terra tremuit, sed incolae

°salvē, salvēte hello

An excavated street in Pompeii shows rather narrow sidewalks, pavement constructed to allow for drainage, and evidences of a second story in many houses.

Pompeiōrum, nihil timentēs, numquam ab urbe fūgērunt."

(p. 55)
"Sed hōc *diē* ipsō," dīxit Mārcus, "nōs ipsī vīdimus fūmum 'et flammās Vesuviī ad caelum ascendentēs."

Rūfus autem interritus cum amīcīs ambulābat in hortum 25 unde Vesuvium spectābat.

(p. 50)
Monte diū *cōnspectō* Rūfus dīxit, "Hodiē nūbēs fūmusque certē sunt lātiōrēs dēnsiōrēsque."

"Quid facere dēbēmus?" quaesīvit Sextus.

(p. 56)
"*Eāmus*° ad forum. Ibi plūra dē hāc rē cognōscere poteri- 30 mus," respondit Rūfus.

Multī cīvēs in forum currēbant. Aliī quaerēbant ex sene,° "Quid dē istā nūbe sentīs? Dēbēmusne fugere? Quid agitur?

(p. 47)
Putāsne *Vesuvium* casās nostrās *dēlētūrūm esse?*"

"Hanc rem nōn timeō," senex dīxit vōce validā. "Meā 35 ex sententiā nōs hīc in oppidō nostrō tūtī erimus. Mōns ille saepissimē ēmīsit nūbēs fūmī in caelum. Nōn ignōrō°

16

(p. 47)
(p. 48)

(p. 50)
(p. 53)

oppidum nostrum sēdecim ante annīs multa vulnera sevēra
sustinuisse. Hodiē autem nihil malī° sustinēbimus."

Lūcius tamen, *hīs verbīs audītīs,* relinquere statim urbem 40
Pompeiōs domumque° *redīre* cōnstituit. Itaque pater atque
duo fīliī Rūfō dīxērunt, "Valē! Fortis es, multō fortior quam
nōs."

"Valē et tū, amīce!" Lūciō respondit Rūfus. "Valēte,
Sexte et Mārce," puerīs dīxit. 45

°**eāmus** (subjunctive) let's go • **ex sene** (abl. sing.) from an
old man • **nōn ignōrō** I am well aware • **malī** (partitive
genitive with **nihil**) no evil • **domum** home, to home

sententia, -ae	F., opinion
*****compluvium, -ī**	N., opening in the roof of a house through which water flowed into the impluvium below; compluvium
*****impluvium, -ī**	N., a square basin in the floor of the atrium; impluvium
*****ōrnāmentum, -ī**	N., decoration
*****pavīmentum, -ī**	N., pavement (of tile)
*****vestibulum, -ī**	N., courtyard
*****dignitās, -ātis**	F., dignity
*****ēruptiō, -ōnis**	F., a breaking forth, eruption
*****facultās, -ātis**	F., opportunity
*****mentiō, -ōnis**	F., mention
vulnus, -eris	N., wound
interritus, -a, -um	unafraid
*****sevērus, -a, -um**	severe
*****exterior, -ius**	outer
iste, ista, istud	this, that (pronoun or adjective)
*****sustineō, -ēre, -tinuī, -tentum**	sustain, endure; support, hold up
*****accidō, -ere, -cidī, —**	happen, occur
ante	previously, before
multō	much
umquam	ever
unde	from where

I Translate each sentence and explain the underlined words and phrases.

(handwritten note: abl. time within which)

(handwritten: At the 1st hour the skilled man killed many beasts.)

1 Prīmā hōrā vir perītus bēstiās plūrimās occīdit.

(handwritten: The terrified children fled from the pirates; — abl. expressing motion from which)

2 Līberī territī ā pīrātīs fūgērunt.

3 Fīliae vestrae cum sociīs suīs in campō lūdunt.

4 Nostrā memoriā virī nōtōs librōs scrībent.

5 Fīnitimōs inimīcōs sagittīs clāvīsque vīcimus.

6 Ex undīs appārēbunt nymphae fōrmōsae.

7 Advenās cum amīcitiā recipite.

The ruins of the Pompeian house known as the House of Castor and Pollux stand around a pool that is open to the sky.

From the air it is possible to see clearly how much of Pompeii has been excavated from the volcanic ashes of Vesuvius. In the foreground is the gladiators' exercise ground with the two theaters nearby.

II Add an appropriate demonstrative adjective from the lettered list to modify each underlined word. Translate.

1 Puerī fēminīs fābulās nōtās nārrābunt.
2 Cibum in cavernā cēlābāmus.
3 Sonus undārum nōs saepe excitat.
4 Fīlius nostrī amīcī nautās timet.
5 Bracchia tua praemia tenēre nōn poterunt.
6 Multae formīcae sub tēctō habitābant.
7 Cum amitā flammās sacrās cūrābitis.
8 Nōnne eris virō benigna?

a) eam c) hic e) illō g) eōs i) hāc k) huic
b) eīs d) hārum f) illud h) haec j) illās l) illōrum

III Change all positive forms of the adjectives to superlatives and superlatives to positives in the same gender, number, and case.

1 aegrīs 3 dēnsissimō 5 fōrmōsae 7 magnum 9 minimam
2 multī 4 optimus 6 pessimōrum 8 sacerrimās 10 tūta

IV Group all verbs that are in the present tense, then all verbs that are in the future. Identify all other forms. Translate.

1 aperīs	5 regam	9 datis	13 afficiunt
2 audiētis	6 manēmus	10 veniēbat	14 eris
3 jubet	7 dūc	11 fugient	15 putābit
4 possumus	8 agēmus	12 esse	16 venīte

V Where necessary complete each sentence by selecting an appropriate preposition from the list. Translate.

1 Dominī (with) optimīs servīs (from) vīcō discēdent.
2 Mendīcus cibum (under) aedificiō dēsertō relinquit.
3 Multās ursās (from) meīs agrīs (with) clāvīs agam.
4 Populus Rōmānus imperium prōvinciārum (in) annō prīmō sūmit.
5 (Without) morā (from) oppidō fugite.
6 Puerī (before) āram (with) audāciā stābant.
7 Deus benignus (down from) caelō flammās portābat.
8 Hoc sacrificium (for) amitā nostrā faciēmus.

ā	ad	apud	dē	ex	prō	sine
ab	ante	cum	ē	in	propter	sub

VI For each noun in the numbered list select from the lettered list a demonstrative which agrees with it.

1 saxī	6 dolōrum	a) haec	e) ejus	i) eō
2 cervōs	7 magistrum	b) hic	f) illae	j) illud
3 sēmitā	8 āram	c) eōrum	g) hōs	k) eam
4 gaudium	9 incolae	d) hunc	h) hāc	l) huic
5 gladius	10 vēstīgia			

VII Change nouns and pronouns from singular to plural or plural to singular whenever possible, and make all other necessary changes. Translate.

1 Incolae hōrum oppidōrum in agrīs suīs labōrant.
2 Ego in silvā dēnsā ambulō; tū in viā lātā curris.
3 Hoc dōnum mihi grātissimum est; illa tibi dabō.
4 Haec dea erat maestissima quod suum speculum āmīserat.
5 Rēgīna huic puerō magna praemia dabit.
6 Dea fābulās ejus audīre nōn cupiet.
7 Fēminae fīliās suās nōn pūniēbant.
8 Illōs nautās laudāmus quod sociī eōrum nōs juvant.

The smoking cone of Vesuvius is seen behind ruined buildings of Pompeii.

VESUVIUS THREATENS

Jam nox erat ubi viātōrēs ad Viam Appiam advēnērunt. Ignēs Vesuviī lūcem dabant incertam. Multōs cīvēs terror cēperat.

"Clārior est lūx majorque ignis," clāmāvit Mārcus.

(p. 47) "Ita," respondit Sextus. "Crēdō *Vesuvium* hāc nocte 5

(p. 50) Pompeiōs *dēlētūrum esse!*"

"Hoc ipse timeō," dīxit pater.

(p. 50) Vix *hīs verbīs dictīs*, subitō dē nūbibus dēnsiōribus atque majōribus saxa atque lapidēs dēscendere incēpērunt. Ē

(p. 53) Vesuviō monte lātissima incendia altaeque flammae *exiērunt.* 10 Vāstīs tremōribus terra tremēbat.

Jam candentēs cinerēs in mare terramque cadēbant. Terra tremēns rīmīs magnīs scissa est°; maria ab ōrīs recessērunt. Flūmina saxōrum liquefactōrum° fluēbant per lītora atque in maria. Ex lateribus montis fluēbant magna flūmina ignis 15 serpentibus similia ārdentibus.

Per tōtam noctem cum multīs aliīs ab eōdem perīculō fugientibus pater puerīque vigilāvērunt. Magnus erat terror

°**scissa est** was split • **saxōrum liquefactōrum** of lava (lit., rocks made liquid)

omnium. Multī auxilium deōrum ōrābant. Lūx sōlis tandem appāruit, obscūra quidem. Omnibus rēbus mūtātīs, 20
terra paene incognita vīsa est.°

(p. 56)
(p. 56)
"Domum *redeāmus*, puerī," dīxit Lūcius. "Mātrī vestrae
haec omnia *nārrēmus*."

(p. 55)
Reditus viātōrum ad oppidum Capuam erat difficilis. In
multīs locīs magnae erant ruīnae. Incolae territī cum uxōri- 25
(p. 55)
bus līberīsque fugiēbant. Plaustrīs, raedīs, *curribus* via
impediēbātur.

Lūcius fīliīque in raedīs suīs senēs et claudōs et līberōs
posuērunt; ipsī jūxtā° raedās ambulābant. Post multās
hōrās fessī viātōrēs ad oppidum Capuam pervēnērunt, ubi 30
maximās deīs grātiās ēgērunt.

"Quam fēlīcēs sumus," dīxit pater, "quī vīvī mortem
paene certam atque horribilem effūgimus! Numquam autem
ruīna Pompeiōrum ē memoriā nostrā excēdet."

°**vīsa est** seemed   •   **jūxtā**   (prep.) beside

rīma, -ae	F., fissure, crack
incendium, -ī	N., fire
plaustrum, -ī	N., wagon
cinis, -eris	M., ashes
***latus, -eris**	N., side, flank
senex, senis	M., old man
***tremor, -ōris**	M., tremor, quake
currus, -ūs	M., chariot, car
reditus, -ūs	M., return
claudus, -a, -um	crippled, lame
***vāstus, -a, -um**	vast, enormous
***horribilis, -e**	horrible
candeō, -ēre, -uī, —	glow with heat
effugiō, -ere, -fūgī, —	escape
***excēdō, -ere, -cessī, -cessum**	leave
***recēdō, -ere, -cessī, -cessum**	recede
***impediō, -īre, -īvī, -ītum**	obstruct, hinder
vix	scarcely, hardly, with difficulty

The tombs outside Pompeii are better preserved than those outside Rome (p. 11) because of their long burial under the ashes of Vesuvius.

REVIEW EXERCISES III

I In each numbered group find three principal parts of one verb and arrange them in order.

1 agō   augēre   ēgī   agitō   agere
2 audīvī   audeō   auxī   audīre   audiō
3 moveō   monuī   mōvī   maneō   movēre
4 capere   cupīvī   cēpī   cupere   cupiō
5 possum   pōnō   potuī   posuī   posse
6 jussī   juvāre   jubēre   juvō   jūvī
7 jactāre   jacēre   jaceō   jēcī   jacuī

II Translate into Latin all (A) relative pronouns; (B) interrogative pronouns; (C) interrogative adjectives.

1 The men who lived in these cottages were farmers.
2 Whose aunt came to school today?
3 Who will end the controversy between the goddesses?
4 What rivers flow into that province?
5 With whom did you come?
6 The men whose homes you see are fighting for you.
7 What did you find in the sack which you have hidden?

23

From plaster poured into the hollows in the ash where victims of the eruption fell it has been possible to make many casts like these of Pompeians of A.D. 79.

III Translate each sentence; then replace the underlined word or phrase with an interrogative pronoun or adjective, rearranging the order if necessary.

1 Illī nautae ad īnsulam nāvigābunt.
2 Virī Rōmānī oppidum Gallōrum cēpērunt.
3 Puella parva apud nōs manēbit.
4 Sine dubiō līberī ursam timent.
5 Fēmina mē cum puerō aegrō vīdit.
6 Magistrīs discipulī suās fābulās nārrābant.
7 Vēla alba procul vīdistī.

IV For each verb give the third principal part and the perfect infinitive active.

1 sentiō	sentīre	5 juvō	juvāre	8 fugiō	fugere
2 cōgō	cōgere	6 mittō	mittere	9 maneō	manēre
3 sum	esse	7 possum	posse	10 stō	stāre
4 volō	volāre				

Excavation of Pompeii has yielded several kinds of food found in shops and homes.

V Supply possible interrogative pronouns for each blank and translate.

1 _____ cum fīliīs nautae pugnābant?
2 _____ cōpiae nostrae prope rīpam fluviī posuērunt?
3 _____ spēluncam mōnstrāverās?
4 _____ in agrō juvābimus?
5 _____ formīcās in incolās mūtāre cupīvit?
6 Prō _____ vir vītam dabit?

V I Select the word which completes each sentence most sensibly and translate.

1 Rēgīna (quā/cujus/quam) nāvem cēperāmus auxilium postulāvit.
2 Agricola (suum/ipsa/huic) equum in agrō relīquit.
3 Discipulī magistrī (ipse/alius/ejusdem) fābulās mīrās didicērunt.
4 Puerī (idem/pauca/hoc) māla (quae/quibus/quās) in hortō vīderāmus edēbant.
5 Anicula (suum/īdem/eōrum) calceum āmīserat.
6 Haec vīta (tibi/mē/eae) nōn grāta erit.

(p. 54) Paucōs post mēnsēs Lūcius negōtium Rōmae° gerere
volēbat. Etiam hāc occāsiōne fīliōs ad iter invītāvit.

Via Appia ab urbe Capuā ad urbem Rōmam dūcit; est
omnium viārum Rōmānārum clārissima. In eā Lūcius fīliīque
multōs viātōrēs vīdērunt. Nocte in tabernā° mānsērunt, ubi ₅
male dormīvērunt. Viātōrēs antīquitus tabernās bonās nōn
saepe inveniēbant.

Tertiō diē in urbem Rōmam ipsam pervēnērunt. "Quam
pulchra est haec urbs!" clāmāvit Sextus. "Ecce collis!"

"Ille est mōns Palātīnus," inquit pater, "in quō Rōma ā ₁₀
Rōmulō prīdem condita est."

Tum Mārcus flūmen dēmōnstrāns dīxit, "Ecce flūmen ā

A glimpse of the Tiber and the island once sacred to Aesculapius, now appropriately
devoted to medical buildings

26

sinistrā, cujus aqua flāva est. Nōnne hoc flūmen Tiberis appellātur?"

"Ita," respondit pater. "Tiberis est maximum hujus 15 regiōnis flūmen. Aqua propter lutum atque arēnam flāva est."

Posteā per Viam Sacram° ad Forum ambulābant Lūcius et fīliī. Puerī Forum Rōmānum vidēre cupiēbant.

(p. 54) "Nōmina omnium templōrum memoriā teneō," inquit Sextus, "sed prīmō templum Jūliī Caesaris vidēre *volō*, dē 20 cujus vītā atque dē cujus morte multa lēgī."

°Rōmae at Rome • **tabernā** inn • **per Viam Sacram** over the Sacred Way

The ruins on the Palatine known as the Palace of the Caesars

A house of the time of the Roman Republic, excavated on the Palatine, contains this elaborately decorated room.

"Estne illud aedificium ōrnātissimum, quod in monte Palātīnō vidēmus, templum Apollinis?" quaesīvit Mārcus.

Pater respondit, "Ita est. Augustus imperātor templum Apollinis in eō monte aedificāvit. Plūrēs diēs manēbimus in 25 urbe, et alia nōta aedificia vidēbimus."

*occāsiō, -ōnis	F., occasion, opportunity
*ōrnātus, -a, -um	ornate, beautiful
*dēmōnstrō, -āre, -āvī, -ātum	show
*invītō, -āre, -āvī, -ātum	invite
condō, -ere, -didī, -ditum	found, establish; store (up)

REVIEW EXERCISES IV

I Complete the following synopses of verbs in all six tenses of the indicative and arrange in proper order.

1 aperueritis   aperītis   4 frangēs   frēgerās
2 occupābat   occupāvit   5 perficiēbam   perfēcerō
3 dēlēvimus   dēlēbimus   6 stābunt   steterant

One of the most familiar monuments in the Roman Forum is the Temple of Saturn, the columns of which are in the foreground. They belong to a fourth-century (A.D.) reconstruction of a building believed to have been built in 497 B.C.

II Arrange the Declension III nouns in proper declension order. Some cases may include more than one form, and any word may be used more than once.

1 altitūdinem	6 genera	11 nāviculīs	16 sorōrum
2 cīvis	7 hostium	12 maria	17 tēcta
3 ducibus	8 iter	13 ōrātiōnēs	18 virtūte
4 equum	9 lapidis	14 pēs	
5 fluviī	10 mīlitī	15 proelium	

III Supply the forms needed to complete the conjugation of each tense indicated, and arrange in proper order. Give the principal parts and meaning of each verb.

1 adīmus/adītis/adīs
2 āfuērunt/āfuistis/āfuī
3 redierit/redierimus/redieris
4 poterunt/poterō/poterit
5 aderam/aderātis/aderant
6 trānsierātis/trānsierās/ trānsierāmus
7 exībis/exībunt/exībit

IV Arrange the present participles to form the declension and identify the gender of each participle. Any form may be used more than once.

a) agentis
b) audientibus
c) cēlantia
d) cupientēs
e) custōdiēns
f) moventem
g) petentium
h) relinquentī
i) volante

V Select the words in each group which, when arranged in proper order, will form the comparison of an adverb. Identify the remaining forms.

1 ācribus/ācriter/ācriōris/ācrius/ācerrimē
2 bene/meliōra/benignius/optimē/melius
3 crūdēliter/crūdēle/crūdēlius/crūdēlitās/crūdēlissimē
4 facillimē/facilius/facilī/faciliōrum/facile
5 libenter/līberē/līberius/līberrimē/līberī
6 majus/maximē/magnopere/magis/magnum

VI Give the gender and genitive of each noun.

1 altitūdō	5 dolor	9 incola	13 moenia
2 arbor	6 flūmen	10 laurus	14 potestās
3 bracchium	7 gēns	11 legiō	15 soror
4 castra	8 hostis	12 mīles	

VII In each group find the one word which does not belong with the others and explain your answer.

1 arma/paucī/leōnēs/moenia/rāmī
2 aperī/juvā/mūnīrī/pōnite/fer
3 antīquitus/dīligēns/idōnea/omnēs/tria
4 animal/corpus/ōmen/īnsigne/rādīx
5 aliter/cum/frūstrā/libenter/tandem
6 cui/quis/quam/ quid/quō
7 apud/contrā/inter/ procul/sine

AT THE CHARIOT RACES

(p. 53)   Posterō diē Lūcius et fīliī ad Circum Maximum iērunt.
(p. 55)   Ibi Rōmānī cursūs equōrum et alia certāmina spectāre solēbant.° Magna multitūdō jam convēnerat; hominēs dē
equōrum celeritāte et arte aurīgārum multa dīcēbant. Puerī
(p. 47)   Capuānī audīverant virum Capuānum inter aurīgās esse.   5

Subitō Sextus exclāmāvit, "Ecce Līber! Vidēsne virum illōs equōs nigrōs agentem? Sine dubiō est Līber, quī ōlim in Capuā habitābat."

Spectātor vīcīnus, quī haec verba Sextī audīverat, dīxit, "Ille Capuānus hīc ignōtus est. Numquam vīcit neque hodiē inter prīmōs erit. Nē ipse quidem victōriam spērat." 10

(p. 47)
"Fortasse errās," inquit Mārcus. "Nōs Capuānī bene scīmus *Līberum* aurīgam perītissimum *esse*. Putō *eum* hodiē *vincere posse.*"

(p. 50)
Jam tuba signum dedit. *Equīs* ē carceribus *ēmissīs*, cer- 15
tāmen inceptum est. Magnus erat fremitus spectātōrum, quī nōmina aurīgārum clāmābant. Vōcēs puerōrum Capuā-
(p. 48)
nōrum vix *audīrī* poterant.

Mox prīmum locum habuit Crēscēns, aurīga Rōmānus, quī plūrimōs fautōrēs° habēre vidēbātur°; secundum locum 20
habuit Hispānus; tertium locum Gallus; locum quārtum Līber, ille Capuānus.

°**solēbant** used to • **fautōrēs** backers, fans • **vidēbātur** seemed

aurīga, -ae	M., charioteer
carcer, -eris	M., starting place of a race course
***spectātor, -ōris**	M., spectator
***cursus, -ūs**	M., race
fremitus, -ūs	M., murmuring, roaring
niger, -gra, -grum	black
***exclāmō, -āre, -āvī, -ātum**	shout
***spērō, -āre, -āvī, -ātum**	hope

This mythological chariot race, with evidence of an accident on the left, is on a sarcophagus now in the Vatican.

31

One of the best-preserved of ancient Roman amphitheaters (at Verona, north Italy)

REVIEW EXERCISES V

I Change each verb from active to passive voice, and make all necessary changes. Translate both sentences.

1 Cīvēs urbem fortiter dēfendent.

2 Ipsī vōs māne excitābimus.

3 Libenter tē semper accipiēbam.

4 Cotīdiē ducēs nōs dē virtūte hostium monent.

5 Custōs mē in forō cognōscet.

II Give the gender and genitive singular/plural of each noun. Which nouns are usually declined only in the plural? Only in the singular? Which can have more than one gender?

1 advena	5 castra	9 dīvitiae	13 lūmen	17 salūs
2 aetās	6 centuriō	10 equus	14 mercātor	18 soror
3 agmen	7 cīvis	11 fortitūdō	15 moenia	19 vellus
4 arbor	8 custōs	12 gaudium	16 regiō	20 virtūs

32

III Change the underlined words from singular to plural or plural to singular. Make all other necessary changes. Translate both versions.

1 <u>Puerī</u> ā patribus crūdēliter aguntur.
2 Fugitīvī magnā cum difficultāte ā mīlite <u>invenientur</u>.
3 <u>Puellae</u> in tergīs arietum trāns mare portābuntur.
4 Saxa <u>ingentia</u> ā servīs movēbantur.

IV Select an appropriate word from the list at the right to replace each blank. Translate the completed sentences.

1 ＿＿ ex illīs ＿＿ puerīs est frāter meus;   ā/ab   mīlle
＿＿ est socius ＿＿.   alter   minus
2 In ＿＿ spēluncā post ＿＿ majōra saxa   brevī   quae
aurum ＿＿ avunculō nostrō ＿＿ est.   cēlātum   suus
3 ＿＿ ovēs in mediō colle ＿＿ poterant.   duōbus   tria
4 ＿＿ flūmina in ＿＿ mare fluunt?   eādem   tribus
5 Mīlitēs sex ＿＿ passuum ＿＿ tempore   ejus   ūnus
iter fēcērunt.   idem   vidērī
                                     mīlia   victum

V Make sensible sentences by supplying the proper case of appropriate words from the lettered list. Translate and explain the use of the words chosen.

1 Hostēs ab ＿＿ nostrīs duōbus ＿＿ vincentur.
2 Rēx mīlia ＿＿ maximā cum ＿＿ rēxit.
3 Līberōs ex ＿＿ currentēs vīdī.
4 Dux iter cum mīlle ＿＿ fēcerat.
5 Nāvem antīquam sub ＿＿ prope ＿＿ jacentem cōnspeximus.
6 Custōdēs prō ＿＿ juvenēs ＿＿ occīdērunt.

a) benignitās   c) gladius   e) incola   g) lītus   i) mīles
b) eques   d) hortus   f) legiō   h) mēnsis   j) unda

VI For all declinable words in the lettered list choose appropriate endings from the numbered list for a complete declension.

1 -a	5 -am	9 -ī	13 -īus	17 -ōrum
2 -ā	6 -ārum	10 -ia	14 -o	18 -ōs
3 -ābus	7 -ās	11 -ibus	15 -ō	19 -um
4 -ae	8 -ēs	12 -ium	16 -ōbus	20 -īs

a) alter   c) mīlle   e) sōlus   g) ūnus
b) duo   d) mīlia   f) trēs   h) vīgintī

One chariot (*quadriga*) has rounded the goal post (*meta*) which marks one end of the oval track; another chariot approaches the *meta*.

CHEERS FOR THE WINNER

In mediō Circō mūrus erat, quī spīna° appellābātur.

(p. 55) Aurīgae circum eam spīnam *cursum* dīrigēbant. Necesse erat septem spatia° circum spīnam cōnficere. In utrōque° fīne spīnae erant mētae.°

(p. 55) Semper is *currus* quī mētīs proximus erat cursum brevissi- 5 mum habēbat. Quārē aurīgae semper locum interiōrem petēbant.

(p. 50) *Prīmō spatiō cōnfectō*, equī Līberī longē post cēterōs currēbant. Spectātōrēs vīcīnī puerōs irrīsērunt, "Ecce

°**spīna** a wall dividing the center of the race course on its longitudinal axis (There was enough room at each end for the chariots to turn for each lap of the course.) • **spatia** laps • **utrōque** each of two, both • **mētae** the posts at each end of the **spīnae** around which the chariots turned

34

vester aurīga Capuānus! Omnēs eum antecēdunt. Num° ₁₀

(p. 47)
etiam nunc *eum* perītissimum *esse* crēditis?"

(p. 55)
Līber autem *spem* nōn āmīserat. Equōs magnā cum arte

(p. 50)
ēgit. Mox, *facultāte datā*, Gallum praeterīvit. Deinde His-
pānum petīvit et eum quoque relīquit. Tum Crēscēns sōlus

(p. 55)
Līberum antecēdēbat neque intervallum inter duōs *currūs* ₁₅
magnum erat. Certāmen fuit inter eōs duōs hominēs, quōs
omnēs intentī° spectābant. Crēscentis fautōrēs ejus nōmen
iterum atque iterum clāmābant.

Dēnique currūs in ultimō spatiō ad mētās appro-
pinquābant. ₂₀

"Nunc contende! Nunc, Līber, mētās pete!" clāmāvit

(p. 47)
Mārcus, *Līberum audīre posse* spērāns.

(p. 50)
Crēscēns nimis° longē mētās vītāvit. Līber *occāsiōne
oblātā* equōs inter Crēscentem et mētās ēgit. Currus Līberī
paene frāctus mētās ultimō mōmentō temporis vītāvit. ₂₅

Līber prīmum locum cēperat. Crēscēns equōs flagellō

(p. 53)
cecīdit,° sed Līberum praeterīre nōn potuit. Līber *trānsī-
vit* prīmus calcem,° quae fīnem certāminis indicābat. Ita
Capuānus ignōtus vīcit.

Puerī et pater clāmāvērunt, "Euge!° Bene fēcistī! Nōs ₃₀
Capuānī tē maximē laudāmus."

°**num** interrogative particle implying that a negative answer is expected • **intentī** intent, anxious • **nimis** too (much), ex-
cessively • **cecīdit** beat • **calcem** goal line • **euge**
well done

*****flagellum, -ī**	N., whip
*****mōmentum, -ī**	N., moment, minute
*****interior, -ius**	inner
*****indicō, -āre, -āvī, -ātum**	mark, indicate
irrideō, -ēre, -rīsī, -rīsum	ridicule, laugh at
*****antecēdō, -ere, -cessī, -cessum**	precede, go ahead (of)
*****dirigō, -ere, -rēxī, -rēctum**	direct
*****offerō, offerre, obtulī, oblātum**	offer
praetereō, -īre, -īvī, -itum	go by, pass by
quārē	wherefore, therefore

I Add each group of endings in the lettered list in proper declension order to the base of an appropriate noun selected from the numbered list. Make any changes necessary in the base of the nouns.

1	animal	6	impetus	a) -ibus, -ū, -ua, -ūs, -uum
2	caedēs	7	liber	b) -ibus, -ū, -uī, -um, -ūs, -uum
3	cornū	8	pēs	c) -ē, -ēbus, -eī, -em, -ērum, -ēs
4	diēs	9	rēs	d) -ī, -ia, -ibus, -is, -ium
5	genus	10	ventus	e) -em, -ēs, -ī, -ibus, -is, -um, -e

II Change from active voice to passive.

1	dēlēbis	4	neglēxerātis	7	vīderint
2	fīnīvit	5	prōvocābam	8	agam
3	mūniunt	6	implōrāmus	9	capiet

III Match all possible verb forms in the numbered list with forms in the lettered list so that each pair corresponds in tense, person, and number. Translate each pair, and identify all forms not used.

1	āctī estis	a)	accipiar
2	cavēbō	b)	crēdēbāminī
3	damus	c)	extīnxistis
4	exiit	d)	fōderint
5	ferte	e)	ībit
6	īnstruētur	f)	jungere
7	latuērunt	g)	mōtus eram
8	prōtegēbātis	h)	pūnīmus
9	sēderam	i)	satum est
10	tracta erunt	j)	vulnerāta sunt

IV Select an appropriate noun for each participle; make the participle agree with the noun in gender, number, and case. Translate the phrases.

1	āmissus	6	frāctus	a) agrōs		g)	jānuā
2	arātus	7	jūnctus	b) aniculae		h)	jūdicī
3	clausus	8	perterritus	c) bovēs		i)	mīlitibus
4	ārsus	9	sessus	d) canem		j)	pontium
5	dēlēctus	10	vulnerātus	e) dolor		k)	prīncipis
				f) grātiās		l)	rāmī

Most charioteers were older than this boy, whose sculptured head is in the Capitoline Museum.

ROMAN HOSPITALITY

(p. 50)   Tum, *Circō Maximō relictō*, Lūcius et fīliī montem Esquilīnum petīvērunt. Amīcus Lūciī, quī in eā regiōne habitābat, eōs in domum suam invītāverat. Ubi pater et fīliī in tēctum pervēnērunt, is amīcus, quī Aulus appellābātur, eōs magnō cum gaudiō accēpit. Servī balneum° ₅ parāre jussī erant. Hospitibus° fessīs balneum erat grātissimum.

Deinde Aulus et hospitēs cēnāvērunt. Post cēnam colloquium fuit breve, quod dormīre cupiēbant viātōrēs.

Aulus, quī vīllam rūsticam° prope Tusculum habēbat, ₁₀
(p. 48) hospitēs eō dūcere cōnstituerat. Carpentum° *parārī* jussit, quod iter erat quīndecim mīlium passuum.°

°**balneum** bath • **hospitibus** (dative with **grātus**) guests
rūsticam rural, rustic, (belonging to the) country • **carpentum** coach • **mīlium passuum** of . . . miles

37

(p. 53)

Per angustās autem viās Rōmae vehicula ab equīs ducta *īre* prohibēbantur ā prīmā lūce usque ad decimam hōram.° Itaque Aulus et amīcī lectīcīs° ad portam urbis vectī sunt, ubi 15 servī cum carpentō adventum eōrum expectābant.

In eā regiōne, per quam via ā tēctō Aulī ad portam urbis dūcēbat, erant multa aedificia altissima. Ea aedificia ā Rōmānīs appellābantur "īnsulae,"° quod viīs undique ab aliīs aedificiīs dīvīsa erant. In eīs īnsulīs multī cīvēs pauperēs° 20 habitābant. Numquam Capuānī in suā urbe tam alta aedificia vīderant.

°**ā prīmā lūce usque ad decimam hōram** from dawn to dusk (What is the literal meaning?) • **lectīcīs** by/on litters • **īnsulae** "islands," i.e., apartment buildings • **pauperēs** poor

Only the bronze fittings inlaid with gold and silver are ancient. They were used to reconstruct this luxurious litter now in the Capitoline Museum in Rome.

38

*domus, -ūs/-ī	F., house; family (See p. 456 for declension.)
*decimus, -a, -um	tenth
cēnō, -āre, -āvī, -ātum	eat
*vehō, -ere, vexī, vectum	carry, (in passive voice) ride
quīndecim	fifteen
eō	there

REVIEW EXERCISES VII

I Supply the other principal parts and arrange in proper order.

1 abesse   āfutūrus
2 cecidī   cāsūrus
3 conjūnxī   conjungō
4 extinguō   extinguere
5 frēgī   frangere
6 nōluī

7 occīdō   occīsum
8 quaesītum   quaerere
9 repellō   repellere
10 scrīpsī   scrībere
11 trānseō   trānsiī
12 velle

II Select the lettered Latin expression which most aptly expresses the underlined word(s) in each English sentence.

1 You told me that they <u>went</u> to the seashore.
2 The names of the rivers must <u>be learned</u> by the pupils.
3 I know you <u>did</u> not <u>believe</u> the scout.
4 We hope that you <u>will be</u> very happy here.
5 The fathers thought their sons <u>could</u> swim.
6 The teachers said the boys <u>had been punished</u> sufficiently.
7 Comrades, <u>don't be afraid</u> of the guards.
8 She didn't want <u>to be seen</u> by her aunts.
9 They thought the little bird <u>would be killed</u> by the fierce eagle.

a) auxisse
b) crēdidisse
c) discī
d) exīre
e) futūrum esse
f) īsse
g) mūnīrī
h) nōlīte
i) occīsum īrī
j) posse
k) pūnītōs esse
l) timēre
m) velle
n) vidērī

The family of a Roman magistrate travels in a litter. A small litter at the rear may be for a child or for a household shrine. (Relief now in the museum at Aquileia)

III Change the ending of the word in parentheses to agree with the other word of each pair, if necessary. Translate the phrases.

1 (rēs) tōtī   4 hujus (diēs)   6 manū (fortis)

2 ātrium (ingēns)   5 (alius) incola   7 minimam (rādīx)

3 (cornū) dextrī

AT A COUNTRY ESTATE

(p. 53)

(p. 55)

Ubi ad portam urbis pervēnērunt, in carpentum ascendērunt et ad vīllam īre incēpērunt. Servī tēla portābant; nam interdum latrōnēs° in viātōrēs *impetūs* faciēbant. Sine comitibus igitur armātīs itinera facere satis tūtē viātōrēs nōn poterant.   5

Per Viam Latīnam° celeriter vectī sunt.° Ab utrōque° latere viae erant sepulchra nōbilium Rōmānōrum, quod Rōmānī mortuōs extrā urbem prope viās sepeliēbant. Aulus sepulchra virōrum clārōrum comitibus mōnstrāvit.

Aulus fundum centum jūgerum° habēbat, in quō erat 10 vīlla magna et pulcherrima. Circum eam vīllam erant fontēs, flōrēs, hortī, arborēs. Vīgintī servī agrum colēbant et animālia cūrābant. Fundus multās rēs ferēbat,° sed maximē vīnum. Hoc vīnum Aulus in urbe vēndēbat. Vīlicus Aulī Capuānīs multa dē fundō narrāvit. Inter aliās rēs magna 15 dōlia° mōnstrāvit, in quibus vīnum conditum erat.

°**latrōnēs** highwaymen, bandits • **per Viam Latīnam** over the Latin Way • **vectī sunt** they rode • **ab utrōque** on each **jūgerum** = gen. pl. of **jūgerum, -ī** N., juger, a measure of land equal to about two thirds of an acre • **ferēbat** was bearing, produced **dōlia** wooden casks

In the country Marcus and Sextus would discard the formal toga for a tunic such as is worn by this Roman boy.

(p. 47)
Rōmānī dīvitēs° exīstimābant *agricultūram esse* optimum
(p. 55)
ūsum pecūniae. Saepe complūrēs fundōs habēbant quōs vīlicī
cūrābant. Dominī in urbe habitābant sed in fundīs multōs
diēs agēbant.

20

Puerī in fundō manēre cupiēbant; invītī igitur cum patre
(p. 53)
atque Aulō ad urbem Rōmam *rediērunt.* Iterum Forum
Rōmānum atque templa deōrum et multa alia aedificia clārissima vīdērunt.

Post trīduum Capuānī amīcō suō "Valē" dīxērunt. Per 25
(p. 53)
Viam Appiam ad urbem Capuam *rediērunt.* Posteā puerī
omnibus amīcīs multa dē itinere nārrāvērunt.

°**dīvitēs**   rich, wealthy

*****fundus, -ī**	M., farm
vīlicus, -ī	M., overseer, foreman, manager
trīduum, -ī	N., (period of) three days
*****flōs, flōris**	M., flower
*****ūsus, -ūs**	M., use

exīstimō, -āre, -āvī, -ātum	think
*****vēndō, -ere, -didī, -ditum**	sell
*****sepeliō, -īre, -īvī, -pultum**	bury

REVIEW EXERCISES VIII

I From the items listed select pairs which may be used to form
ablatives absolute. Any item may be used more than once.

a) noun   e) preposition   h) past participle
b) pronoun   f) infinitive   i) future participle
c) adjective   g) present participle   j) imperative
d) adverb

II Translate each phrase as a clause with the use of one of the
conjunctions listed below.

1 amitā caecā   5 illō aegrō   8 servō fugiente
2 bēstiā dēsultūrā   6 mīlitibus vulnerātīs 9 tē missō
3 eōdem duce   7 nōbīs relictūrīs   10 virō advenā
4 hāc cantante

although   because   since   when   while   after   if

A Roman farm at threshing time is pictured in this mosaic. The sheaves of grain were heaped on the threshing floor, and the feet of the animals driven around trod out the grain. Later it was cleaned by being tossed into the air to blow away chaff and dirt.

III Change from direct quotation to indirect statement, making all necessary changes. Translate both versions.

1 Sacerdōtēs nūntiābunt, "Brevī tempore in ārā sacrificia pōnēmus."

2 Dux monet, "Multī mīlitēs ab hostibus· vulnerantur."

3 Fēmina dīxit, "Propter amōrem Helenae urbs capta est."

IV Change from indirect statement to direct quotation, making all necessary changes. Translate both versions.

1 Nautae nārrāvērunt sē septem annōs trāns maria tempestātibus coāctōs esse.

2 Māter putat patrem fīlium īnfēlīcem saepius laudāre dēbēre.

3 Dux respondit sē pācem factūrum esse.

43

Familiar suffixes that change Latin nouns to adjectives are **-ōsus**, meaning "full of," and **-ālis, -ilis, -ānus, -inus**, all meaning "of" or "pertaining to" whatever the noun designates; e.g., **nātūrālis**, pertaining to **nātūra**. Many of these adjectives were adopted into English with corresponding suffixes -ous/-ose and -al, -il/-ile, -an/-ane, -ine.

Latin Noun		Latin Adjective		English Adjective
verba	words	**verbōsus**	full of words	verbose
urbs	city	**urbānus**	of the city	urban/urbane

Form Latin adjectives from the following nouns and give English equivalents.

caput	**lēx**	**genus**	**canis**	**senex**
cīvis	**Rōma**	**manus**	**puer**	**ratiō**

When the Latin noun contains an **-l-** in either of the two syllables preceding the suffix, the suffix is **-āris**. The English version then shows -ar/-ary.

Latin Noun		Latin Adjective		English
vulgus	common people	**vulgāris**	of the common people	vulgar

Form Latin adjectives in **-āris** from the following nouns and give the English.

familia	**cōnsul**	**mīles**	**populus**	**salūs**	**sōl**

The English suffix -ary also represents Latin **-ārius,** which denotes "of" or "belonging to."

English Adjective	Latin Adjective	Latin Noun
judiciary	**jūdiciārius**	**jūdicium**

The Latin noun means "trial," "judgment," or "court." What is the meaning of the Latin adjective? Of the English adjective?

Some Latin adjectives in **-ārius** were also used as substantives. This use has been carried over into English derivatives in -ary; e.g., "legionary," "notary," "veterinary."

Two such nouns formed from adjectives have found their way into the calendar—"January" and "February." "February" was named from Latin **Februa** (N. pl.), a feast of purification celebrated by the Romans on the fifteenth of that month; **Februa + -ārius = Februārius (mēnsis).** Can you explain the origin of "January"?

The suffix **-ārium** (neuter form of the adjective suffix **-ārius**) was added to Latin nouns to indicate "a place where . . . is found/kept"; e.g., **librārium** (library) is a place where **librī** (books) are kept. A development from this formation is seen in **calendārium,** a book in which moneylenders registered the debts of their clients. It was so named because payment became due on the first of the month **(Calendae/Kalendae).** Later, a **calendārium** came to be simply a book that marked the divisions of the year—a calendar.

LOOK AND THINK What do such adjectives as "amatory," "ambulatory," and "transitory" suggest about the use and meaning of the English/Latin suffix -ory/-**ōrius?** How do "auditorium" and "dormitory" differ in form and meaning from such nouns as "aquarium" and "aviary"?

This silver plate comes from a villa at Boscoreale, which was destroyed at the same time as Pompeii.

AN INTENSIVE REVIEW of late first-year Latin:

Wherever forms and constructions covered by this intensive review occur in the readings of this unit (pages 9-42), the pertinent words appear in italics, and a reference to the appropriate page in this section has been placed in the left-hand margin opposite the italicized word or words.

The intensive review provides all the material necessary for students to gain a thorough knowledge of the forms and constructions covered therein, whether these are being met for the first time or as grammar points introduced late in first-year Latin in which pupils need reinforcement.

See the Summary of Grammar in the back of this book for complete declensions and conjugations and for a concise presentation of Latin usage.

A DIRECT QUOTATION repeats the exact words of a speaker. In writing, we enclose the exact words of a speaker in quotation marks.

Dīcit, "Frāter tuus in rēgiā habitat." She says, "Your brother is living in the palace."

AN INDIRECT QUOTATION repeats the thought, but not the exact words of the original speaker. In writing there are no quotation marks.

Dīcit frātrem tuum in rēgiā habitāre. She says (that) your brother is living in the palace.

The name "indirect statement" is given to this kind of indirect quotation. The verb of indirect statement in Latin is an infinitive and its subject is in the accusative.

In English an indirect statement is often introduced by the conjunction "that"; sometimes the conjunction is omitted. In Latin no conjunction is used to introduce an indirect statement.

INDIRECT STATEMENTS occur in Latin not only with verbs that mean "say," but also with verbs that mean "hear," "know," "believe," "see," "think," and the like.

Dīcit tē errāre. He says (that) you are wrong.
Priamus sēnsit filium vīvere. Priam realized his son was alive.
Paris audivit Helenam in Graeciā habitāre. Paris heard that Helen was living in Greece.

When the subject of an infinitive is the same as the subject of the main verb, the accusative of a reflexive pronoun is used as the subject of the indirect statement.

Putat sē errāre. He thinks (that) he is wrong.

PREDICATE NOUN OR ADJECTIVE IN INDIRECT STATEMENT is in the accusative to agree with the subject of the infinitive.

Dea dixit patrem ejus esse rēgem Trōjae. The goddess said his father was the king of Troy.

PRESENT INFINITIVE IN INDIRECT STATEMENT represents an act as occurring at the time shown by the tense of the main verb.

In these examples **timēre** means "fears" with **dīcit,** but "feared" with **dīxit.**

Dīcit sē perīculum timēre. He says that he fears danger.
Dīxit sē perīculum timēre. He said that he feared danger.

PRESENT INFINITIVES of the four conjugations are patterned after these.

	I	II	III	IV
Active:	**portāre**	**monēre**	**dūcere**	**audīre**
	to carry	to warn	to lead	to hear
Passive:	**portārī**	**monērī**	**dūcī**	**audīrī**
	to be carried	to be warned	to be led	to be heard

In Conjugations I, II, and IV, passive infinitives are like active, except the final letter is **-ī** instead of **-e.** In Conjugation III also, the final letter of the passive infinitive is **-ī,** but in this conjugation alone the preceding syllable **(-er-)** of the active infinitive is dropped.

A PERFECT ACTIVE INFINITIVE consists of the perfect stem of a verb and the ending **-isse.**

I	II	III	IV
portāvisse	**monuisse**	**dūxisse**	**audīvisse**
to have carried	to have warned	to have led	to have heard

A PERFECT PASSIVE INFINITIVE consists of the perfect participle with **esse.**

portātum esse	**monitum esse**	**ductum esse**	**audītum esse**
to have been carried	to have been warned	to have been led	to have been heard

TENSE OF INFINITIVE IN INDIRECT STATEMENT An infinitive expresses relative time. It merely shows the time relationship of its own action to the action of the main verb.

48

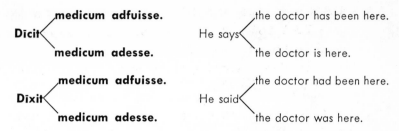

Here, two Latin infinitives may each be translated in two ways in English, depending on the tense of the main verb.

A Latin perfect infinitive always represents an act as completed before the time shown by the tense of the main verb; a present infinitive represents an act as occurring at the same time as that shown by the tense of the main verb.

These principles apply also to passive infinitives.

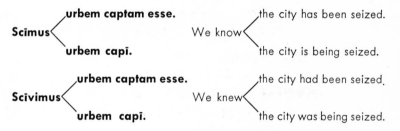

A FUTURE ACTIVE PARTICIPLE in Latin is like a perfect participle in form, except that it has **-ūr-** before the case ending.

portātūrus, -a, -um	about to carry	or going to carry
monitūrus, -a, -um	about to warn	or going to warn
dictūrus, -a, -um	about to say	or going to say
audītūrus, -a, -um	about to hear	or going to hear

Some verbs which have no perfect participle have a future active participle. The future active participle of such verbs is often given as the fourth principal part: **sum, esse, fui, futūrus; stō, stāre, stetī, stātūrus.**

The future active participle of a Latin verb is often combined with a form of **sum** to refer to something which the subject intends to do or is about to do.

Mānsūrus eram.	I was about to remain.	or I intended to remain.
Laudātūrus est.	He is about to praise.	or He intends to praise.

49

A **FUTURE ACTIVE INFINITIVE** also has two parts—a future active participle and infinitive **esse** (to be): **portātūrum esse** to be about to carry.

Putō mē mānsūrum esse.   I think I shall stay.

Putāvit sē mānsūram esse.   She thought she would stay.

In indirect statement, a future active infinitive is translated with "shall" or "will" after a main verb in present or future tense and with "should" or "would" after a main verb in any past tense.

ABLATIVE ABSOLUTE

Trōjā vāstātā, Aenēās ad Thrāciam nāvigāvit.   After Troy had been destroyed Aeneas sailed to Thrace.

In this sentence, **Trōjā vāstātā** is an ablative absolute. The word "absolute" here means "free" or "independent." An ablative absolute is independent of the rest of the sentence; that is, it is not connected with it grammatically. **Trōjā vāstātā** gives additional information, but the rest of the sentence is grammatically complete without these words.

An ablative absolute may consist of any one of several combinations of words. **Trōjā vāstātā**, for example, is made up of a noun and perfect participle.

1 Noun and participle

Ventō surgente, Trōjānī ad īnsulam Crētam nāvigāvērunt.   Since the wind was rising (with the rising wind), the Trojans sailed to the island of Crete.

2 Pronoun and participle

Hōc vīsō, Aenēās territus erat.   When he saw this (having seen this), Aeneas was frightened.

3 Two nouns

Numā rēge, pestilentia erat.   When Numa was king (during Numa's reign), there was a plague.

4 Pronoun and noun

Eō cōnsule, Rōmānī multa proelia commīsērunt.   When he was consul (during his consulship), the Romans undertook many battles.

5 Noun (or pronoun) and adjective

Aenēās, patre praesente, auxilium deī rogāvit.   Aeneas, in the presence of his father (with his father present), asked for the god's help.

50

In English, the use of an absolute phrase is rare. Usually such a phrase is awkward and is therefore avoided; e.g., "The danger past, we went home."

The phrase "The danger past" is absolute, not being connected grammatically to the rest of the sentence.

FREE TRANSLATION OF ABLATIVE ABSOLUTE Since there is no English construction exactly like the ablative absolute, such a Latin phrase may often be translated by a dependent clause introduced by "when," "after," "if," "since," or "although." Occasionally an English phrase is a better translation than a complete clause.

A **Nāvibus parātīs, Aenēās ad Thrāciam nāvigāvit.** When the ships were ready (with the ships ready), Aeneas sailed to Thrace.

B **Paucīs animālibus necātīs, cēnam parāvērunt.** After a few animals had been killed or After killing a few animals (after they had killed a few animals), they prepared a feast.

C **Ventō surgente, Trōjānī ad Crētam nāvigāvērunt.** Since the wind was rising (with the rising wind), the Trojans sailed to Crete.

D **Camillō duce, militēs fortiter pugnant.** Under the leadership of Camillus or When Camillus is the leader, the soldiers fight bravely.

A perfect participle in an ablative absolute phrase indicates time earlier than that of the main verb, as in sentence B. A present participle indicates the same time, as in sentence C.

ABLATIVE WITH PREPOSITION, in general, supplies additional information which would answer such questions as these:

Questions	Answers
1 **Ā quō?** or **Ā quibus?** By whom? (by what person or persons?)	**Ā mātre, ab amitā, ā puerīs**
2 **Quōmodo?** How? (in what manner?)	**Cum gaudiō; sine morā**
3 **Quōcum? Quibuscum?** With whom? (accompanied by whom?)	**Cum patre, cum sociīs; mēcum**
4 **Ubi?** Where? (in, on, under, in front of what?)	**In arcā; sub aquā; prō ārā**
5 **Unde?** Whence? From what place? (away, out, down from what?)	**Ā Forō; ex Āfricā; dē monte**

In Latin a careful distinction is made between "away from" (**ā, ab**), "out from" (**ē, ex**), and "down from" (**dē**) by the use of the appropriate preposition with the ablative.

Nāvis ā terrā mōvit. The ship moved (away) from the land.
Ē rēgiā Aenēās properāvit. Aeneas hurried (out) from the palace.
Dē mūrō saxum jēcit. He threw a stone (down) from the wall.

One of these prepositions (**ā, ab**) also means "by" and introduces agent, that is, the person by whom (**ā quō**) an action is performed. This use occurs only with a passive verb.

Āra ā sacerdōte parāta erat. The altar had been prepared by the priest.

Another preposition with the ablative which serves a two-fold purpose is **cum,** which always means "with." Sometimes a prepositional phrase with **cum** tells in what manner (**quōmodo**) something is done; sometimes it tells with whom (**quōcum**) it is done.

Dīdō Trōjānōs cum benignitāte accēpit. Dido received the Trojans with kindness.
Dīdō trāns mare cum multīs comitibus nāvigāverat. Dido had sailed across the sea with many attendants.

ABLATIVE WITHOUT PREPOSITION supplies additional information which would answer such questions as **Quandō?** "When?" (at or within what time?) and **Quō instrūmentō?** "How?" (by what means?).

Advenae brevī tempore Latīnī appellābuntur. In a short time the strangers will be called Latins.
Aenēās sagittīs septem cervōs occīdit. With arrows Aeneas killed seven stags.

In translating an ablative of time, an English preposition ("at," "in," or "within") is usually supplied.

In translating an ablative of means, "with," "by," or "by means of" must be supplied.

CONJUGATION OF eō, like that of English "go," is irregular. Its principal parts are **eō, īre, iī (īvī), itum.**

Present		Imperfect		Future	
Singular		**Singular**		**Singular**	
1 **e′ō**	I go	**i′bam**	I went	**i′bō**	I'll go
2 **īs**	you go	**i′bās**	you went	**i′bis**	you'll go
3 **it**	he, she goes	**i′bat**	he, she went	**i′bit**	he'll, she'll go
Plural		**Plural**		**Plural**	
1 **i′mus**	we go	**ibā′mus**	we went	**i′bimus**	we'll go
2 **i′tis**	you go	**ibā′tis**	you went	**i′bitis**	you'll go
3 **e′unt**	they go	**i′bant**	they went	**i′bunt**	they'll go

In the perfect, **eō** is conjugated like any other Latin verb (perfect stem + perfect endings): **iī (īvī), iistī (īvistī), iit (īvit); iimus (īvimus), iistis (īvistis), iērunt (īvērunt).**

So also in past perfect: **ieram (īveram), ierās (īverās),** etc.; and in future perfect: **ierō (īverō), ieris (īveris),** etc.

C O M P O U N D S   O F   **eō** are conjugated like **eō**, with a prefixed syllable **(ab-, ad-, ex-, in-, sub-, trāns-,** etc.). There are many compounds of **eō;** e.g., **abeō, adeō, exeō, ineō, subeō, trānseō.** The meaning of these compounds is clear, because each prefix is already familiar as a preposition. The first **(abeō)** means "go away." What do the others mean?

Another compound of **eō (redeō)** has the syllable **red-** (for **re-,** "back" or "again") prefixed.

I N   T R A N S L A T I N G   F O R M S   O F   **eō** in present tense, "I am going," "you are going," "he is going," etc., are often more natural than "I go," etc.

Likewise, in the imperfect, "I was going," "you were going," "he was going," etc., sometimes are preferable to "I went," etc.

Forms of **eō** in future tense may be translated "I shall go," "you will go," "he will go," etc., contractions of which are given above. They may also be translated "I am going," "you are going," etc.

In English, "I am going," "you are going," etc., may be either present or future, depending upon the context. In Latin, the form of the verb **eō** indicates its tense.

Anna ad Eurōpam it. Anna is going (is on the way) to Europe.
Anna ad Eurōpam ībit. Anna is going (intends to go) to Europe.

INFINITIVES OF eō

Present: **ire** to go   Perfect: **isse (iisse)** to have gone

IMPERATIVES OF eō

Singular: **ī** go   Plural: **īte** go

THE VERBS volō AND nōlō are conjugated like most other **-ō** verbs of third conjugation, except for four irregular forms of each verb in present tense.

Nōlō (I do not wish, I am unwilling) combines a negative (**nē**) and **volō** (I wish, I am willing); that is, **nōlō = nōn volō; nōlumus = nōn volumus; nōlunt = nōn volunt.** For the remaining three forms of **nōlō** in present tense **nōn** is used with corresponding forms of **volō: nōn vīs, nōn vult, nōn vultis.**

Principal parts of these verbs are **volō, velle, voluī, ———; nōlō, nōlle, nōluī, ———.**

PRESENT TENSE OF volō AND nōlō

Singular			Plural		
1	**volō**	**nōlō**	1	**volumus**	**nōlumus**
2	**vīs**	**nōn vīs**	2	**vultis**	**nōn vultis**
3	**vult**	**nōn vult**	3	**volunt**	**nōlunt**

IN OTHER TENSES than present, **volō** and **nōlō** are identical (except for the first two letters) in all persons and numbers.

	Imperfect	Future	Perfect	Past Perfect	Future Perfect
	Singular	Singular	Singular	Singular	Singular
1	**volēbam**	**volam**	**voluī**	**volueram**	**voluerō**
2	**volēbās**	**volēs**	**voluistī**	**voluerās**	**volueris**
3	**volēbat**	**volet**	**voluit**	**voluerat**	**voluerit**
	Plural	Plural	Plural	Plural	Plural
1	**volēbāmus**	**volēmus**	**voluimus**	**voluerāmus**	**voluerimus**
2	**volēbātis**	**volētis**	**voluistis**	**voluerātis**	**volueritis**
3	**volēbant**	**volent**	**voluērunt**	**voluerant**	**voluerint**

COMPLEMENTARY INFINITIVE WITH volō AND nōlō often occurs in Latin, as it does also in English in corresponding expressions.

Hīc manēre volō. I am willing to stay here.

Hīc manēre nōlō. I don't wish to stay here.

The infinitive is also used with imperative **nōlī** (singular) or **nōlite** (plural) to express a negative command.

Nōlī manēre hīc, advena! Don't stay here, stranger!

Nōlite manēre hīc, Trōjānī! Don't stay here, Trojans!

FOURTH-DECLENSION NOUNS have genitive singular ending in **-ūs.** Nominative singular of masculine and feminine nouns ends in **-us;** of neuter nouns, in **-ū.**

exercitus (M.) army

	Singular	Plural
Nom.	exercitus	exercitūs
Gen.	exercitūs	exercituum
Dat.	exercituī	exercitibus
Acc.	exercitum	exercitūs
Abl.	exercitū	exercitibus

cornū (N.) horn

	Singular	Plural
Nom.	cornū	cornua
Gen.	cornūs	cornuum
Dat.	cornū	cornibus
Acc.	cornū	cornua
Abl.	cornū	cornibus

Most fourth-declension nouns are masculine; a few are neuter. The most common feminine noun of this declension is **manus** ("hand" or "band").

FIFTH-DECLENSION NOUNS always end in **-ēs** in the nominative singular. The genitive singular ends in **-ēī (-eī** after a consonant).

Rēs (thing) and **diēs** (day) are the only fifth-declension nouns with forms for all cases. The few other nouns of this declension are used mostly in the singular.

rēs (F.) thing

	Singular	Plural
Nom.	rēs	rēs
Gen.	reī	rērum
Dat.	reī	rēbus
Acc.	rem	rēs
Abl.	rē	rēbus

diēs (M. or F.) day

	Singular	Plural
Nom.	diēs	diēs
Gen.	diēī	diērum
Dat.	diēī	diēbus
Acc.	diem	diēs
Abl.	diē	diēbus

Diēs in the singular is sometimes masculine and sometimes feminine; in the plural it is always masculine. Most other nouns of fifth declension are feminine.

THE TERM ''MOOD'' is used to describe the manner in which a verb functions in a sentence. There are three moods: indicative, imperative, subjunctive. To these may be added infinitive and participle, sometimes referred to as moods.

Indicative is used in making a statement or asking a question. Imperative is used to give a command.

Indicative: **Librōs portat.** He is carrying the books.
Imperative: **Portā librōs!** Carry the books!

Indicative: **Mūsicam audiunt.** They hear music.
Imperative: **Audite mūsicam!** Hear the music!

Indicative: **Cūr jacēs?** Why are you lying down?
Imperative: **Jacē!** Lie down!

SUBJUNCTIVE IN PRESENT TENSE used in a main clause often expresses a wish, hope, possibility, or mild command.

	Indicative	Subjunctive
I	**portat** = he is carrying	**portet** = let him carry
II	**habēs** = you have	**habeās** = may you have, I hope you have
III	**vīvimus** = we live	**vīvāmus** = let us live, may we live
IV	**audiunt** = they hear	**audiant** = may they hear

Although the independent subjunctive is often found in Latin, it has almost disappeared from English usage. It survives in a few set phrases: "So be it." "Thy kingdom come." "Come what may."

PRESENT SUBJUNCTIVE FORMS are easy to recognize. In Conjugation I, **-a-** of the indicative is replaced by **-e-**. In Conjugations II, III, IV, and **eō** and its compounds, an **-a-** precedes the person ending in present tense.

I	II	III	III-iō	IV	eō
portem	moneam	dūcam	capiam	audiam	eam
portēs	moneās	dūcās	capiās	audiās	eās
portet	moneat	dūcat	capiat	audiat	eat

Corresponding plural forms end thus: (I) **-ēmus, -ētis,**

-ent; (II) -eāmus, -eātis, -eant; (III) -āmus, -ātis, -ant; (III-iō/IV) -iāmus, -iātis, -iant; (eō) eāmus, eātis, eant.

Passive forms of present subjunctive are like the active except for addition of regular passive endings: **porter, portēris,** etc.; **monear, moneāris,** etc.

Sum and its compounds and **volō** and **nōlō** have -i- before the person ending. **Volō** has another change; its first vowel appears as -e-.

sim/possim	sīmus/possīmus	velim/nōlim	velīmus/nōlīmus
sīs/possīs	sītis/possītis	velīs/nōlīs	velītis/nōlītis
sit/possit	sint/possint	velit/nōlit	velint/nōlint

EXERCISES FOR INTENSIVE REVIEW

I Change from indirect statement to direct quotation, making all necessary changes. Translate.
1 Mīlitēs nūntiant, sacrificiō datō, deōs ventōs secundōs missūrōs esse.
2 Māter dīxit rēgem suam fīliam sacrificāre numquam voluisse.

II Change from direct quotation to indirect statement, making all necessary changes. Translate.
1 Pater servō fīdō dīcit, "Fīlia mea servārī nōn potest."
2 Puella prōmīsit, "Exercitūs Graecī ex portū nāvigābunt."
3 Servus scrībet, "Dominus meus tōtam noctem doluit."

III Change each direct quotation into indirect statement, and each indirect statement into a direct quotation.
1 Ulīxēs dīxit, "Nūllam pecūniam habeō."
2 Eumaeus dīxit, "Tēlemachus Ithacam relīquit."
3 Dīximus Ulīxem reventūrum esse.
4 Ulīxēs nārrāvit, "Decem annōs circum mūrōs Trōjae pugnāvī."
5 Eumaeus dīxit Ulīxem ab uxōre expectārī.

IV Translate the words underlined, using an ablative absolute each time.
1 With Ulysses as leader the Greeks arrived home safe.
2 After Troy had been captured, many Greeks departed.
3 When the cloak has been made, one of the suitors will marry Penelope.

V Give the best possible translation for each ablative absolute, using a clause.

1 Sacrificiō factō, Graecī ventōs secundōs expectāvērunt.

2 Mente mūtātā, puella domī nōn mānsit.

3 Ūndecim labōribus perfectīs, Herculēs fortiter ultimum suscēpit.

VI Supply the correct participle for each blank. Translate the completed sentences.

1 Avēs _____ nōs semper dēlectant. (singing)

2 Puerī dē perīculō _____ dīligentius prōcessērunt. (warned)

3 Quī _____ vīvit, līber numquam erit. (fearing)

4 Omnēs cēnam ā mātre _____ laudant. (prepared)

5 Leō Androclem _____ nōn vulnerāvit. (recognizing)

6 Mīles _____ in castra revēnit. (wounded)

VII Substitute a participle or participial phrase for the part of the sentence underlined, and make other necessary changes. Translate.

1 Castra in lītore posuērunt et statim nūntiōs ad rēgiam mīsērunt.

2 Mīles quī amīcitiam petēbat rēgīnae dōna multa et pretiōsa dedit.

3 Advenam nōn expectāmus, quod ōmina incerta erant.

4 Rēx, quamquam ā deīs monitus erat, tamen mentem nōn mūtāvit.

5 Sī tempestās classem ad vada pellit, nāvēs maximō in perīculō sunt.

VIII Use a form of **volō/nōlō** to replace each word or phrase underlined. Translate.

1 Agricolae avēs ingentēs ex agrīs expellere temptābant.

2 Advenās prope portās dux dēprehendere nōn cupit.

3 Ad arcem in colle sēcrētō appropinquāre nōn temptābō.

4 Signum proeliī tubīs dare cōnstituerāmus.

IX Express in English as wishes.

1 Fāta nōs dēfendant!
2 Dormiās bene!
3 Mittāmus eīs paucōs librōs!
4 Possītis expellere hostēs!
5 Dominī servīs benignī sint!
6 Ad scholam eāmus!

58

X Change each statement to a command by using an imperative.

1 Impetum facitis.   4 Urbem expugnātis.

2 Ad mare īs.   5 Clauditis fenestrās.

3 Nōs ad imperātōrem dūcis.   6 Dēlētis urbēs.

XI Change active verbs to passive and make other changes necessary to construct a sensible sentence. Translate.

1 Dea Athēna vestēs et faciem ejus mūtāverat.

2 Magnā cum difficultāte Eumaeus canēs lapidibus reppulit.

3 Ulīxēs casam Eumaeī petit.

XII Change passive verbs to active and make other changes necessary to construct a sensible sentence. Translate.

1 Decem annōs ā deīs in multīs terrīs errāre coāctus erat.

2 Decem annōs bellum circum mūrōs ā Trōjānīs gerēbātur.

3 Ab amīcīs in casam ductus est ubi eī vīnum datum est.

XIII Change active verbs to passive and vice versa. Make other necessary changes. Translate.

1 Nūntius māne ā mīlite ipsō excitābitur.

2 Mātrēs fīliōs monent.

3 Saxa ā puerīs jaciēbantur.

4 Cīvēs ducem sapientem dēligunt.

5 Pīrātae captīvōs diū tenēbant.

XIV Choose the most appropriate meaning of the verb in each expression, and translate the whole phrase.

1 negōtia gerere	(a) carry
2 galeam gerere	(b) wage
3 bellum gerere	(c) behave
4 sē gerere	(d) wear
5 gerere scūtum	(e) conduct

XV In each pair of phrases, the same verb has two different meanings. Bring out this difference in translating each expression.

1 nautās accipere	3 pecūniam recipere
dōna accipere	sē recipere
2 grātiās agere	4 memoriā tenēre
equōs agere	hastam tenēre

XVI Choose a correct verb form to complete each sentence.

1 Virum hanc epistulam scrīptam/scrībere/scrībentem vīdimus.
2 Incolae arma nova gerēns/gerentem/gerentēs in vincula conjiciuntur.
3 Omnia tēcta urbis nostrae dēlērī/dēlēns/dēlēre nunc sentīs.

XVII Supply a suitable pronoun or adjective for each sentence.

1 _____ oppida dux in animō habet?
2 Frūmentum nōn erat bonum _____ nāvēs portāverant.
3 Ōmina adversa erunt avēs _____ circum umerōs ejus volābunt.
4 _____ dē causā incolae vīcī ā rēge auxilia postulāvērunt?
5 Hic puer est Pūblius _____ avunculus in Galliam iit.

XVIII For each underlined expression choose from the list a word to convey a similar idea and supply proper endings, if necessary.

1 Posterō diē exercitus castra sua relīquit.
2 Hās rēs probō.
3 Sub mūrōs urbis ambulābāmus.
4 Prope locum dēsignātum rēgia erat.
5 Tempore cōnstitūtō cum prīncipibus in medium campum perveniam.
6 Hominēs silentēs circum āram stābant.
7 Mē superante sub potestāte ejus numquam eritis.
8 Furor animōs sociōrum cēpit.

a) **ager**   c) **haec**   e) **dux**   g) **occupō**   i) **tacitus**
b) **dēligō**   d) **mēns**   f) **moenia**   h) **postrīdiē**   j) **victor**

WORD MASTERY 3

Many compound words are made in Latin by adding a prefix to a simple word, usually a verb, noun, or adjective, but sometimes an adverb.

ab + **sum**	= **absum**		**inter** + **rēgnum**	= **interrēgnum**
inter + **diū**	= **interdiū**		**post** + **pōnō**	= **postpōnō**
per + **paucī**	= **perpaucī**		**prae** + **clārus**	= **praeclārus**

However, changes may occur in various ways: in the prefix, the simple word, or in both.

In some compounds the last sound of the prefix changes to the first sound of the word to which it is attached: **ad** +

ferō = **afferō (attulī, allātum)**. This process is called "assimilation" (the act of making similar to), ultimately from Latin **ad** (to) + **similis** (similar/like). Occasionally the last sound of the prefix disappears entirely, as in **ob** + **mittō** = **omittō**.

Combine prefix and verb, making all necessary changes to form compounds.

ad + petō   in + mergō   sub + portō   in + rumpō

Under certain conditions the vowel of the simple word also changes when it serves as part of a compound. The diphthong **-ae-**, for example, becomes **-ī-** (long):

dē + caedō = dēcīdō   re- + quaerō = requīrō

When the word to which a prefix is added has a short **-a-** or **-e-** at the end of the first syllable, this vowel becomes **-i-** (short):

ad + agō = adigō   in + capiō = incipiō
dē + jaciō = dējiciō   re- + teneō = retineō

If the first syllable of the word to which a prefix is added is closed,[1] short **-a-** therein often becomes **-e-**:

ad + captum = acceptum   per + factum = perfectum
dē + jactum = dējectum   retentum   (-e- remains unchanged)

Four common inseparable[2] prefixes are **dis-/dī-** (apart/away), **in-** (not/un-), **re-/red-** (again/against/back), and **sē-/sēd-** (apart/aside/away).

dis- + facilis = difficilis   in- + amīcus = inimīcus
red- + agō   = redigō (redāctum)   sē- + parō   = sēparō

Sē- is a part of the adjective **sēcūrus** (free from care/safe/secure), which is derived from the phrase **sē** (old preposition = **sine**) **cūrā** (without care). The prefix is also found in **sēditiō** (sedition/insurrection—lit., act of going apart), made up of prefix **sēd-** + **-itiō** (from **eō/itum**).

Give the principal parts of the compound formed from **sē-** + **cēdō**. Explain the meaning and give English derivatives.

---

[1]A syllable is closed when it ends in one or more consonants; it is open if it ends in a vowel or diphthong.

[2]i.e., that do not occur independently.

61

Both the Colosseum and the Arch of Constantine demonstrate Roman use of the arch.

ROMAN ARCHITECTURE

As in other fields, the Romans learned much from the Greeks and their building techniques. Sulla, for instance, removed some columns from the temple of Olympian Zeus at Athens and brought them to Rome, where they served as a model for the Roman-Corinthian order of architecture.

However, Roman buildings are generally not considered as beautiful as Greek buildings, because their proportions are less perfect. The Romans, moreover, tended to use excessive ornamentation without making it an integral part of the structure. Thus it was a peculiarly Roman practice to use columns for merely decorative (as opposed to constructive) purposes.

Greek architects adopted the post-and-lintel system, relegating the arch to subterranean structures. Roman architects, on the other hand, employed arches wherever possible. They had developed an excellent cement that hardened to strong and durable concrete. Since the pouring of concrete requires wooden forms, and since it is economical to use the same forms again and again, the arch became a popular structural element at Rome. The most striking example is no doubt the Colosseum, where every story is supported by a huge arcade. The same principle is observed in Roman aqueducts. Depending on the height required, these may consist of one or several rows of arches, one on top of another.

Their excellent concrete enabled Roman architects to build vaults and domes whose daring grandeur remains impressive to this day. The dome of the Pantheon, for example, measures more than a hundred and forty feet in diameter. Enough has survived of the Baths of Caracalla and of Diocletian, also, to let us imagine their former spaciousness and splendor.

A type of Roman building that continued for centuries to be a model for Christian churches and cathedrals was the basilica. It was a rectangular roofed hall, sometimes divided into aisles by pillars supporting the spectators' galleries. Basilicas served as law courts, exchanges, and bazaars; in short, they were indoor forums. Although many were later converted into Christian churches, these structures are still often called "basilicas."

Except for domed or vaulted structures, basilicas and temples had either flat or pitched roofs upheld by columns. To top their columns the Romans adopted mainly the Corinthian capital, although the Greeks from whom they borrowed the design had also developed two other, simpler capitals, the Ionic and the Doric. The more ornate design of the Corinthian capital, resembling the leaf of the acanthus plant, appealed to the Roman taste for elaborate ornamentation.

With adaptations to locally available materials, buildings in all parts of the Roman world were much alike. Local slaves or a branch of the Roman army comparable to a corps of engineers constructed many splendid public buildings, which were financed from the State Treasury.

From early times, permanent buildings were made of stone and unfired brick, but no examples of such brick have survived. In Augustus' time, fired bricks were in general use. In fact, buildings can often be dated rather accurately from their bricks, especially since such bricks frequently were stamped with identifying marks by their makers.

Walls of Roman buildings were not made of bricks alone, however, even after firing made the bricks more durable. Basically, walls were made of stonework or concrete, and the concrete was usually faced with stone or brick. Unfaced concrete was used in foundations and substructures that would not be visible when the building was completed.

Stone and brick facings might in turn be covered with plaster or stucco. The latter became a natural ground for decorations, especially in the interiors of houses. The finest kind of stucco was made of lime, sand, white marble dust, water or milk, and an albuminous substance. This *caementum marmoreum* was hard to distinguish from marble itself. Both marble cement and marble slabs were widely used for decoration, and various kinds of colored marble were imported from all parts of the empire. Pertinent to this practice is Augustus' often quoted remark that he found Rome a city of brick and left it a city of marble.

Staircases and remnants of upper stories that were excavated at Herculaneum and Pompeii show that the Romans sometimes built houses several stories high. Overcrowding led Roman builders to pile up buildings to dangerous heights. Because of this practice, Augustus was forced to decree that no building was to exceed seventy feet in height.

Above: A hut urn of pottery in the form of the earliest and simplest Roman house.

Below: The Italian artist Giovanni Paolo Pannini (1691-1765) painted *The Interior of the Pantheon at Rome,* which is in The National Gallery in Washington, D.C. The outstanding characteristics of Roman building, the dome and the arch, are evident, as are ornate Corinthian capitals on the columns that ring the edifice.

Above: Some of the mosaic facing has fallen away from the wall of this Pompeian building. Marble slabs or stone were more commonly used than mosaic. Right: An acanthus plant. The leaves of this plant form the motif for much Roman architectural decoration. In the Pantheon painting on the facing page, note the motif on the columns.

Below: These temples are in the Forum Boarium in Rome. The smaller round building, more properly a shrine sacred to a secondary divinity, has Corinthian capitals. The rectangular temple was once coated with stucco. Though its columns are of Greek style, the rear five are freestanding, in Roman fashion.

How many complete Latin words can you find in the inscription? The first two letters D M stand for DIS MANIBUS (To the spirits of the departed).

YOU CAN
READ LATIN

In learning to read Latin you must master the signals which carry meanings. Recognizing the signals of a language is as important as knowing its vocabulary.

In English you automatically recognize certain meaningful signals. For example, when you see or hear the word "dogs" you know that it refers to more than one dog; the -s on the end is a plural signal. Similarly, when you see or hear the Latin word for "dogs" (**canēs**) you know it is plural from the ending **-ēs,** which on a noun or adjective is nearly always a plural signal. (Exception: **nūbēs,** cloud/clouds)

English has comparatively few signals, while Latin, being a highly inflected language, has many. In Latin, therefore, more than in English, familiarity with all the signals is essential. This familiarity is acquired through a thorough knowledge of conjugations and declensions.

Important as signals are, it is often essential also to make a careful analysis of other grammatical features of a language. The more complicated the language is, the more necessary such an analysis becomes.

Yet to read the Latin in this book you do not have to be able to give names to ablatives or accusatives when they are accompanied by prepositions, nor to clauses that have conjunctions to introduce them. But you must understand how the various case and verb forms relate to each other and to the rest of the sentence.

In reading or speaking English you automatically divide sentences into thought units. For the most part, these thought groups coincide with grammatical structure. Read aloud the following paragraph, which explains and illustrates this point.

In reading a text‖you must separate‖the various subdivisions‖or thought units‖of the text.‖In fact‖your skill in reading‖and comprehending your own language‖depends very largely‖on your ability‖to identify the thought units‖as your eyes meet them‖in the text.‖In this very paragraph‖the thought units‖have been separated‖from each other‖by double bars.‖This kind of separation‖is somehow made automatically‖by the rapid reader.‖In reading another language‖you have to learn‖to do exactly‖the same thing.

Here is a Latin passage divided into thought units. As you read it aloud, notice how much easier it appears to be when thus arranged.

Prīmā lūce‖summus mōns‖ā Labiēnō tenēbātur.‖Ipse‖ab hostium castrīs‖nōn longius‖mīlle et quīngentīs passibus aberat, ‖neque‖ut posteā ex captīvīs comperit‖aut ipsīus adventus‖ aut Labiēnī‖cognitus erat. . . .

Multō dēnique diē‖per explōrātōrēs‖Caesar cognōvit‖et montem ā suīs tenērī‖et Helvētiōs castra mōvisse‖et Cōnsidium timōre perterritum‖quod nōn vīdisset‖prō vīsō‖sibi renūntiāsse.

You can easily learn to form such thought units. When the meaning of a single unit is not clear you can at least isolate it from the others and try to make an intelligent guess as to what it may mean.

Stretch

Actors in ancient plays wore masks and costumes designed to reveal what characters they portrayed. A typical tragic mask is at the left. The comic slave at the right is probably a runaway who has taken refuge at the altar on which he is seated.

THE ALCESTIS STORY

Alcestis was the wife of Admetus, king of Pherae in Thessaly. The story develops from the circumstances under which Admetus might prolong his life. The Fates had promised the god Apollo that Admetus need not die at the appointed time if he could find someone willing to die in his stead. But all refuse to serve as his substitute: strangers in the land, his soldiers, slaves, even his parents. Finally, Admetus' wife, Alcestis, unselfishly offers to die in his place.

A comic element is added to the story by Hercules, who, unaware of Alcestis' death, drinks and makes merry in the palace. Upon learning of her self-sacrifice, Hercules rushes off to fight with Death and later restores Alcestis to her husband and children. The story was dramatized by the Greek poet Euripides and produced in 438 B.C.

The Greek myth of Alcestis and Admetus deals with the separation by death of the royal couple. On this Etruscan vase their farewell to each other is pictured, with demons from the underworld looking on.

Thessalia maxima atque pulcherrima regiō Graeciae an-
tīquae erat. Rēgēs hujus regiōnis magnās dīvitiās habēbant
et in rēgiīs pulchrīs habitābant. In agrīs atque in vīllīs Thessaliae multī servī erant, quī bellō captī erant.

Ūna ex urbibus Thessaliae erat Pherae; hujus urbis Admētus 5
erat rēx. Ubi Admētus Alcestem pulchram in mātrimōnium
dūxit, magnum fuit in rēgnō gaudium. Dīvitiae Admētī
magnopere augēbantur atque, incolīs contentīs dīligenter
labōrantibus, agrī magnam cōpiam frūmentī reddēbant. Mox
Admētus erat rēx Thessaliae potentissimus.   10

Brevī tempore autem rūmōrēs sēcrētō vulgābantur verbīs
ōrāculī vītam Admētī brevem futūram esse. Admētus ipse
quidem hoc ōrāculī dictum adhūc ignōrāvit.

Interim ā Jove Apollō dē Olympō dēscendere et mortālī
per ūnum annum servīre jussus erat. Juppiter enim pūnīre 15
Apollinem in animō habuit, quod ille Cyclōpēs innocentēs
interfēcerat.

Apollō ex caelō terrās beātās Thessaliae dēspexerat. Itaque,
omnibus īnsignibus dīvīnīs dēpositīs, cum lyrā tantum ad
Admētī rēgnum vēnit. Tōtum annum Apollō pāstor gregum 20
rēgiōrum erat.

Dolēns dē morte Admētī appropinquante, Apollō prō rēge
dōnum vītae aeternae ā Fātīs petīvit. Fāta, quamquam
Apollinī concessērunt, tamen monuērunt sē diē cōnstitūtā
alterīus vītam prō vītā rēgis postulātūra esse.   25

vulgābantur were being spread abroad • **ignōrāvit** did not
know • **mortālī ... servīre** be a slave to (serve) a mortal
Cyclōpēs, -um M. pl., Cyclopes, legendary one-eyed giants of Sicily
beātās rich, fertile • **dēspexerat** had looked down upon
grex, gregis M., flock, herd • **concessērunt** yielded • **diē
cōnstitūtā** on the appointed day (note fem. gender)

LIFE IS DEAR

Diēs mortis cōnstitūta jam appropinquat. Apollō, quī
annum servitūtis cōnfēcit, Admētō dīcit.

Apollō. Tōtum annum gregēs tuōs cūrāvī, deum dissimulātus. Nōn sum pāstor; deus Apollō sum. Cognōvī igitur
perīculum mortis tibi maximum esse. Properā! Temptā 5
sine morā hominem invenīre prō tē mortem dēligentem.
Valē! Ad Olympum redeō. (Exit Apollō.)

Admētus (servīs dīcēns). Īte! Petite omnēs advenās urbis!
Dūcite eōs ad rēgiam!

Servī. Haec, ō rēx, quam celerrimē faciēmus. (Exeunt 10
servī.)

Servī reveniunt, dūcentēs advenās.

Admētus (advenīs convocātīs). Vōs convocāvī, quod advenae adestis in hāc terrā. Hīc neque uxōrēs neque līberōs
habētis. Auxilium ā vōbīs petō. Diēs mortis mihi cōn- 15
stitūta jam appropinquat. Sī quis ē numerō vestrō mortem
prō mē dēlēgerit, in ejus honōre magnum sepulchrum
aedificābō atque dōna splendida ad ejus parentēs mittam.

Prīmus Advena. Hoc praemium mortis numquam accipiam!

Advenae Secundus Tertiusque. Hoc praemium mortis num- 20
quam accipiēmus!

Advenae Omnēs (ūnā vōce). Nēmō hoc praemium mortis
accipiet! (Exeunt advenae.)

Admētus (mīlitibus). Saepe prō mē, rēge vestrō, in proeliō
vōs vītam dare velle dīxistis. Nōnne melius est pāce 25
dēcēdere dē vītā et in patriā sepelīrī?

Mīles. Bellō mors mīlitis in longinquā terrā pugnantis
glōriōsa est, sed pāce mortem petere nōlō. Vultisne,
comitēs, mortem petere?

Mīlitēs Omnēs. Minimē! Minimē! (Exeunt mīlitēs.) 30

Admētus (servīs). Bonī servī estis. Cotīdiē multās hōrās
in agrīs vīllīsque labōrātis. Saepe vōs vītam prō dominō
dare velle dīxistis. Sī quis ē numerō vestrō mortem prō
mē dēlēgerit, līberīs ejus lībertātem, domum, dīvitiās dabō.
Servus ipse magnum sepulchrum et nōmen nōtum habēbit. 35

Servus (capite dējectō). Servō sīcut rēgī vīta cāra est.

deum dissimulātus concealing my divinity, pretending not to be a
god • **quam celerrimē** as quickly as possible • **sī quis** if
anyone • **dējectus, -a, -um** lowered, bowed

Līberī nostrī suam lībertātem petant. Mortem prō tē dēligere nōn possum.

Servī Omnēs (capitibus dējectīs). Mortem dēligere nōn possumus. (Exeunt servī omnēs.) ₄₀

ADMETUS' PARENTS REFUSE DEATH

Admētus dēspērāns parentēs suōs vocāvit.

Admētus (patrī dīcēns). Aetāte jam cōnfectus es neque tuae tempus mortis longē abest. Utram dēligēs? Vītamne tuam an fīliī tuī? Tū omnēs laetitiās vītae habuistī, quās deī hominibus dant. Per multōs annōs rēx fuistī, ₅ cui ego, fīlius tuus, honōrem dedī. Sapientēs senēs, aetāte exanimātōs, mortem sibi saepe petere . . .

Pater (interrumpēns). Morte proximā, mī fīlī, nēmō ad Orcum īre dēsīderat neque senectūs jam onus est. Ubi mihi succēdēns rēx hujus terrae factus es, laetus fuī. ₁₀ Mortem autem prō tē dēligere nōlō. Lūcem diēī amās. Num eandem lūcem patrī odiōsam esse putās? Saepe mihi dīcō vītam brevem sed cāram esse atque nōs omnēs diū in sepulchrō futūrōs esse.

Admētus (mātrī dīcēns ācriter). Quam crūdēlia sunt verba ₁₅ patris! Māter mea, mihi cārissima, ego tibi ūnus fīlius sum. Mihi semper bene voluistī. Vīta brevis est atque . . .

Māter (multīs cum lacrimīs). Rēs domesticae meae gravēs sunt. Officia mea sunt multa. Prīmō familiam ōrdināre dēbeō. Quamquam fīlius meus es, tamen prō tē mortem ₂₀ nōndum petere possum. (Exeunt māter paterque.)

---

uter, utra, utrum which (of the two) • **laetitia, -ae** F., joy
exanimātōs weakened, exhausted • **senectūs, -ūtis** F., old age • **officium, -ī** N., duty • **familia, -ae** F., household

A WILLING SUBSTITUTE

Alcestis invenit Admētum quī morī aequō animō parat.

Alcestis. Tū es rēx, conjūnx mī; morī parāre nōn dēbēs.

aequō animō calmly • **morior, morī, mortuus sum** die

Admētus (maestus). Diēs ā Fātīs cōnstitūta paene adest, conjūnx mea!

Alcestis. Rēx populum cūrat, rem pūblicam tōtam adminis- 5 trat, exercitum in proelium dūcit, fīnēs ab hostibus dē- fendit. Praetereā rēx deīs dōna sacrificiaque nōmine cīvitātis dat.

Admētus. Mox alius rēx mihi succēdet populumque meum cūrābit. 10

Alcestis. Quis reget, tē mortuō? Fīlius tuus puerulus est, quī haec facere nōn potest. Laeta meam vītam prō tē dabō.

Admētus (vōce territā). Minimē! Minimē! Tantum sacri- ficium accipere nōn possum. Ego ipse mortem dēligam! 15

Alcestis (aequō animō). Ego fēmina populum cūrāre, rem pūblicam administrāre, exercitum in proelium dūcere, fīnēs ab hostibus dēfendere, deīs dōna sacrificiaque nōmine cīvitātis dare nōn possum. Servāre autem vītam tuam possum; prō tē mortem petere possum. 20

Admētus (lacrimāns). Vae! Vae! Quantum sacrificium deī postulant! Nōlī mē relinquere!

Alcestis. Jam morī parāre dēbeō. Gemmīs pretiōsīs et pallā pulcherrimā adōrnāta mortem petam. (Exit Alcestis.)

Admētus. Vae! Vae! Prō mē Alcestis vītam suam dare 25 vult.

A TIME OF MOURNING

Stāns prope āram Admētus, capite dējectō, expectat Alcestem. Appropinquat Alcestis dūcēns fīlium fīliamque. Rēgīna, gemmīs pretiōsīs adōrnāta, pulcherrimam pallam gerit.

Alcestis. Venīte, līberī; ad patrem vestrum eāmus. Pater 5 bene vōs cūrābit.

Admētus (līberōs accipiēns). Vae! Vae! Prō mē, mī fīlī, fīlia mea, māter vestra mortem dēligit.

Līberī lacrimāre incipiunt.

Alcestis. Nōlīte lacrimāre, līberī meī. Meā voluntāte 10 mortem petō. Nōlī dolēre, conjūnx mī. Bene līberōs nostrōs cūrā. Nōlī in mātrimōnium fēminam alteram

73

dūcere. Nōlī eīs, tuō fīliō, tuae fīliae, novercam dare.
Sīs līberīs et pater et māter.

Admētus. Bene līberōs nostrōs cūrābō. Līberīs et pater 15
et māter erō. Numquam novercam . . .

Alcestis līberīs suāvia dat; deinde ad āram prōcēdit, in
quā manum dextram pōnit.

Alcestis (magnā vōce). Meā voluntāte vītam prō conjuge dō.
Ō Apollō, dā signum, et populus meum arbitrium probābit. 20

Apollō (dē caelō). Lēx perfecta est. Haec fēmina prō ārā
deōrum stāns vītam prō conjuge prōmīsit. Brevī tempore
Alcestis ē vītā excēdet.

Exeunt līberī cum Alceste. Admētus vocat nūntium.

Admētus (nūntiō dīcēns). Ī! Nūntiā omnibus ea quae 25
nunc jubeō. Fūnera rēgīnae idōnea celebrārī jubeō. Ut
omnēs crīnibus tōnsīs atque vestibus ātrīs dolōrem dēmōns-
trent. Tondeant etiam equīs[1] jubās atque currūs ōrnā-
mentīs nūdātōs agant. Nōn erit sonus tībiārum aut lyrārum
in hōc rēgnō per duodecim mēnsēs. Alcestī, quae maximum 30
amōrem atque maximam pietātem dēmōnstrāvit, quae sōla
mortem prō mē dēlēgit, summōs honōrēs dabimus. Hōc
diē ipse corpus Alcestis in sepulchrō extrā moenia urbis
pōnam, quod rēgīna ante tempus nātūrā cōnstitūtum
moritūra est. 35

noverca, -ae F., stepmother • **suāvium, -ī** N., kiss (with **dare** =
to kiss) • **arbitrium, -ī** N., decision • **fūnus, -eris** N.,
funeral, funeral rites • **ut** (with subjunctive) introduces a wish
crīnis, -is M., hair • **tondeō, tondēre, totondī, tōnsum** shear,
crop • **juba, -ae** F., mane • **tībia, -ae** F., flute • **pie-
tās, -ātis** F., sense of duty, devotion

A STRANGER AT THE GATES

Herculēs, quī ā rēge Eurystheō ad Thrāciam īre jussus
erat, in Thessaliam pervēnit.

Herculēs (ad rēgiam veniēns). Estne domī rēx Admētus?

[1]Dative of reference; translate as a genitive.

Custōs. Admētus domī est. Quō nōmine appellāris? Cūr in hanc urbem vēnistī?   5

Herculēs. Tū servus īnsolēns! Herculēs sum, rēgis Admētī amīcus.

Hōc mōmentō temporis Admētus, vestēs ātrās gerēns, crīnibus dētōnsīs, lentē ē rēgiā ambulat.

Admētus. Salvē, Herculē, fīlī Jovis!   10
Herculēs. Salvē, Admēte, rēx Thessaliae!
Admētus. Cognōvī, Herculē, tē mihi velle bene.
Herculēs (cōnspectū rēgis perturbātus). Quid haec signa dolōris indicant?
Admētus. Rēgia hodiē est dolōris domus.   15
Herculēs. Quis mortuus est? Num fīlius? Num fīlia?
Admētus. Līberī meī vīvunt.
Herculēs. Estne pater longaevus mortuus?
Admētus. Pater meus vīvit māterque mea.
Herculēs. Estne rēgīna Alcestis mortua?   20
Admētus. Alcestis et vīvit et nōn vīvit.
Herculēs. Quid significant haec verba ancipitia?
Admētus. Nōnne sortem Alcestī cōnstitūtam intellegis?
Herculēs. Intellegō eam prō tē vītam dare velle.
Admētus. Nōnne igitur Alcestis jam mortua est?   25
Herculēs. Nōlī dē uxōre mātūrius dolēre!
Admētus. Alcestis mortua est! Quae moritūra est nōn jam vīvit.
Herculēs. Dissimillimae inter sē sunt mors et vīta.
Admētus. Haec tū sentīs; alia ego.   30
Herculēs. Quae jam est dolōris causa? Quī amīcus mortuus est?
Admētus. Hodiē fēminam in sepulchrō positūrus. . . .
Herculēs (interrumpēns). Cōnsanguineane an aliēnigena?
Admētus. Aliēnigena, sed ā familiā magnopere amāta. . . .   35
Herculēs (interrumpēns iterum). Adventus hospitis dolentibus incommodus est. Ad aliam domum ībō.

---

anceps, gen., **ancipitis** ambiguous • **sors, sortis** F., lot, fate
mātūrius (adv.) too early • **cōnsanguineus, -a, -um** related
(by blood) • **aliēnigenus, -a, -um** foreign(-born) • **hospes,**
-itis M./F., guest • **incommodus, -a, -um** inconvenient

75

Admētus. Minimē! Servus tē dūcet in penetrālia, quae sonīs dolōris longē absunt. (Herculēs et servus exeunt.)

penetrālia, -ium N. pl., the interior (part of a building)

AN UNTIMELY GUEST

Pompa fūneris ad sepulchrum extrā moenia prōcēdit. Servus Admētī, vestēs ātrās gerēns, ex penetrālibus ad apertās rēgiae portās lentē ambulat.

Servus. Advenae ē multīs terrīs longinquīs ad rēgiam vēnērunt. Mēnsās omnibus viātōribus extrūxī, sed num- 5 quam pejōrem hospitem quam istum vīdī.

Custōs. Tibi bene volō, quod iste hospes est maximus et ferōcissimus et fortissimus virōrum quōs vīdī. Dīcit sē nūdīs manibus leōnem interfēcisse. Pellem leōnis ab umerō pendentem gerit atque clāvam ingentem portat. 10

Servus (magnopere perturbātus). Is vir quidem est mendāx! Mihi sē ad Thrāciam iter facere dēclārat; sē ā quōdam rēge equōs Diomēdis ā Thrāciā redūcere jussum esse; hōs equōs carnem hominum edere; Diomēdem, virum crūdē- lissimum, equīs terribilibus omnēs advenās prōjicere; sē 15 autem ipsum paucīs mēnsibus cum equīs reditūrum esse.

Custōs (acerbē). Eum ad Thessaliam umquam revenīre nōlō!

Servus (violenter). Hunc hominem nōn amō. Rēgiam sertīs fūneris ōrnātam videt, sed in portās intrāre audet. Deinde, calamitāte nostrā cognitā, hospitium rēgis bonō animō nōn 20 accēpit. Maximam cēnam parārī jussit; in capite ingentem myrtī sertam posuit. Etiam ex hāc portā canēns audīrī potest! Nōnne hunc hospitem jūstē ōdī? Sed nunc mē vocat. (Exit servus.)

pompa, -ae F., procession • **mēnsa, -ae** F., table • **ex- trūxī** I have loaded, spread (with food) • **istum** (acc. sing.) that guy • **pendēns,** gen., **pendentis** hanging • **mendāx, -ācis** M., liar • **quōdam** (abl. sing.) a certain • **carō, carnis** F., flesh • **prōjicere** drive out, expel • **homō, -inis** M., fel- low, guy • **serta, -ae** F., wreath, garland • **hospitium, -ī** N., hospitality • **bonō animō** in the proper spirit, with good grace • **myrtus, -ī** F., myrtle • **ōdī** I hate

Herculēs, sertam ā capite removēns, servō in penetrālia intrantī īrātissimus exclāmat.

Herculēs. Cūr tam maestus atque ānxius es? Bonus servus trīstis nōn est, sed laetō animō hospitibus dominī administrat. 5

Servus. Magnus dolor nōs tenet; itaque capita tōnsa et vestēs ātrās et vultūs maestōs vidēs.

Herculēs. Nunc mihi vērum dīc! Ā fenestrā penetrālium pompam fūneris vīdī—rēgem, fīlium rēgis, omnēs Thessaliae prīncipēs, multitūdinem cīvium—omnēs dōna ferentēs. 10 Tū ipse cum custōde jānuae modo lacrimābās. Quid cēlāre temptās?

Servus (perterritus). Fēlīx hospes ad hanc rēgiam vēnistī. Dolōris nostrī causam vēram nōn intellegis, quod dominus meus lēgēs hospitiī observat. 15

Herculēs. Quem Admētus in sepulchrō positūrus est?

Servus (lacrimāns). Ō advena, uxor Admētī nōn jam vīvit!

Herculēs (dolōre permōtus). Cūr mihi deōs mīsisse tantum dolōrem ad hanc domum mātūrius nōn nārrāvistī? Ubi Admētus Alcestem sepelit? 20

Servus. Extrā moenia urbis prope viam Lārissam dūcentem est sepulchrum marmoreum. In hōc sepulchrō Alcestis rēgīna sepeliētur.

Herculēs. Dā mihi clāvam meam! Immō manūs nūdae meliōrēs erunt! Remanē hīc! Tacē! (Exit Herculēs.) 25

trīstis, -e sad, glum • **administrat** (with dative) serves, waits on • **vultus, -ūs** M., face, expression • **modo** just now **mātūrius** (adv.) sooner • **marmoreus, -a, -um** (of) marble **immō** (adv.) no, rather; on the contrary • **tacē!** be silent!/quiet!

HERCULES FIGHTS WITH DEATH

Admētus et comitēs maestī ad urbem redeunt. Rēx in rēgiae līmine stat.

Admētus. Relinquite mē, amīcī, dolōrī meō! Sors uxōris

līmen, -inis N., threshold, doorway

meae fēlīcior est quam sors mea. Fātum jūstum effūgī; posthāc vītam miseram agam. 5

Admētus dolēns prō līmine sedet. Comitēs maestī lentē excēdunt.

Servus. Ecce, domine! Iste Herculēs fēminam vēlātam dūcēns ad rēgiam appropinquat. 10
Herculēs. Vir amīcō, Admēte, sine dolō dīcere dēbet. Tū mihi nōn dīxistī fēminam mortuam uxōrem tuam esse.
Admētus. Sortem uxōris meae īnfēlīcem cēlāvī, nōlēns tē ad domum aliam īre.
Herculēs. Dūcō hanc fēminam. . . . 15
Admētus (interrumpēns). Dūc eam ex cōnspectū meō! Fōrma hujus fēminae meam uxōrem mortuam in memoriam redūcit.
Herculēs. Dūc eam ipse, Admēte, quaesō, in rēgiam tuam. Aliquandō gaudēbis. 20
Admētus. Minimē! Dīmitte fēminam!
Herculēs. Magnam victōriam tulī! Haec mātrōna praemium fuit. Jam, quaesō, cūrā eam, dum in Thrāciā absum. Hoc enim est magnī labōris praemium.
Admētus (invītus). Bene est. Servam vocābō; serva in 25 penetrālia rēgiae eam dūcet.
Herculēs. Ipse eam dūcere dēbēs. Tibi sōlī eam committam.
Admētus. Minimē! Eam tangere recūsō!
Herculēs. Ipse manū eam dūcere dēbēs! Prōtende dextram tuam! Tange manum advenae!

Admētus manum lentē prōtendit; manum fēminae invītus 30 tangit.

Herculēs. Tenēsne manum ejus?
Admētus. Teneō.
Herculēs (vēlāmen fēminae removēns). Ecce, uxor tua vīvit!
Admētus (attonitus). Quōmodo Alcestis vīvere potest? Ego 35

---

posthāc (adv.) after this, hereafter • **vēlātus, -a, -um** veiled
quaesō (used parenthetically) I beg you, please • **gaudēbis**
you will be glad • **victōriam ferre** win a victory • **mātrōna,**
-ae F., lady • **tangō, -ere, tetigī, tāctum** touch • **vēlā-**
men, -inis N., veil • **quōmodo** (adv.) how

78

ipse corpus conjugis meae in sepulchrō posuī. Quōmodo
eam ab Orcō redūxistī?

Herculēs. Lībātiōnēs deum Mortem occupātum tenēbant.
Subitō in eum saluī et balteō meō alligāvī. Sīc Mortem
vīcī. Alcestis, vīva incolumisque, praemium victōriae ₄₀
est. Cum uxōre amātā, Admēte, longam atque beātam
vītam agās. Jam necesse est mē labōrem mihi ā rēge Eurystheō impositum perficere. Valē!

Admētus (laetissimus). Manē apud nōs, Herculē, et accipe
praemia tuōrum labōrum.   ₄₅

Herculēs. In deōrum manibus est. Valē! Reveniam!

Admētus. Bene vertat! Tūtus reveniās!

Herculēs ē rēgiā discēdit. Admētus et Alcestis in rēgiam
eunt; populus laetus signa dolōris removēre incipit.

lībātiō, -ōnis F., libation, drink-offering • **saluī** I leapt
balteus, -ī M., sword-belt • **alligāvī** I tied, bound • **impositum** (with **mihi**) set, imposed (on me) • **vertat** may it turn out

WORD MASTERY 4

A number of Latin adjectives denoting capacity or quality
end in **-ilis/-bilis.** These suffixes are added sometimes to the
verb base and sometimes to the base of the perfect participle.
Corresponding English adjectives end in -ile/-ble. Example:
from **agō** comes **agilis**/agile (quick to move); from **flectō/flexum**
comes **flexibilis**/flexible (able to be bent).

Give the Latin adjectives in **-ilis** based on **faciō, dūcō,
mittō,** and their English derivatives. Name the Latin verbs
from which the following adjectives were formed and give
the corresponding English adjectives.

docilis   **fragilis**   **textilis**   **volātilis**

The suffix **-bilis** was applied more widely than **-ilis.** When
joined to the vowel **-ā-** or **-i-** to form **-ābilis/-ibilis,** the suffix
came into English as -able/-ible. Example: from **arō** comes
arābilis/arable (able to be plowed).

79

Name the Latin verbs from which the following Latin adjectives were formed and give the corresponding English adjectives.

plācābilis   **comprehēnsibilis**   **crēdibilis**   **terribilis**

The English suffix -able has in some cases been borrowed from French where it can be attached to any verb stem; e.g., "comfortable," from French *confortable*, from *conforter* (to comfort). It is also added to nouns of French/Latin origin to form English adjectives, as "fashionable," "seasonable," and to native English verbs, as in "breakable," "understandable."

Other common Latin adjectives end in the suffixes **-cus/ -icus/-ticus/-ius**. These generally mean "of" or "pertaining to" and are added to the base of a noun. Give the corresponding English word for each Latin adjective and the Latin noun that supplies the base. Example: **rūsticus**/rustic, from **rūs** (country) + **-ticus**.

cīvicus   **Ītalicus**   **aquāticus**   **uxōrius**

The Latin suffix **-uus**, meaning "inclined to," forms adjectives from verbs. What are the corresponding English adjectives and the Latin verb from which each Latin adjective is derived? Example: **dēciduus**/deciduous, from **dēcidō** (fall off).

continuus   **cōnspicuus**   **nocuus**   **innocuus**

Another suffix that has the same function and meaning as **-ōsus** (full of) is **-lentus/-lent**. This is joined to a noun base by a stem or connecting vowel (**-i-, -o-, -u-**); e.g., **turba** (commotion/crowd) + **-u-** + **-lentus** = **turbulentus**/turbulent (full of commotion). Form similar Latin/English adjectives from the following nouns.

vīs   **fraus**   **opēs** (pl.)   **succus**

LOOK AND THINK   Under the influence of the English adjective suffix -ous from Latin **-ōsus**, many derivatives of Latin words that ended in **-us/-ius/-uus** have become -ous/-ious/-uous in English.

odōrus/odorous   **varius**/various   **arduus**/arduous

Mosaic of a Carthaginian ship found near Sousse (ancient Hadrumetum)

ROME AND CARTHAGE

In the third century B.C. two great cities, one in Africa, the other in Italy, were rivals for the supremacy of the Mediterranean world. Carthage was already an important trading post for the western part of the Mediterranean when Rome, according to tradition, was founded in 753 B.C.

Established in the ninth century B.C. by Phoenician merchants from Tyre and Sidon, Carthage later became the most powerful commercial center in the Mediterranean area. As the Carthaginians, in expanding their trade, set up trading posts throughout the Mediterranean, they closed the sea to the commerce of all other nations.

Meanwhile the Romans were emerging as masters of Italy. They subdued neighboring tribes, founded colonies throughout the Italian peninsula, and formed alliances with other communities, including Greek settlements in southern Italy **(Magna Graecia)**. Rome's influence had not yet extended beyond the Italian peninsula, however, when the Carthaginians took possession of Sardinia, Corsica, and western Sicily.

As long as Carthaginian holdings were limited to western Sicily, Roman interests were reasonably safe. In 265 B.C., however, Rome and Carthage became involved in a dispute over Messana (modern Messina), a city in eastern Sicily. Control of this city by Carthage would close the Sicilian

81

straits to all foreign ships and cut off the important sea route between Rome and her Greek allies in southern Italy.

War broke out the following year between the Romans and the Carthaginians. Known as the First Punic War, the fighting dragged on for more than twenty years, ending in 241 B.C. in a Roman victory. The Carthaginians not only lost Sicily but also had to return all prisoners and pay a heavy indemnity.

With the winning of Sicily began Rome's expansion outside the Italian peninsula. Sicily became the first Roman province. A few years after the end of the first war, the Romans responded to an appeal for protection made by mutinous mercenaries on Sardinia. Eventually Rome took possession of both Sardinia and Corsica, and these islands became the second Roman province.

The Carthaginians meanwhile were establishing a stronghold in Spain, with a city named for their African capital— New Carthage (modern Cartagena). A treaty between Carthage and Rome made the Ebro (**Hibērus/Ibērus**) river the northern limit of Carthaginian influence in Spain and also guaranteed the independence of Saguntum, a town south of the Ebro that was friendly to Rome.

In 219 B.C., ignoring the treaty between Carthage and Rome, Hannibal—the most formidable general the Romans ever had to face—attacked and took Saguntum after a siege of eight months. Thus began the Second Punic War.

With the home government in Africa supporting his action, Hannibal then moved swiftly to take the Romans by surprise. Early the next year, leaving his brother Hasdrubal in command of a covering force in Spain, he marched rapidly north and crossed the Pyrenees mountains. His purpose was to carry the war into Italy.

The Romans had hoped to turn Hannibal back at the Rhone, but the Carthaginians had already crossed that river before the Roman consul Publius Cornelius Scipio could transport his two legions by ship from Italy to the mouth of the Rhone. Although Hannibal met no opposition from the Romans, he nevertheless suffered other delays, and his plan to reach the Alps by late summer failed. It was November when the Carthaginians, with an army of 50,000 infantry, 9000 cavalry, and about forty elephants, began their ascent of the Alps.

UNIT I

An imaginative portrait of the Carthaginian general, Hannibal—being a detail from a painting in the Louvre by Giovanni Battista Tiepolo (1696-1770)

THE CARTHAGINIANS

Reliable information about the Carthaginians is hard to obtain. The view presented by ancient historians is undoubtedly prejudiced, since both Greeks and Romans were bitter enemies of Carthage. Even literature written in the Punic language adds little to our knowledge of the people who produced it, since Carthaginian writings consist almost entirely of records and inventories.

The Carthaginians and their ancestors, the Phoenicians, were primarily traders, who by the nature of their business came into contact with the people of many countries. We are indebted to the Phoenicians for the development and diffusion of their alphabet, which is the basis of written language throughout the Western world.

For centuries the Phoenicians flourished in what is now Syria and Lebanon. They carried on trade all over the Mediterranean, bringing silver and tin from Spain, spices, perfume, and incense from Arabia, and copper and timber from Cyprus, and selling their own textiles and metal- and glasswork. Phoenician ships ventured as far west as the Scillies (off Southwest England) and perhaps reached Ireland. They may even have circumnavigated the continent of Africa in the sixth century B.C.

In 814 B.C., according to tradition, under the Tyrian princess Elissa (also called Dido), the Phoenicians founded Carthage (in Latin, *Carthago/Karthago*), whose Punic name (*Kart-Hadasht*) means "new city." In the *Aeneid*, Vergil called the Phoenician princess Dido and made her a contemporary of Aeneas, although historically the fall of Troy preceded the founding of Carthage by nearly four centuries.

The new Phoenician city pursued a policy of trade monopoly in the western Mediterranean. To this end it established outposts in Spain, Majorca and Minorca, Malta, Sicily, Sardinia, and Corsica. The Carthaginians supplied the ancient world with slaves, ivory, and gold dust from other parts of Africa. They also traded their own pottery and a crimson dye made from a sea snail (*murex*). Having almost no art of their own, the Carthaginians admired and collected art objects of other nations. They made and sold inferior wine, but themselves consumed large quantities of the better wines imported from Rhodes.

Their chief god seems to have been Baal. His name is often mentioned in the Old Testament, and the names of two famous Carthaginian generals, Hannibal and Hasdrubal, in Punic mean "favored by Baal" and "my help is Baal," respectively. Unlike most ancient religions, the beliefs of the Carthaginians forbade them to make images of either gods or human beings. On the other hand, the Carthaginian practice of sacrificing humans to Baal and other gods was looked upon with horror by most other peoples of ancient times.

Archaeological discoveries in Carthaginian Africa are too recent to be widely known. One important discovery was a whole Carthaginian town or colony (Dar Essafi) that had been built in the fifth century B.C. The outside walls of its well-built houses are white; the interior walls are covered with purple-colored stucco. Pink and white terrazzo floors, and baths, lavatories, sewers, and drains found in these houses are evidences of an advanced civilization.

This city has been excavated and found to be in much the same condition as it must have been when deserted by its inhabitants in 146 B.C. after the Romans had destroyed Carthage. The furnishings of the houses were simple, consisting mainly of large pottery jars for storage and of rough wooden chests which, after serving as storage pieces, eventually became their owners' coffins.

In 46 B.C. Julius Caesar, while in Africa for the purpose of completing the overthrow of his political enemies, ordered the reconstruction of Carthage. This city, which had been destroyed by the Romans one hundred years earlier, was destined to rise to prominence once more and to become the third city after Rome and Alexandria because of its strategic location in the Mediterranean.

The descendants of the original Carthaginians were by Caesar's time widely scattered throughout Africa. Because they had intermingled with other native populations, their language and customs had changed. They were no longer a united people, but they still retained certain qualities of stubbornness and persistence that caused them to resist at first the Roman program of restoration. Eventually, however, many of them began to see the advantages of coöperating with the Romans.

Gradually Latin replaced the Punic language, but early in the fifth century St. Augustine still quoted numerous Punic words. St. Augustine was a native African, having been born near Carthage, where he later studied and taught.

Other Africans who played a prominent part in the early Christian church are Tertullian, a native Carthaginian, who served as the Bishop of Carthage, and St. Cyprian, who was the first to write in Latin a major work on Christianity. Moreover, the Carthaginian town of Leptis Magna was the birthplace of the Roman Emperor Septimius Severus.

From 442 to 533 Carthage was under the rule of the Vandals, a Germanic people. During this period the Western Roman Empire passed out of existence (476), and only the Eastern (Byzantine) Roman Empire with Constantinople as its capital remained. Finally, in 533, when Justinian was emperor, the Roman general Belisarius landed in Africa and destroyed the Vandal kingdom.

Carthage was once more under Roman control, but then the Arabs invaded North Africa, and in 698 burned Carthage to the ground. Carthage has never been rebuilt.

85

Above: The remains of Carthaginian buildings, perhaps warehouses, on the North African coast. Left: A figure of the Punic goddess Tanit bears an inscription in Punic characters.

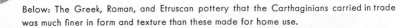

Below: The Greek, Roman, and Etruscan pottery that the Carthaginians carried in trade was much finer in form and texture than these made for home use.

Above: Carthaginian ships resembled Roman vessels of the same period. This mosaic is now in the museum at Sousse, near the site of ancient Carthage.

Above: Small Carthaginian amulets of colored glass paste in the form of masks of gods were popular trade objects and have been found around the Mediterranean.

Left: Small shrine sacred to Demeter, characterized by the figure of her sacred animal, the pig, and by the Greek style of the pillars. The worship of Demeter (Ceres) was adopted from the Greeks and Romans.

Hannibal ad Alpēs cum bonā pāce° Gallōrum ea loca incolentium pervēnit. Ubi ascendit in prīmōs clīvōs, montānōs
vīdit tumulōs īnsidentēs.° Hannibal signa cōnsistere jussit;
Gallōs mīsit quī loca explōrārent.

Postquam comperit sē trānsitum facere nōn posse, castra 5
in valle quam lātissimā potest° posuit. Tum per eōsdem
Gallōs quī cum montānīs colloquia habuerant Hannibal
doctus est° interdiū tantum° angustiās obsidērī, nocte in sua
quemque tēcta discēdere.

°**cum bonā pāce** with friendly toleration • **īnsidentēs** occupy-
ing • **quam lātissimā potest** the widest possible (valley)
doctus est learned, was informed • **tantum** only

angustiae, -ārum	F. pl., narrow pass
clīvus, -ī	M., slope
montānus, -ī	M., mountaineer
signum, -ī	N., (military) standard; signal
vallēs, -is	F., valley
trānsitus, -ūs	M., passage; crossing
quisque/quidque	each/every (one) (see page 432)
obsideō, -ēre, -sēdī, -sessum	besiege; obstruct
cōnsistō, -ere, -stitī, —	halt; **signa cōnsistere** = halt
incolō, -ere, -coluī, —	inhabit, live (in)
comperiō, -īre, -perī, -pertum	find out, discover

Lūce prīmā exercitus Poenōrum ad tumulōs subiit ut 10
hostēs crēderent sē interdiū impetum per angustiās factūrum
esse. Deinde eī castra mūnīvērunt eōdem locō quō
cōnstiterant.

Hannibal, ubi prīmum° montānōs nocte dē tumulīs discessisse laxātāsque custōdiās esse sēnsit, impedīmentīs cum 15

°**ubi prīmum** as soon as

[1]All but the last of the Latin selections in this unit are adaptations from the Roman historian Titus Livius (59 B.C.—A.D. 17). Livy began publishing under the Emperor Augustus a
history of Rome (Ab Urbe Condita) from its founding to 9 B.C. Only 35 of 142 books survive (1–10 and 21–45).

A village in the Alps in the region of Hannibal's crossing

equite et maximā parte peditum relictīs, ipse cum expedītīs celeriter ex angustiīs ēvāsit ut eōs ipsōs tumulōs quōs hostēs tenuerant occupāret.

custōdia, -ae	F., guard, watch
expedītus, -ī	M., light-armed soldier
impedīmenta, -ōrum	N. pl., baggage
laxō, -āre, -āvī, -ātum	relax, reduce
subeō, -īre, -iī, -itum	go or come up to, approach
quō	where, to/in which place

THE IMPERFECT SUBJUNCTIVE of all Latin verbs, both active and passive, is made up of the present active infinitive plus regular person endings.

I	II	III	III-iō	IV
portāret	monēret	dūceret	caperet	audīret
portārētur	monērētur	dūcerētur	caperētur	audīrētur

Imperfect subjunctive of irregular verbs is formed likewise by adding regular person endings to the present infinitive.

eō	sum	possum	volō	nōlō
īret	esset	posset	vellet	nōllet

For complete conjugations of verbs in the imperfect subjunctive, see the Summary of Grammar at the back of this book.

The Carthaginians were surprised by the Gallic mountain dwellers in a steep defile like this.

PURPOSE may be expressed in Latin by a subordinate clause with its verb in the subjunctive.

1 **Vēnī ut tē vidērem.** I came to see you/that I might see you/in order to see you.
2 **Mīlitēs missī sunt nē urbs caperētur.** Soldiers were sent that/in order that the city might not be captured.
3 **Hannibal mīsit Gallōs quī loca explōrārent.** Hannibal sent Gauls to explore the region.

A purpose clause is usually introduced by the conjunction **ut** (sentence 1) or, when negative, by **nē** (sentence 2).

Sometimes a relative pronoun introduces a purpose clause with verb in the subjunctive (sentence 3). As in other relative clauses, the introductory pronoun agrees in gender and number with the antecedent, but its case is determined by its use in the relative clause.

Caution: In classical Latin an infinitive is not used to express purpose. An English infinitive is regularly used in this way and is often the best translation of a clause of purpose.

I From the lettered list select a verb or verbs to complete each sentence. Translate.

1 Hannibal peditēs mīsit quī nātūram locī _____ .
2 Custōdiae _____ loca quam altissima _____ obsidēre.
3 Ut colloquium cum montānīs _____ , Gallōs eandem vallem incolentēs ad eōs mīsit.
4 Prīmā lūce exercitus ē castrīs _____ ut in hostēs impetum per angustiās _____ .
5 Expedītī quī tumulōs _____ prīmōs clīvōs explōrābant.

a) ascenderant
b) comperīrent
c) discessit
d) faceret
e) habērētur
f) īnsidērent
g) jubēbuntur
h) mittēs
i) potest

II Arrange the imperfect subjunctive forms in the list below according to person and number (1st, 2nd, 3rd singular and plural). Identify the remaining forms.

1 mūnīrētur
2 discessisse
3 essent
4 ēvāderēmus
5 factūrum esse
6 incolentium
7 jubērēminī
8 mittere
9 obsidērī
10 occupārem
11 pōnerēris
12 relictīs

91

Prīmā lūce ā Poenīs castra mōta sunt et agmen incēdere coepit. Jam montānī, signō datō, ex castellīs ad statiōnem solitam conveniēbant. Subitō eī cōnspexērunt aliōs hostēs arcem suam occupāvisse, aliōs per angustiās trānsīre. Deinde, cum vīdissent agmen Poenōrum in angustiīs suō tumultū° ₅ terrērī, ipsī dē dīversīs rūpibus dēcurrērunt.

Tum vērō Poenī simul ab hostibus simul° inīquitāte° locōrum oppugnābantur. Mīlitēs contendentēs ut ē perīculō ēvāderent inter ipsōs magis quam cum hostibus certābant. Equī, clāmōribus territī, agmen maximē perīculōsum° faciē- ₁₀ bant. Nam equī vulnerātī, cum maximē territī essent, ingentem strāgem° hominum et sarcinārum omnis generis fēcērunt. Cum praecipitēs angustiae essent, turba° multōs dē rūpibus dējēcit, quōsdam etiam armātōs; multa jūmenta cum oneribus dēvolvēbantur.° ₁₅

°**tumultus, -ūs** M., commotion, confusion • **simul ... simul** at the same time as • **inīquitāte locōrum** by the unevenness of the ground • **maximē perīculōsum faciēbant** greatly endangered (the marching column) • **strāgem** havoc • **turba, -ae** F., crowd; tumult • **dēvolvēbantur** rolled down

sarcinae, -ārum	F. pl., baggage, packs
jūmenta, -ōrum	N. pl., beasts of burden (mules)
onus, -eris	N., burden, load, pack
rūpēs, -is	F., rock, cliff
statiō, -ōnis	F., military post
quīdam, quaedam, quiddam	a certain one, someone; pl., some (see page 433)
dīversus, -a, -um	different; separate
solitus, -a, -um	customary, usual
praeceps, gen., **-cipitis**	steep
certō, -āre, -āvī, -ātum	fight, struggle
coepī, coepisse, coeptum	began (see page 455)
dēcurrō, -ere, -currī, -cursum	run down
dējiciō, -ere, -jēcī, -jectum	throw or hurl down
incēdō, -ere, -cessī, -cessum	advance, march; seize

One of the treasures of the French National Library is this bronze statuette of a Carthaginian warrior.

Cum haec speciēs horribilis esset, tamen Hannibal parumper° stetit atque suōs continuit nē tumultum ac trepidātiōnem augēret. Postquam interruptum° agmen perīculumque exercitūs vīdit, ex superiōre locō dēcurrit. Cum impetū ipsō hostēs fūdisset, tamen suīs quoque tumultum 20 auxit.

Mōmentō temporis, postquam itinera fugā montānōrum līberāta sunt, is tumultus sēdātus° est. Mox omnēs trāductī sunt, nōn sōlum per ōtium, sed prope silentiō. Hannibal

°**parumper** (adv.) for a little while • **interruptum** (perf. part.) cut in two • **sēdātus est** was checked

93

castellum quod caput° ejus regiōnis erat vīcōsque circum- 25
jectōs° cēpit. Per trīduum pecoribus ac cibō captō exercitum aluit.

°**caput** main town • **circumjectus, -a, -um** surrounding •
captō captured (modifies both **pecoribus** and **cibō,** but agrees with
the nearest noun.)

fuga, -ae	F., rout, flight; (means of) escape
ōtium, -ī	N., leisure; quiet, peace
pecus, -oris	N., cattle; herd, flock
trepidātiō, -ōnis	F., confusion; agitation
speciēs, -ēī	F., sight; appearance, semblance
superior, -ius	(comp. of **superus**) higher
līberō, -āre, -āvī, -ātum	clear, free
contineō, -ēre, -uī, -tentum	check, restrain; contain, hold
alō, -ere, -uī, altum	support; nourish
fundō, -ere, fūdī, fūsum	rout, put to flight
trādūcō, -ere, -dūxī, -ductum	bring or lead across/through/over
prope	(adv.) almost, nearly
ac	(conj.) and; and also (used in place of **atque** before consonants)

THE PAST PERFECT SUBJUNCTIVE of all
Latin verbs in active voice is made up of the perfect active
infinitive plus regular person endings. Passive forms of past
perfect subjunctive consist of the perfect participle with imperfect subjunctive of **sum.** (The participle agrees with the
subject in gender and number.)

I	II	III	IV
portāvisset	**monuisset**	**dūxisset**	**audīvisset**
portātus esset	**monitus esset**	**ductus esset**	**audītus esset**

Past perfect subjunctive of irregular verbs is formed by
adding regular person endings to the perfect active infinitive.

eō	sum	possum	volō	nōlō
isset/iisset	**fuisset**	**potuisset**	**voluisset**	**nōluisset**

A landslide foiled an attempt in recent years to take this elephant, borrowed from the Turin Zoo, over the Alps by one of the passes Hannibal may have used. A guild of Scottish linen weavers made the blanket and leggings for Jumbo.

THE CONJUNCTION cum, when used to introduce a subordinate clause with verb in the subjunctive, may mean "since," "when," or "although."

1 **Cum praecipitēs angustiae essent, turba multōs dē rūpibus dējēcit.** Since the pass was steep, the crowding together caused many to fall (lit., hurled many down) from the cliffs.

2 **Cum montānī vīdissent agmen Poenōrum terrērī, ipsī dē rūpibus dēcurrērunt.** When the mountaineers saw (had seen) that the marching line of the Carthaginians was terrified, they themselves ran down from the cliffs.

3 **Cum impetū ipsō hostēs fūdisset, tamen suīs quoque tumultum auxit.** Although he had routed the enemy by this very attack, yet for his own men too he increased the confusion. *when tamen is used, trans. Cum as Although.*

95

No one knows exactly where Hannibal crossed the Alps, but he undoubtedly encountered obstacles as forbidding as these Alpine cliffs.

The verb in a **cum** clause is translated as an indicative.

With **cum** meaning "since" or "although" any tense of the subjunctive may occur. When **cum** means "although," **tamen** is frequently found in the main clause.

With **cum** meaning "when" the imperfect or past perfect subjunctive is generally used if the verb of the main clause is past tense.

For convenience a **cum** clause is sometimes referred to as a **cum** causal clause (sentence 1, page 95), a **cum** descriptive clause of situation (sentence 2), or a **cum** concessive clause (sentence 3).

III Replace each infinitive in parentheses by the appropriate form of that verb. Explain the use, and translate each sentence.

1 Cum montānī Poenōs **(cōnspicere)**, custōdiās in angustiīs posuērunt.

2 Hannibal arcem ab auxiliīs Gallīs **(occupāre)** jusserat.

3 Cum multī equī vulnerātī **(esse)**, tamen mīlitēs territī incolumēs erant.

4 Cum multī peditēs ab hostibus (**interficere**), omnēs expedītī incessērunt ut auxilium (**dare**).

IV Distinguish between the two verb forms of each pair below.

1 augērētur/auxissem   6 mōta esse/mōta esset
2 certārī/certārētur   7 potuisse/posuissent
3 cōnsistī/cōnstitī   8 relinquere/relinquerēre
4 fūdissent/fuissent   9 sēdārēris/sēdārēs
5 īnsidēns/īnsēdisse   10 trānsitūrōs esse/trānsīsse

NATIVE TREACHERY AND AMBUSH

The chieftains of the next canton on the route of the Carthaginians assured Hannibal of their friendship and offered him provisions, guides, and hostages as evidence of their good faith. Hannibal accepted all these, but remained alert to whatever else the natives might do.

Hannibal, cum temere prīncipibus nōn crēderet,° tamen benignē respondit. Obsidēs quōs prīncipēs dabant° et commeātum quem ipsī dētulerant accēpit, nē repudiātī° apertē hostēs fierent.

Deinde, agmine nēquāquam ut° inter pācātōs compositō, 5 post ducēs eōrum prōcessit. Prīmum agmen° elephantī et equitēs erant. Post eōs Hannibal ipse, circumspectāns omnia, cum peditibus incēdēbat.

Ubi in angustiōrem viam ventum est,° undique ex īnsidiīs barbarī Poenōs ā fronte et ab tergō° petīvērunt atque saxa 10 ingentia in agmen dēvolvērunt. Tum quoque ad extrēmum perīculī° ac prope ad perniciem ventum est.

Nam, dum cunctātur° Hannibal, nōlēns dēmittere agmen in angustiās, montānī, interruptō mediō agmine,° viam īnsēdērunt°; noxque ūna sine equitibus atque impedīmentīs ab 15 Hannibale ācta est.°

°**nōn crēderet** did not trust (The object of **crēdō** is in the dative.)
dabant offered • **repudiātī** if scorned • **nēquāquam ut** by no means as • **prīmum agmen** van(-guard) • **ventum est** (impersonal expression) they came • **ab tergō** from behind **extrēmum perīculī** utmost danger • **dum cunctātur** while... hesitated • **interruptō mediō agmine** having cut the marching column in half • **īnsēdērunt** occupied • **ācta est** was spent

īnsidiae, -ārum	F. pl., ambush
barbarus, -ī	M., stranger, barbarian
frōns, frontis	F., front; forehead
obses, -sidis	M./F., hostage
commeātus, -ūs	M., supplies
perniciēs, -ēī	F., ruin, destruction
pācātus, -a, -um	peaceful
circumspectō, -āre, -āvī, -ātum	look around at/for
compōnō, -ere, -posuī, -positum	draw up, arrange; put, place
dēmittō, -ere, -mīsī, -missum	send or let (down); drop
dēvolvō, -ere, -volvī, -volūtum	roll down
dēferō, -ferre, -tulī, -lātum	bring (down)

Know fero and fio

THE VERB ferō is a Conjugation III verb that is irregular in its principal parts and in five forms of the present indicative. Otherwise, the entire present system of **ferō** is conjugated regularly.

Principal parts: **ferō ferre tulī lātum**

Present Indicative Active/Passive		Present Subjunctive Active/Passive
Singular		Singular
ferō/feror	I carry/am being carried	**feram/ferar**
fers/ferris	you carry/are being carried	**ferās/ferāris**
fert/fertur	he carries/is being carried	**ferat/ferātur**
Plural		Plural
ferimus/ferimur	we carry/are being carried	**ferāmus/ferāmur**
fertis/feriminī	you carry/are being carried	**ferātis/ferāminī**
ferunt/feruntur	they carry/are being carried	**ferant/ferantur**

The perfect system active of **ferō,** as in all Latin verbs, is based on the third principal part (**tulī, tulistī, tulit,** etc.), and the perfect system passive on the fourth principal part combined with the forms of **sum** (**lātus sum, lātus es, lātus est,** etc.).

For the complete conjugation of **ferō** and for a list of its most frequently used compounds, see the Summary of Grammar at the back of this book.

Carthaginian amulets like these, made of glass paste in the form of masks of gods, were popular in all the Carthaginian trade area, and have been found in many parts of the Mediterranean world. These two are in the Louvre.

THE IRREGULAR VERB fīō takes the place of the passive voice of **faciō**, which has no passive forms in the present system except in compounds; e.g., **cōnficiō/cōnficior.**

Principal parts: **fīō . fierī . factus sum**

Present Indicative		Present Subjunctive	
Singular	Plural	Singular	Plural
fīō	_____¹	**fīam**	**fīāmus**
fīs	_____¹	**fīās**	**fīātis**
fit	**fīunt**	**fīat**	**fīant**

In the present system **fīō** is active in form, though passive in meaning. **Fīō** is conjugated as a regular Conjugation III verb, except that two forms are missing from the present indicative.¹ The perfect system of **faciō** is formed regularly in the passive: **factus sum, factus eram,** etc.

For the complete conjugation of **fīō,** see the Summary of Grammar at the back of this book.

In addition to passive meanings of **fīō,** (e.g., **fit,** it is being

¹The forms **fīmus** and **fītis** do not occur in classical Latin.

made/done; **fīēbat,** it was being made/done; **fīet,** it will be made/done), forms of **fīō** may sometimes be translated "I become," "I became," "I shall become," etc.

Third person singular forms **(fīt, fīēbat, fīet)** often may be translated "it happens," "it happened," "it will happen," or "it comes about," etc.

V In the lettered list find one possible English translation of each numbered Latin expression.

1 cum fieret   a) although you had carried
2 cum lāta essent   b) I shall be made
3 cum tulissētis   c) lest we become
4 dum fertis   d) because it was happening
5 ferētur   e) that you be brought
6 fīam   f) while you were bearing
7 nē fierēmus   g) it will be endured
8 ut ferrēminī   h) since they had been brought

THE VIEW FROM THE SUMMIT

Posterō diē, cum jam barbarī tardius aggrederentur, cōpiae Hannibalis jūnctae sunt et per angustiās sine proeliō iter fēcērunt. Elephantī tardē prōgressī per viās angustās praecipitēsque magnā morā agēbantur; sed ita agmen tūtum erat quod montānī hās bēstiās maximās mīrāsque multum 5 timēbant.

Nōnō diē in jugum° Alpium perventum est.° Bīduum° Poenī in jugō morātī sunt mīlitibusque labōre ac pugnandō° fessīs quiēs data est. Hīc jūmenta aliquot, quae in rūpibus prōlāpsa° erant, sequendō° vēstīgia agminis in castra per- 10 vēnērunt.

Cāsus etiam nivis° exercituī ingentem terrōrem adjēcit. Quārē, cum, signīs mōtīs, prīmā lūce agmen incēderet, dēspērātiō in omnium vultū° appārēbat.

Itaque Hannibal jussit mīlitēs in quōdam prōmontōriō 15

°**jugum, -ī** N., top, summit • **perventum est** (impersonal expression) they came • **bīduum** (for) two days • **pugnandō** from fighting • **prōlāpsa erant** had fallen • **sequendō** by following • **nivis** of snow • **in vultū** on the face

cōnsistere, unde longē ac lātē prōspectus° erat. Ostendit eīs
Ītaliam et agrōs Alpīnīs montibus subjectōs.° Dīxit eōs tum
trānscendere moenia nōn sōlum Ītaliae sed etiam urbis
Rōmae; cētera itinera aut plāna aut prōclīva° futūra esse;
eōs arcem et caput Ītaliae in manū ac potestāte° habitūrōs esse. 20

°**prōspectus, -ūs** M., view • **subjectōs** lying at the foot of
prōclīva (adj.) downhill • **in manū ac potestāte** in their power
and control

prōmontōrium, -ī	N., promontory, headland
dēspērātiō, -ōnis	F., despair
quiēs, -ētis	F., rest
plānus, -a, -um	level
aliquot	(indecl. adj.) some, several
moror, -ārī, -ātus sum	delay
adjiciō, -ere, -jēcī, -jectum	add; throw (into)
aggredior, -gredī, -gressus sum	attack
prōgredior, -gredī, -gressus sum	advance
trānscendō, -ere, -scendī, -scēnsum	climb, scale
tardē	(adv.) slowly
tardius	more slowly; less vigorously
signa movēre	break camp

A DEPONENT VERB is passive in form but active in
meaning.

1 **Rēgnum in cīvitāte suā occupāre cōnābātur.** He was trying to
seize the power in his own state.

2 **Dux pollicitus est sēsē cum eīs pācem factūrum esse.** The leader
promised that he would make peace with them.

3 **Mīlitēs suā voluntāte ducem sequuntur.** The soldiers are following
their leader of their own accord.

4 **Nostrī in locum inīquiōrem nōn prōgrediēbantur.** Our men were
not advancing into a more unfavorable position.

5 **Dux partīrī et lātius distribuere exercitum dēsīderāvit.** The
leader wanted to divide his army and distribute it more widely.

There are deponent verbs in each of the four regular conjugations (I, II, III, III-iō, IV). The conjugation of each deponent corresponds to the passive of a regular verb of the same conjugation; e.g., (I) **cōnor/portō**; (II) **polliceor/moneō**; (III) **sequor/dūcō**; (III-iō) **prōgredior/capiō**; (IV) **partior/audiō**.

It may have been snowy slopes like these above the famous Hospice of St. Bernard that brought desperate hardships to the Carthaginians when they crossed the Alps.

	Present Indicative	Present Infinitive	Perfect Indicative
I	**cōnor**	**cōnārī**	**cōnātus (sum)**
II	**polliceor**	**pollicērī**	**pollicitus (sum)**
III	**sequor**	**sequī**	**secūtus (sum)**
III-**iō**	**prōgredior**	**prōgredī**	**prōgressus (sum)**
IV	**partior**	**partīrī**	**partītus (sum)**

A deponent verb has only two stems (present and participial) and three principal parts, the latter corresponding to the first, second, and fourth principal parts of a regular verb.

A deponent verb has a few active forms; e.g., present and future active participles and future active infinitive.

Present Active Participles	Future Active Participles
cōnāns, -antis/trying	**cōnātūrus, -a, -um**/about to try
pollicēns, -entis/promising	**pollicitūrus, -a, -um**/about to promise
sequēns, -entis/following	**secūtūrus, -a, -um**/about to follow
prōgrediēns, -ientis/advancing	**prōgressūrus, -a, -um**/about to advance
partiēns, -ientis/dividing	**partītūrus, -a, -um**/about to divide

As in other verbs, the future active infinitive is made up of the future active participle and **esse;** e.g., **cōnātūrus esse**/to be about to try.

Caution: Other infinitives (present and perfect) of a deponent verb are passive in form, but active in meaning; e.g., **sequī**/to follow; **prōgressus esse**/to have advanced. Although the perfect participle of a deponent verb (a passive form) generally has an active meaning, it sometimes is used as a passive; e.g., **partītus**/divided.

A DIFFICULT DESCENT

Prōcēdere inde agmen coepit, sed iter fuit multō difficilius quam in ascēnsū fuerat. Omnis enim fermē° via erat praeceps, angusta, lūbrica°; quārē Poenī sē ab lāpsū° sustinēre nōn poterant. Aliī super aliōs° et jūmenta in hominēs occidēbant.

Deinde ventum est ad multō angustiōrem rūpem. Locus, 5

°**fermē** almost • **lūbrica** slippery • **lāpsū** sliding, falling
aliī super aliōs one on top of the other

jam ante° nātūrā praeceps, recentī lāpsū terrae° abruptus° erat
in altitūdinem mīlle pedum.° Ibi cum equitēs cōnstitissent,
quasi ad fīnem viae, Hannibalī nūntiātum est rūpem inviam°
esse.

°**ante** (adv.) previously • **lāpsū terrae** landslide • **abrup-
tus erat** had been sheared off • **in . . . pedum** to a depth
of a thousand feet • **inviam** impassable

ascēnsus, -ūs	M., ascent
recēns, gen., **recentis**	recent, new
inde	(adv.) then; from there
multō	(abl. of **multus**) much, by far
quasi	(adv./conj.) as if, as though

AN ABLATIVE WITHOUT PREPOSITION
in Latin usually requires an English connective in translation. Such prepositions as "with," "by," "at," "in,"
"from," or "of," and phrases like "by means of" or "because
of" may be tried for sense.

Occasionally, however, idiomatic usage is the same in both
languages. With comparative adjectives and some adverbs
the degree of difference is expressed without a preposition in
both Latin and English.

Iter multō difficilius est. The journey is far more difficult.
Paucīs ante diēbus castra mōverant. They had broken camp a few
days before.

VI Identify each form. Give principal parts of all deponents.

1 aggressūrum esse   4 fierem   7 morārēminī
2 cōnstitisse   5 funderis   8 prōgredī
3 ēvāsum esset   6 īnsiderent   9 sequēns

VII Translate each sentence. Explain underlined words/phrases.
1 Mox exercitus ad vallem multō lātiōrem perveniet.
2 Cum jūmenta in clīvīs prōlāpsa essent, sarcinae tamen dē-
jectae nōn sunt.
3 Dux, monte ab hostibus obsessō, nostrōs in valle continēbat.

4 Cum id eī nūntiātum esset, ex urbe posterō diē discessit.

5 Ut montānī laxātī fierent, sē obsidēs eōrum acceptūrum esse nūntiāvit.

6 Aliī hostēs agmen Poenum secūtī sunt, ut id ā fronte et ā tergō aggrederentur.

7 Equitēs ad omnēs urbēs mīsimus quī Rōmānīs auxilium ferrent.

8 Hannibal custōdiās circum castra compōnī jussit nē undique impetus fieret.

REMOVING AN OBSTACLE

Hannibal went to see for himself. He thought his troops might make a detour, but that proved impracticable. The snow, slush, and ice prevented any further advance, since the feet of both men and animals kept slipping from under them. Sometimes the baggage animals sank through

This pass, called La Traversette, is the point at which some scholars believe Hannibal crossed the Alps.

the snow to the lowest crust and were trapped by the hard snow around them.

At last, when men and beasts had been worn out in vain, the soldiers made camp as best they could on the ridge. Men were sent to clear away the snow and to construct a road. In making the road, they had to cut through rock. To do this the soldiers first chopped down and trimmed big trees and with the logs built a large fire to heat the rocks. When the rocks were very hot, the men poured vinegar on them, causing them to disintegrate.[1] A passage was made through the rocks, and a zigzag road constructed to lessen the steepness of the descent.

[1]This means of softening rock had long been used in the Spanish mines. Limestone would readily yield to vinegar thus employed. Hannibal may have had a few skins of sour wine in his baggage train. There is nothing inherently improbable in this report, if the operation was carried out on a small scale.

Snowy Alpine peaks such as these lend beauty to a picture, but to inexperienced mountain climbers like the Carthaginians they became a desperate reality.

Hōc modō nōn sōlum jūmenta sed etiam elephantī dēdūcī poterant. Quattuor diēs circā hanc rūpem cōnsūmptī sunt; jūmenta prope famē° mortua sunt. Dēscendērunt tamen in īnferiōra loca ubi erant flūmina et silvae. Ibi jūmenta in pābulum° Hannibalī mittenda erant; quiēs hominibus pug- 5 nandō labōrandōque fessīs danda erat.

Ita, quīntō mēnse ā Carthāgine Novā, Alpibus quīntō decimō diē superātīs, in Ītaliam perventum est. Hannibal, postquam Rhodanum trānsiit, trīgintā sex mīlia hominum ingentemque numerum equōrum et aliōrum jūmentōrum 10 āmīsit.

°**famē** (irregular abl.) of hunger • **in pābulum** to pasture

īnferior, -ius	(comp. of **īnferus**) lower
dēdūcō, -ere, -dūxī, -ductum	lead down/away
morior, morī, mortuus sum	die
circā	(prep. with acc./adv.) around, about, near (by)

THE FUTURE PASSIVE PARTICIPLE is formed on the present stem and has endings **-ndus, -nda, -ndum** in the nominative singular. It is declined like **bonus, -a, -um.**

I	**portandus, -a, -um**		III-iō	**capiendus, -a, -um**
II	**monendus, -a, -um**		IV	**audiendus, -a, -um**
III	**dūcendus, -a, -um**			

In **-iō** verbs of Conjugation III and in Conjugation IV verbs, the present stem has **-ie-** in the future passive participle, as in the present active participle. The table below shows differences and similarities of participial forms.

	Present Active	Future Passive	Perfect Passive	Future Active
I	**portāns**	**portandus**	**portātus**	**portātūrus**
II	**monēns**	**monendus**	**monitus**	**monitūrus**
III	**dūcēns**	**dūcendus**	**ductus**	**ductūrus**
III-iō	**capiēns**	**capiendus**	**captus**	**captūrus**
IV	**audiēns**	**audiendus**	**audītus**	**audītūrus**

107

Ostendit id faciendum esse. He explained that this had to be done.
Rēx dēfendendus est. The king must be defended.

The future passive participle is often used with forms of **sum** to denote an act which must be done or ought to be done.

DATIVE OF AGENT to denote the person by whom an act must be done or ought to be done is often used with the future passive participle. (geRUNDIVE)

Id Rōmānīs faciendum est. This must/ought to be done by the Romans. or The Romans must/ought to do this.

Sentences containing a future passive participle with dative of agent are often best translated by an active verb with the "agent" as the subject of the English sentence.

VIII Match verbs in the same tense and mood. Identify the forms.

1 aggrediēre	6 mortua erō	11 sequeris
2 ēgissēs	7 mūnīrētur	12 subībunt
3 facta sunt	8 petītum esset	13 tulistis
4 fertis	9 poterat	14 vidērent
5 morābiminī	10 relīquerimus	15 vincēris

The Rhone River in the area where Hannibal crossed it

Carthaginians stored milk and oil in pottery jars such as these.

IX Complete each sentence with an appropriate form from the lettered list. Translate.

1. Prīmā lūce rūpēs expedītīs ⸺ erunt.
2. Vēstīgia agminis ⸺ prīncipēs hostium castra Poena invēnērunt.
3. Jūmenta in pābulum ⸺ erant, nē famē ⸺ .
4. Cum bēstiās mīrās ⸺ , barbarī fūgērunt.
5. Elephantī per angustiās mīlitibus Hannibalis ⸺ .

a) agentium
b) cōnsūmerētur
c) dūcendī erant
d) mittenda
e) morerentur
f) obsidendās
g) sequendō
h) trānscendendae
i) vīdissent

THE ROMANS INTERCEPT

Meanwhile the Roman consul Publius Cornelius Scipio had landed with his army at Pisa and was swiftly marching north toward the Po River. His purpose was to intercept Hannibal before he could invade the Italian peninsula.

The opposing armies were almost within sight of each other at the Po, the Romans on one side, the Carthaginians on the other. Scipio, first to cross the river, brought his army up to another river, the Ticinus.

There Scipio delivered a speech of encouragement to his men, expressing a confidence in them which he probably did not feel. These were raw recruits, his own consular army being in Spain under the command of his brother, Gnaeus Scipio.

109

Hannibal also had words of encouragement for his men. The Carthaginian general, however, prefaced his speech with an object lesson. To some of the mountaineers they had captured he offered the opportunity of fighting each other to the death—in pairs. Freedom was the prize for each winner, who would also receive weapons and a horse. After watching several pairs of volunteer contestants in bloody combat, his soldiers were sufficiently stirred to satisfy Hannibal.

HANNIBAL ADDRESSES HIS TROOPS

"Nesciō an° majōra vincula majōrēsque necessitātēs vōbīs quam captīvīs vestrīs Fortūna circumdederit.°

"Dextrā sinistrāque duo maria vōs claudunt quī nūllam ad effugiendum nāvem habētis. Circā vōs est Padus flūmen; ab tergō° Alpēs vōs urgent, vix ab integrīs vōbīs trānsitae.   5

"Hīc vōbīs vincendum aut moriendum est, mīlitēs, ubi prīmum hostibus occurristis. Et eadem Fortūna, quae vōbīs necessitātem pugnandī imposuit, vōbīs victōribus prōpōnit praemia ampliōra quam ea quae hominēs ab dīs immortālibus petere solent."   10

°**an** whether (with **nesciō** = I rather think that . . .) • **circum-dederit** has given (perf. subjunctive in an indirect question) • **ab tergō** in the rear

necessitās, -ātis	F., necessity, constraint, need
amplus, -a, -um	great; splendid
integer, -gra, -grum	fresh, vigorous; unharmed
soleō, -ēre, solitus sum	be accustomed
urgeō, -ēre, ursī, ——	press (upon); hem in, confine
impōnō, -ere, -posuī, -positum	set (upon); impose (on)
prōpōnō, -ere, -posuī, -positum	offer, propose

A GERUND is a verbal noun; that is, it is a noun formed on the present stem of a verb. A Latin gerund is found only in the singular, and is declined like a neuter Declension II noun, except that it has no nominative. (The present infinitive is used in place of the nominative.)

This so-called bust of Hannibal is now in the National Museum of Naples. The clothing is of Roman rather than Carthaginian style.

	I	II	III	III-iō	IV
Nom.	(portāre)	(monēre)	(dūcere)	(capere)	(audīre)
Gen.	portandī	monendī	dūcendī	capiendī	audiendī
Dat.	portandō	monendō	dūcendō	capiendō	audiendō
Acc.	portandum	monendum	dūcendum	capiendum	audiendum
Abl.	portandō	monendō	dūcendō	capiendō	audiendō

1 **Quiēs hominibus pugnandō labōrandōque fessīs danda erat.**
Rest had to be given to the men worn out from (by) fighting and working.

In sentence 1 "fighting" and "working" are gerunds, as are also **pugnandō** and **labōrandō**.

2 **Quiēs hominibus pugnantibus labōrantibusque danda erat.** Rest
had to be given to the men fighting and working.

In sentence 2 "fighting" and "working" are present participles, as are **pugnantibus** and **labōrantibus.**

Latin makes a distinction in form as well as in usage between the gerund and the present participle. Both are formed
on the present stem of the verb, but the distinguishing sign
of the gerund is **-nd-,** to which Declension II noun endings
are added, while the sign of the present participle is **-nt-,** to
which Declension III adjective endings are added.

An English gerund ends in -ing, as does also the English
present participle; e.g., "carrying," "warning," "leading,"
etc. If it is used as a noun, the word ending in -ing is a
gerund; if it is used as an adjective, it is a participle.

C A S E   U S E S   O F   A   G E R U N D are similar to those
of any other noun, with certain limitations.

1 **Modus operandī nōbīs ignōtus erat.** The method of working was
unknown to us.

A Roman cavalryman is represented in this bronze statuette.

2 **Puer studiōsus discendī est.** The boy is desirous of learning.

3 **Hostēs effugiendī causā discessērunt.** The enemy withdrew for the purpose of escaping.

4 **Tempestās pugnandō idōnea est.** The weather is suitable for fighting.

5 **Nūllam ad effugiendum nāvem habētis.** You have no ship for (the purpose of) escaping.

6 **Docendō discimus.** We learn by teaching.

The genitive of a gerund is used with a noun (sentence 1), an adjective (sentence 2), and the ablative **causā** (sentence 3).

The dative of a gerund is rarely used. It occasionally occurs with a verb or adjective that regularly takes the dative (sentence 4).

The accusative of a gerund occurs only with prepositions, mainly **ad,** but sometimes with **inter, ob,** and a few others. The gerund with **ad** often expresses purpose (sentence 5).

In the ablative case the gerund occurs both with and without a preposition. Without a preposition a gerund often expresses means or cause, and the English translation requires "by," "with," "from," or some other connecting word (sentence 6).

DATIVE WITH COMPOUND VERBS Many compound verbs which are formed from a verb and a prefix take a dependent noun or pronoun in the dative case to complete their meanings. The most important prefixes whose compounds take the dative are **ante, ob, prae,** and **sub.**

1 **Hostibus occurristis.** You have met the enemy.

Hostibus (sentence 1) is in the dative case because it is dependent on a verb which is a compound of **ob.** Other prefixes whose compounds sometimes take the dative are **ad, circum, com- (con-), in, inter, post, prō, super.**

2 **Fortūna vōbīs victōribus prōpōnit praemia ampliōra.** Fortune offers greater rewards to you as victors.

If the simple verb is transitive, the compound may take both an accusative and a dative. In sentence 2, **vōbīs** is the dative and **praemia** the accusative that complete the meaning of the compound verb **prōpōnit.**

X One form of each group in parentheses will give a sensible meaning to the sentence. Select the appropriate word or phrase and translate.

1 Mihi major multō vidētur necessitās (pugnandō/pugnantem/ pugnāre/pugnandī).

2 Cum vōs victōrēs esse (solitī eritis/solētis/solērētis/solitī essētis), vōbīs tamen Fortūna necessitātem vincendī prōposuit.

3 Cum nūllam nāvem ad (effugiēns/effugiendum/effugiendō/ effugienda) habeātis, (vōs/tibi/tē/vōbīs) vincendum aut moriendum erit.

4 Commeātum ab hostibus lātum accēpit (nē/ut/quī/quod) mīlitēs suī aegrī famē (fierent/fīam/factī essētis/fierī).

5 Vincula (obsidis/obsidem/obsidibus/obsidēs) imposuimus, nē ēvādere (cōnābuntur/cōnārentur/cōnātī essent/cōnantis).

BATTLE IMPROMPTU

The opposing armies had set up their camps about five miles apart, and each general had gone out with his cavalry to reconnoiter the other's position. Coming upon each other unexpectedly, they were forced into combat earlier than either had planned.

The Romans were already losing ground, when the situation was made even worse by the wounding of their general. As the Roman army was retreating, Scipio was joined near the Trebia River by the other consul, Tiberius Sempronius.

Against the better judgment of Scipio, his fellow-consul arrogantly insisted upon their granting protection against the invading Carthaginians to the Gallic inhabitants of the land between the Trebia and the Po.

Hannibal, who had hardly dared hope for such rashness, was ready and eager for an early battle. Although the Romans at first met with some success, much to the delight of the reckless and headstrong Sempronius, their complete defeat in the end justified Scipio's more cautious judgment.

Scipio immediately led his army into winter quarters at Cremona, while Sempronius and his army were quartered at Placentia. Even in winter quarters, however, the Romans had no peace. The enemy was busily engaged in cutting them off from their supplies.

A terra cotta statuette in the National Museum of Naples, probably representing one of Hannibal's elephants

MORE MOUNTAINS TO CROSS

Hannibal ex hībernīs prōfectus est, quia jam Flāminium cōnsulem Arrētium pervēnisse fāma erat. Cum aliud longius sed commodius ostenderētur iter, tamen propiōrem viam per palūdēs petīvit.

Hispānōs et Āfrōs et omne rōbur° veterānī exercitūs prī- 5 mōs īre jussit, Gallōs sequī, ut eī agminis medium essent, equitēs īre novissimōs.° Numidās expedītōs inde cōgere agmen° jussit.

°**rōbur** choice troops, flower (of an army) • **novissimōs** last
cōgere agmen bring up the rear

Ipse Hannibal, aeger oculīs prīmum ex vernā intemperiē,° elephantō quī ūnus superfuerat° vectus est. Tamen et nocturnō ūmōre gravante caput,° et quia medendī nec locus° nec tempus erat, alterō oculō capitur.°

Multīs hominibus jūmentīsque āmissīs, Hannibal tandem ē palūdibus ēmersit° et castra locāvit. Certum per praemissōs explōrātōrēs habuit° exercitum Rōmānum circā moenia Arrētiī esse.

°**ex vernā intemperiē** as a result of bad spring weather • **quī ūnus superfuerat** the only surviving • **nocturnō . . . caput** because the dampness at night aggravated his head (condition) • **medendī . . . locus** opportunity for healing • **alterō oculō capitur** became blind in one eye • **ēmersit** came out, emerged • **certum habuit** he was assured

fāma, -ae	F., rumor, report; reputation
hīberna, -ōrum	N. pl., winter quarters
medium, -ī	N., the middle (part), center
palūs, -ūdis	F., swamp, marsh
commodus, -a, -um	convenient, suitable
expedītus, -a, -um	light-armed (also as noun)
veterānus, -a, -um	veteran, old
propior, -ius	nearer
praemittō, -ere, -mīsī, -missum	send ahead
proficīscor, -fīcīscī, -fectus sum	depart, set out
sequor, sequī, secūtus sum	follow, pursue; accompany
nec . . . nec/neque . . . neque	neither . . . nor
quia	(conj.) because

G E R U N D I V E is the term applied to a future passive participle when it is used as a verbal adjective. A gerundive agrees with its noun or pronoun in gender, number, and case.

1 **Cupidus oppidī expugnandī dux castra posuit.** Desirous of the town being stormed/Desirous of storming the town, the general pitched camp.

2 **Difficultātēs bellī gerendī erant magnae.** The difficulties of war being waged/The difficulties of waging war were great.

3 **Puerī ad urbem vēnērunt ad lūdōs spectandōs.** The boys came to the city for the purpose of the games being seen/for the purpose of seeing the games.

4 **Rōmānī auxilium mīsērunt ad cōnficiendum proelium.** The Romans sent aid for the purpose of the battle being ended/for the purpose of ending the battle.

5 **Dux cōnsultus est dē auxiliō mittendō.** The general was consulted about aid being sent/about sending aid.

6 **Lapidibus portandīs moenia urbis cōnstrūxērunt.** By stones being carried/By carrying stones they constructed the walls of the city.

Although a gerundive is passive in both form and meaning, it is usually best translated as active, and the noun or pronoun that it modifies then is translated as its object. In the sentences above, the literal (passive) translation of the gerundive is given first, followed by its translation as active.

C A S E   U S E S   O F   A   G E R U N D I V E are in general like those of a gerund.

Sentences 1 and 2 illustrate the use of the genitive of the gerundive with an adjective (1) and a noun (2). The ablatives **grātiā** and **causā** also occur with the genitive of a gerundive, as with the genitive of a gerund. (See page 113.)

The dative of a gerundive is rarely used. The accusative of a gerundive occurs only with prepositions, mainly **ad.** **Ad** with the gerundive construction often expresses purpose (sentences 3 and 4), as does **ad** with a gerund. (See page 113.)

In the ablative case the gerundive occurs both with and without a preposition (sentences 5 and 6). Without a preposition a gerundive construction expresses means or cause, as does the gerund. (See page 113.)

G E R U N D S   A N D   G E R U N D I V E S   D I F F E R

Gerund:	A noun	Neuter gender	Singular only
Gerundive:	A participle	All genders	Singular and plural
Gerund:	No nominative[1]	Active voice	Transitive or intransitive
Gerundive:	All cases[2]	Passive voice	Always transitive

[1]Nominative of gerund is replaced by present infinitive.
[2]Nominative of future passive participle has no gerundive use.

117

XI Explain all phrases or clauses which express purpose. Translate all the sentences.

1 Mox in palūdibus perīcula toleranda erunt.
2 Mīlitēs missī sunt quī urbem oppugnārent.
3 Ad explōrandum locum castrīs idōneum praemittēris.
4 Peditēs ad agmen dūcendum missī sunt.
5 Cum ingentis impetūs fāma esset, paucī tamen vulnerātī erant.
6 Prīmum agmen hostibus occurrere jubēbitur.
7 Exercitum barbarōrum fūdimus, nē flūmen prope castra nostra trānsīret.

XII For each numbered verb find a lettered verb of the same conjugation and give the corresponding form.

1 comperiēbās	4 līberāvissent	a) morior	d) polliceor
2 dējiciendum	5 urgēret	b) moror	e) sequor
3 fundere		c) partior	

A RECKLESS LEADER

In the spring of 217 B.C. Hannibal was devastating Etruria. Meanwhile at Rome two new consuls had been elected. Gaius Flaminius—like his predecessor Sempronius—was headstrong and impatient; he would neither seek advice nor take it when it was given.

While the other consul, Gnaeus Servilius, stayed in Rome to assume his consulship there in the customary way, Flaminius slipped away to Ariminum. In that Adriatic city Flaminius took over the command of his army and entered upon his consulship at the same time.

In a council of war at Arretium in Etruria, Flaminius was the only one to advocate quick, drastic action against Hannibal, for he considered it a personal affront that the Carthaginians should be allowed to roam unchecked through Italy, destroying and plundering at will. The majority of the council, however, recommended caution. When he was advised to wait for Servilius to arrive and join forces with him, the fiery Flaminius stalked out of the meeting.

PRIDE BEFORE A FALL

Īrātus Flāminius sē ex cōnsiliō prōripuit° signumque simul itineris pugnaeque cum dedisset, "Immō° Arrētiī ante moenia sedeāmus," inquit; "hīc enim patria et penātēs° sunt. Hannibal ēmissus ē manibus° populētur Ītaliam vāstandōque et incen-

The Etruscans whose land Hannibal devastated were highly civilized and very artistic. This gold vase, now in the Louvre, is a fine example of their handicraft.

dendō omnia ad Rōmāna moenia perveniat. Nec nōs hinc 5
mōverīmus° antequam C. Flāminium ab Arrētiō patrēs vocā-
verint, sīcut ōlim Camillum ā Veiīs vocāvērunt.''

Haec simul increpāns signa convellī° Flāminius jussit et
ipse in equum īnsiluit. Subitō equus concidit cōnsulemque
super caput jēcit. Omnēs quī circā erant velut malō ōmine 10
incipiendae reī territī sunt; praetereā Flāminiō nūntiātum est
signum ā labōrante omnī vī signiferō convellī nōn posse.

°sē . . . prōripuit rushed out • immō by all means • pe-
nātēs, -ium M. pl., penates, guardian deities of the household
ēmissus ē manibus if (Hannibal) slips through our fingers • nec
(= et nē) nōs . . . mōverīmus and let us not move (independent use
of perfect subjunctive with nē to express a strong negative wish)
convellī be pulled out

119

Turning to the messenger, "Go away," he said. "tell them to dig out

Conversus ad nūntium, "Abī," inquit, "nūntiā ut effodiant°

the sign ·
ever it they have become numb will fear digit up anyway
signum, sī ad convellendum manūs propter metum obtorpuērunt.°"

Then the marching column began to march   The milites were joyful with the boldn[es]
of their leader. since they felt hope itself more than cause of hope
Incēdere inde agmen coepit. Mīlitēs ferōciā° ducis laetī 15
erant, cum spem ipsam magis quam causam speī sentīrent.

°nūntiā ut effodiant   tell them to dig out   •   **obtorpuērunt**
have become numb   •   **ferōcia, -ae**   F., rashness, boldness

pugna, -ae	F., battle, fight
signifer, -ferī	M., standardbearer
cōnsilium, -ī	N., council (of war); plan; advice
patrēs, -um	M. pl., senators, senate; fathers
vīs, ——	F., strength (see page 456)
metus, -ūs	M., fear
increpō, -āre, -āvī, -ātum	speak scornfully; rebuke
populor, -ārī, -ātus sum	devastate, lay waste
concidō, -ere, -cidī, ——	fall (down)
convertō, -ere, -vertī, -versum	turn, change
īnsiliō, -īre, -siluī, ——	leap
hinc	(adv.) from here
sīcut/sīcutī	(adv./conj.) just as, just as if
simul	(adv.) at the same time
velut	(adv.) as, just as, as it were
antequam	(conj.) before, until

THE PERFECT SUBJUNCTIVE   active of all verbs
is formed on the perfect stem with the tense sign **-erī- (-eri-**
before final **-m, -t, -nt).**   Perfect subjunctive passive consists of
the perfect participle with present subjunctive of **sum.** (The
participle agrees with the subject in number and gender.)

portāverit	**monuerit**	**dūxerit**	**cēperit**	**audīverit**
portātus sit	**monitus sit**	**ductus sit**	**captus sit**	**audītus sit**

The perfect subjunctive of irregular verbs is formed likewise by adding the tense sign **-erī-/-eri-** to the perfect stem
and then adding regular person endings.

eō	sum	possum	volō	nōlō	ferō
ierit/īverit	**fuerit**	**potuerit**	**voluerit**	**nōluerit**	**tulerit**

120

In a recently discovered Etruscan city in the extreme northern part of Etruria this bronze statuette was found. A goddess is holding a libation bowl as she sends a warrior off to combat.

For complete conjugation of verbs in the perfect subjunctive, see the Summary of Grammar at the back of this book.

ANTICIPATORY SUBJUNCTIVE is often used in subordinate clauses introduced by conjunctions meaning "until" or "before." Such a clause denotes an act that is anticipated or expected.

1 **Expectābam dum frāter redīret.** I was waiting until my brother should return/for my brother to return.

2 **Rōmānī clāmōre undique ortō, priusquam satis cernerent, sē circumventum esse sēnsērunt.** From the shouting that arose on every side the Romans learned, before they could clearly see, that they were surrounded.

In sentence 1 **redīret** is subjunctive because it denotes an act that is expected. In sentence 2 **cernerent** likewise de-

121

notes an act that is anticipated or expected and is therefore in the subjunctive.

Observe that in sentence 1 the conjunction **dum,** used with the subjunctive, means "until." The same conjunction, when used with the present indicative, means "while."

Dum haec geruntur, nūntiī ad castra pervēnērunt. While these things were going on, messengers arrived at the camp.

XIII Translate each pair of sentences and explain the difference (if any) in construction and/or meaning.

1 Equitēs illās regiōnēs explōrābant, dum peditēs castra pōnunt.
 Equitēs illās regiōnēs explōrābant, dum hostēs invenīrent.

2 Prīnceps pābulum petīvit, nē jūmenta famē morerentur.
 Prīnceps pābulum petīvit, quō jūmenta alerentur.

3 Exercitus ē castrīs ad urbem oppugnandam discessit.
 Impedimenta ad proficīscendum colligentur.

4 Cum eōrum prīncipem cēpissēmus, hostēs nōn ēvādere cōnātī sunt.
 Cum prīncipem eōrum cēpissēmus, tamen hostēs ēvādere cōnātī sunt.

5 Prīmā lūce castra moveāmus, nē hostēs per angustiās effugiant.
 Prīmā lūce proficīscēmur, antequam hostēs nostra cōnsilia comperiant.

AMBUSH

Near Lake Trasumennus the Romans under Flaminius were trapped between the lake and the mountains, with the Carthaginians in front of and behind them. Attacked suddenly and from all sides, the Romans were unable to effect any regular battle formation.

Livy reports that the three-hour battle which followed was so fierce that neither side was aware of an earthquake that partially destroyed nearby towns, altered the courses of rivers, and caused landslides.

In this battle the consul Flaminius was fatally wounded. Many of the soldiers fled in panic; others surrendered to the Carthaginians upon being given the assurance that they would be allowed to go free if they gave up their weapons. Livy sarcastically reports that Hannibal kept

Roman mosaic from the Capitoline Museum picturing Rome's harbor at Ostia. During the wars with Carthage, Ostia became an important Roman naval base. This ancient city was located about fifteen miles southwest of Rome, near the mouth of the Tiber River.

this pledge with "true Punic reverence" **(Pūnicā religiōne),**[1] for they were all thrown into chains. The Carthaginian general did, however, release prisoners "of the Latin name" **(Latīnī nōminis),**[2] while keeping the Romans as captives.

---

[1]This is the usual Roman sneer at Punic honor, even though for a modern historian there is little to choose between Roman and Punic honor.

[2]i.e., Roman allies and colonists, but without full Roman citizenship. Hannibal discriminated in the treatment of prisoners, in the hope of alienating the allies of Rome.

Rōmae ad prīmum nūntium calamitātis ejus cum ingentī
terrōre ac tumultū concursus populī in forum est factus.
Mātrōnae vagae° per viās obviōs° rogābant quae repentīna
calamitās aut quae fortūna exercitūs esset.

Et cum turba, in comitium° et cūriam conveniēns, magis- 5
trātūs vocāret, tandem paulō ante sōlis occāsum M. Pompōnius praetor dīxit, "Pugnā magnā victī sumus."

Quot cāsūs exercitūs victī fuerant, tot in cūrās distractī
erant animī eōrum quōrum propinquī sub C. Flāminiō cōn-
sule pugnāverant; nam ignōrābant quae suōrum fortūna esset. 10

Posterō diē ad portās major prope mulierum quam virōrum
multitūdō stetit expectāns suōrum aliquem aut nūntiōs dē
eīs. Fēminārum praecipuē et dolōrēs et gaudia īnsignia
erant. Ūna in ipsā portā subitō fīlium incolumem tūta° in
complexū ejus expīrāvit; altera, cui mors fīliī falsō nūntiāta 15
erat, sedēns domī° ad prīmum cōnspectum fīliī redeuntis
gaudiō exanimāta est.°

°**vagae** wandering • **obviōs** those whom they met • **comitium** place of assembly • **tūta** having seen • **domī** at
home • **exanimāta est** died

cūria, -ae	F., senate house
turba, -ae	F., crowd; tumult
propinquus, -ī	M., relative
mulier, -eris	F., woman, wife
praetor, -ōris	M., praetor (a Roman magistrate)
complexus, -ūs	M., embrace
concursus, -ūs	M., a running together, meeting
occāsus, -ūs	M., a falling, setting
	(with **sōlis** = sunset; the west)
tumultus, -ūs	M., commotion, confusion
aliquis, aliquid	(pron.) someone, something; any-one, anything
repentīnus, -a, -um	sudden
īnsignis, -e	marked, remarkable

124

quot	(indecl. adj.) as many (as); how many?
tot	(indecl. adj.) so many (**quot . . . tot** as many . . . as)
ignōrō, -āre, -āvī, -ātum	not know, be unaware of; overlook
distrahō, -ere, -trāxī, -tractum	divide, distract; remove
falsō	(adv.) falsely
paulō	(adv.) (by) a little
praecipuē	(adv.) especially

A N I N D I R E C T Q U E S T I O N in Latin has its verb in the subjunctive, but is translated in the same way as the indicative.

1 **Mātrōnae obviōs rogābant quae fortūna exercitūs esset.** Matrons asked those whom they met what the fortune of the army was.

2 **Ignōrābant quae suōrum fortūna esset.** They did not know what the fortune of their own men was.

An indirect question depends on words meaning "ask," "know," "perceive," and the like, and repeats the thought, but not the exact words, of the speaker. (A direct question repeats the speaker's exact words, which in writing are enclosed in quotation marks.)

T H E T E N S E O F A S U B J U N C T I V E in a subordinate clause is determined by the tense of the main verb.

1 **It ut praemium accipiat.** He goes to/that he may receive a reward.

2 **Hostēs fūgērunt cum victī essent.** The enemy fled because they had been defeated.

3 **Vīdērunt quid faciam.** They have seen what I am doing.

4 **Hostēs ācriter pugnāvērunt nē vincerentur.** The enemy have fought fiercely in order that they might not be conquered.

When the main verb denotes present or future time, a subjunctive in a subordinate clause is regularly in the present or perfect tense (sentence 1).

When the main verb denotes past time, a subjunctive in a subordinate clause is regularly in the imperfect or past perfect (sentence 2).

125

When the main verb is a perfect that is equivalent to an English present perfect (translated with "have" or "has"), a dependent subjunctive may be in the present (sentence 3) or in the imperfect (sentence 4).

XIV Change the underlined forms to subjunctives and make other necessary changes. Translate both versions of each sentence.

1 "Quot tēcta montānōrum incēnsa sunt?" mīlitēs rogant.
2 Cōpiās ad commeātūs petendōs auxit.
3 Dum frāter parvus dormit, puella parvā vōce cantat.
4 Cōnsul rogāvit, "Quid ille obses cupit?"
5 "Quis est illa mulier?" omnēs rogābant.
6 Nōlī rogāre, "Quō itinere Poenī in Ītaliam pervēnērunt?"

XV For each verb in the lettered list select a verb of similar meaning from the numbered list and give the corresponding form.

1 aggredior   a) incēdāmus
2 cōnor   b) oppugnāverant
3 polliceor   c) prōmīsit
4 populor   d) temptāret
5 prōgredior   e) vāstāvissent

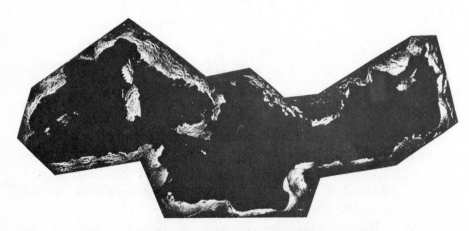

The area in which the Punic Wars occurred is encompassed in this photograph of the Mediterranean Sea and its shores. Taken by radar, it has the effect of a relief map. Can you find Italy, Sicily, North Africa, and Spain?

In the late Middle Ages, Francisco Sforza, a boastful Italian leader of professional soldiers, wrote a treatise on military matters. As a tactician he considered himself equal to the great generals of antiquity. This highly imaginative illumination from his manuscript pictures Sforza himself with Caesar on the left, Hannibal on the right, and Quintus Fabius Maximus at far left, next to Scipio. Also included are the Greek generals Epaminondas and Themistocles. The name of the character at the far right is unknown. The man at Caesar's right may be Marius, Caesar's uncle, who was leader of the popular party at Rome.

TIME FOR A DICTATOR

The four thousand cavalry sent by Servilius were still on their way north when they learned of the Roman defeat at Lake Trasumennus. They turned aside into Umbria, but Hannibal captured them.

This second disaster called for extreme measures in an effort to try to stem the tide of Carthaginian victories. For the first time a Roman dictator was chosen by popular election. Quintus Fabius Maximus was given the task of defending Rome, after the defense of Italy had broken down.

Fabius ordered unfortified towns and villages to be evacuated, and he applied a "scorched earth" policy by burning all the farms and crops in Hannibal's path. He enlisted enough Roman citizens and allies to form two new legions. Then he set out by the Flaminian Way to take over the command of Servilius' army.

127

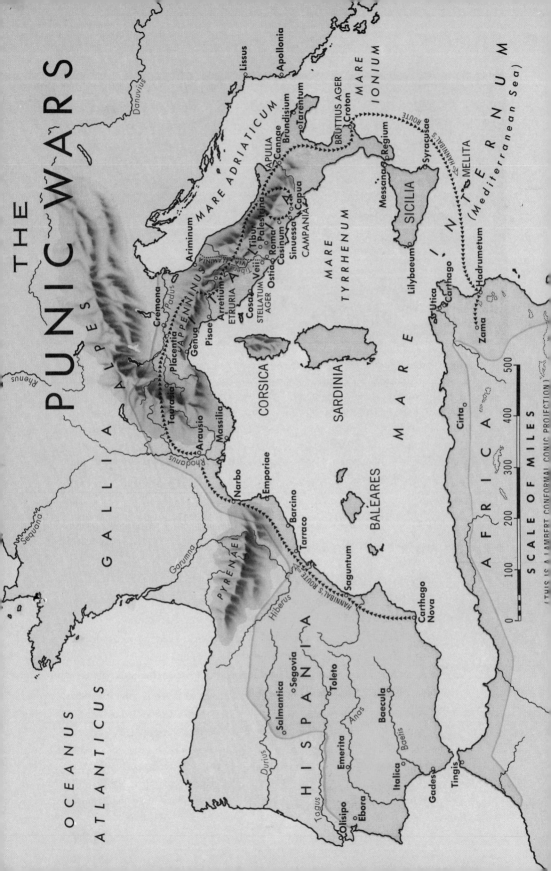

Most Latin perfect participles were used also as adjectives. English adopted many of them simply by dropping the Latin endings or replacing them by -e.

English	Latin			
temperate	**temperātum**	perf. part. of **temperō**	(I)
tacit	**tacitum**	perf. part. of **taceō**	(II)
abrupt	**abruptum**	perf. part. of **abrumpō**	(III)
definite	**dēfinītum**	perf. part. of **dēfiniō**	(IV)

Give the Latin perfect participle and the corresponding English adjective of each of the following verbs.

appōnō   compleō   dēspērō   ōrnō   quiēscō   removeō

The perfect participle **concrētum** (from **concrēscō,** grow together/stiffen/harden) has given English "concrete"— adjective, noun, and verb.

Some of these participles had assumed verb duties in English as early as the fifteenth/sixteenth century; e.g., "content," "complete." While the examples just given show no difference in form between adjective and verb, many English words derived from Conjugation I verbs distinguish between verb and adjective by pronunciation rather than by spelling. For instance, "separate," as a verb, is pronounced to rhyme with "gate"; as an adjective, it rhymes with "Margaret."

With the help of a dictionary (if necessary), give the first and fourth principal parts of the Latin verbs from which these English words were derived.

alternate   consummate   elaborate   moderate   predicate

Another large group of Latin perfect participles now occur only as verbs in English; e.g., "navigate" from **nāvigātum.** Verbs of all four conjugations are represented in this class. For each Latin verb give the perfect participle and the English verb derivative.

agitō	**creō**	**injiciō**	**inveniō**	**prohibeō**
cōgitō	**dēleō**	**instruō**	**obsideō**	**subtrahō**

Fabius, cum prōspexisset agmen cōnsulemque cum equitibus ad sē prōgredientem, viātōrem° mīsit quī cōnsulī nūn-
tiāret ut sine lictōribus ad dictātōrem venīret.

Cōnsul dictō pāruit° congressusque eōrum° ingentem spe-
ciem° dictātūrae apud cīvēs sociōsque jam vetustāte prope 5
oblītōs ejus imperiī° fēcit.° Epistulā ab urbe allātā Fabius
certior factus est nāvēs onerāriās commeātum ab Ōstiā in
Hispāniam ad exercitum portantēs ā classe Pūnicā circā
portum Cosānum° captās esse.

Itaque statim ā dictātōre cōnsul Ōstiam proficīscī jussus 10
est nāvibusque quae ad urbem Rōmānam aut Ōstiae essent
complētis mīlitibus ac nāvālibus sociīs° persequī hostium
classem ac lītora Ītaliae dēfendere.

°**viātōrem** courier, messenger attached to the service of a Roman
magistrate • **dictō pāruit** obeyed the order • **eōrum** i.e.,
of the consul and the dictator • **speciem . . . fēcit** created an
impression • **oblītōs ejus imperiī** who had forgotten that
supreme command • **Cosānum** of Cosa, a town in Etruria •
nāvālibus sociīs sailors (chosen from freedmen of colonists and
allies)

dictātūra, -ae	F., dictatorship
dictātor, -ōris	M., dictator
lictor, -ōris	M., lictor (attendant of a magis-trate)
vetustās, -ātis	F., passage of time; (great) age
congressus, -ūs	M., meeting
onerārius, -a, -um	suitable for freight (**nāvis one-rāria** freight ship, transport)
Pūnicus, -a, -um	Carthaginian
compleō, -ēre, -plēvī, -plētum	(with abl.) fill; man (verb)
persequor, -sequī, -secūtus sum	pursue
prōspiciō, -ere, -spexī, -spectum	see, look (out), watch
afferō, -ferre, attulī, allātum	bring, deliver; advance
certior fierī	be informed

130

PLACE is expressed without a preposition with the names of cities, towns, and small islands, and also with **domus** (when it means "home").

1 **Rōmae concursus in forum populī est factus.** At Rome the people rushed together into the forum. (Lit., A rushing together of people into the forum was made.)

Place where is denoted by the locative case, which in singular nouns of Declensions I and II has the same form as genitive singular; in singular nouns of Declension III, the same form as ablative singular; and in all plural nouns, the same form as ablative plural.

Rōmae/at Rome	**Tarentī**/at Tarentum	**Athēnīs**/at Athens
domī/at home	**Bibracte**/at Bibracte	**Vēiīs**/at Veii

2 **Rōmā statim dictātor ēgressus est.** The dictator departed from Rome immediately.
3 **Itaque ā dictātōre cōnsul Ōstiam proficīscī jussus est.** Therefore the consul was ordered by the dictator to set out for Ostia.
4 **Cōnsul domum rediit.** The consul returned home.

Place from which is denoted by the ablative case (sentence 2) and place to which by the accusative case (sentences 3 and 4).

A **Cōnsul in domum rediit.** The consul went back into the house.
B **Nūntius ad domum cōnsulis rediit.** The messenger returned to the consul's house.

When **domus** means "house," a preposition is used with the accusative case to express place to which, as in sentences A and B.

C **In urbe cōnsul nōn manēre nōluit.** The consul did not want to remain in the city.
D **Epistula ab urbe allāta est.** A letter was brought from the city.
E **Nāvēs commeātum in Hispāniam ad exercitum portābant.** Ships carried provisions to Spain for the army.

With other words prepositions are used to express place where **(in)**, as in sentence C; place from which **(ā/ab, dē, ē/ex)**, as in sentence D; and place to which **(in, ad)**, as in sentence E.

131

XVI From the list select all words which, with/without the preposition, may replace each underlined expression. Translate all versions and explain the case and use of every choice.

Alpium	domī	Hispāniā	locō	palūdis	Rōmam
angustiās	domō	īnsidiae	monte	portū	rūpibus
Carthāgine	domum	jugō	Ōstiae	Rhodanus	Vēiīs

1 In illō oppidō fāmam audīvimus multōs famē mortuōs esse.
2 Proximō diē mīlitēs ab hībernīs profectī sunt.
3 Hominēs in sua tēcta redīre cupiēbant.
4 Barbarī saxa dē clīvīs in agmen dējiciēbant.
5 Castra exercituī Rōmānō ē valle movenda erant.

A NOUN CLAUSE with its verb in the subjunctive may be the object or the subject of certain verbs.

1 **Ille cōnsulī nūntiāvit ut sine lictōribus ad dictātōrem venīret.** He reported to the consul that he should come to the dictator without lictors.

2 **Cōnsulī nūntiātum est nē cum lictōribus ad dictātōrem venīret.** It was reported to the consul that he should not come to the dictator with lictors.

3 **Dictātor cōnsulī imperāvit[1] ut hostium classem persequerētur.** The dictator commanded the consul to pursue the enemy's fleet.

A noun clause of desire may occur with a verb signifying or implying desire or purpose; e.g., **admoneō/moneō** (admonish/warn), **adhortor/hortor** (encourage/urge), **imperō/mandō** (command/order), and **suādeō/persuādeō** (persuade). In sentences 1 and 2 the force of a command is implied in **nūntiāvit** and **nūntiātum est.**

Verbs of wishing, permitting, deciding, and decreeing are sometimes completed by a noun clause of desire and sometimes by an infinitive with subject accusative.

The subjunctive in a clause of desire may often be translated by an English infinitive, as in sentence 3.

4 **Hoc effēcit ut castra tūta essent.** This fact made the camp safe. (Lit., This fact brought about that the camp was safe.)

[1]**Jubeō** (order) is regularly completed by an infinitive with subject accusative.

132

5 **Hoc effēcit ut castra tūta nōn essent.** This fact made the camp not safe. (Lit., This fact brought about that the camp was not safe.)

6 **Saepe accidit ut frātrem tuum in urbe videam.** It often happens that I see your brother in the city.

A noun clause of fact occurs with a verb signifying accomplishment or result. With a verb meaning "to bring about," "to make," or "to cause" (e.g., **committō, faciō, efficiō, cōnficiō**), the noun clause is the object of the verb (sentences 4 and 5).

With a verb in the third person singular meaning "it happens," "it comes about," "it results," "it remains," or "it follows" (e.g., **accidit, ēvenit, fit, fierī potest, efficitur, relinquitur, sequitur**), the noun clause is the subject.

A noun clause of desire/fact is introduced by **ut** unless it is negative. When negative, a noun clause of desire is introduced by **nē** (sentence 2), while a negative noun clause of fact is introduced by **ut . . . nōn** (sentence 5).

XVII To complete each sentence select an appropriate form from the group in parentheses. Translate the sentences.

1 Prīncipēs mīlitibus veterānīs ut agmen Gallōrum (secūtī sunt/sequī/sequerentur/secūtūrōs esse) imperāverant.

2 Cōnsulī nūntiāvērunt ut ducem dē sitū castrōrum hostium (docuissent/docēret/docērī/doceant).

3 Cōnsul cupiet ut tribūnus ex urbe statim (proficīscī/proficīscēns/proficīscerētur/proficīscātur).

4 Magistrātus quaesīvit cūr viātor lēgātō nōn (pāruerat/pāruisset/pārēre/pāreant).

5 Propter rūpēs altōs accidit ut expedītī hostēs nōn (vidērī/vidērent/vīdērunt/videat).

NEW GENERAL, NEW TACTICS

Dictātor exercitū cōnsulis acceptō ā Fulviō Flaccō lēgātō per agrum Sabīnum Tībur vēnit. Inde Praeneste ac trānsversīs līmitibus° in viam Latīnam est ēgressus, unde itineribus summā cum cūrā explōrātīs ad hostem dūxit.°

°**trānsversīs līmitibus** by means of crossroads • **dūxit** advanced

133

The French artist Jean Baptiste Camille Corot (1796-1875) painted this view of Tivoli (ancient Tibur). The painting is in the Louvre.

Quō prīmum diē in cōnspectū hostium posuit castra, nūlla ⁵ mora facta est quīn Hannibal ēdūceret in aciem cōpiamque° pugnandī faceret. Sed quiēta erant omnia apud hostēs, nec castra ūllō tumultū mōta vīdit. Increpāns quidem Rōmānōs, Hannibal in castra rediit. Tacita cūra animum incessit, quod jam doctī malīs Rōmānī ducem Hannibalī parem quaesī- ¹⁰ vissent.° Et prūdentiam quidem novī dictātōris statim timuit.

Fabius per loca alta agmen dūcēbat mediocrī ab hoste intervallō, ut neque omitteret eum neque congrederētur.

°**cōpiamque** and ... an opportunity • **quaesīvissent** had chosen (subjunctive; this is Hannibal's rather than the author's opinion)

prūdentia, -ae	F., foresight, prudence
Via (-ae) Latīna (-ae)	F., Latin Way (famous Roman road)
aciēs, -ēī	F., line of battle; battle
Sabīnus, -a, -um	Sabine, of the Sabines; **ager Sabīnus,** Sabine territory
ūllus, -a, -um	any
mediocris, -e	moderate, ordinary

pār, gen., **paris**	equal (to), like; a match for
congredior, -gredī, -gressus sum	meet (in battle), encounter
ēdūcō, -ere, -dūxī, -ductum	lead out (troops); (of a general) march out
ēgredior, -gredī, ēgressus sum	come out, march out, leave
omittō, -ere, -mīsī, -missum	let go, lose; disregard
nec/neque	and not; nor

NEGATIVE EXPRESSIONS OF DOUBT

1 **Nōn erat dubium quīn hūc vēnisset.** There was no doubt that he had come here.

2 **Nōn dubitō quīn veniat.** I have no doubt that he is coming.

3 **Nūlla mora facta est quīn Hannibal ēdūceret in aciem cōpiamque pugnandī faceret.** Without delay Hannibal led out (his troops) into battle formation and offered an opportunity for fighting. (Lit., No delay was made in that Hannibal led out [his troops] etc.)

Words and phrases of doubt or hindrance, when accompanied by a negative, are followed by **quīn** and the subjunctive.

XVIII Combine each clause or phrase from the lettered list with one in the numbered list to make sensible sentences. Translate the completed sentences. Explain the uses of all subjunctives.

a) mīlitibus imperat   e) dux prohibēre nōn potuit
b) quārē accidit ut   f) multa jūmenta mortua sunt
c) nōn dubitāvī   g) obsidēs monitī sunt
d) senātus cōnstituerat   h) statim dux jussit

1 dictātōrem dīcendum esse
2 priusquam commeātus invenīrētur
3 ut agmen hostium omittant
4 quīn exercitus noster ēgrederētur
5 ut ante occāsum sōlis redīrent
6 signifer certior nōn factus esset
7 quīn mīlitēs fortēs fuissent
8 peditēs ūnam aciem efficere

By means of little skirmishes, rather than in an all-out battle, Fabius helped his men to regain some of the courage and self-confidence that they had lost through their earlier defeats. Fabius continued his plan of merely following the enemy, although Hannibal tried by every means to provoke the Roman general into engaging in a pitched battle.

Hannibal deliberately destroyed the lands and cities of Roman allies in his attempt to make Fabius angry enough to fight on equal terms. His army moved into Campania, burning and plundering everywhere, while Fabius continued to watch and wait all through the summer.

Even while the dictator's measures were unpopular to a growing number of Romans, they were exasperating to Hannibal. For northern Campania could not supply him indefinitely, so that he was forced to find a more suitable place for winter quarters.

THE ROMANS GUARD THE PASS

Haec° per explōrātōrēs relāta Fabiō sunt. Cum satis scīret° Hannibalem per eāsdem angustiās quibus intrāverat Falernum agrum° reditūrum, Calliculam montem et Casilīnum occupāvit mediocribus praesidiīs.

Eō forte diē Minucius[1] sē conjūnxerat° Fabiō, missus ad 5
firmandās praesidiō angustiās, nē ab Sinuessā Hannibal Viā
Appiā pervenīre in agrum Rōmānum posset.

Conjūnctīs exercitibus dictātor ac Minucius castra in viam dētulērunt quā Hannibal ductūrus erat. Duo inde mīlia passuum hostēs aberant.   10

°**haec**   this (namely Hannibal's intentions)   •   **satis scīret**   felt sure
Falernum agrum   Falernian territory (in Campania)   •   **sē conjūnx-erat**   (with dative) had joined

praesidium, -ī	N., garrison, guard
firmō, -āre, -āvī, -ātum	strengthen
referō, -ferre, rettulī, relātum	report, mention; bring back

[1]Minucius was the "master of the horse," that is, he commanded the cavalry. In practice he also served as lieutenant to the dictator Fabius.

Viā ad Casilīnum obsessā, inclūsus inde Hannibal vīsus est. Itaque cum per Casilīnum ēvādere nōn posset, montēs Hannibalī petendī erant et jugum Calliculae superandum erat.

Hannibal timēbat nē Rōmānī impetum facerent in agmen, vallibus inclūsum.° Lūdibrium° oculōrum, igitur, ad dēcipiendum hostem invēnit.

Facēs° undique ex agrīs collēctae fascēsque° virgārum praeligātī sunt° cornibus circiter duōrum mīlium bovum quōs inter praedam agēbat. Hasdrubalī negōtium datum est ut nocte id armentum,° accēnsīs° cornibus, ad montēs ageret, maximē super angustiās ab hoste obsessās.

Castra silentiō mōta sunt. Bovēs quī facēs in cornibus ferēbant ante signa āctī sunt. Ubi ad rādīcēs montium° viāsque angustās ventum est, signum datum est. Accēnsīs cornibus, bovēs in adversōs° montēs agēbantur. Timor calorque flammārum hōs bovēs velut furōre stimulābant. Capitum quassātiō° flammās excitābat et speciem hominum passim currentium praebēbat. Rōmānī, ubi in summīs montibus ac super sē ignēs cōnspexērunt, sē circumventōs esse ratī fūgērunt.

Intereā Hannibal tōtum agmen per angustiās trādūxit et ultrā montēs castra posuit. Fabius quoque mōvit castra trānsgressusque angustiās locō altō ac mūnītō cōnsēdit.

°**vallibus inclūsum** (modifies **agmen**) as it was marching through the gorges • **lūdibrium, -ī** N., mockery, trick • **facēs** F. pl., torches • **fascēs** M. pl., bundles (**virgārum** of twigs) **praeligātī sunt** were tied (to) • **armentum, -ī** N., herd **accēnsīs** aflame • **ad rādīcēs montium** to the foot of the mountains • **in adversōs montēs** up the mountains • **quassātiō, -ōnis** F., shaking

praeda, -ae	F., booty, plunder
jugum, -ī	N., ridge, summit
calor, -ōris	M., heat
timor, -ōris	M., fear
stimulō, -āre, -āvī, -ātum	rouse, spur on, stimulate

137

This bronze belt of Campanian workmanship was found in a Carthaginian grave. Some soldier probably carried it back to Carthage as booty from the fighting in Campania.

praebeō, -ēre, -uī, -itum	give; show, display
reor, rērī, ratus sum	think, believe; reckon
videor, -ērī, vīsus sum	seem, appear
cōnsīdō, -ere, -sēdī, -sessum	encamp, settle; sit down
dēcipiō, -ere, -cēpī, -ceptum	deceive
inclūdō, -ere, -clūsī, -clūsum	shut or hem in
trānsgredior, -gredī, -gressus sum	cross; go through/over
circumveniō, -īre, -vēnī, -ventum	surround

circiter	(adv./prep. with acc.) about
maximē	(adv.) especially, mostly
passim	(adv.) everywhere, in every direction
ultrā	(adv./prep. with acc.) beyond

A DEPENDENT CLAUSE OF FEAR with its verb in the subjunctive may be used with a verb of fearing or with other expressions of fear to tell what the subject fears will happen.

1 **Hannibal timēbat nē Rōmānī impetum facerent in agmen.**
Hannibal was afraid (that) the Romans would make an attack on (his) line of march.

138

2 **Timeō ut hodiē perveniat.** I am afraid (that) he will not arrive today.

A clause of fear is introduced by **nē**/that or by **ut**/that ... not. (Occasionally **nē ... nōn** is used instead of **ut.**)

With English expressions of fear the conjunction "that" is sometimes omitted. (See sentences 1 and 2.) In Latin the conjunction **ut/nē** or **nē ... nōn** is necessary in a clause of fear.

Caution: With other subjunctive clauses **ut** means "that" and **nē** means "that ... not," exactly the reverse of usage in clauses of fear.

In this kind of clause the Latin present subjunctive has the same force as the English future. (See sentence 2.)

XIX Complete each sentence with an appropriate verb from the lettered list. Translate the completed sentences, and explain the form and use of each chosen verb.

1 Incolae vallis magnum metum habent nē sua tēcta _____ .

2 Rōmānī timēbant nē explōrātor Poenus facilius iter per palūdēs _____ .

3 Cum Hannibal ex hībernīs nōn _____ , tamen fāma erat illum urbem _____ .

4 Gallī praemissī erunt antequam equitēs Hannibalis nostrum agmen _____ .

5 Timeō ut ignēs urbis _____ .

a) comperīret
b) ēvāserīs
c) fierem
d) incendantur
e) morārī
f) obsidēre
g) profectus esset
h) subeant

AN INJUSTICE IS DONE

Hannibal now pretended that he was going to march on Rome, while Fabius led his troops along the ridges between the enemy and the city. Suddenly Hannibal turned and marched back toward Apulia till he came to an abandoned town.

When Fabius had been recalled to Rome to take care of religious matters, word came that the Romans under Minucius had engaged in a successful battle against Hannibal. Actually the losses had been about equal on both sides, and the report of a Roman victory was highly exaggerated. Nevertheless, the people at Rome—already impatient with Fabius' cautious methods and anxious for more active military measures—were encouraged by the falsified report of Minucius' success

139

to pass a bill making the master of the horse equal in power to the dictator.

News of the passage of the bill reached Fabius as he was returning to his army, but the unwarranted action bothered the dictator little. He was confident of his superior ability, in spite of the equalization of authority of the two commanders. On the dictator's return, Minucius and Fabius decided to divide the army, with each commanding one half.

Hannibal was doubly pleased by this arrangement, since it halved Fabius' strength and at the same time increased the possibility of the rest of the army being involved in unfavorable action because of Minucius' rashness.

After concealing five thousand men in the hollow cliffs near his camp, Hannibal enticed Minucius and his men into what appeared to be a fight with a small force of Carthaginian soldiers sent to occupy the hill. The Romans were completely demoralized by the sudden appearance of the troops that were in ambush.

FABIUS TO THE RESCUE

Tum Fabius prīmō clāmōre timentium audītō, deinde cōnspectā procul turbātā aciē, "Ita est," inquit; "nōn celerius quam timuī dēprehendit fortūna temeritātem. Fabiō aequātus° imperiō Hannibalem et virtūte et fortūnā superiōrem Minucius videt. Sed aliud jūrgandī° suscēnsendīque° tempus nōbīs erit; nunc signa extrā vallum prōferte; victōriam hostī extorqueāmus,° cōnfessiōnem errōris cīvibus." 5

Jam magnā ex parte° caesīs aliīs, aliīs circumspectantibus fugam Fabiāna sē aciēs subitō velut caelō dēmissa auxiliō ostendit. Itaque, priusquam ad conjectum° tēlī venīret aut manum cōnsereret,° et suōs ā fugā effūsā° et ab ferōcī pugnā hostēs continuit. 10

°aequātus (modifies **Minucius**) made equal • **jūrgō** 1 quarrel **suscēnseō** 2 be angry • **extorqueō** 2 (with dative of person) wrest away (from) • **magnā ex parte** in large part, to a great extent • **ad conjectum** within range • **manum cōnsereret** engaged in hand-to-hand fighting • **effūsā** headlong

140

Ac jam prope ūna aciēs facta erat victī atque integrī exer-
citūs° īnferēbantque signa in hostem, cum Poenus receptuī
cecinit,° palam ferente° Hannibale ab sē Minucium, sē ab 15
Fabiō victum esse.

°**victī atque integrī exercitūs** of the beaten and the fresh army (This
genitive depends on **aciēs.**) • **signa receptuī cecinit** gave the
signal for retreat • **ferente** stating, declaring

vallum, -ī	N., entrenchment, rampart
cōnfessiō, -ōnis	F., confession, admission
error, -ōris	M., error; wandering
temeritās, -ātis	F., rashness
Fabiānus, -a, -um	of Fabius, Fabian
celer, celeris, celere	swift, sudden
turbō, -āre, -āvī, -ātum	disturb, confuse
caedō, -ere, cecīdī, caesum	kill, slay
īnferō, -ferre, intulī, illātum	bring on/in/forward; with **signa** = advance, attack
prōferō, -ferre, -tulī, -lātum	carry/bring out; with **signa** = advance, march
palam	(adv.) openly; in public

DATIVE OF PURPOSE

1 **Hunc librum dōnō mīsī.** I sent this book as a gift (lit., for a gift).
2 **Equitātum auxiliō mīserant.** They had sent the cavalry as aid (lit., for aid).
3 **Haec fāma auxiliō erit.** This reputation will be a help.

Sometimes a noun in the dative denotes the purpose which
something serves or is intended to serve; e.g., **dōnō** (sentence
1), **auxiliō** (sentence 2).

A dative of purpose is sometimes employed when English
usage would require a predicate nominative (sentence 3).

141

DATIVE OF REFERENCE

1 **Legiō equitātuī auxiliō missa est.** The legion was sent as aid (lit., for aid) to the cavalry.

2 **Equitātum auxiliō Caesarī Haeduī mīserant.** The Haeduī had sent the cavalry as aid (lit., for aid) to/for Caesar.

The dative sometimes denotes the person/thing with reference to whom/which an act is done or a situation exists; e.g., **equitātuī** (sentence 1), **Caesarī** (sentence 2).

This use is especially important in expressions which contain also a dative of purpose, such as **auxiliō** in both sentences 1 and 2.

DATIVE OF POSSESSION

1 **Magistrō multī librī sunt.** The teacher has many books.

2 **Puerō nōmen Mārcus est.** The boy's name is Marcus. (Lit., To the boy the name is Marcus.)

A noun or pronoun in the dative case may denote the possessor of something. The thing that is possessed is then denoted by a word in the nominative case—the subject of a form of the verb **sum.**

A dative of possession emphasizes the fact of ownership rather than the owner.

Chests, such as the one above, and huge pottery jars constituted most of the furnishings in a Carthaginian house. When the owner died he was buried in the chest.

XX Supply a suitable ending for each noun in parentheses and explain the case and use of underlined words. Translate completed sentences.

1 Equitātus illī <u>legiōnī</u> (auxilium) mittētur.

2 Nāvēs <u>expedītīs</u> complētae (classis) <u>praesidiō</u> imperātae sunt.

3 Flammae in boum <u>cornibus</u> ārdentēs <u>mīlitibus</u> Rōmānīs (dolus) fuērunt.

4 Sunt (Poenī) mīlitēs fortēs quī <u>ducī</u> (praesidium) sunt.

5 Speciēs <u>eārum</u> fīliōrum (mulier) <u>reī</u> gaudiī vīsa est.

6 <u>Minuciō</u>, quī (Fabius) aequātus erat, imperium magnum erat.

7 Vallēs lāta <u>exercituī</u> (hīberna) dēligenda erat.

A GOOD LOSER

Cum in castra reditum esset, Minucius convocātīs mīlitibus, "Saepe ego," inquit, "audīvī, mīlitēs, eum prīmum esse virum quī ipse cōnsulat quid in rem sit°; secundum eum quī bene monentī pāreat; eum quī nec ipse cōnsulere nec alterī pārēre possit esse extrēmī ingeniī.°

"Nōbīs quoniam prīma animī ingeniīque sors negāta est, secundam ac mediam sortem teneāmus, et dum imperāre discimus, pārēre prūdentī in animum indūcāmus.° Castra cum Fabiō jungāmus. Cum ad praetōrium° ejus signa tulerimus, ubi ego eum parentem appellāverō, vōs, mīlitēs, eōs 10 quōrum arma ac dextrae vōs modo tēxērunt patrōnōs° salūtābitis; et sī nihil aliud, grātōrum certē nōbīs animōrum glōriam diēs hic dederit."

°**quid in rem sit** what is of advantage • **extrēmī ingeniī** of the lowest intelligence • **in animum indūcāmus** let us resolve **praetōrium, -ī** N., (a general's) tent, headquarters • **patrōnōs** as patrons (protectors)

parēns, -entis	M./F., parent, mother, father; relative
sors, sortis	F., lot, destiny
prūdēns, gen., **-entis**	wise, intelligent
imperō, -āre, -āvī, -ātum	command; rule
negō, -āre, -āvī, -ātum	deny, refuse, say . . . not

143

pāreō, -ēre, -uī, _____	obey, listen to
cōnsulō, -ere, -suluī, -sultum	take thought for, look out for
tegō, -ere, tēxī, tēctum	protect, defend; cover
modo	(adv.) just now
quoniam	(conj.) since, because

DATIVE WITH SPECIAL VERBS

cēdō	yield (to)	**pāreō**	obey/be obedient
cōnfīdō	trust/give trust	**placeō**	please/be pleasing
crēdō	believe/trust	**resistō**	resist/offer resistance
faveō	favor/show favor	**studeō**	desire/study/be favorable/
imperō	order/command		be eager
noceō	harm/do harm	**suādeō/persuādeō**	persuade/
parcō	spare/show mercy		make pleasing

The object of the action of verbs of special meaning is in the dative case, although the English equivalents of these verbs require a direct object.

1 **Līberī parentibus pārēre dēbent.** Children ought to obey their parents.

2 **Rōmānī hostibus cēdere recūsāvērunt.** The Romans refused to yield to the enemy.

In sentence 1 the dative **parentibus** is the object of **pārēre**, and in sentence 2 the dative **hostibus** is the object of **cēdere**.

PRAISE FROM BOTH SIDES

Reports of this incident, confirmed by letters from both commanders and from their soldiers, came to Rome. Immediately Fabius was given the highest praise by those who had so recently insulted him. Hannibal, too, became acutely aware of the kind of general he was opposing.

Pār glōria apud Hannibalem hostēsque Poenōs erat; ac tum dēmum sēnsērunt bellum esse cum Rōmānīs atque in Italiā. Nam bienniō ante adeō et ducēs Rōmānōs et mīlitēs sprēverant ut vix cum eādem gente bellum esse crēderent cujus terribilem fāmam ā patribus accēpissent. Hannibal ex 5

144

aciē rediēns dīxit tandem eam nūbem quae in jugīs montium sedēre solita esset° cum tempestāte imbrem° dedisse.

°**sedēre solita esset** had (customarily) sat (subjunctive in relative clause within indirect statement) • **imber, -bris** M., rain

biennium, -ī	N., two years
terribilis, -e	dreadful, terrible
spernō, -ere, sprēvī, sprētum	scorn, despise
adeō	(adv.) so, to such an extent
dēmum	(adv.) at last

R E S U L T may be expressed in Latin by a subordinate clause with its verb in the subjunctive.

1 **Biennō ante adeō et ducēs Rōmānōs et mīlitēs sprēverant ut vix cum eādem gente bellum esse crēderent.** Two years ago they had despised both the Roman generals and the soldiers so much that they scarcely believed that the (present) war was with the same people.

2 **Tempestātēs tantae erant ut ex portū proficīscī nōn audērēmus.** The storms were so great that we did not dare to set out from the harbor.

A result clause is regularly introduced by the conjunction **ut** (sentence 1). When the clause is negative, **ut . . . nōn** is used (sentence 2).

The verb in a result clause is translated as an indicative.

XXI Translate each sentence and explain the tense and use of all subjunctives.

1 Trepidātiō tanta fuit ut jūmenta terrērentur.

2 Dictātor imperāvit ut omnia oppida frūmentumque in agrīs vāstārentur.

3 Minucius tam audāx erat ut salūtem suī exercitūs nōn cōnsuleret.

4 Terram populābimur adeō ut hostēs nūllōs commeātūs invenīre possint.

5 Equitēs jugum tegēbant dum cōpiae integrae ab hībernīs pervenīrent.

6 Cum dux virōs dē īnsidiīs monuerit, in angustiīs tamen inclūdentur.

7 Explōrātor comperīre cōnābitur quot castra hostēs habeant.

8 Sequāminī agmen novissimum maximā cum cūrā ut Poenī īnsidiās nostrās ignōrent.

END OF THE DICTATORSHIP

Realizing that his six-month term of office as dictator was nearly at an end, Fabius sent for the two consuls, Gnaeus Servilius and Marcus Atilius, so that they might take over his armies.

The two new generals, upon taking over the dictator's armies, carried on the war for the rest of the autumn in accordance with Fabius' policies. Their success was apparent when Hannibal considered retreating into Gaul. He had given up hope of supporting his army in Italy, unless the next consuls should change the tactics of the Roman forces.

THEY CHOSE TO FIGHT

In the spring of 216 Hannibal captured the Roman supply depot at Cannae. He had also cut off the Roman army from Apulia and the early grain harvest there. Faced with the choice of retreating, fighting, or drawing supplies from more distant depots, the Romans chose to fight.

In command of the Roman army were Aemilius Paulus and Terentius Varro, newly elected consuls. Of the two, Paulus was more experienced and cautious, while Varro was impatient and overconfident in the superior numbers of Roman troops. Each consul commanded the entire army on alternate days. On August 3, 216 B.C. Terentius Varro was in command, and on that day the battle of Cannae was fought.

Varro drew up his line of battle in the customary Roman fashion. He placed cavalry on each flank and heavy infantry in the center. His entire front line was made up of light-armed troops. The infantry was under the command of Servilius and Atilius, the two proconsuls (i.e., consuls of the preceding year whose authority was extended so that they could hold a military command). Varro and Paulus were in charge of the cavalry—Paulus on the right flank and Varro on the left.

The monument in the foreground marks the site of the battle of Cannae.

Hannibal drew up his army in a similar manner. The location of Cannae on an open plain was favorable to him, since his strength was in his cavalry. On the left flank (opposite Paulus' cavalry on the Roman right flank) Hannibal placed his Gallic and Spanish cavalry and, on the right, his Numidian cavalry (opposite Varro's cavalry on the Roman left flank).

After his troops had formed into a straight line, Hannibal ordered the center companies of his infantry to advance, thus forming a crescent-shaped bulge extending out from the heavy infantry on each side. (See diagram.)

BATTLE OF CANNAE

Clāmōre factō, prōcursum est ab auxiliīs et pugna prīmum levibus armīs° commissa est. Deinde sinistrum cornū equitum Gallōrum Hispānōrumque cum cornū dextrō Rōmānō concurrit.° Concurrendum erat adversīs frontibus,°

°**levibus armīs** with light-armed troops • **concurrit** engaged in battle, clashed • **adversīs frontibus** head on

147

quod nūllō spatiō ad ēvagandum° relictō hinc flūmen hinc 5
aciēs peditum claudēbant. Dēnique in turbā equōrum
stantium° vir virum amplexus° dē equō dētrahēbat. Pedestre
certāmen jam magnā ex parte factum erat. Ācrius tamen
quam diūtius[1] pugnātum est, Rōmānīque equitēs pulsī terga
vertunt. 10

As the cavalry skirmish was nearing an end, the infantry got into
action. At first the two sides were evenly matched. Then, with a determined thrust, the Roman front line pushed forward in a straight, deep
formation, flattening the bulge of the enemy's line. As the thin line of
troops that had formed the bulge continued to give way, a crescent-
shaped hollow was formed in the center.

The Africans, who had already begun a flanking operation with their
cavalry on either side, were able to close in on the Romans and surround them. Thus the Romans, caught at a disadvantage, not only were
forced to fight shut in by their enemies, but their already exhausted
soldiers faced troops that were fresh and strong. The Romans were,
moreover, the victims of a clever Carthaginian trick.

Sinistrō cornū Rōmānō sociōrum equitēs adversus Numidās steterant. Circiter quīngentī Numidae, habentēs
(praeter cētera arma tēlaque) gladiōs occultōs sub lōrīcīs,°
suōs dēserunt, ex equīs dēsiliunt, scūtīs et tēlīs ante pedēs
Rōmānōrum prōjectīs. Hī, in mediam aciem° acceptī 15
ductīque ad ultimōs mīlitēs, cōnsīdere jubentur.

Dum proelium ab omnī parte geritur, quiētī mānsērunt.
Cum autem certāmen oculōs animōsque omnium occupāret,
arreptīs scūtīs Rōmānam aciem aggressī sunt, terga ferientēs.°
Ita strāgem° ingentem ac majōrem terrōrem ac tumultum 20
fēcērunt.

°**ad ēvagandum** for maneuvering • **stantium** standing still
(because they had no room to move) • **amplexus** having grap-
pled • **lōrīca, -ae** F., leather cuirass • **in mediam aciem**
into their midst • **ferientēs** striking • **strāgēs, -is** F.,
slaughter

[1]Latin can have the comparative also in the second element of a comparison, where
English uses only the positive.

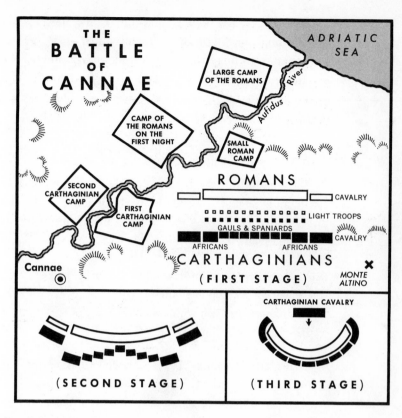

This diagram of the battle of Cannae shows the three stages of the action.

occultus, -a, -um	hidden, concealed
pedester, -tris, -tre	on foot, (of) infantry
arripiō, -ere, -ripuī, -reptum	seize hurriedly
dētrahō, -ere, -trāxī, -tractum	pull or draw down/away
prōcurrō, -ere, -currī, -cursum	run forward; charge
prōjiciō, -ere, -jēcī, -jectum	throw forward/down
hinc ... hinc	on this side ... on that side; here ... there
adversus	(prep. with acc.) opposite, facing
praeter	(prep. with acc.) in addition to, besides; beyond; except
terga vertere	flee, run away

IMPERSONAL VERBS are so called because they have no personal subject. In Latin an impersonal verb has only one person ending (third person singular), but is used in all six tenses of the indicative and in all four tenses of the subjunctive. An impersonal verb also has infinitive forms. In English the subject of an impersonal verb is always "it."

ningit/it is snowing   **pluit**/it is raining   **tonat**/it thunders

Verbs denoting weather conditions are impersonal in both Latin and English. In Latin each of such verbs may stand alone, since it requires no subject, object, infinitive, or clause to complete it.

1 **Diū atque ācriter pugnātum est.** It was a long and bitter fight. (Lit., It was fought long and bitterly.)
2 **Ad extrēmum perīculī ventum est.** They came (lit., it was come) to the utmost danger.

Intransitive Latin verbs, which do not have regular passive forms, occur in the passive only as impersonal verbs (sentences 1 and 2).

3 **Licēbit nōbīs in urbe manēre.** We shall be permitted (lit., it will be permitted to us) to stay in the city.
4 **Nōbīs placuit in urbe manēre.** We decided (lit., it was pleasing to us) to stay in the city.
5 **Oportet nōs in urbe manēre.** We ought (lit., it is necessary for us) to stay in the city.

Certain Latin verbs are often used impersonally. Unlike the verbs denoting weather and the intransitive passives, however, these verbs frequently require an infinitive (sentences 3 and 4) or infinitive with subject accusative (sentence 5).

6 **Accidit ut duae cohortēs ante castra essent.** It happens that there were two cohorts in front of the camp.

Some verbs, when used impersonally, are completed by a noun clause of fact (sentence 6), introduced by **ut/ut . . . nōn,** with its verb in the subjunctive. (See also page 133.)

IMPERSONAL EXPRESSIONS are sometimes completed by an infinitive or by an infinitive with subject accusative (sentence 7), and sometimes by a subordinate (noun) clause (sentences 8 and 9).

7 **Nōs manēre in urbe necesse est.** We must (lit., it is necessary for us to) stay in the city.

8 **Necesse est (ut)[1] in urbe maneāmus.** We must (lit., it is necessary for us to) stay in the city.

9 **Mōs est ut ex equīs pugnent.** It is their custom to fight on horseback.

In addition to **necesse est** and **mōs est,** such impersonal expressions include **cōnsilium est** (the plan is), **cōnsuētūdō est** (the custom is), **facile est** (it is easy), **fās est** (it is lawful), **jūs est** (it is the law), **nefās est** (it is unlawful/a crime), **satis est** (it is enough).

XXII Translate the sentences. Explain fully the form and use of the underlined words.

1 Ducī nūntiātum est rūpem inviam futūram esse.
2 Diē alterō in jugum super flūmen perventum est.
3 Senātuī placuit dictātōrem dīcere.
4 Vōbīs vincendum aut moriendum est.
5 Accidit ut portās urbis jam oppugnārent.
6 Satis erit ut nōs fortitūdinem patrum memoriā teneāmus.

DEFEAT FOR THE ROMANS

Parte alterā pugnae, Paulus, cum prīmō statim proeliō° fundā° graviter vulnerātus esset, tamen cum suīs mīlitibus saepe Hannibalī occurrit et in aliquot locīs proelium restituit. Equitēs Paulum prōtegentēs dē equīs dēsiluērunt, quod vīrēs ad regendum equum cōnsulem dēficiēbant. 5

Pedestre proelium fuit, in quō equitēs nūllam spem victōriae habēbant. Victī tamen mālēbant morī in vēstīgiō°

°**prīmō . . . proeliō** at the start of the fighting • **fundā, -ae** F., sling • **in vēstīgiō** at their post

[1]With **necesse est** and with some verbs the conjunction **ut** is regularly omitted from the noun clause.

quam fugere. Victōrēs īrātī interfēcērunt eōs quōs pellere nōn poterant. Paucōs, labōre et vulneribus fessōs, pepulērunt. Rōmānī omnēs fūgērunt; eī quī poterant equōs ad fugiendum repetēbant.° 10

Gnaeus Lentulus, tribūnus mīlitum,[1] praetervehēns° equō, cum vīdisset Aemilium Paulum cōnsulem in saxō sedentem, cruōre opplētum,° dīxit, "Cape hunc equum; ego comes tē prōtegere possum. Nē fūnestam° hanc pugnam morte cōnsulis 15 fēcerīs. Etiam sine hōc lacrimārum dolōrisque satis est."

Cui° respondit cōnsul, "Tū quidem, macte virtūte estō!° Sed exiguum tempus est ēvādendī ē manibus hostium. Abī, patribus Rōmānīs persuādē ut mūniant urbem Rōmānam priusquam victor hostis adveniat. Prīvātim Q. Fabiō nūntiā 20 L. Aemilium, praeceptōrum ejus memorem,° et vīxisse adhūc et morī,"

Vix hōc dictō, hostēs cōnsulem obruērunt° tēlīs, ignōrantēs quis esset; inter tumultum Lentulum abripuit° equus.

Tum undique omnēs fūgērunt. Septem mīlia hominum 25 in minōra castra, decem° in majōra, duo° in vīcum ipsum Cannās perfūgērunt. Varrō, cōnsul alter, cum quīnquāgintā equitibus Venusiam perfūgit.

°**repetēbant** tried to recover • **praetervehēns** riding by **cruōre opplētum** covered with blood • **fūnestus, -a, -um** mournful • **cui** to him (Lentulus) • **macte virtūte estō!** good luck to your bravery! • **memor,** gen., **-oris** (with gen.) mindful of **obruērunt** overwhelmed • **abripuit** carried away • **decem** (**mīlia** is understood) • **duo** (**mīlia** is understood)

praeceptum, -ī	N., order, instruction, precept
exiguus, -a, -um	little, scanty
persuādeō, -ēre, -suāsī, -suāsum	(with dat. of person) persuade
dēficiō, -ere, -fēcī, -fectum	fail
perfugiō, -ere, -fūgī, ____	flee for refuge
restituō, -ere, -uī, -ūtum	renew, restore
mālō, mālle, māluī, ____	prefer, choose
prīvātim	(adv.) privately, in private

[1] Each legion had six military tribunes, who rotated the chief command. The rest probably commanded groups of cohorts or performed administrative duties.

A Carthaginian goddess. The clothes reflect the typical dress of a Carthaginian woman.

THE VERB MĀLŌ is a compound of **volō** (**magis** + **volō**), and its conjugation is similar to that of **volō**. (See page 450.) **Mālō** means "prefer/choose" (lit., wish more).

> **Victī mālēbant morī in vēstīgiō quam fugere.** Defeated, they preferred to die in their tracks rather than to flee.

Like **volō** and **nōlō, mālō** is completed by a complementary infinitive.

A NEGATIVE WISH may be expressed by **nē** with an independent subjunctive.

> **Nē fūnestam hanc pugnam morte cōnsulis fēcerīs.** Don't (May you not) make this battle mournful by the death of the consul.

XXIII For each numbered singular verb find the plural of the corresponding tense in the lettered list.

1 nōllet	5 nōluistī	a) mālēmus	e) mālueritis
2 nōluerim	6 nōn vult	b) māllent	f) māluistis
3 nōluerīs	7 velīs	c) mālītis	g) māluissent
4 nōluisset	8 volam	d) māluerīmus	h) mālunt

XXIV Translate these sentences with particular attention to underlined words and phrases. Use all possible English expressions in the lettered list.

1 Cōnsulem legiōnēsque duās flūmen trānsīsse fāma erat.
2 Cum peditēs signa intulissent tardius, veterānī tamen pugnāre cupiēbant.
3 Virī solēbant signa noctū movēre.
4 Gallī rettulērunt agmen Poenum ad occāsum sōlis profectum esse.
5 Mīlitēs certiōrēs fīent sibi aut vincendum aut moriendum esse.
6 Cum exercitus signa cōnstitisset in angustiīs, quiēs virīs fessīs danda erat.

a) had advanced	g) had halted	m) there was a rumor
b) were accustomed	h) will be informed	
c) it was rumored	i) usually	n) they must . . .
d) to break camp	j) rather slowly	o) will learn
e) were eager	k) reported	
f) broke camp	l) westward	

WORD MASTERY 6

Although many English verbs have been formed on the fourth principal part of Latin verbs, often the same Latin verb has supplied English with two separate words: one based on the perfect participle, the other on the present stem. Thus, the verb "transfer" comes from **trānsferō**, while "translate" derives from **trānslātum**. Give the first and fourth principal parts of the Latin verbs from which the following English pairs originate.

construe	construct	deduce	deduct
refer	relate	repel	repulse
convert	converse	convince	convict

The first and fourth principal parts of the same Latin verb may be used with different prefixes to form compounds that supply English derivatives. **Mittō** appears in "admit," "commit," "emit," "permit," "remit," etc., and **missum** in "dismiss" and "promise." **Cēdō** supplies the verbal element of "concede," "precede," "proceed," "recede," "secede," "succeed," etc., just as **cessum** can be seen in "process" and "recess."

Give pairs of English verbs, with or without prefix, derived from the first and fourth principal parts of **aestimō, mergō, moveō, sedeō, veniō,** and **videō;** e.g., **in** + **veniō/ventum** = **inveniō/inventum** = invent.

The perfect participle of **capiō (captum/-ceptum)** has come into English in such compounds as "accept," "intercept"; the present stem, by way of French, appears in "deceive," "perceive," "receive." Through French, too, comes "pursue" (from the present stem of **prōsequor**), while English "prosecute" is derived directly from Latin **prōsecūtus** (perf. part. of **prōsequor**).

Of special interest are Latin verbs compounded from a noun and a verb, such as these.

animus + **advertō**	= **animadvertō**		turn the mind to/observe
bellum + **gerō**	= **belligerō**	(I)	wage war
fūmus + **agō**	= **fūmigō**	(I)	make smoke/smoke

With the help of a dictionary (if necessary), give English derivatives of these Latin compounds. Explain derivation of manumit/manumission; navigate/navigation/navigator.

With the present stem of the Latin verb as your starting point, draw up a set of principles to cover the formation and meaning of the following nouns:

ōrnāmentum   nūtrīmentum   īnstrūmentum   impedīmentum

What are their English derivatives? the form of the Latin/English suffix? the (probable) meaning of the suffix? Has this suffix produced other nouns in Latin? in English?

LOOK AND THINK

What change besides spelling occurred when **gerō** was combined with **bellum,** and **agō** with **fūmus** to form compound verbs? The Latin compound from which "navigate" was derived went through a similar change. To what conjugation does the compound belong? To what conjugation does the basic verb belong?

155

Hannibalī victōrī cum cēterī congrātulārentur suādē-
rentque ut ipse sibi quiētem sūmeret et fessīs mīlitibus daret,
Maharbal, dux equitum, minimē cessandum° esse arbitrātus
est.

"Immō, ut sciās,°" inquit, "quid hāc pugnā āctum sit, 5
quīntō diē in Capitōliō Rōmānō cēnābis. Sequere° mē; cum
equitibus praecēdam, ut Rōmānī tē vēnisse priusquam tē ventūrum esse sciant!"

Hannibal dīxit sē laudāre Maharbalis voluntātem; sed
temporis opus esse° ad cōnsilium capiendum. 10

Tum Maharbal respondit, "Nōn omnia eīdem deī dedērunt.
Vincere scīs, Hannibal, sed victōriā ūtī nescīs."

Mora ejus diēī satis crēditur salūtī fuisse urbī atque imperiō.

°**cessō** 1 stop, delay • **ut sciās** that you may know • **se-
quere** (imperative 2nd pers. sing.) • **temporis opus esse** (that)
there was need of time

arbitror, -ārī, -ātus sum	think
congrātulor, -ārī, -ātus sum	(with dat.) wish joy; congratulate
suādeō, -ēre, suāsī, suāsum	(with dat. of person) advise, rec-ommend
praecēdō, -ere, -cessī, -cessum	go ahead/before; excel, surpass
ūtor, ūtī, ūsus sum	take advantage of; use
nesciō, -scīre, -īvī, _____	not know (how)
immō	(adv.) on the contrary, by no means; yes indeed, by all means

ABLATIVE WITH DEPONENT VERBS

1 **Eā urbe Graecī potītī sunt.** The Greeks got possession of this city.
2 **Manū dextrā semper ūtitur.** He always uses his right hand.

Two deponent verbs often used in this book—**ūtor**/use and
potior/get possession of—take objects in the ablative case.

Other deponents whose objects are in the ablative case
are **fruor**/enjoy, **fungor**/perform, and **vescor**/eat.

XXV From the list below select appropriate endings for the incomplete nouns and justify your choice. Translate all completed sentences. Explain the form and use of all underlined verbs.

1 Fessī mīlitēs duc__ suādēre nōn potuērunt ut cib__ atque quiēt__ fruerentur.
2 Cum hostēs urb__ <u>potītī essent</u>, tamen victōri__ ūtī nesciēbant.
3 Ōsti__ tam diū morātī sunt ut ā nostrīs undique <u>inclūderentur</u>.
4 Nē <u>dīxerīmus</u> vōs offici__ exiguā prūdentiā <u>functōs esse</u>.
5 Timēbāmus ut lictōrēs dictātōr__ <u>pārērent</u>.

-ā	-am	-em	-ī	-ō
-ae	-e	-ēs	-īs	-um

MARCHING THROUGH ITALY

After their disastrous defeat at Cannae the Romans expected Hannibal to march on Rome. Instead he spent the next twelve years marching through Italy, ravaging the land.

Many Italian towns went over to him, but Hannibal found these to be liabilities rather than assets. He had the responsibility of garrisoning them to protect them against Roman counterattack. Consequently, the mobility and size of his army were greatly reduced. Moreover, while the loss of the defecting towns reduced Rome's resources, their gain did not add materially to Hannibal's strength, since most of them had stipulated that they would not provide any aid to him.

In 211 the Romans besieged Capua, one of the defecting towns, in an attempt to recapture it from the Carthaginians. Hannibal, knowing he could not break the siege by force, attempted to draw off the Romans by making a swift march toward Rome itself. In this way he hoped to force the Roman armies at Capua to lift the siege and rush to the protection of their city.

The two Roman generals at Capua decided that one of them, Appius Claudius, would continue the siege there, while the other, Quintus Fulvius Flaccus, would set out with 15,000 infantry and 1000 cavalry to defend Rome. Having obtained reliable information as to Hannibal's route, Fulvius chose another. They arrived in the vicinity of Rome at about the same time.

157

Diagram of Rome showing the "Servian" Wall, now known to belong to a later period than the Roman king (Servius Tullius) for whom it was named. Can you locate the gates mentioned in lines 1-3 on this page?

HANNIBAL AT THE GATES

As Hannibal approached Rome, the panic of the city increased. More and more refugees tried to escape from the threatened city, and many were killed or taken prisoner by Hannibal.

In hōc tumultū Fulvius Flaccus portā Capēnā[1] cum exercitū Rōmam ingressus est. Inde ēgressus inter Esquilīnam Collīnamque portam posuit castra.

Inter haec Hannibal ad Aniēnem fluvium tria mīlia passuum ab urbe castra admōvit. Ibi custōdiīs positīs, ipse cum duōbus 5

[1]The *Porta Capena*, like the *Porta Esquilina* and *Porta Collina*, was a gate in the so-called Servian Wall of Rome.

mīlibus equitum ad portam Collīnam usque ad templum
Herculis prōgressus est atque, unde proximē poterat,° moenia
situmque urbis contemplābātur.

Id factum audāx Rōmānīs indignum esse vīsum est; itaque
Fulvius Flaccus mīsit equitēs quī equitātum hostium sum- 10
movērent atque in castra repellerent. Equestre proelium
secundum° fuit, summōtīque hostēs sunt.

Quia multīs locīs comprimendī tumultūs erant, placuit°
omnēs quī dictātōrēs aut cōnsulēs aut cēnsōrēs fuissent° cum
imperiō esse,° dōnec hostēs ā mūrīs recessissent. 15

Posterō diē Hannibal Aniēnem fluvium trānsgressus omnēs
cōpiās in aciem ēdūxit. Exercitūs utrimque īnstrūctī sunt
in cāsum° ejus pugnae, in quā urbs Rōma victōrī praemium
erat. Subitō imber ingēns, grandine mixtus,° ita utramque
aciem turbāvit, ut mīlitēs, armīs cum difficultāte retentīs, in 20
castra sēsē recēperint.

Posterō diē aciēs īnstrūctās eōdem locō eadem tempestās
dirēmit. Cum recēpissent sē in castra, mīra serēnitās cum
tranquillitāte oriēbātur. Hannibal ad Tūtiam fluvium cōpiās
remōvit, sex mīlia passuum ab urbe. Inde in Bruttium 25
agrum ad fretum° ac Rēgium contendit.

°**unde proximē poterat** from the closest place possible • **secundum** successful • **placuit** it was decreed (that) • **fuissent**
had been (subjunctive because dependent on indirect statement after
placuit) • **cum imperiō esse** hold the supreme command
in cāsum for the outcome • **grandine mixtus** mixed with hail
fretum, -ī N., strait (of Messina)

cēnsor, -ōris	M., censor (a Roman magistrate responsible for the census)
imber, imbris	M., rain, rainstorm, shower
serēnitās, -ātis	F., clearness, clear weather
tranquillitās, -ātis	F., calmness, calm
equitātus, -ūs	M., cavalry
situs, -ūs	M., site, situation
indignus, -a, -um	shameful, intolerable
uterque, utraque, utrumque	(adj./pron.) each (of two); both
equester, -tris, -tre	(of) cavalry

contemplor, -ārī, -ātus sum	survey, gaze upon, observe
admoveō, -ēre, -mōvī, -mōtum	move; bring (to)
placeō, -ēre, -uī, -itum	please, be pleasing (to)
placet	(impers.) it is decided/resolved
summoveō, -ēre, -mōvī, -mōtum	drive away, remove
comprimō, -ere, -pressī, -pressum	check, restrain
dirimō, -ere, -ēmī, -ēmptum	break up, part; interrupt
ingredior, -gredī, -gressus sum	enter
orior, orīrī, ortus sum	arise, rise; appear
modo . . . modo	now . . . now; at one time . . . at another
dōnec	(conj.) until

GENITIVE OF DESCRIPTION

1 **Imperātor fuit vir magnae virtūtis.** The general was a man of great courage.

2 **Militēs mūrum trium pedum aedificābant.** The soldiers were building a three-foot wall (lit., a wall of three feet).

3 **Hostēs exercitum fortium virōrum habuērunt.** The enemy had an army of brave men.

The genitive with an adjective may be used to describe a person or thing (sentence 1).

The genitive is also used to express measure (sentence 2) and composition or material (sentence 3).

The ablative without a preposition is also employed in descriptive phrases such as that in sentence 1: **Imperātor fuit vir magnā virtute.**

Measure and composition are always expressed by the genitive, as in sentence 2.

Phrases describing physical characteristics are usually expressed by the ablative; e.g., **Ille corpore fuit rōbustō et faciē laetā.** He had (lit., he was with) a strong body and a happy face.

RETURN TO AFRICA

Hannibal not only failed to lay siege to Rome, but also failed in his attempt to divert the Romans from the siege of Capua; for that city eventually surrendered to the Romans.

In the foreground is what remains of the harbor of Carthage, which was artificially constructed. The irregular basin at the left and center was the commercial harbor. The smaller, more irregular basin to the right was walled in antiquity for security reasons, and naval headquarters occupied an artificial island in the center of this naval harbor.

After campaigning in Italy for fifteen years, Hannibal was at last recalled to Africa in 203 B.C. His aid was desperately needed to defend Carthage from Roman invasion. Publius Cornelius Scipio the Younger, a dynamic young general, had been given command of the Roman troops for such an invasion. He had already captured some African towns and was becoming a serious threat to Carthage.

Scipio had grown up in the Second Punic War; he had fought at Cannae and learned much from Hannibal's methods. He had particularly distinguished himself as commander of Roman armies in Spain. Thus, when the time came, he eagerly welcomed the opportunity to cross into Africa.

Hannibal left Italy with reluctance and disappointment. In spite of the damage inflicted on Italy, he had not accomplished his purpose. He was returning to Carthage as the defender of his own city, not as the conqueror of Rome.

161

Gemēns° ac vix lacrimās retinēns lēgātōrum verba Hannibal audīvit. Postquam mandāta ēdita sunt, "Jam nōn cōnfūsē," inquit, "sed palam revocant quī vetandō commeātum et pecūniam mittī jam prīdem retrahēbant. Vīcit ergō Hanni- balem nōn populus Rōmānus, sed senātus Carthāginiēnsis 5 obtrectātiōne° atque invidiā. Neque hōc dēdecore° reditūs meī tam P. Scīpiō exultābit quam Hannō,[1] quī domum nos- tram, quandō aliā rē° nōn potuit, ruīnā Carthāginis oppressit."

Jam hoc ipsum praesentiēns animō praeparāverat anteā nāvēs. Itaque inūtilī mīlitum turbā praesidiī speciē pauca in 10 oppida Bruttiī agrī quae° metū magis quam fidē continēbantur dīmissā,° quod rōboris in exercitū erat° in Āfricam trānsvexit.

Rārō° quisquam alius patriam exiliī causā relinquēns tam maestus abīvit quam Hannibal hostium terrā excēdēns. Respexit saepe Italiae lītora, et deōs hominēsque accūsāns in 15 sē quoque ac suum ipsīus caput exsecrātus est,° quod nōn cruentōs° ab Cannēnsī victōriā mīlitēs Rōmam dūxisset.

Haec accūsāns querēnsque ex diūtinā possessiōne Italiae est dētractus.

°**gemēns** groaning • **obtrectātiōne** with detraction • **dē-decus, -oris** N., disgrace • **aliā rē** by other means • **quae** which (refers to **pauca oppida**) • **dīmissā** (abl. abs. with **inūtilī turbā**) having been distributed • **quod rōboris in exercitū erat** the flower of the army • **rārō** rarely • **exsecrātus est** uttered a curse • **cruentus, -a, -um** covered with blood

mandātum, -ī	N., order; message
possessiō, -ōnis	F., occupation; possession
fidēs, -eī	F., loyalty; trust
quisquam, quicquam/quidquam	(indef. pron.) anyone, anything
diūtinus, -a, -um	long, of long standing
Carthāginiēnsis, -e	Carthaginian, of Carthage
inūtilis, -e	useless

[1]Hanno was formerly a leader of the opposition to Hannibal.

exultō, -āre, -āvī, -ātum	rejoice, exult
praeparō, -āre, -āvī, -ātum	prepare
vetō, -āre, vetuī, vetitum	forbid
ēdō, -ere, -didī, -ditum	disclose; give out, state
queror, querī, questus sum	complain (of)
retrahō, -ere, -trāxī, -tractum	drag or bring back
trānsvehō, -ere, -vexī, -vectum	transport; carry across
praesentiō, -īre, -sēnsī, -sēnsum	feel beforehand, foresee
anteā	(adv.) before, previously
ergō	(adv.) therefore
tam . . . quam	so much as, so . . . as
causā	(abl., with preceding genitive) for the sake of, on account of
quandō	(conj.) since, when

A DEPENDENT CLAUSE IN INDIRECT STATEMENT

1 **Prōmīsit sē magna praemia datūrum esse sī ille remedium repperisset.** He promised that he would give great rewards if that man found a remedy.

In an indirect statement, what is indirectly quoted may contain a dependent clause. The verb in the main clause of the quotation is still an infinitive, with subject in the accusative case. However, the verb of the dependent clause is in the subjunctive, even though in a direct quotation it would be in the indicative (sentence 1).

2 **Hannibal in sē ac suum caput exsecrātus est, quod nōn cruentōs ab Cannēnsī victōriā mīlitēs Rōmam dūxisset.** Hannibal uttered a curse upon himself and his own head, because (as he said) he had not led his soldiers, covered with blood from the victory at Cannae, to Rome.

Even when an indirect statement is only implied (as in sentence 2), the verb of a dependent clause is in the subjunctive mood.

163

In this page from an illuminated manuscript in the French National Library, Scipio's fleet is pictured setting out for Africa and the defeat of Carthage. The written passage beneath the ships is in French, as is the word Sipion (Scipio) on the cabin of the large ship. Also notice the letters S P Q R (*Senatus Populusque Romanus*) on the masthead. As in so many medieval paintings, costume and objects are in the style of the period.

After landing at Leptis Magna, Hannibal set up camp at Hadrumetum. At that time Carthage had already accepted Scipio's severe terms for an armistice. However, the presence of a large Punic army with its victorious general caused the Carthaginians to violate the agreement and to fight the Romans anew. A conference between Hannibal and Scipio did not settle anything, either.

Ambō ducēs, ubi in castra vēnērunt, prōnūntiāvērunt, ut arma animōsque parārent mīlitēs ad suprēmum certāmen.

"Nōn in ūnum diem," dīxērunt, "sed in perpetuum,° sī fēlīcitās adfuerit, erimus victōrēs. Utrum Rōma an Carthāgō jūra gentibus det, ante crāstinam noctem sciēmus. Neque 5 enim Āfrica aut Ītalia, sed orbis terrārum victōriae praemium erit. Pār praemiō perīculum eīs erit quibus adversa pugnae fortūna fuerit."

Nam neque Rōmānīs effugium ūllum patēbat in aliēnā ignōtāque terrā, et Carthāginī, suprēmō auxiliō° effūsō, 10 adesse vidēbātur ruīna.

°**in perpetuum** forever • **auxiliō** resources

effugium, -ī	N., means of escape; escape
fēlīcitās, -ātis	F., success, good fortune, happiness
jūs, jūris	N., law, right; pl., legal rights
aliēnus, -a, -um	foreign; another's, others'
crāstinus, -a, -um	(of) tomorrow; tomorrow's
suprēmus, -a, -um	(superl. of **superus**) last, final; highest, greatest
ambō, -ae, -ō	(adj./pron.) both
prōnūntiō, -āre, -āvī, -ātum	announce, order; make known publicly
pateō, -ēre, -uī, ____	be or lie open
effundō, -ere, -fūdī, -fūsum	pour out/forth; exhaust
utrum	(conj.) whether; **utrum . . . an** (used in double questions) whether . . . or

165

Ad hoc discrīmen° prōcēdunt posterō diē duōrum opulen-
tissimōrum populōrum duo longē clārissimī ducēs, duo fortissimī exercitūs. Anceps° igitur spēs et metus miscēbant
animōs. Contemplantibusque° modo suam modo hostium
aciem, cum oculīs magis quam ratiōne exāminārent vīrēs, 5
simul laeta, simul trīstia obversābantur.°

Quae mīlitibus suā sponte nōn succurrēbant,° ea ducēs
admonendō atque hortandō subjiciēbant. Hannibal sēdecim
annōrum in Ītaliā rēs gestās, tot ducēs Rōmānōs, tot exercitūs
occīsōs referēbat. Referēbat Scīpiō Hispāniās° et recentia 10
in Āfricā proelia et cōnfessiōnem hostium, quod° neque nōn
petere pācem propter metum neque manēre in eā° propter
perfidiam potuissent.

°**discrīmen, -inis** N., crisis, decisive battle • **anceps,** gen.,
-cipitis uncertain • **contemplantibus** to those who looked
carefully (indirect object of **obversābantur)** • **obversābantur**
appeared • **succurrēbant** occurred • **Hispāniās** the
Spanish provinces • **quod** that (The **quod** clause gives the con-
tents of **cōnfessiōnem.)** • **in eā = in pāce**

perfidia, -ae	F., treachery, dishonesty, perfidy
ratiō, -ōnis	F., reason, judgment, consideration; account, business
rēs gesta	F., deed, act
sponte	F. (abl.), of one's own accord; voluntarily (used with **suā, meā,** etc.)
opulentus, -a, -um	wealthy, rich
trīstis, -e	sad, glum, grim
exāminō, -āre, -āvī, -ātum	weigh
hortor, -ārī, -ātus sum	encourage, urge
admoneō, -ēre, -uī, -itum	warn
misceō, -ēre, miscuī, mixtum	confuse, disturb; mix, mingle
subjiciō, -ere, -jēcī, -jectum	suggest, add
simul . . . simul	not only . . . but at the same time

SUMMARY OF SUBJUNCTIVE FORMS

	Present	Imperfect	Perfect	Past Perfect
	Active	Active	Active	Active
I	portet	portāret	portāverit	portāvisset
II	moneat	monēret	monuerit	monuisset
III	dūcat	dūceret	dūxerit	dūxisset
III-iō	capiat	caperet	cēperit	cēpisset
IV	audiat	audīret	audīverit	audīvisset

	Passive	Passive	Passive	Passive
I	portētur	portārētur	portātus sit	portātus esset
II	moneātur	monērētur	monitus sit	monitus esset
III	dūcātur	dūcerētur	ductus sit	ductus esset
III-iō	capiātur	caperētur	captus sit	captus esset
IV	audiātur	audīrētur	audītus sit	audītus esset

SEQUENCE OF TENSES

1 **Rogō (Rogābō/Rogāverō) eum ut epistulam scrībat.** I am asking (I shall ask/I shall have asked) him to write a letter.

2 **Rogō (Rogābō/Rogāverō) eum cūr epistulam scrīpserit.** I am asking (I shall ask/I shall have asked) him why he wrote/has written the letter.

When the main verb of a sentence denotes present or future time, a subjunctive in a subordinate clause is regularly in the present (sentence 1) or perfect tense (sentence 2).

3 **Rogābam (Rogāvī/Rogāveram) eum ut epistulam scrīberet.** I was asking (I asked/I had asked) him to write a letter.

4 **Rogābam (Rogāvī/Rogāveram) eum cūr epistulam scrīpsisset.** I was asking (I asked/I had asked) him why he had written the letter.

When the main verb denotes past time, the subjunctive in a subordinate clause is regularly in the imperfect (sentence 3) or the past perfect tense (sentence 4).

5 **Vidērunt quid faciam.** They have seen what I am doing.

6 **Hostēs ācriter pugnāvērunt nē vincerentur.** The enemy have fought fiercely in order that they might not be conquered.

If the main verb is a perfect that is equivalent to an English present perfect (i.e., translated with "have" or "has"), a de-

167

pendent subjunctive may be in the present (sentence 5) or in the imperfect (sentence 6).

A result clause after a main verb denoting past time sometimes has its verb in the perfect subjunctive.

THE BATTLE OF ZAMA

Carthāginiēnsium sociōrumque caesa sunt eō diē suprā vīgintī mīlia. Pār fermē numerus captus est cum signīs mīlitāribus centum trīgintā duōbus, elephantīs ūndecim. Ad mīlle et quīngentī victōrēs cecidērunt.

Hannibal cum paucīs equitibus inter tumultum ēlāpsus 5 Hadrūmētum perfūgit. Omnia et ante aciem et in proeliō expertus erat, priusquam ē pugnā excēderet. Et cōnfessiōne etiam Scīpiōnis omniumque perītōrum mīlitiae Hannibal laudābātur quod singulārī arte aciem eō diē īnstrūxisset.°

Hōc factō quasi ultimō virtūtis opere, Hannibal, cum 10 Hadrūmētum fūgisset, inde Carthāginem sextō ac trīcēsimō annō postquam puer inde profectus erat rediit. In cūriā cōnfessus est nōn proeliō modo sē sed bellō victum,° nec spem salūtis alibī quam° in pāce impetrandā esse.

°**īnstrūxisset** had drawn up (subjunctive because the opinion expressed is Scipio's and the experts' rather than Livy's) • **victum = victum esse** • **nec . . . alibī quam** and nowhere else than

mīlitia, -ae	F., warfare
opus, -eris	N., deed, work
mīlitāris, -e	military
singulāris, -e	extraordinary
impetrō, -āre, -āvī, -ātum	obtain, secure, effect; obtain by asking
cōnfiteor, -ērī, -fessus sum	admit, confess
ēlābor, ēlābī, ēlāpsus sum	escape, slip away
experior, -īrī, expertus sum	try
⁺**ad**	(adv./prep.) about, nearly, approximately
alibī	(adv.) elsewhere, in/at another place
fermē/ferē	(adv.) almost

In spite of Hannibal's skill, the battle ended in a complete Roman victory. The Carthaginians then sent thirty envoys to negotiate terms of peace. Many Romans would have preferred to see the complete destruction of Carthage itself. A siege of the fortified city, however, might be long and costly; the war had already lasted for so many years that the desire for peace prevailed.

Posterō diē revocātīs lēgātīs° et dē perfidiā monitīs, condiciōnēs pācis dictae sunt, ut° līberī lēgibus suīs vīverent; quās urbēs quōsque agrōs quōsque fīnēs ante bellum tenuissent tenērent, populandīque fīnem eō diē Rōmānī facerent; perfugās fugitīvōsque et captīvōs omnēs redderent Rōmānīs, 5
et nāvēs longās praeter decem trirēmēs° trāderent elephantōsque quōs habērent domitōs,° neque domārent aliōs; bellum nēve° in Āfricā nēve extrā Āfricam injussū populī Rōmānī gererent; decem mīlia talentum° argentī, dīvīsa pēnsiōnibus aequīs in annōs quīnquāgintā,° solverent; obsidēs centum arbitrātū Scīpiōnis° darent. 10

Payment of the war indemnity was no extraordinary hardship for the wealthy Carthaginians. After only a few years their nation prospered again as it had before the war.

°**revocātis lēgātis** when the (Carthaginian) envoys had been recalled (by Scipio) • **ut** namely, that (introducing a noun clause of desire; the following clauses depend on implied **ut.**) • **trirēmēs** triremes, warships with three rowers to a bench • **domō, -āre, -uī, -itum** train, tame • **nēve...nēve** (after **ut** or **nē**) neither...nor **talentum** (gen. pl.) talents (One talent = about 55 pounds of silver.) **dīvīsa...quīnquāgintā** divided into equal payments over fifty years • **arbitrātū Scīpiōnis** according to Scipio's choice

perfuga, -ae	M., deserter
argentum, -ī	N., silver
injussū	(abl.), without command/permission
aequus, -a, -um	equal; even
solvō, -ere, solvī, solūtum	pay; loosen; release
trādō, -ere, -didī, -ditum	surrender; give over/up

XXVI Find and identify the verbs in the list as follows:

    a) Special verbs whose objects are regularly in the dative case

    b) Compound verbs which are generally completed by a noun/ pronoun in the dative case

    c) Deponent verbs which may be completed by objects in the ablative case

    d) All remaining verbs, explaining any special characteristics each may have.

1 antepōnō	7 hortor	13 pāreō
2 cōnfīdō	8 imperō	14 potior
3 crēdō	9 jubeō	15 quaerō
4 dēsum	10 nesciō	16 praesum
5 faveō	11 occurrō	17 suādeō
6 fīō	12 oportet	18 ūtor

XXVII Translate the sentences, omitting the words in parentheses. Then substitute the verbs in parentheses for those in the original sentences, changing underlined verbs to conform to rules for sequence of tenses. (See page 167.) Translate the altered sentences.

1 Equitātus quī commeātūs <u>comperīret</u> ad vīcōs fīnitimōs missus erat (mittitur).

2 Hīc vōs <u>expectābimus</u> dōnec hostēs angustiās obsideant (obsidērent).

3 Explōrātor nescit (nescīvit) utrum sociī an hostēs oppidum <u>oppugnāverint</u>.

4 Dubium nōn erat (erit) quīn equitēs hostium flūmen trānsīre <u>possent</u>.

5 Arbitrātus sum (Arbitror) peditēs quī vāllum <u>custōdīrent</u> signiferum hortātūrōs esse.

6 Cum cīvēs cōnsulibus <u>cōnfīderent</u>, tamen timēbant (timent) nē urbs ab hostibus <u>vāstārētur</u>.

7 Tam ācriter <u>pugnābātur</u> ut paucī ex nostrīs ēlābī cōnārentur (cōnentur).

8 Nōnne satis est (fuit) ut parentēs nostrī vītā magnae fēlīcitātis <u>frūctī sint</u>?

9 Cum victōria incerta <u>fuisset</u>, Rōmae nūllus nūntius exitum proeliī rettulit (referet).

ornelly?

HANNIBAL'S DEATH[1]

After Zama, Hannibal had a hand in reorganizing the Carthaginian state and proved himself an able administrator. Soon, however, envy and Roman intrigue drove him away. For some years he found refuge in Asia Minor, but even there he could not avoid the long arm of Rome indefinitely. Hannibal's last host, King Prusias of Bithynia, did not surrender the Carthaginian outright (that would have violated the laws of hospitality), but neither did he protect him from the Roman agents who tracked him down.

Hannibal enim ūnō locō sē tenēbat, in castellō quod eī ā rēge[2] dātum erat mūnerī, idque ita aedificāverat, ut in omnibus partibus aedificiī exitūs habēret. Hūc cum lēgātī Rōmānōrum vēnissent ac multitūdine domum ejus circumdedissent, puer ab jānuā prōspiciēns Hannibalī dīxit plūrēs praeter cōnsuē- 5 tūdinem° armātōs appārēre. Puer cum celeriter, quid esset,° renūntiāvisset omnēsque exitūs occupātōs ostendisset, Hannibal sēnsit id nōn forte factum, sed sē petī neque sibi diūtius vītam esse retinendam. Quam nē aliēnō arbitriō° dīmitteret, memor prīstinārum virtūtum venēnum, quod semper sēcum 10 habēre cōnsuēverat, sūmpsit.

°**praeter cōnsuētūdinem** than usual • **quid esset** what was going on • **arbitrium, -ī** N., judgment, authority

mūnus, -eris	N., gift, present; service, duty
exitus, -ūs	M., exit, passage; outcome; end
prīstinus, -a, -um	former, early
memor, gen., **-oris**	(with gen.) mindful of, remembering
circumdō, -āre, -dedī, -datum	surround
renūntiō, -āre, -āvī, -ātum	report, bring back word
cōnsuēscō, -ere, -suēvī, -suētum	become accustomed; (perf.) be accustomed
circumeō, -īre, -īvī, (-iī) -itum	go around; inspect

[1]This account is from C. Cornelius Nepos (about 100–25 B.C.), of whose works only part of the book *De Viris Illustribus* is extant.

[2]King Prusias provided separate living quarters for the Carthaginian general.

The name "inchoative" is given to Latin verbs that have the infix[1] **-sc-** in the present stem. This name comes from the verb **inchoāre** (to begin) and is used because these inchoative verbs stress the beginning aspect of a verbal action. For example, in addition to the verb **flōreō** (blossom/flower), there is **efflōrēscō** (begin to blossom); **alō** (nourish/rear/make grow) has the inchoative **coalēscō** (grow together). The adjective **altus** (high/deep), by the way, was originally the perfect participle of **alō** and meant "well-fed," "grown," "tall."

Give English derivatives of **crēscō (creō), effervēscō (ferveō,** boil), **convalēscō (valeō), incandēscō (candeō,** shine).

Common English derivatives of **adolēscō** are "adolescent" (from **adolēscēns,** pres. part.), a person who is growing up, and "adult" (from **adultus,** perf. part.), a grown-up.

"Adolescent," "crescent," etc., are English adoptions, usually nouns or adjectives, from Latin present participles.

Latin present participle	base	English
adolēscēns, adolēscentis	**adolēscent-**	adolescent

The English spelling normally follows the Latin conjugation; i.e., -ant for Conjugation I; -ent/-ient for all other conjugations. Exceptions come through French, where all present participles end in -ant; e.g., "tenant" (from **teneō**).[2]

The Latin suffix **-ia** is often added to a present participle base to form nouns expressing quality or state. The ending **-tia** becomes English -ce/-cy.

cōnstāns, cōnstantis	**cōnstant-** + **-ia** =	**cōnstantia/**
standing together		constancy
prōvidēns, prōvidentis	**prōvident-** + **-ia** =	**prōvidentia/**
foreseeing		providence

Give the English noun or adjective derived from the present participle of these verbs.

agere	**applicāre**	**inhaerēre**	**latēre**	**studēre**
fluere	**complacēre**	**mīlitāre**	**rōdere**	**vigilāre**

[1]A formative element inserted within the body of a word.

[2]Both Latin and French spellings occur in persistent/resistant and pendent/pendant.

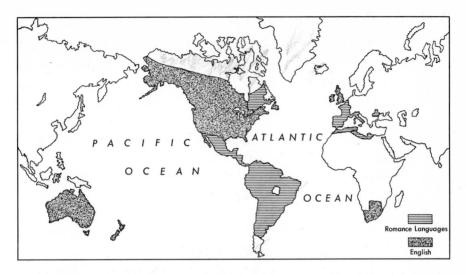

This map shows the extent to which Latin has influenced the languages of the world.

LATIN THROUGH
THE AGES

After the fall of the Roman Empire in the west in the fifth century A.D., there was a general economic, political, and educational decline until the reforms instituted under Charlemagne in the late eighth century. Because Latin was the official language of church and state in Europe, however, and because scholars everywhere used it, the language of the Romans was kept alive. Latin was an international language, understood and spoken by all educated Europeans.

In this unit you will find selections of Latin writings showing how Latin has persisted through the ages. These writings, extending from the first century A.D. to the twentieth, include an excerpt from the first Roman emperor's account of his own reign. Another selection tells of Charlemagne and his efforts to promote education by founding a school devoted mainly to the teaching of Latin. Still another selection—an

173

extract from the famous *Magna Charta* drawn up in A.D. 1215, which guaranteed the personal and political liberties of the English people—is of special interest to us, since much of our law is based directly on English law.

Wherever the Romans went they took their language and made it the official language of the Roman world. Even after the fall of Rome, Latin continued to be spoken in regions that had once been Roman provinces—regions such as those now known as Italy, Spain, France, Portugal, and Romania. Gradually variations developed in the spoken Latin of these areas, as travel and communications decreased with the decline and fall of Rome. The differences eventually became so great that instead of one language (Latin) there were several —Italian, Spanish, French, Portuguese, and Romanian.[1] These new forms of Latin (neo-Latin) are called Romance languages, since they are variations of the language once used by the Romans.

The influence of Latin on English was less direct. When England was conquered in 1066 by the inhabitants of Normandy in northern France, the Normans (a mixture of Scandinavian and French) introduced their version of Latin. Thus Norman-French neo-Latin mingled with Anglo-Saxon to form the basis of the English language as we know it. Several other linguistic elements were introduced from time to time, but Latin has continued to be a predominant source of English word origins. Although English is not one of the neo-Latin or Romance languages, about fifty per cent of the words in a large English dictionary are of Latin origin.

To illustrate the survival of Latin words and Latin derivatives in modern languages, a short extract from Cicero's essay on friendship is given at the end of this section—first in Latin, then in three neo-Latin languages (French, Italian, and Spanish), and finally in English.

Latin, then, still lives today in three ways. The original language is still read, written, and sometimes spoken; several modern languages are direct descendants of it; and a large percentage of English words are derived from Latin.

[1]The language of the pre-Roman populations and large-scale migrations (e.g., the Frankish invasion of Gaul, the Arabic invasion of Spain) also played a part in the differentiation of an area's language.

Before the invention of printing, books existed as handwritten documents. Much of the material in this unit was first published in manuscript books. Some were elaborately and beautifully illuminated, like this page of the Book of John in the New Testament.

1 To a Ballplayer: **Epaphra! Pilicrepus nōn es!**[1]
Epaphra! You're no ballplayer!

2 To a Blonde: **Candida mē docuit nigrās ōdisse puellās.**[1]
The blonde has taught me to dislike brunettes.

3 New Year's Wish: **Jānuāriās nōbīs fēlīcēs multīs annīs!**[1]
Happy New Year for many years (to come)!

4 Election Appeal: **Aulum Vettium Firmum aedīlem ōrō vōs faciātis, dignum rēpūblicā virum! Ōrō vōs faciātis! Pilicrepī, facite!**[1]
Vote for Aulus Vettius Firmus as aedile, a man worthy of the republic! Vote for him, you ballplayers!

5 Sold Out:

Circus plēnus	The circus is jammed.
Jānuae clausae	The gates are shut.
Clāmor ingēns[2]	The cheers are loud.

A RECORD OF ACHIEVEMENT

In his will, the Emperor Augustus directed that his own account of his reign should be engraved on monuments in different parts of the Empire. One copy, called the *Monumentum Ancyranum*, was found at Ancyra, in Asia Minor.

Annōs ūndēvīgintī nātus,[3] exercitum prīvātō cōnsiliō et prīvātā impēnsā° comparāvī, per quem rem pūblicam oppressam in lībertātem restituī. Quās ob rēs senātus in ōrdinem suum mē allēgit,° imperiumque mihi dedit.

Quī parentem[4] meum interfēcērunt, eōs in exilium expulī, 5
et posteā bellum īnferentēs reī pūblicae vīcī aciē. Bella terrā
et marī cīvīlia externaque° tōtō in orbe terrārum suscēpī
victorque omnibus cīvibus veniam° petentibus pepercī.°
Nāvēs cēpī DC.

Ob rēs ā mē aut per lēgātōs meōs auspiciīs meīs° terrā 10
marīque prōsperē° gestās quīnquāgiēns et quīnquiēns° dē-

[1] From wall inscriptions found in Pompeii and Rome (*Corpus Inscriptionum Latinarum*, Vol. 4)
[2] Stone found in Spain, now in the British Museum
[3] The usual way of expressing age in Latin. Augustus was nineteen on September 23, 44 B.C.
[4] Julius Caesar. Having no legitimate son, Caesar adopted his grandnephew.

crēvit senātus supplicandum esse dīs immortālibus. In tri-
umphīs meīs ductī sunt ante currum meum rēgēs aut rēgum
līberī novem.

Capitōlium et Pompeium theātrum[1] impēnsā magnā refēcī 15
sine ūllā īnscrīptiōne nōminis meī. Rīvōs° aquārum complūribus locīs vetustāte lābentēs° refēcī. Forum Jūlium[2] et
basilicam, quae fuit inter templum Castoris et templum
Sāturnī, coepta° ā patre meō, perfēcī. Duo et octōgintā templa deōrum in urbe refēcī; Viam Flāminiam ab urbe Arīmi- 20
num[3] fēcī et pontēs omnēs praeter Mulvium et Minucium.

In prīvātō solō° Mārtis Ultōris templum forumque Augustī
fēcī. Lūdōs gladiātōriōs dedī quibus in lūdīs pugnāvērunt
hominum circiter decem mīlia.

Nāvālis proeliī spectāculum populō dedī trāns Tiberim 25
cavātō solō° in longitūdinem mīlle et octingentōs pedēs, in
lātitūdinem mīlle et ducentōs. In quō spectāculō trīgintā
nāvēs inter sē cōnflīxērunt.

Mare pācāvī° ā pīrātīs. Eō bellō[4] servōrum, quī fūgerant ā
dominīs suīs et arma contrā rem pūblicam cēperant, trīgintā 30
ferē mīlia capta dominīs trādidī ad supplicium sūmendum.

Omnium prōvinciārum populī Rōmānī, quibus fīnitimae
fuērunt gentēs quae nōn pārērent° imperiō nostrō, fīnēs auxī.

Classis mea per Ōceanum ab ōstiō Rhēnī ad orientem
sōlem usque ad fīnēs Cimbrōrum nāvigāvit. Hūc neque terrā 35
neque marī quisquam° Rōmānus ante id tempus adiit.

°**impēnsa, -ae** F., expense • **allēgit** elected • **externus,
-a, -um** foreign • **venia, -ae** F., pardon • **parcō, -ere,
peperci** spare • **auspiciīs meīs** under my direction • **prōs-**
perē successfully • **quīnquāgiēns et quīnquiēns** fifty-five
times • **rīvus, -ī** M., channel • **vetustāte lābentēs** falling
down from old age • **coepta** begun • **solum, -ī** N.,
ground, property • **cavātō solō** after the ground had been dug
up • **pācāvī** cleared (pacified) • **quae nōn pārērent** who
did not submit • **quisquam** any

[1]The first theater in Rome built of stone
[2]Forum of Julius Caesar. Caesar had begun to build a forum next to the Forum Romanum.
[3]To Ariminum (modern Rimini), a city of northern Italy
[4]His war with Sextus Pompeius, terminated in 36 B.C. Pompey's following was made up
largely of runaway slaves. His fleet interfered with the Roman grain supply.

Augustus is shown sitting beside the goddess Roma on this cameo, which is now in the Kunsthistorisches Museum of Vienna.

Aegyptum imperiō populī Rōmānī adjēcī. Prōvinciās omnēs quae trāns Adriāticum Mare vergunt° ad orientem recuperāvī.

°**vergunt** face

PSALM XXIII

As early as A.D. 383 the whole Bible had been translated into Latin.

Dominus regit mē, et nihil mihi dēerit.
In locō pascuae° ibi mē collocāvit; super aquam refectiōnis° ēducāvit mē.
Animam meam convertit. Dēdūcit mē super sēmitās jūstitiae, propter nōmen suum.

5

°**pascua, -ae** F., pasture • **refectiō, -ōnis** F., restoration

Nam, etsī ambulāverō in mediō[1] umbrae mortis, nōn timēbō mala; quoniam tū mēcum es, virga° tua, et baculus° tuus, ipsa mē cōnsōlāta sunt.°

Parāstī° in cōnspectū meō mēnsam, adversus eōs quī trībulant° mē; impinguāstī° in oleō caput meum; et calix° meus inēbriāns° quam praeclārus est!

Et misericordia° tua subsequētur mē omnibus diēbus vītae meae; et ut inhabitem in domō Dominī in longitūdinem diērum.

°**virga, -ae** F., rod • **baculus, -ī** M., staff • **cōnsōlor, -ārī, cōnsōlātus sum** comfort • **parāstī = parāvistī** • **trībulant** trouble • **impinguāstī** thou hast anointed • **calix, -icis** M., cup • **inēbriāns** brimming • **misericordia, -ae** F., mercy

PORTRAIT OF A KING

In the ninth century A.D., Charlemagne ruled over a large territory, including what had once been Gaul. He considered himself a successor to the Roman emperors and liked to be called Emperor of the Holy Roman Empire. Einhard, his secretary, wrote a life of Charlemagne, from which this description is taken.

Corpore fuit amplō atque rōbustō, statūrā ēminentī—septem suōrum pedum—oculīs magnīs, nāsō° paulum° mediocritātem excēdentī, faciē laetā, vōce clārā quidem sed quae minus corporis fōrmae convenīret.

Exercēbātur assiduē° equitandō ac vēnandō° et frequentī nātandō. In cibō et potū temperāns.° Inter° cēnandum lēctōrem audiēbat. Legēbantur eī historiae et antīquōrum rēs gestae. Dēlectābātur et° librīs Sānctī Augustīnī praecipuēque° hīs quī "Dē Cīvitāte Deī" nōminātī sunt.

°**nāsus, -ī** M., nose • **paulum** (adv.) a little • **assiduē** incessantly • **equitandō ac vēnandō** by riding and hunting • **in potū temperāns** (he was) temperate in drinking • **inter** while • **et =etiam** • **praecipuēque** and especially

[1]Classical Latin would say **in mediā mortis umbrā.**

Charlemagne is pictured here enthroned and wearing the crown of Emperor of the Holy Roman Empire. The sword and orb in his hands are other symbols of his imperial power. This picture illustrates a medieval devotional book, called Book of Hours, which is in The Cloisters, New York City.

Erat ēloquentiā cōpiōsus poteratque quicquid° vellet aper- 10
tissimē exprimere°. Nec patriō° sermōne contentus, etiam
peregrīnās° linguās didicit. In quibus Latīnam ita didicit ut
aequē illā ac° patriā linguā ōrāre sit solitus; Graecam vērō
melius legere quam prōnūntiāre poterat.

°**quicquid** whatever • **exprimere** to express • **patrius,
-a, -um** native • **peregrīnus, -a, -um** foreign • **ac** (with
aequē) as well as

Rēx quīdam nārrātōrem habuit suum, quī singulīs noctibus quīnque sibi nārrāre fābulās cōnsuēverat. Accidit ut rēx cūrīs quibusdam sollicitus minimē posset dormīre, plūrēsque quaesīvit audīre fābulās. Fābulātor tum trēs ēnārrāvit fābulās. Quaesīvit rēx etiam plūrēs. 5

Ille, "Plūrimās jam nārrāvī," dīxit. Ad haec rēx: "Plūrimās jam nārrāstī,° sed brevissimās, vellem vērō tē aliquam rem nārrāre, quae multa habet verba, et sīc tē dormīre permittam." Concessit nārrātor, et sīc incēpit:

"Erat quīdam rūsticus, quī pecūniam multam habuit. Hic 10 autem in negōtiātiōne comparāverat mīlle ovēs. Accidit eō redeunte ut magna esset inundātiō aquārum. Quī cum neque vadō neque per pontem trānsīre posset, invēnit tandem parvam nāvem, et necessitāte coāctus duās ovēs impōnēns aquam trānsiit." 15

Hīs dictīs nārrātor obdormīvit. Rēx illum excitāns monuit ut fābulam quam incēperat fīnīret. Nārrātor ad haec:

"Flūmen illud magnum est, nāvicula autem parva, et numerus ovium magnus. Permitte ergō rūsticum suās trānsferre ovēs; tum fābulam quam incēpī ad fīnem perdūcam." 20

°for **nārrāvistī**

Dionȳsius, vir crūdēlissimus, Syrācūsās, urbem Siciliae, rēgnābat. Omnēs Syrācūsānī ejus mortem maximē dēsīderābant praeter quandam fēminam summae senectūtis.° Quae sōla prō Dionȳsiō mātūtīnīs hōrīs deōs ōrābat. Ea sōla eum vīvere cupiēbat. 5

Cujus ōrātiōnis° causam Dionȳsius admīrāns ab eā quaesīvit.

°**senectūs, senectūtis** F., age, old age • **ōrātiō, -ōnis** F., prayer, praying

[1]From *Disciplina Clericalis*, by Petrus Alfonsi, who lived in Spain in the tenth century
[2]From *Gesta Romanorum*, a collection of stories popular in the Middle Ages

Fēmina respondit, "Mē puellā nōs Syrācūsānī gravem tyrannum habēbāmus. Alium rēgem cupientēs pejōrem recēpimus. Eum magnō cum dolōre tolerāvimus. Nunc 10 tertium dūriōrem habēmus. Nōlō quārtum dēteriōrem° tibi succēdere. Prō vītā tuā igitur omnī diē deōs ōrō."

Dionӯsius haec audiēns amplius° molestiam nōn fēcit.

°**dēterior, dēterius** worse • **amplius** (adv.) more, longer

King John is about to sign the Magna Charta in the presence of the barons. This mural by Albert Herter adorns the Court Chamber in the Capitol at Madison, Wisconsin.

THE GREAT CHARTER

One of the earliest documents in history which recognized the rights of the common man was the *Magna Charta.* It was given by King John of England to the barons, at Runnymede, in 1215.

Nūllus līber homō capiātur, vel imprisonētur;° . . . nec super eum mittēmus[1] nisi per lēgāle jūdicium parium° suōrum, vel per lēgem terrae. Nūllī vēndēmus, nūllī negābimus, aut

°**imprisonētur** (independent subjunctive) let . . . be imprisoned
pār, gen., **paris** equal, like; (as noun) peer, equal

[1]"We shall not pass sentence on him." The subject is really the author, since kings customarily speak of themselves in the plural.

differimus° rēctum° aut jūstitiam. Omnēs mercātōrēs habeant salvum et sēcūrum exīre[1] ab Angliā, et venīre[1] in Angliam, morārī[1] et īre[1] per Angliam, tam per terram quam per aquam, ad emendum et vēndendum. . . . Quārē volumus et firmiter praecipimus . . . quod[2] hominēs in rēgnō nostrō habeant et teneant omnēs . . . lībertātēs, jūra et concessiōnēs, bene et in pāce, līberē et quiētē, plēnē et integrē,[3] sibi et haerēdibus° suīs . . . in omnibus rēbus et locīs, in perpetuum. . . . Jūrātum est autem, tam ex parte nostrā, quam ex parte barōnum,° quod haec omnia . . . bonā fidē et sine malō ingeniō servābuntur. . . . Data per manum nostram, in prātō° quod vocātur Runnimede . . . quīntō decimō diē Jūniī, annō rēgnī nostrī septimō decimō.

°differō, differre, distulī, dīlātum delay, postpone • **rēctum, -ī** N., right • **haerēs, -ēdis** M./F., heir • **barō, -ōnis** M., baron • **prātum, -ī** N., meadow

THE SAINT AND THE BIRDS

This story tells how St. Francis loved all mankind devotedly and how he extended his charity even to birds.

Franciscus ad quendam locum vēnit in quō maxima multitūdō avium dīversī generis convēnerat. Quās cum vir sānctus vīdisset, alacriter° ad avēs accessit.

Omnibus convertentibus sē ad eum, omnēs monuit ut verbum Deī audīrent, dīcēns, "Frātrēs meī, avēs, multum dēbētis laudāre Creātōrem vestrum quī plūmīs° vōs induit et pennās° dedit ad volandum, et sine cūrā vestrā vōs gubernat.°"

°alacriter eagerly • **plūma, -ae** F., feather • **penna, -ae** F., (wing-)feather • **gubernat** guides

[1]The infinitive is used as a noun, modified by **salvum** and **sēcūrum**.

[2]In Medieval Latin **quod** often takes the place of **ut** in introducing noun clauses.

[3]The meaning of these four adverbs can be figured out from adjectives that you have already learned.

This painted wooden statue of St. Francis is in The Cloisters, New York City.

Cum autem eīs haec verba et similia loquerētur, avēs mīrō modō coepērunt prōtendere° ālās, aperīre rōstra, et illum spectāre. Ipse vērō cum spīritūs fervōre per mediās avēs 10 trānsiēns, tunicā suā contingēbat eās. Nūllae mōvērunt ā locō dum signum crucis faceret. Tum cum benedictiōne virī Deī, omnēs simul āvolāvērunt.

°**coepērunt prōtendere** began to stretch

Tum per vīcīna loca prōcēdēns, vēnit ad locum ubi congregātō populō° audīrī vix poterat propter hirundinēs° nīdi- 15
ficantēs.°

Quās vir Deī, omnibus audientibus, ita allocūtus est, dīcēns,
"Sorōrēs meae, hirundinēs, jam tempus est ut loquar; audīte
verbum Deī, tenentēs silentium, dum sermō Deī compleātur."

Illae subitō tacuērunt nec mōvērunt dē locō. Omnēs igitur 20
quī vīdērunt glōrificāvērunt Deum. Istīus mīrāculī fāma
volāvit.

°**congregātō populō** dative of agent • **hirundō, -inis** F.,
swallow • **nīdificantēs** (pres. part.) building nests

CITY AND COUNTRY LIFE[1]

Sōcratēs philosophus clārus urbēs amābat. "Cupiō
discere," dīcēbat, "et mē multum urbēs docent. In agrīs
sunt arborēs et hortī et fontēs. Oculōs dēlectant, sed nōn
dīcunt, et nihil docent. In urbe igitur nōn in agrīs vīvere
cupiō." 5

Amīcus respondit, "Meā sententiā nōn est mūta nātūra, sed
multa docet. Nōnne omnis nātūra magnā vōce sapientiam
et benevolentiam Creātōris clāmat?"

Multa tamen in urbe discēbat docēbatque Sōcratēs.

Hodiē hominēs multī in urbe labōrāre et in agrīs vīvere 10
cupiunt.

WHERE ARE YOU?[1]

Petrus (pulsat forēs). Heus, heus, puer. Ubi tū es?
Mārcus. Nōlī, sīs,° frangere forēs. Salvē, Petre.
Petrus. Et tū. Gaudeō tē vidēre. Quid agis hodiē?
Mārcus. Nihil. Num quid vīs?

°**sīs (= sī vīs)** please, if you please

[1]Based on Erasmus (Desiderius Erasmus Roterodamus), a famous Dutch humanist (1466?-
1536), whose serious works include a translation of the Greek New Testament into Latin
published in 1516, the same year in which his *Colloquia* appeared.

This picture, which shows Erasmus writing, is in the Louvre. It is one of several portraits which Hans Holbein the Younger (1497-1543) painted of the Dutch humanist. Another portrait of Erasmus by Holbein is also in France. It is in the Museum Beaux-Arts at Chartres. One of the portraits is in the Metropolitan Museum of Art in New York City.

Petrus. Estne Jōannēs domī?

Mārcus. Incertus sum, sed inveniam.

Petrus. Abī intrō, sīs, et rogā ipsum.

Mārcus. Immō abī tū.

Petrus. Clāmābō. Heus, Jōannē, esne domī?

Jōannēs. Nōn sum.

Petrus. Impudēns, nōnne tē audiō? Domī tū es.

Jōannēs. Immō tū impudēns. Hesternō diē tē vīsitāvī. Servus tuus dīxit, "Petrus nōn domī est." Per fenestram autem tē vīdī. Ego igitur discessī. Nunc ego dīcō, "Domī nōn sum." Nōnne tū crēdis mihi ipsī?

Petrus. Periī.° Ego quoque discēdō. Valē, Jōannē. Valē, Mārce.

Mārcus et Jōannēs. Venī crās iterum, Petre. Valē.

°**Periī** I've had it!

186

Eight girls at New York's Dalton School had translated President Kennedy's Inaugural Address of 1961 into Latin and sent their translation to the White House. This is the reply they received from the President.

Jōhannēs Fīliusgeraldī Kennediēnsis, Rēspūblicae Praesidēns, puellīs Scholae Daltōnī salūtem plūrimam dīcit.

Eximiae puellae, litteram vestram, in quā dē interpretātiōne ōrātiōnis meae mentiōnem facitis, accēpī, eandemque interpretātiōnem percurrī. Multaque in eā mē placent et 5 dēlectant. Cognitiōnem linguae Latīnae et artem ēloquentiamque scrībendī vehementer admīror. Stilus interpretātiōnis vestrae mihi laudābilis probandusque vidētur; habet enim et cōpiam et varietātem.

Quid ā vōbīs fierī potest, nōn probātū° dignum? Grātiās 10 vōbīs agō, cum ob vestram benevolentiam, tum quod labōribus vestrīs efficitur ut ōrātiōnem meam linguam Latīnam loquentem nunc legere possem.

Valēte optimē! Ex urbe Washingtoniī, diē XXVII Māiī annō dominī MDCCCCLXI. 15

°**nōn probātū dignum** that is not deserving of approbation

DĒ AMĪCITIĀ

This selection is from Cicero's essay on friendship. The translations resemble each other because of the Latin origin of many of the words. Italics indicate words occurring in Latin and the Romance languages; small capitals show that there is a related word in English also.

Quanta autem vīs *amīcitiae* sit, ex hōc intellegī maximē potest, quod ex INFĪNĪTĀ societāte generis HŪMĀNĪ, quam conciliāvit ipsa NĀTŪRA, ita contracta rēs est et adducta in angustum, ut omnis cāritās aut inter *duōs* aut inter paucōs jungerētur. 5

Est enim *amīcitia* nihil aliud nisi omnium DĪVĪNĀRUM HŪMĀNĀRUMque rērum cum *benevolentiā* et cāritāte cōnsēnsiō; quā quidem haud sciō an, EXCEPTĀ sapientiā, nihil melius hominī sit ā *dīs* IMMORTĀLIBUS *datum*. Dīvitiās aliī praepōnunt, bonam aliī valētūdinem, aliī potentiam, aliī HONŌRĒS, multī 10

187

etiam voluptātēs. *Quī* autem in VIRTŪTE summum *bonum*
pōnunt, praeclārē illī quidem, sed haec ipsa VIRTŪS *amīcitiam*
et gignit et continet, nec sine VIRTŪTE *amīcitia* esse ūllō
pactō potest.

DE L'AMITIÉ

On peut comprendre toute la force de l'*amitié*, en observant
que de l'INFINIE société du genre HUMAIN, formée par la NA-
TURE, l'amitié véritable tire et compose une société infiniment
restreinte, qui ne comprend que *deux* hommes, ou tout au
plus un très petit nombre d'amis. 5

L'*amitié* en elle-même n'est autre chose qu'un accord
parfait de sentiments sur toutes les choses DIVINES et HU-
MAINES, joint à une *bienveillance* et une tendresse mutuelle.
Et certes, je crois que, la sagesse EXCEPTÉE, c'est le don le
plus précieux que les *dieux* IMMORTELS aient fait à l'homme. 10
Il en est qui préfèrent les richesses, d'autres la santé, ceux-ci
la puissance, ceux-là les HONNEURS, le plus grand nombre les
plaisirs. Pour ceux *qui* mettent le souverain *bien* dans la
VERTU, on ne peut que leur applaudir; mais c'est la VERTU
qui enfante et entretient l'*amitié*, et sans VERTU point d'*amitié*. 15

DELL'AMICIZIA

Come sia grande la forza dell'*amicizia* si può immaginare
da quanto segue: nella società INFINITA delle razze UMANE,
che la NATURA stessa ha formata, la scelta degli amici così si
restringe ed è stata ridotta, che si offrono i nostri affetti sia a
due sia a poche persone. 5

L'*amicizia* non è che l'accordo con *buona volontà* ed affezione
di ogni cosa DIVINA ed UMANA. Mi pare che, ECCETUATO il
senno, niente di meglio ci sia stato *dato* dai *dei* IMMORTALI.
Alcuni preferiscono la richezza, altri la salute, altri la potenza,
altri gli ONORI, molti il piacere. *Chi* crede, dunque, che la 10
VIRTÙ sia il *bene* più importante, ha ragione; ma altresì
la VIRTÙ stessa produce e sostiene l'*amicizia*, la quale, senza
VIRTÙ, è impossibile.

188

Además, cuanto más grande es la fuerza de la *amistad* puede reconocerse especialmente por esto: que de las INFINITAS relaciones de la raza HUMANA que la misma NATURALEZA provee, ésta que se llama *amistad* sea tan restringida y esté encerrada dentro de tan estrechos límites que todo afecto sea un nexo 5 que existe entre *dos* personas o entre unas pocas.

Porque la *amistad* no es más que el estar de acuerdo con otros en todo, en lo DIVINO y en lo HUMANO, en combinación con la *benevolencia* y el amor; en verdad, apenas sé si, con la EXCEPCIÓN de la sabiduría, nada mejor que ella haya sido 10 *dado* al hombre por los *dioses* INMORTALES. Algunos prefieren las riquezas; otros, la salud; algunos, el poder; algunos, los HONORES; muchos, aun el placer sensual. También hay otros para *quienes* el «más alto *bien*» es la VIRTUD, cosa admirable; pero esta misma VIRTUD produce y mantiene la *amistad*, y sin 15 la VIRTUD la *amistad* no puede existir.

ON FRIENDSHIP

Moreover, how great the strength of friendship is can be recognized especially from this fact, that out of the INFINITE relationships of the HUMAN race which NATURE herself has provided, this thing has been so restricted and brought into narrow limits, that every affection is a bond either between 5 two persons or among a few.

For friendship is nothing else than agreement on all matters, DIVINE and HUMAN, combined with kindliness and love; indeed, with the EXCEPTION of wisdom, perhaps nothing better (than friendship) has been given to man by the IMMORTAL 10 gods. Some prefer wealth, some good health, some power, some HONORS, many even sensual pleasures. However, there are those who place the highest good in VIRTUE, and indeed admirably; but this very VIRTUE both produces and maintains friendship, and without VIRTUE friendship 15 cannot exist at all.

A remarkable relationship prevails between a large number of Latin verbs (chiefly of Conjugation II) that express state or condition and corresponding Latin adjectives in **-idus** and nouns in **-or**.

-eō		-idus	-or, -ōris, M.	
caleō	be warm	calidus	calor[1]	warmth/heat
doleō	suffer	dolidus[2]	dolor	pain/grief
faveō	favor	———	favor	good will
hūmeō	be moist	hūmidus	hūmor	liquid/moisture
liqueō	be fluid	liquidus	liquor	fluid/liquid
paveō	fear	pavidus	pavor	a trembling/fear
placeō	please	placidus	placor[2]	pleasure
rubeō	be red	rubidus	rubor	redness
valeō	be strong	validus	valor[3]	worth/value
vigeō	be lively	vigidus[2]	vigor	liveliness/force

English has not borrowed any of these verbs, but has adopted most of the adjectives and many of the nouns related to them. A few verbs of Conjugation III have corresponding adjectives in **-idus** or nouns in **-or**.

cupiō   cupidus   fluō   fluidus   fluor   rapiō   rapidus

Which of the adjectives listed above have familiar English equivalents? which of the nouns? Give Latin adjectives and nouns and their English counterparts or meanings for the following verbs.

candeō   ferveō   horreō   palleō   rigeō   stupeō   timeō

Since these verbs denote state or condition rather than action, as shown by the translation, many of them form inchoatives, often with a prefix; e.g., **rubēscō** (turn red).

calēscō become warm   **effervēscō** boil up
incandēscō turn white/glow   **liquēscō** become fluid/melt

Form the inchoatives of **horreō, paveō, stupeō,** and **vigeō,** and give the meaning of each. (See also page 172.)

---

[1]All **-or** words in this list have genitive in **-ōris**.
[2]Late Latin.   [3]Medieval Latin.

This deity of the Gauls, who is holding a hammer in one hand and a rustic flute in the other, became identified under Roman influence with either Jupiter or a forest god, Silvanus. This representation of the Gallic god is in the form of a relief in the Calvet Museum in Avignon, France.

French sculptor Frémiet made this bronze statue of a Gallic warrior. It stands in the museum in Saint-Germain-en-Laye, near Paris.

LIFE IN GAUL AND GERMANY

In his sixth book (out of the seven on the Gallic Wars) Caesar had only a short military account to give. So it is there, among the events of the year 53 B.C., that he described the manners and customs of the Gauls and the Germans, among whom he had waged campaigns for several years.

Caesar was a keen observer, and his description of the peoples with whom he was fighting is of historical importance even now. Caesar was the first to set down the names of a number of Gallic and Germanic tribes which had up to that time remained outside the sphere of recorded history.

In omnī Galliā eōrum hominum quī aliquō sunt numerō°
atque honōre genera sunt duo; nam plēbēs paene servōrum
habētur locō,° quae nihil audet per sē, nūllī adhibētur cōnsiliō.

Plērīque, cum aut aere aliēnō aut magnitūdine tribūtōrum
aut injūriā potentiōrum premuntur, sēsē in servitūtem dicant° 5
nōbilibus; quibus° in hōs eadem omnia sunt jūra quae
dominīs° in servōs.

Sed dē hīs duōbus generibus alterum est druidum,[1] alterum
equitum.[2] Illī rēbus dīvīnīs intersunt, sacrificia pūblica ac
prīvāta cūrant, religiōnēs° interpretantur; ad eōs magnus 10
adulēscentium numerus disciplīnae° causā concurrit, magnōque hī° sunt apud eōs° honōre.

°**aliquō . . . numerō** of any account/importance • **paene . . .
locō** are regarded almost as slaves • **sēsē dicant** give themselves up (**dicō, -āre,** not **dīcō, -ere**) • **quibus/dominīs** datives with **sunt = quī/dominī habent** • **rēbus . . . intersunt**
have charge of sacred rites • **religiōnēs** questions of religion
disciplīnae (gen. with **causā**) for training • **hī** Druids
eōs the Gauls

adhibeō	2 admit (to)	**plēbēs**	F., common people
aes aliēnum	N., debt	**plērīque**	M. pl., a great many
+eques[3]	M., knight	**premō**	3 oppress; press (hard)
+habeō	2 regard	**servitūs**	F., slavery

*****magnitūdō**[4] F.   **tribūtum** N.   **nōbilis** M. (also adj.)   **pūblicus** (adj.)
prīvātus (adj.)   **interpretor** 1   **adulēscēns** M.

[1]The Druid priests wore a distinguishing robe of white. They held the oak tree and the
mistletoe in greatest reverence, and performed their sacrifices in oak groves.

[2]This term applies to both the class and the occupation of Gallic knights. Members of
the Roman equestrian order were by this time chiefly men engaged in commerce and trade,
while the calvalry was made up of military men, many of whom were foreigners.

[3]Latin words which have occurred in earlier vocabularies and appear in Caesar with
a new meaning or function bear the symbol (+) in lesson vocabularies.

[4]Latin words not previously taught that have common English derivatives similar in form
and meaning are listed (*) in order of occurrence following lesson vocabularies. Students
should consult the General Vocabulary for more information about words in either the
vertical or horizontal listings.

Both mistletoe and the oak were sacred to the Druids. Mistletoe found growing as a parasite on oak—a rare occurrence—was specially venerated.

PRIESTS AS JUDGES

Nam ferē dē omnibus contrōversiīs pūblicīs prīvātīsque cōnstituunt; et, sī quod est facinus admissum, sī caedēs facta, sī dē hērēditāte, dē fīnibus contrōversia est, eīdem dēcernunt, praemia poenāsque cōnstituunt; sī quī aut prī-

vātus aut populus eōrum dēcrētō nōn stetit,° sacrificiīs 5
interdīcunt.°

Haec poena apud eōs est gravissima. Quibus ita est inter-
.dictum, hī numerō° impiōrum ac scelerātōrum habentur; hīs
omnēs dēcēdunt,° aditum eōrum sermōnemque dēfugiunt nē

°**nōn stetit** (with **dēcrētō**)   does not abide by (their decision)   •   **interdīcunt**   they exclude (Supply dative of reference **eī.**)   •   **numerō**   (with gen.) among, as   •   **dēcēdunt**   avoid, withdraw from

This ancient statue of a Gallic peasant was found at Cavaillon, southern France.
It is now in the Calvet Museum at Avignon.

quid ex contāgiōne incommodī° accipiant, neque eīs petenti- 10
bus jūs redditur neque honōs ūllus commūnicātur.

Hīs autem omnibus druidibus praeest ūnus, quī summam
inter eōs habet auctōritātem. Hōc mortuō, aut, sī quī ex
reliquīs excellit dignitāte, succēdit, aut, sī sunt plūrēs parēs,
suffrāgiō druidum, nōn numquam etiam armīs dē prīncipātū 15
contendunt.

Hī certō annī tempore in fīnibus Carnutum, quae regiō
tōtīus Galliae media habētur, cōnsīdunt° in locō cōnsecrātō.
Hūc omnēs undique quī contrōversiās habent conveniunt
eōrumque dēcrētīs jūdiciīsque pārent. 20

°**quid . . . incommodī** any harm from contact • **cōnsīdunt** hold
their meetings

¹**aditus**	M., approach	⁺**jūs**	N., justice
admittō	3 commit	**jūs reddere/**	
auctōritās	F., authority	**dīcere**	administer justice
commūnicō	1 bestow; share²	**nōn numquam**	(adv.) sometimes
dēcernō	3 decide (a dis-	**praesum**	be in charge of/
	pute)		be over
dēfugiō	3 flee from, shun.	**prīncipātus**	M., chief position
facinus	N., crime	⁺**quī/quis**³	(indef. adj.) any
hērēditās	F., inheritance	**scelerātus**	(adj.) accursed
impius	(adj.) wicked	**sermō**	M., conversation
		suffrāgium	N., vote

*excellō 3 succēdō 3 cōnsecrō 1

¹Beginning with the lesson vocabularies of this unit, words are listed in alphabetical
order instead of by parts of speech as in earlier sections of this book. The numeral preceding the meaning of each verb indicates the conjugation to which it belongs. If more
help is needed than is given in these shorter listings, students should consult the General
Vocabulary.

²Lesson vocabularies—here as in the preceding lessons—give the meaning of the Latin
word in its context. Where space permits, additional meanings are sometimes given in
order to cover later occurrences of the same word. For example, in this lesson commūnicō has the meaning "bestow"; in later lessons it can be more appropriately translated
"share." However, it is impossible to include in the lesson vocabularies all the meanings
or connotations of words that students must use for effective translation into English.
Students should consider the meaning of each word carefully in its context and consult
the General Vocabulary for additional meanings of Latin words.

³Often used after **sī**; for declension, see page 433.

Disciplīna° in Britanniā[1] reperta atque inde in Galliam trānslāta esse exīstimātur, et nunc quī dīligentius eam rem cognōscere volunt plērumque illō° discendī causā proficīscuntur.

Druidēs ā bellō abesse cōnsuērunt neque tribūta ūnā cum reliquīs pendunt. Tantīs excitātī praemiīs et suā sponte° multī in disciplīnam conveniunt et ā parentibus propinquīsque mittuntur. [5]

Magnum ibi numerum versuum° ēdiscere dīcuntur. Itaque annōs nōnnūllī xx in disciplīnā permanent. Neque fās [10] esse exīstimant ea° litterīs mandāre, cum in reliquīs ferē rēbus, pūblicīs prīvātīsque ratiōnibus, Graecīs litterīs ūtantur. Id mihi duābus dē causīs īnstituisse videntur, quod neque in vulgus disciplīnam efferrī velint, neque eōs quī discant litterīs cōnfīsōs° minus memoriae studēre°; quod ferē [15] plērīsque accidit, ut praesidiō° litterārum dīligentiam in discendō ac memoriam remittant.

°**disciplīna** the system • **illō** there, i.e., to Britain • **suā sponte . . . conveniunt** come voluntarily (contrast with **ā parentibus . . . mittuntur**) • **versuum** of verses (lines of poetry containing the substance of Druidical teaching) • **ea** things they learn **litterīs cōnfīsōs** relying on writing • **minus studēre** pay less attention to • **praesidiō** = auxiliō

ēdiscō	3 memorize	**pendō**	3 pay
efferō	make known	**permaneō**	2 continue
fās	N. (indecl.) right	**plērumque**	(adv.) generally
fās est	it is proper	+**ratiō**	F., record, account
īnstituō	3 adopt	**remittō**	3 relax
littera	F., a letter (of the	**reperiō**	4 develop; find
	alphabet); pl., let-	**trānsferō**	bring over
	ter, epistle; writing	**ūnā**	(adv.) together
mandō	1 commit	**vulgus**	N., common peo-
nōnnūllus	(pron./adj.) some		ple; the crowd

*****dīligentia** F.

[1] It is more probable that the Britons had originally received the Druidical teaching from the Continent, but little is positively known about Druidism.

Imprīmīs hoc volunt persuādēre,° nōn interīre animās, sed ab aliīs post mortem trānsīre ad aliōs°; atque hōc maximē ad virtūtem excitārī° putant, metū mortis neglēctō. Multa praetereā dē stellīs atque eōrum mōtū, dē mundī ac terrārum magnitūdine, dē rērum nātūrā, dē deōrum immortālium vī ac potestāte disputant et juvenibus trādunt. 20

°**hoc persuādēre** to convince (men) of this • **ab aliīs...ad aliōs** from one body to another • **excitārī** that (men) are incited

anima	F., soul	**mōtus**	M., motion
imprīmīs/		**mundus**	M., universe, world
in prīmīs	especially	**⁺trādō**	3 teach
intereō	die		

KNIGHTS IN GAUL[1]

Alterum genus est equitum. Hī, cum est ūsus° atque aliquod bellum incidit (quod° ferē ante Caesaris adventum quotannīs accidere solēbat, utī aut ipsī injūriās īnferrent aut illātās repellerent), omnēs in bellō versantur, atque eōrum ut quisque° est genere cōpiīsque amplissimus, ita plūrimōs 5 circum sē ambactōs° clientēsque habet. Hanc ūnam grātiam potentiamque nōvērunt.

°**ūsus** need • **quod** subject of **solēbat,** explained by the clause **utī...repellerent** • **ut quisque est...amplissimus, ita plūrimōs...** the more distinguished one of them is..., the more... **ambactōs** paid servants, retainers

⁺cōpiae	F. pl., wealth	**nōscō**	3 learn; (perf.)
⁺genus	N., family		know
⁺grātia	F., influence	**quotannīs**	(adv.) annually
incidō	3 occur	**utī**	(conj./adv.) = **ut**
⁺inferō	cause, inflict	**versor**	1 engage (in)

*cliēns M.

[1]Caesar is our chief source for the class of Gallic knights. See T. Rice Holmes' *Caesar's Conquest of Gaul* (2nd ed., Oxford University Press, 1911), pages 512-513. For a discussion of Roman knights and their careers during the time of Caesar, see pages 40-41 of Johnston's *Roman Life* (Scott, Foresman and Company, 1957).

Nātiō est omnis Gallōrum admodum dēdita religiōnibus,° atque ob eam causam quī sunt affectī graviōribus morbīs quīque in proeliīs perīculīsque versantur aut prō victimīs hominēs° immolant aut sē immolātūrōs vovent. Administrīs ad ea sacrificia druidibus ūtuntur, quod, prō vītā[1] hominis 5 nisi hominis vīta reddātur, nōn posse deōs immortālēs plācārī arbitrantur; pūblicēque° ejusdem generis habent īnstitūta sacrificia.

Aliī ingentī magnitūdine simulācra° habent, quōrum contexta vīminibus membra° vīvīs hominibus complent; quibus 10 incēnsīs, circumventī flammā exanimantur hominēs.

Supplicia eōrum quī in fūrtō° aut in latrōciniō aut in aliquā noxiā° sint comprehēnsī grātiōra° dīs immortālibus esse arbitrantur; sed cum ejus generis cōpia dēficit, etiam ad innocentium supplicia dēscendunt. 15

°**dēdita religiōnibus** devoted to religious observances; superstitious
hominēs object of **immolant** and **immolātūrōs** • **pūblicē** on behalf of the state • **simulācra** images (of men) • **contexta vīminibus membra** limbs made of wickerwork • **fūrtō** theft
noxiā crime • **grātiōra** especially pleasing

administer	M., assistant	latrōcinium	N., robbery
admodum	(adv.) very much	nisi	(conj.) unless,
comprehendō	3 catch, seize		except
exanimō	1 kill; (pass.) die	supplicium	N., punishment
immolō	1 sacrifice	voveō	2 vow

*nātiō F. victima F. plācō 1 innocēns (adj.)

GALLIC GODS

Deōrum[2] maximē Mercurium colunt; hujus sunt plūrima

---

[1] Primitive tribes often sacrificed animals—and even human beings—in connection with funeral rites or ceremonies designed to cure diseases.

[2] From what Caesar could learn of the Gallic gods he thought that they corresponded to certain Roman gods, and he gives them Roman names. In the same way the Romans identified their gods with those of the Greeks, though they were not really the same.

simulācra; hunc omnium inventōrem artium ferunt°; hunc
viārum atque itinerum ducem; hunc ad quaestūs° pecūniae
mercātūrāsque° habēre vim maximam arbitrantur.

Post hunc Apollinem° et Mārtem et Jovem et Minervam. 5
Dē hīs eandem ferē quam reliquae gentēs habent opīniōnem:
Apollinem morbōs dēpellere, Minervam operum atque arti-
ficiōrum° initia trādere, Jovem imperium caelestium tenēre,
Mārtem bella regere. Huic, cum proeliō dīmicāre cōnstitu-
ērunt, ea quae bellō cēperint plērumque dēvovent. Cum 10
superāvērunt, animālia capta immolant reliquāsque rēs in
ūnum locum cōnferunt.

Multīs in cīvitātibus hārum rērum exstrūctōs cumulōs°
locīs cōnsecrātīs cōnspicārī licet; neque saepe accidit ut neg-
lēctā quisquam religiōne aut capta apud sē occultāre aut 15
posita° tollere audēret, gravissimumque eī reī supplicium cum
cruciātū cōnstitūtum est.

°**ferunt** they call • **quaestūs** acquisition (plural indicates different kinds of moneymaking and business) • **mercātūrās** trade
Apollinem object of **colunt** (to be supplied from line 1) • **ope-**
rum atque artificiōrum of handicrafts and trades • **cumulōs**
mounds • **posita** what has been deposited (in sacred places)

caelestis	(adj.) heavenly;	cruciātus	M., torture
	M. pl., gods	dēvoveō	2 vow
cīvitās	F., state	dīmicō	1 fight
+colō	3 worship	exstruō	3 build/pile up
cōnferō	collect	occultō	1 conceal
cōnspicor	1 see, observe	tollō	3 take away; remove

*inventor M.   opīniō F.

STRANGE GALLIC CUSTOMS

Gallī sē omnēs ab Dīte[1] patre prōgnātōs° praedicant idque
ab druidibus prōditum dīcunt. Ob eam causam spatia omnis

°**ab Dīte patre prōgnātōs** sprang from Pluto as their ancestor

[1]The name Dis is sometimes used for the god of the underworld. The Gauls asserted
that they were aborigines, that they had not immigrated from any other region.

temporis nōn numerō diērum sed noctium[1] fīniunt°; diēs nātālēs° et mēnsium et annōrum initia sīc observant ut noctem diēs subsequātur.

In reliquīs vītae īnstitūtīs hōc ferē ab reliquīs differunt, quod suōs līberōs,° nisi cum adolēvērunt ut° mūnus mīlitiae° sustinēre possint, palam ad sē adīre nōn patiuntur; fīliumque puerīlī aetāte in pūblicō in cōnspectū patris assistere° turpe dūcunt.

°**fīniunt** measure • **diēs nātālēs** birthdays • **līberōs** subj. of **adīre** • **ut** so that • **mīlitiae** of military service • **in cōnspectū patris assistere** to appear at his father's side

adolēscō	3 grow up	**praedicō**	1 claim; declare
⁺dūcō	3 consider	**prōdō**	3 hand down; reveal
īnstitūtum	N., custom	**subsequor**	3 follow (closely)
patior	3 permit; suffer	**turpis**	(adj.) shameful

*__observō__ 1   **differō** 3   **puerīlis** (adj.)   **pūblicum** N.

Virī,° quantās pecūniās° ab uxōribus dōtis nōmine° accēpērunt, tantās ex suīs bonīs, aestimātiōne factā, cum dōtibus° commūnicant. Hujus omnis pecūniae conjūnctim ratiō habētur,° frūctūsque° servantur. Uter° eōrum vītā superāvit, ad eum pars utrīusque cum frūctibus superiōrum temporum pervenit.

Virī in uxōrēs,[2] sīcutī in līberōs, vītae necisque habent potestātem; et cum pater familiae illūstriōre locō nātus dēcessit, ejus propinquī conveniunt et, dē morte sī rēs in suspīciōnem vēnit, dē uxōribus in servīlem modum quaestiōnem[3] habent et, sī compertum est,° ignī atque omnibus tormentīs excruciātās° interficiunt.

°**virī** husbands • **pecūniās/dōtibus** plural because **virī** is plural • **dōtis nōmine** as dowry • **conjūnctim ratiō habētur** an account is kept jointly • **frūctūs** income • **uter** whichever (of two) • **sī compertum est** if guilt is discovered • **excruciātās** tortured

[1]English "fortnight" (fourteen nights) is a survival of this method of reckoning time.

[2]According to Roman law the head of the family had such power over his children, but not over his wife.

[3]An inquiry after the manner practiced on slaves.

+**bona**	N. pl., property	**quantus**	(rel. adj.) as great;
nāscor	3 be born; arise	**tantus . . . quantus** =	
nex	F., death		as much . . . as

*****aestimātiō** F. **illūstris** (adj.) **servīlis** (adj.) **tormentum** N.

Fūnera° sunt prō cultū Gallōrum magnifica et sūmptuōsa;
omniaque quae vīvīs cordī fuisse° arbitrantur in ignem īnferunt, etiam animālia; ac paulō suprā hanc memoriam° servī   25
et clientēs quōs ab eīs dīlēctōs° esse cōnstābat, jūstīs fūnebribus cōnfectīs,° ūnā cremābantur.[1]

Quae cīvitātēs commodius suam rem pūblicam administrāre
exīstimantur habent lēgibus sānctum,° sī quis quid dē rē
pūblicā ā fīnitimīs rūmōre ac fāmā° accēperit, utī ad magis-   30
trātum dēferat nēve cum quō aliō commūnicet, quod saepe
hominēs temerāriōs atque imperītōs falsīs rūmōribus terrērī
et ad facinus impellī et dē summīs rēbus cōnsilium capere
cognitum est. Magistrātūs quae vīsa sunt° occultant, quae
esse ex ūsū jūdicāvērunt multitūdinī prōdunt. Dē rē pūblicā   35
nisi per concilium loquī nōn concēditur.

°**fūnera** funerals • **cordī fuisse** to have been dear • **suprā hanc memoriam** before our time • **dīlēctōs esse** to have
been beloved • **jūstīs fūnebribus cōnfectīs** with proper funeral rites • **habent lēgibus sānctum** have a legal enactment
fāmā by current report (which may be true) • **quae vīsa sunt**
what seems best

+**accipiō**	3 hear, learn	**jūdicō**	1 decide
commodē	(adv.) well; easily	**loquor**	3 speak
concēdō	3 permit	**nēve**	(conj.) and not,
cōnstō	1 stand together;		nor
	agree	+**prō**	(prep.) in view of
cōnstat	(impers.) it is known	**rēs pūblica**	F., government,
cultus	M., civilization		public affairs
imperītus	(adj.) inexperienced	**temerārius**	(adj.) imprudent

*****sūmptuōsus** (adj.) **cremō** 1 **administrō** 1 **rūmor** M. **falsus**
(adj.) **impellō** 3

[1]Cremation was not the universal practice. Many Gallic skeletons have been found
in France.

Caesar subjugated the Treveri in 53 B.C. At their capital, Augustus later founded the colony Augusta Treverorum, modern Trier/Trèves. The Porta Nigra, a fortified gate, is one of the most impressive Roman remains at Trier.

THE GERMANS WERE DIFFERENT

Germānī multum ab hāc cōnsuētūdine differunt; nam neque druidēs[1] habent quī rēbus dīvīnīs praesint, neque sacrificiīs student. Deōrum numerō eōs sōlōs dūcunt quōs cernunt et quōrum apertē° opibus juvantur, Sōlem et Vulcānum et Lūnam. Reliquōs nē fāmā quidem accēpērunt. 5

Vīta omnis in vēnātiōnibus atque in studiīs reī mīlitāris cōnsistit. Ā parvīs° labōrī ac dūritiae student.

°**apertē** obviously • **ā parvīs** from childhood

cernō	3 see	**rēs mīlitāris**	F., warfare
cōnsuētūdō	F., way of life, custom	+**studeō**	2 attach importance to; be eager (for)
dūritia	F., hardship	+**studium**	N., pursuit, interest
(ops), opis	F., aid; power; pl., power, resources	**vēnātiō**	F., hunting, hunt

[1]The Germans had no exclusive priestly class, but they had priests and priestesses who offered sacrifices and interpreted omens.

Agricultūrae nōn student, majorque pars eōrum vīctūs in lacte, cāseō, carne cōnsistit.

Neque quisquam agrī modum certum aut fīnēs habet proprios; sed magistrātūs ac prīncipēs in annōs singulōs° gentibus cognātiōnibusque hominum, quīque[1] ūnā coiērunt° quantum 5 et quō locō vīsum est agrī° attribuunt, atque annō post aliō° trānsīre cōgunt.

Ejus reī multās afferunt causās[2]: nē assiduā cōnsuētūdine captī studium bellī gerendī agricultūrā° commūtent; nē lātōs fīnēs parāre studeant potentiōrēs° atque humiliōrēs° posses- 10 siōnibus expellant; nē accūrātius° ad frīgora atque aestūs vītandōs aedificent; nē qua oriātur pecūniae cupiditās, quā ex rē factiōnēs dissēnsiōnēsque nāscuntur; ut animī aequi-tāte[3] plēbem contineant, cum suās quisque opēs cum poten-tissimīs aequārī videat. 15

°in annōs singulōs every year • **gentibus cognātiōnibusque hominum** to families and (groups of) relatives • **quīque ūnā coiērunt** and (to those) who have united together • **agrī** (gen. with **quantum**) as much land as • **aliō** to another place **agricultūrā** for agriculture • **potentiōrēs** (subject of **studeant**) **humiliōrēs** (object of **expellant**) • **accūrātius** with greater care, too carefully

aequō	1 make equal, equal- ize; adjust	**frīgus**	N., cold
		+humilis	(adj.) weak
aestus	M., heat	**lac**	N., milk
assiduus	(adj.) continual	**+modus**	M., amount
attribuō	3 assign	**+parō**	1 acquire, get
carō	F., meat, flesh	**+post**	(adv.) after(wards)
cāseus	M., cheese	**proprius**	(adj.) one's own, pri- vate; characteristic
commūtō	1 change, exchange		
cupiditās	F., desire	**vīctus**	M., food; life

*factiō F. **dissēnsiō** F. **aequitās** F.

[1] Individuals and small groups of men who did not belong to the same stock united them-selves for this purpose.

[2] For this annual move, four reasons are each introduced by **nē** and a fifth by **ut.**

[3] i.e., a contented frame of mind, which kept the common people in their place.

Cīvitātibus maxima laus est quam lātissimē circum sē, vāstātīs fīnibus, sōlitūdinēs habēre. Hoc° proprium virtūtis exīstimant, expulsōs agrīs fīnitimōs cēdere neque quemquam prope sē audēre cōnsistere. Simul hōc sē fore tūtiōrēs arbitrantur, repentīnae incursiōnis timōre sublātō.° 5

Cum bellum cīvitās aut illātum dēfendit aut īnfert, magistrātūs quī eī bellō praesint et vītae necisque habeant potestātem dēliguntur. In pāce nūllus est commūnis magistrātus, sed principēs regiōnum atque pāgōrum inter suōs jūs dīcunt contrōversiāsque minuunt. 10

Latrōcinia nūllam habent īnfāmiam quae extrā fīnēs cujusque cīvitātis fīunt, atque ea juventūtis exercendae ac dēsidiae° minuendae causā fierī praedicant. Atque ubi quis ex principibus in conciliō dīxit sē ducem fore, quī sequī velint profiteantur,° cōnsurgunt eī quī et causam et hominem probant, 15 suumque auxilium pollicentur, atque ā multitūdine laudantur maximē; quī ex hīs secūtī nōn sunt in dēsertōrum ac prōditōrum° numerō dūcuntur, omniumque hīs rērum posteā fidēs dērogātur.°

Hospitem violāre fās nōn putant; quī° quācumque dē causā 20 ad eōs vēnērunt ab injūriā prohibent, sānctōsque habent; hīsque omnium domūs patent, vīctusque commūnicātur.°

°**hoc** explained by **expulsōs ... cōnsistere** • **sublātō** from **tollō** • **dēsidia, -ae** F., idleness • **profiteantur** let them **(eī quī sequī velint)** speak up • **prōditor** M., traitor • **omnium ... rērum ... fidēs dērogātur** all confidence is taken away (from them) • **quī** those who • **commūnicātur** (i.e., **cum hīs**)

cēdō	3 go away	**minuō**	3 settle; lessen
commūnis	(adj.) general	**pāgus**	M., district, canton
cōnsurgō	3 stand up, arise	+**prohibeō**	2 protect
+**dēfendō**	3 ward off, repel	**qui-/quae-/**	(indef.) whoever,
exerceō	2 train, exercise	**quodcumque**	whatever
hospes	M./F., guest	+**quis/quid**	(indef.) any(one),
incursiō	F., raid, invasion		anything
juventūs	F., youth	**sānctus**	(adj.) inviolable
laus	F., glory, praise	**sōlitūdō**	F., wilderness

īnfāmia F.   *__dēsertor__ M.   **violō** 1

205

As previously pointed out, many Latin words have been taken over unchanged into English. The spelling is exactly the same, and the connection in meaning is usually easy to see. The English word, however, is often a different part of speech from the Latin.

Examples include English nouns that come from varied forms of Latin verbs.

affidavit	from **affidāre** (state on oath)	written statement
	perf. indic. act./3rd sing.	sworn to be true
caveat	from **cavēre** (beware)	warning//legal notice
	pres. subj. act./3rd sing.	to stop action
fiat	from **fierī** (be done/be made)	authoritative decree/
	pres. subj./3rd sing.	command//permission
imprimatur	from **imprimere** (print)	license to print/pub-
	pres. subj. pass./3rd sing.	lish//approval
innuendo	from **innuere** (give a nod/hint)	indirect hint/sugges-
	abl. of gerund	tion against someone
memento	from **meminisse** (remember)	something that serves
	fut. imperative/2nd sing.	to remind or warn
veto	from **vetāre** (forbid)	refusal of consent//
	pres. indic. act./1st sing.	prohibition

Identify each Latin verb form below and give its meaning as an English noun.

caret	**dēficit**	**habitat**	**interest**	**posse**
crēscendō	**exit**	**ignōrāmus**	**mandāmus**	**tenet**

Some English nouns in frequent use come from Latin gerundives.

memorandum	from **memorāre**	note to aid one's memory
	(call to mind)	(lit., thing to be remembered)
propaganda	from **propāgāre**	ideas or doctrines spread abroad
	(spread)	by an organization or movement

From what Latin verb does each of the following come? Give the meaning of the English.

agenda	legend	multiplicand	reverend
dividend	Miranda	referendum	subtrahend

THE ETERNAL CITY

No one knows who first called Rome *urbs aeterna*. The phrase was used in the reign of Augustus by the poets Tibullus and Ovid, who naturally considered Rome an eternal city. After seven centuries their city was then greater, more prosperous, more splendid than ever before. Nor was there any reason to doubt that Rome would continue to keep would-be invaders at a comfortable distance.

Rome was on the salt route from the salt marshes north of the Tiber to the inland hills. In fact, one of the roads leading north from Rome was called *Via Salaria* (the Salt Road) because salt was transported on it. Moreover, Rome was located at an advantageous point on the Tiber River where an island facilitated a crossing from Latium to Etruria. The Tiber is unsuitable for navigation, and so the town of Ostia fifteen miles away serves as the port of Rome, as it did also in ancient times. Bridges now spanning the river all are modern or medieval, with the exception of the Ponte Fabricio (*Pons Fabricius*), which was constructed in the first century B.C.

The earliest Roman settlement was on the Palatine Hill, well fortified on three sides by steep cliffs. The town gradually spread until it enclosed all seven of the hills (Palatine, Capitoline, Quirinal, Viminal, Esquiline, Caelian, and Aventine) which gave to Rome the name "City of the Seven Hills." The temple of Jupiter and the citadel were on the Capitoline, the only part of the city that escaped being sacked by the Gauls in 387 B.C.

To prevent further destruction the Romans built a massive stone wall around the city. This wall, commonly known as the Servian Wall, probably followed the line of earlier defenses constructed by Servius Tullius, the sixth king of Rome. It did not enclose the low-lying land along the Tiber, but did include the Seven Hills. Rome soon outgrew the boundaries of the Servian Wall, but no new fortifications were built for over five hundred years. About A.D. 275 a sense of insecurity caused the Emperor Aurelian to build a new wall, which also enclosed the Janiculum, a hill on the west bank of the Tiber not counted with the Seven Hills of Rome. Large sections of both the Servian and the Aurelian Walls are still visible today.

Rome's first emperor, Augustus, claimed credit for beautifying the city and leaving it a city of marble. He was responsible for the forum named for him "Forum of Augustus" and dedicated in 2 B.C. Augustus also built a temple of Apollo on the Palatine and a temple of Jupiter on the Capitoline. He encouraged wealthy Romans to follow his example in constructing new temples and monuments and repairing old ones. Succeeding emperors also left reminders of their reigns in the form of arches, bridges, monuments, temples, and other public buildings.

Rome has suffered destruction many times in the course of its long history—from fires, from floods, and from invaders. Especially destructive was the great fire in A.D. 64, when Nero was emperor. Invasions by Gauls, by Goths, and by Vandals also took a heavy toll.

Most of the ancient buildings did not survive the ravages of time, wars, and vandalism. They were buried by tons of debris from collapsing walls or by the slow accumulation of dirt and rubbish. Since the Renaissance, antiquarians and archaeologists have dug out and partly reconstructed a great many ancient monuments. Before the days of enlightened and careful archaeological procedures, however, reconstruction often began with grading an entire area and filling in and leveling the ruins. Builders who used the ancient ruins as quarries also are responsible for much mutilation and destruction.

While even the names and uses of many buildings are forgotten, structures like the Colosseum, the Pantheon, and Hadrian's Tomb still remain and continue to be used, although for purposes other than those for which they were built. The most impressive of the excavated sites is no doubt the *Forum Romanum*. In fact, the whole triangle between the Capitoline, the Palatine, and the Colosseum is one great outdoor museum.

The Eternal City, where all historical periods have left their monuments side by side, lives on. For hundreds of years Rome was the capital of the ancient world, the center of a mighty empire. Later came the division of the Empire, with two capitals, one at Rome, the other at Constantinople. Still later came the fall of the Roman Empire and eventually the political separation of Rome from the rest of Italy. Through the adversities of all the ages, however, Rome did survive. Also, since 1871, when Victor Emmanuel II made it the national capital of the restored and reunited Italian kingdom, Rome has been the center of a politically united Italy.

It has been estimated that under the Empire Rome's population numbered at least a million persons, including foreigners as well as Roman citizens, their families, and their slaves. This figure dropped to twenty or thirty thousand during the Middle Ages, when only a small area inside the Aurelian Wall and at the Vatican was inhabited. Now, with its suburbs, greater Rome has a population of more than two million.

Thus, while no longer the capital of the world, modern Rome, with her architectural, cultural, and linguistic heritage from ancient Rome, is still the City of the Seven Hills, is still the Eternal City.

The map shown on the facing page is a small reproduction of "Rome Today: A Visitor's Guide," a map by Don Almquist which appeared as a double spread (pages 80-81) in the April 1960 issue of *Holiday*. In the printed key accompanying the map, an asterisk (*) denotes the name of a church.

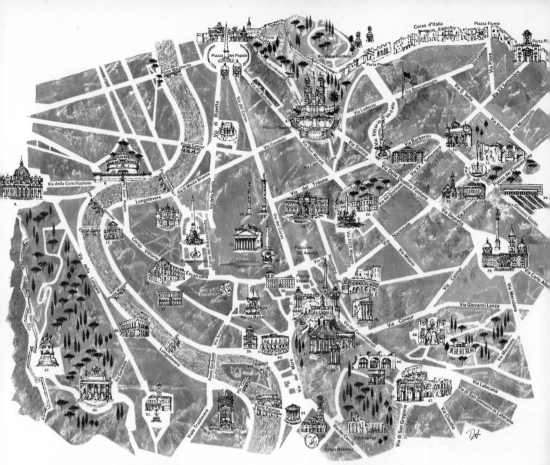

Top: The spectacular monument to King Victor Emmanuel, founder of modern Italy, is at left; Trajan's Column with its spiral band of reliefs of Roman military activity at right. Left: The pyramid tomb of Cestius, of Egyptian inspiration, was outside ancient Rome, but is near the railway station of the modern city. Right: Remains of the Temple of Vesta in the Forum.

Above: The ruined three stories of the so-called *Domus Augustana*, thought to be the home of Caesar's successor, the Emperor Augustus, are on the Palatine Hill. Below: The Colosseum is so familiar that it might be called the trademark of Rome. Here occurred the gladiatorial games that were the favorite spectacle of the ancient Romans.

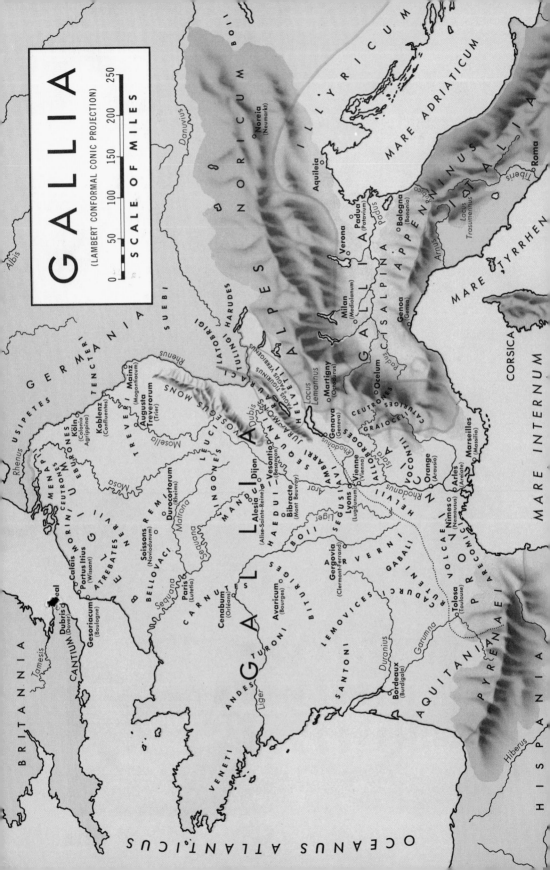

GALLIA

(LAMBERT CONFORMAL CONIC PROJECTION)

SCALE OF MILES

0 50 100 150 200 250

GERMANIA

BRITANNIA

OCEANUS ATLANTICUS

HISPANIA

MARE INTERNUM

MARE ADRIATICUM

MARE TYRRHEN

ILLYRICUM

NORICUM

ITALIA

GALLIA CISALPINA

APPENNINUS

CORSICA

ALPES

GALLIA

AQUITANIA

PYRENAEI

Roma
Tiberis
Arnus
Lacus Trasumennus
Bologna (Bononia)
Padus
Padua (Patavium)
Genoa (Genua)
Ocelum
Milan (Mediolanum)
Verona
Aquileia
Noreia (Neumarkt)
Danuvius
Albis

Martigny (Octodurus)
Ocelum
CEUTRONES
CATURIGES
GRAIOCELI
VOCONII
Genava (Geneva)
Lacus Lemannus
Rhodanus
Isara
Arles (Arelate)
Orange (Arausio)
Vienne (Vienna)
Marseilles (Massilia)
Nimes (Nemausus)
VOLCAE
AREA COMICI

HELVETII
Lyons (Lugdunum)
SEGUSIAVI
AMBARRI
SEQUANI
Vesontio (Besançon)
Dubis
Arar
Bibracte (Mont Beuvray)
Dijon
Alesia (Alise-Sainte-Reine)
HAEDUI
BOII
LINGONES
MANDUBII
JURA-MONS
VOSEGUS MONS
Moselle
Mosella
Augusta Treverorum (Trier)
TREVERI
Koblenz (Confluentes)
Köln (Colonia Agrippina)
Mainz (Mogontiacum)
Rhenus
Rhenus
EBURONES
CEUTRONES
MENAPI
MORINI
NERVII
ATREBATES
BELLOVACI
REMI
Soissons (Noviodunum)
Durocortorum (Rheims)
Matrona
Sequana
Seguana
Paris (Lutetia)
CARNUTES
Cenabum (Orléans)
TURONI
ANDES
VENETI
Liger
BITURIGES
Avaricum (Bourges)
Gergovia (Clermont-Ferrand)
ARVERNI
GABALI
RUTENI
CADURCI
LEMOVICES
SANTONI
Duranius
Bordeaux (Burdigala)
Garumna
Tolosa (Toulouse)
Hiberus

Gesoriacum (Boulogne)
Portus Itius (Wissant)
Calais
Dubris (Dover)
CANTIUM
Tamesis

SUEBI
USIPETES
TENCTERI
LATOBRIGI
TULINGI
HARUDES
Paris (Paris)
Lacus Figulinus

SEDUNI
PENNINUS

On the left is a portrait bust of Marius, Caesar's uncle, who was leader of the plebeian party. On the right is a bust of Sulla, Caesar's enemy, who was leader of the aristocratic party.

PROLOGUE TO POWER

Gaius Julius Caesar spent his life in the midst of political and military actions which led to the decline of the Roman Republic and to dictatorship and, shortly after his death, to empire.

At nineteen he was captured by pirates and ransomed. While a captive he told the pirates that he would return and destroy them. He did.

At the time of Caesar's birth (102 or 100 B.C.) his uncle Marius had turned back an invasion of Teutonic tribes. Marius was the champion of the popular party and later engaged in civil war with Sulla, the leader of the patricians. Marius'

213

defeat meant danger for his nephew, too. Yet Caesar escaped, and from 82 to 78 he served with the army in Asia.

On his return to Rome, Caesar practiced law for a time; then he studied oratory on the island of Rhodes. In 68 he was appointed quaestor in Spain. As such he was an assistant to the governor and also gained experience in conducting military campaigns.

As aedile in 65, Caesar provided Rome with sumptuous spectacles and festivals. To do this he went heavily into debt, but the money was well spent. In 63 B.C. the people showed Caesar their appreciation by electing him Pontifex Maximus (chief priest).

Caesar returned to Spain as praetor in 62, and the following year he was governor of Farther Spain. Having thus complied with **cursus honorum**—the sequence of public offices leading to the consulship, Caesar intended to run for this office. Encountering opposition from the Senate, however, Caesar allied himself with Crassus, a man of great wealth and influence, and with the popular military leader Pompey. The marriage of the latter to Caesar's daughter Julia helped to cement relations between Caesar and Pompey.

Caesar, Pompey, and Crassus formed the coalition known as the First Triumvirate for the purpose of dividing among themselves the government of the Roman world. Caesar became consul in 59, and in 55 Pompey and Crassus shared the consulship. The same triumvirate secured the passage of laws that were to their mutual advantage.

Caesar was by now well established in the favor of the people. At the end of his consulship, passage by the Senate of the Lex Vatinia made Caesar governor of the Roman Province in Gaul for the unusually long period of five years. (This term was later extended to ten years.)

Caesar's territories included Cisalpine Gaul (Italy between the Alps and the Apennines), Illyricum (Albania and Dalmatia), and Transalpine Gaul (which eventually included all the land between the Mediterranean Sea and the Pyrenees Mountains in the south, the Atlantic in the west, the Rhine in the east, and of unknown limits to the north).

With four legions (at full strength about 24,000 men), five staff officers **(legati)**, and a quaestor, Caesar left for Gaul in 58.

UNIT III

This narrow mountain pass, now called Pas de l'Ecluse, was the only road open to the Helvetians after Caesar had refused their request to let them through the Province. Caesar's description of the route as *angustum* and *difficile* is confirmed by this modern photograph.

ᵀA statue of C. Julius Caesar, Imperator, who appears here dressed in the full splendor of his general's uniform

CAESAR AND THE HELVETIANS¹

Caesar, the newly appointed governor of the Roman Province, faced some restless neighbors. The Helvetians, a large tribe of Celtic Gauls living in what is now Switzerland, decided to migrate westward in search of living space for an expanding population.

It must have been an exciting moment in Rome when word came of the Helvetians' move in an area too close to the Roman Province to be ignored. After all, the Helvetians could muster nearly 100,000 armed men.

¹Beginning with Unit III, both lesson vocabulary and all special helps keyed to the text by the symbol (°) will be found at the end of each section of the reading.

Gallia est omnis° dīvīsa in partēs trēs, quārum ūnam incolunt Belgae, aliam Aquītānī, tertiam quī ipsōrum linguā
Celtae, nostrā Gallī appellantur. Hī omnēs linguā, īnstitūtīs,
lēgibus inter sē differunt. Gallōs ab Aquītānīs Garunna
flūmen, ā Belgīs Matrona et Sēquana dīvidit.°   5

Hōrum omnium fortissimī sunt Belgae, proptereā quod ā
cultū atque hūmānitāte prōvinciae longissimē absunt; mini-
mēque ad eōs mercātōrēs saepe° commeant atque ea quae ad
effēminandōs animōs pertinent° important; proximīque sunt
Germānīs, quī trāns Rhēnum incolunt, quibuscum conti-   10
nenter bellum gerunt.

Quā dē causā Helvētiī quoque reliquōs Gallōs virtūte
praecēdunt, quod ferē cotīdiānīs proeliīs cum Germānīs contendunt, cum aut suīs fīnibus eōs prohibent, aut ipsī in
eōrum fīnibus bellum gerunt.   15

Eōrum ūna pars, quam Gallōs obtinēre dictum est, initium
capit ā flūmine Rhodanō; continētur Garunnā flūmine,
Ōceanō, fīnibus Belgārum; attingit etiam ab° Sēquanīs et
Helvētiīs flūmen Rhēnum; vergit ad septentriōnēs.

Belgae ab extrēmīs Galliae fīnibus oriuntur; pertinent ad 20
īnferiōrem partem flūminis Rhēnī; spectant in septentriōnēs
et orientem sōlem.

Aquītānia ā Garunnā flūmine ad Pȳrēnaeōs montēs et eam
partem Ōceanī quae est ad Hispāniam pertinet; spectat inter
occāsum sōlis et septentriōnēs.   25

°**omnis** as a whole • **dīvidit** (singular, because the Marne and
the Seine are thought of as one boundary) • **minimē saepe**
very seldom • **ad effēminandōs animōs pertinent** tend to
weaken character • **ab** on the side of

attingō	3 touch/border (on)	**hūmānitās**	F., refinement
commeō	1 (with **ad**) visit	**proptereā**	(adv.) on this account
continenter	(adv.) continually	**proptereā quod**	because
cotīdiānus	(adj.) daily; usual	**septentriōnēs**	M. pl., the north
extrēmus	(adj.) farthest	**vergō**	3 (with **ad**) face

*importō 1

Bronze figure of the goddess Sequana, patroness of the Seine River and the Sequani

A NATION OUTGROWS ITS BOUNDARIES

Apud Helvētiōs longē nōbilissimus fuit et dītissimus Orgetorīx. Is, M. Messālā M. Pīsōne cōnsulibus,° rēgnī cupiditāte inductus, conjūrātiōnem nōbilitātis fēcit et cīvitātī persuāsit[1] ut dē fīnibus suīs cum omnibus cōpiīs exīrent: perfacile° esse, cum virtūte omnibus praestārent, tōtīus Galliae 5 imperiō potīrī.

Id hoc facilius eīs persuāsit quod undique locī nātūrā Helvētiī continentur; ūnā ex parte° flūmine Rhēnō lātissimō atque altissimō, quī agrum Helvētium ā Germānīs dīvidit,

---

[1] **Persuādeō** commonly takes a dative (indicating the person persuaded), and is usually followed by a noun clause of desire, whose verb is best translated by an infinitive.

alterā ex parte monte Jūrā altissimō, quī est inter Sēquanōs 10
et Helvētiōs; tertiā ex parte lacū Lemannō et flūmine Rhodanō, quī prōvinciam nostram ab Helvētiīs dīvidit.

Hīs rēbus fīēbat ut minus lātē vagārentur et minus facile
fīnitimīs bellum īnferre possent; quā dē causā hominēs bellandī cupidī magnō dolōre afficiēbantur. Prō multitūdine 15
autem hominum et prō glōriā bellī atque fortitūdinis angustōs
sē fīnēs habēre arbitrābantur, quī in longitūdinem mīlia
passuum CCXL, in lātitūdinem CLXXX patēbant.

Hīs rēbus adductī et auctōritāte Orgetorīgis permōtī, cōn-
stituērunt ea° quae · ad proficīscendum pertinērent com- 20
parāre, jūmentōrum et carrōrum quam[1] maximum numerum
coëmere, sēmentēs° quam maximās facere ut in itinere cōpia
frūmentī suppeteret,° cum proximīs cīvitātibus pācem et

[1]The superlative is often strengthened by **quam**, with or without a form of **possum**,
as **quam maximum (potest) numerum**, as great a number as possible/the greatest
possible number.

At this point the Rhone begins its course, flowing out of Lake Geneva.

219

The head of a young Gallic chief portrayed in bronze

amīcitiam cōnfirmāre. Ad eās rēs cōnficiendās biennium sibi
satis esse dūxērunt; in tertium annum profectiōnem lēge 25
cōnfirmant.

Ad eās rēs cōnficiendās Orgetorīx dēligitur. Is sibi lēgā-
tiōnem ad cīvitātēs suscipit. In eō itinere persuādet Casticō,
Sēquanō (cujus pater rēgnum in Sēquanīs multōs annōs
obtinuerat et ā senātū populī Rōmānī[1] amīcus appellātus 30
erat), ut rēgnum in cīvitāte suā occupāret quod pater ante
habuerat. Itemque Dumnorīgī Haeduō, frātrī Dīviciācī, quī
eō tempore prīncipātum in cīvitāte obtinēbat ac maximē
plēbī acceptus erat, ut idem cōnārētur persuādet, eīque fīliam
suam in mātrimōnium dat. 35

°**cōnsulibus** in the consulship of . . . (61 B.C.) • **perfacile** very
easy. (As a predicate adjective, **perfacile** modifies **potīrī,** itself the subject of **esse.**) • **ūnā ex parte** on one side (See map on page
314.) • **ea** (object of **comparāre**) • **sēmentēs** sowings
suppeteret might be available

[1]The genitive **populī Rōmānī** is to be taken with **senātū.**

220

acceptus	(adj., with dative) acceptable	**item**	(adv.) also, likewise
bellō	1 carry on war	**lēgātiō**	F., office of ambassador
bellum †īnferre	(with dative) make war on	**permoveō**	2 move strongly; influence
carrus	M., cart		
coëmō	3 buy (up)	**potior**	4 get control of
comparō	1 provide; gain	**praestō**	1 surpass, excel
conjūrātiō	F., conspiracy	**profectiō**	F., departure
cōnor	1 attempt	**suscipiō**	3 take (up/on); undertake
dītissimus	(superl. of **dives**) richest	**vagor**	1 range, wander

*nōbilitās F.

Perfacile factū° esse illīs probat cōnāta perficere, proptereā quod ipse suae cīvitātis imperium obtentūrus esset; nōn esse dubium quīn tōtīus Galliae plūrimum Helvētiī possent°; sē suīs cōpiīs suōque exercitū illīs rēgna conciliātūrum° cōnfirmat.

Hāc ōrātiōne adductī inter sē fidem et jūs jūrandum dant° et, rēgnō occupātō, per trēs potentissimōs ac firmissimōs populōs tōtīus Galliae imperiō sēsē potīrī posse spērant.

Ea rēs est Helvētiīs per indicium° ēnūntiāta. Mōribus suīs Orgetorīgem ex vinculīs causam dīcere° coēgērunt; damnātum° poenam sequī oportēbat, ut ignī cremārētur.

40

45

Representation of a Helvetian cart, here being used to transport wine in skins. The carts the Helvetians prepared for their migration may have been similar.

Diē cōnstitūtā causae dictiōnis,° Orgetorīx ad jūdicium omnem suam familiam, ad° hominum mīlia decem, undique coēgit, et omnēs clientēs obaerātōsque° suōs, quōrum magnum numerum habēbat, eōdem condūxit; per eōs, nē causam 50 dīceret, sē ēripuit.

Cum cīvitās, ob eam rem incitāta, armīs jūs suum exsequī° cōnārētur multitūdinemque hominum ex agrīs magistrātūs cōgerent, Orgetorīx mortuus est; neque abest suspīciō, ut Helvētiī arbitrantur, quīn ipse sibi mortem cōnscīverit.° 55

°**perfacile factū** very easy to do • **plūrimum possent** were the most powerful (people) • **conciliātūrum (esse)** would win **inter sē . . . dant** they gave a pledge and (swore) an oath to one another • **per indicium** through information, i.e., by informers **ex vinculīs causam dīcere** to plead his case in chains • **damnātum . . . cremārētur** the punishment of being burned by fire must be inflicted upon (lit., follow) him if condemned ⟶ **diē . . . dictiōnis** on the day set for the trial • **ad** about • **obaerātōs** debtors **exsequī** to enforce • **quīn . . . cōnscīverit** that he committed suicide

cōnātum	N., attempt	**mōs**	M., custom
ēnūntiō	1 disclose, report	**ōrātiō**	F., speech;
eōdem	(adv.) to the same		argument
	place	+**probō**	1 show
ēripiō	3 save; take away;	+**ut**	(conj./adv.) as,
	sē ēripere = escape		just as

*incitō 1

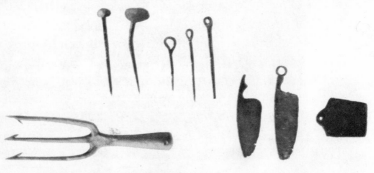

Gallic implements, including a fishing spear, pins and needles, and chopping blades. The Helvetians probably took such items with them.

Another view of the narrow road by which the Helvetians planned to travel west into Gaul.

LET US PASS

Post ejus mortem nihilō minus° Helvētiī id quod cōn-stituerant facere cōnantur, ut ē fīnibus suīs exeant. Ubi jam sē ad eam rem parātōs esse arbitrātī sunt, oppida sua omnia numerō ad° duodecim, vīcōs ad quadringentōs, reliqua prīvāta aedificia incendunt; frūmentum omne, praeter quod sēcum 5 portātūrī erant, combūrunt, ut, domum reditiōnis° spē sub-lātā, parātiōrēs ad omnia perīcula subeunda essent. Trium mēnsium° molita cibāria° sibi quemque domō efferre jubent.

Persuādent Rauracīs et Tulingīs et Latobrīgīs, fīnitimīs, utī eōdem ūsī cōnsiliō, oppidīs suīs vīcīsque incēnsīs, ūnā 10 cum eīs proficīscantur. Boiōs, quī trāns Rhēnum incoluerant et in agrum Nōricum trānsierant Nōreiamque oppugnābant, receptōs ad sē sociōs sibi ascīscunt.°

Erant omnīnō itinera duo quibus itineribus° domō exīre possent; ūnum per Sēquanōs, angustum et difficile, inter montem Jūram et flūmen Rhodanum, vix quā singulī carrī dūcerentur°; mōns autem altissimus impendēbat ut facile perpaucī prohibēre[1] possent; alterum per prōvinciam nostram, multō facilius atque expedītius, proptereā quod inter fīnēs Helvētiōrum et Allobrogum, quī nūper pācātī erant, Rhodanus fluit, isque nōnnūllīs locīs vadō trānsitur. Extrēmum oppidum Allobrogum est proximumque Helvētiōrum fīnibus Genava. Ex eō oppidō pōns ad Helvētiōs pertinet.

Helvētiī exīstimābant Allobrogibus sēsē vel persuāsūrōs, quod nōndum bonō animō° in populum Rōmānum vidērentur, vel vī coāctūrōs ut per suōs fīnēs eōs īre paterentur. Omnibus rēbus ad profectiōnem comparātīs, diem dīcunt quā diē ad rīpam Rhodanī omnēs conveniant. Is diēs erat a.d. v Kal. Apr.,° L. Pīsōne A. Gabīniō cōnsulibus.

Up to this point Caesar has been reporting exclusively on non-Roman matters. He wants the people back home to be informed as to whom and what he encounters as he advances into unknown territories. His desire to impress his readers with a sense of adventure and daring is partially achieved by his mere mention of names of faraway places and tribes.

Now at last the general brings himself by name into the story. With three or four exceptions, Caesar refers to himself in the third person.

Caesarī cum id nūntiātum esset eōs per prōvinciam nostram iter facere cōnārī, mātūrat ab urbe° proficīscī et quam maximīs potest itineribus° in Galliam Ulteriōrem contendit et ad Genavam pervenit.

Prōvinciae tōtī quam maximum potest mīlitum numerum imperat° (erat omnīnō in Galliā Ulteriōre legiō ūna); pontem quī erat ad Genavam jubet rescindī.°

Ubi dē ejus adventū Helvētiī certiōrēs factī sunt, lēgātōs ad eum mittunt, nōbilissimōs cīvitātis. Hī dīxērunt Helvētiōs habēre in animō sine ūllō maleficiō iter per prōvinciam facere,

[1]Supply **eōs** as object of **prohibēre** = intercept them.

proptereā quod aliud iter habērent nūllum; rogāvērunt ut 40
ejus voluntāte id sibi facere licēret.

Caesar, quod memoriā tenēbat L. Cassium cōnsulem occīsum[1] exercitumque ejus ab Helvētiīs pulsum et sub jugum[2]
missum, concēdendum nōn putābat; neque hominēs inimīcō
animō, datā facultāte per prōvinciam itineris faciendī, tem- 45
perātūrōs ab injūriā et maleficiō exīstimābat.

Tamen, quod mīlitēs quōs imperāverat nōndum convēnerant, lēgātīs respondit diem sē ad dēlīberandum sūmptūrum; sī quid vellent, ad Īd. Apr. reverterentur.

°**nihilō minus** none the less • **numerō ad duodecim** about
twelve in number • **reditiōnis** of returning • **trium mēnsium**
for three months • **molīta cibāria** ground food, i.e., meal, flour
sociōs sibi ascīscunt admit (the Boii) to themselves as allies
quibus itineribus by which (English does not repeat the antecedent.)
dūcerentur could be drawn • **bonō animō** well disposed
a.d. V Kal. Apr. March 28 (See page 361.) (The Helvetians laid their
plans in 61 B.C.) • **urbe** the city (Rome) • **quam ... itineribus** by the longest possible marches • **prōvinciae tōtī imperat**
he levied on the entire province • **rescindī** to be broken down
ut sibi licēret that they be allowed • **temperātūrōs (esse)**
would refrain • **diem ... sūmptūrum (esse)** that he would take
time to deliberate • **ad Īd. Apr.** by April 13 (See page 361.)

combūrō	3 burn (up)	**perpaucī**	(adj.) very few; (as
+expedītus	(adj.) free, un-		noun) a very few
	obstructed	**+quā**	(adv. = **quā viā**)
impendeō	2 overhang		where
mātūrō	1 make haste,	**revertor**	3 return
	hasten	**singulī**	(num. adj.) one at a
nūper	(adv.) recently		time, single; one
omnīnō	(adv.) in all; al-		each
	together; in	**+subeō**	undergo, endure
	general	**ulterior**	(adj.) farther
pācō	1 subdue, pacify	**vel ... vel**	(conj.) either ... or

[1] In this sentence, **esse** is omitted with all the perfect passive infinitives.

[2] This yoke was made of three spears, two planted in the ground and the third fastened
across their tops. As a sign of submission and degradation, soldiers of the captured army
were compelled to pass under such a yoke.

The Rhone River near its source at Lake Geneva

YOU SHALL NOT PASS

The time gained was well spent by Caesar, who used it to make sure the Helvetians would not pass through the Province. There was no longer any direct danger to Roman territory.

Intereā ā lacū Lemannō ad montem Jūram, quī fīnēs Sēquanōrum ab Helvētiīs dīvidit, mīlia passuum xix mūrum[1] in altitūdinem pedum sēdecim fossamque perdūcit. Eō opere perfectō, praesidia dispōnit,° castella mūnit, quō° facilius, sī sē invītō trānsīre cōnārentur, prohibēre posset.   5

Ubi lēgātī ad eum diē cōnstitūtā revertērunt, negat sē mōre et exemplō populī Rōmānī posse iter ūllī per prōvinciam dare et, sī vim facere cōnentur, prohibitūrum° ostendit.

Helvētiī eā spē dējectī° nōn numquam interdiū, saepius noctū, perrumpere° cōnābantur. Aliī nāvibus jūnctīs ratibusque complūribus factīs, aliī vadīs Rhodanī, quā minima   10

[1]Not a stone wall, but an earthwork made by cutting down the top of the river bank so as to leave a steep front.

altitūdō flūminis erat, trānsīre cōnābantur; sed operis mū-
nītiōne° et mīlitum concursū° et tēlīs repulsī hōc cōnātū
dēstitērunt.

Relinquēbātur ūna per Sēquanōs via, quā Sēquanīs invītīs 15
propter angustiās[1] īre nōn poterant. Hīs cum suā sponte
persuādēre nōn possent, lēgātōs ad Dumnorīgem Haeduum
mittunt ut eō dēprecātōre° ā Sēquanīs impetrārent.°

Dumnorīx grātiā et largītiōne° apud Sēquanōs plūrimum
poterat et Helvētiīs erat amīcus, quod ex eā cīvitāte Orge- 20
torīgis fīliam in mātrimōnium dūxerat; et cupiditāte rēgnī
adductus novīs rēbus° studēbat et quam plūrimās cīvitātēs
suō beneficiō habēre obstrictās° volēbat.

Itaque rem suscipit et ā Sēquanīs impetrat ut per fīnēs
suōs Helvētiōs īre patiantur, obsidēsque utī inter sēsē dent 25
perficit°—Sēquanī, nē itinere Helvētiōs prohibeant; Helvētiī,
ut sine maleficiō et injūriā trānseant.

Caesarī nūntiātur Helvētiōs habēre in animō per agrum
Sēquanōrum et Haeduōrum iter in Santonum fīnēs facere; hī
nōn longē[2] ā Tolōsātium fīnibus absunt, quae° cīvitās est in 30
prōvinciā. Id sī fieret,° hominēs bellicōsī, populī Rōmānī
inimīcī, locīs patentibus maximēque frūmentāriīs° fīnitimī
futūrī erant.°

Ob eās causās eī mūnītiōnī quam fēcerat T. Labiēnum
lēgātum praeficit.[3] Ipse in Ītaliam magnīs itineribus contendit 35
duāsque ibi legiōnēs cōnscrībit, et trēs, quae circum Aquileiam
hiemābant, ex hībernīs ēdūcit, et proximō itinere in Ulteriōrem Galliam per Alpēs cum hīs quīnque legiōnibus īre
contendit.

Ibi Ceutronēs et Graiocelī et Caturīgēs, locīs superiōribus
occupātīs, itinere exercitum prohibēre cōnantur.

Complūribus° hīs proeliīs pulsīs,° ab Ocelō, quod est
oppidum citeriōris prōvinciae extrēmum, in fīnēs Voconti-
ōrum ulteriōris prōvinciae diē septimō pervenit; inde in
Allobrogum fīnēs, ab Allobrogibus in Segusiāvōs exercitum 45
dūcit. Hī sunt extrā prōvinciam trāns Rhodanum prīmī.[4]

[1]The narrow passage along the bank of the Rhone, described in the preceding section.
[2]The distance is really about 130 miles.
[3]What cases does the verb **praeficiō** take?
[4]Caesar has now led an armed force into foreign territory without an order of the
Roman Senate.

°**dispōnit** he distributed • **quō facilius** so that more easily
prohibitūrum = sē eōs prohibitūrum esse • **eā spē dējectī**
disappointed in that hope • **perrumpere** to force a passage
operis mūnītiōne by the strength of the fortification (lit., by the fortification of the siege work) • **concursus, -ūs** M., attack, onset
eō dēprecātōre through his intercession (lit., with him as mediator)
ā Sēquanīs impetrārent prevail on the Sequanians • **grātiā
et largītiōne** because of his popularity and liberality • **novīs
rēbus** (dat. with **studēbat**) revolution • **obstrictās** obligated
(to him) • **obsidēsque . . . perficit** and brought it about that
they exchanged hostages • **quae** (relative pronoun with **cīvitās**
as antecedent) • **id sī fieret** if this should be done/happen
locīs . . . frūmentāriīs open territory and (country) especially fruitful
in grain • **futūrī erant** would be • **complūribus . . . proeliīs** (abl. of means) • **hīs . . . pulsīs** (abl. absolute)

citerior	(adj.) nearer	+**impetrō**	1 obtain one's re-
cōnātus	M., attempt		quest; prevail on
cōnscrībō	3 levy, enroll	+**magnum iter**	forced march
fossa	F., trench	**perdūcō**	3 construct; conduct
hiemō	1 winter, pass	**praeficiō**	3 put in command of
	the winter	**ratis**	F., raft

*__exemplum__ N.   **bellicōsus** (adj.)

HELP FOR THE INVADED

Caesar was eager to answer the pleas for help that he received from
several tribes. These pleas gave him still more justification for going
outside the Province.

Helvētiī jam per angustiās et fīnēs Sēquanōrum suās
cōpiās trādūxerant et in Haeduōrum fīnēs pervēnerant eōrumque agrōs populābantur.[1]

[1]While Caesar was marching to Aquileia and back, the Helvetians—though they had
kept their pledge to the Sequanians (see p. 227)—invaded and began devastating
Dumnorix' homeland, the country of the Haedui.

Such mountains as these in the Province lay between troubled Gaul and Italy, where Caesar went to collect reinforcements.

Haeduī, cum sē suaque° ab eīs dēfendere nōn possent, lēgātōs ad Caesarem mittunt quī auxilium rogent.   5

"Ita nōs," inquiunt, "omnī tempore dē populō Rōmānō meritī sumus° ut paene in cōnspectū exercitūs vestrī° agrī vāstārī, līberī in servitūtem abdūcī, oppida expugnārī nōn dēbuerint.°"

Eōdem tempore Ambarrī, necessāriī et cōnsanguineī   10 Haeduōrum, Caesarem certiōrem faciunt sēsē, dēpopulātīs agrīs, nōn facile ab oppidīs vim hostium prohibēre. Item Allobrogēs quī[1] trāns Rhodanum vīcōs possessiōnēsque habēbant fugā sē ad Caesarem recipiunt et dēmōnstrant sibi praeter agrī solum° nihil esse reliquī.°   15

Quibus rēbus adductus Caesar nōn expectandum sibi

[1] Most of the Allobroges were south of the Rhone and were not troubled; but some were north of the river and on the route of the Helvetians.

229

Remains of a Roman road in the Alps. Caesar's soldiers built many such roads.

statuit dum, omnibus fortūnīs sociōrum cōnsūmptīs, in Santonōs Helvētiī pervenīrent.

Flūmen est Arar, quod per fīnēs Haeduōrum et Sēquanōrum in Rhodanum fluit incrēdibilī lēnitāte° ita ut oculīs in utram° partem fluat jūdicārī nōn possit. Id Helvētiī ratibus ac lintribus jūnctīs trānsībant, trēsque jam partēs cōpiārum trādūxerant. 20

Caesar dē tertiā vigiliā[1] cum legiōnibus tribus ē castrīs profectus ad eam partem pervēnit quae nōndum flūmen trānsierat. Eōs impedītōs et inopīnantēs° aggressus[2] magnam partem eōrum concīdit; reliquī sēsē fugae mandārunt atque in proximās silvās° abdidērunt. 25

[1]The Romans divided the night into four equal divisions or watches (**vigiliae**); e.g., **dē tertiā vigiliā** = during/in the third watch, just past midnight; **dē quārtā vigiliā** = between 2 and 3 A.M.

[2]The Helvetians did not know that the Roman army was in the vicinity.

230

Is pāgus appellābātur Tigurīnus; nam omnis cīvitās Helvētia in quattuor pāgōs dīvīsa est. Hic pāgus ūnus, cum 30 domō exīsset patrum nostrōrum memoriā, L. Cassium cōnsulem interfēcerat et ejus exercitum sub jugum mīserat.[1]

Ita sīve cāsū sīve cōnsiliō deōrum immortālium, quae pars° cīvitātis Helvētiae īnsignem calamitātem populō Rōmānō intulerat, ea prīnceps poenās persolvit.° 35

Quā in rē Caesar nōn sōlum pūblicās, sed etiam prīvātās injūriās ultus est; nam L. Pīsōnem lēgātum, avum L. Pīsōnis, socerī° Caesaris, Tigurīnī eōdem proeliō quō Cassium interfēcerant.

°**suaque** N. pl., and their possessions • **ita nōs … meritī sumus** we have always so deserved of the Roman people • **vestrī** (agreeing with **exercitūs**) • **vāstārī nōn dēbuerint** ought not to have been devastated • **solum** N., soil • **sibi nihil esse reliquī** they had nothing left • **lēnitās, -ātis** F., slowness • **uter, utra, utrum** (interr. adj.) which (of two) • **inopīnāns, -antis** (adj.) off guard • **silvās** (acc. because of the motion implied in **abdidērunt**) • **quae pars … ea = ea pars quae** • **prīnceps poenās persolvit** was the first to pay the penalty • **socer, -erī** M., father-in-law

abdō	3 (also, **sē abdere**) hide; withdraw	**inquiunt**	they say
abdūcō	3 carry off; lead away	**linter**	F., boat, skiff
avus	M., grandfather	**necessārius**	M., friend, relative; (adj.) necessary; critical
cāsū	(abl. as adv.) by chance	**sīve/seu**	(conj.) or (if); whether
certiōrem facere	inform	**sīve … sīve**	whether … or; either … or
concīdō	3 kill		
cōnsanguineus	M., kinsman, relative; (adj.) related by blood	**statuō**	3 decide; pass sentence
dēpopulor	1 devastate	**ulcīscor**	3 avenge; punish

[1]This refers to the disaster inflicted nearly fifty years earlier, mentioned on page 225, lines 42-46.

Soldiers are shown crossing a river by means of a bridge built on boats.

Hōc proeliō factō, reliquās cōpiās Helvētiōrum ut cōn- 40
sequī posset, pontem in Ararī faciendum cūrāvit° atque ita
exercitum trādūxit. Helvētiī repentīnō ejus adventū com-
mōtī sunt; ille enim ūnō diē flūmen trānsierat, id quod° ipsī
diēbus xx aegerrimē cōnfēcerant.

Posterō diē castra ex eō locō Helvētiī movent. Idem facit 45
Caesar, equitātumque omnem ad numerum quattuor mīlium,
quem ex omnī prōvinciā et Haeduīs atque eōrum sociīs¹
coāctum habēbat,° praemittit quī videant quās in partēs
hostēs iter faciant. Quī,° cupidius° novissimum agmen īnsecūtī, aliēnō locō cum equitātū Helvētiōrum proelium com- 50
mittunt, et paucī dē nostrīs cadunt.

Quō proeliō sublātī° Helvētiī, quod quīngentīs equitibus
tantam multitūdinem equitum prōpulerant, audācius sub-

¹Caesar has now joined forces with the Gallic tribes which were threatened by the
Helvetians. Caesar's soldiers were mainly infantry.

sistere nōn numquam et novissimō agmine° proeliō nostrōs
lacessere coepērunt.

Caesar suōs ā proeliō continēbat ac satis habēbat in praesentiā hostem rapīnīs populātiōnibusque prohibēre.°

Ita diēs circiter xv iter fēcērunt ut inter novissimum
hostium agmen et nostrum prīmum° nōn amplius quīnīs°
aut sēnīs° mīlibus passuum interesset.

°**pontem faciendum cūrāvit** arranged for a bridge to be built (**in,**
over) • **id quod** a task which • **quem coāctum habēbat =**
quem coēgerat • **quī** these • **cupidius** too eagerly
quō proeliō sublātī elated by this battle • **novissimō agmine**
with/from their rear line • **satis habēbat ... prohibēre** regarded it as sufficient for the present to prevent the enemy from plundering and pillaging • **prīmum (agmen)** front line • **quīnīs**
five (each day) • **sēnīs** six (each day)

aegerrimē	(adv.) with the utmost difficulty	**īnsequor**	3 pursue
amplius	N., more, a greater distance	**intersum**	be/lie between
		lacessō	3 challenge, attack
commoveō	2 excite, alarm	**prōpellō**	3 repel, rout
cōnsequor	3 pursue; overtake, reach	**subsistō**	3 make a stand; halt

AN ARMY TRAVELS ON ITS STOMACH

In general, the armies of antiquity lived on whatever they could find
or levy wherever they happened to be. It was up to the soldier to feed
himself. This was not true of the Roman army of citizen-soldiers. About
twice a month the legionary was supplied with a specified quantity of
grain, from which he baked his bread.

Caesar, as is evident in this chapter, devoted a great deal of attention
to having his soldiers supplied regularly. This concern for their welfare
was an important reason why the legionaries were so loyal to their commander.

Interim cotīdiē Caesar frūmentum quod Haeduī essent
pūblicē pollicitī flāgitābat. Nam propter frīgora, quod Gallia

sub septentriōnibus posita est, nōn modo frūmenta in agrīs
mātūra nōn erant, sed nē pābulī quidem satis magna cōpia
suppetēbat.° Eō autem frūmentō quod flūmine Ararī nāvi- 5
bus subvexerat,° proptereā° ūtī minus[1] poterat, quod iter ab
Ararī Helvētiī āverterant, ā quibus discēdere nōlēbat.

Diem ex diē dūcunt° Haeduī; cōnferrī, comportārī, adesse°
dīcunt. Ubi sē diūtius° dūcī intellēxit et diem īnstāre, quō
diē frūmentum mīlitibus mētīrī oportēret, convocāvit eōrum 10
prīncipēs, quōrum magnam cōpiam in castrīs habēbat.

In hīs erant Dīviciācus et Liscus, quī summō magistrātuī
praeerat, quem vergobretum° appellant Haeduī, quī creātur
annuus° et vītae necisque in suōs° habet potestātem.

Tum Caesar graviter eōs accūsat, quod, cum frūmentum 15
neque emī neque ex agrīs sūmī possit, hostibus tam propinquīs,° ab eīs nōn sublevētur, praesertim cum, magnā ex parte
eōrum precibus adductus, bellum suscēperit.

Tum dēmum Liscus, ōrātiōne Caesaris adductus, quod°
anteā tacuerat prōpōnit: Esse nōnnūllōs quōrum auctōritās 20
apud plēbem plūrimum valeat,° quī prīvātim° plūs possint°
quam ipsī magistrātūs. Hōs sēditiōsā atque improbā° ōrātiōne multitūdinem dēterrēre° nē frūmentum cōnferant
quod dēbeant.

[1]The adverb **minus** is often used as the equivalent of **nōn.**

A modern representation of a Roman cavalryman

Liscus addidit: " 'Praestat,'° inquiunt,[1] 'sī jam prīncipātum 25
Galliae obtinēre nōn possumus, Gallōrum quam Rōmānōrum
imperia perferre; sī Helvētiōs superāverint Rōmānī, ūnā cum
reliquā Galliā Haeduīs° lībertātem sine dubiō ēripient.'

"Ab eīsdem tua cōnsilia quaeque in castrīs geruntur hostibus ēnūntiantur; hōs coercēre nōn possum. Quīn etiam° 30
intellegō quantō cum perīculō hanc necessāriam rem tibi
ēnūntiāverim, et ob eam causam quam diū° potuī tacuī."

°**suppetēbat** was available • **subvexerat** he had conveyed
proptereā (to be taken with following **quod**) • **diem ex diē
dūcunt** put (him) off day after day • **cōnferrī . . . adesse** (supply
frūmentum) • **diūtius** too long • **vergobretus, -ī** M.,
vergobret (title of chief magistrate of the Haedui) • **annuus**
(adj.) annually, for one year • **in suōs** over his fellow citizens
hostibus tam propinquīs (abl. abs.) with the enemy so near
quod = id quod • **plūrimum valeat** is very great • **prīvātim** (adv.) as private citizens • **plūs possint** have more influence • **improbus, -a, -um** disloyal • **dēterrēre nē cōnferant** were preventing . . . from collecting • **praestat . . . perferre** it is better to endure • **Haeduīs** from the Haedui
quīn etiam more than that • **quam diū** as long as

āvertō	3 turn away, divert	**praesertim**	(adv.) especially, chiefly
coerceō	2 restrain		
comportō	1 collect, bring to-gether	**precēs**	F. pl., entreaties, prayers
emō	3 buy	**pūblicē**	(adv.) in the name
flāgitō	1 demand, entreat, ask		of the state/peo-ple; publicly
+**frūmenta**	N. pl., growing crops, standing grain	+**quantus**	(interr. adj.) how great? how much?
īnstō	1 be at hand; press on	**sublevō**	1 aid, assist, sup-port
mētior	4 distribute, measure out		
pābulum	N., forage, fodder	**taceō**	2 keep silent/ secret; be silent

*__mātūrus__ (adj.) **sēditiōsus** (adj.) **dēterreō** 2 **addō** 3
lībertās F.

[1]The subject of **inquiunt** is the troublemakers referred to in the preceding lines.

This representation of a mechanical reaper in Gaul was discovered in recent years.

TWO BROTHERS

Caesar hāc ōrātiōne Liscī Dumnorīgem, Dīviciācī frātrem, dēsignārī° sentiēbat, sed quod plūribus praesentibus
eās rēs jactārī° nōlēbat, celeriter concilium dīmittit, Liscum
retinet. Quaerit ex sōlō° ea quae in conventū dīxerat. Liscus
dīcit līberius atque audācius.   5

Eadem sēcrētō ab aliīs quaerit, quī ita respondērunt,
"Ipse est Dumnorīx, summā audāciā, magnā apud plēbem
propter līberālitātem grātiā, cupidus rērum novārum. Complūrēs annōs portōria° reliquaque omnia Haeduōrum vectīgālia[1] parvō pretiō redēmpta° habet, proptereā quod, illō   10

[1]Instead of collecting taxes directly from the taxpayers, the government accepted bids
from wealthy men or corporations, who paid a lump sum to the treasury and then collected
as much as they could from the people. Presumably the bidding was open, but Dumnorix
was so powerful that no one dared bid against him, and he won the right for a small price.

Left: A Gallic helmet encrusted with gold. Right: A Gallic helmet of bronze

licente,° contrā licērī audet nēmō. Hīs rēbus et suam rem familiārem° auxit et facultātēs ad largiendum° magnās comparāvit.

"Magnum numerum equitātūs suō sūmptū° semper alit et circum sē habet; neque sōlum domī, sed etiam apud fīnitimās cīvitātēs plūrimum potest, atque hujus potentiae causā mātrem in Biturīgibus hominī illīc° nōbilissimō ac potentissimō in mātrimōnium dedit.

"Ipse ex Helvētiīs uxōrem habet, sorōrem ex mātre° et propinquās suās in aliās cīvitātēs in mātrimōnium dedit. Favet Helvētiīs propter eam affīnitātem°; ōdit etiam suō nōmine° Caesarem et Rōmānōs, quod eōrum adventū potentia ejus dēminūta° et Dīviciācus frāter in antīquum locum grātiae atque honōris est restitūtus. Rōmānīs superātīs, summam spem per Helvētiōs rēgnī obtinendī habet; imperiō° populī Rōmānī nōn modo dē rēgnō, sed etiam dē eā grātiā quam habet dēspērat."

Initium fugae equitātūs paucīs ante diēbus, ut Caesar in quaerendō repperit, factum erat ā Dumnorīge atque ejus equitibus (nam equitātuī quem auxiliō Caesarī Haeduī mīserant Dumnorīx praeerat); eōrum fugā reliquus equitātūs erat perterritus.

Ad hās suspīciōnēs certissimae rēs° accēdēbant, quod Dumnorīx per fīnēs Sēquanōrum Helvētiōs trādūxerat, quod obsidēs inter eōs dandōs cūrāverat,° quod ea omnia nōn modo 35
injussū Caesaris et cīvitātis, sed etiam īnscientibus ipsīs°
fēcerat, quod ā magistrātū Haeduōrum accūsābātur. Hīs
rēbus cognitīs, Caesar priusquam quicquam cōnārētur, Dīviciācum ad sē vocārī jubet et, cotīdiānīs interpretibus remōtīs,
per C. Valerium Troucillum, prīncipem Galliae prōvinciae, 40
familiārem suum, cui summam omnium rērum fidem habēbat,°
cum eō colloquitur; simul° commonefacit° quae ipsō praesente
in conciliō dē Dumnorīge sint dicta, et ostendit quae sēparātim
quisque dē eō apud sē° dīxerit. Petit atque hortātur ut sine
ejus° offēnsiōne animī vel ipse dē eō,° causā cognitā, statuat, 45
vel cīvitātem statuere jubeat.
      Dīviciācus multīs cum lacrimīs Caesarem complexus°
ōrāvit nē quid gravius in frātrem statueret. Haec cum plūribus verbīs flēns ā Caesare peteret, Caesar ejus dextram pre-
hendit; cōnsōlātus rogat ut fīnem ōrandī faciat. Caesar tantī 50
ejus apud sē° grātiam esse° ostendit ut et reī pūblicae injūriam
et suum dolōrem ejus voluntātī ac precibus° condōnet.°
Dumnorīgem ad sē vocat, frātrem adhibet; quae in eō repre-
hendat° ostendit; quae ipse intellegat, quae cīvitās querātur
prōpōnit. Monet ut in reliquum tempus omnēs suspīciōnēs 55
vitet; praeterita sē Dīviciācō frātrī° condōnāre dicit. Dumnorīgī custōdēs pōnit, ut quae agat, quibuscum loquātur,
scīre possit.

°**dēsignārī** was meant • **jactārī** (to be) discussed • **ex
sōlō = ex eō sōlō** (from) him in private • **portōria** N. pl., im-
posts (taxes on imports and exports; contrasted with **vectīgālia**, N. pl.,
general taxes and revenues) • **redēmpta** bought up • **licente**
(pres. part. of **liceor, -ērī,** bid) • **rēs familiāris** private property
facultātēs ad largiendum resources for bribery • **suō sūmptū**
at his own expense • **illic** (adv.) there • **sorōrem ex mātre**
half sister (sister on his mother's side) • **affīnitās, -ātis** F., relationship (by marriage) • **suō nōmine** on his own account
dēminūta (est) was lessened • **imperiō** under the rule

[1]At this time Caesar could not afford to stir up a possible revolt of the Haedui by punish-
ing their most popular noble. A few years later, however, Caesar was forced to put the
disobedient Dumnorix to death. (See pages 302-304.)

certissimae rēs most clearly proved facts (explained by **quod** clauses) • **obsidēs . . . cūrāverat** he had arranged for an exchange of hostages between them (i.e., the Helvetians and Sequanians) **ipsīs** i.e., Caesar and the Haedui • **cui . . . habēbat** in whom he had the highest confidence in all matters • **simul . . . et = et . . . et** • **commonefacit** reminded (of) • **apud sē** to himself (i.e., Caesar) • **ejus** Diviciacus' • **ipse** (Caesar) **dē eō** (Dumnorix) • **complexus** embracing • **tantī . . . esse** (that) his friendship was worth so much to him • **ejus . . . precibus** out of regard for his wish and prayers • **condōnet** pardoned **reprehendat** blamed • **frātrī** for the sake of his brother

accēdō	3 be added; draw or come near	**insciēns**	(adj.) unaware, not knowing
colloquor	3 speak (with)	**ōdī**	(defective) hate
+**contrā**	(adv.) against him		(For conjugation,
conventus	M., meeting		see page 454.)
familiāris	(adj.) personal, private; M., personal friend	+**praeteritus**	(adj.) past; N. pl., the past
		prehendō	3 take, grasp
faveō	2 (with dat.) favor	+**propinqua**	F., female relative
fleō	2 weep	**rēs novae**	F. pl., revolution

*__liberālitās__ F. **interpres, -etis** M. **sēparātim** (adv.) **offēnsiō** F. **cōnsōlor** 1

AN OFFICER'S ERROR

Caesar's military ability was equal to his talent as a politician and statesman. Careful planning usually prevented unexpected crises; but even when a crisis arose Caesar kept control of the situation. Many later generals, among them Napoleon himself, have studied Caesar's strategy, trying to learn from the Roman commander.

Caesar selected his subordinates for their ability, and then trusted them. His chief legatus, Labienus, was a gifted staff officer to whom Caesar could confidently assign the most dangerous and difficult tasks. In the case of Considius, whose intelligence mission is the topic of this chapter, Caesar pointed out that the officer's record indicated that he should have been able to carry out his orders.

Statue of a Gallic chief

Eōdem diē ab explōrātōribus certior factus° hostēs sub monte cōnsēdisse mīlia passuum ab ipsīus castrīs octō, quālis esset nātūra montis et quālis in circuitū ascēnsus quī cognōscerent mīsit. Renūntiātum est facilem esse. Dē tertiā vigiliā T. Labiēnum, lēgātum prō praetōre,° cum duābus 5 legiōnibus et eīs ducibus quī iter cognōverant summum jugum montis ascendere jubet; quid suī cōnsiliī sit° ostendit.

Ipse dē quārtā vigiliā eōdem itinere quō hostēs ierant ad eōs contendit equitātumque omnem ante sē mittit. P. Cōnsidius, quī reī mīlitāris° perītissimus habēbātur et in exercitū L. 10 Sullae et posteā in° M. Crassī fuerat, cum explōrātōribus praemittitur. ~ The hicos tmonter was held be L.

Prīmā lūce summus mōns ā Labiēnō tenēbātur. Ipse ab hostium castrīs nōn longius mīlle et quīngentīs passibus

aberat, neque,° ut posteā ex captīvīs comperit, aut ipsīus 15
adventus aut Labiēnī cognitus erat.

Tum Cōnsidius, equō admissō,° ad eum accurrit atque dīcit
montem quem ā Labiēnō occupārī voluerit ab hostibus tenērī;
id sē ā Gallicīs armīs atque īnsignibus cognōvisse. Caesar
suās cōpiās in proximum collem subdūcit et aciem īnstruit. 20
Labiēnus, monte occupātō, nostrōs expectābat proeliōque
abstinēbat; Caesar enim eum adventum suum expectāre jusserat ut undique ūnō tempore in hostēs impetus fieret.

Multō° dēnique diē per explōrātōrēs Caesar cognōvit et
montem ā suīs tenērī et Helvētiōs castra mōvisse et Cōn- 25
sidium timōre perterritum quod nōn vīdisset prō vīsō° sibi
renūntiāsse.

Eō diē quō cōnsuērat° intervāllō° hostēs sequitur et mīlia
passuum tria ab eōrum castrīs castra pōnit.

Postrīdiē ejus diēī,° quod omnīnō bīduī frūmentum° super- 30
erat, reī frūmentāriae° prōspiciendum exīstimāns, iter ab
Helvētiīs āvertit, ac Bibracte, oppidum Haeduōrum, īre contendit. Nam hoc oppidum longē maximum et cōpiōsissimum°
erat atque nōn amplius mīlibus passuum XVIII aberat. Ea rēs
per fugitīvōs° L. Aemiliī, decuriōnis° equitum Gallōrum, hosti- 35
bus nūntiātur. Helvētiī, commūtātō cōnsiliō atque itinere
conversō, nostrōs ā° novissimō agmine īnsequī ac lacessere
coepērunt.

°**certior factus** (a phrase taking indirect statement) • **prō praetōre** with praetorian rank (an honorary designation, since Labienus had
not held the office of praetor) • **quid . . . sit** what his plan was
reī mīlitāris (gen. with **perītissimus**) • **in** (supply **exercitū**)
neque . . . aut . . . aut and neither . . . nor • **equō admissō**
with his horse at a gallop • **multō diē** late in the day • **prō
vīsō** as seen • **cōnsuērat** (contraction of **cōnsuēverat**)
quō . . . intervāllō at the customary interval (i.e., five or six miles)
postrīdiē ejus diēī = **postrīdiē** (This idiom gives somewhat the effect
of "the very next day" in English.) • **bīduī frūmentum** a two days'
supply of grain • **reī frūmentāriae** (dat. with **prōspiciendum
[esse]**, he must look out for) • **cōpiōsissimus, -a, -um** best
supplied • **fugitīvōs** runaway slaves • **decuriō, -ōnis** M.,
decurion (commander of a group of ten horsemen) • **ā** on (The
Helvetians were now following Caesar.)

accurrō	3 hasten or run (to)	frūmentārius	(adj.) of grain;
bīduum	N., (a period of)	rēs frūmentāria	
	two days		grain supply
circuitus	M., a going around;	quālis	(interr. adj.) of
	circumference; in		what sort? what?
	circuitū = on all sides	supersum	remain; survive

*Gallicus (adj.)   abstineō 2

BATTLE AND VICTORY

Postquam id animum advertit, cōpiās suās Caesar in proximum collem subdūxit equitātumque quī sustinēret hostium
impetum mīsit.

Ipse interim in colle mediō° triplicem aciem° īnstrūxit
legiōnum quattuor veterānārum; in summō jugō duās legiōnēs 5
quās in Galliā Citeriōre proximē cōnscrīpserat et omnia
auxilia collocāvit; impedīmenta sarcināsque in ūnum locum
cōnferrī et eum° ab hīs quī in superiōre aciē cōnstiterant
mūnīrī jussit. Helvētiī cum omnibus suīs carrīs secūtī
impedīmenta in ūnum locum contulērunt; ipsī cōnfertissimā° 10
aciē, rejectō nostrō equitātū, phalange[1] factā, sub° prīmam
nostram aciem successērunt.

Caesar prīmum suum deinde omnium ex cōnspectū remōvit equōs ut, aequātō omnium perīculō, spem fugae tolleret.
Cohortātus inde suōs proelium commīsit. Mīlitēs, ē locō 15
superiōre pīlīs missīs, facile hostium phalangem perfrēgē-
runt. Eā disjectā,° gladiīs dēstrictīs,° in eōs impetum fēcērunt.

Gallīs magnō ad pugnam erat impedīmentō quod° plūra[2]
eōrum scūta ūnō ictū pīlōrum trānsfīxa et colligāta° erant;
nam cum ferrum sē īnflexisset,[3] neque id ēvellere° neque 20

[1]The Helvetian phalanx was a close formation of infantry, in which the men of each
rank were protected by the shields of the men in front of them as well as by their own
shields. It probably resembled the Roman testūdō.

[2]Plūra, in many cases. In the phalanx formation shields were overlapped, so that it
was possible for one javelin to pierce two of the wicker or wooden shields carried by
the Gauls.

[3]Cum . . . īnflexisset, when the iron head had become bent. After several shields
had been pierced by one javelin, the pulling and tugging of those who carried the shields
would bend the long iron tip.

sinistrā impedītā satis commodē pugnāre poterant. Multī igitur, diū jactātō bracchiō,° praeoptāvērunt° scūtum manū ēmittere et nūdō° corpore pugnāre.

Tandem vulneribus dēfessī et pedem referre et, quod mōns suberat° circiter mīlle passuum spatiō, eō sē recipere coepē- 25 runt.

°**in colle mediō** halfway up the hill (See diagram.) • **triplicem aciem** a triple line of battle (i.e., each legion in three lines, with each of the lines consisting of about eight ranks) • **eum** (supply **locum**) **cōnfertissimā aciē** in very close formation • **sub** up to **eā disjectā** when that was dispersed • **dēstrictis** drawn **quod** that (introducing a noun clause, the subject of **erat**) • **colligāta** fastened together • **ēvellere** pull out • **jactātō bracchiō** after their arms had been jerked about • **praeoptāvērunt** preferred • **nūdō corpore** with unprotected bodies **suberat** was close by

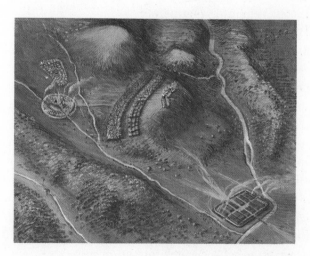

The Roman triple line (red) successfully opposes the solid Helvetian phalanx.

advertō	3 turn to; **animum advertere** or **animadvertere** = observe, notice	**collocō**	1 station
cohortor	1 encourage	**⁺commodē**	**satis commodē** = with sufficient ease, very easily
		dēfessus	(adj.) worn out

ferrum	N., iron	**+referō**	**pedem referre** =
ictus	M., blow, stroke		withdraw, retire
perfringō	3 break up/through; shatter	**rejiciō**	3 repel; throw or hurl back
pilum	N., javelin	**+succēdō**	3 advance, come up
proximē	(adv.) lately		(to)

*triplex (adj.)   **phalanx** F.   **impedīmentum** N.

Captō° monte et succēdentibus nostrīs, Boiī et Tulingī, quī hominum mīlibus circiter xv agmen hostium claudēbant et novissimīs praesidiō erant, ex itinere° nostrōs ab latere apertō aggressī circumveniēbant. Id cōnspicātī Helvētiī, quī 30 in montem sēsē recēperant, rūrsus īnstāre et proelium redintegrāre° coepērunt. Rōmānī signa bipertītō° intulērunt; prīma et secunda aciēs ut victīs ac summōtīs° resisteret; tertia, ut venientēs sustinēret.

Ita ancipitī proeliō diū atque ācriter pugnātum est. 35 Diūtius cum sustinēre nostrōrum impetūs nōn possent, alterī° sē, ut coeperant, in montem recēpērunt; alterī° ad impedīmenta et carrōs suōs sē contulērunt. Nam hōc tōtō proeliō, cum ab hōrā septimā ad vesperum pugnātum sit, āversum hostem° vidēre nēmō potuit. 40

Ad multam noctem° etiam ad impedīmenta pugnātum est, proptereā quod prō vāllō° carrōs objēcerant° et ē locō superiōre in nostrōs venientēs tēla conjiciēbant, et nōnnūllī inter carrōs trāgulās subjiciēbant nostrōsque vulnerābant. Diū cum esset pugnātum, impedīmentīs castrīsque nostrī 45 potītī sunt. Ibi Orgetorīgis fīlia atque ūnus ē fīliīs captus est. Ex eō proeliō circiter hominum mīlia cxxx superfuērunt eāque tōtā nocte continenter iērunt. In fīnēs Lingonum diē quārtō pervēnērunt, cum et propter vulnera mīlitum et propter sepultūram occīsōrum nostrī eōs sequī nōn potuis- 50 sent.

Caesar ad Lingonēs litterās nūntiōsque mīsit, nē eōs frūmentō nēve° aliā rē juvārent°; aliter sē eōs eōdem locō quō° Helvētiōs habitūrum.° Ipse, trīduō intermissō,° cum omnibus cōpiīs eōs sequī coepit. 55

°captō reached • **ex itinere** at once (lit., from the march; i.e., without waiting for the usual battle formation) • **redintegrāre** to renew • **bipertītō** (adv.) in two directions • **victīs ac summōtīs** (referring to the Helvetians, while **venientēs** refers to the Boii and Tulingi) • **alterī . . . alterī** one party (the Helvetians) . . . the other (the Boii and the Tulingi) • **āversum hostem** an enemy in flight • **ad multam noctem** until late at night • **prō vāllō** as a rampart • **objēcerant** had picked up/placed in front **nēve** or (lit., and not/nor) • **nē . . . juvārent** (ordering them) not to assist (a noun clause depending on the idea of command in **litterās . . . mīsit**) • **eōdem locō quō** in the same position as **habitūrum (esse)** (infinitive in indirect statement depending on verb of saying implied in **litterās . . . mīsit**) • **trīduō intermissō** after a three days' interval

agmen ⁺claudere	bring up the rear	**rūrsus**	(adv.) again
		sē ⁺cōnferre	retreat, go
anceps	(adj.) double	**sepultūra**	F., burial
conjiciō	3 throw, hurl	**trāgula**	F., javelin, dart
novissimus	(adj.) last; M. pl., the rear		(used by Gauls)
		vesper	M., evening

In the first stage of the battle (see page 243), the Romans were fighting only the Helvetians. In the second stage, there were two fronts, with the first two Roman lines opposing the Helvetians, and the third opposing the Boii and Tulingi. The Helvetian camp is at the left; the Roman camp is in the foreground.

Helvētiī omnium rērum inopiā adductī lēgātōs dē dēdi-
tiōne ad eum mīsērunt. Quī cum eum in itinere convēnissent,° sē ad pedēs prōjēcērunt suppliciterque° locūtī flentēs
pācem petīvērunt. Caesar eōs in eō locō quō tum essent
suum adventum expectāre jussit. Eō postquam pervēnit, 5
obsidēs, arma, servōs quī ad eōs perfūgissent, poposcit.

Dum ea conquīruntur et cōnferuntur, circiter hominum
milia VI ejus pāgī quī Verbigenus appellātur prīma nocte ē
castrīs Helvētiōrum ēgressī ad Rhēnum fīnēsque Germānōrum
contendērunt. 10

Quod° ubi Caesar resciit,° quōrum per fīnēs ierant, hīs°
ut conquīrerent et redūcerent,[1] sī sibi pūrgātī esse vellent,°
imperāvit; reductōs° in hostium numerō habuit°; reliquōs
omnēs, obsidibus, armīs, perfugīs trāditīs, in dēditiōnem
accēpit. 15

Helvētiōs, Tulingōs, Latobrīgōs in fīnēs suōs, unde erant
profectī, revertī jussit et, quod omnibus frūgibus° āmissīs[2]
domī nihil erat quō famem tolerārent,° Allobrogibus imperāvit
ut eīs frūmentī cōpiam facerent. Ipsōs[3] oppida vīcōsque quōs
incenderant restituere jussit. 20

Id eā maximē ratiōne° fēcit, quod nōluit eum locum unde
Helvētiī discesserant vacāre nē° propter bonitātem agrōrum
Germānī, quī trāns Rhēnum incolunt, ex suīs fīnibus in
Helvētiōrum fīnēs trānsīrent et fīnitimī Galliae, prōvinciae,
Allobrogibusque essent. Boiōs[4] in fīnibus Haeduōrum collo- 25
cāvit; id enim petēbant Haeduī, quī Boiōs ēgregiā virtūte
esse cognōverant; posteā eōs in parem jūris lībertātisque
condiciōnem atque° ipsī erant recēpērunt.

In castrīs Helvētiōrum tabulae repertae sunt litterīs
Graecīs[5] cōnfectae et ad Caesarem relātae, quibus in tabulīs 30
nōminātim ratiō° cōnfecta erat, quī numerus domō exīsset

---

[1]Supply **eōs** as object.

[2]They had burned all the grain except what they took with them. (See page 223, lines 5-6.)

[3]To whom does **ipsōs** refer? Explain the difference in construction required by **imperō** and **jubeō**.

[4]The Boii had no fixed home.

[5]The Gauls had no alphabet of their own, but they had learned the Greek letters from traders. The language of the records was Gallic.

eōrum quī arma ferre possent, et item sēparātim quot puerī, senēs, mulierēsque.

Quārum omnium ratiōnum summa erat capitum° Helvētiōrum mīlium CCLXIII, Tulingōrum mīlium XXXVI, Latobrīgōrum XIV, Rauracōrum XXIII, Boiōrum XXXII; ex hīs, quī arma ferre possent, ad mīlia nōnāgintā duo. Summa omnium fuērunt ad mīlia CCCLXVIII. 35

Eōrum quī domum rediērunt cēnsū habitō, ut Caesar imperāverat, repertus est numerus mīlium C et X. 40

°**convēnissent** (usually intransitive, but transitive here with **eum** as direct object) had met • **suppliciter** (adv.) humbly • **dum ea conquīruntur** while these were being hunted up • **quod** this (object of **resciit**, discovered) • **hīs** (object of **imperāvit** and antecedent of **quōrum**) • **sī ... vellent** if they wished to be free from guilt in his sight • **reductōs** (agreeing with **eōs** [to be supplied]) • **in ... habuit** treated (them) as enemies (i.e., he had them put to death or sold into slavery) • **frūgēs, -um** F. pl., crops • **quō famem tolerārent** to live on (lit., whereby they could endure hunger) • **eā ratiōne** for this reason (explained by the following **quod** clause) • **nē** for fear that • **parem ... atque** the same ... as • **nōminātim ratiō** detailed record **capitum** of persons (Compare our use of "head" in speaking of cattle.)

bonitās	F., fertility; goodness	**poscō**	3 demand
cēnsus	M., count, enumeration	**summa**	F., (sum) total; general conduct, control
dēditiō	F., surrender	**vacō**	1 be unoccupied/empty/idle
inopia	F., lack, need		

The Helvetians probably carried their emergency food supply in wagons like this.

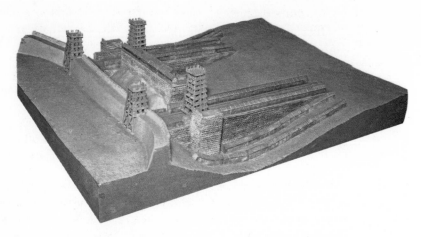

Model of a rampart *(agger)* used by the Romans in a formal siege.

THE ARMY IN ACTION

The principal unit of the Roman army in Caesar's time was the heavy infantry legion. Ideally it was composed of ten cohorts, each numbering six hundred men. The cohort was divided into three maniples of two hundred men, and each maniple was further broken down into two centuries. Actually, a legion rarely attained its full strength of six thousand, being continually reduced by the casualties of war as well as by ordinary illness, natural death, and military leaves.

In addition to the legion there were auxiliary troops of cavalry and light-armed infantry. These *auxilia* were made up almost entirely of foreigners, many of whom continued to wear their own national dress and to use their own methods of fighting. Such was the basic organization of the fighting force with which Caesar subjugated Gaul.

On the march, the arrangement of a Roman army varied according to the tactical situation. Usually the main body of troops was preceded by a van of reconnaissance cavalry and light infantry. The army followed at a convenient distance, marching in a column of centuries. Each legion was followed by its baggage. Several cohorts, detailed by the last legion as a guard for its baggage, also served as a rear guard for the entire army.

In the presence of the enemy the army marched with its baggage train collected; that is, three quarters of the legions preceded the baggage and the rest formed a rear guard. During a normal marching day a Roman army covered not more than twelve to fifteen miles, since it was necessary to halt early in the afternoon to make camp for the night. The rate of march was also slowed by the encumbrance of equipment, both military and personal. In an emergency, of course, the marching period might be lengthened and a greater distance covered.

General baggage consisted of tents, tools, and various other supplies carried by pack animals. The personal baggage of a Roman soldier included clothing, rations, cooking utensils, entrenching tool, and one or two stakes to be used in building a rampart. To protect the upper part of his body and head the soldier wore a leather corselet and a leather helmet, both reinforced with metal. He also carried a shield of leather or cloth-covered wood.

A Roman general preferred to draw up his army in a triple line of battle on higher ground than the enemy. The legions advanced slowly until they were about two hundred yards from the enemy; then they broke into a run. About fifty feet from the enemy they hurled their javelins. Then with swords drawn they charged into the confused enemy ranks. What followed was often a series of individual duels. The first line of troops, as they began to tire, fell back and were replaced by the second line. These two lines alternately relieved each other while the third line was kept in reserve.

The Romans were as effective at capturing fortified places as they were at fighting in the field. The three methods used were assault, blockade, and siege.

In an assault the enemy was driven from the walls by a barrage from archers, slingers, and heavy artillery consisting of machines called catapults, scorpions (small catapults), onagers, and ballistas. The catapults were capable of throwing javelins, arrows, and darts, while the onagers and ballistas hurled large stones. Battering rams were moved into position under cover of wooden sheds; scaling ladders and towers were moved forward, and the storming parties with shields locked together over their heads advanced to scale the walls. This last formation was called *testudo* (tortoise).

In a blockade, strong fortifications were erected around the city so that no reinforcements or supplies could enter. The inhabitants were thus forced to surrender. If the city was a seaport, ships were also used to enforce the blockade.

The formal siege was used only in the most difficult cases. It involved the use of all the ordinary war machines plus the construction of an *agger*. This was a rampart which, beginning about five hundred feet from the wall, extended with a gradual incline toward it until the rampart topped the fortifications. It served as a broad roadway along which the legions could advance to the top of the enemy's walls.

The advantage the Roman army enjoyed over most of its enemies was undoubtedly the result of organization and discipline. Long after ease and luxury had sapped the strength of Rome itself, the army continued to hold the empire together.

Left: This bronze statuette shows a cavalry-man in typical Roman military uniform.

Above: Model of standard surmounted by an eagle. Below the eagle are the various decorations of honor which the legion had won.

Below: Model of a battering ram encased in a protective shed on wheels shows how the real device could be moved up to walls and operated forcefully by ropes and pulleys.

Above: A watchtower similar to this model was built by the Romans beside the Danube River as the only means of aerial surveillance possible at that time.

Below: From Trajan's column comes this relief of Romans and barbarians in hand-to-hand combat. Compare the cavalryman with the statuette on page 250. Caesar's cavalrymen were often recruited from foreign allies. Sometimes non-Roman soldiers continued to wear their own native clothing.

Above: Models of typical Roman armor. Helmets were of bronze or iron, the tunic of leather or metal strips sewn to a cloth foundation. The sword was of iron, the shield of leather and metal. Leather sandals completed the equipment. Right: A model of a more elaborate standard than that on page 250.

Left: Bronze statuette of a legionary. Feathers or horse-hair could be inserted in a slot in the helmet for parades. Right: Bronze pots and an iron trivet used in a Roman camp.

Above: The clothing and some of the shields, swords, and helmets of typical Roman soldiers are evident on this relief now in the Berlin Museum.

Right: This portrait bust of Julius Caesar, one of the most famous in existence, is in the British Museum.

Below: Successful Roman generals on their return to Rome rode in a parade (called a triumph) of soldiers, prisoners, and booty. This triumphal chariot with a yoke for harnessing two horses is Etruscan. Roman chariots were similar except that four horses were used in a triumph.

If the Gauls had been united, they could have driven the Romans out of their country. However, there were always rivalries between various factions—a constant struggle for supremacy. The Sequanians had enlisted the aid of German tribes to help them overthrow the Haedui. After this was accomplished, the Germans preferred settling in Gaul to returning across the Rhine. Their king, Ariovistus, held many Gallic hostages and was in full control of the Sequanians' land. When he demanded additional land for still more Germans, the leaders of the Gauls appealed to Caesar, whose recent victory over the Helvetians had established his prestige in Gaul.

Omnēs quī aderant multīs lacrimīs auxilium ā Caesare petere coepērunt. Animadvertit Caesar autem Sēquanōs nihil eārum rērum facere quās cēterī facerent, sed trīstēs, capite dēmissō, terram spectāre. Ejus reī° quae causa esset[1] mīrātus, ex ipsīs quaesīvit. Nihil Sēquanī respondērunt sed 5 in eādem trīstitiā tacitī permānsērunt.

Dīviciācus Haeduus respondit, "Fortūna Sēquanōrum est miserior et gravior quam reliquōrum, quod sōlī nē in occultō quidem querī neque auxilium implōrāre audent absentisque Ariovistī crūdēlitātem sīcut praesentis° horrent.° 10

"Reliquīs enim Gallīs fugae facultās datur, Sēquanīs° vērō, quī intrā fīnēs suōs Ariovistum recēpērunt, quōrum oppida omnia in potestāte ejus sunt, omnēs cruciātūs sunt perferendī."

Hīs rēbus cognitīs, Caesar Gallōrum animōs verbīs cōn- 15 firmāvit pollicitusque est sibi[2] eam rem cūrae futūram°: magnam sē habēre spem et beneficiō[3] suō et auctōritāte adductum Ariovistum fīnem injūriīs factūrum. Hāc ōrātiōne habitā, concilium dīmīsit.

Secundum ea° multae rēs eum hortābantur ad eam rem 20 cōgitandam et suscipiendam: imprīmīs, quod° Haeduī, frātrēs cōnsanguineīque saepenumerō ā senātū appellātī, in servitūte atque in diciōne° Germānōrum tenēbantur, eōrumque obsidēs

---

[1]The subjunctive **esset** is in an indirect question depending on **mīrātus.**

[2]Notice that **sibi** (dative of reference) and **cūrae** (dative of purpose) are used in the so-called "double dative" construction.

[3]As consul, Caesar had granted favors to Ariovistus. Diviciacus knew this.

(1.19) They decided to prepare everything which is necessary

to set up to buy a large number of pack animals + carriages + seed

so that they might have sufficient supplies + grain also they wanted to begin

strengthen their friendship with neighboring states.

To complete these arrangements, they were lead to believe 2 years

they confirmed this that the departure would be in the 3rd year

To make these arrangements, Orye was selected. He himself under

---

(7) Movies are inconvenient.
a) Stay at home + watch TV.
b) Movie theaters are far away.
c) Movie houses are too big ⊙

(5) Movie houses are dangerous.
a) Things hang out there
b) Movie houses are fire traps
c) Radio has all the news that movies give

(3) T.V + Radio are taking movies place.
a) Pictures usually shown at movies are shown on TV
b) Normally objectionable. Inconvenient

(1) They are getting worse.
a) Less money making them.

Now that I have told you these things I hope you
can see why movies are so
undesirable in life today.

As I sat in a movie house last Sunday
watching a couple prehistoric monsters
battle it out and I really did not could
see the same picture on television, without the expense.

He said it would be easy to do because he is quite size(?), there is no doubt except that the Helvetians are very powerful of all the Gauls.; he very strongly told them that he would join them in taking the rules by with his own resorce and also with his horses.

By his speech they were influenced they swore their faith with a oath and after this is accomplished the hoped to be able to sew(?) the rule of Gaul.

This conspiracy was announce to the Helvetians through an informer. Acording to their custans they forced Orgen. to plead his case and then if he was condemned it aught to follow with punishment, he was going to be burned

on the day of the pleing of the case Orge. got all his (?) men together from all sides and also all pegle he did bour(?) with everyone who owed him money; with these he escaped les the pleade his case.

When the state, on account of this, they tried to enforce the right by arms. they gathered a multitude of peple while (?) did this Orgetorix.   As the Helutan thought suspise(?) was that he comited suicide.

apud Ariovistum ac Sēquanōs erant; quod° in tantō imperiō populī Rōmānī turpissimum° sibi et reī pūblicae esse arbitrā- ₂₅ bātur.°

As in the case of the Helvetians, Caesar was not reluctant to intervene in the affairs of Ariovistus and the Gauls. He saw and seized another opportunity for distinguishing himself.

Ariovistus was not intimidated; he rejected Caesar's demands. Since negotiations showed no result, Caesar put his legions in motion.

Paulātim autem Germānōs cōnsuēscere Rhēnum trānsīre et in Galliam magnam eōrum multitūdinem venīre populō Rōmānō perīculōsum° vidēbat; exīstimābat autem hominēs ferōs ac barbarōs, omnī Galliā occupātā, ut° ante Cimbrī ₃₀ Teutonīque fēcissent, in prōvinciam atque inde in Ītaliam exitūrōs esse, praesertim cum Sēquanōs ā prōvinciā nostrā Rhodanus dīvideret; quibus rēbus quam mātūrrimē occurrendum putābat.° Ipse autem Ariovistus tantōs sibi spīritūs,° tantam arrogantiam sūmpserat ut ferendus nōn vidērētur. ₃₅

°**ejus reī** (depends on **causa**) • **sīcut praesentis** as if (he were) present • **horrent** dread • **Sēquanīs** (dat. of agent with **perferendī**) • **sibi . . . futūram** that he would give attention to their case (lit., that this thing would be [for] a care to him) **secundum ea** in addition to these things • **quod** (conj.) the fact that • **diciōne** power • **quod** (rel. pron.) and . . . that (lit., a thing which) • **turpissimum** (predicate adj. after **esse**) • **sibi . . . arbitrābātur** (**Sibi** = Caesar, the implied subject of **arbitrābātur**.) • **perīculōsum** (predicate adj. after **esse** [to be supplied]; the subjects of **esse** are the infinitive phrases **Germānōs cōnsuēscere** and **multitūdinem venīre**) • **ut** as (**Fēcissent** is subjunctive because the clause occurs in indirect statement.) • **quibus . . . putābat** he thought that this state of affairs must be met as soon as possible • **spīritūs** pride

cōgitō	1 consider (carefully)	**ōrātiōnem**	
		⁺**habēre**	deliver a speech
⁺**dēmissus**	(adj.) bowed, low	**perferō**	endure; report
mātūrē	(adv.) soon, early	**saepenumerō**	(adv.) often
mīror	1 wonder	**trīstitia**	F., sadness

***absēns** (adj.)   **arrogantia** F.

Quam ob rem, lēgātīs ad Ariovistum missīs, ab eō postulāvit
ut aliquem locum medium utrīusque° colloquiō dēligeret:
velle° sēsē dē rē pūblicā et summīs utrīusque rēbus° cum eō
agere.

Eī lēgātiōnī Ariovistus respondit, "Sī quid mihi ā Caesare 5
opus esset,° ad eum vēnissem; sī quid ille mē vult,° illum ad
mē venīre oportet. Praetereā neque sine exercitū in eās
partēs Galliae venīre audeō quās Caesar possidet, neque exercitum sine magnō commeātū atque mōlīmentō° in ūnum
locum contrahere possum. Mihi autem mīrum vidētur quid 10
in meā Galliā, quam bellō vīcī, aut Caesarī aut omnīnō populō
Rōmānō negōtiī sit.°"

Hīs respōnsīs ad Caesarem relātīs, iterum ad eum Caesar
lēgātōs cum hīs mandātīs mittit.

"Quoniam in cōnsulātū Caesaris rēx atque amīcus ā senātū 15
appellātus nunc in colloquium venīre invītātus gravāris°
atque dē commūnī rē dīcere et cognōscere nōn vīs, haec°
sunt quae ā tē postulat: prīmum, nē quam multitūdinem
hominum amplius trāns Rhēnum in Galliam trādūcās; deinde
ut obsidēs quōs habēs ab Haeduīs reddās Sēquanīsque per- 20
mittās ut idem faciant; nēve Haeduōs injūriā° lacessās nēve
hīs sociīsque eōrum bellum īnferās.

"Sī id ita fēceris, Caesarī° populōque Rōmānō° perpetua
grātia atque amīcitia tēcum erit; sī Caesar nōn impetrāverit,
Haeduōrum injūriās nōn negleget. 25

"Nam ex senātūs cōnsultō, quod paucīs ante annīs factum
est, quīcumque Galliam prōvinciam obtinet Haeduōs cēte-
rōsque amīcōs populī Rōmānī dēfendere dēbet."

Ad haec Ariovistus respondit, "Jūs est bellī ut victōrēs
victīs quem ad modum° velint imperent. Item populus 30
Rōmānus victīs nōn ad alterīus praescrīptum,° sed ad suum
arbitrium° imperāre cōnsuēvit.

"Sī ego populum Rōmānum in ejus jūre nōn imp ediō,
nōn oportet mē ā populō Rōmānō in meō jūre impedīrī.
Haeduī, bellī fortūnā temptātā, superātī sunt mihique stīpen- 35
diāriī° sunt factī.[1]

---

[1]When Caesar arrived in Gaul, the Haedui had ceased to pay the tribute demanded
by Ariovistus, who blames Caesar for his reduced revenues. (See the next paragraph.)

"Magnam Caesar injūriam facit, quī suō adventū vectī-
gālia° mihi dēteriōra° facit. Haeduīs obsidēs nōn reddam,
neque eīs neque eōrum sociīs injūriā bellum īnferam, sī in
eō manēbunt quod convēnit° stīpendiumque quotannīs pen-   40
dent; sī id nōn fēcerint, longē eīs frāternum nōmen populī
Rōmānī aberit.°

"Quod° mihi Caesar dēnūntiat sē Haeduōrum injūriās nōn
neglēctūrum, nēmō mēcum sine suā perniciē contendit.
Cum vult, congrediātur.° Intelleget quid° invictī Germānī,   45
exercitātissimī° in armīs, quī inter annōs XIV tēctum nōn
subierint, virtūte possint."

°**medium utrīusque** midway between them • **velle sēsē dē...
agere** (he said that) he wished to discuss • **summīs utrīusque
rēbus** matters of the greatest importance to both • **sī quid...
opus esset** if I (had) needed anything from Caesar • **sī quid
...vult** if he wishes anything from me • **mōlīmentō** trouble
quid Caesarī negōtiī sit what business Caesar has (**Caesarī** is dative
of possession; **negōtiī** is partitive genitive with **quid.**) • **gravāris**
you are unwilling • **haec** (defined by subjunctive noun clauses
depending on **postulat**) • **injūriā** F. (abl.), unjustly • **Caesarī, populō Rōmānō** (datives of possession) • **quem ad
modum** as • **praescrīptum** direction • **arbitrium**
judgment • **stīpendiāriī** tributaries • **vectīgālia** revenues • **dēteriōra** less • **sī in eō...convēnit** if they abide
by our agreement • **longē eīs...aberit** the title of brothers of
the Roman people will be of little value to them • **quod...dē-
nūntiat** as for Caesar's threat to me that • **congrediātur** let
him come on • **quid...virtūte possint** what...can accomplish by valor • **exercitātissimī** thoroughly trained

amplē	(adv.) generously	**contrahō**	3 bring together
amplius	more gener-	**+grātia**	F., good will
	ously; more	**+inter**	(prep.) during, for
cōnsulātus	M., consulship	**invictus**	(adj.) invincible
cōnsultum	N., decree; **ex**	**+opus**	N. (indecl.) need
	senātūs cōnsultō,	**opus est**	there is need
	by decree of the	**possideō**	2 occupy, possess
	senate	**stipendium**	N., tribute, tax

*****respōnsum** N. **permittō** 3 **frāternus** (adj.)

This photograph of Besançon (ancient Vesontio) shows how the Doubs (Dubis) River encircles the town site as if drawn with a pair of compasses.

THE RACE FOR VESONTIO

Haec eōdem tempore Caesarī mandāta referēbantur, et lēgātī ab Haeduīs et ā Trēverīs veniēbant. Haeduī querē- bantur, quod Harūdēs, quī nūper in Galliam trānsportātī essent, fīnēs eōrum populārentur: sēsē nē obsidibus quidem datīs pācem Ariovistī redimere potuisse. Trēverī autem 5 dīcēbant pāgōs centum Suēbōrum ad rīpās Rhēnī cōnsēdisse, quī Rhēnum trānsīre cōnārentur.

Quibus rēbus Caesar vehementer commōtus mātūrandum° sibi exīstimāvit nē, sī nova manus Suēbōrum cum veteribus cōpiīs Ariovistī sēsē conjūnxisset, minus facile resistī posset.° 10

Itaque rē frūmentāriā quam celerrimē potuit comparātā, magnīs itineribus ad Ariovistum contendit.

Cum trīduī viam prōcessisset, nūntiātum est eī Ariovistum

cum suīs omnibus cōpiīs ad occupandum Vesontiōnem, quod
est oppidum maximum Sēquanōrum, contendere.   15

Id magnopere sibi praecavendum° Caesar exīstimābat.
Namque omnium rērum quae ad bellum ūsuī° erant summa
erat in eō oppidō facultās, idque nātūrā locī sīc mūniēbātur
ut magnam ad dūcendum° bellum daret facultātem, proptereā
quod flūmen Dūbis, ut circinō circumductum,° paene tōtum 20
oppidum cingit. Reliquum spatium, quod est nōn amplius°
pedum DC, quā flūmen intermittit, mōns continet magnā
altitūdine, ita ut rādīcēs¹ montis ex utrāque parte rīpae
flūminis contingant. Hunc mūrus circumdatus° arcem efficit
et cum oppidō conjungit.   25

Hūc Caesar magnīs nocturnīs diurnīsque° itineribus contendit, occupātōque oppidō, ibi praesidium collocat.

Dum paucōs diēs ad Vesontiōnem reī frūmentāriae com-
meātūsque causā morātur, nostrī Gallōs ac mercātōrēs dē
Germānīs interrogant. Illī Germānōs ingentī magnitūdine 30
corporum, incrēdibilī virtūte atque exercitātiōne in armīs
esse praedicābant. Quibus ex vōcibus tantus subitō timor
omnem exercitum occupāvit ut nōn mediocriter° omnium
mentēs animōsque perturbāret.

Hic prīmum ortus est ā tribūnīs mīlitum,² praefectīs,³ 35
reliquīsque⁴ quī ex urbe amīcitiae causā Caesarem secūtī
nōn magnum in rē mīlitārī ūsum habēbant. Hī, variīs causīs
domum proficīscendī illātīs, petēbant ut ejus voluntāte discēdere licēret; nōnnūllī pudōre adductī, ut timōris suspīciōnem vītārent, remanēbant.   40

Hī neque vultum fingere° neque interdum lacrimās tenēre
poterant; abditī in tabernāculīs aut suum fātum querēbantur
aut cum familiāribus suīs commūne perīculum miserābantur.°
Vulgō tōtīs castrīs testāmenta obsignābantur.° Hōrum vōcibus ac timōre paulātim etiam eī quī magnum in castrīs ūsum 45
habēbant, mīlitēs centuriōnēsque quīque equitātuī praeerant,
perturbābantur.

---

¹rādīcēs is the object of **contingant, rīpae** the subject.

²Military tribunes, less experienced than **lēgātī,** are not to be confused with tribunes
of the people (**tribūnī plēbis**). See note on page 263.

³Prefects were officers of auxiliary forces; some were of the same nationality as their
troops.

⁴Sons of influential families accompanied Caesar without performing military service.

Gravestone of a centurion. Centurions were seasoned veterans who had been promoted from the ranks.

Quī sē ex hīs° minus timidōs exīstimārī volēbant, dīcēbant, "Nōn hostem verēmur, sed angustiās itineris et magnitūdinem silvārum quae inter nōs atque Ariovistum intercēdunt; 50 timēmus etiam ut° rēs frūmentāria satis commodē supportārī° possit."

Nōnnūllī etiam Caesarī nūntiābant mīlitēs propter timōrem neque castra mōtūrōs neque signa lātūrōs.

°**mātūrandum sibi** that he must make haste • **minus...posset** resistance could not easily be made • **sibi praecavendum** that he must prevent • **ūsuī** of use/useful • **dūcendum** prolong **ut circinō circumductum** as if drawn by a compass • **amplius** (often used instead of **amplius quam**) • **mūrus circumdatus** an

260

encircling wall (**Hunc [montem]** is the object of **efficit; arcem** is predicate accusative.) • **diurnīsque** and (by) day • **nōn mediocriter** considerably • **vultum fingere** to control their expressions • **miserābantur** were deploring • **Vulgō ... obsignābantur.** Everywhere in the whole camp wills were being signed and sealed. • **quī ... ex hīs** those who • **ut** that ... not (a fear clause introduced by **ut** is negative) • **supportārī** be brought up

cingō	3 surround	**perturbō**	1 disturb; alarm
contingō	3 touch, reach	**pudor**	M., (sense of) shame
exercitātiō	F., experience	**+rādīcēs**	F. pl. (with **montis/**
+facultās	F., supply[1]		**collis),** foot, base
intercēdō	3 be/lie between	**redimō**	3 purchase
intermittō	3 leave off, cease	**+ūsus**	M., experience
namque	(conj.) for	**vereor**	2 fear
nocturnus	(adj.) (by/at) night	**vetus**	(adj.) old, veteran

*interrogō 1 **praefectus** M. **remaneō** 2 **fātum** N. **testāmentum** N.

A BOLD DECISION

The exaggerated rumors of German valor and the subsequent panic in the Roman camp created a difficult situation. There was, however, a capable general in command. The speech that Caesar delivered to his troops was a masterpiece; he reasoned, exhorted, criticized, argued, flattered. He aroused the spirit of competition by singling out his favorite tenth legion.

Caesar accomplished what he wanted; panic gave way to optimistic enthusiasm.

Caesar, cum haec° animadvertisset, convocātō cōnsiliō omniumque ōrdinum ad id cōnsilium adhibitīs centuriōnibus, vehementer eōs incūsāvit.

[1]Through this lesson Latin words that have appeared in earlier vocabularies and then occur in a later lesson with a new meaning or function have been listed again, with the symbol (+). For example, students have previously met **facultās** in the sense "opportunity"; here it is more appropriately translated "supply." In order to encourage students to consult the General Vocabulary and to exercise their own judgment, hereafter such words will not be repeated in lesson vocabularies, except in special instances.

Soldiers' rations of unground grain were weighed on steelyard scales like the two above. The two balance scales were used for weighing lighter commodities.

"Vestrum nōn officium est," inquit, "aut quam in partem aut quō cōnsiliō dūcāminī° quaerere aut cōgitāre. Cūr Ger- 5 mānōs timētis? Hī sunt eīdem quōs saepenumerō Helvētiī nōn sōlum in suīs sed etiam in illōrum fīnibus superāvērunt; quī° tamen parēs esse nostrō exercituī nōn potuērunt. Quī suum timōrem in reī frūmentāriae simulātiōnem° angustiās- que itineris cōnferunt faciunt arroganter, cum aut dē officiō 10 imperātōris dēspērāre aut praescrībere videantur.

"Haec mihi sunt cūrae; frūmentum Sēquanī, Leucī, Lingonēs subministrant, jamque sunt in agrīs frūmenta mātūra; dē itinere ipsī brevī tempore jūdicābitis. Quod° vōs signa nōn lātūrōs esse dīcitur, nihil eā rē commoveor; cui- 15 cumque[1] ducī enim exercitus nōn pāruit, aut male rē gestā eī fortūna dēfuit aut alicujus sceleris vel avāritiae damnātus est; mea innocentia perpetuā vītā, fēlīcitās Helvētiōrum bellō est perspecta.°

"Itaque quod in longiōrem diem collātūrus fuī reprae- 20

[1]Caesar is giving the reasons that might justify disobedience to a leader's orders: poor management, bad luck, conviction for criminal acts, guilt in taking bribes.

sentābō,° et proximā nocte dē quārtā vigiliā castra movēbō,
ut quam prīmum intellegere possim utrum apud vōs pudor
atque officium an timor plūs valeat. Quod sī praetereā
nēmō sequētur, tamen cum sōlā decimā legiōne ībō, dē quā
nōn dubitō, mihique ea praetōria cohors° erit." 25

Huic legiōnī Caesar et favēbat praecipuē et propter virtūtem cōnfīdēbat maximē.

Hāc ōrātiōne habitā, mīrum in modum° conversae sunt
omnium mentēs, summaque alacritās et cupiditās bellī gerendī
innāta est°. Prīnceps decima legiō per tribūnōs mīlitum[1] eī 30
grātiās ēgit, quod dē sē optimum jūdicium fēcisset, sēque esse
ad bellum gerendum parātissimam cōnfirmāvit.

Deinde reliquae legiōnēs cum tribūnīs mīlitum[1] et prīmō-
rum ōrdinum centuriōnibus ēgērunt° ut Caesarī satisfacerent.
Dīxērunt sē neque umquam dubitāsse neque timuisse neque 35
jūdicium dē summā bellī suum, sed imperātōris esse exīstimā-
visse.° Caesar, eōrum satisfactiōne° acceptā et itinere ex-
quīsītō per Dīviciācum, quod ex Gallīs eī maximam fidem
habēbat, dē quārtā vigiliā, ut dīxerat, profectus est. Septimō
diē, cum iter nōn intermitteret, ab explōrātōribus certior 40
factus est Ariovistī cōpiās ā nostrīs mīlia passuum IV et XX
abesse.

°**haec** (N. pl. acc., referring to evidences of panic described in the
last section) • **dūcāminī** (subjunctive in indirect question after
quaerere and **cōgitāre**) • **quī** these (the Helvetians) • **simulātiō, -ōnis** F., pretense (about) • **quod** (conj.) as to the fact
that • **mea innocentia ... est perspecta** my integrity has been
observed throughout my life, my good fortune (has been observed) in
the Helvetian war • **quod ... repraesentābō** I shall do at once
what I had intended to put off for a (longer) time • **praetōria cohors**
praetorian cohort, i.e., a (general's) bodyguard, composed of the bravest
troops • **mīrum in modum** in a marvelous manner • **innāta
est** arose • **ēgērunt** arranged • **sed ... exīstimā-
visse** but did think it was the commander's (decision) • **satis-
factiō, -ōnis** F., apology, excuse

[1]Tribunes of the soldiers received complaints of the men and acted as their spokesmen
with the commander; centurions of the first rank had the confidence of soldiers and
commander; ordinarily only centurions of the first rank were called to a council. Why do
you think Caesar summoned centurions of every rank to the council just ended? (See
page 261, lines 1-2.)

confīdō	3 have confidence (in)	+plūs	(adv.) more
		plūs valēre	be stronger
damnō	1 condemn, convict	praescrībō	3 dictate to, direct
dēsum	be lacking, fail		
dubitō	1 hesitate; doubt	quam prīmum	(adv.) as soon as possible
incūsō	1 censure, upbraid		
officium	N., duty; service	quod sī	(conj.) but if
ōrdō	M., rank; order; row	satisfaciō	3 apologize
+parātus	(adj.) ready, prepared	scelus	N., crime
		subministrō	1 supply

*arroganter (adv.) avāritia F. alacritās F.

PLAYING FOR TIME

Cognitō Caesaris adventū, Ariovistus per lēgātōs eī nūntiāvit sē jam in colloquium venīre velle; quoniam Caesar propius accessisset, sē id sine perīculō facere posse exīstimāre.

Nōn respuit° condiciōnem Caesar jamque eum ad sānitātem revertī arbitrābātur. Diēs colloquiō dictus est ex eō diē quīntus. 5

Interim cum lēgātī saepe ultrō citrōque inter eōs mitterentur, Ariovistus dīxit sē īnsidiās verērī postulāvitque ut uterque cum sōlō equitātū ad colloquium venīret; aliā ratiōne° sēsē nōn esse ventūrum. 10

Caesar, hāc condiciōne acceptā, salūtem suam tamen Gallōrum equitātuī[1] committere nōn audēbat. Itaque legiōnāriōs[2] mīlitēs legiōnis decimae in equōs Gallōrum equitum imposuit ut praesidium quam amīcissimum habēret.

Quod cum fieret, nōn irrīdiculē° quīdam ex mīlitibus 15 decimae legiōnis dīxit, "Plūs quam pollicitus est Caesar facit. Pollicitus sē in cohortis praetōriae locō decimam legiōnem habitūrum, ad equum[3] rescrībit."

[1]Caesar's cavalry was composed at various times of Gauls, Germans, and Spaniards. Caesar had never found the cavalry very reliable.

[2]Legionaries were infantrymen. It must have been interesting to see these heavily armed soldiers, who had no experience with horses, riding off to meet the enemy.

[3]A pun, since **ad equum rescrībere** can mean either to transfer to the cavalry (**equitēs**) or to raise to the rank of knights (also **equitēs),** the name of the wealthy middle class in Roman society.

Plānitiēs erat magna, et in eā tumulus terrēnus satis grandis°. Hic locus aequum ferē spatium ā castrīs utrīusque 20 aberat. Eō, ut erat dictum, ad colloquium vēnērunt. Legiōnem Caesar quam equīs dēvexerat° passibus CC ab eō tumulō cōnstituit.

Item equitēs Ariovistī parī intervāllō cōnstitērunt. Ariovistus ex equīs ut° colloquerentur et praeter sē dēnōs ut° ad 25 colloquium addūcerent postulāvit.

Ubi eō ventum est, Caesar initiō ōrātiōnis sua senātūsque in eum beneficia commemorāvit, quod° rēx appellātus esset ā senātū, quod° amīcus, quod° mūnera amplissima missa.

"Haec rēs," inquit, "et paucīs contigit et prō magnīs homi- 30 num officiīs cōnsuēvit tribuī.° Beneficiō ac līberālitāte meā ac senātūs ea praemia cōnsecūtus es.

"Veterēs jūstāsque causās necessitūdinis° Rōmānī cum Haeduīs habent. Multa senātūs cōnsulta honōrifica° in eōs facta sunt. Omnī tempore tōtīus Galliae prīncipātum Haeduī 35 tenuērunt, prius etiam quam° nostram amīcitiam appetī- vērunt."

Postulāvit deinde eadem quae lēgātīs in mandātīs dederat: nē aut Haeduīs aut eōrum sociīs bellum īnferret; ut obsidēs redderet; sī nūllam partem Germānōrum domum remittere 40 posset, at nē quōs amplius Rhēnum trānsīre paterētur.

Ariovistus ad postulāta Caesaris pauca respondit; dē suīs virtūtibus multa praedicāvit.

"Trānsiī Rhēnum," inquit, "nōn meā sponte, sed rogātus et arcessītus ā Gallīs; nōn sine magnā spē magnīsque praemiīs 45 domum propinquōsque relīquī. Sēdēs habeō in Galliā ab ipsīs° concessās, obsidēs ipsōrum voluntāte datōs. Stīpendi- um capiō jūre bellī, quod victōrēs victīs impōnere cōnsuērunt.

"Nōn ego° Gallīs, sed Gallī mihi bellum intulērunt. Omnēs Galliae cīvitātēs ad mē oppugnandum vēnērunt ac contrā mē 50 castra habuērunt. Eae omnēs cōpiae ā mē ūnō proeliō pulsae ac superātae sunt.

"Sī iterum experīrī volunt, iterum parātus sum dēcertāre; sī pāce ūtī° volunt, inīquum est dē stīpendiō recūsāre, quod suā voluntāte ad hoc tempus pependērunt. Amīcitiam populī 55 Rōmānī mihi ōrnāmentō et praesidiō, nōn dētrīmentō esse oportet, atque hāc spē petīvī.

"Sī per populum Rōmānum stīpendium remittētur et

dēditiciī° subtrahentur, nōn minus libenter recūsābō populī Rōmānī amīcitiam quam appetīvī. Quod° multitūdinem Ger- 60 mānōrum in Galliam trādūcō, id meī mūniendī, nōn Galliae oppugnandae causā faciō. Ejus reī testimōnium° est quod nisi rogātus nōn vēnī et quod bellum nōn intulī sed dēfendī.

"Ego prius in Galliam vēnī quam populus Rōmānus. Numquam ante hoc tempus exercitus populī Rōmānī Galliae 65 prōvinciae fīnibus ēgressus est. Quid tibi vīs?° Cūr in meās possessiōnēs venīs? Prōvincia mea haec est Gallia,° sīcut illa vestra.°

"Ut mihi concēdī nōn oportēret sī in vestrōs fīnēs impetum facerem, sīc item vōs estis inīquī, quod in meō jūre 70 mē interpellātis.°

"Quod frātrēs ā senātū Haeduōs appellātōs dīcis, neque bellō[1] Allobrogum proximō Haeduī Rōmānīs auxilium tulērunt neque ipsī in hīs contentiōnibus° quās Haeduī mēcum et cum Sēquanīs habuērunt auxiliō populī Rōmānī ūsī sunt. 75

"Neque tam barbarus neque tam imperītus sum rērum ut haec nōn sciam. Dēbeō suspicārī tē, simulātā amīcitiā, exercitum in Galliā meī opprimendī causā habēre.

"Nisi dēcēdēs atque exercitum dēdūcēs ex hīs regiōnibus, tē nōn prō amīcō sed prō hoste habēbō.° Quod sī tē inter- 80 fēcerō, multīs nōbilibus prīncipibusque populī Rōmānī grātum° faciam. Id ab ipsīs per eōrum nūntiōs compertum habeō,° quōrum omnium grātiam atque amīcitiam tuā morte redimere possum.[2]

"Quod sī dēcesseris et līberam possessiōnem Galliae mihi 85 trādideris, magnō tē praemiō remūnerābor,° et quaecumque bella gerī volēs sine ūllō tuō labōre et perīculō cōnficiam."

°**nōn respuit** did not reject • **aliā ratiōne** otherwise, on other terms • **irrīdiculē** without humor; with **nōn**=wittily • **grandis** large • **equīs dēvexerat** had brought on horseback • **ut ... ut** (placed out of their normal order to emphasize other words: **ex equīs** [on horseback] in one case, and **praeter sē dēnōs** [besides themselves ten men each] in the other) • **quod** that (The **quod** clauses define **beneficia**.) • **quod amīcus** (supply **appellātus**

[1] i.e., the recent war with the Allobroges, in 62-61 B.C.

[2] Caesar has many political enemies among the nobles; Ariovistus is implying that he has contacts with these enemies.

esset) • **quod ... missa** (supply **essent**) • **cōnsuēvit tribuī**
is usually granted • **necessitūdō, -inis** F., alliance, friendship
honōrificus, -a, -um honorable (**in eōs** = in their behalf) • **prius**
... quam = **priusquam** • **ipsīs** = **Gallīs** • **ego** (supply
bellum intulī) • **ūtī** enjoy • **dēditicius, -ī** M., captive
quod ... trādūcō as for my leading (over) • **ejus reī testimō-**
nium est quod proof of this is that • **quid tibi vīs?** what do
you mean/intend? • **haec Gallia** this part of Gaul • **vestra**
(referring to the whole Roman nation, not to Caesar alone) • **in-**
terpellātis hinder • **contentiō, -ōnis** F., struggle • **prō**
... habēbō I shall treat/regard ... as • **grātum** a favor
compertum habeō (emphasizing the resulting fact; translate as if
comperī) • **remūnerābor** I will repay

appetō	3 seek; approach	**propius**	(adv./prep. with
arcessō	3 summon; invite		acc.) nearer
commemorō	1 mention	**rescrībō**	3 transfer; enroll
+**cōnsequor**	3 obtain	**sēdēs**	F., home; seat
+**contingō**	3 happen	**simulō**	1 pretend
dēcertō	1 fight (to the	**subtrahō**	3 take away
	end)	**suspicor**	1 suspect
dētrīmentum	N., loss, harm	**terrēnus**	(adj.) earthen
inīquus	(adj.) unfair, un-	**ultrō**	(adv.) beyond; **ultrō**
	just		**citrōque** = back and
plānitiēs	F., plain		forth
+**postulātum**	N., demand	**ut ... sīc**	just as ... so

*****sānitās** F. **legiōnārius** (adj.; also noun) **testimōnium** N.[1]

MANEUVERING FOR THE ADVANTAGE

Dum haec in colloquiō geruntur, Caesarī nūntiātum est
equitēs Ariovistī propius tumulum accēdere et ad nostrōs
adequitāre° et lapidēs tēlaque in nostrōs conjicere. Caesar
loquendī fīnem fēcit sēque ad suōs recēpit suīsque imperāvit
nē quod omnīnō tēlum in hostēs rejicerent. Nam etsī sine 5
ūllō perīculō legiōnis dēlēctae proelium cum equitātū futū-

---

[1]Hereafter the horizontal listing (*) of new vocabulary words that have common
English derivatives is omitted. Since these words—both the Latin and English—are in-
variably included in one's permanent "mastery" vocabulary, students are encouraged to
keep notebook lists of all such words met in future lessons.

rum esse vidēbat, tamen nōlēbat hostēs dīcere posse, sī pulsī essent, sē ā Rōmānīs per fidem[1] in colloquiō circumventōs esse. Ita colloquium dirēmptum est°.

Postquam mīlitēs[2] dē hīs rēbus certiōrēs factī sunt, multō 10 major alacritās studiumque pugnandī majus exercituī injectum est.°

Ariovistus had proved himself a shrewd bargainer. Who was in the right? Both Germans and Romans came to Gaul as conquerors; both tried to justify their presence there on the basis of Gallic appeals for help.

Two days after their summit meeting Ariovistus sent word that he would like to meet with Caesar again. This time, however, the suspicious Caesar did not go himself; he sent only Procillus, the Romanized son of a Gaul, and another emissary.

Caesar's report indicates that Ariovistus spoke Gallic fluently. We may therefore infer that the first meeting was conducted in Gallic, with Caesar communicating presumably through his interpreter Procillus.

Angry because Caesar did not come himself, Ariovistus had the two emissaries thrown into chains on arrival. After this incident both sides began to prepare for battle.

Ubi Ariovistum castrīs sē tenēre Caesar intellēxit, nē diūtius commeātū prohibērētur, ultrā eum locum quō in locō Germānī cōnsēderant, idōneum locum castrīs minōribus[3] 15 dēlēgit. Hic locus ab hoste circiter passūs DC aberat. Eō circiter hominum XVI mīlia expedīta cum omnī equitātū Ariovistus mīsit quae cōpiae nostrōs perterrērent et mūnītiōne prohibērent. Nihilō minus mīlitēs Caesaris opus perfēcērunt.

Proximō diē Caesar iterum hostibus pugnandī potestātem 20 fēcit.° Ubi nē tum quidem eōs prōdīre intellēxit, circiter merīdiē exercitum in castra redūxit. Tum dēmum Ariovistus partem suārum cōpiārum quae castra minōra oppugnāret mīsit. Ācriter utrimque usque ad vesperum pugnātum est. Sōlis occāsū suās cōpiās Ariovistus, multīs illātīs et 25 acceptīs vulneribus, in castra redūxit.

[1]Through their faith (in Caesar's honor), i.e., treacherously. Notice the relationship between the phrase **per fidem** and the noun **perfidia,** meaning "treachery, perfidy."

[2]i.e., the main body of soldiers left at camp.

[3]Caesar's plan is to have a small camp on his road of communication while keeping the main body in the larger camp. This leaves Ariovistus between the two camps.

An ancient representation of a Roman camp and its fortifications

Cum ex captīvīs quaereret Caesar quam ob rem Ariovistus
proeliō nōn dēcertāret, illī respondērunt, "Apud Germānōs
mātrēs familiae dēclārant° utrum proelium committī ex
ūsū° sit necne.° Eae ita dīxērunt, 'Nōn est fās Germānōs 30
superāre, sī ante novam lūnam proeliō contenderint.' "

Postrīdiē ejus diēī Caesar praesidiō utrīsque castrīs quod
satis esse vīsum est relīquit; omnēs ālāriōs° in cōnspectū
hostium prō castrīs minōribus cōnstituit. Ipse, triplicī aciē
īnstrūctā,[1] usque ad castra hostium accessit. Tum dēmum 35
necessāriō Germānī suās cōpiās castrīs ēdūxērunt cōnstituē-
runtque generātim° paribus intervāllīs, omnemque aciem
suam raedīs et carrīs circumdedērunt, nē qua spēs in fugā
relinquerētur. Eō mulierēs imposuērunt, quae ad proelium
proficīscentēs mīlitēs, passīs manibus,° flentēs implōrābant 40
nē sē in servitūtem Rōmānīs trāderent.

[1]Normal battle formation; the first line served as shock troops, the others as reserves.

°**adequitāre** ride up to • **dirēmptum est** was broken off
injectum est was inspired (in) • **potestātem fēcit** gave a
chance • **mātrēs familiae dēclārant** (their) matrons predict
ex ūsū of advantage/advantageous • **necne** or not
ālāriōs auxiliaries • **generātim** (adv.) by tribes • **passīs
manibus** with outstretched hands (**passum** = perf. part. of **pandō**)

mūnītiō	F., fortification	**nihilō minus**	nevertheless
necessāriō	(adv.) of necessity, necessarily	**prōdeō**	come out/forward, advance

This plaything, made of terra cotta in the form of a Gallic cavalryman, must have delighted some child of long ago, as toy soldiers still bring pleasure to children today.

Utrimque diū atque ācriter pugnātum est. Dēnique omnēs
hostēs terga vertērunt neque prius fugere dēstitērunt quam
ad flūmen Rhēnum circiter v mīlia passuum ex eō locō pervēnērunt. Ibi perpaucī aut vīribus° cōnfīsī trānāre° contendērunt aut lintribus inventīs sibi salūtem reppererunt. 5
In hīs fuit Ariovistus, quī nāviculam dēligātam ad rīpam
nactus° eā profūgit. Reliquōs omnēs nostrī equitēs cōnsecūtī
interfēcērunt.

Duae fuērunt Ariovistī uxōrēs,[1] ūna Suēba nātiōne, quam
domō sēcum dūxerat, altera Nōrica, quam in Galliā in mātri- 10
mōnium dūxerat; utraque in eā fugā periit. Fuērunt duae
fīliae; hārum altera occīsa, altera capta est.

Hōc proeliō trāns Rhēnum nūntiātō, Suēbī, quī ad rīpam
Rhēnī vēnerant, domum revertī coepērunt; ubi eī quī proximī
Rhēnum incolunt eōs perterritōs sēnsērunt, īnsecūtī magnum 15
ex eīs numerum occīdērunt.

Caesar, ūnā aestāte duōbus maximīs bellīs cōnfectīs,
mātūrius paulō quam tempus annī postulābat, in hīberna in
Sēquanōs exercitum dēdūxit. Hībernīs Labiēnum praeposuit;
ipse in Citeriōrem Galliam ad conventūs agendōs° profectus est. 20

Caesar reported that his joy at finding Procillus again was as great
as the pleasure he felt at gaining the victory.

The results of one summer's campaigning were truly remarkable. The
defeated Helvetians had been sent home; central Gaul was under Roman
control; and the legions were garrisoned at Vesontio for the winter.

The first book of the Gallic War ends abruptly. Caesar had done all
there was to do in Gaul; so he returned to northern Italy, there to sit as
judge in his provincial courts.

°**vīribus** abl. with **cōnfīsī** = trusting in their strength • **trānāre**
swim across • **nactus** (perf. part. of **nancīscor**) finding (lit.,
having found) • **ad conventūs agendōs** to hold the (provincial)
courts

aestās	F., summer	praepōnō	3 put in command of
dēligō	1 tie (down), fasten	profugiō	3 escape
nancīscor	3 find; get		

[1]Polygamy was not common among the Germans, though the chiefs practiced it.

THE ARMY IN CAMP

Roman generals recognized the importance of rest and security for soldiers off duty in the field. An army on the march sent ahead scouts to find a suitable location for, and mark off the boundaries of, a camp. A preferred site was a hillside sloping toward the enemy. An adequate supply of water and wood for fuel was necessary. Such forethought for the safety and comfort of the men contributed to the usually high morale of Roman armies.

A Roman camp was regularly laid out in a square or rectangle. A trench (*fossa*) about seven feet deep and nine or ten feet wide was dug around the camp. The excavated earth was piled up to form a wall (*vallum*) about six feet high on the camp side of the trenches. The exterior of the wall was faced with turf and bundles of stakes (fascines) and was steep enough to discourage scaling by the enemy.

The interior face sloped gradually and sometimes had log steps leading to the top, which was flat and broad enough to accommodate the soldiers. At the outer edge of the wall a fence of stakes about four feet high served as a breastwork. When stronger fortifications were needed, towers were erected at intervals along the walls.

A Roman camp was divided into three parts. The two principal streets running parallel to the front of the camp separated the sections. The general's quarters (*praetorium*) were in the center of the camp with the other officers' quarters nearby. Between the *praetorium* and the rear gate were storehouses and the paymaster's office (*quaestorium*). The remaining space was allotted to the tents of the soldiers with about ten men assigned to each tent (*tabernaculum*). A camp was laid out according to a fixed system so that a soldier could always find his place. In winter quarters, straw-thatched huts were substituted for the leather tents to provide better protection.

A permanent camp usually had a central meeting place (*forum*). Sometimes there was a platform where the general addressed the troops or sat to perform judicial duties. In every camp there was a sacrificial altar in front of the general's quarters. Here was kept, as in a shrine, the legionary standard with its characteristic eagle— wings outspread. To lose the "eagle" was the ultimate disgrace.

The gates of the camp were designated as follows: front gate, *Porta Praetoria*; rear gate, *Porta Decumana*; side gates, *Porta Principalis Dextra* and *Porta Principalis Sinistra*. The right and left designations correspond to the right and left of a person leaving the camp by the front gate. The gates were defended by outposts of infantry and cavalry, and sentries patrolled the walls. Guards were changed at each of the four watches (*vigiliae*) during the night. The length of a watch varied with the length of the days and nights during the year, the hours of darkness being always divided into four watches.

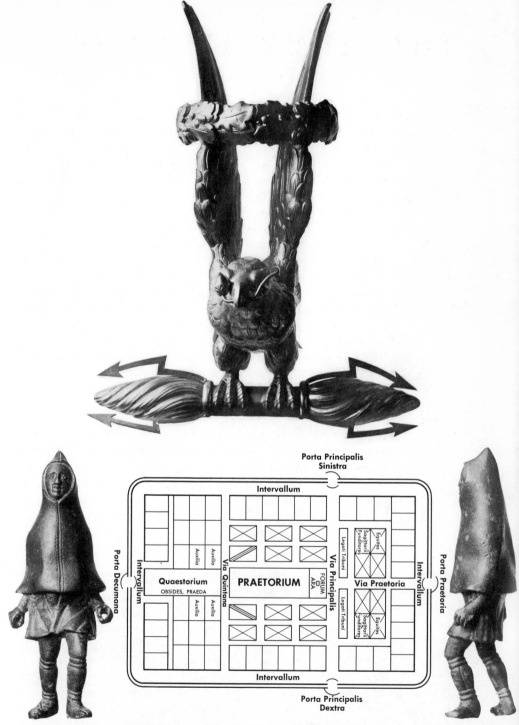

The labels within the figure:

Porta Principalis Sinistra

Intervallum

Porta Decumana

Intervallum

Quaestorium
OBSIDES, PRAEDA

Via Quintana

PRAETORIUM

FORUM ARA

Auxilia

Auxilia

Legati Tribuni

Sagittarii Fundifores

Equites

Via Principalis

Legati Tribuni

Sagittarii Fundifores

Equites

Via Praetoria

Intervallum

Porta Praetoria

Intervallum

Porta Principalis Dextra

Regular plan for the arrangement of a Roman military camp. Left and right: Two views of a soldier wearing the paenula, a cloak for bad weather. Above: A model of the eagle that symbolized Roman military power. His upthrust wings are encircled with a laurel wreath and he clutches a stylized thunderbolt in his talons.

Above: Model of a relief in which the general attended by other officers is addressing his troops from a raised platform within the camp. The signifers have a place of honor in the first ranks.

Left: Model of a signifer carrying his massive standard, and wearing an animal pelt on his head and shoulders.

Below: This list of Roman soldiers shows some Roman names. Others, obviously foreign, reflect the enlistment of allies.

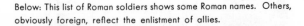

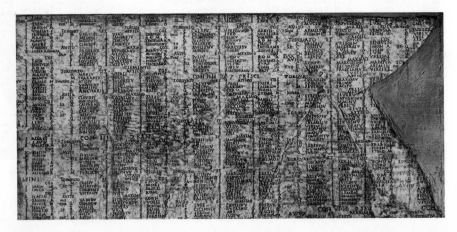

Above: This condensed relief from Trajan's Column shows many features of a permanent camp. Masonry instead of stakes surrounds the camp. Inside are a tent and a frame building. A soldier guards hostages or prisoners while sentries guard the ditch and wall. Right: In permanent camps such sundials, adapted from the Greeks, could be used.

The following year, in 57 B.C., Caesar extended his conquest farther to the north. After the Gauls, it was the Belgians' turn to succumb to the superior discipline and leadership of the Roman legions. Like the Gauls, the Belgians made it easy for Caesar to conquer them. Instead of making one common all-out effort, they were defeated, one or two tribes at a time.

Particularly strong resistance was offered by the Nervii, one of the northernmost Belgian tribes. They had heard that the Roman army marched in a certain way: first a legion and its baggage train, then another legion and its baggage, and so on. What the Nervii did not know, however, was the Roman custom of changing this marching order when they approached an enemy. Caesar had six legions march in front without their packs. Then followed the baggage train, and two more legions brought up the rear.

When the Romans began constructing their camp, the Nervii rushed out of a forest and took them somewhat by surprise. The Nervii in turn were surprised to find not one but six legions fighting them.

THE GENERAL HAS HIS HANDS FULL

Caesarī omnia ūnō tempore erant agenda: vexillum° prōpōnendum,° quod erat īnsigne cum ad arma concurrī oportēret, signum° tubā dandum, ab opere revocandī mīlitēs, quī
paulō longius° aggeris petendī causā prōcesserant arcessendī,
aciēs īnstruenda, mīlitēs cohortandī, signum° dandum. 5
Quārum rērum magnam partem temporis brevitās et incursus
hostium impediēbat.

Hīs difficultātibus duae rēs[1] erant subsidiō: scientia atque
ūsus mīlitum, quod, superiōribus proeliīs exercitātī, quid fierī
oportēret nōn minus commodē ipsī sibi praescrībere quam ab 10
aliīs docērī poterant; et quod ab opere singulīsque legiōnibus
singulōs° lēgātōs Caesar discēdere nisi mūnītīs castrīs° vetuerat. Hī propter propinquitātem et celeritātem hostium nihil°
jam Caesaris imperium expectābant, sed per sē quae vidē-
bantur° administrābant. 15

---

[1]**Duae rēs** is explained by two appositives: (1) **scientia atque ūsus** (i.e., theoretical knowledge and practical experience) and (2) **et quod . . . vetuerat** (a noun clause of fact).

Caesar necessāriīs rēbus imperātīs ad cohortandōs mīlitēs, quam partem fors obtulit,° dēcucurrit, et ad legiōnem decimam dēvēnit. Mīlitēs nōn longiōre ōrātiōne cohortātus quam utī suae prīstinae virtūtis memoriam retinērent neu[1] perturbārentur animō hostiumque impetum fortiter sustinērent, 20 quod nōn longius hostēs aberant[2] quam quō tēlum adigī posset, proelī committendī signum dedit. Atque in alteram partem[3] item cohortandī causā profectus pugnantibus° occurrit.

Temporis tanta fuit exiguitās hostiumque tam parātus ad 25 dīmicandum animus ut nōn modo ad īnsignia accommodanda,° sed etiam ad galeās induendās[4] scūtīsque tegimenta° dētrahenda, tempus dēfuerit.[5] Quam quisque ab opere in partem° cāsū dēvēnit quaeque prīma signa cōnspexit, ad haec cōnstitit, nē in quaerendīs suīs° pugnandī tempus dīmitteret. 30

°**vexillum, -ī** N., banner, standard • **prōpōnendum (erat)** had to be displayed (Supply **erat** or **erant** with the following future passive participles.) • **signum** signal (to form ranks) • **paulō longius** a little too far • **signum** signal (to attack) • **singulīs . . . singulōs** particular/respective . . . each/his several • **nisi . . . castrīs** until (lit., unless) the camp had been fortified • **nihil** = an emphatic **nōn** • **vidēbantur** seemed best • **quam . . . obtulit** that part (of the soldiers) which chance offered • **pugnantibus** (his men already) fighting • **ad . . . accommodanda** to put on their decorations (e.g., badges, crests on their helmets) • **tegimentum, -ī** N., leather covering • **quam in partem** to whatever place • **suīs** = **suīs signīs**

adigō	3 throw; drive	**fors**	F., chance
agger	M., rampart; materials	**incursus**	M., attack
	for a rampart, timber	**induō**	3 put on
dēveniō	4 come, go	**neu**	(conj.) = **nēve,**
exercitātus	(adj.) well trained		and (that) not
exiguitās	F., shortness, smallness	**subsidium**	N., assistance

[1]Since **et nē** is not used, **neu/nēve** serves as the negative connective for **ut/nē**.

[2]**Quod . . . aberant** is a causal clause, explaining the following **signum dedit.**

[3]to the other section; i.e., the right wing

[4]On the march, a soldier's helmet was hanging at his breast; the helmet was laid aside, however, while a soldier was working on the fortifications.

[5]What is the usual sequence of tenses after a perfect indicative in the main clause?

The legionaries on this crude tombstone are dwarfed by their equipment.

ENCOURAGEMENT BY EXAMPLE

With forces thus hastily arranged, the ninth and tenth legions, which were stationed on the Roman left, made short work of the enemy and drove them across the river. The Roman center held fast, but, on the right, the seventh and twelfth legions were outflanked by the Nervii, while enemy soldiers were penetrating the Roman camp itself.

Roman auxiliary forces, never the best in a fight, panicked. Some of the cavalry even rode directly home and told of a tremendous defeat. We are not told what they did when the news of a Roman victory arrived later or how they explained their own cowardice.

Caesar ab decimae legiōnis cohortātiōne ad dextrum cornū profectus, suōs urgērī signīsque in ūnum locum collātīs duo-decimae legiōnis cōnfertōs° mīlitēs sibi ipsōs ad pugnam esse impedīmentō vīdit. Quārtae cohortis omnibus centuriōnibus occīsīs, signiferō interfectō, signō āmissō, reliquārum co- 5 hortium omnibus ferē centuriōnibus aut vulnerātīs aut occīsīs, in hīs prīmipīlō° P. Sextiō Baculō, fortissimō virō, multīs gravibusque vulneribus cōnfectō, ut jam sē sustinēre nōn posset, reliquōs esse tardiōrēs et nōn nūllōs ab novissimīs° dē-sertō locō° proeliō excēdere ac tēla vītāre° vīdit. Hostēs 10 neque ā fronte ex īnferiōre locō subeuntēs intermittere° et ab utrōque latere īnstāre, et rem esse in angustō° vīdit neque ūllum esse subsidium quod submittī posset.

Scūtō ab novissimīs mīlitī dētractō,° quod ipse eō sine scūtō vēnerat, in prīmam aciem prōcessit; centuriōnibusque 15 nōminātim appellātīs, reliquōs cohortātus mīlitēs signa īn-ferre et manipulōs laxāre° jussit, quō° facilius gladiīs ūtī possent. Cujus adventū spē illātā mīlitibus ac redintegrātō animō, cum prō sē quisque° in cōnspectū imperātōris etiam in extrēmīs suīs rēbus operam nāvāre° cuperet, paulum hostium 20 impetus tardātus est.

°**cōnfertōs** crowded together • **prīmipīlus, -ī** M., chief cen-turion • **ab novissimīs** in the rear (with **nōn nūllōs**) • **dē-sertō locō** deserting their posts • **tēla vītāre** were getting out of the range of weapons • **hostēs neque subeuntēs inter-mittere** that the enemy were continually coming up • **esse in angustō** was in a critical situation • **scūtō mīlitī dētractō** snatching a shield from a soldier • **manipulōs laxāre** to open out the ranks • **quō** (introducing a purpose clause containing a comparative) • **prō sē quisque** each one according to his ability • **operam nāvāre** to do his best (**nāvō** = do diligently)

cohors	F., cohort (one tenth of a Roman legion)	**redintegrō**	1 renew, restore
		sē ⁺sustinēre	stand up
cohortātiō	F., encouragement	**submittō**	3 send (under/
nōminātim	(adv.) by name		up/as aid)
opera	F., work; attention	**tardō**	1 check, hinder;
paulum	(adv.) a little,		slow
	somewhat	**tardus**	(adj.) slow

Tombstone of a Roman standardbearer, a soldier who carried the cherished "eagle"

THE GOOD JUDGMENT OF LABIENUS

Caesar cum septimam legiōnem, quae jūxtā cōnstiterat, item urgērī ab hoste vīdisset, tribūnōs mīlitum monuit ut paulātim sēsē legiōnēs conjungerent° et conversa signa[1] in hostēs īnferrent. Quō factō, cum aliīs aliī subsidium ferrent neque timērent nē āversī° ab hoste circumvenīrentur, audācius 5 resistere ac fortius pugnāre coepērunt.

Interim mīlitēs legiōnum duārum quae in novissimō agmine

---

[1]Probably only the rear line was to face about **(signa convertere)**, and the cohorts on the wings turned half around. Thus an oblong would be formed, facing the enemy on all sides.

praesidiō impedīmentīs fuerant, proeliō nūntiātō, in summō
colle ab hostibus cōnspiciēbantur; et T. Labiēnus castrīs hostium potītus et ex locō superiōre quae rēs in nostrīs castrīs 10
gererentur cōnspicātus decimam legiōnem subsidiō nostrīs
mīsit. Quī cum° ex equitum et cālōnum° fugā quō in locō°
rēs esset quantōque in perīculō et castra et legiōnēs et imperātor versārētur cognōvissent, nihil ad celeritātem sibi
reliquī fēcērunt.°   15

Hōrum adventū tanta rērum commūtātiō est facta ut nostrī,
etiam quī vulneribus cōnfectī prōcubuissent, scūtīs innīxī
proelium redintegrārent; cālōnēs perterritōs hostēs cōnspicātī
etiam inermēs armātīs° occurrerent; equitēs vērō, ut turpi-
tūdinem fugae virtūte dēlērent, omnibus in locīs pugnandī 20
studiō sē legiōnāriīs mīlitibus praeferrent.°

These timely reinforcements turned the tide. The Nervii were prac-
tically annihilated.

At about the same time more Belgian states on the Atlantic coast gave
hostages. Thus Caesar had a proud record to show after his second
year in Gaul. In recognition of Caesar's achievements, the Senate
decreed a public thanksgiving of fifteen days.

°**sēsē conjungerent** should unite (i.e., close up the gap between
them) • **āversī** in the rear (lit., turned away) • **quī cum**
when they (i.e., the soldiers of the tenth legion) • **cālō, -ōnis**
M., a soldier's servant, noncombatant • **quō in locō** in what condition • **nihil ... fēcērunt** made all possible speed • **armātīs** the armed (enemy) • **sē praeferrent** (with dat.) surpassed

commūtātiō	F., change	**jūxtā**	(adv.) nearby, near
inermis	(adj.) unarmed	**prōcumbō**	3 fall or lie down
innītor	3 lean on	**turpitūdō**	F., disgrace

A heavy missile such as this Roman dart was probably launched from a catapult.

In English a group of words may have a common root.

love   lovely   loving   lovable   unlovely

In Latin also several words can come from the same root. Such a group of words is often called a "word family."

amō   amor   amābilis   amīcus   inimīcus

Give the meaning of each word in this word family and tell what part of speech it is:

rēx (rēg-)   rēgius   regō   regiō
rēgina   rēgia   rēgnō   rēgnum

List some English words from each word family below.

audeō	bellum	pars	pellō	expellō
audāx	bellō	partim	appellō	impellō
audācia	bellicōsus	particula	compellō	prōpellō
audācter	rebelliō	partior	dēpellō	repellō

Give as many members as you can of the Latin word family for each of the following verbs.

faciō   ferō   jaciō   stō

What do the following words mean? Some have related English words. What are they? How does the meaning "sharp" enter into each of these words?

ācer   acerbē   aciēs   acidus   acūmen   acūtus

Latin word families provide the basis for English word families, too. Give the Latin root word for each English word family below and tell what Latin prefix appears in each word.

accept	appetite	acquire
intercept	competitive	inquiry
perception	impetus	prerequisite
recipient	repetition	requirement

Make an English word family for **mittō**. Think of the primary meaning (let go) and the connection of such words as "missile" will be clear.

At Dover, England, near Caesar's landing place stands this Roman lighthouse tower. It was built after Caesar's time, about A.D. 50, but is considered the oldest structure standing in Britain.

In 56 B.C. the Romans spent a great deal of time conquering the Veneti. These experienced mariners lived in the western part of the area now called Brittany. They owed their prosperity to their fleet which carried on trade with Britain. In fact, they monopolized Gallic-British trade.

The decisive naval battle was won by the Romans, aided by the weather. A dead calm immobilized the fleet of the Veneti but not the Roman galleys, which were rowed by oarsmen.

A campaign against the Belgian Morini and Menapii, whose lands extended from modern Calais to the lower Rhine, was cut short by bad weather and approaching winter.

The following year (55 B.C.), Caesar was compelled to ward off another German invasion—this time by the tribes of the Usipetes and the Tencteri. Caesar contrived to arrest their leaders and then almost completely massacred the two tribes. His conduct was condemned by the Senate, but, unperturbed by the censure, the general crossed the Rhine for the first time. His purpose was to intimidate still other German tribes with a show of Roman strength. On this occasion his engineers built a bridge which the Romans themselves destroyed after they had returned to the left bank. Then Caesar turned his attention to Britain, separated from Gaul only by the Channel.

Caesar realized that he could be assured of continued control over Gaul only if he neutralized Britain. He also wanted to punish the southern British tribes who had helped their kinsmen in Gaul resist the Romans.

PREPARATION FOR AN INVASION

Exiguā parte aestātis reliquā, Caesar, etsī in hīs locīs, quod omnis Gallia ad septentriōnēs vergit, mātūrae sunt hiemēs, tamen in Britanniam proficīscī contendit, quod omnibus ferē Gallicīs bellīs hostibus nostrīs inde subministrāta° auxilia intellegēbat; et, sī tempus annī[1] ad bellum gerendum 5 dēficeret, tamen magnō sibi ūsuī fore° arbitrābātur sī modo īnsulam adīsset, genus hominum perspexisset, loca, portūs, aditūs cognōvisset; quae omnia ferē Gallīs erant incognita.[2]

[1]It was customary for Roman soldiers to go into winter quarters (hiberna) before cold weather set in.

[2]This statement is not quite accurate. The coastal tribes, at least, had some knowledge of Britain.

Neque enim temere praeter mercātōrēs illō° adit quisquam,
neque hīs ipsīs quicquam praeter ōram maritimam atque eās 10
regiōnēs quae sunt contrā Galliam nōtum est.

Itaque vocātīs ad sē undique mercātōribus, neque quanta
esset īnsulae magnitūdō neque quae aut quantae nātiōnēs
incolerent neque quem ūsum bellī habērent aut quibus īnstitūtīs ūterentur neque quī essent ad majōrem nāvium multi- 15
tūdinem idōneī portūs reperīre¹ poterat.

Ad haec cognōscenda, priusquam perīculum faceret,° idōneum esse arbitrātus C. Volusēnum° cum nāve longā praemittit. Huic mandat ut explōrātīs omnibus rēbus ad sē quam
prīmum revertātur. 20

Ipse cum omnibus cōpiīs in Morinōs proficīscitur, quod inde
erat brevissimus in Britanniam trājectus.° Hūc² nāvēs undique ex fīnitimīs regiōnibus et quam° superiōre aestāte ad
Veneticum bellum³ fēcerat classem jubet convenīre.

Interim, cōnsiliō ejus cognitō et per mercātōrēs perlātō ad 25
Britannōs, ā complūribus īnsulae cīvitātibus ad eum lēgātī
veniunt quī polliceantur obsidēs dare atque imperiō populī
Rōmānī obtemperāre.

Quibus audītīs, līberāliter pollicitus hortātusque ut in eā
sententiā permanērent, eōs domum remittit et cum eīs ūnā 30
Commium, quem ipse, Atrebātibus superātīs, rēgem ibi° cōnstituerat, cujus et virtūtem et cōnsilium° probābat et quem
sibi fidēlem esse arbitrābātur,⁴ cujusque auctōritās in hīs
regiōnibus magnī habēbātur,° mittit.

Huic imperat⁵ quās possit adeat cīvitātēs° hortēturque ut 35
populī Rōmānī fidem sequantur,° sēque celeriter eō ventūrum
nūntiet. Volusēnus, perspectīs regiōnibus, quantum eī facul-
tātis darī potuit° quī nāve ēgredī ac sē barbarīs committere
nōn audēret, quīntō diē ad Caesarem revertitur quaeque ibi
perspexisset renūntiat. 40

---

¹The indirect questions (**quanta . . . portūs**) depend on **reperīre.** Before invading
Britain, Caesar was trying to get information from Gallic traders.

²This harbor was Gesoriacum (now Boulogne). See map on page 314.

³This refers to a minor revolt of some coastal tribes of Gaul. See map on page 314.

⁴Caesar gives his reasons for entrusting Commius with an important mission. Later,
Commius disappointed him by leading a revolt (52 B.C.).

⁵The orders are expressed by the subjunctives **adeat, hortētur, nūntiet,** in noun
clauses. Note that verbs of commanding often take the subjunctive without **ut.**

Relief from Trajan's column showing Roman soldiers loading a ship.

Model of a Roman military standard, a symbol of the pride of the Roman army

Dum in hīs locīs Caesar nāvium parandārum causā morātur,
ex magnā parte Morinōrum ad eum lēgātī vēnērunt quī sē dē
superiōris temporis cōnsiliō° excūsārent, quod° hominēs barbarī et nostrae cōnsuētūdinis imperītī bellum populō Rōmānō fēcissent, sēque ea quae imperāsset factūrōs polli- 45
cērentur.

Hoc sibi Caesar satis opportūnē accidisse arbitrātus, quod
neque post tergum hostem relinquere volēbat neque bellī
gerendī propter annī tempus facultātem habēbat neque hās
tantulārum° rērum occupātiōnēs Britanniae antepōnendās 50
jūdicābat, magnum eīs numerum obsidum imperat. Quibus
adductīs, eōs in fidem recipit.

Nāvibus circiter LXXX onerāriīs coāctīs, quot satis esse ad duās trānsportandās legiōnēs exīstimābat, quod praetereā nāvium longārum habēbat° quaestōrī, lēgātīs praefectīsque distribuit. Hūc accēdēbant° XVIII onerāriae nāvēs, quae ex eō locō ā° mīlibus passuum VIII[1] ventō tenēbantur quōminus in eundem portum venīre possent°; hās equitibus tribuit. 55

Reliquum exercitum Q. Titūriō Sabīnō et L. Aurunculeiō Cottae lēgātīs in Menapiōs atque in eōs pāgōs Morinōrum ā quibus ad eum lēgātī nōn vēnerant dūcendum dedit. P. Sulpicium Rūfum lēgātum cum eō praesidiō quod satis esse arbitrābātur portum tenēre jussit. 60

°**hostibus ... subministrāta (esse)** had been supplied from there to our enemies • **fore** (=**futūrum esse**) it would be (of great advantage to him) • **illō** (adv.) to that place • **perīculum faceret** should incur any risk • **idōneum ... Volusēnum** = **C. Volusēnum quem idōneum** (a suitable man) **esse arbitrābātur** • **trājectus, -ūs** M., passage • **quam** (agreeing with **classem,** its antecedent) • **ibi** (i.e., among the Atrebates) • **cōnsilium** discretion • **magnī habēbātur** was highly regarded **quās ... cīvitātēs** to go to whatever states he could • **fidem sequantur** put themselves under the protection • **quantum ... potuit** as much as a man could (lit., as much of opportunity as could be given to one) • **dē ... cōnsiliō** for their attitude in the past • **quod** on the ground that • **tantulārum** unimportant **quod ... habēbat** the additional warships which he (Caesar) had (lit., whatever of warships he had besides) • **hūc accēdēbant** in addition to these, there were • **ā** away, off • **quōminus possent** so that they could not

antepōnō	3 place ahead	**obtemperō**	1 obey
distribuō	3 assign, divide	**perspiciō**	3 observe; explore
excūsō	1 excuse; **sē excūsāre** = offer excuses	**quaestor**	M., quaestor[2]
		tribuō	3 assign; pay
hiems	F., winter; storm		

[1]Caesar sailed from Gesoriacum; the cavalry, from Portus Itius, eight miles north of there. See map on page 314.

[2]The number of quaestors varied from an original two to forty in Caesar's time. In Rome, a quaestor served as a magistrate in charge of finances; in the field, as paymaster and staff officer.

On this relief, picturing a Roman warship filled with soldiers, the steersman stands by the rudder, in front of the shelter he used in bad weather. (Vatican)

OPERATION CHANNEL

Since Britain was almost completely unknown, Caesar exercised great caution, trying to gain as much information as possible before committing his fleet. The submission of the Veneti, which had been enforced the previous summer, was a further advantage. Some of the ships built then were useful for this expedition. And since the Morini had also been subdued, he could set sail for Britain.

Hīs cōnstitūtīs rēbus, nactus idōneam ad nāvigandum tempestātem tertiā ferē vigiliā solvit equitēsque in ulteriōrem portum prōgredī et nāvēs cōnscendere et sē sequī jussit. Ā quibus cum paulō tardius[1] esset administrātum, ipse hōrā diēī circiter quārtā[2] cum prīmīs nāvibus Britanniam attigit atque 5 ibi in omnibus collibus[3] expositās hostium cōpiās armātās cōn-

[1] i.e., too slowly to take advantage of the favoring winds which carried Caesar to Britain. A change of wind kept the cavalry in port for three days.

[2] About 10 A.M.

[3] The cliffs at Dover, 28 miles across the Channel from Boulogne (Gesoriacum).

spexit. Cujus locī haec° erat nātūra, atque ita montibus mare continēbātur utī ex locīs superiōribus in lītus tēlum adigī posset. Hunc ad ēgrediendum nēquāquam° idōneum locum arbitrātus, dum reliquae nāvēs° eō convenīrent, ad hōram 10 nōnam in ancorīs expectāvit.

Interim lēgātīs tribūnīsque mīlitum convocātīs, et quae ex Volusēnō cognōvisset et quae fierī vellet ostendit monuitque, ut reī mīlitāris ratiō maximēque ut maritimae rēs postulārent,° ut, cum celerem atque īnstabilem mōtum habērent,° ad nūtum° 15 et ad tempus° omnēs rēs ab eīs administrārentur.[1]

Hīs dīmissīs, et ventum et aestum ūnō tempore nactus secundum, datō signō et sublātīs ancorīs, circiter mīlia passuum VII ab eō locō prōgressus apertō ac plānō lītore nāvēs cōnstituit.   20

At barbarī, cōnsiliō Rōmānōrum cognitō, praemissō equitātū et essedāriīs,° quō plērumque genere° in proeliīs utī cōnsuērunt, reliquīs cōpiīs subsecūtī nostrōs nāvibus ēgredī prohibēbant.

Caesar's men were utterly untrained for an amphibious landing, while the enemy enjoyed all the natural advantages of being based on dry land. It was only the support of their "naval artillery" which gave the Romans a more even chance.

Erat ob hās causās summa difficultās, quod nāvēs propter 25 magnitūdinem nisi in altō° cōnstituī nōn poterant, mīlitibus°

---

[1] The noun clause **ut . . . omnēs rēs administrārentur** (that . . . all things be done) is the object of **monuit.**

British arrowheads of bronze

autem ignōtīs locīs, impedītīs manibus magnō et gravī onere armōrum pressīs, simul et dē nāvibus dēsiliendum° et in flūctibus cōnsistendum° et cum hostibus erat pugnandum, cum illī° aut ex āridō aut paulum in aquam prōgressī, omnibus 30 membrīs expedītīs, nōtissimīs locīs audācter tēla conjicerent et equōs īnsuēfactōs° incitārent.

Quibus rēbus nostrī perterritī atque hujus omnīnō generis pugnae imperītī non eādem alacritāte ac studiō quō in pedestribus ūtī proeliīs cōnsuērant ūtēbantur. 35

Quod ubi Caesar animadvertit, nāvēs longās,[1] quārum et speciēs erat barbarīs inūsitātior° et mōtus ad ūsum expedītior,° paulum removērī ab onerāriīs nāvibus et rēmīs incitārī et ad latus apertum hostium cōnstituī atque inde fundīs, sagittīs, tormentīs hostēs prōpellī ac submovērī jussit;° quae rēs° 40 magnō ūsuī nostrīs fuit. Nam et nāvium figūrā et rēmōrum mōtū et inūsitātō genere tormentōrum permōtī barbarī cōnstitērunt ac paulum etiam pedem rettulērunt.

Atque nostrīs mīlitibus cūnctantibus, maximē propter altitūdinem maris, quī° x legiōnis aquilam ferēbat, obtestātus° 45 deōs, ut ea rēs legiōnī fēlīciter ēvenīret, "Dēsilīte," inquit, "commīlitōnēs, nisi vultis aquilam hostibus prōdere. Ego certē meum reī pūblicae atque imperātōrī officium praestiterō.°"

Hoc cum vōce magnā dīxisset, sē ex nāve prōjēcit atque in 50 hostēs aquilam ferre coepit. Tum nostrī, cohortātī inter sē° nē tantum dēdecus° admitterētur, ūniversī ex nāve dēsiluērunt. Hōs item ex proximīs nāvibus cum cōnspexissent,° subsecūtī hostibus appropinquāvērunt.

°**haec** such • **nēquāquam** in no way • **reliquae nāvēs** (i.e., the cavalry transports) • **ut reī ... postulārent** as the rules of war and especially as naval operations demand • **cum ... habērent** inasmuch as they have (to do with) rapid and irregular movements • **ad nūtum** at a nod • **ad tempus** on the instant **essedārius, -ī** M., charioteer • **quō genere** a kind (of troops) which • **in altō** in deep water • **mīlitibus ... dēsiliendum** our soldiers, however, in unfamiliar places, with hands encumbered (by

[1]The warships of the Romans had oars and differed in shape from the trading vessels that visited Britain. The Britons themselves used small wicker boats covered with skins.

weapons) and weighed down by a great (heavy) weight of armor, had to leap down from the ships • **cōnsistendum** had to get a foothold **cum illī** while they (i.e., the Britons) • **īnsuēfactus, -a, -um** well-trained • **inūsitātior** (comp. of **inūsitātus, -a, -um,** unfamiliar) less familiar • **(quārum) mōtus . . . expedītior** which were more easily managed (lit., whose motion was freer for use) **jussit** (governing five infinitives, the first three with **nāvēs** as subject, the last two with **hostēs**) • **quae rēs** this maneuver • **quī** the man who • **obtestātus** having called on • **praestiterō** I shall have performed • **inter sē** one another • **dēdecus** N., disgrace • **Hōs . . . cōnspexissent** Also when (the soldiers) from the nearest ships had seen these

commilitō	M., fellow soldier	**membrum**	N., limb, part
cūnctor	1 hesitate, delay		of the body
expōnō	3 draw up; land	⁺**tormentum**	N., military
flūctus	M., wave, flood		machine; pl.,
funda	F., sling (shot)		artillery
⁺**incitō**	1 spur on; propel;	**ūniversus**	(adj.) all, all
	(with **rēmīs**) row		together

The scouting boats Caesar used in his invasion of Britain were similar to the fishing boat seen in this mosaic.

291

A relief from Trajan's column of small boats loaded with Roman soldiers

WINNING A BEACHHEAD

Once more the tenth legion had set the example. The legionaries were now on the beach, but the Britons still held a firm position on higher ground. It took all the soldiers' skill and Caesar's brilliant leadership to overcome this handicap.

Caesar pointed out that, inasmuch as the cavalry transports did not arrive, his usual good luck—which every successful general needs—had failed him.

Pugnātum est ab utrīsque ācriter. Nostrī tamen, quod neque ōrdinēs servāre neque firmiter īnsistere neque signa

subsequī poterant, atque alius aliā ex nāve,° quibuscumque
signīs occurrerat sē aggregābat,° magnopere perturbābantur.

Hostēs vērō, nōtīs omnibus vadīs, ubi ex lītore aliquōs 5
singulārēs ex nāve ēgredientēs cōnspexerant,[1] incitātīs equīs,
impedītōs adoriēbantur, plūrēs paucōs circumsistēbant, aliī
ab latere apertō in ūniversōs° tēla conjiciēbant.

Quod cum animadvertisset Caesar, scaphās° longārum
nāvium, item speculātōria nāvigia° mīlitibus complērī jussit 10
et, quōs° labōrantēs cōnspexerat, hīs subsidia submittēbat.

Nostrī, simul° in āridō cōnstitērunt, suīs omnibus cōnse-
cūtīs, in hostēs impetum fēcērunt atque eōs in fugam dedērunt, neque° longius prōsequī potuērunt, quod equitēs
cursum tenēre atque īnsulam capere° nōn potuerant. Hoc 15
ūnum ad prīstinam fortūnam Caesarī dēfuit.°

Hostēs proeliō superātī, simul atque sē ex fugā recēpērunt,
statim ad Caesarem lēgātōs dē pāce mīsērunt; obsidēs sēsē
datūrōs quaeque imperāsset factūrōs pollicitī sunt.

Ūnā cum hīs lēgātīs Commius Atrebās vēnit, quem suprā 20
dēmōnstrāveram ā Caesare in Britanniam praemissum.

Hunc illī ē nāve ēgressum, cum ad eōs ōrātōris modō°
Caesaris mandāta dēferret, comprehenderant atque in vincula
conjēcerant. Tum, proeliō factō, remīsērunt et in petendā
pāce ejus reī culpam in multitūdinem[2] contulērunt et propter 25
imprūdentiam° ut ignōscerētur° petīvērunt.

More bad luck was yet to come for the Romans. In addition to the
high tide at full moon (more than sixteen feet at Deal as against a few
inches in the Mediterranean), a violent storm struck. The effect on the
fleet was all but disastrous.

Caesar's mention of the full moon (p. 295, l. 3) has made it possible
for astronomers to determine the exact date: the moon was full on
August 30; Caesar had first landed on August 26, 55 B.C.

Caesar questus quod, cum ultrō in continentem, lēgātīs
missīs, pācem ab sē petīssent, bellum sine causā intulissent,

---

[1]The past perfect is used instead of the usual perfect after **ubi** in order to express
repeated action: "whenever the enemy saw (had seen)." The following imperfects also
express repeated action, an idea that can often be conveyed in English by use of the
auxiliary "would"; e.g., "several (of the enemy) would surround a few."

[2]Probably the leaders had been equally responsible.

ignōscere sē imprūdentiae dīxit obsidēsque imperāvit; quōrum
illī partem statim dedērunt, partem ex longinquiōribus locīs 30
arcessītam paucīs diēbus sēsē datūrōs dīxērunt.

Intereā suōs remigrāre in agrōs jussērunt, prīncipēsque
undique convenīre et sē cīvitātēsque suās Caesarī commendāre
coepērunt.

°**alius aliā ex nāve** men from different ships (lit., one from one ship,
another from another) • **quibuscumque . . . aggregābat** gathered about whatever standards they happened on • **in ūniversōs**
against the main body • **scaphās** skiffs (small messenger boats
belonging to the warships) • **speculātōria nāvigia** scouting
boats (light, swift-sailing vessels used in reconnoitering. They were
camouflaged with green paint, and the sailors wore green clothing.
Both the **scaphae** and the **speculātōria nāvigia** could be rowed into
shallow water.) • **quōs** (having **hīs** as its antecedent) • **simul**
= simul atque • **neque** but . . . not • **capere** reach
Hoc . . . dēfuit In this (respect) alone did Caesar's usual good fortune
fail him. • **ōrātōris modō** as (in the character of) an ambassador
imprūdentia F., ignorance (of the rights of envoys) • **ut ignōsce-**
rētur that they be pardoned. (Verbs governing the dative are used
impersonally in the passive. What would be the form of the subject
"they," if expressed?)

adorior	4 attack	**īnsistō**	3 stand, take
circumsistō	3 surround		a stand
commendō	1 surrender, entrust	**prōsequor**	3 pursue
continēns	F., continent	**remigrō**	1 return
culpa	F., blame, guilt	+**ultrō**	(adv.) voluntarily

A TEMPORARY SETBACK

Hīs rēbus pāce cōnfirmātā, post diem quārtum quam° est in
Britanniam ventum nāvēs XVIII, dē quibus suprā dēmōnstrā-
tum est, quae equitēs sustulerant, ex superiōre portū lēnī
ventō solvērunt. Quae cum appropinquārent Britanniae et ex
castrīs vidērentur, tanta tempestās subitō coörta est ut nūlla 5
eārum cursum tenēre posset, sed aliae eōdem unde erant pro-
fectae referrentur, aliae ad īnferiōrem partem īnsulae, quae
est propius sōlis occāsum, magnō suō cum perīculō dējiceren-
tur; quae tamen, ancorīs jactīs, cum flūctibus complērentur,

A cargo ship *(nāvis onerāria)* was carved in relief on the front of a Roman burial chest now in the Museum of Antiquities in Beirut, Lebanon.

necessāriō adversā nocte° in altum prōvectae° continentem 10 petīvērunt.

Eādem nocte accidit ut esset lūna plēna, quī diēs maritimōs aestūs[1] maximōs in Ōceanō efficere cōnsuēvit;° nostrīsque[2] id erat incognitum. Ita ūnō tempore et longās nāvēs, quās Caesar in āridum subdūxerat, aestus complēbat, et onerāriās, 15 quae ad ancorās erant dēligātae, tempestās afflīctābat, neque ūlla nostrīs facultās aut administrandī° aut auxiliandī° dabātur.

Complūribus nāvibus frāctīs, reliquae cum essent, fūnibus,° ancorīs, reliquīsque armāmentīs° āmissīs, ad nāvigandum inūtilēs, magna,° id quod necesse erat accidere, tōtīus exer- 20 citūs perturbātiō facta est.

Neque enim nāvēs erant aliae° quibus reportārī possent, et° omnia dēerant quae ad reficiendās nāvēs erant ūsuī, et,° quod

---

[1]The tides rise to the height of nineteen feet at Dover and twenty-five feet at Boulogne. In the Mediterranean the tides are so slight as to be hardly noticeable.

[2]Caesar could not have known this either. A more modest writer might have written **Caesarī** instead of **nostrīs**.

This figure of a Roman soldier, originally on his tomb, was found in London. It had been used in the fill of a wall.

omnibus cōnstābat° hiemārī in Galliā oportēre, frūmentum in
hīs locīs in hiemem prōvīsum nōn erat. 25

When the Britons saw Caesar's plight, they resumed fighting. In
particular they harassed one legion that was on a supply mission, and
also tried to attack the Roman camp.

Quibus rēbus cognitīs, prīncipēs Britanniae, quī post proelium ad Caesarem convēnerant, inter sē collocūtī, cum et
equitēs et nāvēs et frūmentum Rōmānīs dēesse intellegerent
et paucitātem mīlitum ex castrōrum exiguitāte cognōscerent,°
quae hōc° erant etiam angustiōra, quod sine impedīmentīs 30

Caesar legiōnēs trānsportāverat, optimum factū° esse dūxērunt,° rebelliōne factā, frūmentō commeātūque nostrōs prohibēre et rem in hiemem prōdūcere, quod, hīs superātīs aut°
reditū interclūsīs, nēminem posteā bellī īnferendī causā in
Britanniam trānsitūrum cōnfīdēbant. Itaque paulātim ex 35
castrīs discēdere et suōs clam ex agrīs dēdūcere coepērunt.

°post . . . quam = quārtō diē postquam • **adversā nocte** in
the face of the night (lit., with the night against them) • **prōvectae**
having set out • **quī diēs efficere cōnsuēvit** a time which always
causes • **administrandī** of managing (the ships) • **auxiliandī** of
aiding • **fūnis, -is** M., rope • **armāmenta** N. pl., rigging
magna (modifying **perturbātiō**) • **Neque . . . aliae** For on the
one hand there were no other ships • **et . . . et** on the other
hand . . . then, too • **omnibus cōnstābat** it was evident to all
(The subject of the impersonal **cōnstābat** is the infinitive **oportēre.**)
cognōscerent (depending on **cum**) • **hōc** (abl. of degree of
difference) on this account; **hōc . . . quod** = because • **optimum
factū** the best thing to do • **dūxērunt = putāvērunt** (with
prīncipēs as subject) • **aut** or at least

afflictō	1 damage greatly	**perturbātiō**	F., alarm, disturbance
clam	(adv.) secretly	**prōdūcō**	3 prolong; lead out
coörior	4 arise	**prōvideō**	2 care for, provide
interclūdō	3 cut or shut off	**rebelliō**	F., renewal of war,
lēnis	(adj.) gentle		revolt, rebellion
paucitās	F., small number	**reficiō**	3 repair; renew

C A E S A R   R E O R G A N I Z E S

At Caesar, etsī nōndum eōrum cōnsilia cognōverat, tamen
et ex ēventū° nāvium suārum et ex eō, quod° obsidēs dare
intermīserant, fore id quod accidit suspicābātur. Itaque ad
omnēs cāsūs subsidia comparābat. Nam et frūmentum ex
agrīs cotīdiē in castra cōnferēbat et quae gravissimē afflīctae 5
erant nāvēs, eārum° māteriā atque aere ad reliquās reficiendās
ūtēbātur et quae° ad eās rēs erant ūsuī ex continentī comparārī jubēbat.

Itaque, cum summō studiō ā mīlitibus administrārētur, XII
nāvibus āmissīs, reliquīs° ut nāvigārī satis commodē posset 10
effēcit.°

Carpenters like these on a relief from the Vatican must have been among the skilled workmen who repaired vessels of Caesar's fleet damaged by the storm.

Lēgātī ab hostibus missī ad Caesarem dē pāce vēnērunt. Hīs Caesar numerum obsidum quem ante imperāverat duplicāvit eōsque in continentem addūcī jussit, quod propinquā diē aequinoctiī,[1] īnfirmīs nāvibus, hiemī nāvigātiōnem subjiciendam nōn exīstimābat.

When Caesar had his fleet in sufficient repair to venture back across the Channel, he left Britain after only about three weeks on the island.

°**ēventus** M., disaster • **ex eō, quod** from the fact that **quae . . . nāvēs, eārum** = **eārum nāvium quae** • **quae** (As antecedent, supply **ea,** subject of **comparārī.**) • **reliquīs** (in earlier than normal position for emphasis) by/with the rest • **ut nāvigārī posset effēcit** made it possible for the voyage to be made

aes	N., copper	**īnfirmus**	(adj.) weakened, weak
afflīgō	3 damage, break	**māteria**	F., material; timber
duplicō	1 double	**nāvigātiō**	F., voyage; sailing

[1]The time of the equinox was drawing near (**propinquā diē** = abl. abs.). Severe storms often occur about this time of year.

ROMAN BRITAIN

Although Caesar's landings in Britain were not a full-scale invasion, they were the forerunners of the occupation of the island which began almost one hundred years later under the Emperor Claudius. Moreover, between the time of Caesar's landings and the invasion of Claudius, the Belgae from the mainland had partially conquered Britain and had brought with them a degree of Romanization.

Claudius gave the order which initiated the Roman invasion of A.D. 43 and subsequent occupation of Britain. Later, under the Flavian emperors, the frontier was pushed far into Scotland. The Romans, however, were never able to hold this northernmost line, and after Scotland had been lost and reoccupied several times it was decided to establish a definite frontier farther south. So it was that Hadrian's Wall came to be built.

The Roman army remained in Britain until the first part of the fifth century, when the empire was crumbling under the attacks of the barbarians. During the Roman occupation of Britain there was a great difference in the life and customs of the southeastern part of the country and those of the remainder of the island. The people of the southeast had been the first to feel the effects of the Roman civilization that was then spreading throughout Gaul. Therefore they were more receptive to Romanization than the rest of the inhabitants of Britain.

The degree to which civilization spread to various parts of Roman Britain can best be seen in the towns and villas of the island. Scattered about southeast England were numerous small towns, all more or less Roman in character. Some seem to have been market towns or posting stations located along Roman roads. London apparently was a town that was purely Roman and probably did not exist before the coming of the Romans. Its inhabitants were highly Romanized, and there are many indications that Latin was the spoken language of ancient Londinium.

Towns such as Exeter and Canterbury were allowed to remain organized on a tribal basis with local government matters left in the hands of the tribal aristocracy. Even on such towns as these, however, Rome imposed her ideas of town planning.

An adaptation of the Roman villa came to be a status symbol in Britain. These houses were not copies of those built in Italy at that time, nor were they normally the homes of Italians settled in Britain by the Roman government. They were the homes of Romanized native landowners. Built for comfort and convenience, they contained such modern features as baths and central heating. Landowners who lived in these villas were better housed than any other Britons until the seventeenth century.

Above: A bit of the wall of Roman Londinium is incorporated into the structure of a London office building. Right: A shrine containing this figure of the Oriental god Mithras, favorite of Roman soldiers, was dug up and reconstructed in London. Below: Jars for ashes of the dead have crude human faces.

Facing page: An artist trained in archaeology made this reconstruction of Roman Caister, a port city recently unearthed in eastern Britain. The buildings are typical Romano-British villas unlike those of Italy. The protective ditches and bridge, the wall with its gates, the roads and buildings outside the town, and the harbor installations have all been substantiated by excavation. The wall dates from the second half of the second century A.D. Evidence for the lighthouse in the left background is not complete. The whole represents civilization in Britain after Caesar's invasions had been followed up. Under the Emperor Claudius the Romans began an occupation of Britain that lasted several centuries.

The fact that only two of the British tribes sent Caesar the hostages they had promised was ample proof that nothing more than a preliminary reconnaissance had been accomplished. Caesar realized that he needed a much larger force to conquer Britain. Therefore he quartered his army for the winter in places suitable for shipbuilding and issued orders for the construction of a large fleet; he himself went to Cisalpine Gaul.

On his return in June 54 B.C., he found a fleet of 800 vessels. This he concentrated near modern Wissant. He had yet to quiet the Treveri (in the Moselle area on the left bank of the Rhine), who threatened to make trouble. He also required the less reliable Gallic chiefs to accompany him, so that he could keep an eye on them.

A GALLIC CHIEF BIDS FOR POWER

Erat ūnā cum cēterīs[1] Dumnorīx Haeduus, dē quō ante ā nōbīs dictum est. Hunc sēcum habēre in prīmīs Caesar cōnstituerat, quod eum cupidum rērum novārum, cupidum imperī, magnī animī,° magnae inter Gallōs auctōritātis cognōverat. Accēdēbat hūc quod° in conciliō Haeduōrum Dumnorīx 5 dīxerat sibi ā Caesare rēgnum cīvitātis dēferrī; quod dictum Haeduī graviter ferēbant,[2] neque° recūsandī aut dēprecandī causā lēgātōs ad Caesarem mittere audēbant.

Id factum ex suīs hospitibus Caesar cognōverat. Ille omnibus prīmō precibus petere contendit° ut in Galliā relinquerē- 10 tur, partim quod īnsuētus nāvigandī mare timēret, partim quod religiōnibus impedīrī sēsē dīceret.

Posteāquam id obstinātē sibi negārī vīdit, omnī spē impetrandī adēmptā, prīncipēs Galliae sollicitāre, sēvocāre singulōs, hortārīque coepit utī in continentī remanērent: Nōn 15 sine causā fierī ut Gallia omnī nōbilitāte spoliārētur; id esse cōnsilium Caesaris, ut quōs in cōnspectū Galliae interficere verērētur hōs omnēs in Britanniam trāductōs necāret; fidem reliquīs interpōnere,° jūs jūrandum poscere ut quod esse ex ūsū Galliae intellēxissent commūnī cōnsiliō administrārent. 20

Haec ā complūribus ad Caesarem dēferēbantur.

---

[1] i.e., the other Gallic chiefs.

[2] The Haedui were angry because they had no king and wanted none. They were prepared to believe the statement, because Caesar had set up kings in a few other states.

A model of a Roman centurion and a bronze statuette of a Gallic chief

°**magnī animī**   (gen. of description) of haughty spirit   •   **accēdēbat hūc quod** and besides (lit., there was added to this the fact that) **neque** but . . . not   •   **petere contendit** earnestly begged **fīdem interpōnere** he pledged his word/honor (**Interpōnere** and **poscere,** like **hortārī,** depend on **coepit.**)

adimō	3 take away	**obstinātē**	(adv.) firmly,
⁺dēferō	offer; report		resolutely
dēprecor	1 protest	**partim**	(adv.) partly
dictum	N., statement	**posteāquam**	(conj.) when, after
graviter ferre	be annoyed (at)	**sēvocō**	1 call apart/aside
īnsuētus	(adj.) unaccus-	**sollicitō**	1 stir up; incite;
	tomed		disturb
jūs jūrandum	N., oath	**spoliō**	1 strip, despoil

A GALLIC MENACE IS REMOVED

Quā rē cognitā Caesar, quod tantum cīvitātī Haeduae dignitātis tribuēbat, coërcendum atque dēterrendum quibuscumque rēbus posset Dumnorīgem statuēbat°; et, quod longius ejus

These terra-cotta tiles of Gallic workmanship may have decorated a building. The one on the right is thought to be the likeness of a Gallic chief.

āmentiam prōgredī vidēbat, prōspiciendum nē quid sibi° ac reī pūblicae nocēre posset.

Itaque diēs circiter xxv in eō locō commorātus, quod Cōrus ventus nāvigātiōnem impediēbat, quī magnam partem omnis temporis in hīs locīs flāre cōnsuēvit, dabat operam ut in officiō Dumnorīgem continēret, nihilō tamen sētius° omnia ejus cōnsilia cognōsceret.

Tandem idōneam nactus tempestātem mīlitēs equitēsque cōnscendere nāvēs jubet. At omnium animīs impedītīs[1] Dumnorīx cum equitibus Haeduōrum ā castrīs, īnsciente Caesare, domum discēdere coepit.

Quā rē nūntiātā, Caesar, intermissā profectiōne atque omnibus rēbus postpositīs, magnam partem equitātūs ad eum īnsequendum mittit retrahīque imperat[2]; sī vim faciat neque pāreat, interficī jubet, nihil hunc sē absente prō sānō° factūrum arbitrātus quī° praesentis imperium° neglēxisset.

Ille autem revocātus resistere ac sē manū° dēfendere suōrumque fidem implōrāre coepit, saepe clāmitāns līberum sē līberaeque esse cīvitātis. Illī, ut erat imperātum, circumsistunt hominem atque interficiunt; at equitēs Haeduī ad Caesarem omnēs revertuntur.

[1] i.e., occupied by preparations for embarking
[2] Note the unusual infinitive with **imperō;** only a passive (or deponent) infinitive is so used.

°**coërcendum ... statuēbat**   decided that Dumnorix must be restrained
and checked by whatever means he could (**Prōspiciendum,** also, is
dependent on **statuēbat.**) • **sibi** Caesar • **nihilō sētius**
nonetheless • **prō sānō** like a sane man • **qui** since he
(Dumnorix) • **praesentis imperium** (lit., the authority of him
[Caesar] present) • **manū** (i.e., with the weapons in his hands)

āmentia	F., folly, madness	**flō**	1 blow
clāmitō	1 exclaim, cry	**noceō**	2 injure; harm
	out repeatedly	⁺**operam dare**	take pains/care
commoror	1 stay, wait,	**postpōnō**	3 lay aside; disre-
	stop		gard

A VICTORY FOR THE FLEET

Now at last the five legions and 2000 cavalry set sail for Britain,
while Labienus stayed behind with three legions and 2000 cavalry. With
these he was to protect the ports, keep up regular supplies, and be alert
to whatever might happen among the Gauls.

Accessum est ad Britanniam omnibus nāvibus merīdiānō
ferē tempore,° neque in eō locō hostis est vīsus. Ut posteā
Caesar ex captīvīs cognōvit, cum magnae manūs eō convēnissent, multitūdine nāvium perterritae, quae cum annōtinīs°
prīvātīsque, quās suī quisque commodī causā fēcerat, amplius 5
DCCC ūnō erant vīsae tempore, ā lītore discesserant ac sē in
superiōra loca abdiderant.

°**merīdiānō tempore** =**merīdiē** • **annōtinīs** last year's (ships)

FIRST CONTACT WITH THE ENEMY

Caesar, expositō exercitū et locō° castrīs idōneō captō, ex
captīvīs cognōvit quō in locō hostium cōpiae cōnsēdissent.
Cohortibus X ad mare relictīs et equitibus CCC quī praesidiō
nāvibus essent, dē tertiā vigiliā ad hostēs contendit, eō minus
veritus nāvibus° quod in lītore mollī atque apertō dēligātās ad 5
ancorās relinquēbat. Eī praesidiō nāvibusque Q. Ātrium
praefēcit.

Ipse noctū prōgressus mīlia passuum circiter XII hostium
cōpiās cōnspicātus est. Illī equitātū atque essedīs ad flūmen

prōgressī ex locō superiōre nostrōs prohibēre et proelium 10
committere coepērunt.

Repulsī ab equitātū sē in silvās abdidērunt, locum nactī
ēgregiē et nātūrā et opere° mūnītum, quem domesticī bellī, ut
vidēbātur, causā jam ante praeparāverant; nam crēbrīs arbori-
bus succīsīs omnēs introitūs erant praeclūsī.   15

The Romans easily defeated the Britons and pursued them some distance inland. They were recalled, however, by the news of the fleet's
partial destruction by a storm during the night. Though time was precious,
Caesar decided to have the fleet drawn up on the shore and protected
by a fortification. His soldiers, working day and night, completed this
task in ten days.

After the fleet was secured on the beach, Caesar began marching
his troops back to their camp near modern Canterbury.

°**locō** (i.e., a place near the seashore) • **nāvibus** (indirect
object of **veritus**) • **opere** by art

crēber	(adj.) numerous; thick	**mollis**	(adj.) smooth; soft
ēgregiē	(adv.) excellently	**praeclūdō**	3 shut/close (in
essedum	N., two-wheeled war		front)
	chariot (of the Britons)	**succīdō**	3 cut down/from
introitus	M., entrance		under

A COSTLY LESSON IN WARFARE

Equitēs hostium essedāriīque ācriter proeliō cum equitātū
nostrō in itinere° cōnflīxērunt, ita tamen ut nostrī omnibus
partibus superiōrēs fuerint atque eōs in silvās collēsque com-
pulerint; sed complūribus interfectīs cupidius īnsecūtī nōn
nūllōs ex suīs āmīsērunt.   5

At illī, intermissō spatiō, imprūdentibus° nostrīs atque
occupātīs° in mūnītiōne castrōrum, subitō sē ex silvīs ēje-
cērunt impetūque in eōs factō quī erant in statiōne prō castrīs
collocātī ācriter pugnāvērunt; duābusque missīs subsidiō[1]
cohortibus ā Caesare, atque hīs prīmīs° legiōnum duārum, 10
cum hae perexiguō° intermissō locī spatiō inter sē cōnstitis-

[1] Apparently the two cohorts left the camp by the two side gates and got around in the
rear of the enemy who were attacking in front of the camp, intending to cut off their
retreat. But as the two cohorts did not quite meet, the enemy escaped between them.

sent, novō genere pugnae perterritīs nostrīs, per mediōs
audācissimē perrūpērunt sēque inde incolumēs recēpērunt.

Eō diē Q. Laberius Dūrus, tribūnus mīlitum, interficitur.
Illī plūribus submissīs cohortibus repelluntur.   15

The Britons were beaten twice in succession. Then their leader
Cassivellaunus avoided any further pitched battles, but tried to wear the
Romans out by harassing them and by cutting off their supplies.

Caesar marched farther inland, crossing the Thames west of Londinium.
In a last effort Cassivellaunus tried an attack on the fleet—with disastrous results for the Britons, who were forced to surrender. Caesar
compelled them to give hostages and pay an annual tribute.

°**in itinere** (i.e., on the march from the sea to the camp near Canterbury) • **imprūdentibus** off their guard • **occupātīs**
engaged • **atque hīs prīmīs** and these the first (cohorts—which
contained the best officers and men) • **perexiguō ... sē** with a
very little space between them

compellō	3 drive, force	**essedārius**	M., charioteer
cōnflīgō	3 contend, fight	**perrumpō**	3 force a passage
ējiciō	3 drive out, expel	**sē ējicere**	rush (out)

Caesar's initial conquest of Britain had been extended by Roman emperors when
Legion II erected this tablet in Northumberland to display its name and symbols.

Obsidibus acceptīs, exercitum redūcit ad mare, nāvēs invenit refectās. Hīs dēductīs, quod et captīvōrum magnum numerum habēbat et nōn nūllae tempestāte dēperierant nāvēs, duōbus commeātibus° exercitum reportāre īnstituit.

Ac sīc accidit utī, ex tantō nāvium numerō, tot nāvigā- 5 tiōnibus,° neque hōc neque superiōre annō ūlla omnīnō nāvis quae mīlitēs portāret dēsīderārētur; at ex eīs quae inānēs ex continentī ad eum remitterentur, priōris° commeātūs expositīs mīlitibus, et quās posteā Labiēnus faciendās cūrāverat, numerō LX, perpaucae locum caperent,° reliquae ferē omnēs 10 rejicerentur.

Quās cum aliquamdiū Caesar frūstrā exspectāsset, nē annī tempore ā nāvigātiōne exclūderētur, quod[1] aequinoctium suberat, necessāriō angustius mīlitēs collocāvit ac summā tranquillitāte cōnsecūtā, secundā initā cum solvisset vigiliā, prīmā 15 lūce terram attigit omnēsque incolumēs nāvēs perdūxit.

It is not known whether the tribute was actually paid or not. Caesar left no troops in Britain, which was not invaded again until A.D. 43, nearly a century later.

°**commeātibus** voyages, trips • **nāvigātiōnibus** (supply **et ex**) and out of/despite so many voyages • **priōris** first • **locum caperent** reached their destination (i.e., Britain)

[1]It was, therefore, somewhere near September 20, and Caesar had been in Britain more than two months.

The Druids used a ceremonial ax such as this to cut the sacred mistletoe.

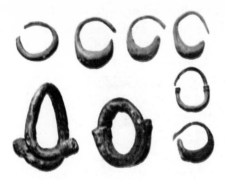

This ancient gold jewelry is of British workmanship.

aliquamdiū	(adv.) for some time	**exclūdō**	3 prevent; shut out,
angustē	(adv.) closely		cut off
dēpereō	be lost; perish	**inānis**	(adj.) empty
+dēsīderō	1 (pass.) be lost or	**+ineō**	begin, start
	missing	**subsum**	be near/at hand

ORIGIN AND CUSTOMS OF THE BRITONS

Britanniae pars interior ab eīs incolitur quōs nātōs° in īnsulā ipsā memoriā prōditum dīcunt,[1] maritima pars ab eīs quī praedae ac bellī īnferendī causā ex Belgiō trānsiērunt (quī omnēs ferē īsdem nōminibus cīvitātum appellantur quibus ortī ex cīvitātibus eō pervēnērunt) et bellō illātō ibi permānsērunt 5 atque agrōs colere coepērunt.

Hominum est īnfīnīta multitūdō crēberrimaque aedificia ferē Gallicīs cōnsimilia, pecoris magnus numerus. Ūtuntur aut nummō aureō aut tāleīs° ferreīs ad certum pondus exāminātīs prō nummō. Nāscitur ibi plumbum album° in medi- 10 terrāneīs[2] regiōnibus, in maritimīs ferrum, sed ejus exigua est cōpia; aere ūtuntur importātō.

Māteria cujusque generis ut in Galliā est praeter fāgum° atque abietem.° Leporem et gallīnam et ānserem gustāre fās

[1]The meaning is that they were descended from ancestors who sprang from the soil of Britain. A similar belief about themselves was held by other ancient races.

[2]The mines are in Cornwall, the extreme southwestern part of the island, so that Caesar is mistaken as to their location. Centuries before this time the Phoenicians had obtained tin which came from these mines.

nōn putant; haec tamen alunt animī voluptātisque° causā. 15
Loca° sunt temperātiōra quam in Galliā, remissiōribus
frīgoribus.

Caesar has given us a glimpse of the customs of the Britons. He also
attempted to give the dimensions of the island, though his statements are
far from accurate; for example, he said that the western part is opposite
Spain. On other points we can consider him more reliable. He stated
that the inhabitants of the area now called Kent (Latin **Cantium**) were
the most civilized. People in the interior of the island did not grow grain,
but lived on milk and meat and wore skins. All Britons dyed their bodies
blue in order to look ferocious in battle. They wore beards and mus-
taches, probably for the same reason.

°**quōs nātōs ... dīcunt** whose origin upon the island itself is handed
down, they say, by tradition; **quōs nātōs (esse)** = subj. of **prōditum
(esse).** • **tāleīs ferreīs** iron bars (many of which have been
found) • **plumbum album** tin (lit., white lead) • **fāgus, -ī**
F., beech tree (The beech, probably unnoticed by Caesar, is native to
Britain.) • **abiēs, -ietis** F., fir tree • **animī voluptātisque
causā** for amusement and pleasure (i.e., as pets) • **loca** N. pl.,
climate

ānser	M., goose	**⁺nāscor**	3 be produced/
cōnsimilis	(adj.) very like,		found
	similar	**nummus**	M., coin
gallīna	F., hen	**pondus**	N., weight
lepus	M., hare	**⁺remissus**	(adj.) mild
⁺mediterrāneus	(adj.) inland	**remissior**	less severe

Leather sandals found in London (*Londīnium*) are reminders of a Roman past.

310

ROMAN GAUL

When Caesar became governor of Gaul, Cisalpine Gaul—now northern Italy—had long been a Roman province and was thoroughly Romanized. The part of southern France which Caesar called Provincia (now Provence) and the lands on the borders of Spain called Gallia Narbonensis had also been under Roman authority for more than half a century.

Soon after Caesar's conquest of the rest of Gaul, emigrants from Italy pressed into Gaul, finding it full of opportunity. Trade flourished; towns grew and became wealthy. Splendid public buildings of Roman design were built, as were aqueducts and bridges. Roman roads came into Gaul, as they did everywhere Roman armies went. Roman engineers were equal even to road building in the Alps—a real test of their skill. They took advantage of natural, easy slopes instead of resorting to the switchbacks and hairpin turns of modern road builders.

Though tribal wrangling and the feudal power of tribal kings weakened Gallic unity, Gallic civilization was far from primitive, and even the Gauls most remote from Rome were not savages. They accepted what was forced on them of Roman civilization. Many good soldiers of the Roman armies came from Gaul, and famous Roman authors such as Vergil, Livy, Catullus, Nepos, Pliny the Elder, and his nephew Pliny the Younger came to Rome from towns of Cisalpine Gaul.

The original Gallic tribal organization was broken up by the Romans, and municipalities consisting mainly of Roman citizens were established to rule the territories around them. Nemausus (modern Nîmes), for example, was established as a capital in the land of the Volcae, and Vienna (Vienne, not the Austrian Vienna) ruled the country of the Allobroges.

Transalpine Gaul, of course, was not Romanized until after Caesar's time, and never so thoroughly as Cisalpine Gaul. Roman government of Transalpine Gaul was organized differently, with a single capital established at Lugdunum (modern Lyons).

Modern place names of central and northern Europe testify to Gallo-Roman influence there. Amiens recalls the name of the Ambiani, Paris the Parisii, Rheims the Remi, Soissons the Suessiones, Sens the Senones, Bourges the Bituriges, Trier (on the borders of Germany) the Treveri, and Besançon Vesontio.

One factor which helped to preserve the power of the Romans was the great admiration the Gauls felt for Augustus, Caesar's successor, which later grew into outright worship. Educated Gauls spoke and wrote Latin, and Gallic civilization retained its Roman aspect until after the death of Charlemagne and the dissolution of his empire in the ninth century.

Above: Fine pottery and well-finished metal trappings were found in this grave of a Gallic chieftain.

Below: The excellently preserved Roman arena and theater, seen among the buildings of modern Arles, testify to the fine quality of Romano-Gallic buildings.

Above: Modern Alpine road utilizing hairpin turns where the elevations are steep

The Alpine road below, which utilizes easy grades, follows a route that was originally laid out by the Romans.

ROMAN TERRITORY
at the
End of the Republic

COLCHIS

Phasis

Tigris

ARABIA

SARMATIA

PONTUS EUXINUS

CILICIA

CYPRUS

Sidon
Tyrus

RHODUS

AEGY

Nilus

THRACIA

ASIA

CRETA

Mare Aegaeum

MACEDONIA

Larisa

Pharsalus

ACHAIA

Dyrrachium

Mare Ionium

INTERNUM

(Mediterranean Sea)

Mare
Libycum

MARE

SICILIA

MELITA

Mare Suebicum

Vistula

GERMANIA

Danuvius

Albis

Rhenus

ALPES

Mare Adriaticum

Brundisium

APULIA

Mare
Adriaticum

Ravenna

Ariminum

Arretium

Sentinum

Ancona

ITALIA

SAMNIUM

APENNINUS

Roma

Mare Tyrrhenum

Thapsus

AFRICA

Mare
Germanicum

BRITANNIA

Camulodunum

Londinium

Dubris

Portus Itius

Gesoriacum

Fretum Gallicum

Tamesis

CANTIUM

Aquae
Sulis

OCEANUS
BRITANNICUS

HIBERNIA

Sequana

Liger

GALLIA

Locus
Lemannus

Rhodanus

Massilia

ALLOBROGES

GALLIA
CISALPINA

Padus

Narbo

Sinus
Gallicus

NARBONENSIS

CORSICA

SARDINIA

BALIARES

Garunna

PYRENAEI

Tarraco

HISPANIA
CITERIOR

Hiberus

Mare
Cantabricum

Durius

Anas

HISPANIA

Italica

Corduba

Carmo

Munda

Baetis

ULTERIOR

Gades

Mare Ibericum

MAURETANIA

OCEANUS ATLANTICUS

SCALE OF MILES

(LAMBERT CONFORMAL CONIC PROJECTION)

0 100 200 300 400 500 600

A large, well-organized rebellion of the conquered Gallic tribes against Caesar was led by Vercingetorix, whose portrait and name ornament this Gallic coin. Part of this unit deals with the siege of Alesia, the center of Vercingetorix' rebellion.

AN UNEASY WINTER

Returning from Britain, Caesar established a series of camps throughout Belgian territory. Since the grain harvest had been exceptionally small, Caesar dispersed his army for the winter more widely than usual. Nevertheless he kept his several detachments within (what he considered) easy reach of each other.

A legion of recruits, reinforced by five veteran cohorts, was under the command of officers Sabinus and Cotta. At the instigation of Indutiomarus, a chief of the Treveri, the Eburones made a sudden attack on that camp. When they were repulsed, Ambiorix, one of the leaders, asked for a conference. He promised the Romans not to hinder their march, if they agreed to withdraw from camp. The treacherous Eburones, however, caught the Romans in an ambush and almost annihilated them.

Only fifty miles away there was another camp, under the command of Quintus Cicero, brother of the famous orator. Before the great disaster became known to the Romans, Ambiorix joined the Nervii and persuaded them to attack Cicero's camp. The methods used by the Gauls in their siege of this camp show that they were quick to learn and imitate Roman techniques. Cicero's only hope lay in getting word to Caesar.

RESISTANCE AGAINST ODDS

Mittuntur ad Caesarem cōnfestim ā Cicerōne[1] litterae, magnīs prōpositīs praemiīs, sī pertulissent.° Obsessīs omnibus viīs, missī° intercipiuntur. Noctū ex eā māteriā quam mūnītiōnis causā comportāverant turrēs admodum cxx excitantur; incrēdibilī celeritāte quae dēesse operī vidēbantur 5 perficiuntur.

Hostēs posterō diē, multō majōribus coāctīs cōpiīs, castra oppugnant; fossam complent. Ā nostrīs eādem ratiōne quā prīdiē resistitur. Hoc idem reliquīs deinceps fit diēbus.

Nūlla pars nocturnī temporis ad labōrem intermittitur; 10 nōn aegrīs, nōn vulnerātīs facultās quiētis datur. Quaecumque ad proximī diēī oppugnātiōnem opus sunt, noctū comparantur. Multae praeustae sudēs,° magnus mūrālium pīlōrum° numerus īnstituitur; turrēs contabulantur°; pinnae lōrīcaeque° ex crātibus° attexuntur.° 15

Ipse Cicerō, cum tenuissimā valētūdine° esset, nē noc-

---

[1]Quintus Cicero, younger brother of the orator Marcus Cicero

turnum quidem sibi tempus ad quiētem relinquēbat, ut ultrō°
mīlitum concursū ac vōcibus sibi parcere cōgerētur.

Tum ducēs prīncipēsque Nerviōrum, quī aliquem sermōnis
aditum° causamque amīcitiae cum Cicerōne habēbant, collo- 20
quī sēsē velle dīcunt.

Factā potestāte, eadem quae Ambiorīx[1] cum Titūriō ēgerat
commemorant: omnem Galliam esse in armīs; Germānōs
Rhēnum trānsīsse; Caesaris reliquōrumque hīberna oppug-
nārī. Addunt etiam dē Sabīnī morte; Ambiorīgem ostentant° 25
fideī faciendae causā.

Errāre eōs° dīcunt, sī quicquam ab eīs praesidiī spērent
quī suīs rēbus diffīdant°; sēsē tamen hōc esse in Cicerōnem
populumque Rōmānum animō° ut nihil nisi hīberna recūsent
atque hanc inveterāscere° cōnsuētūdinem nōlint; licēre illīs 30
per sē° incolumibus ex hībernīs discēdere et quāscumque in
partēs velint sine metū proficīscī.

Cicerō ad haec ūnum modo respondet: nōn esse cōnsuētūdinem populī Rōmānī accipere ab hoste armātō condiciōnem;
sī ab armīs discēdere° velint, sē adjūtōre ūtantur lēgātōsque 35
ad Caesarem mittant; spērāre sē prō ejus jūstitiā quae petī-
verint impetrātūrōs.

°**sī pertulissent** if they (the messengers) should deliver them • **missī**
the messengers; lit., (those) sent • **praeustae sudēs** stakes burned
at the end (serving in place of javelins) • **mūrālium pīlōrum** of
wall javelins; i.e., large pikes hurled from the walls • **contabulō,
-āre** build up in stories • **pinnae lōrīcaeque** battlements and
breastworks • **crātibus** interwoven branches, wickerwork
attexuntur were fastened (to the towers) • **tenuissimā valētūdine** in/of very delicate health • **ultrō** actually • **sermōnis aditum** pretext for talking • **ostentō, -āre** show, display • **eōs** these (Cicero's men) • **ab eīs quī . . . diffīdant**
from those who were in doubt of their own safety; i.e., the legions in the
other camps • **hōc esse animō** were of this mind • **invete-
rāscere** become ·established; lit., grow old • **per sē** so far as
they were concerned • **ab armīs discēdere** to lay down their
arms

[1]Ambiorix had actually on that occasion spoken to (**ēgerat cum**) envoys, not to Titurius
Sabinus himself. Later, after killing Sabinus and his men by treachery, Ambiorix joined the
Nervii, who were attacking Cicero's camp.

Left: A model of siege works made from Caesar's description. Right: A barbarian chieftain. Above: A cavalryman's tombstone shows him riding over a fallen enemy. Can you find a word in the inscription that tells his nationality?

318

adjūtor	M., helper	intercipiō	3 intercept
+admodum	(adv., with num.) fully	oppugnātiō	F., assault, attack, siege
cōnfestim	(adv.) at once	+praesidium	N., relief, help
deinceps	(adv.) in succession	prīdiē	(adv.) (on) the day before
+excitō	1 erect		
+īnstituō	3 provide	turris	F., tower

THE GAULS HAD THEIR TROUBLES, TOO

Ab hāc spē[1] repulsī Nerviī vāllō pedum x et fossā pedum
xv hīberna cingunt. Haec et° superiōrum annōrum cōnsuētūdine ā nōbīs cognōverant et, quōsdam dē exercitū nactī
captīvōs, ab hīs docēbantur; sed, nūllā ferrāmentōrum° cōpiā
quae essent ad hunc ūsum idōnea, gladiīs caespitēs° circum- 5
cīdere,° manibus sagulīsque terram exhaurīre° cōgēbantur.

Quā quidem ex rē hominum multitūdō cognōscī potuit;
nam minus hōrīs tribus mīlium passuum III in circuitū mūnītiōnem perfēcērunt. Reliquīs diēbus turrēs ad° altitūdinem
vāllī, falcēs° testūdinēsque,° quās eīdem captīvī docuerant, 10
parāre ac facere coepērunt.

Septimō oppugnātiōnis diē, maximō coörtō ventō, ferventēs
fūsilī ex argillā glandēs[2] fundīs et fervefacta jacula° in casās,
quae mōre Gallicō strāmentīs° erant tēctae, jacere coepērunt.
Hae celeriter ignem comprehendērunt et ventī magnitūdine 15
in omnem locum castrōrum distulērunt.° Hostēs maximō
clāmōre, sīcutī partā jam atque explōrātā victōriā,° turrēs
testūdinēsque agere et scālīs° vāllum ascendere coepērunt.

At tanta mīlitum virtūs atque ea° praesentia animī fuit ut,
cum undique flammā torrērentur° maximāque tēlōrum multi- 20
tūdine premerentur suaque omnia impedīmenta atque omnēs
fortūnās cōnflagrāre° intellegerent, nōn modo dē vāllō dēcē-
deret nēmō, sed paene nē respiceret quidem quisquam, ac
tum omnēs ācerrimē fortissimēque pugnārent.

Hic diēs nostrīs longē gravissimus fuit; sed tamen hunc 25
habuit ēventum,° ut eō diē maximus numerus hostium vul-

---

[1]i.e., hope of trapping Cicero and his men if they left their camp

[2]Experiments have shown that "red-hot balls of molded clay" (ferventēs . . . glandēs)
can set fire to straw. It has been suggested that the slings from which these balls were
thrown must have been lined with metal.

Left: Gauls were excellent workers in metal, as evidenced by this bronze dagger.
Above: These Gallic spear points and sword, which were found at the site of Alesia, are in the Museum of Saint Germain-en-Laye, near Paris.
Below: A chest containing an elaborate collection of jewelry and valuables of a Roman woman were found at Alesia. Notice the lock.

nerārētur atque interficerētur, ut sē sub ipsō vāllō cōnstī-
pāverant° recessumque° prīmīs ultimī nōn dabant.

Paulum quidem intermissā flammā et quōdam locō turrī
adāctā et contingente° vāllum, tertiae cohortis centuriōnēs ex 30
eō quō stābant locō recessērunt suōsque omnēs remōvērunt.

Nūtū° vōcibusque hostēs, sī introīre° vellent, vocāre coepērunt; quōrum prōgredī ausus est nēmō. Tum ex omnī parte
lapidibus conjectīs dēturbātī,° turrisque incēnsa est.

°**et** (correlative with the following **et;** may be omitted in translation)
ferrāmentum N., iron tool • **caespitēs** M. pl., sod • **cir-
cumcidere** to cut • **manibus . . . exhaurīre** to take out the
earth with (their) hands and (carry it away) in (their) cloaks • **ad** in
proportion to • **falcēs** F. pl., (wall) hooks (for pulling down the
palisades of the rampart) • **testūdinēs** F. pl., sheds • **fervefacta jacula** N. pl., heated javelins • **strāmentīs** with straw
distulērunt (from **differō**) spread; i.e., the embers from the huts spread
the fire. • **sīcutī . . . victōriā** as if victory were already won and
certain • **scālae** F. pl., scaling ladder(s) • **ea** such
torreō, -ēre scorch, burn • **cōnflagrō, -āre** be on fire
ēventus, -ūs M., outcome • **cōnstīpō, -āre** crowd (What is
the meaning of **ut** with the indicative?) • **recessus, -ūs** M.,
(chance to) retreat • **turrī . . . contingente** (abl. abs.) • **nūtū**
by a nod/sign • **introeō, -īre** come in, enter • **dēturbātī
(sunt)** they (the enemy) were driven back

GOOD NEWS—HELP IS ON THE WAY!

Cum gravior atque asperior° fieret oppugnātiō, magnā
parte mīlitum cōnfectā vulneribus, crēbriōrēs litterae nūntiī-
que ad Caesarem mittēbantur; quōrum pars capta in cōnspectū nostrōrum mīlitum cum cruciātū necābātur. Gallus
quīdam autem, nōmine Verticō, quī ad Cicerōnem fūgerat, 5
servō suō spē lībertātis magnīsque praemiīs persuāsit ut
litterās ad Caesarem dēferret. Hās litterās ille in jaculō
illigātās° effert, et Gallus inter Gallōs sine ūllā suspīciōne
versātus° ad Caesarem pervenit.

Caesar, acceptīs litterīs, nūntium in Bellovacōs ad M. 10
Crassum mittit; jubet mediā nocte legiōnem proficīscī celeriterque ad sē venīre. Alterum° ad C. Fabium lēgātum mittit

ut in Atrebātium fīnēs legiōnem addūcat. Scrībit Labiēnō ut, sī possit, cum legiōne ad fīnēs Nerviōrum veniat. Labiēnus autem veritus nē hostium impetum sustinēre nōn posset, litterās Caesarī remittit[1] quantō cum perīculō legiōnem ex hībernīs ēductūrus esset; docet omnēs equitātūs peditātūsque cōpiās Trēverōrum tria mīlia passuum ā suīs castrīs cōnsēdisse.[2]

Caesar, cōnsiliō ejus probātō, etsī opīniōne trium legiōnum dējectus° ad duās reciderat,° tamen ūnum commūnī salūtī auxilium in celeritāte pōnēbat.

Venit magnīs itineribus in Nerviōrum fīnēs. Ibi ex captīvīs cognōscit quae apud Cicerōnem gerantur quantōque in perīculō rēs sit. Tum cuidam ex equitibus Gallīs magnīs praemiīs persuādet utī ad Cicerōnem epistulam dēferat.

Hanc Graecīs cōnscrīptam litterīs[3] mittit nē, interceptā epistulā, nostra ab hostibus cōnsilia cognōscantur. Sī adīre° nōn possit, monet ut trāgulam cum epistulā ad ammentum° dēligātā intrā mūnītiōnēs castrōrum abjiciat.

In litterīs scrībit sē cum legiōnibus profectum celeriter affore°; hortātur ut prīstinam virtūtem retineat. Gallus perīculum veritus, ut erat praeceptum, trāgulam mittit.

Haec cāsū ad turrim adhaesit neque ā nostrīs bīduō° animadversa tertiō diē ā quōdam mīlite cōnspicitur; ad Cicerōnem dēfertur. Ille perlēctam° in conventū mīlitum recitat maximāque omnēs laetitiā afficit.

Tum fūmī incendiōrum[4] procul vidēbantur; quae rēs omnem dubitātiōnem° adventūs legiōnum expulit.

°**asperior** more violent • **in jaculō illigātās** tied on/to his javelin; i.e., rolled around the shaft and wrapped with cord, as if the shaft had been mended • **versātus** mingling • **alterum =
alterum nūntium** • **opīniōne dējectus** disappointed in his expectation (of) • **reciderat** had been reduced • **adīre** i.e., **(ad) Cicerōnem** • **ammentum** N., thong (The letter could not be rolled around the shaft, as was Cicero's letter to Caesar, for it

[1]Supply "explaining" or "telling" to introduce the indirect question which follows.

[2]Although Gaul was nominally under Roman control, the occupation forces held only key points and could not afford to take chances.

[3]The Latin words were probably written with the corresponding Greek characters. Evidently some of the Nervii understood Latin.

[4]Caesar was burning villages as he advanced.

had to be seen by Cicero's men.) • **affore =adfutūrum esse** (fut. inf. of **adsum**) • **bīduō** for two days • **perlēctam** (the letter which he had) read (himself) =having read the letter (himself) **dubitātiō** F., doubt, uncertainty

abjiciō	3 throw (down); hurl	**laetitia**	F., joy, rejoicing
adhaereō	2 stick (to)	**recitō**	1 read aloud
+cōnscrībō	3 write		

BETWEEN TWO FIRES

Once communication was established, Cicero and Caesar kept each other well informed. Since the enemy was numerically stronger, Caesar lured them into a disadvantageous position for fighting.

Gallī, rē cognitā per explōrātōrēs, obsidiōnem relinquunt; ad Caesarem omnibus cōpiīs contendunt. Haec erant armāta circiter mīlia LX.[1]

Cicerō, datā facultāte, Gallum alium ab eōdem Verticōne quem suprā dēmōnstrāvimus petit quī litterās ad Caesarem 5 dēferat. Hunc° admonet iter cautē° dīligenterque faciat.° Perscrībit in litterīs hostēs ab sē discessisse omnemque ad eum° multitūdinem convertisse.

Quibus litterīs circiter mediā nocte Caesar allātīs suōs facit certiōrēs eōsque ad dīmicandum animō cōnfirmat.° 10

Posterō diē lūce prīmā movet castra et circiter mīlia passuum quattuor prōgressus trāns vallem magnam et rīvum° multitūdinem hostium cōnspicātur.

Erat magnī perīculī rēs tantulīs° cōpiīs inīquō locō dīmicāre. Tum, quoniam obsidiōne līberātum Cicerōnem sciēbat, aequō 15 animō° remittendum dē celeritāte° exīstimābat.

Cōnsīdit et quam aequissimō potest locō castra commūnit, atque haec, etsī erant exigua per sē, vix hominum mīlium septem,[2] praesertim nūllīs cum impedīmentīs, tamen angustiīs viārum quam maximē potest contrahit eō cōnsiliō, ut in 20 summam contemptiōnem hostibus veniat.

---

[1]Caesar had scarcely seven thousand men to meet this formidable number of Gauls.

[2]This is a rather small number for two legions. Possibly those soldiers who were unfit for rapid marching had been left to guard the camp, and veterans may have been granted leave for the winter.

Interim, speculātōribus° in omnēs partēs dīmissīs, explōrat quō commodissimē itinere vallem trānsīre possit.

Prīmā lūce hostium equitātus ad castra accēdit proeliumque cum nostrīs equitibus committit. Caesar cōnsultō° equitēs 25 cēdere sēque in castra recipere jubet; simul ex omnibus partibus castra altiōre vāllō mūnīrī portāsque obstruī atque in hīs administrandīs rēbus quam maximē concursārī° et cum simulātiōne timōris agī jubet.

Quibus omnibus rēbus hostēs invītātī cōpiās trādūcunt 30 aciemque inīquō locō cōnstituunt, nostrīs vērō etiam dē vāllō dēductīs[1] propius accēdunt et tēla intrā mūnītiōnem ex omnibus partibus conjiciunt. Ac sīc nostrōs contempsērunt ut aliī vāllum manū scindere, aliī fossās complēre inciperent. Tum Caesar, omnibus portīs ēruptiōne factā equitātūque 35 ēmissō, celeriter hostēs in fugam dat, sīc ut pugnandī causā resisteret nēmō, magnumque ex eīs numerum occīdit atque omnēs armīs exuit.°

Even though Cicero's men were saved, the situation continued difficult for the Romans. The effect produced by the annihilation of a Roman legion could not quickly be undone. Caesar therefore decided to spend the winter 54-53 B.C. in Gaul.

Indutiomarus, eager to carry on the revolt, attacked still another camp. Labienus, the officer in charge, by pretending fear of the besiegers, got them to advance all the way to the wall of the camp. The Romans then suddenly charged out, took the Gauls by surprise, and put them to flight. Indutiomarus was killed by the pursuing Roman cavalry.

°**hunc** (referring to the messenger) • **cautē** (adv.) cautiously • **iter . . . faciat** = obj. of **admonet** (note the simple subjunctive without introductory **ut**) • **eum** = Caesar • **animō cōnfirmat** encouraged • **rivus, -ī** M., brook • **tantulīs** such small • **aequō animō** without anxiety • **remittendum dē celeritāte** that he ought to/could relax his speed • **speculātor** M., scout • **cōnsultō** (adv.) deliberately, on purpose • **concursārī** (that his men) run about • **omnēs armīs exuit** disarmed all (the rest); i.e., they threw away their weapons in their flight

[1]By withdrawing defenders from the rampart, he could give an even greater impression of fear.

+**angustiae**	F. pl., narrowness	**obsidiō**	F., blockade, siege
commūniō	4 fortify strongly, entrench	**obstruō**	3 barricade
		perscrībō	3 write, report
contemnō	3 despise, disdain	**scindō**	3 tear down, destroy
contemptiō	F., contempt	**simulātiō**	F., pretense
+**ēruptiō**	F., sortie, sally	+**tum**	(adv.) moreover

AN INTREPID LEADER IN GAUL

Early in 52 B.C. rumors of trouble in Rome reached Gaul. The Gauls, thinking that Caesar would be detained in Rome, believed that in his absence they could defeat the legions and rid themselves of the Romans.

The Carnutes struck the first blow, killing some Romans near Cenabum (modern Orléans). Encouraged by the first success, Vercingetorix, a great leader of the Arvernians, urged other tribes to revolt, and soon was regarded as the head of a group of Gallic states.

Contrary to Gallic expectation, Caesar returned at once to Gaul, and, with some difficulty, managed to join his troops. He then marched on Avaricum, the capital of the Bituriges.

Vercingetorix wished to burn Avaricum according to his "scorched earth" policy, so that the Romans would find nothing of use to them. The Bituriges, however, believed their town was impregnable and did not destroy it. After a siege of twenty-five days the Romans destroyed the town, putting to death nearly 40,000 men, women, and children.

Caesar turned next to Vercingetorix' own capital, Gergovia (near modern Clermont-Ferrand), but this town successfully resisted all attacks. Because some soldiers were too eager for booty, the Romans even suffered a minor defeat. This Roman reverse encouraged the Haedui to break their alliance with the Romans and to join Vercingetorix. Plundering one of their own towns, the Haedui got possession of Caesar's hostages. This stroke of luck was the signal for a general revolt.

THE FIRES OF REVOLT BLAZE UP

Dēfectiōne Haeduōrum cognitā, bellum augētur. Lēgā-tiōnēs in omnēs partēs circummittuntur; quantum grātiā, auctōritāte, pecūniā valent,° ad sollicitandās cīvitātēs nītun-tur.° Nactī obsidēs quōs Caesar apud eōs dēposuerat, hōrum suppliciō dubitantēs terrent. Petunt ā Vercingetorīge Haeduī 5 ut ad sē veniat ratiōnēsque bellī gerendī commūnicet. Rē impetrātā, contendunt ut ipsīs summa imperiī trādātur; et rē in contrōversiam dēductā, tōtīus Galliae concilium Bibracte indīcitur.

Conveniunt undique frequentēs.° Multitūdinis suffrāgiīs 10 rēs permittitur; ad ūnum omnēs Vercingetorīgem probant imperātōrem. Ab hōc conciliō Rēmī, Lingonēs, Trēverī āfuērunt: illī,° quod amīcitiam Rōmānōrum sequēbantur; Trēverī, quod aberant longius et ā Germānīs premēbantur, quae fuit causa quārē tōtō abessent bellō et neutrīs auxilia mitterent. 15 Magnō dolōre Haeduī ferunt° sē dējectōs prīncipātū. Queruntur fortūnae commūtātiōnem et Caesaris indulgentiam in sē requīrunt,° neque tamen, susceptō bellō, suum cōnsilium ab reliquīs sēparāre audent.

Invītī summae speī° adulēscentēs, Eporēdorīx et Virido- 20 mārus, Vercingetorīgī pārent.

Ille° imperat reliquīs cīvitātibus obsidēs, diemque eī reī cōnstituit. Omnēs equitēs, quīndecim mīlia numerō, celeriter convenīre jubet. Peditātū quem anteā habuerit sē fore contentum dīcit neque fortūnam temptātūrum aut aciē dīmicā- 25 tūrum. Sed, quoniam abundet equitātū, perfacile esse Rōmānōs dēterrēre nē pābulentur; aequō modo animō sua ipsī frūmenta corrumpant° aedificiaque incendant, quā reī familiāris jactūrā° perpetuum imperium lībertātemque sē consequī videant. 30

Hīs cōnstitūtīs rēbus, Haeduīs Segusiāvīsque, quī sunt fīnitimī prōvinciae, decem mīlia peditum imperat; hūc° addit equitēs DCCC. Hīs praeficit frātrem Eporēdorīgis bellumque īnferre Allobrogibus jubet.

Alterā ex parte Gabalōs proximōsque pāgōs Arvernōrum in 35 Helviōs, item Rutēnōs Cadūrcōsque ad fīnēs Volcārum Arecomicōrum dēpopulandōs mittit. Nihilō minus clandestīnīs nūntiīs lēgātiōnibusque Allobrogēs sollicitat, quōrum mentēs nōndum ab superiōre bellō resēdisse° spērābat. Hōrum prīncipibus pecūniās, cīvitātī autem imperium tōtīus prōvinciae 40 pollicētur.

Since the whole of Gaul was mobilizing against Caesar, the Province was seriously threatened. Caesar tried to march back closer to the Province, partly to defend it, partly to improve his supply situation. Then Vercingetorix abandoned his successful harassing technique and made the mistake of attacking the Romans openly.

°**quantum valent** so far as they could do so • **nītor, -ī** strive
frequentēs in great numbers • **illī** the former; i.e., the Remi and
the Lingones • **magnō dolōre ferunt** were greatly annoyed
requīrō, -ere miss, long for • **summae speī** of (very) great
promise = most promising • **ille** = Vercingetorix • **aequō modo animō corrumpant** only they must not hesitate to destroy
quā . . . jactūrā for by this loss/sacrifice of private property
hūc to these • **resēdisse** had settled down/become calm

aequō animō	(abl.) calmly;	**indīcō**	3 call, proclaim
	without anxiety	**neuter**	(adj./pron.) neither;
circummittō	3 send around		M. pl., neither side
commūtātiō	F., change	**pābulor**	1 forage
corrumpō	3 destroy	**peditātus**	M., infantry
dēfectiō	F., revolt, desertion	**perfacilis**	(adj.) very easy
+**dēpōnō**	3 station, place	+**permittō**	3 leave, entrust

HIGH HOPES PROVE VAIN

Ad hōs omnēs cāsūs prōvīsa erant praesidia cohortium
duārum et vīgintī, quae ex ipsā coācta prōvinciā ab L. Caesare[1]
lēgātō ad omnēs partēs oppōnēbantur.°

Helviī, suā sponte cum fīnitimīs proeliō congressī, pelluntur; et C. Valeriō Domnotaurō, Cabūrī fīliō, prīncipe cīvitātis, 5
complūribusque aliīs interfectīs, intrā oppida mūrōsque com-
pelluntur. Allobrogēs, crēbrīs ad Rhodanum dispositīs praesidiīs, magnā cūrā et dīligentiā suōs fīnēs tuentur.

Caesar, quod hostēs equitātū superiōrēs esse intellegēbat et,
interclūsīs omnibus itineribus, nūllā rē ex prōvinciā atque 10
Ītaliā sublevārī poterat, trāns Rhēnum in Germāniam mittit
ad eās cīvitātēs quās superiōribus annīs pācāverat, equitēsque
ab hīs arcessit et levis armātūrae peditēs° quī inter eōs pugnāre cōnsuērant. Eōrum adventū, quod minus idōneīs equīs
ūtēbantur, ā tribūnīs mīlitum reliquīsque equitibus Rōmānīs 15
atque ēvocātīs° equōs sūmit Germānīsque distribuit.

Intereā, dum haec geruntur, hostium cōpiae ex Arvernīs
equitēsque quī tōtī Galliae erant imperātī conveniunt. Magnō
hōrum coāctō numerō, cum Caesar in Sēquanōs per extrēmōs
Lingonum fīnēs iter faceret quō facilius subsidium prōvinciae 20

---

[1]A distant relative of the commander

ferre posset, circiter mīlia passuum decem ab Rōmānīs trīnīs[1]
castrīs° Vercingetorīx cōnsīdit; convocātīsque ad concilium
praefectīs equitum, vēnisse tempus victōriae dēmōnstrat:
fugere in prōvinciam Rōmānōs Galliāque excēdere. Id sibi
ad praesentem obtinendam lībertātem satis esse; ad reliquī 25
temporis pācem atque ōtium parum prōficī; majōribus enim
coāctīs cōpiīs, reversūrōs° neque fīnem bellandī factūrōs.°

Proinde in agmine° impedītōs adoriantur.[2] Sī peditēs suīs
auxilium ferant atque in eō morentur,° iter facere nōn posse;
sī, id quod magis futūrum cōnfīdat, relictīs impedīmentīs, 30
suae salūtī cōnsulant, et ūsū rērum necessāriārum° et dignitāte spoliātum īrī°; nam dē equitibus hostium, quīn nēmō
eōrum prōgredī modo extrā agmen audeat, nē ipsōs quidem
dēbēre dubitāre. Id quō majōre faciant animō, cōpiās sē
omnēs prō castrīs habitūrum et terrōrī hostibus futūrum. 35

Conclāmant equitēs sānctissimō jūre jūrandō cōnfirmārī
oportēre nē tēctō recipiātur,[3] nē ad līberōs, ad parentēs, ad
uxōrem aditum habeat quī nōn bis per agmen hostium perequitārit.°

Probātā rē atque omnibus ad jūs jūrandum adāctīs,° posterō 40
diē in trēs partēs distribūtō equitātū, duae sē aciēs ab duōbus
lateribus ostendunt; ūna ā prīmō agmine iter impedīre coepit.
Quā rē nūntiātā, Caesar suum quoque equitātum tripertītō°
dīvīsum contrā hostem īre jubet. Pugnātur ūnā° omnibus in
partibus. Cōnsistit agmen; impedīmenta intrā legiōnēs re- 45
cipiuntur.

Sī quā in parte nostrī labōrāre aut gravius premī vidēbantur,
eō signa īnferrī Caesar aciemque convertī° jubēbat; quae rēs
et hostēs ad īnsequendum tardābat et nostrōs spē auxiliī
cōnfirmābat. 50

Tandem Germānī[4] ab dextrō latere summum jugum nactī
hostēs locō dēpellunt; fugientēs usque ad flūmen, ubi Vercingetorīx cum pedestribus cōpiīs cōnsēderat, persequuntur
complūrēsque interficiunt. Quā rē animadversā, reliquī, nē

[1]With nouns that are plural in form but singular in meaning, such as **castra,** the dis-
tributive numbers (see p. 456) are used instead of the cardinals; e.g., **trīnīs,** three, is
used here instead of **tribus.**

[2]For a subjunctive expressing an exhortation in the direct form ("let us attack")

[3]The subject is the implied antecedent of the following **quī.**

[4]i.e., the German cavalry, skilled horsemen who were of great assistance to Caesar

circumvenīrentur veritī, sē fugae mandant. Omnibus locīs 55
fit caedēs.

Trēs nōbilissimī Haeduī captī ad Caesarem perdūcuntur:
Cotus, praefectus equitum, quī contrōversiam cum Convictoli-
tāve proximīs comitiīs° habuerat, et Cavarillus, quī post dēfec-
tiōnem Litaviccī pedestribus cōpiīs praefuerat, et Eporēdorīx,[1] 60
quō duce ante adventum Caesaris Haeduī cum Sēquanīs bellō
contenderant.

°**ad ... oppōnēbantur** were being opposed (to the enemy) in every
quarter • **levis ... peditēs** light infantry; lit., infantry of light
equipment • **ēvocātus** M., (reënlisted) veteran • **trīnīs castrīs** in three camps • **reversūrōs/factūrōs** (having **Rōmānōs**
as subject) • **in agmine** on the march • **in eō morentur**
should be delayed in/by (doing) this • **et ūsū ... necessāriārum**
both their property; lit., the enjoyment of the necessities (of life)
spoliātum īrī (fut. pass. inf.) (the Romans) would lose/be deprived of
perequitārit (= perequitāverit) had ridden • **ad jūs ... adāctīs**
bound by oath • **tripertītō** (adv.) in(to) three parts • **ūnā**
= ūnō tempore • **convertī** to wheel about • **proximīs**
comitiīs in the last/recent elections

bis	(adv.) twice	**prōficiō**	3 accomplish
conclāmō	1 shout, cry out	**proinde**	(adv.) therefore
+**modo**	(adv.) even; only	+**quō**	(conj.) so that
parum	(adv.) little, too little	**tueor**	2 guard, protect

P R E P A R I N G   F O R   A   S I E G E

Alesia, near modern Dijon, was a strongly fortified town, and Vercingetorix apparently was confident that he could hold it indefinitely.
Otherwise he would not have abandoned his usually successful strategy
of fighting in the open. After a brief survey of the terrain, Caesar at
once made preparations for the siege of Alesia.

Fugātō omnī equitātū Vercingetorīx cōpiās suās redūxit
statimque Alesiam, quod° est oppidum Mandubiōrum, iter facere coepit celeriterque impedīmenta ex castrīs ēdūcī et sē

[1]To be distinguished from the other Haeduan leader of the same name

329

subsequī jussit. Caesar, impedīmentīs in proximum collem
ductīs, duābus legiōnibus praesidiō relictīs, secūtus hostēs 5
quantum diēī tempus est passum, circiter tribus mīlibus ex
novissimō agmine interfectīs, alterō diē ad Alesiam castra
fēcit. Perspectō urbis sitū perterritīsque[1] hostibus, quod
equitātū°, quā maximē parte exercitūs cōnfīdēbant,[2] erant
pulsī, adhortātus ad labōrem mīlitēs Alesiam circumvāllāre° 10
īnstituit.[3]

Ipsum erat oppidum in colle summō admodum altō locō,°
ut nisi obsidiōne expugnārī nōn posse vidērētur; cujus collis
rādīcēs duo duābus ex partibus flūmina[4] subluēbant. Ante
oppidum[5] plānitiēs circiter mīlia passuum tria in longitūdinem 15
patēbat; reliquīs ex omnibus partibus collēs, mediocrī inter-
jectō spatiō, parī altitūdinis fastīgiō° oppidum cingēbant. Sub
mūrō,[6] quae pars° collis ad orientem sōlem spectābat, hunc
omnem locum° cōpiae Gallōrum complēverant fossamque et
mūrum in altitūdinem sex pedum praedūxerant. Ejus mūnī- 20
tiōnis[7] quae ab Rōmānīs īnstituēbātur circuitus decem mīlia
passuum tenēbat.° Castra opportūnīs locīs erant posita octō
castellaque tria et vīgintī facta; quibus in castellīs interdiū
statiōnēs pōnēbantur, nē qua subitō ēruptiō fieret; haec
eadem noctū firmīs praesidiīs tenēbantur. 25

°**quod** (agreeing with the predicate noun, **oppidum,** instead of with
its antecedent, **Alesiam**) • **equitātū** (abl. of respect) with **erant
pulsī** = the cavalry had been routed • **circumvāllāre** to surround with a rampart • **admodum altō locō** in a very high place
parī altitūdinis fastīgiō with equal elevation (i.e., the tops of the
hills were on about the same level) • **quae pars . . . , hunc omnem locum** all that part (of the hill) which • **tenēbat** extended

[1]The **quod** clause depends upon **perterritīs,** modifying **hostibus.** Supply **perspectīs**
as the participle in ablative absolute with **hostibus.**

[2]Note that Caesar often uses the ablative instead of the dative with **cōnfīdō.**

[3]Caesar's circumvallation actually consisted of two walls, more or less parallel to each
other, which completely surrounded the town. The inner wall was a defense against the
Gauls inside the city; the outer protected the Romans from the Gallic reinforcements summoned by Vercingetorix.

[4]The two streams are the Ose and the Oserain.

[5]The plain of Les Laumes is to the west of Alesia (near modern Alise-Sainte-Reine).

[6]i.e., the wall of the town

[7]This refers to the inner wall and ditch which eventually encircled the town.

adhortor	1 encourage	praedūcō	3 construct in front
fugō	1 rout	+quantum	(rel. adv.) as much
interjectus	(adj.) lying		as, as long as, as
	between		far as
interjiciō	3 interpose	+statiō	F., sentry, picket
opportūnus	(adj.) favorable	subluō	3 wash, flow along

DESPERATE MEASURES

Opere īnstitūtō fit equestre proelium in eā plānitiē. Summā
vī ab utrīsque contenditur. Labōrantibus nostrīs Caesar Germānōs submittit legiōnēsque prō castrīs cōnstituit, nē qua
subitō irruptiō° ab hostium peditātū fīat. Hostēs in fugam
conjectī sē ipsī multitūdine impediunt. Fit magna caedēs. 5
Eī quī intrā mūnītiōnēs erant Gallī perturbantur.

Vercingetorīx, priusquam mūnītiōnēs ab Rōmānīs perfician-
tur, cōnsilium capit omnem ab sē equitātum noctū dīmittere.
Discēdentibus mandat ut suam quisque eōrum cīvitātem adeat
omnēsque quī per aetātem arma ferre possint° ad bellum cō- 10
gant; mīlia hominum dēlēcta° octōgintā sēcum interitūra° dēmōnstrat; sē frūmentum vix diērum trīgintā habēre. Hīs
datīs mandātīs, quā° erat nostrum opus intermissum, secundā
vigiliā silentiō equitātum dīmittit.

Caesar had to construct a complex system of fortifications. He set
up two concentric rings, one of nearly ten miles' circumference and the
other, fourteen. Only in this way could Caesar hope to prevent Vercingetorix' 80,000 infantry from breaking out of Alesia, and at the same
time to repel any army of relief summoned by Vercingetorix.

Quibus rēbus cognitīs ex perfugīs et captīvīs Caesar haec 15
genera mūnītiōnis īnstituit. Fossam pedum[1] vīgintī dūxit.
Reliquās omnēs mūnītiōnēs ab eā fossā pedēs quadringentōs
redūxit, nē dē imprōvīsō° aut noctū ad mūnītiōnēs multitūdō
hostium advolāret,° aut interdiū tēla in nostrōs labōrantēs
conjicere posset. Hōc intermissō spatiō duās fossās quīn- 20
decim pedēs lātās, eādem altitūdine[2] perdūxit. Post eās aggerem ac vāllum° duodecim pedum cōnstrūxit.

---

[1] i.e., in width

[2] i.e., the two trenches were of the same depth, about eight or nine feet.

°**nē qua irruptiō**   so that no attack   •   **per aetātem ... possint**
were of military age   •   **dēlēcta**   (modifying **milia** but to be translated with **hominum**)   •   **interitūra (esse)**   would perish   •   **quā**
where   •   **dē imprōvīsō**   unexpectedly   •   **advolō, -āre**   sally
out/forth   •   **vāllus, -ī**   M., palisade

COUNCIL OF WAR

Meanwhile the Gallic states held a big council of war. They decided
to dispatch to the relief of Alesia an army of 8000 cavalry and a quarter
of a million infantry. Four generals were chosen to lead the relieving
army, for there was no one leader besides Vercingetorix who could
command universal confidence. It took more than a month to assemble
such an impressive force and move it to Alesia.

Inside the walls of Alesia, Vercingetorix and his men, now completely
isolated, had exhausted their food supply. The situation of the besieged
was desperate. What joyful excitement when at last they sighted the
large mass of the relieving army!

At eī quī Alesiae obsidēbantur, cōnsūmptō omnī frūmentō,
īnsciī° quid ab aliīs Gallīs gererētur, conciliō coāctō dē suīs
fortūnīs cōnsultābant. Variīs dictīs sententiīs, quārum pars
dēditiōnem, pars, dum vīrēs suppeterent,° ēruptiōnem facien-
dam cēnsēbat, Critognatus, quī magnam in Arvernīs auctōri- 5
tātem habēbat, dīxit: "In cōnsiliō capiendō, omnem Galliam
respiciāmus, quam ad nostrum auxilium concitāvimus.° Nōlīte hōs vestrō auxiliō spoliāre quī vestrae salūtis causā
suum perīculum neglēxērunt. Dē eōrum fidē cōnstantiāque
dubitātis? Quid, ergō, meum est cōnsilium? Facere quod 10
nostrī majōrēs fēcērunt.

"Quī in oppida compulsī eōrum corporibus quī aetāte ad
bellum inūtilēs vidēbantur vītam tolerāvērunt neque sē hostibus trādidērunt. Respicite fīnitimam Galliam quae perpetuā
premitur servitūte." 15

Sententiīs dictīs cōnstituunt ut eī quī inūtilēs sint bellō
ex oppidō exeant. Hī, cum ad mūnītiōnēs Rōmānōrum ac-
cessissent, flentēs ōrābant ut sē in servitūtem reciperent. At
Caesar, dispositīs in vāllō custōdiīs, eōs recipī prohibēbat.[1]

---

[1]This was not a purposeless cruelty, but an attempt to force the Gauls to use up their
supplies.

°**īnscius, -a, -um**   not knowing   •   **suppeterent**   held out
concitō, -āre   arouse, stir up

cēnseō | 2 think; propose   **cōnsultō** | 1 deliberate
cōnstantia | F., constancy   **majōrēs** | M. pl., ancestors

RELIEF IN SIGHT

Intereā Commius reliquīque ducēs cum omnibus cōpiīs ad
Alesiam perveniunt et, colle exteriōre occupātō, nōn longius
mīlle passibus ā nostrīs mūnītiōnibus cōnsīdunt. Posterō
diē, equitātū ex castrīs ēductō, omnem eam plānitiem, quam
in longitūdinem mīlia passuum tria patēre dēmōnstrāvimus, 5
complent, pedestrēsque cōpiās in locīs superiōribus cōnstituunt. Erat ex oppidō Alesiā dēspectus° in campum.° Concur-
runt hīs auxiliīs vīsīs; fit grātulātiō° inter eōs atque omnium
animī ad laetitiam excitantur. Itaque prōductīs cōpiīs ante
oppidum cōnsistunt sēque ad ēruptiōnem atque omnēs cāsūs 10
comparant.

°**dēspectus, -ūs**   M., a view (down)   •   **in campum**   over the
plain   •   **grātulātiō**   F., congratulation, rejoicing (**fit . . . eōs,** they
congratulated one another)

THE BATTLE

Caesar, omnī exercitū ad utramque partem mūnītiōnum[1]
dispositō, equitātum ex castrīs ēdūcī et proelium committī
jubet. Cum suōs pugnā superiōrēs esse Gallī cōnfīderent et
nostrōs multitūdine premī vidērent, ex omnibus partibus et eī
quī mūnītiōnibus continēbantur et eī quī ad auxilium convē- 5
nerant clāmōre et ululātū° suōrum animōs cōnfirmābant.
Quod in cōnspectū omnium rēs gerēbātur neque rēctē aut
turpiter factum° cēlārī poterat, utrōsque et laudis cupiditās
et timor ignōminiae° ad virtūtem excitābat.

Cum ā merīdiē prope ad sōlis occāsum dubiā victōriā° pug- 10
nārētur, Germānī ūnā in parte in hostēs impetum fēcērunt
eōsque prōpulērunt; quibus in fugam conjectīs sagittāriī
circumventī interfectīque sunt. Item ex reliquīs partibus

[1]Of the two lines of defense, one faced the town, the other faced the relieving army.

nostrī hostēs cēdentēs usque ad castra īnsecūtī suī colligendī°
facultātem nōn dedērunt. At eī quī Alesiā prōcesserant, 15
maestī, prope victōriā dēspērātā, sē in oppidum recēpērunt.

The ever victorious German cavalry had won for the Romans. The
defenders of Alesia were discouraged and withdrew behind the walls.

°**ululātus** M., yelling • **neque . . . factum** and no brave or
cowardly act • **ignōminia** F., disgrace • **dubiā victōriā**
without decisive result • **suī colligendī** of rallying

UNDER COVER OF NIGHT

Ūnō diē intermissō Gallī,[1] mediā nocte silentiō ex castrīs
ēgressī, ad mūnītiōnēs Rōmānās accēdunt. Subitō clāmōre
sublātō ut eī quī in oppidō obsidēbantur dē suō adventū
cognōscere possent, fundīs, sagittīs, lapidibus nostrōs dē
vāllō prōturbābant. Eōdem tempore, clāmōre exaudītō, dat 5
tubā signum suīs Vercingetorīx atque ex oppidō ēdūcit.
Nostrī ad mūnītiōnēs accēdunt.

Gallī, multīs undique vulneribus acceptīs, nūllā mūnītiōne
Rōmānōrum perruptā, cum lūx venīret, veritī nē ab latere
apertō circumvenīrentur, sē ad suōs recēpērunt. At eī quī 10
ex oppidō vēnerant priōrēs fossās explent; diūtius in hīs
rēbus administrandīs morātī, suōs discessisse cognōvērunt
priusquam mūnītiōnibus appropinquārent. Ita, rē īnfectā,°
in oppidum revertērunt.

°**rē īnfectā** without accomplishing anything

exaudiō	4 hear (from a distance)	**prōturbō**	1 drive in confusion; dislodge
expleō	2 fill up	**revertō**	3 return

ALESIA — FORTRESS OR PRISON?

After two unsuccessful attempts the prospects of the Gauls were
even more dubious. Though the leadership of Vercingetorix was lacking,
the four generals of the relieving army formed the sound plan of attack
from the north, where Roman fortifications were weakest, owing to the
difficult terrain. This was to be the decisive battle.

[1] i.e., the relieving army

Bis magnō cum dētrīmentō repulsī, Gallī quid agant cōn-
sulunt. Erat ā septentriōnibus collis, quem propter magnitūdinem circumvāllāre° nōn potuerant nostrī, necessāriōque
paene inīquō locō castra fēcerant. Haec C. Antistius Rēgīnus
et C. Canīnius Rebilus lēgātī cum duābus legiōnibus obtinē- 5
bant. Cognitīs per explōrātōrēs regiōnibus, ducēs Gallōrum
sexāgintā mīlia ex omnī numerō dēligunt eārum cīvitātum
quae maximam virtūtis opīniōnem° habēbant; quid agī
placeat, occultē inter sē cōnstituunt; adeundī tempus dēfī-
niunt, cum merīdiēs esse videātur. Hīs cōpiīs Vercassivella- 10
unum, ūnum ex quattuor ducibus, praeficiunt. Ille ex castrīs
prīmā vigiliā ēgressus, post montem sē occultāvit. Cum jam
merīdiēs appropinquāre vidērētur, ad ea castra[1] contendit;
eōdemque tempore equitātus ad mūnītiōnēs accēdere et
reliquae cōpiae[2] prō castrīs[3] sēsē ostendere coepērunt. 15

Vercingetorīx ex arce Alesiae suōs cōnspicātus ex oppidō
ēgreditur. Pugnātur ūnō tempore omnibus locīs atque omnia
temptantur. Exercitus Rōmānus tantīs mūnītiōnibus dis-
tinētur° nec facile plūribus locīs occurrit.° Multum ad ter-
rendōs nostrōs valet° clāmor quī post tergum[4] orītur. 20

Caesar idōneum locum nactus quid quāque in parte° gerā-
tur cognōscit; labōrantibus[5] subsidium submittit. Utrīsque
ad animum occurrit° ūnum esse illud tempus, quō maximē
contendī necesse sit: Gallī, nisi perfrēgerint mūnītiōnēs, dē
omnī salūte dēspērant; Rōmānī, sī rem obtinuerint,° fīnem 25
labōrum omnium expectant.

°**circumvāllāre** to surround with a rampart • **opīniō** F., reputation (for) • **distineō, -ēre** divide • **occurrit** (supply **hostibus**) • **multum valet** had a strong tendency • **quāque in
parte** everywhere (i.e., wherever there was fighting) • **utrīsque
. . . occurrit** both sides realized • **sī rem obtinuerint** if they
won the victory

[1]i.e., the Roman camp on the north where attack would be the easiest, because the
fortifications were the weakest.

[2]These amounted to about 190,000 men, but they were so poorly commanded that
Caesar says nothing more of them. Their bad generalship saved Caesar.

[3]i.e., their own (Gallic) camp

[4]As the Romans formed two lines placed back to back, each line had the enemy behind it.

[5]What has been the usual meaning of **labōrō** in Caesar?

⁺adeō	attack	**occultē**	(adv.) secretly;
dēfīniō	4 determine		obscurely

A GENERAL AND HIS STRATEGY

Hīs rēbus cognitīs, Caesar Labiēnum cum cohortibus sex subsidiō labōrantibus mittit; imperat, sī sustinēre nōn possit, dēductīs[1] cohortibus ēruptiōne pugnet; id,° nisi necessāriō, nē faciat. Ipse adit reliquōs[2]; cohortātur nē labōrī succumbant.°

Mittit[3] prīmum Brūtum adulēscentem cum cohortibus 5 Caesar, post cum aliīs C. Fabium lēgātum; postrēmō° ipse, cum vehementius pugnārētur, integrōs subsidiō addūcit. Restitūtō proeliō ac repulsīs hostibus, eō quō Labiēnum mīserat contendit; cohortēs quattuor ex proximō castellō dēdūcit, equitum partem sē sequī, partem circumīre exteriōrēs 10 mūnītiōnēs et ā tergō hostēs adorīrī jubet.

Labiēnus, postquam neque aggerēs neque fossae vim hostium sustinēre poterant, coāctīs XI cohortibus, quās ex proximīs praesidiīs dēductās fors obtulit, Caesarem per nūntiōs facit certiōrem quid faciendum exīstimet. Accelerat Caesar 15 ut proeliō intersit.

°**id** (refers to the phrase **ēruptiōne pugnet**) • **succumbō, -ere** yield, succumb • **postrēmō** (adv.) at last, finally

FOR WANT OF A GENERAL

Caesar threw every soldier within reach into the critical battle. Finally almost half of the Roman troops were concentrated in one place. The Gauls should now have attacked with full force at other points along the fourteen-mile front. In that case they could almost certainly have broken through the weakened Roman lines. As it was, when they saw the Roman cavalry behind them, the Gauls turned to flee.

Ejus° adventū ex colōre vestītūs° cognitō, turmīsque° equitum et cohortibus vīsīs quās sē sequī jusserat, hostēs proe-

[1] i.e., from the rampart

[2] i.e., those defending the siege works in the plain. Caesar galloped down from his position on the hill.

[3] i.e., to points of the fortifications where the besieged Gauls were trying to break through.

The area of Caesar's main camp as viewed from the air. The edge of the Gallic town is seen in upper left.

lium committunt. Utrimque clāmōre sublātō excipit° rūrsus ex vāllō atque omnibus mūnītiōnibus clāmor. Nostrī ēmissīs pīlīs gladiīs rem gerunt. Repente post tergum° equitātus 5 cernitur; cohortēs aliae appropinquant. Hostēs terga vertunt; fugientibus equitēs occurrunt. Fit magna caedēs.

Sedulius, dux et prīnceps Lemovīcum, occīditur; Vercassivellaunus Arvernus vīvus in fugā comprehenditur; signa mīlitāria septuāgintā quattuor ad Caesarem referuntur; paucī 10 ex tantō numerō sē incolumēs in castra recipiunt. Cōnspicātī ex oppidō° caedem et fugam suōrum dēspērātā salūte cōpiās ā mūnītiōnibus redūcunt. Fit prōtinus° hāc rē audītā ex castrīs Gallōrum fuga.

Quod nisi° crēbrīs subsidiīs° ac tōtīus diēī labōre mīlitēs 15 essent dēfessī, omnēs hostium cōpiae dēlērī potuissent. Dē mediā nocte missus equitātus novissimum agmen cōnsequitur: magnus numerus capitur atque interficitur; reliquī ex fugā in cīvitātēs discēdunt.

°**ejus** Caesar's • **vestītus** M., garment, clothing (Caesar wore a scarlet cloak.) • **turma** F., troop, squadron (about thirty cavalrymen) • **excipiō, -ere** follow • **repente post tergum**

suddenly in the rear (of the Gauls) • **cōnspicātī ex oppidō = eī
(Gallī), quī in oppidō erant, cōnspicātī** • **prōtinus** (adv.)
immediately • **quod nisi** and unless, and if . . . not • **crēbrīs
subsidiīs** (by sending) frequent reinforcements (to relieve points of
danger)

SURRENDER

Posterō diē Vercingetorīx conciliō convocātō id bellum
sē suscēpisse nōn suārum necessitātum sed commūnis lībertātis causā dēmōnstrat; et quoniam sit fortūnae cēdendum, ad
utramque rem sē illīs offerre, seu morte suā Rōmānīs satisfacere seu° vīvum trādere velint. Mittuntur dē hīs rēbus ad 5
Caesarem lēgātī. Jubet arma trādī, prīncipēs prōdūcī. Ipse
in mūnītiōne prō castrīs cōnsīdit; eō ducēs prōdūcuntur;
Vercingetorīx dēditur°; arma prōjiciuntur. Reservātīs
Haeduīs atque Arvernīs, sī° per eōs cīvitātēs recuperāre°
posset,° ex reliquīs captīvīs tōtī exercituī capita singula° 10
praedae nōmine distribuit.

°**seu . . . seu = sīve . . . sīve** • **dēdō, -ere** surrender • **sī
posset** (to see) whether he could • **recuperō, -āre** win back,
regain • **capita singula** a man apiece

Vercingetorix was sent as a prisoner to Rome. There he remained
in captivity for six years, until Caesar returned to celebrate a formal
triumph. Then, after being led before the victor's chariot, he was put to
death in a dungeon in the Capitol. Many believe that Vercingetorix was
the greatest soldier who ever fought against Caesar. He gave up first
his liberty, then his life, for his people.

The conquest of Alesia, which put an end to serious resistance in Gaul,
concludes Caesar's commentaries. One of his officers, Aulus Hirtius,
wrote what has been called an "Eighth Book" of the Gallic Wars. This
book describes some minor uprisings which Caesar put down one by one
and so quickly that no chance was given for several tribes to act together. There was never again any threat to Roman power in Gaul.

Caesar had already laid the groundwork for turning Gaul into a
Roman province, and this was accomplished in the following years. Thus
Gaul was destined to become thoroughly Romanized and to inherit Latin
as the language of the people.

Some Latin words yield a particularly large number of English derivatives. For example, the noun **labor, -ōris** and its verb **labōrō** (work).

labor	noun or verb	work
laborer	noun made with suffix	one who works
laborious	adj. made with suffix	requiring work
laboratory	noun made with suffix	place where work is done
elaborate	adj. made with prefix	worked out with care
elaborately	adv. made with suffix	in an elaborate way

Add other derivatives to this list.

From **currō** (run) come several English words.

current	adj. from pres. part.	running/passing
currency	noun from pres. part.	money/circulation
course	noun from perf. part.	progress/way
concur	verb made with prefix	agree (run with)
excursion	noun made with prefix/suffix	trip (a running out)

Explain the derivation of the following words.

cursory   discourse   incur   occur   precursor   recur

Give several English words from each of the following Latin verbs and explain the meaning of each word.

cadō   cāsūrus   nāscor   nātus   sequor   secūtus
loquor   locūtus   patior   passus   videō   vīsum

Many Latin nouns also have English derivatives. Give the meaning of each word.

terra		**nāvis**	
terrace	terrestrial	naval	navigation
terrain	terrier	nave	navigator
terrarium	territory	navigate	navy

What English words are connected with each of the following Latin nouns?

arma	**caput, -itis**	**tempus, -oris**
ignis	**salūs, -ūtis**	**voluntās, -ātis**

339

LATIN WORDS AND PHRASES serve a useful purpose in English. Here are a few with their translations or meanings. The list can easily be extended from your daily reading.

ad hoc	with reference to this/special
ad litteram	to the letter/exact/exactly
ad valorem	according to the value
a fortiori	with the greater force
alma mater	one's school/college/university (literally, fostering mother)
alter ego	a second self/a close friend
ars gratia artis	art for art's sake
bona fide	in good faith/honest/genuine
ceteris paribus	other things being equal
cui bono	for whose benefit?/of what good?
cum laude	with praise/honor
de facto	in fact/actual(ly)/in reality
Deo volente	God willing
ergo	therefore
festina lente	make haste slowly
fiat lux	let there be light (Genesis 1:3)
hic et ubique	here and everywhere
in loco parentis	in the place of a parent
magna cum laude	with high honors
me judice	in my judgment
mirabile dictu	wonderful to tell
modus operandi	manner of operating
nolens volens	willy-nilly (literally, unwilling willing)
non sequitur	an unwarranted conclusion (literally, it does not follow)
onus probandi	the burden of proof
per annum/centum	by the year/hundred
per se	by itself
persona grata	an acceptable person
post-mortem	after death (adj.)/autopsy (noun)
sine die	without (appointing) a day (for future action)
sine qua non	something essential (literally, without which not)
summa cum laude	with the highest honor
una voce	with one voice/unanimously
volens et potens	willing and able

THE ROMAN STATE

By Caesar's time Roman government had undergone radical changes in a continuing struggle of the common people (plebeians) to wrest political freedom from the aristocracy (patricians). Kings gave way to two consuls, elected yearly, who later lost some of their power to tribunes chosen to safeguard the rights of the common people. Gradually plebeians gained access to offices originally restricted to patricians. They could become aediles (supervisors of business, public health, and public amusements), praetors and censors (judges), and even consuls.

The popular party, led by Marius and Cinna, was determined to preserve the political gains of the people; the senatorial party, led by Sulla, was dedicated to restoring power to the Senate and to the aristocrats. Though patrician by birth, Caesar was firmly attached to the popular party. When Sulla's party won, the powers of the Senate were restored, and Caesar and others of his party were driven out of Rome for a while.

The government, already shaken by earlier upheavals, was further weakened by this conflict, and an ideal climate was created for Caesar's ambition for power. The First Triumvirate, a secret alliance of Caesar with Pompey and Crassus, was formed. Pompey annulled the Sullan constitution, and Caesar was given the consulate, which he shared with a colleague too weak to oppose his aims. Caesar's five-year appointment as governor of Gaul followed his consulship. Former consuls and praetors regularly became governors of provinces, and were expected to enrich themselves there. Caesar did so in Gaul.

The senatorial party continued its fight at Rome, and Caesar's enemies, who now included Pompey, connived to have him ordered home from Gaul without his army. His decision to bring his army with him into Italy was in defiance of the Senate and a declaration of civil war.

Popular support and a succession of military victories culminated in Caesar's becoming dictator. In the disordered condition of the government, Caesar undoubtedly thought he was saving Rome from anarchy. The conspirators who became his assassins neither trusted nor understood him. Though jealousy motivated some of them, there is no doubt that others, including his friend Brutus, were honest patriots.

The republic came to an end with Caesar's death. Eventually C. Octavius (called C. Julius Caesar Octavianus after adoption by his great-uncle Caesar) became the first emperor of Rome. He is better known by the title Augustus, granted to him in 27 B.C. by a grateful Senate for his achievements in putting down the enemies of Rome. Indirectly, therefore, through his grandnephew Augustus, Caesar contributed to the establishment of the Roman Empire.

341

CIVIL WAR

While Caesar was conquering Gaul and gradually transforming it into a province, one of his fellow triumvirs (Crassus) was killed in the east (53 B.C.). Between Caesar and the other surviving triumvir (Pompey) there was already open rivalry. The death of Julia had severed the family ties between Caesar (her father) and Pompey (her husband).

Pompey allied himself with the Senate and the aristocrats, while Caesar continued to find support among the plebeians and their tribunes. A serious quarrel arose over the exact date when each was to give up his proconsular command.

Caesar had a strong army, while both legions available to Pompey in Italy had fought under Caesar. On the other hand, Pompey's position was less critical, since he had remained at the center of political events in Rome, leaving the administration of his province (Spain) to his lieutenants.

It was to Caesar's advantage to keep his command in Gaul till the end of 49. If he should return to Rome before he could begin his consulship in 48, he would temporarily be a private citizen and as such open to indictment by his enemies. By retaining his Gallic command Caesar could retain also his political immunity to civil law.

However, in order to step directly into the consulship from his post in Gaul he must get permission to run *in absentia* for that office. Caesar's petition to be allowed to do this was denied by the Senate, which voted that he must retire from his command on July 1, 49[1] or be declared a public enemy.

Caesar's friend, the tribune Mark Antony, promptly vetoed the measure. For days Cicero and other conservatives tried to work out a compromise. On January 7, disregarding the tribune's veto, the Senate passed the "last decree," ordering the magistrates to take measures for the safety of the state. The consul—in a symbolic gesture—handed a sword to Pompey, commissioning him defender of the state. Although the act was without legal authority, Pompey accepted the challenge. That night the tribunes left Rome to join Caesar.

[1]According to some historians, on March 1, 49.

This view shows the Basilica Julia on the south of the *Forum Romanum*. Before the emperors built their larger fora to the east, the *Forum Romanum* remained the center of political activity through the Civil War and till the end of the Republic.

Quibus rēbus cognitīs, Caesar mīlitēs ad cōntiōnem convocat. Is omnēs injūriās inimīcōrum in sē commemorat.

"Ab inimīcīs meīs Pompēius dēductus ac dēprāvātus est.° Novum exemplum in rē pūblicā intrōductum est, ut tribūnicia intercessiō° armīs opprimerētur. Sulla, tribūniciā 5 potestāte omnibus rēbus nūdātā,° tamen intercessiōnem tribūnōrum līberam relīquit. Pompēius, quī restituisse āmissa dōna° vidētur, adēmit° etiam dōna quae ante habuērunt.°

"Quotiēnscumque° est dēcrētum magistrātūs darent 10 operam, nē quid rēs pūblica dētrīmentī caperet, factum est in° perniciōsīs lēgibus, in° vī tribūniciā, in° sēcessiōne populī. Quārum rērum hōc tempore nihil° factum est, nē cōgitātum° quidem."

Caesar hortātur ut ejus exīstimātiōnem dignitātemque ab 15 inimīcīs dēfendant, cujus imperātōris ductū° IX annīs rem pūblicam fēlīcissimē gesserint plūrimaque proelia secunda fēcerint. Conclāmant mīlitēs legiōnis XIII, quae aderat, sēsē parātōs esse imperātōris suī tribūnōrumque plēbis injūriās dēfendere. 20

°**dēprāvātus est** was corrupted • **tribūnicia intercessiō** intercession of the tribunes • **nūdātā** stripped • **dōna** privileges • **adēmit** took away • **habuērunt** (supply **tribūnī**) **quotiēnscumque** every time (however often) • **in** in the case of • **quārum rērum ... nihil** none of these things • **cōgitātum** thought of • **cujus imperātōris ductū** of the general under whose leadership (**cujus** resumes **ejus** of preceding line)

THE RUBICON INCIDENT[1]

Neque senātū interveniente et adversāriīs negantibus ūllam sē dē rē pūblicā factūrōs pactiōnem, trānsiit Caesar in citeriōrem Galliam. Ravennae substitit, ad bellum parātus sī quid° dē tribūnīs plēbis intercēdentibus prō sē° gravius° ā senātū cōnstitūtum esset. 5

[1]The account given here is that of Suetonius, a second century A.D. biographer.

Cum igitur sublātam° tribūnōrum intercessiōnem ipsōsque tribūnōs urbe cessisse nūntiātum esset, praemissīs sēcrētō cohortibus, paucīs cum comitibus Caesar profectus est. Tandem cōnsecūtus° cohortēs praemissōs ad Rubicōnem flūmen, quī° prōvinciae ejus fīnis erat, paulum cōnstitit, 10 putāns quanta rēs esset.

Conversus° ad proximōs, "Etiam nunc," inquit, "regredī possumus; quod sī° hoc flūmen trānsierimus, omnia armīs agenda erunt."

Tunc Caesar, paulum cunctātus, "Eātur,°" inquit, "quō 15 deōrum voluntās et inīquitās inimīcōrum vocat. Jacta ālea est."[1]

°**sī quid dē . . . gravius** if something too serious concerning • **prō sē** on his (Caesar's) behalf (goes with **intercēdentibus**) • **sublātam** (from **tollō**) set aside • **cōnsecūtus** having overtaken **quī** which (refers to **Rubicōnem**, not to **flūmen**) • **conversus** turning • **quod sī** but if • **eātur** let us go (let it be gone)

NEGOTIATIONS

Cognitā mīlitum voluntāte Arīminum cum legiōne XIII[2] proficīscitur ibique convenit tribūnōs plēbis, quī ad eum cōnfūgerant; reliquās legiōnēs ex hībernīs ēvocat et subsequī jubet.

Eō L. Caesar adulēscēns venit, cujus pater Caesaris erat 5 lēgātus. Is reliquō sermōne cōnfectō, cujus reī causā vēnerat,° sē habēre ā Pompēiō ad eum prīvātī officiī° mandāta dēmōnstrat. Eadem ferē atque eīsdem verbīs praetor Roscius agit cum Caesare sibique Pompēium haec commemorāsse dēmōnstrat. 10

Quae rēs etsī nōn ad levandās injūriās pertinēre vidēbantur, tamen Caesar idōneōs esse habuit° hominēs, per quōs mandāta sua ad Pompēium perferrentur.

[1]Caesar himself does not report the famous words **Jacta ālea est!** (The die is cast!). They are found in Plutarch's *Parallel Lives,* originally written in Greek, and in Suetonius' *The Lives of the Twelve Caesars.* Caesar does not even mention the Rubicon River, although the crossing of that small stream symbolized his decision to undertake civil war.

[2]To the last, Caesar had hoped for a compromise. Otherwise he would have had more than one legion with him in Cisalpine Gaul. As it was, six legions were in Transalpine Gaul, while two were on the way to join him.

Acceptīs mandātīs Roscius cum L. Caesare Capuam pervenit ibique cōnsulēs Pompēiumque invenit; postulāta 15 Caesaris nūntiat. Illī respondent scrīptaque ad eum mandāta per eōs mittunt, quōrum haec erat summa: "Caesar in Galliam revertātur, Arīminō excēdat, exercitūs dīmittat; quae sī fēcerit, Pompēius in Hispāniās° ībit."

°**cujus reī causā vēnerat** which was the reason for his coming
prīvātī officiī of a private nature • **habuit** considered • **Hispāniās** the (two) Roman provinces of Spain

CAESAR'S DECISION

Erat inīqua condiciō postulāre° ut Caesar Arīminō excēderet atque in prōvinciam reverterētur, ipsum Pompēium et prōvinciās et legiōnēs aliēnās tenēre°; exercitum Caesaris velle° dīmittī, dēlēctūs habēre°; pollicērī° sē in prōvinciam itūrum neque dēfīnīre° ante quem diem itūrus sit. 5

Itaque Caesar ab Arīminō M. Antōnium cum cohortibus v Arrētium mittit; ipse Arīminī cum duābus legiōnibus subsistit ibique dēlēctum habēre īnstituit; Pisaurum, Fānum, Ancōnam singulīs cohortibus occupat.

Continuing southward, as he moved swiftly into the heart of Italy, Caesar met with great success in winning support for his cause. Three entire legions went over to him.

°**postulāre** to demand (infinitive used as subject of **erat,** with the **ut** clause as its own object) • **tenēre** to keep (infinitive with subject accusative—**ipsum Pompēium**—and two direct objects, the entire phrase being another subject of **erat**) • **velle, habēre, pollicērī, dēfīnīre** to wish, to hold, to promise, to set a limit (four infinitives with the same subject accusative as **tenēre,** and all, like **postulāre** and **tenēre,** part of the series of subjects belonging to **erat**)

POMPEY GOES EAST

With his own position thus weakened, Pompey decided to leave Italy. Caesar arrived too late to attempt a blockade of his rival's fleet at Brundisium (modern Brindisi). Pompey sailed to northern Greece with five legions. He could hope to strengthen his army in the East because he had many friends and allies there. Moreover, the generals who controlled Spain with seven legions were Pompey's men. Caesar, in Italy, was caught between two arms of Pompeian forces—on the west by those in Spain and on the east by those in Greece.

CAESAR GOES WEST

For lack of a navy Caesar could not immediately follow Pompey to Greece. Instead he turned to Spain, which could be reached by land. On the land route from Italy to Spain lay Massilia (modern Marseilles). There Caesar found the city gates closed and the Massilians ready for defense. Pompey, through his agents, had already secured Massilian support.

Anxious to reach Spain as soon as possible, Caesar wasted no time at Massilia. He put Decimus Brutus in charge of the blockade by sea, and left C. Trebonius in command of land operations.

MASSILIA BESIEGED

C. Trebōnius lēgātus, quī ad oppugnātiōnem Massiliae relictus erat, duābus ex partibus aggerem, vīneās turrēsque ad oppidum agere īnstituit.

Ūna° erat proxima portuī nāvālibusque,° altera° ad partem quā est aditus ex Galliā atque Hispāniā ad id mare, quod 5 adigitur° ad ōstium Rhodanī. Massilia enim ferē ex tribus oppidī partibus marī adluitur; reliqua quārta est, quae aditum habet ab terrā. Hujus quoque spatiī pars ea quae ad arcem pertinet, locī nātūrā et valle¹ altissimā mūnīta, longam et difficilem habet oppugnātiōnem. 10

Ad ea perficienda opera C. Trebōnius magnam jūmentōrum atque hominum multitūdinem ex omnī prōvinciā vocat; vīmina° māteriamque comportārī jubet. Quibus comparātīs rēbus aggerem in altitūdinem pedum LXXX exstruit.

Sed magnitūdō operum, altitūdō mūrī atque turrium, 15 multitūdō tormentōrum omnem administrātiōnem tardābat. Crēbrae etiam per Albicōs ēruptiōnēs fiēbant° ex oppidō ignēsque aggerī et turribus īnferēbantur. Haec facile nostrī mīlitēs repellēbant, magnīsque ultrō illātīs° dētrīmentīs, eōs quī ēruptiōnem fēcerant in oppidum rejiciēbant. 20

---

¹This deep valley to the north of the old citadel is now filled with dirty, narrow streets leading to the new port.

°**Ūna . . . altera** One position . . . the other position (referring to **duābus ex partibus** in line 2) • **nāvālibusque** and the dockyards • **mare . . . adigitur** the sea into which (the mouth of the Rhone) runs; lit., the sea which runs into (the mouth of the Rhone); i.e., **Sinus Gallicus** (now the Gulf of Lions) • **vīmina** willow twigs **fiēbant** (Translate as passive of **faciō.**) • **illātis** (perf. part. of **inferō**)

SEA OPERATIONS

A first attempt to break the blockade ended in a costly failure for the Massilians. They lost nine out of seventeen ships. A little later, however, the Massilians received word that Pompey had sent to their support a fleet of seventeen ships under the command of L. Nasidius. With other ships that had been saved or repaired after the first battle and with a number of converted fishing vessels, the Massilians felt strong enough to risk another naval engagement.

The ships under Nasidius, however, after fighting only a short time, made off for Spain before suffering any losses. After a hard battle, the Massilians were defeated once more, again with a loss of nine ships—five sunk and four captured. This Roman victory was so decisive that the Massilians no longer challenged Brutus' sea blockade.

TREACHERY

Caesar's land forces under Trebonius had not been idle in the meantime. Concealed by a movable shed that had been rolled up to the city wall, Roman engineers were making a breach into the wall. Unable to defend their crumbling fortifications, the Massilians asked for a truce. Trebonius granted generous terms. Hostilities were to be suspended till Caesar's arrival from Spain on his return trip to Italy.

At hostēs sine fidē tempus atque occāsiōnem fraudis ac dolī quaerunt. Interjectīs aliquot diēbus, nostrīs languentibus atque animō° remissīs, subitō merīdiānō tempore, cum alius discessisset, alius ex diūtinō labōre in ipsīs operibus quiētī sē dedisset, arma vērō omnia reposita contēctaque essent, 5 portīs sē forās ērumpunt, secundō magnōque ventō ignem operibus īnferunt. Hunc° sīc distulit ventus, utī ūnō tempore agger, pluteī, testūdō, turris, tormenta flammam

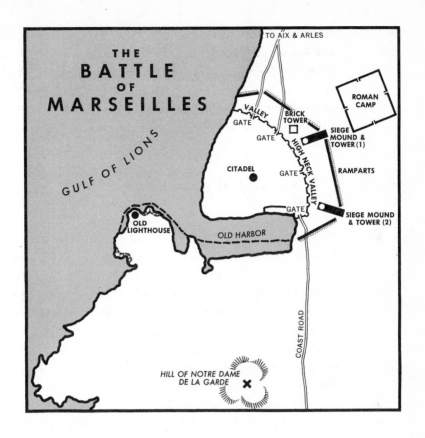

THE
BATTLE
OF
MARSEILLES

conciperent et haec omnia cōnsūmerentur, priusquam
animadvertī posset quemadmodum accidisset. 10

Nostrī repentīnā fortūnā permōtī arma, quae possunt,
arripiunt; aliī ex castrīs sēsē incitant. Fit in hostēs impetus;
sed ē mūrō sagittīs tormentīsque fugientēs persequī pro-
hibentur.° Illī sub mūrum sē recipiunt ibique musculum
turrimque laterīciam līberē incendunt. Ita multōrum 15
mensium labor hostium perfidiā et vī tempestātis punctō
temporis° interiit.

Temptāvērunt hoc idem Massiliēnsēs posterō diē. Eandem
nactī tempestātem majōre cum fidūciā° ad alteram turrim
aggeremque ēruptiōne pugnāvērunt multumque ignem in- 20
tulērunt. Sed ut superiōris temporis contentiōnem nostrī
omnem remīsērunt,° ita proximī diēī casū admonitī omnia
ad dēfensiōnem parāverant. Itaque multīs interfectīs reliquōs infectā rē° in oppidum reppulērunt.

349

SURRENDER OF MASSILIA

Trebonius reorganized the siege. The damage to the siege works
was repaired, and once more the Massilians found themselves hopelessly
shut in. The entire siege lasted about three months.

On his return trip to Rome, Caesar arrived at Massilia in time to
accept the city's surrender. It was at Massilia that Caesar learned of
his appointment as dictator of Rome.

Ibi lēgem dē dictātōre lātam° sēsēque dictātōrem dictum ā
M. Lepidō praetōre cognōscit.

Massiliēnsēs omnibus dēfessī malīs, reī frūmentāriae ad
summam inopiam adductī, bis nāvālī proeliō superātī, crēbrīs
ēruptiōnibus fūsī, gravī etiam pestilentiā afflīctī, dējectā ⁵
turrī, labefactā magnā parte mūrī, auxiliīs prōvinciārum et
exercituum dēspērātīs, quōs in Caesaris potestātem vēnisse
cognōverant,° sēsē dēdere sine fraude cōnstituunt.

Sed paucīs ante diēbus L. Domitius, cognitā Massiliēnsium
voluntāte, nāvēs III comparāverat, ūnam ex quibus ipse ¹⁰
cōnscenderat; nactus turbidam tempestātem profectus est.
Hunc° cōnspicātae nāvēs, quae ad portum excubābant,
sublātīs ancorīs sequī coepērunt. Ex hīs° ūnum ipsīus°
nāvigium contendit et fugere persevērāvit auxiliōque tempestātis ex cōnspectū abiit; duo nāvigia perterrita concursū ¹⁵
nostrārum nāvium sēsē in portum recēpērunt.

Massiliēnsēs arma tormentaque ex oppidō, ut est imperātum, prōferunt, nāvēs ex portū nāvālibusque ēdūcunt,
pecūniam ex pūblicō° trādunt. Quibus rēbus cōnfectīs,
Caesar, magis eōs prō nōmine et vetustāte quam prō meritīs ²⁰
in sē cīvitātis° cōnservāns, duās ibi legiōnēs praesidiō relinquit; cēterās in Italiam mittit; ipse ad urbem proficīscitur.

°**lēgem . . . lātam (esse)** that a law had been passed (**Lātam** is from **ferō.**) • **cognōverant** had been informed • **hunc** = **Domitium** • **hīs** (the three ships that tried to get away) • **ip- sīus** = **Domitiī** • **ex pūblicō** from the public treasury • **cīvi- tātis** (gen. with **prō nōmine et vetustāte** and also with **prō meritīs**)

ELEVEN DAYS IN ROME

After leaving Massilia, Caesar went to Rome, where he spent a busy period of eleven days discharging his duties as dictator. At the elec- tions, over which he presided, he won the consulship for the second time. (His first consulship had been eleven years earlier, in 59 B.C.)

He also took measures to improve economic conditions by having real estate and personal property assessed at prewar valuations and by stabilizing credit (particularly the payment of loans), which had been threatened by wartime conditions.

TO BRUNDISIUM AGAIN

Hīs rēbus et fēriīs° Latīnīs comitiīsque omnibus perficiendīs XI diēs tribuit dictātorque sē abdicat et ab urbe proficīscitur Brundisiumque pervenit. Eō legiōnēs XII, equitātum omnem venīre jusserat. Sed tantum nāvium° repperit ut angustē XV mīlia legiōnāriōrum mīlitum, DC equitēs trānsportārī possent. 5

Hoc ūnum Caesarī ad celeritātem cōnficiendī bellī dēfuit. Atque hae ipsae cōpiae hōc īnfrequentiōrēs° impōnuntur, quod multī Gallicīs tot bellīs dēfēcerant, longumque iter ex Hispāniā magnum nūmerum dēminuerat, et gravis autumnus in Āpūliā circumque Brundisium ex salūberrimīs Galliae et 10 Hispāniae regiōnibus omnem exercitum valētūdine temptā- verat.°

°**fēriīs**[1] festival • **tantum nāvium** only enough ships • **īn- frequentiōrēs** with thinner ranks (than their full complement) **omnem exercitum valetūdine temptāverat** had been a trial to the whole army in the matter of health

---

[1]**Feriae Latīnae** were religious ceremonies commemorating the old Latin federation. Every Roman magistrate was expected to observe the rites of this festival before proceed- ing with his duties.

Pompey meanwhile was organizing his forces in Greece. He now had nine legions under his command, and two more were on their way from Asian provinces. The kings on the eastern frontier of the Roman Empire furnished him with their finest horsemen. Pompey's fleet controlled the Eastern Mediterranean, especially the Adriatic Sea.

Although Caesar had found transport for only half his army, he nevertheless crossed the Adriatic in January 48 B.C. With about 20,000 men he dashed for Pompey's important supply depots at Dyrrachium (modern Durazzo); but Pompey, who was returning from Thessaly, reached them first. Caesar remained in serious danger till Antony was at last able to bring the remnant of his army safely through Pompey's naval patrols.

An attempt to besiege Pompey in Dyrrachium failed. Pompey broke through the fortifications, which were too extensive for Caesar's weak forces to cover. Thereupon Caesar withdrew his troops to Thessaly, where supplies could be more easily obtained than from across the Adriatic.

Pompey followed Caesar into Thessaly. In July 48 B.C. Pompey's army, about 50,000 strong, was encamped on a ridge near Pharsalus. Caesar, with only about 22,000 men, could not hope to attack that position with any degree of success.

BATTLE OF PHARSALUS

One day Pompey yielded to the urging of his impatient friends and moved his battle formation farther downhill than usual. Caesar was quick to notice and seize this opportunity.[1]

Between the two lines there was only enough space left for each army to charge. Pompey had ordered his men to await Caesar's attack without moving from their position. He hoped that the javelins would fall with less effect than if his men advanced; also that Caesar's soldiers, having to run twice as far, would be breathless and exhausted.

Nostrī mīlitēs datō signō suīs īnfestīs pīlīs° prōcucur-rērunt atque animadvertērunt Pompēiānōs nōn concurrere. Ūsū perītī ac superiōribus pugnīs exercitātī, suā sponte cursum repressērunt et ad medium ferē spatium cōnstitērunt,

---

[1] Caesar had already given orders to move camp when he noticed this chance to do battle.

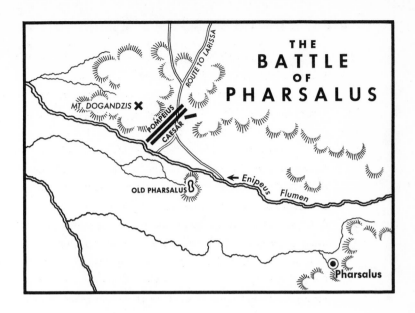

nē cōnsūmptīs vīribus appropinquārent. Parvō intermissō 5
temporis spatiō ac rūrsus renovātō cursū pīla mīsērunt
celeriterque, ut erat praeceptum ā Caesare, gladiōs strīnxērunt.

Neque vērō Pompēiānī huic reī dēfuērunt. Nam et tēla
missa excēpērunt et impetum legiōnum tulērunt et ordinēs
cōnservāvērunt pīlīsque missīs ad gladiōs rediērunt.° 10

Eōdem tempore equitēs ab sinistrō Pompēī cornū, ut erat
imperātum, ūniversī prōcucurrērunt, omnisque multitūdō
sagittāriōrum sē profūdit. Quōrum impetum noster equitātus
nōn tulit, sed paulātim locō mōtus° cessit, equitēsque Pompēī
hōc ācrius īnstāre et sē turmātim explicāre° aciemque nostram 15
ā latere apertō circumīre coepērunt.

Quod ubi Caesar animadvertit, quārtae aciēī, quam īnstitu-
erat sex cohortium, dedit signum. Illī celeriter prōcucurrērunt īnfestīsque signīs° tantā vī in Pompēī equitēs impetum
fēcērunt, ut eōrum nēmō cōnsisteret omnēsque conversī nōn 20
sōlum locō excēderent, sed prōtinus incitātī fugā montēs
altissimōs peterent.

Quibus submōtīs° omnēs sagittāriī funditōrēsque dēstitūtī
inermēs sine praesidiō interfectī sunt. Eōdem impetū cohortēs sinistrum cornū, pugnantibus etiam tum ac resistenti- 25

353

bus in aciē Pompēiānīs, circumiērunt eōsque ā tergō adortī
sunt.

Eōdem tempore Caesar tertiam aciem, quae quiēta fuerat
et sē ad id tempus locō tenuerat, prōcurrere jussit. Ita cum
recentēs atque integrī dēfessīs successissent, aliī autem ā 30
tergō adorīrentur, sustinēre Pompēiānī nōn potuērunt atque
ūniversī terga vertērunt.

°**infestīs pīlis**   with javelins ready for the throw; lit., with hostile javelins   •   **ad gladiīs rediērunt**   they resorted to their swords
paulātim locō mōtus   gradually forced (lit., moved) from their position   •   **sē turmātim explicāre**   to deploy in successive squadrons
infestīsque signīs   in hostile array   •   **Quibus submōtīs**   with
these out of the way   [What is the literal meaning?]

POMPEY'S DEFEAT AND FLIGHT

Caesar, Pompēiānīs ex fugā intrā vallum compulsīs,
nūllum spatium perterritīs dare oportēre exīstimāns, mīlitēs
cohortātus est, ut beneficiō fortūnae ūterentur castraque
oppugnārent.

Castra ā cohortibus, quae ibi praesidiō erant relictae, 5
industriē dēfendēbantur, multō etiam ācrius ā Thrācibus
barbarīsque auxiliīs. Nam quī aciē refūgerant mīlitēs, et
animō perterritī et lassitūdine cōnfectī, missīs plērīque armīs°
signīsque mīlitāribus magis dē reliquā fugā quam dē castrōrum
dēfēnsiōne cōgitābant. Neque vērō diūtius, quī in vallō 10
cōnstiterant, multitūdinem tēlōrum sustinēre potuērunt, sed
cōnfectī vulneribus locum relīquērunt prōtinusque omnēs
ducibus° ūsī centuriōnibus tribūnīsque mīlitum in altissimōs
montēs, quī ad castra pertinēbant, cōnfūgērunt.

Pompēius, jam cum intrā vallum nostrī versārentur, equum 15
nactus dētractīs īnsignibus imperātōris decumānā portā sē
ex castrīs ējēcit prōtinusque equō citātō° Lārīsam contendit.
Neque ibi cōnstitit, sed eādem celeritāte paucōs suōs ex fugā
nactus nocturnō itinere nōn intermissō° comitātū equitum
trīgintā ad mare pervēnit nāvemque frūmentāriam cōnscendit. 20

°**missīs armīs**   having thrown away their weapons   •   **ducibus**   as
leaders   •   **equō citātō**   driving his horse hard   •   **nocturnō itinere
nōn intermissō**   without interrupting his journey at night

An ancient statue of Julius Caesar completely restored in modern times

In concluding his *Commentaries on the Civil War*, Caesar mentions Pompey's flight to Egypt. Since Pompey's father had helped Ptolemy's father regain the throne of Egypt, Pompey hoped for a friendly welcome. The Egyptians, however, treacherously killed him as he was landing.

In pursuit of Pompey, Caesar also went to Egypt. There the Romans became involved in Egyptian internal affairs. Although Caesar's comments break off at this point, we know from other sources that he stayed on for several months and was instrumental in gaining the throne of Egypt for Cleopatra.

On his way back to Rome, Caesar stopped in Asia, where he defeated King Pharnaces after a five days' campaign. Suetonius, writing about the triumph that took place to celebrate this victory, says:

Ponticō triumphō inter pompae fercula° trium verbōrum praetūlit titulum VENI • VIDI • VICI nōn ācta bellī significantem sīcut cēterīs,° sed celeriter cōnfectī nōtam.°

The battle of Thapsus in Africa (46 B.C.) regained that country for Caesar. In Spain the last of Pompey's men, including Labienus, Caesar's favorite staff officer of the Gallic wars, were defeated at Munda.

°**fercula** triumph biers; i.e., platforms or litters for carrying the trophies of war in triumphal procession • **sīcut cēterīs** as in other (triumphs) • **celeriter ... nōtam** as the mark of a swiftly completed war.

SUETONIUS, THE BIOGRAPHER

Other aspects of Caesar's life have come down to us in *The Lives of the Twelve Caesars*, by C. Suetonius Tranquillus. (See below.)

About Suetonius himself very little is known. He was certainly alive from A.D. 69 to 121, but he may have lived considerably longer. He is supposed to have been a secretary to Emperor Hadrian. Suetonius was a literary man, writing on antiquities, natural history, and grammar in addition to biography and history.

A list of his many writings has survived, but only two of his works have come down to us. Suetonius has been called the great gossip of antiquity, because he included many trivial details about his subjects, while ignoring or minimizing great events in their lives and times.

CAESAR'S APPEARANCE

Caesar fuisse trāditur excelsā statūrā,° colōre candidō, ōre plēniōre, nigrīs oculīs, valētūdine prosperā. Calvitiī° vērō dēfōrmitātem inīquissimē tulit. Ideōque et dēficientem capillum revocāre ā vertice adsuēverat et ex omnibus dēcrētis sibi ā senātū populōque honōribus nōn aliud recēpit libentius 5 quam jūs laureae corōnae perpetuō gerendae.

Eum vīnī parcissimum° esse nē inimīcī quidem negāvērunt. M. Catō dīxit ūnum ex omnibus Caesarem ad ēvertendam° rem pūblicam sōbrium accessisse.

°**excelsā statūrā** (abl. of specification, describing a physical quality of Caesar; as also each of the four phrases following) • **calvitiī dēfōrmitātem** the disfigurement of baldness • **eum vīnī parcissimum esse** he drank very little wine; lit., he was very thrifty with wine **ad ēvertendam rem pūblicam** for the purpose of overthrowing the government (state)

CAESAR AS ORATOR AND AUTHOR

Ēloquentiā mīlitārīque rē° aut aequāvit praestantissimōrum glōriam aut excessit. Post accūsātiōnem Dolābellae[1] haud dubiē prīncipibus patrōnīs° adnumerātus est. Certē Cicerō negat sē vidēre, cui dēbeat Caesar cēdere. Aitque eum ēlegantem, splendidam quoque atque etiam magnificam ra- 5 tiōnem dīcendī° tenēre.

Caesar relīquit et rērum suārum commentāriōs Gallicī cīvīlisque bellī Pompēiānī. Dē commentāriīs Caesaris Cicerō sīc refert: "Commentāriōs scrīpsit valdē quidem probandōs; nūdī sunt, rēctī et venustī, omnī ōrnātū ōrātiōnis tamquam 10 veste dētractā."

°**ēloquentiā mīlitārīque rē** in eloquence and in military skill **prīncipibus patrōnīs** first-rate lawyers (dat. with **adnumerātus est**) **ratiōnem dīcendī** style of speaking

[1]Cn. Cornelius Dolabella, consul for 81 B.C., and afterwards proconsul in Macedonia. In 77 B.C. he was tried on the charge of extortion in his province, with the twenty-three-year-old Caesar as his prosecutor and with Cotta and Hortensius as attorneys for the defense.

After Caesar had defeated the last of Pompey's group, he was in fact the sole ruler in Rome. He was dictator, imperator, and pontifex maximus at the same time. His portrait appeared on coins. The name of the month **Quīnctīlis** was changed in his honor to **Jūlius** (July).

Nobody claims, however, that Caesar rested on his laurels. With great energy he set about reconstructing the devastations of the civil war. In all areas of Roman life he initiated many reforms, the most lasting of which has been that of the calendar. Instead of the lunar year of 355 days and an occasional extra month for correction, he introduced the solar year of 365 days with an extra day every fourth or leap year.

Caesar's almost kinglike rule did not go unchallenged by the Roman people, who were traditionally tyrant haters. Suetonius reports the following about a conspiracy against him.

CAUSES OF THE CONSPIRACY

Tanta tamen cētera facta dictaque ejus° sunt, ut et abūsus[1] dominātiōne et jūre caesus[1] exīstimētur. Nōn enim honōrēs modo nimiōs recēpit (continuum cōnsulātum, perpetuam dictātūram, praenōmen Imperātōris, cognōmen Patris patriae, statuam inter rēgēs, sēdem auream in cūriā et prō tribūnālī, 5 templa, ārās, simulācra jūxtā deōs); appellātiōnem mēnsis ē suō nōmine cēpit.

Cōnspīrātum est igitur in eum ā sexāgintā virīs, Gāiō Cassiō Mārcōque et Decimō Brūtō prīncipibus cōnspīrātiōnis. Postquam senātus Īdibus Mārtiīs in Pompēī cūriam 1 convocātus est, facile tempus et locum° inventa sunt.

°**ejus** = **Caesaris** • **tempus et locum** the time and place (for an assassination)

THE IDES OF MARCH

Caesarī futūra caedēs multīs prōdigiīs dēnūntiāta est. Ob haec et ob īnfirmam valētūdinem diū cunctātus est, an sē domī continēret. Tandem Decimō Brūtō adhortante, quīntā hōrā prōgressus est et introiit cūriam.

[1]Supply **esse.** Remember that **abūsus** (deponent) is active in meaning and that **caesus** is passive in both form and meaning.

Assīdentem cōnspīrātī speciē officiī° circumstetērunt, et 5
Tillius Cimber, quī prīmās partēs° suscēperat, quasi aliquid
rogātūrus propius accessit et ab utrōque umerō togam appre-
hendit; deinde Caesarem clāmantem, "Ista quidem vīs est!"
alter vulnerat paulum īnfrā jugulum.

Caesar bracchium arreptum[1] stylō suō trājēcit cōnātusque 10
prōsilīre aliō vulnere tardātus est. Utque animadvertit
undique sē strictīs sīcīs petī, togā caput obvolvit, simul
sinistrā manū sinum ad īma crūra° dēdūxit, quō honestius
caderet etiam īnferiōre corporis parte vēlātā.

Atque ita tribus et vīgintī vulneribus cōnfossus est° sine 15
vōce ēditā, etsi trādidērunt quīdam Mārcō Brūtō dīxisse: "Et
tū, Brūte?"

Trēs serviolī eum domum rettulērunt.

Sunt quī putent Caesarem neque voluisse diūtius vīvere
neque cūrāvisse, quod aeger esset; itaque et quae religiōnes 20
et quae amīcī monērent neglēxisse.

°**speciē officiī** with a show of courtesy • **prīmās partēs** the
lead; i.e., the leading role (as on the stage) • **īma crūra** the lowest part of his legs • **cōnfossus est** (from **cōnfodiō**) he was
stabbed

THE DEIFIED JULIUS

Periit sextō et quīnquāgēsimō aetātis annō atque in deōrum
numerum relātus est voluntāte nōn modo senātūs sed etiam
vulgī. Stella crīnīta° per septem continuōs diēs fulsit,°
crēditumque est animam esse Caesaris in caelum receptī; et
hāc dē causā simulācrō ejus in vertice additur stella. 5

Cūriam, in quā occīsus est, obstruī placuit Īdūsque Mārtiās
Parricīdium nōminārī, ac nē umquam eō diē senātus agerētur.

°**stella crīnīta** a comet; lit., a star with long hair • **fulsit** (from
fulgeō) shone

[1]Caesar grasped the attacker's forearm and stabbed it with his pen; lit., Caesar stabbed
with his pen the grasped forearm.

SPECIAL VOCABULARY

Words in this list occur only in Units VI-VII. For other words in these sections see page 363.

*accūsātiō, -ōnis, F., trial

*adnumerō 1, reckon in the number of

adsuēscō, -ere, -suēvī, -suētum, grow accustomed (to)

Albicī, -ōrum, M., a Gallic tribe

*appellātiō, -ōnis, F., (act of) naming

assīdō, -ere, -sēdī, -sessum, sit down

*candidus, -a, -um, fair (complexion)

*capillus, -ī, M., hair (of head)

Cimber, L. Tillius, a conspirator

*cognōmen, -inis, N., family name

comitātus, -ūs, M., retinue, train

*commentārius, -ī, M., notebook, diary

*cōnspīrātī, -ōrum, M., conspirators

*cōnspīrō 1, form a plot, conspire

contegō, -ere, -tēxī, -tēctum, cover

*dēfēnsiō, -ōnis, F., protection

*dēminuō 3, reduce, diminish

*dēnūntiō 1, declare, announce

*dēstitūtus, -a, -um, deserted

*dominātiō, -ōnis, F., power

*ēlegāns, -antis (adj.), choice, fine

excubō 1, be watchful/vigilant

forās (adv.), out of doors

*fraus, fraudis, F., deceit, deception

funditor, -ōris, M., slinger

haud dubiē, certainly, undoubtedly

*honestē (adv.), respectably, properly

ideō(que) (adv.), on that account

*industriē (adv.), industriously

*jugulum, -ī, N., throat

*jūxtā (with acc.), close by, near

*labefaciō 3, cause to totter, shake

*languēns, -entis (adj.), faint, languid

laterīcius, -a, -um, (of) brick

Lepidus, Mārcus, consul for 79 B.C.

*Mārtius, -a, -um, of/sacred to Mars

*meritum, -ī, N., merit; service

musculus, -ī, M., movable shed

*nāvigium, -ī, N., vessel, ship

nimius, -a, -um, very great/much

*obvolvō, -ere, -volvī, -volūtum, wrap up

*parracīdium, -ī, N., murder of a parent

*perpetuō, (adv.), uninterruptedly

*persevērō 1, persist, persevere

pluteus, -ī, M., shield (on wheels)

*Ponticus, -a, -um, Pontic, of Pontus

*praenōmen, -inis, N., first name

*prōdigium, -ī, N., ominous sign

*prōfundō, -ere, -fūdī, -fūsum, pour forth

prōsiliō, -īre, -siluī, spring up

*prosperus, -a, -um, favorable

quemadmodum (adv.), how

*salūber, -bris, -bre, healthful

*serviolus, -ī, M., little slave

sīca, -ae, F., dagger

*significāns, -antis, distinct, clear

*simulācrum, -ī, N., image, likeness

*sinus, -ūs, M., fold, pleat

*sobrius, -a, -um, sober, moderate

*stringō, -ere, strīnxī, strictum, unsheathe, draw (a weapon)

Thrācēs, -ium, M., Thracians

*titulus, -ī, M., inscription

*turbidus, -a, -um, confused, agitated

valdē (adv.), intensely, very much

venustus, -a, -um, charming, lovely

*vertex, -icis, M., crown (of the head)

THE ROMAN CALENDAR had three points in each month from which the days were counted backward in giving dates.

Kalendae (the Kalends) were the first of each month.
Īdūs (the Ides) were the thirteenth or the fifteenth.
Nōnae (the Nones) were nine days before the Ides. (We would say eight days, whereas the Romans counted both the first and the last days of a series.)

In March, May, July, and October the Ides were the fifteenth; in all other months, the thirteenth. Thus, the Nones of March, May, July, and October were the seventh; of all other months, the fifth.

The day before each date-point was given as **prīdiē.**

December 31 = **pr. Kal. Jān. (prīdiē Kalendās Jānuāriās)**
March 6 = **pr. Nōn. Mār. (prīdiē Nōnās Mārtiās)**
April 12 = **pr. Īd. Apr. (prīdiē Īdūs Aprīlēs)**

In other dates a Roman numeral shows the number of days before each date-point. Why does the Roman numeral II never appear in a date? (Remember the Roman method of counting both ends of a series.)

Latin words used to designate the months are adjectives. In the form given here they modify **mēnsis** (often omitted); e.g., **(mēnsis) Aprīlis; (mēnsis) Jūnius.**

Jānuārius	Aprīlis	Jūlius[1]	Octōber
Februārius	Māius	Augustus[1]	November
Mārtius	Jūnius	September	December

These adjectives may also modify a date-point.

K. Apr. or **Kal. Apr. (Kalendae Aprīlēs)** = April 1
pr. Kal. Apr. (prīdiē Kalendās Aprīlēs) = March 31
a. d. III Kal. Apr. (ante diem tertium Kalendās Aprīlēs) = ?
Īd. Mār. (Īdibus Mārtiīs) = on March 15 (on the Ides of March)
pr. Īd. Mār. (prīdiē Īdūs Mārtiās) = ?
a. d. VIII Kal. Jān. = December 25; **a. d. IV Nōn. Jūl.** = ?

Say in Latin: March 1, 5, 6, 7; January 1, 10, 13.

[1]Earlier names were **Quīntīlis** for **Jūlius** and **Sextīlis** for **Augustus.**

PRONUNCIATION OF LATIN is determined by the sounds of the letters (vowels, diphthongs, consonants) and by the number and length of syllables in a word.

SOUNDS OF VOWELS AND DIPHTHONGS

Long Vowels	Short Vowels	Diphthongs
ā (father)	a (aha)	ae (like)
ē (they)	e (met)	au (round)
ī (meet)	i (pin)	eu (ĕ+oo)
ō (lone)	o (obey)	oe (boil)
ū (cool)	u (full)	ui (ruin)

CONSONANTS are in general the same as in English. Note, however, these sounds of letters and groups of letters.

g is hard (good)	c = k (cook)	bs = ps (cups)
s is soft (say)	i = y (yes)	bt = pt (kept)
ngu (language)	qu = kw (quick)	ch = k (look)
p (spin)	x = ks (extra)	ph = p (put)
t (stop)	v = w (wet)	th = t (ten)

SYLLABLES A Latin word has as many syllables as it contains vowels or diphthongs. A syllable is long if it contains a long vowel or a diphthong or if it ends in a consonant; otherwise it is short: **mo ne ō, au di ē tis, vi a, pic tū rae.**

WORD DIVISION If there are not more than two consonants between vowels, one goes with the vowel that follows: **la cū na, por tō, al tus, ve ni ō.**

If there are more than two consonants, the division is usually made after the first consonant: **ob scū rus, tem plum, mōn strum, pul chra.** Exception: **temp tō**

Compound words are separated into their elements: **ex it, ab est, in e ō, post e ā.**

When **x** occurs between two vowels, it goes with the first: **max i mum, dīx it, dūx i mus.**

ACCENT falls on the first syllable of a two-syllable word. In a longer word the accent falls on the next to last syllable if it is long. If that syllable is short, the one immediately preceding it is stressed: **al′tus, an ti′qua, a gri′co la.**

GENERAL VOCABULARY

This word list is a combined Latin-English and English-Latin vocabulary, including proper names and their definitions. It contains all the words required for the readings and excercises of this book, except words which occur only in Units VI and VII (Civil War). For these words, see the special vocabulary provided at the end of Unit VII (page 360).

A

ā, ab (with abl.), from, by, at; away from; on; since, after; away, off

abdō, -ere, -didī, -ditum, put away, hide; **sē abdere,** hide, withdraw

abdūcō, -ere, -dūxī, -ductum, lead/ take away; carry off

abeō, -ire, -iī, -itum, go away, retire

abjiciō, -ere, -jēcī, -jectum, cast away, throw (down), hurl

abripiō, -ere, -ripuī, -reptum, snatch/ carry away; drag off

absēns, gen., **-entis,** absent, away

abstineō, -ēre, -tinuī, -tentum, hold back, refrain/abstain from

absum, -esse, āfuī, āfutūrus, be absent/distant (from)

abundō, -āre, -āvī, -ātum, overflow

ac = atque, (conj.), and; and also

accēdō, -ere, -cessī, -cessum, come near/to, approach; be added (to)

accelerō, -āre, -āvī, -ātum, hasten

accendō, -ere, -cendī, -cēnsum, set fire to, light; inflame

acceptus, -a, -um, acceptable, pleasing, welcome

accidō, -ere, -cidī, occur; happen (to)

accipiō, -ere, -cēpī, -ceptum, take (in), receive; hear, learn; endure

accurrō, -currere, -currī/-cucurrī, -cursum, run to, come up hurriedly

accūsō, -āre, -āvī, -ātum, blame

ācer, ācris, ācre, sharp; eager, fierce

acerbē (adv.), bitterly, harshly

aciēs, aciēī, F., tip, edge; battle line; battle; **aciēs media,** the center

acquirō, -ere, -quisīvī, -quisītum, get, acquire

ācriter (adv.), sharply, fiercely

ācrius, more fiercely

ad (with acc.), to, against, toward, according to, up to; near (to), at, beside; for; until, on; (adv.), about

addō, -ere, -didī, -ditum, add, attach; give

addūcō, -ere, -dūxī, -ductum, lead/ bring (to), lead against, conduct; draw to/tight; induce, influence

adeō, -ire, -iī, -itum, go/come up to, approach; visit; face; attack

adeō (adv.), to such an extent; so

adhaereō, -ēre, -haesī, -haesum, hang/stick to, adhere

363

adhibeō, -ēre, -hibuī, -hibitum, apply; summon, admit, invite; bring

adhortor, -ārī, -ātus sum, encourage

adhūc (adv.), until now, as yet; still

adigō, -ere, -ēgī, -āctum, drive (to), compel, urge; hurl, drive in, ram in; haul, move, bring up; bind

adimō, -ere, -ēmī, -ēmptum, take away, remove

aditus, -ūs, M., approach, access

adjiciō, -ere, -jēcī, -jectum, hurl toward/on, throw (into); add (to)

adjūtor, -ōris, M., helper, assistant

Admētus, -ī, M., Adme'tus, ruler of Pher'ae in Thess'aly

administer, -trī, M., assistant, priest

administrātiō, -ōnis, F., the giving of help; direction, government

administrō, -āre, -āvī, -ātum, manage, administer, do; govern

admīror, -ārī, -ātus sum, wonder/be surprised at; admire

admittō, -ere, -mīsī, -missum, admit, receive; let go; commit; incur

admodum (adv.), fully; very (much)

admoneō, -ēre, -monuī, -monitum, admonish, remind, warn; urge, incite

admoveō, -ēre, -mōvī, -mōtum, move, bring (to)

adolēscō, -ere, adolēvī, adultum, grow up

adorior, -orīrī, -ortus sum, rise against, attack

adornō, -āre, -āvī, -ātum, adorn

Adriāticus, -a, -um, A'driat'ic

adsum, -esse, -fuī, -futūrus, be present/here/near; come

adulēscēns/adolēscēns, gen., **-entis,** young; (as noun) M., young man

adulēscentia, -ae, F., youth

advena, -ae, M./F., stranger

adveniō, -īre, -vēnī, -ventum, come to/up; arrive

adventus, -ūs, M., approach, arrival

adversārius, -a, -um, turned against; (as noun) M./F., antagonist, rival

adversus, -a, -um, facing, in front, opposite; unfavorable, hostile

adversus (prep. with acc.), against, opposite, facing; (adv.), to meet

advertō, -ere, -vertī, -versum, turn to; proceed against; **animum advertere,** observe, notice

aedificium, -ī, N., building, house

aedificō, -āre, -āvī, -ātum, build

aeger, aegra, aegrum, sick, feeble

aegrē (adv.), painfully; with difficulty; **aegrē ferre,** be indignant, resent

Aegyptus, -a, -um, Egyp'tian; M. pl., **Aegyptiī, -ōrum,** the Egyp'tians

Aemilius, -ī, L., M., Lu'cius Aemil'ius, an officer of the Gall'ic cavalry; also see **Paulus, L. Aemilius**

aequinoctium, -ī, N., the equinox

aequitās, -ātis, F., fairness, equity

aequō, -āre, -āvī, -ātum, equalize, make even/equal; adjust

aequus, -a, -um, even, level; equal; just, favorable; calm; **aequō animō,** calmly; without anxiety

aerārium, -ī, N., treasury, especially the public treasury at Rome

aes, aeris, N., copper, bronze; money; **aes aliēnum** (another's money), debt

aestās, -ātis, F., summer; **initā aestāte,** at the beginning of summer

aestimātiō, -ōnis, F., valuation, estimation

aestus, -ūs, M., a boiling; heat; tide

aetās, -ātis, F., age; generation

aeternus, -a, -um, eternal, everlasting

Āfer, Āfra, Āfrum, Af'rican; (as noun) M. pl., the Af'ricans

afferō, -ferre, attulī, allātum, bring, deliver; advance; report

afficiō, -ere, -fēcī, -fectum, do to; affect, treat; afflict; influence

afflīctō, -āre, -āvī, -ātum, damage greatly; afflict

afflīgō, -ere, -flīxī, -flīctum, strike, dash down; break, damage; afflict

afraid (be afraid), **timeō 2**

Āfrica, -ae, F., Af'rica

after, **postquam** (conj.)

ager, agrī, M., field, land, farm; country, territory, district

agger, aggeris, M., earthwork; (materials for) a rampart; timber

aggredior, -gredī, -gressus sum, advance against, attack; approach

agitō, -āre, -āvī, -ātum, drive (about); vex, agitate, disturb; consider; toss about

agmen, agminis, N., marching army/ column; army; **agmen claudere/ cōgere,** bring up the rear; **novissimum agmen,** the rear (line); **prīmum agmen,** van

agō, -ere, ēgī, āctum, drive; bring up; do, act; discuss, speak; **conventūs agere,** hold courts/assemblies; **grātiās agere,** give thanks, thank; **vītam agere,** live

agricola, -ae, M., farmer

agricultūra, -ae, F., agriculture

ait, he/she says, asserts; see p. 455

āla, -ae, F., wing; squadron (of cavalry)

alacritās, -ātis, F., activity, energy, eagerness

albus, -a, -um, white

Alcestis, -is, F., Alces'tis, wife of Adme'tus, king of Pher'ae

ālea, -ae, F., die (pl., dice); chance, risk; uncertainty

Alesia, -ae, F., Ale'sia, a Gallic town, scene of Ver'cinget'orix' final stand

alibī (adv.), elsewhere, at another place

aliēnus, -a, -um, another's, others'; foreign, strange; unfavorable; **aes aliēnum** (another's money), debt

aliquamdiū (adv.), for some time

aliquandō (adv.), at some time/any time, sometimes; at last

aliquī, -qua, -quod (adj.), some, any

aliquis, aliquid (pron.), someone, something; anyone, anything

aliquot (indecl. adj.), some, several

aliter (adv.), otherwise, differently; **aliter . . . ac,** otherwise than

alius, -a, -ud, another, other; different, else; **alius . . . alius,** one . . . another; pl., some . . . others

Allobrogēs, -um, M. pl., the Allob'-roges, a Gallic tribe

alloquor (adloquor), -loquī, -locūtus sum, address, speak to

alō, -ere, aluī, altum, nourish, support; rear; sustain; increase

Alpēs, Alpium, F. pl., the Alps

Alpīnus, -a, -um, of the Alps, Al'pine

alter, altera, alterum, the other, another; **alter . . . alter,** the one . . . the other; **diē alterō,** the next day

although, **cum** (conj. with subjunctive); **quamquam** (conj. with indicative)

altitūdō, -tūdinis, F., height; depth

altus, -a, -um, high, tall; deep; (as noun) N., the deep/sea

amātus, -a, -um, beloved

Ambarrī, -ōrum, M. pl., the Ambar'ri, a tribe of southern Gaul

Ambiorix, -īgis, M., Ambi'orix, king of the Eb'uro'nes in Bel'gic Gaul

ambō, -ae, -ō (adj./pron.), both

ambulō, -āre, -āvī, -ātum, walk

āmentia, -ae, F., folly, madness

amīcitia, -ae, F., friendship

amīcus, -a, -um, friendly, loving, kind; pleasing; (as noun) M., friend

amita, -ae, F., aunt

āmittō, -ere, -mīsī, -missum, lose; let slip, miss; send away; let go

amō, -āre, -āvī, -ātum, love, like

amor, -ōris, M., love

amplē (adv.), largely, generously; **amplius,** more, farther

amplus, -a, -um, large; great; noted, distinguished; splendid, generous

an (conj. used in double questions), or; **utrum . . . an,** whether . . . or; (used alone, introducing a question), or is it that? can it be that?

anceps, gen., **ancipitis,** ambiguous, uncertain; double

Ancōna, -ae, F., Anco'na, a town of the Pice'ni in Italy

ancora, -ae, F., anchor; **in ancorīs,** at anchor; **ancoram tollere,** weigh anchor, set sail

Andēs, Andium, M. pl., the An'des, a Gallic tribe

Androclēs, -is, M., An'drocles, a Roman slave

anew, **dē integrō/dē novō**

Anglia, -ae, F., Eng'land

angustē (adv.), narrowly, closely

angustia, -ae, F., narrowness; usually pl., narrow place, pass; narrows; difficulties

angustus, -a, -um, narrow

anicula, -ae, F., little old woman

anima, -ae, F., soul, mind

animadvertō, -ere, -vertī, -versum, turn the mind to, observe, notice

animal, -ālis (-ium), N., animal

animus, -ī, M., soul, mind; courage; spirit; feeling, heart; **aequus animus,** calmness; **animum advertere,** observe, notice, **ex animō,** sincerely; **in animō habēre,** intend (to . . .), have in mind

Aniō, Aniēnis, M., the An'io (river), a tributary of the Ti'ber

annus, -ī, M., year

ānser, -eris, M., goose

ante (prep. with acc.), before, in front of; (adv.), before, formerly, previously, ago

anteā (adv.), previously, before

antecēdō, -ere, -cessī, -cessum, go before, precede; (in time) precede (with dat.); excel, surpass (with dat./acc. of what/whom is surpassed)

antepōnō, -ere, -posuī, -positum, prefer, put before, place ahead

antequam (conj.), before, until (with indicative, especially in pres./perf.; with subjunctive to denote anticipation)

antīquitus (adv.), in former times, long ago, in ancient times

antīquus, -a, -um, old, former, ancient; (as noun) M. pl., the ancients

Antōnius, -ī, M., M., Mark An'tony, quaestor with Caesar in Gaul for two years; general/commander in the campaign in Greece

ānxius, -a, -um, anxious, uneasy

aper, aprī, M., wild boar

aperiō, -īre, aperuī, apertum, open (up), make accessible; reveal

apertē (adv.), obviously, openly

apertissimē (adv.), most openly

apertus, -a, -um, open, exposed, unprotected; plain, frank; **ab latere apertō,** on the unprotected flank

Apollō, Apollinis, M., Apol′lo, god of the sun

appāreō, -ēre, -pāruī, -pāritum, become visible, appear

appellō, -āre, -āvī, -ātum, call by name, address; appeal to; name

appellō, -ere, pulī, -pulsum, drive/ bring to; (with/without **nāvem)** bring to land, bring up, land

appetō, -ere, -petīvī, -petītum, strive after, seek; approach, attack

apple, **pōmum, -ī,** N.

appōnō, -ere, -posuī, -positum, serve; put on the table

appropinquō, -āre, -āvī, -ātum, come near, approach

apud (with acc.), at, near, before; among, in, with; to; in the possession of; at the home/house of

Āpūlia (Appūlia), -ae, F., Apu′lia, a region in southern Italy

aqua, -ae, F., water; aqueduct

aquila, -ae, F., eagle

Aquileia, -ae, F., Aq′uile′ia, a city in Cisal′pine Gaul

Aquitānia, -ae, F., Aq′uita′nia, southwestern Gaul, between the Garonne′ River and the Pyr′enees Mountains

Aquitānus, -a, -um, Aq′uita′nian; (as noun) M. pl., Aq′uita′nians

āra, ārae, F., altar

Arar, Araris, M., the A′rar, a river in Cel′tic Gaul, now called the Saône

arbitror, -ārī, -ātus sum, judge, believe, think, consider

arbor, arboris, F., tree

arcessō, -ere, -cessīvī, -cessītum, send for, summon, invite; seek

ārdēns, gen., **-entis,** burning, blazing

ārdeō, -ēre, ārsī, ārsūrus, be on fire, burn (up), glow, be consumed; be inflamed (with emotion)

Arelās, Arelātis, F., a town in Gal′lia Nar′bonen′sis, now Arles

arēna, -ae, F., sand; arena

argentum, -ī, N., silver

āridus, -a, -um, dry, parched, arid; (as noun) N., dry land

ariēs, arietis, M., ram; battering ram

Ariminum, -ī, N., Arim′inum, a town in Um′bria on the A′driat′ic coast

Ariovistus, -ī, M., Ar′iovis′tus, king of a German tribe

arma, -ōrum, N. pl., arms, weapons, implements, equipment

armātus, -a, -um, armed, equipped; (as noun) M. pl., armed men; troops

armō, -āre, -āvī, -ātum, equip, arm

arō, -āre, -āvī, -ātum, plow

Arrētium/Ārētium, -ī, N., Arre′tium, a town in Etru′ria, now Arez′zo

arripiō, -ere, -ripuī, -reptum, seize (on), lay hold of, snatch (hurriedly)

arrive, **perveniō** 4

arroganter (adv.), arrogantly

arrogantia, -ae, F., arrogance

ars, artis (-ium), F., skill, art; business, profession; craft, cunning

Arvernī, -ōrum, M. pl., the Arver′ni a tribe of Cel′tic Gaul

arx, arcis (-ium), F., citadel, fortress

ascendō, -ere, ascendī, ascēnsum, climb, mount, ascend; go aboard

ascēnsus, -ūs, M., ascent, approach

Asculum, -ī, N., As′culum, chief town of Pice′num

asinus, -ī, M., ass; dolt, blockhead

aspectus, -ūs, M., aspect, view

assiduus, -a, -um, continual

at (conj. used to contradict or introduce objections), but, yet, at least

āter, ātra, ātrum, black, dead black

Athēna, -ae, F., Athe′na, goddess of wisdom and of war

atque (conj.); and; and also; (after words of likeness/unlikeness) as, than, from; **simul atque,** as soon as

Atrebās, Atrebātis (-ium), M., an At′reba′tian, one of the At′reba′tes, a tribe of Bel′gic Gaul

ātrium, ātriī, N., atrium (principal room of a Roman house), hall, main room

Ātrius, -ī, M., Quin′tus A′trius, one of Caesar's officers

attingō, -ere, -tigī, -tāctum, touch, reach; border on; arrive at

Attius, -ī, M., Pub′lius At′tius Var′us, an officer in charge of Pompey's forces in Africa

attonitus, -a, -um, stunned, terrified

attribuō, -ere, -tribuī, -tribūtum, allot, assign, hand over; attribute

auctōritās, -ātis, F., influence, authority, prestige, dignity

audācia, -ae, F., boldness; audacity

audācter (adv.), boldly, fiercely

audāx, gen., **-ācis,** daring, bold

audeō, -ēre, ausus sum, dare; be courageous; see p. 444

audiō, -īre, -īvī, -ītum, hear, listen to; learn; **dictō audiēns,** obedient

auferō, -ferre, abstulī, ablātum, carry away, remove; destroy

augeō, -ēre, auxī, auctum, enlarge, grow, increase, add to

Augustīnus, -ī (Sānctus), M., St. Au′gustine (354-430 A.D.), Bishop of North Africa, and a leader in early Christianity

Augustus, -ī, M., Augus′tus, title granted to Octa′vian as emperor

Aulus, -ī, M., Au′lus, a given name

aunt, **amita, -ae,** F.; **mātertera, -ae,** F.

aureus, -a, -um, of gold, golden

aurīga, -ae, M., charioteer

aurum, -ī, N., gold

aut (conj.), or; **aut . . . aut,** either . . . or

autem (conj./adv.), but, however; moreover (never first in clause)

auxilium, -ī, N., help, aid, support; pl., auxiliary troops, reinforcements

Auximum, -ī, N., Aux′imum, a town of the Pice′ni, now Os′imo

avāritia, -ae, F., greed, avarice

āvehō, -ere, āvexī, āvectum, carry off/away; take away

āvertō, -ere, āvertī, āversum, turn away/aside, avert, divert; (perf. part.) with back turned

avis, avis (-ium), F., bird

āvolō, -āre, -āvī, -ātum, fly away

avunculus, -ī, M., uncle

avus, -ī, M., grandfather

B

Baculus, -ī, M., Pub′lius Sex′tius Bac′ulus, one of Caesar's centurions

balneum, -ī, N., bath, bathing place

barbarus, -a, -um, uncivilized, rude; (as noun) M. pl., barbarians, strangers

basilica, -ae, F., basilica (a building used as a public meeting place and hall of justice)

be, **sum, esse, fuī, futūrus**

be afraid (of), **timeō 2**

bear (carry), **ferō, ferre, tulī, lātum**

beātus, -a, -um, happy, fortunate

because, **quod, cum** (conjs.)

become, **fīō, fierī, factus sum**

before, **ante** (prep. with acc.); **prius-quam/antequam** (conjs.)

behave, **sē gerere 3**

be informed, **certior fierī;** see **fīō**

Belgae, -ārum, M. pl., the Bel'gians, one of three divisions of Gauls

Belgium, -ī, N., Bel'gium, country of the Bel'gae

believe, **crēdō 3** (with dative)

bellicōsus, -a, -um, warlike, bellicose

bellō, -āre, -āvī, -ātum, carry on/wage war

Bellovacī, -ōrum, M. pl., the Bellov'-aci, a tribe of Bel'gic Gaul

bellum, -ī, N., war; **bellō ac pāce,** in war and peace; **bellum gerere,** wage war; **bellum īnferre,** make war on (with dat.)

bellus, -a, -um, beautiful, lovely

bene (adv.), well, rightly, successfully; quite; **melius,** better; **optimē,** best

benedictiō, -ōnis, F., blessing

beneficium, -ī, N., kindness, favor, benefit, good deed, service; honor

benevolentia, -ae, F., kindliness

benignē (adv.), kindly, courteously

benignitās, -ātis, F., kindness, mild-ness; liberality, generosity

benignus, -a, -um, kind

be rumored, **fāmam esse**

bēstia, -ae, F., (wild) beast, animal

be sure, **certum habēre 2**

between, **inter** (with acc.)

bibō, -ere, bibī, drink

Bibracte, -is, N., Bibrac'te, town of the Haed'ui

Bibrax, Bibractis, F., Bi'brax, town of the Re'mi

biduum, -ī, N., (period of) two days

biennium, -ī, N., (period of) two years

bird, **avis, avis (-ium),** F.

bis (adv.), twice, doubly, in two ways

Biturigēs, -um, M. pl., the Bit'uri'ges, a tribe of central Gaul

Boiī, -ōrum, M. pl., the Boi'i, a tribe once very powerful in southern Germany and Cisal'pine Gaul

bonitās, -ātis, F., goodness; fertility

bonus, -a, -um, good; (as noun) N., good, advantage; N. pl., goods, property; **melior, -ius,** better; **op-timus, -a, -um,** best, excellent

bōs, bovis, M./F., bull, ox, cow; pl., cattle, oxen; see p. 456

boy, **puer, puerī,** M.

bracchium, -ī, N., forearm, arm

break camp, **castra movēre 2**

brevis, -e, short, brief, small; **brevī/brevī tempore,** briefly, quickly, soon

brevitās, -ātis, F., brevity, shortness

bring, **ferō, ferre, tulī, lātum**

Britannia, -ae, F., Brit'ain

Britannus, -ī, M., Brit'on

Brundisīnus, -a, -um, Brundis'ian, of Brundis'ium

Brundisium, -ī, N., Brundis'ium (now Brin'disi'), port at southeastern ex-tremity of Italian peninsula

Bruttius, -a, -um, Bru'ttian, of the Bru'ttii, inhabitants of southern Italy

Brūtus, -ī, M., De'cius Ju'nius Bru'tus, Caesar's admiral in the siege of Massi'lia

Brūtus, -ī, L. Jūnius, -ī, M., Lu'cius
Ju'nius Bru'tus, leader of revolt
against Tar'quin

but, **sed** (conj.)

by, **ā/ab** (with abl.); by means of, (abl.
without prep.)

C

C. (abbr. for **Gāius, -ī**), M., Ga'ius, a
given name

Cabūrus, -ī, C. Valerius, -ī, M.,
Ga'ius Vale'rius Cabu'rus, a Gaul
who had received Roman citizenship

cadō, -ere, cecidī, cāsūrus, fall, happen; fall (dead), be slain, perish

Cadūrcī, -ōrum, M. pl., the Cadur'ci,
a tribe of southwestern Gaul

caecus, -a, -um, blind; hidden; dark

caedēs, -is (-ium/-um), F., murder,
slaughter, bloodshed

caedō, -ere, cecīdī, caesum, cut
(down), kill, slay; rout

caelestis, -e, heavenly; (as noun) M.
pl., the gods

caelum, -ī, N., heaven; air; sky

Caesar, -aris, C. Jūlius, -ī, M., Ga'-
ius Jul'ius Cae'sar, Roman general
and author

Caesar, -aris, L., M., Lu'cius Cae'sar,
a distant relative of Jul'ius Cae'sar,
who served on his staff in Gaul

calamitās, -ātis, F., disaster, calamity

calceus, -ī, M., shoe

calidus, -a, -um, warm, hot; violent

Callicula, -ae, F., Calli'cula, a mountain in Campa'nia near Casili'num

calor, -ōris, M., warmth, heat, glow

Camillus, -ī, M., Mar'cus Fu'rius
Camil'lus, who took Ve'ii and freed
Rome from the Gauls

Campānus, -a, -um, Campa'nian

campus, -ī, M., plain, field

can, **possum, posse, potuī**

candeō, -ēre, canduī, shine, glitter;
glow with heat

canis, canis (-um), M./F., dog, hound

Cannae, -ārum, F. pl., Cann'ae, a
town in Apu'lia, scene of Roman
defeat by Hann'ibal in 216 B.C.

Cannēnsis, -e, of/from Cann'ae

canō, -ere, cecinī, sing, play; **receptuī
canere,** sound the signal for retreat

cantō, -āre, -āvī, -ātum, sing

Capēna, -ae, F., Cape'na, a town in
Etru'ria; **Porta Capēna,** gate in
"Servian" Wall at Rome at the be-
ginning of the Appian Way; see p. 158

capiō, -ere, cēpī, captum, take, capture, seize; receive; reach; attract;
cōnsilium capere, form/adopt a
plan; **initium capere ā/ab,** begin at

Capitōlium, -ī, N., the Cap'itol, a
temple of Ju'piter in Rome on Cap'-
itoline' Hill; also the Cap'itoline',
one of the Seven Hills of Rome

captīvus, -a, -um, captive; (as noun)
M., prisoner, captive

capture, **capiō** 3

Capua, -ae, F., Cap'ua, a city in Italy

Capuānus, -a, -um, Cap'uan, of
Cap'ua; (as noun) M./F., Capuan, a
resident of Capua

caput, capitis, N., head; top; source
or mouth (of a river); person, citizen,
individual; citizenship; chief city/
town; capital; **capite dēmissō/
dējectō,** with bowed/downcast head

carcer, -eris, M., prison; starting place
(of a race course)

cāritās, -ātis, F., dearness, love, esteem

carmen, carminis, N., song, tune; poetry; prediction, oracular declaration; incantation, magic formula

Carnutēs, -um, M. pl., the Car'nutes, a tribe of Cel'tic Gaul

carō, carnis, F., meat, flesh

carrus, -ī, M., cart

carry, **portō** 1, **ferō, gerō** 3

Carthāginiēnsis, -e, of Car'thage, Car'thagin'ian; (as noun) M. pl., Car'thagin'ians

Carthāgō, -inis, F., Car'thage, city in North Af'rica; **Carthāgō Nova** (now Car'tage'na), New Car'thage, a Car'thagin'ian colony in Spain founded in 228 B.C.

cārus, -a, -um, dear, beloved; **cārum habēre,** love, esteem

casa, -ae, F., cottage, hut

cāseus, -ī, M., cheese

Casilīnum, -ī, N., Casili'num, a town in Campa'nia

Casīnās, gen., **Casīnātis,** of/belonging to Casi'num

Casīnum, -ī, N., Casi'num, town in La'tium (near the present Mon'te Casi'no)

Cassiānus, -a, -um, Cas'sian, referring to Lu'cius Cas'sius, a consul, conquered and killed by the Helve'tii; **Bellum Cassiānum,** war in which Cas'sius was slain

Cassius, -ī, L., M., Lu'cius Cas'sius, consul in 107 B.C.

castellum, -ī, N., fort, fortress

Casticus, -ī, M., Cas'ticus, a Sequa'nian noble

Castor, -oris, M., Cas'tor, brother of Helen and twin brother of Pol'lux

castra, -ōrum, N. pl., camp, military encampment; **castra facere/pōnere,** pitch camp; **castra habēre,** encamp; **castra movēre,** break camp

cāsus, -ūs, M., fall; accident, chance, happening, occurrence; emergency; disaster, fate; **cāsū,** by chance

catēna, -ae, F., chain, shackle

Caturigēs, -um, M. pl., the Cat'uri'ges, a Gall'ic tribe of the Province

caupō, -ōnis, M., innkeeper

caupōna, -ae, F., tavern, inn

causa, -ae, F., cause, reason, excuse; a cause, interest; **causā** (abl. with preceding genitive) for the sake of, on account of; **causam dīcere,** plead a case; **quā dē causā/quam ob causam,** why

Cavarillus, -ī, M., Cav'aril'lus, a Haed'uan noble

caveō, -ēre, cāvī, cautum, beware of, take care

caverna, -ae, F., cavern, cave

cēdō, -ere, cessī, cessum, go away, abandon; give up, withdraw; yield

celebrō, -āre, -āvī, -ātum, solemnize; publish; honor

celer, celeris, celere, swift, sudden

celeritās, -ātis, F., speed, swiftness

celeriter (adv.), swiftly, quickly

celerrimē (adv.), very quickly; **quam celerrimē,** as quickly as possible

cēlō, -āre, -āvī, -ātum, conceal, hide

Celtae, -ārum, M. pl., the Celts, inhabitants of Cel'tic Gaul; the Gauls

cēna, -ae, F., dinner

cēnō, -āre, -āvī, -ātum, eat

cēnseō, -ēre, cēnsuī, cēnsum, assess; think; propose, vote, judge

cēnsor, -ōris, M., censor (a Roman magistrate responsible for the census)

cēnsus, -ūs, M., census (an enumeration of the people according to wealth for purposes of taxation and military service); count

centum (indecl. adj.), hundred

centuriō, -ōnis, M., centurion (commander of a hundred men); non-commissioned officer

cernō, -ere, crēvī, crētum, separate, distinguish; discern, see

certāmen, certāminis, N., struggle, battle; contest, trial

certē (adv.), surely; at least,

certō, -āre, -āvī, -ātum, settle by contest; fight, struggle, vie with

certus, -a, -um, definite, settled, certain, fixed; sure; **aliquem certiōrem facere,** inform someone; **certior fierī,** be informed; **certum habēre,** be certain (about/that)

cervus, -ī, M., stag, deer

cēterī, -ae, -a, pl., the rest of, the other/remaining; (as noun) M., the rest, others, all the rest

Ceutronēs, -um, M. pl., the Ceu'trones, a Gall'ic tribe

cibus, -ī, M., food

Cicerō, -ōnis, M., Quin'tus Cic'ero, one of Caesar's officers in Gaul

Cimbrī, -ōrum, M. pl., the Cim'bri, a people of northern Germany

cingō, -ere, cīnxī, cīnctum, surround, encircle; gird on

cinis, cineris, M. (rarely F.,) usually pl., ashes; remains of a corpse after cremation

circā (adv./prep. with acc.), around, round about, near(by)

circiter (adv./prep. with acc.), around, about, near(by)

circuitus, -ūs, M., a going around; circumference; **in circuitū,** all around, on all sides

circum (with acc.), around, about

circumdō, -dare, -dedī, -datum, place/put around; surround

circumeō, -ire, -iī, -itum, go around (to); inspect

circumjiciō, -ere, -jēcī, -jectum, throw/put around; surround

circummittō, -ere, -mīsī, -missum, send/put around

circumsistō, -ere, -stetī, stand around, surround

circumspectō, -āre, -āvī, -ātum, look around at/for; wait/watch for

circumstō, -stāre, -stetī, stand around/ in a circle; surround

circumveniō, -ire, -vēnī, -ventum, surround, outflank; deceive

Circus (-ī) Maximus (-ī), M., the Cir'cus Max'imus, the great circus/ race course in Rome

citerior, -ius, on this side; nearer

cīvilis, -e, of a citizen, civil, civic

cīvis, cīvis (-ium), M./F., citizen

cīvitās, -ātis, F., citizenship; the/a state, nation, city

clam (adv.), secretly, privately

clāmitō, -āre, -āvī, -ātum, cry out repeatedly, exclaim

clāmō, -āre, -āvī, -ātum, cry/shout

clāmor, -ōris, M., loud cry, shout, clamor; shout of approval; **clāmōrem tollere,** set up a shout/cry

clandestinus, -a, -um, hidden, secret

clārus, -a, -um, bright, clear; loud; famous

classis, -is (-ium), F., division, class; fleet

claudō, -ere, clausī, clausum, shut, close, fasten; hem in; **agmen claudere,** bring up the rear

claudus, -a, -um, lame; crippled

clāva, -ae, F., club, stick

cliēns, -entis (-ium), M., dependent, follower, client

clīvus, -ī, M., slope, rise; ascent

cloak, **palla, -ae,** F.

coëmō, -emere, -ēmī, -ēmptum, buy (up)

coepī, coepisse, coeptum, have begun, began; see p. 455

coërceō, -ēre, -uī, -itum, check

cōgitātiō, -ōnis, F., meditation

cōgitō, -āre, -āvī, -ātum, consider carefully, think over; plan, intend

cognitiō, -ōnis, F., knowledge, acquaintance (with)

cognōscō, -nōscere, -nōvī, -nitum, become acquainted with, investigate, learn (about); (perf.) know, be aware (of); recognize

cōgō, -ere, coēgī, coāctum, bring together, collect; compel, force; **agmen cōgere,** bring up the rear

cohors, cohortis (-ium), F., cohort (tenth part of a Roman legion); **cohors praetōria,** guard of honor

cohortātiō, -ōnis, F., encouragement

cohortor, -ārī, -ātus sum, encourage

collēga, -ae, M., colleague, partner

colligō, -ere, -lēgī, -lēctum, gather/bring together, collect; gain, acquire

Collina, -ae (Porta Collina), F., Porta Colli'na, a gate in the "Servian" Wall at Rome; see p. 158

collis, -is (-ium), M., hill, height

collocō, -āre, -āvī, -ātum, station, arrange; establish; place

colloquium, -ī, N., conference, conversation, interview

colloquor, -loquī, -locūtus sum, talk with, converse, confer

colō, -ere, coluī, cultum, cultivate, till; live/dwell in; honor, worship

colōna, -ae, F., country woman

color, -ōris, M., color, hue

columen, -inis, N., height, summit, crown; support

coma, -ae, F., hair

combūrō, -ere, combussī, combustum, burn up

come, **veniō 4**

comes, comitis, M./F., companion, comrade, associate; attendant

comitium, -ī, N., place of assembly; meeting place in the Roman Forum; pl., assembly; elections

commeātus, -ūs, M., communication; trip; supply train; supplies

commemorō, -āre, -āvī, -ātum, mention, relate, state

commendō, -āre, -āvī, -ātum, entrust; commend; surrender

commeō, -āre, -āvī, -ātum, go back and forth; (with **ad**) visit

commīlitō, -ōnis, M., fellow soldier

committō, -ere, -mīsī, -missum, send/bring together; commit; entrust, trust to; **proelium committere,** begin/engage in battle

Commius, -ī, M., Com'mius, chief of the At'reba'tes

commodē (adv.), conveniently, easily, well; **satis commodē,** with sufficient ease, very easily

commodus, -a, -um, convenient, suitable; (as noun) N., convenience, advantage

commoror, -ārī, -ātus sum, stop, stay, wait

commoveō, -ēre, -mōvī, -mōtum, excite, arouse, stir up, disturb, alarm

commūnicō, -āre, -āvī, -ātum, make common; communicate, impart; share, divide; (with prep. **cum**) add to

commūniō, -īre, -īvī, -ītum, fortify strongly, entrench

commūnis, -e, common, in common, general, public

commūtātiō, -ōnis, F., change

commūtō, -āre, -āvī, -ātum, change, exchange

comparō, -āre, -āvī, -ātum, prepare (for), provide; secure, obtain

compellō, -ere, -pulī, -pulsum, drive together, collect; force, compel

comperiō, -īre, -perī, -pertum, find out, discover, learn

compleō, -ēre, -plēvī, -plētum (with abl.), fill (up), man (with)

complexus, -ūs, M., embrace; love

complūrēs, -plūra/-plūria, pl., several, a number of, many; a great many

compluvium, -ī, N., compluvium (a quadrangular opening in roof of atrium to admit light and rain water)

compōnō, -ere, -posuī, -positum, arrange; draw up, bring together; collect together, compose; put, place

comportō, -āre, -āvī, -ātum, bring together, collect

compositiō, -ōnis, F., orderly arrangement; settlement of differences

comprehendō, -ere, -hendī, -hēnsum, seize, catch, grasp

comprimō, -ere, -pressī, -pressum, press/squeeze together; hold back, restrain, check

comrade, **socius, -ī,** M.; **comes, comitis,** M.

cōnātum, -ī, N., attempt

cōnātus, -ūs, M., attempt, effort

concēdō, -ere, -cessī, -cessum, go away, yield; grant, permit; (impers.) **concēditur,** it is granted/admitted

concessiō, -ōnis, F., concession

concidō, -ere, -cidī, fall (down)

concīdō, -ere, -cīdī, -cīsum, cut down/to pieces; kill

concilium, -ī, N., meeting, council

conclāmō, -āre, -āvī, -ātum, cry out together, shout, exclaim

concurrō, -ere, -currī/-cucurrī, -cursum, assemble hurriedly, come / run together; engage in battle

concursus, -ūs, M., a running together; meeting; attack; collision

condiciō, -ōnis, F., terms; condition

condō, -dere, -didī, -ditum, found, establish; store (up)

condūcō, -ere, -dūxī, -ductum, bring together; escort, lead, conduct

conduct (lead), **dūcō, condūcō, dēdūcō, perdūcō** 3; (manage), **gerō** 3

cōnferō, -ferre, contulī, collātum, bring (together), collect, gather; compare; ascribe; **sē cōnferre,** proceed, withdraw, go

cōnfessiō, -ōnis, F., acknowledgment, confession, admission

cōnfestim (adv.), at once, immediately

cōnficiō, -ere, -fēcī, -fectum, make; finish, accomplish; consume; weaken, exhaust; (of troops) muster, raise; **ad eās cōnficiendās,** to accomplish/complete this

cōnfīdō, -ere, -fīsus sum, be confident, have confidence (in), rely on

cōnfirmō, -āre, -āvī, -ātum, strengthen, confirm; establish; encourage, reassure, assert, assure

cōnfiteor, -fitērī, -fessus sum, confess, admit, acknowledge

cōnflīgō, -ere, -flixī, -flictum, come together, collide; contend, fight

cōnfugiō, -ere, -fūgī, flee, take refuge

cōnfūsē (adv.), confusedly, obscurely

congrātulor, -ārī, -ātus sum (with dat.), wish . . . joy, congratulate

congredior, -gredī, -gressus sum, encounter, meet; engage in battle with, contend

congregō, -āre, -āvī, -ātum, come together

congressus, -ūs, M., meeting

conjiciō, -ere, -jēcī, -jectum, throw/put together; throw, hurl

conjungō, -ere, -jūnxī, -jūnctum, join/fasten together, join, unite

conjūnx, -jugis, M./F., husband/wife; spouse

conjūrātiō, -ōnis, F., conspiracy

cōnor, -ārī, -ātus sum, try, attempt

conquīrō, -ere, -quīsīvī, quīsītum, search/hunt for

cōnsanguineus, -a, -um, related by blood; (as noun) M. pl., kinsmen, relatives

cōnscendō, -ere, -scendī, -scēnsum, climb/go aboard, embark on

cōnscrībō, -ere, -scrīpsī, -scrīptum, write; enroll, levy

cōnsecrātus, -a, -um, consecrated

cōnsēnsiō, -ōnis, F., agreement, harmony

cōnsequor, -sequī, -secūtus sum, follow up/after, pursue; overtake; obtain, accomplish

cōnservō, -āre, -āvī, -ātum, save, spare; observe

Cōnsidius, -ī, P., M., Pub'lius Consid'ius, an officer in Caesar's army

cōnsīdō, -ere, -sēdī, -sessum, sit down; halt; encamp, settle

cōnsilior, -ārī, -ātus sum, hold a consultation, consult, take counsel

cōnsilium, -ī, N., deliberation; counsel; advice; judgment; plan, purpose; council; cōnsilium capere, form/adopt a plan

cōnsimilis, -e, very like, similar

cōnsistō, -ere, -stitī, take one's stand, halt, stop, settle, make a stand; consist (in); signa cōnsistere, halt

cōnsōlor, -ārī, -ātus sum, comfort, console

cōnspectus, -ūs, M., sight, view

cōnspiciō, -ere, -spexī, -spectum, catch sight of, look at, observe

cōnspicor, -ārī, -ātus sum, catch sight of, see, observe, behold

cōnstantia, -ae, F., steadiness, firmness, constancy

cōnstituō, -ere, -stituī, -stitūtum, place, station; set up, establish; arrange; appoint; decree, decide

cōnstō, -stāre, -stitī, -stātūrus, stand together/with; consist; agree; (impers.) cōnstat, it is known/certain/agreed/evident

cōnstruō, -ere, -strūxī, -strūctum, build, construct

cōnsuēscō, -ere, -suēvī, -suētum, become accustomed; (perf.) be accustomed/in the habit (of)

cōnsuētūdō, -inis, F., custom, habit, way (of life), manner of living

cōnsul, cōnsulis, M., consul

cōnsulāris, -e, relating to a consul, consular; (as noun) M., ex-consul

cōnsulātus, -ūs, M., consulship

cōnsulō, -ere, -suluī, -sultum, deliberate, consult; look out for; take thought for

cōnsultō, -āre, -āvī, -ātum, deliberate

cōnsultum, -ī, N., decree; **ex senātūs cōnsultō,** by decree of the senate

cōnsūmō, -ere, -sūmpsī, -sūmptum, consume, destroy; spend

cōnsurgō, -ere, -surrēxī, -surrēctum, stand up, arise (together/in a body)

contemnō, -ere, -tempsī, -temptum, scorn, despise

contemplor, -ārī, -ātus sum, gaze upon, observe, look at attentively, survey, regard, contemplate

contemptiō, -ōnis, F., contempt

contendō, -ere, -tendī, -tentum, attempt; contend, fight; hurry; insist

contentus, -a, -um, satisfied, contented

contexō, -ere, -texuī, -textum, weave together

continēns, -entis, F., continent

continenter (adv.), continually

contineō, -ēre, -tinuī, -tentum, hold together; shut in, bound; contain, maintain, restrain, check

contingō, -ere, -tigī, -tāctum, extend to, touch; adjoin; happen to

continuō, -āre, -āvī, -ātum, join; continue

continuus, -a, -um, uninterrupted, successive, continuous

cōntiō, -ōnis, F., assembly of the people/soldiers; public meeting

contrā (adv.), on the contrary, on the opposite side; against (him/them); (prep. with acc.) against, opposite

contrahō, -ere, -trāxī, -tractum, gather, draw together, bring together

contrōversia, -ae, F., dispute, quarrel controversy, **contrōversia, -ae,** F.

convehō, -ere, -vexī, -vectum, bring together, carry into one place

convellō, -ere, -vellī, -vulsum, tear, pull up/away/out; **signa convellere,** pull out/up the standards

conveniō, -īre, -vēnī, -ventum, come (together), meet (with), assemble; convene; come to, arrive; (impers.) **convenit,** an agreement is made, it is agreed/fitting

conventus, -ūs, M., meeting, court

convertō, -ere, -vertī, -versum, turn, change, convert; wheel about; **aciem/signa convertere,** face about

Convictolitāvis, -is, M., Convic'-tolita'vis, a chief of the Haed'ui

convivium, -ī, N., feast, entertainment, banquet; the company assembled

convocō, -āre, -āvī, -ātum, call (together), summon

coörior, -orīrī, -ortus sum, arise

cōpia, -ae, F., abundance, supply; plenty; opportunity; amount, number; pl., resources, wealth, supplies, provisions; forces, troops; **pedestrēs cōpiae,** infantry forces, infantry

cōpiōsus, -a, -um, copious, plentiful, rich, full, well supplied

cor, cordis, N., heart; **cordī esse,** be dear (to)

Corfinium, -ī, N., Corfin'ium, capital of the Paelig'ni, headquarters of Italian Confederacy in Social War

cornū, -ūs, N., wing (of an army); flank; horn (of an animal)

corōna, -ae, F., crown

corpus, corporis, N., body; corpse

corripiō, -ere, -ripuī, -reptum, seize, take hold of; attack

Cōrus, -ī, M., Cor'us, the northwest wind

Cosānus, -a, -um, of/belonging to Co'sa, an ancient town in Etru'ria

cotīdiānus, -a, -um, daily; usual

cotīdiē (adv.), every day, daily

Cotta, -ae, M., Lu'cius Aurun'cule'ius Cott'a, one of Caesar's generals

cottage, **casa, -ae,** F.

Cotus, -ī, M., Co'tus, a Haed'uan

could; see can

crās (adv.), tomorrow; in the future

Crassus (-ī), M. Licinius (-ī), M., Mar'cus Licin'ius Crass'us, triumvir with Caesar and Pompey; also, his son, one of Caesar's quaestors

crāstinus, -a, -um, of tomorrow

Creātor, -ōris, M., the Crea'tor; God

crēber, crēbra, crēbrum, thick, numerous, frequent

crēdō, -ere, -didī, -ditum, entrust, commit; believe, think; trust in

cremō, -āre, -āvī, -ātum, burn, cremate

Cremōna, -ae, F., Cremo'na, town in northern Italy

creō, -āre, -āvī, -ātum, create; elect

Crēs, Crētis, M., inhabitant of Crete

Crēscēns, Crēscentis, M., Cres'cent, name of a charioteer

crēscō, -ere, crēvī, crētum, grow, thrive, increase

Critognātus, -ī, M., Crit'ogna'tus, a chief of the Arver'ni

cruciātus, -ūs, M., torture; cruelty

crūdēlis, -e, cruel, unmerciful

crūdēlitās, -ātis, F., cruelty

crūdēliter (adv.), cruelly

crūs, crūris, N., shin, shin bone, leg

crux, crucis, F., cross

cubiculum, -ī, N., bedroom

culpa, -ae, F., blame, guilt

cultus, -ūs, M., cultivation; training, education; refinement, civilization

cum (prep. with abl.), with, along with; **-cum** (attached to pron.), with

cum (conj.), when, whenever; because, since; although, though; **cum . . . tum,** both . . . and; not only . . . but also; **cum prīmum,** as soon as

cūnctor, -ārī, -ātus sum, delay, hesitate; be reluctant

cupiditās, -ātis, F., desire, eagerness, enthusiasm

cupidus, -a, -um, desirous (of), eager (for), fond (of)

cupiō, -ere, -īvī, -ītum, wish eagerly, desire, be eager, wish (for)

cūr (interrog. adv.), why?

cūra, -ae, F., care, attention; anxiety

cūria, -ae, F., curia, senate house

cūrō, -āre, -āvī, -ātum, care (for), take care of, cure; cause (to be done)

currō, -ere, cucurrī, cursum, run

currus, -ūs, M., chariot, car

cursus, -ūs, M., a running, race; pace, speed; course, way; journey

custōdia, -ae, F., watch, garrison, guard

custōdiō, -īre, -īvī, -ītum, watch, guard, defend, protect

custōs, custōdis, M./F., guard, spy

Cyclōps, -clōpis, Cy'clops, one-eyed giant, a workman of Vul'can

D

damnō, -āre, -āvī, -ātum, condemn, convict

dē (with abl.), from, down from, away from; of, on account of, in accordance with; concerning, about

dea, deae, F., goddess

dēbeō, -ēre, -uī, -itum, owe; be under obligation to; ought, must

dēcēdō, -ere, -cessī, -cessum, withdraw/retire from; depart; avoid; die

decem (indecl. adj.), ten

dēcernō, -ere, -crēvī, -crētum, decide, decree, resolve, vote

dēcertō, -āre, -āvī, -ātum, fight out/ to the end; fight, contend

decimus, -a, -um, tenth

dēcipiō, -ere, -cēpī, -ceptum, take in, deceive

dēclārō, -āre, -āvī, -ātum, make clear/distinct, reveal, declare

dēclīnō, -āre, -āvī, -ātum, turn aside, deviate; shun

dēcurrō, -ere, -cucurrī/-currī, -cursum, run down, hurry along

decus, decoris, N., distinction, honor

dēdecus, dēdecoris, N., shame, dishonor, disgrace

dēditiō, -ōnis, F., surrender

dēdō, -ere, -didī, -ditum, give up; devote (to); **sē dēdere,** surrender

dēdūcō, -ere, -dūxī, -ductum, lead away/down, bring; withdraw; settle; launch (ships); unfurl (sails)

dēfectiō, -ōnis, F., revolt, desertion

dēfendō, -ere, -fendī, -fēnsum, keep /ward off, repel; defend, protect

dēferō, -ferre, -tulī, -lātum, bring (down/away), offer; confer; report

dēfessus, -a, -um, exhausted, weary

dēficiō, -ere, -fēcī, -fectum, fail, run out, be missing; desert; revolt

dēfīgō, -ere, -fīxī, -fīxum, fasten (down), fix (in); secure, plant firmly

dēfīniō, -īre, -īvī, -ītum, limit, mark off; determine

dēfugiō, -ere, -fūgī, flee from, shun

deinceps (adv.), in succession, in turn

deinde (adv.), next, then; afterwards

dēiciō, -ere, -jēcī, -jectum, throw/ hurl down; drive away/down/out; disappoint; **capite dējectō,** with bowed head

dēlectō, -āre, -āvī, -ātum, divert, attract, delight, please

dēlēctus, -ūs, M., choice; draft

dēleō, -ēre, -ēvī, -ētum, blot out, destroy, overthrow; erase

dēligō, -āre, -āvī, -ātum, bind down, fasten, tie (up), moor

dēligō, -ere, -lēgī, -lēctum, choose

dēmittō, -ere, -mīsī, -missum, send/ drop; let/put down; bow (the head)

dēmōnstrō, -āre, -āvī, -ātum, point out, show; state, explain, mention

dēmum (adv.), at last, at length

dēnique (adv.), at last, finally

dēnsus, -a, -um, close, thick, dense

depart, **dēcēdō** 3

dēpellō, -ere, -pulī, -pulsum, drive, drive from/away

dēpereō, -īre, -iī, -itum, be lost; perish

dēpōnō, -ere, -posuī, -positum, lay down/aside; give up; put, station

dēpopulor, -ārī, -ātus sum, lay waste, plunder, ravage, devastate

dēportō, -āre, -āvī, -ātum, carry down/away; take away, remove

dēprecor, -ārī, -ātus sum, try to avert by entreaty; deprecate; protest

dēprehendō, -ere, -hendī, -hēnsum, seize upon; catch, detect, overtake

dēscendō, -ere, -scendī, -scēnsum, climb down, descend; resort (to)

dēserō, -ere, -seruī, -sertum, abandon, desert

dēsertor, -ōris, M., deserter

dēsertus, -a, -um, deserted, solitary

dēsīderō, -āre, -āvī, -ātum, long for, wish, desire; demand, require; (pass.) be lost/missing

dēsignātus, -a, -um, designated

dēsiliō, -īre, -siluī, -sultum, jump/leap down

dēsistō, -ere, -stitī, -stitum, stop, cease; desist from, abandon

dēspērātiō, -ōnis, F., despair

dēspērō, -āre, -āvī, -ātum, despair (of), lack confidence (in)

dēspiciō, -ere, -spexī, -spectum, look down on, scorn, despise

dēsum, -esse, -fuī, -futūrus, be wanting/lacking, fail

dēterreō, -ēre, -terruī, -territum, prevent, hinder, deter

dētondeō, -ēre, -tondī, -tōnsum, shear, clip

dētrahō, -ere, -trāxī, -tractum, draw/pull down/away, remove

dētrimentum, -ī, N., loss; harm

deus, deī, M., god; nom. pl., **deī/dī;** (dat./abl. pl.), **deīs/dīs; Deus,** God

dēveniō, -īre, -vēnī, -ventum, come, go

dēvertō, -ere, -vertī, -versum, turn away/aside

dēvolvō, -ere, -volvī, -volūtum, roll down/headlong

dēvorō, -āre, -āvī, -ātum, swallow, gulp down, devour

dēvoveō, -ēre, -vōvī, -vōtum, consecrate, devote; vow (away)

dexter, -tra, -trum, right, right-hand, on the right (side)

dextra, -ae, F., right hand; **ā dextrā,** on the right

dī; see **deus**

dīcō, -ere, dīxī, dictum, say, tell, state, speak; mention; call; set, appoint; **mīrābile dictū,** strange to say

dictātor, -ōris, M., dictator

dictātūra, -ae, F., dictatorship

dictum, -ī, N., word; statement

didicī (perf. of **discō**)

diēs, diēī, M./F., day; time, period; **ad diem,** at the appointed time, punctually; **diē alterō,** on the next day; **multō diē,** late in the day; **postrīdiē ejus diēī/posterō diē/ proximō diē,** on the following day, tomorrow; **priōre diē,** yesterday; **diēs nātālis,** birthday

differō, -ferre, distulī, dilātum, carry apart, scatter; postpone, delay; differ, be different

difficilis, -e, difficult, troublesome

difficultās, -ātis, F., difficulty, trouble

diffīdō, -ere, -fīsus sum, distrust

dignitās, -ātis, F., merit; dignity, reputation; prestige, honor

diligēns, gen., **-entis,** careful

diligenter (adv.), carefully

diligentia, -ae, F., diligence, care

dīmicō, -āre, -āvī, -ātum, fight, contend, struggle

dīmidius, -a, -um, halved, half

dīmittō, -ere, -mīsī, -missum, send out/away, dismiss; give up, lose

Diomēdēs, -is, M., Di'ome'des, king of the Bis'tones in Thrace, who gave his captives to his horses as food

Dionȳsius, -ī, M., Di'ony'sius the elder, tyrant of Syr'acuse

dīrigō, -ere, -rēxī, -rēctum, direct

dirimō, -ere, dirēmī, dirēmptum, part, divide; break up/off; interrupt

dīripiō, -ere, -ripuī, -reptum, tear into pieces; plunder

dīs (dat./abl. of **deus**)

Dīs, Dītis, M., Plu'to, god of the lower world

discēdō, -ere, -cessī, -cessum, go away, withdraw, leave, depart

disciplīna, -ae, F., instruction, training, teaching, doctrine; system

discipulus, -ī, M., pupil, student

discō, -ere, didicī, learn, be taught

dispōnō, -ere, -posuī, -positum, arrange, distribute, dispose; station

disputātiō, -ōnis, F., arguing, debate

disputō, -āre, -āvī, -ātum, discuss, debate (on), dispute, argue

dissēnsiō, -ōnis, F., dissension

dissentiō, -īre, -sēnsī, -sēnsum, disagree, differ, dissent

dissimilis, -e, unlike, dissimilar

distō, distāre, be apart/separate/distant; differ, be distinct

distrahō, -ere, -trāxī, -tractum, pull apart; divide; distract; remove

distribuō, -ere, -tribuī, -tribūtum, assign, divide, distribute

dītissimus, -a, -um, richest

diū (adv.), long, a long time, for a long time; **diūtius,** longer, too long; **diūtissimē,** for a very long time

diūtinus, -a, -um, long, longtime

dīversus, -a, -um, different; separate

dīves, dīvitis, rich

Dīviciācus, -ī, M., Divi'cia'cus, a Haed'uan chief; also, a chief of the Suess'io'nes

Dīvicō, -ōnis, M., Div'ico, a Helve'tian chieftain

dīvidō, -ere, -vīsī, -vīsum, part, divide, separate; distribute, share

dīvīnus, -a, -um, divine, sacred

dīvitiae, -ārum, F. pl., riches, wealth

dō, dare, dedī, datum, give, concede, afford, grant, offer; pay; **in mātrimōnium dare,** give in marriage; **poenās dare,** pay the penalty

doceō, -ēre, docuī, doctum, teach, inform, instruct; explain

doleō, -ēre, doluī, dolitūrus, grieve, suffer; be sorry/indignant

dolor, -ōris, M., sorrow, pain; **dolōrem ferre,** be indignant; **magnō dolōre afficere,** annoy greatly

dolus, -ī, M., fraud, deceit; trick

domesticus, -a, -um, civil, domestic

dominātus, -ūs, M., mastery, absolute power

dominus, -ī, M., master, lord; **Dominus,** the Lord

Domitiānus, -a, -um, of Domi'tius; (as noun) M. pl., men/soldiers of L. Domi'tius Ahe'nobar'bus

Domitius, -ī, M., Lu'cius Domi'tius Ahe'nobar'bus, general and follower of Pompey

Domnotaurus, -ī, M., Ga'ius Vale'rius Dom'notaur'us, son of C. Vale'rius Cabu'rus

domus, -ūs (-ī), F., house, home; family; (locative) **domī,** at home; **domum,** (to) home

dōnec (conj.), until; so long as

dōnō, -āre, -āvī, -ātum, give

don't/do not (in negative command), **nōlī/nōlīte** (with infinitive)

dōnum, -ī, N., gift, present, offering

dormiō, -īre, -īvī, -ītum, sleep

dōs, dōtis (-ium), F., marriage gift

druidēs, -um, M. pl., Dru'ids, ancient order of priests in Gaul and Britain

Dūbis, -is, M., the Doubs, a river in Gaul

dubitō, -āre, -āvī, -ātum, be uncertain, doubt; hesitate, delay

dubium, -ī, N., doubt; **nōn est dubium quīn,** there is no doubt that

ducentī, -ae, -a, two hundred

dūcō, -ere, dūxī, ductum, lead, conduct; bring, carry; make; think, consider; reckon, count; construct; prolong; (of a general) march; **in mātrimōnium dūcere,** marry (said of bridegroom)

ductus, -ūs, M., command, leadership

dum (conj.), while, during the time that, as long as; till, until; provided

Dumnorīx, -īgis, M., Dum'norix, a Haed'uan chieftain, brother of Divi'cia'cus

duo, duae, duo, two

duodecim (indecl. adj.), twelve

duodecimus, -a, -um, twelfth

duodēvīgintī (indecl. adj.), eighteen

duplex, gen., **duplicis,** double

duplicō, -āre, -āvī, -ātum, double, increase

dūritia, -ae, F., hardness, hardship

Dūrus, -ī, M., Quin'tus Labe'rius Du'rus, a tribune

dūrus, -a, -um, hard, harsh; difficult

duumvir, -ī, M., one of a pair or commission of two magistrates

dux, ducis, M., leader, commander

Dyrrachium, -ī, N., Dyrrach'ium, town on the coast of Illy'ria, now Durrës

E

ē; see **ex**

eagle, **aquila, -ae,** F.

ecce (adv.), behold! lo! see!

ēdiscō, -ere, ēdidicī, learn thoroughly/by heart, memorize

ēdō, -ere, ēdidī, ēditum, give out, put forth, state, disclose

edō, -ere, ēdī, ēsum, eat, consume

ēducō, -āre, -āvī, -ātum, bring up, rear, train

ēdūcō, -ere, -dūxī, -ductum, lead out (troops); draw (a sword); (of a general) march out

efferō, efferre, extulī, ēlātum, bring/carry out, carry; make known

efficiō, -ere, -fēcī, -fectum, make, accomplish; perform, cause, effect

effugiō, -ere, -fūgī, flee (from), escape

effugium, -ī, N., (means of) escape, flight

effundō, -ere, -fūdī, -fūsum, pour out/forth, shed; (of weapons) discharge; exhaust, squander; **effūsa fuga,** headlong flight

ego (1st pers. pron.), I; pl., **nōs,** we

ēgredior, ēgredī, ēgressus sum, go/come out; march out; leave, depart; disembark, land

ēgregiē (adv.), excellently

ēgregius, -a, -um, remarkable, unusual; distinguished, excellent

ēiciō, -ere, ēiēcī, ēiectum, drive out, expel; **sē ēicere,** rush (out)

ēlābor, ēlābī, ēlāpsus sum, slip out/away; escape

381

elephantus, -ī, M., elephant

ēloquentia, -ae, F., eloquence

ēminēns, gen., **-entis,** outstanding

ēmittō, -ere, -mīsī, -missum, send out, release, drop; give forth

emō, -ere, ēmī, ēmptum, buy

ēnārrō, -āre, -āvī, -ātum, explain

end (noun), **fīnis, -is (-ium),** M./F.; (verb), **fīniō** 4

endure, **ferō, ferre, tulī, lātum; tollō, tollere, sustulī, sublātum**

enim (conj.), for; really, in fact, indeed

ēnūntiō, -āre, -āvī, -ātum, assert; proclaim, reveal, disclose; report

eō, īre, iī/īvī, itum, go, advance, pass; march

eō (adv.), on that account, therefore, for that reason; to that place, there

eōdem (adv.), to the same place

epistula, -ae, F., letter, epistle

Eporēdorix, -īgis, M., Ep′ored′orix, the name of two Haed′uan leaders

eques, equitis, M., cavalryman, knight; pl., cavalry

equester, -tris, -tre, of a horseman, of the cavalry, equestrian, cavalry

equitātus, -ūs, M., cavalry, horsemen

equus, equī, M., horse

ergō (adv.), therefore, then

ēripiō, -ere, ēripuī, ēreptum, take away; rescue; **sē ēripere,** escape

errō, -āre, -āvī, -ātum, wander; go astray, stray; be mistaken, err

error, -ōris, M., wandering; error

ērudiō, -īre, -īvī, -ītum, train, teach

ēruptiō, -ōnis, F., a breaking out, sortie, sally; eruption

Esquilīnus, -a, -um, Es′quiline; of the Esquiline, one of the Seven Hills of Rome

essedārius, -ī, M., charioteer

essedum, -ī, N., British war chariot

et (conj.), and; **et . . . et,** both . . . and; not only . . . but also; (adv.), also, even, too

etiam (adv.), yet, even yet; still; also, even; **etiam atque etiam,** again and again, repeatedly; **nōn modo . . . sed etiam,** not only . . . but also; **nōn sōlum . . . sed (etiam),** not only . . . but also

Etrūria, -ae, F., Etru′ria, a country in central Italy

etsī (conj.), even if, and if, although; and yet

Eumaeus, -ī, M., Eumae′us, swineherd of Ulyss′es

Eurystheus, -ī, M., Eurys′theus, king of Myce′nae, who imposed the twelve labors on Her′cules

ēvādō, -ere, ēvāsī, ēvāsum, go away, escape

ēveniō, -īre, ēvēnī, ēventum, come forth/out; result, happen

ēvocō, -āre, -āvī, -ātum, call forth/ out, summon; evoke

ex/ē (**ex** before vowels and some consonants; **ē** only before consonants) (with abl.), from, out of; according to, by, of; on the side of, on; because of, in accordance with

examinō, -āre, -āvī, -ātum, weigh

exanimō, -āre, -āvī, -ātum, exhaust, weaken; kill; (pass.) die; (perf. part.) breathless, exhausted; dead

exaudiō, -īre, -īvī, -ītum, hear (from a distance)

excēdō, -ere, excessī, excessum, go out, withdraw, depart, leave; exceed; **ē vītā excēdere,** die

excellō, -ere, excelluī, excelsum, excel

excīdō, -ere, -cīdī, -cīsum, cut out; destroy, demolish; root out, banish

excipiō, -ere, -cēpī, -ceptum, take out, except; capture; meet, greet, receive; follow

excitō, -āre, -āvī, -ātum, stir up, arouse, awaken; erect (towers), raise

exclāmō, -āre, -āvī, -ātum, shout, cry aloud; exclaim

exclūdō, -ere, -clūsī, -clūsum, prevent; shut out, cut off

excūsātiō, -ōnis, F., plea, defense

excūsō, -āre, -āvī, -ātum, excuse; **sē excūsāre,** offer excuses

exemplum, -ī, N., example, precedent

exeō, -īre, -iī, -itum, go out/away/ forth, withdraw, leave

exerceō, -ēre, -uī, -itum, employ; train, drill, exercise; administer

exercitātiō, -ōnis, F., exercise, training, experience

exercitātus, -a, -um, well trained

exercitus, -ūs, M., army

exigō, -ere, -ēgī, -āctum, drive out/ away; force out, exact, demand

exiguitās, -ātis, F., shortness, smallness

exiguus, -a, -um, limited, small, short

exilium, -ī, N., exile, banishment

eximius, -a, -um, exceptional

existimātiō, -ōnis, F., judgment, opinion; reputation; character

existimō, -āre, -āvī, -ātum, estimate; consider, judge, believe, think

exitus, -ūs, M., passage; exit; conclusion, end, result, outcome

expectō, -āre, -āvī, -ātum, await, wait for; expect, hope for, look forward to

expediō, -īre, -īvī, -ītum, extricate, free

expedītus, -a, -um, unimpeded, free; light-armed; open, easy; (as noun) M., light-armed soldier

expellō, -ere, -pulī, -pulsum, drive (from/out), expel, remove, banish

experior, -īrī, expertus sum, try; experience; prove, test

expīrō (exspīrō), -āre, -āvī, -ātum, breathe out, exhale; emit; die

expleō, -ēre, -plēvī, -plētum, fill up

explōrātor, -ōris, M., scout

explōrō, -āre, -āvī, -ātum, investigate, examine; reconnoiter, explore

expōnō, -ere, -posuī, -positum, put/set forth; expose; abandon; set ashore, land; draw up, explain

expugnō, -āre, -āvī, -ātum, assault, take by storm, capture, overcome

exquīrō, -ere, -quīsīvī, -quīsītum, investigate, seek (out)

exstō, -āre, stand out, project; appear; be extant

exstruō, -ere, -strūxī, -strūctum, heap/pile up, construct

exterior, -ius, outer, further

extinguō, -ere, -tīnxī, -tīnctum, put out, extinguish; kill; abolish; destroy

extrā (adv./prep. with acc.), outside, beyond

extrahō, -ere, -trāxī, -tractum, drag/draw out, draw forth, extract

extrāordinārius, -a, -um, extraordinary; (with **equitēs/cohortēs**) picked troops of auxiliary forces

extrēmus, -a, -um, outermost, extreme, farthest, last; lowest

extruī = exstrūxī; see **exstruō**

exultō, -āre, -āvī, -ātum, rejoice

F

Fabiānus, -a, -um, Fa'bian, of Fabius

Fabius, -ī, C., M., Ga'ius Fa'bius, one of Caesar's generals in Gaul

Fabius, Quin'tus Fa'bius Max'imus, named dictator by the people after Roman defeat at Cann'ae

fābula, -ae, F., tale, story, fable

fābulātor, -ōris, M., storyteller

faciēs, faciēī, F., face, expression

facile (adv.), easily, readily

facilis, -e, easy; agreeable, courteous

facinus, -ōris, N., act, deed; misdeed, crime

faciō, -ere, fēcī, factum, make, do, form, construct, accomplish; act; **aliquem certiōrem facere,** inform someone; **iter facere,** march, travel, make a journey; **potestātem facere,** grant permission, give a chance; **proelium facere,** engage in battle; **vim facere,** use force

factiō, -ōnis, F., faction, party

factum, -ī, N., act, event; exploit

facultās, -ātis, F., ability; means, opportunity; supply; pl., resources

Falernus, -a, -um, Faler'nian; (with **ager),** Faler'nian country, in Campa'nia

falsō (adv.), falsely

falsus, -a, -um, false, misleading

fāma, -ae, F., report; rumor; reputation, fame; **fāma est,** it is rumored

famēs, -is; (abl. sing.) **famē,** F., hunger, starvation

familia, -ae, F., household; family

familiāris, -e, private, personal; (as noun) M., intimate friend; **rēs familiārēs,** private property

fānum, -ī, N., temple with surrounding land; a holy place

Fānum, -ī, N., Fa'num, a town on the coast of Um'bria, in central Italy

farmer, **agricola, -ae,** M.

fās (indecl.), N., divine law; the right/ lawful thing; the will of Heaven; **fās est,** it is right/proper

fascis, -is (-ium), M., a bundle/ packet; pl., fasces (bundles of sticks with an ax projecting, carried by lictors before chief Roman magistrates); high office, consulship

father, **pater, patris,** M.

fātum, -ī, N., utterance; fate, doom, destiny; **Fātum, -ī,** Fate, Destiny (personified); pl., the Fates

Faustus, -ī, M., Lu'cius Cornel'ius (Faus'tus) Sull'a, son of the dictator

fautor, -ōris, M., patron, fan

faveō, -ēre, fāvī, fautum, favor

fear (be afraid of), **timeō** 2

fēlicior, -ius, happier, more fortunate

fēlicitās, -ātis, F., good fortune, happiness, success

fēliciter (adv.), happily, favorably

fēlix, gen. **-icis,** happy, fortunate

fēmina, -ae, F., female, woman

fenestra, -ae, F., window

fer/ferte (imperative sing./pl. of **ferō)**

ferē/fermē (adv.), almost, nearly; usually, generally; (with negatives) hardly, scarcely

ferō, ferre, tulī, lātum, bear, carry, bring; endure; report, say, state; propose, enact (laws); (impers.) **fertur,** it is said; **ferunt,** they say; **aegrē/molestē ferre,** be indignant, resent; **signa ferre,** advance (the standards)

ferōx, gen., **-ōcis,** fierce, ferocious

ferrum, -ī, N., iron; spearhead; sword

ferus, -a, -um, wild; cruel, fierce

fervēns, gen., **-entis,** glowing, hot

fervor, -ōris, M., ardor, fervor

fessus, -a, -um, tired, weary

fidēlis, -e, faithful, loyal

fidēs, fideī, F., faith, confidence; loyalty, honor; trust; **fidem facere,** give a pledge; **in fidem recipere,** take under one's protection

fīdus, -a, -um, faithful, loyal

fierce, **ferus, -a, -um; ferōx, -ōcis**

fight (verb), **pugnō** 1; (noun), **pugna, -ae,** F.

figūra, -ae, F., shape, form, figure

filia, -ae, F., daughter

filius, -ī, M., son

find, **inveniō** 4

finiō, -īre, -īvī, -ītum, bound, define, limit, mark off, measure; end, finish

finis, -is (-ium), M./F., limit, boundary; end; pl., boundaries; territory

finitimus, -a, -um, bordering, neighboring; (as noun) M. pl., neighbors

fīō, fierī, factus sum, be made/done, become; occur, happen, result; **certior fierī,** be informed

firmiter (adv.), strongly, firmly

firmō, -āre, -āvī, -ātum, strengthen

firmus, -a, -um, strong, firm

Flaccus, -ī, M., Quin'tus Ful'vius Flacc'us, four-time consul and leader of Roman forces at Capua

flagellum, -ī, N., whip; scourge

flāgitō, -āre, -āvī, -ātum, demand

Flāminius, -ī, C., M., Ga'ius Flamin'ius Ne'pos, consul with Gnae'us Servil'ius, defeated by Hann'ibal at Lake Tra'sumenn'us

flamma, -ae, F., blaze, fire, flame

flāvus, -a, -um, yellow

fleō, -ēre, flēvī, flētum, weep, cry

flō, -āre, -āvī, -ātum, blow

flōs, flōris, M., blossom, flower

flow, **fluō** 3

flūctus, -ūs, M., wave, flood; pl., sea

flūmen, flūminis, N., river, stream

fluō, -ere, flūxī, flūxum, flow

fluvius, -ī, M., stream, river

fodiō, -ere, fōdī, fossum, dig

foedus, foederis, N., pledge, compact, agreement; treaty, league

folium, -ī, N., leaf

fōns, fontis (-ium), M., spring, well

for, **prō** (prep. with abl.)

fore = futūrum esse

foris, -is (-ium), F., door

fōrma, -ae, F., form, figure, shape; appearance; beauty

formīca, -ae, F., ant

fōrmōsus, -a, -um, handsome, beautiful

fors, fortis, F., chance; **forte** (abl. as adv.), by chance; perhaps

fortasse (adv.), perhaps

fortis, -e, strong, powerful; brave

fortiter (adv.), bravely, gallantly

fortitūdō, -inis, F., bravery, courage

fortūna, -ae, F., fortune, fate, luck, good fortune, misfortune; pl., property, possessions; **Fortūna,** Chance, Fortune (personified)

forum, -ī, N., open space; market place; forum; **Forum (Rōmānum),** the Roman Forum

fossa, -ae, F., ditch, trench

Franciscus, -ī, M., St. Francis of Assi'si, founder of the Francis'can Order

frangō, -ere, frēgī, frāctum, break, wreck, shatter; weaken, wear out

frāter, frātris, M., brother

frāternus, -a, -um, brotherly

fremitus, -ūs, M., a roaring, murmuring, growling

frīgus, -oris, N., cold, coolness, coldness; cold weather/spells

from (away from), **ā/ab** (with abl.)

from (down from), **dē** (with abl.)

from (out from), **ē/ex** (with abl.)

frōns, frontis (-ium), F., forehead, brow; front; (military) van; **ā fronte,** in front

frūmentārius, -a, -um, of/pertaining to grain/provisions; productive of grain; **rēs frūmentāria,** grain supply, provisions

frūmentum, -ī, N., grain; pl., growing crops, standing grain

fruor, fruī, frūctus sum (with abl.), enjoy

frūstrā (adv.), in vain, without effect

fuga, -ae, F., rout, flight; (means of) escape; **fugae sē mandāre,** flee

fugiō, -ere, fūgī, fugitūrus, flee, escape, run away (from); avoid

fugitīvus, -ī, M., fugitive; runaway slave; deserter

fugō, -āre, -āvī, -ātum, rout, put to flight

Fulvia, -ae, F., Ful'via, a given name

Fulvius; see **Flaccus**

fūmus, -ī, M., smoke

funda, -ae, F., sling, slingshot

fundō, -ere, fūdī, fūsum, pour (out); rout, defeat; put to flight

fundus, -ī, M., ground; the bottom/base of a thing; soil; a farm, estate

fūnus, fūneris, N., funeral (rites)

fūr, fūris, M., thief

furor, -ōris, M., rage, fury

G

Gabalī, -ōrum, M. pl., the Gab'ali, clients of the Arver'ni

Gabīnius, -ī, A., M., Au'lus Gabin'ius, consul with Lu'cius Calpur'nius Pi'so in 58 B.C.; with Caesar in Civil War

galea, -ae, F., helmet

Gallia, -ae, F., Gaul; **Gallia Citerior/Cisalpīna,** Nearer /Cisal'pine Gaul (northern Italy); **Gallia Narbōnēnsis,** Nar'bonese' Gaul (the Province); **Gallia Ulterior,** Farther/Transal'pine Gaul

Gallicus, -a, -um, Gall'ic, of Gaul

gallīna, -ae, F., hen

Gallus, -ī, M., a Gaul, inhabitant of Gaul; pl., the Gauls

Garunna, -ae, M., the Garonne', a river of Gaul

gaudeō, -ēre, gāvīsus sum, rejoice, be glad, take pleasure

gaudium, -ī, N., joy, delight

gemma, -ae, F., jewel, gem

Genava, -ae, F., Gene'va, a Gallic city on Lake Gene'va

gēns, gentis (-ium), F., tribe, people, nation; clan, house, family

genus, -eris, N., birth, race, origin; sort, class, kind, character, nature

Gergovia, -ae, F., Gergo'via, chief town of the Arver'ni

Germānia, -ae, F., Ger'many

Germānus, -a, -um, Ger'man; M. pl., the Germans

gerō, -ere, gessī, gestum, wear, carry (on); conduct; manage, administer; do, perform; (pass.) go on, take place; **bellum gerere,** wage war; **sē gerere,** conduct oneself

gignō, -ere, genuī, genitum, beget, bear, give birth to; produce; spring

gladiātōrius, -a, -um, gladiatorial

gladius, -ī, M., sword

glōria, -ae, F., glory, reputation

glōrificō, -āre, -āvī, -ātum, glorify

glōriōsus, -a, -um, glorious

go, **eō, īre, iī/īvī, itum**

goddess, **dea, -ae,** F.; (dat./abl. pl.), **deābus**

golden, **aureus, -a, -um**

gradior, gradī, gressus sum, step, walk, go

Graecia, -ae, F., Greece

Graecus, -a, -um, Greek; (as noun) M., a Greek; F., the Greek language

Graioceli, -ōrum, M. pl., the Graioc'-eli, a Gallic tribe

grātia, -ae, F., favor, friendship; influence, good will, popularity; gratitude, thanks; **grātiās agere,** thank; **grātiam referre,** requite, repay

grātus, -a, -um, pleasing; grateful; **grātior,** especially pleasing

gravis, -e, heavy; hard (to bear), severe, serious, grave, important

graviter (adv.), heavily; deeply; severely, gravely, seriously; hard; **graviter ferre,** be annoyed (at)

Greek; see **Graecus**

guard (noun), **custōs, -ōdis,** M./F.; (verb), **custōdiō** 4

gustō, -āre, -āvī, -ātum, taste, take a little of, eat; partake of; enjoy

H

habeō, -ēre, habuī, habitum, have, hold; consider, regard; **castra habēre,** encamp; **in animō habēre,** intend; **(in) memoriā habēre,** remember; **ōrātiōnem habēre,** make/deliver a speech

habitō, -āre, -āvī, -ātum, live, dwell

Hadrūmētum, -ī, N., Had'rume'tum, a town on the north coast of Africa

Haeduus, -a, -um, Haed'uan; (as noun) M., a Haed'uan; pl., the Haed'ui, a tribe of Celtic Gaul

Hannibal, Hannibalis, M., Hann'ibal, leading Car'thagin'ian general in Second Punic War

Hannō, Hannōnis, M., Hann'o, prominent Car'thagin'ian general, leader of opposition to Hann'ibal

happen, **accidō** 3; **fīō** (See p. 451)

happy, **laetus, -a, -um; fēlīx,** gen., **-īcis; beātus, -a, -um** (adjs.)

Harūdēs, -um, M. pl., the Haru'des, a German tribe

Hasdrubal, Hasdrubalis, M., Has'-drubal, Hann'ibal's nephew, general with him in Second Punic War; also, one of Hann'ibal's officers in charge of engineers at Calli'cula

hasta, -ae, F., spear, javelin, dart

haud (adv.), not (at all), by no means

hauriō, -īre, hausī, haustum, draw

Helena, -ae, F., Helen (Men'ela'us' wife), whose abduction by Paris was a cause of the Trojan War

Helvētius, -a, -um, Helve'tian, of the Helve'tians; (as noun) M. pl., the Helve'tians, a tribe of Celtic Gaul

Helviī, -ōrum, M. pl., the Hel'vii, a Gall'ic tribe

her (when reflexive), **suus, -a, -um;** (when not reflexive), **ejus** (gen. sing. of **ea**)

herba, -ae, F., grass, herb, plant

Herculēs, -is, M., Her'cules, a hero famous for his great strength

here, **hīc** (adv.)

hērēditās, -ātis, F., inheritance

hesternus, -a, -um, yesterday's, of yesterday; **hesternō diē,** yesterday

heus! (interjection), Hello! Hi there!

hīberna, -ōrum, N. pl., winter quarters/camp

hic, haec, hoc (demonstr. adj.), this (pl., these); the following; the first/ the last named, the former, the latter; (demonstr. pron.), this, this man/ woman/thing; (pers. pron.), he, she, it; pl., they

hīc (adv.), here, on this occasion

hide, **cēlō** 1; hide oneself, **sē cēlāre**

hiemō, -āre, -āvī, -ātum, spend the winter, winter

hiems, hiemis, F., winter; storm; wintry/stormy weather

hinc (adv.), from here, hence; **hinc . . . hinc,** on this side . . . on that side, here . . . there

Hispānia, -ae, F., Spain

Hispāniae, -ārum, F., pl., the two Roman provinces in Spain

Hispānus, -a, -um, Spanish; (as noun) M., Spaniard

historia, -ae, F., historical narration

hodiē (adv.), today; now

home, **domus, -ūs (-ī),** F.; at home, **domī;** (to) home, **domum**

homō, hominis, M., human being, man, person; pl., mankind, people

honor/honōs, -ōris, M., honor, esteem, reputation, distinction; office

hope (noun), **spēs, speī,** F.; (verb), **spērō** 1

hōra, -ae, F., hour, time

horribilis, -e, dreadful, horrible

hortor, -ārī, -ātus sum, encourage, cheer, exhort, urge, advise

hortus, -ī, M., garden

hospes, -itis, M., host; guest, stranger, visitor; friend

hostis, -is (-ium), M., enemy, public enemy, foe; pl., the enemy

hūc (adv.), to this place, here; besides, in addition (to these)

hūmānitās, -ātis, F., human nature/ feeling; kindliness; civilization, refinement, culture

hūmānus, -a, -um, of man, human; kind; civilized

humilis, -e, low; humble, unknown; weak; M. pl., the weak (ones)

humilitās, -ātis, F., nearness to the ground; lowness; insignificance, obscurity; submissiveness

hūmor, -ōris, M., moisture, fluid; dew

I

I, **ego** (1st pers. pron.); see p. 430

ibi (adv.), there, in that place; then

ictus, -ūs, M., thrust, blow; wound

īdem, eadem, idem (identifying pron./ adj.), the same, the very one

idōneus, -a, -um, suitable, favorable, fit, capable, deserving

Īdūs, -uum, F., the Ides, a day in the Roman month; see p. 361

igitur (adv.), therefore, then, consequently, accordingly

ignis, -is (-ium), M., fire; signal fire

ignōrō, -āre, -āvī, -ātum, not know, be unaware of; ignore, overlook

ignōtus, -a, -um, unknown, unfamiliar

Īlerda, -ae, F., Iler'da, city in northeastern Spain, now Lé'rida

ille, illa, illud (demonstr. adj.), that (pl., those); the well-known/famous; (demonstr. pron.), that one; the other/former/latter; (pers. pron.) he, she, it; they

illūc (adv.), there, to that place

illūstris, -e, illustrious, distinguished

Īllyricum, -ī, N., Illyr′ia, territory northeast of the A′driat′ic

imber, imbris (-ium), M., rain storm

imitor, -ārī, -ātus sum, copy; be like

immittō, -ere, -mīsī, -missum, send in; let go

immō (adv.), on the contrary, by no means; no indeed; by all means; yes indeed

immolō, -āre, -āvī, -ātum, sacrifice, offer as a sacrifice

immortālis, -e, immortal, eternal

impedīmentum, -ī, N., impediment, hindrance; pl., (heavy) baggage (of an army), baggage train

impediō, -īre, -īvī, -ītum, entangle, hinder, obstruct; prevent

impedītus, -a, -um, encumbered, hindered; at a disadvantage; (of military persons) hindered by baggage

impellō, -ere, -pulī, -pulsum, drive/urge on; incite; impel

impendeō, -ēre, impend, overhang

imperātor, -ōris, M., general; commander (in chief); emperor

imperātum, -ī, N., order, command; **imperāta facere,** obey orders

imperītus, -a, -um, inexperienced, unskilled, unacquainted with, ignorant

imperium, -ī, N., command, order; power, control, authority; supreme power/command; sovereignty, rule, government, empire

imperō, -āre, -āvī, -ātum, command, order, direct; demand; levy; control; rule, govern; impose

impetrō, -āre, -āvī, -ātum, obtain one's request, secure, effect

impetus, -ūs, M., attack, raid; force, violence; **impetum facere,** (with **in** and acc.) make an attack (on)

impius, -a, -um, evil, wicked

implōrō, -āre, -āvī, -ātum, wail, beseech, entreat, beg, implore

impluvium, -ī, N., impluvium (pool for catching rain water in the atrium of a Roman house)

impōnō, -ere, -posuī, -positum, place/set/put on; impose (on); put on board, mount

importō, -āre, -āvī, -ātum, import

imprīmīs (adv.), especially, chiefly

impudēns, gen., **-entis,** without shame

īmus; see **infimus**

in (on), **in** (with abl.)

in (with abl.), in, in the midst of, on, upon, among, at, over; in view of; (with acc.), into, toward, against, on; for, to, till; over; upon

inānis, -e, empty, idle, vain

incēdō, -ere, -cessī, -cessum, move on/through; advance, march; seize

incendium, -ī, N., fire, conflagration

incendō, -ere, -cendī, -cēnsum, set fire to, burn; inflame, enrage

incertus, -a, -um, uncertain

incidō, -ere, -cidī, fall into/on, fall; happen, occur

incipiō, -ere, -cēpī, -ceptum, begin

incitō, -āre, -āvī, -ātum, urge on; incite; propel; **rēmīs incitāre,** row; **sē/sēsē incitāre,** hasten

inclūdō, -ere, -clūsī, -clūsum, hem in

incognitus, -a, -um, unknown

incola, -ae, M./F., inhabitant, resident

incolō, -ere, -coluī, live (in), inhabit

incolumis, -e, unharmed, safe

incommodum, -ī, N., inconvenience; loss, disaster, misfortune; harm

incrēdibilis, -e, incredible, extraordinary, unbelievable

increpō, -āre, -uī/-āvī, -itum/-ātum, speak angrily/scornfully (against); rebuke

incursiō, -ōnis, F., invasion, raid

incursus, -ūs, M., attack

incūsō, -āre, -āvī, -ātum, accuse, complain of; upbraid, censure

inde (adv.), then, therefore; from that place; after that, next; in consequence; from/of it

indicō, -āre, -āvī, -ātum, make known, mark, indicate

indīcō, -ere, -dīxī, -dictum, proclaim, set, call (for)

indignus, -a, -um, unworthy; shameful; intolerable

indulgentia, -ae, F., indulgence

induō, -ere, -duī, -dūtum, put on

ineō, -īre, -iī, -itum, go into, enter; begin, start, undertake; **cōnsilium inīre,** form/make a plan; **grātiam inīre,** gain favor

inermis, -e, unarmed, defenseless

īnfāmia, -ae, F., disgrace

īnfectus, -a, -um, undone, unfinished

īnfēlīx, gen., **-fēlīcis,** unhappy

īnferior, -ius, lower (down); weaker

īnferō, -ferre, -tulī, illātum, bring/carry in; inflict; offer; bring on/forward, cause; **bellum īnferre,** wage war on; **sē īnferre,** advance; **signa īnferre,** advance, attack

īnferus, -a, -um, down, low, below; (as noun) M. pl., those of the lower world, the dead

īnfimus/īmus, -a, -um (superl. of **īnferus**), lowest, deepest

īnfīnitus, -a, -um, infinite, endless

īnfirmus, -a, -um, weak, weakened

īnflectō, -ere, -flexī, -flexum, bend down; **sē īnflectere,** become bent

īnfrā (adv./prep. with acc.), below, under, underneath, beneath

ingenium, -ī, N., understanding; ability, talent, genius

ingēns, gen., **-gentis,** enormous, huge

ingredior, -gredī, -gressus sum, go into, enter, advance; engage in

inhabitō, -āre, -āvī, -ātum, dwell in

inimīcus, -a, -um, unfriendly, hostile; (as noun) M., enemy (personal); rival

inīquitās, -ātis, F., unevenness; unfavorableness, difficulty; injustice

inīquus, -a, -um, unfair, unjust; unfavorable, disadvantageous

initium, -ī, N., going in; beginning; **initium capere,** begin (at); **initium trānseundī facere,** be first to cross

injūria, -ae, F., injustice; harm, injury; **injūriā** (abl. used as adverb), unjustly

injussū (only in abl.), M., without (the) command/order/permission

innītor, -nītī, -nīxus sum, lean upon

innō, -āre, -āvī, -ātum, swim, float

innocēns, gen., **-entis,** innocent; M. pl., the innocent (ones)

inopia, -ae, F., lack, need, scarcity

inquam (defective verb), I say; **inquit,** he/she says; **inquiunt,** they say

īnsciēns, gen., **-entis,** not knowing, ignorant, unaware

īnscrīptiō, -ōnis, F., inscription

īnsequor, -sequī, -secūtus sum, follow after/on/up; pursue; attack

īnsideō, -ēre, -sessī, -sessum, occupy

īnsidiae, -ārum, F. pl., treachery, ambush, plot

īnsīdō, -ere, -sēdī, -sessum, sit, settle, perch upon; occupy, beset

īnsigne, -is (-ium), N., mark, badge, signal; pl., decorations, insignia

īnsignis, -e, marked, remarkable

īnsiliō, -īre, -siluī, leap/jump (into/on)

īnsistō, -ere, -stitī, stand firm, take a stand

īnsolēns, gen., **-entis,** contrary to custom, unusual; haughty, arrogant

īnsolentia, -ae, F., inexperience; excess; pride, arrogance, insolence

īnstituō, -ere, -stituī, -stitūtum, set in place; draw up, arrange, provide; erect, build; establish, begin, adopt

īnstitūtum, -ī, N., principle, custom

īnstō, -āre, -stitī, -stātūrus, stand on; be near, be at hand; press on, pursue

īnstruō, -ere, -strūxī, -strūctum, build up, construct; equip; draw up

īnsuētus, -a, -um, unaccustomed

īnsula, -ae, F., island; block of flats; apartment building

integer, -gra, -grum, untouched, unharmed; fresh, vigorous, whole

integrē (adv.), wholly, entirely

intellegō, -ere, -lēxī, -lēctum, understand, perceive, know; see, realize

intendō, -ere, -tendī, -tentum, stretch to; extend, direct, bend

inter (with acc.), between, among, through; during; **inter sē,** with/to each other; among themselves

intercēdō, -ere, -cessī, -cessum, go/come/be between, intervene

intercessiō, -ōnis, F., going bail; exercise by tribunes of their veto

intercipiō, -ere, -cēpī, -ceptum, intercept, catch up

interclūdō, -ere, -clūsī, -clūsum, shut/cut off

interdiū (adv.), during the day, by day

interdum (adv.), sometimes

intereā (adv.), meanwhile

intereō, -īre, -iī, -itum, be lost, die

interficiō, -ere, -fēcī, -fectum, kill, slay; **sē interficere,** commit suicide

interim (adv.), meanwhile

interior, -ius, inner, interior

interjiciō, -ere, -jēcī, -jectum, interpose; (perf. part.) lying between

intermittō, -ere, -mīsī, -missum, leave off, cease; interrupt, suspend; let pass; neglect; intervene, separate; (perf. part.) intervening

interpres, -pretis, M/F., interpreter

interpretor, -ārī, -ātus sum, interpret

interritus, -a, -um, unafraid

interrogō, -āre, -āvī, -ātum, ask, inquire of, question, interrogate

interrumpō, -ere, -rūpī, -ruptum, interrupt; cut in two/half

intersum, -esse, -fuī, -futūrus, be/lie between; be present (at); (with dat.), have charge of; (impers.) **interest,** it is to the advantage; it concerns

intervāllum, -ī, N., intervening space, distance, interval (of time/space)

interveniō, -īre, -vēnī, -ventum, come between, intervene

into, **in** (with acc.)

intrā (with acc.), within, inside (of)

intrō (adv.), inwards, within

intrō, -āre, -āvī, -ātum, go into, enter

intrōdūcō, -ere, -dūxī, -ductum, lead into, introduce

introitus, -ūs, M., entrance, approach

inundātiō, -ōnis, F., flood

inūtilis, -e, useless, unprofitable

invādō, -ere, -vāsī, -vāsum, enter; (with **in** and acc.), invade

inveniō, -īre, -vēnī, -ventum, come upon, find, discover, learn

inventor, -ōris, M., inventor, author

invictus, -a, -um, unconquered, unconquerable, invincible

invidia, -ae, F., envy, hatred

invītō, -āre, -āvī, -ātum, invite, summon, urge; influence; allure

invītus, -a, -um, against one's will, unwilling, reluctant

ipse, ipsa, ipsum (intensive pron./adj.), himself, herself, itself (pl., themselves); he, she, it; they; (the) very

īra, -ae, F., anger, rage, ire, wrath

īrātus, -a, -um, angry, irate

irrīdeō, -ēre, -rīsī, -rīsum, laugh, laugh at, ridicule

irrumpō, -ere, -rūpī, -ruptum, break in/into; burst (into)

is, ea, id (demonstr. adj.), that, this (pl., those, these); such, of such a sort/kind; (demonstr. pron.), that (one), this (one) (pl., those, these); (pers. pron.), he, she, it; they

iste, ista, istud (demonstr. adj.), that of yours, that, this; (demonstr. pron.), that (one), this (one); (pers. pron.), he, she, it; they

ita (adv.), so, thus, in this way, as follows; to such an extent, in such a way; accordingly, thus; yes; **ut . . . ita,** just as . . . so/while . . . yet

Ītalia, -ae, F., Italy

itaque (conj.), and so, therefore

item (adv.), also, likewise, too

iter, itineris, N., way, road; journey, march; passage; route, line of march; **iter facere,** march, make a journey; **magnum iter,** rapid/forced march

iterum (adv.), again, a second time

Ithaca, -ae, F., Ith'aca, a Greek island

it is rumored, **fāma est**

J

jaceō, -ēre, jacuī, lie (down), recline; be prostrate/fallen; lie dead

jaciō, -ere, jēcī, jactum, throw, hurl, fling; construct; drop (anchor)

jactō, -āre, -āvī, -ātum, toss about, shake, hurl

jaculum, -ī, N., javelin, dart

jam (adv.), already, now, by this time; soon, directly; at last; furthermore; besides; **jam jamque,** now at last; **jam prīdem,** long ago, for a long time now; **nōn jam,** no longer

jānua, -ae, F., door

Jānuārius, -a, -um, (of) January; see p. 361

Jōannes/Jōhannēs, -is, M., John

Jove; see **Juppiter**

jubeō, -ēre, jussī, jussum, order, command

jūcundus, -a, -um, pleasant

jūdex, -icis, M., judge

jūdicium, -ī, N., (legal) trial; judgment; **jūdicium facere,** express an opinion

jūdicō, -āre, -āvī, -ātum, decide, judge, consider

jūgerum, -ī, N. (pl. in Decl. III), a measure of land (28,000 sq. ft.), slightly less than ⅔ of an acre (juger)

jugum, -ī, N., yoke; ridge, summit

jūmenta, -ōrum, N. pl., beasts of burden, pack animals; mules

jungō, -ere, jūnxī, jūnctum, join, fasten together, unite, yoke

Jūnius, -a, -um, (of) June; see p. 361

Jūnō, -ōnis, F., Ju'no, queen of the gods

Juppiter, gen., **Jovis,** M., Ju'piter, king of the gods

Jūra, -ae, M., the Ju'ra, mountains between the Rhine and the Rhone Rivers

jūrō, -āre, -āvī, -ātum, take an oath

jūs, jūris, N., right, justice, law; rights; **jūre** (abl. as adv.), by right, justly; **jūs dīcere/reddere,** administer justice, act as judge

jūs jūrandum, jūris jūrandī, N., an oath

jussū (abl.), M., by order/command

jūstē (adv.), justly, rightly

jūstitia, -ae, F., justice, uprightness

jūstus, -a, -um, just, fair; proper

juvenis, -is (-um), young, youthful; (as noun) M./F., young person, youth

juventūs, -ūtis, F., youth; young men

juvō, -āre, jūvī, jūtum, aid, help

jūxtā (adv.), close, near(by); (prep. with acc.), close/near to, beside

K

kill, **necō** 1; **interficiō** 3

know, **sciō,** 4; also perf. of **cognōscō (cognōvī)** 3

L

L. (abbr. for **Lūcius, -ī**)

Labiēnus, -ī, T., M., Ti'tus La'bie'nus, Caesar's most trusted general in the Gallic War, who later defected to Pompey at Arim'inum

labor, -ōris, M., labor, work, exertion, effort; hardship; trouble, difficulty

labōrō, -āre, -āvī, -ātum, work, labor; be in trouble/difficulty

lac, lactis, N., milk

lacessō, -ere, -īvī, -ītum, harass, provoke, attack, challenge

Lacōnia, -ae, F., Laco'nia, a country of Greece, of which Sparta was the capital

lacrima, -ae, F., tear

lacrimō, -āre, -āvī, -ātum, weep, cry

lacūna, -ae, F., pond, pool

lacus, -ūs, M., lake, pond

laetitia, -ae, F., joy, rejoicing

laetus, -a, -um, joyful, glad, happy

lapis, lapidis, M., stone

Lārisa/Lārissa, -ae, F., La'rissa, a town in Thess'aly

lāssitūdō, -inis, F., weariness

lātē (adv.), widely, far and wide

latēns, gen., **-entis,** hidden

lateō -ēre, -uī, lie/be hidden; hide

Latīnus, -a, -um, Latin; (as noun) M. pl., the Latins, people of La'tium; F. sing., the Latin language

lātitūdō, -inis, F., width, breadth

Latobrīgī, -ōrum, M. pl., the Lat'obri'gi, a Gallic tribe east of the Rhine

latrō, -ōnis, M., robber, brigand

latrōcinium, -ī, N., robbery

latus, lateris, N., side; flank, wing (of an army)

lātus, -a, -um, broad, wide, extensive

laudābilis, -e, praiseworthy

laudō, -āre, -āvī, -ātum, praise

laurus, -ī, F., laurel tree; victory

laus, laudis, F., praise, fame, glory

laxō, -āre, -āvī, -ātum, relax, reduce, extend, open (out)

leader, **dux, ducis,** M.

learn, **discō** 3

lectīca, -ae, F., litter

lēgālis, -e, legal, of/pertaining to law

lēgātiō, -ōnis, F., embassy, legation; mission; office of ambassador

lēgātus, -ī, M., representative; envoy; ambassador; staff officer; lieutenant general

legiō, -ōnis, F., legion

legiōnārius, -a, -um, of the legion, legionary; (as noun) M., legionary

lēgitimus, -a, -um, lawful, legitimate

legō, -ere, lēgī, lēctum, read (aloud), collect, gather together

Lemannus, -ī, M., (Lake) Lemann'us, Lake Gene'va

Lemovīcēs, -um, M. pl., the Lem'ovī'-ces, a people of Cel'tic Gaul

lēnis, -e, smooth, gentle; kind, soft

lēniter (adv.), smoothly

lentē (adv.), slowly

Lentulus, -ī, M., Lu'cius Cornel'ius Len'tulus Crus, consul in 49 B.C.

Lentulus (-ī), Spinther (-eris), M., Pub'lius Cornel'ius Len'tulus Spin'-ther, one of Pompey's party

Lentulus, Gnaeus, -ī, M., Gnae'us Cornel'ius Len'tulus, a Roman tribune of soldiers in Second Punic War

leō, -ōnis, M., lion

lepidus, -a, -um, pleasant, charming

lepus, -oris, M., hare

lest, **nē** (conj. with subjunctive)

Leucī, -ōrum, M. pl., the Leu'ci, a people of eastern Gaul

levis, -e, light, slight; easy

leviter (adv.), slightly, lightly, softly

levō, -āre, -āvī, -ātum, raise, lift up; make light, relieve, ease

lēx, lēgis, F., law, enactment; terms

libēns, gen., **-entis,** willing, with pleasure, with good will

libenter (adv.), willingly, gladly

liber, librī, M., book

līber, lībera, līberum, free, independent; permitted

Līber, Līberī, M., Li'ber, a given name

līberālitās, -ātis, F., generosity, liberality

līberāliter (adv.), generously, liberally

līberē (adv.), freely

līberī, -ōrum, M. pl., children

līberō, -āre, -āvī, -ātum, (set) free, release; liberate; clear

lībertās, -ātis, F., liberty, freedom

licet, -ēre, licuit/licitum est (impers.) it is allowed 'permitted; one may

lictor, -ōris, M., lictor, one of the public attendants who carried the fasces before principal Roman magistrates to indicate their rank and authority

lignum, -ī, N., wood; pl., firewood

Liguria, -ae, F., Ligur'ia, a district of Cisal'pine Gaul

līmus, -ī, M., mud

Lingonēs, -um, M. pl., the Ling'ones, a tribe of Cel'tic Gaul

lingua, -ae, F., tongue; language

linter, lintris, F., boat, skiff

liqueō, -ēre, līquī/licuī, be liquid

Liscus, -ī, M., Lis'cus, a chief magistrate of the Haed'ui

Litaviccus, -ī, M., Lit'avicc'us, a Haed'-uan nobleman

littera, -ae, F., letter (of the alphabet); pl., letter, epistle, literature, writing

little, **parvus, -a, -um,**

lītus, -oris, N., shore, seashore, beach

live, **vīvō** 3; live (in), **habitō** 1

locō, -āre, -āvī, -ātum, place, put; locate; **castra locāre,** encamp

locus, -ī, M. (pl. usually N., **loca, -ōrum**), place, situation; chance; (abl. **locō** with gen.), in place of, as

longaevus, -a, -um, aged, old

longē (adv.), far (away/off); at/to a distance; by far; for a long time

longinquus, -a, -um, distant, far off

longitūdō, -inis, F., length

longus, -a, -um, long; long-continued; distant; **nāvis longa,** warship

loquor, loquī, locūtus sum, say, speak, talk

lōrīca, -ae, F., coat of mail; breastwork

Lūcius, -ī, M., Lucius/Luke

lūdō, -ere, lūsī, lūsum, play

lūdus, -ī, M., game, sport

lūmen, -inis, N., light, lamp, torch

lūna, -ae, F., moon; **Lūna,** F., Lu'na, the moon-goddess

lutum, -ī, N., mud, dirt

lūx, lūcis, F., light, daylight; **ortā lūce/prīmā lūce,** at daybreak

lyra, -ae, F., lyre, lute

M

M. (abbr. for **Mārcus, -ī**)

maestus, -a, -um, sad

magis (compar. of **magnopere**), more, in a greater degree, rather

magister, -trī, M., chief, master, teacher; **magister equitum,** master of the horse, cavalry commander

magistrātus, -ūs, M., public office, magistracy; magistrate, official

Magius (-ī), Numerius (-ī), M., Nume'rius Ma'gius, chief engineer for Pompey

magnificus, -a, -um, magnificent

magnitūdō, -inis, F., greatness, magnitude; size, extent; **magnitūdō ventī,** violent wind

magnopere/magnō opere (adv.), greatly, exceedingly; especially

magnus, -a, -um, great, large, loud; **magnum iter,** rapid/forced march; **magnā vōce,** in a loud voice

Maharbal, -alis, M., Mahar'bal, a Carthaginian official under Hann'ibal

major, majus (compar. of **magnus**), greater, larger; (as noun) M. pl., ancestors; **major nātū,** older

make, **faciō** 3

male (adv.), badly, wickedly

malefactor, -ōris, M., evildoer

maleficium, -ī, N., evil deed; injury

mālō, mālle, māluī, prefer, choose rather/instead of; see p. 450

mālum, -ī, N., apple

malum, -ī, N., evil, misfortune, harm

malus, -a, -um, bad, evil, wicked

man, **vir, virī,** M.; **homō, hominis,** M.

mandātum, -ī, N., command, order; mandate; demand; message

mandō, -āre, -āvī, -ātum, commit; command; **fugae sē mandāre,** flee

Mandubiī, -ōrum, M. pl., the Mandu'bii, a Gallic tribe

māne (adv.), in the morning; early

maneō, -ēre, mānsī, mānsum, remain, stay

mānēs, -ium, M. pl., spirits, ghosts

manus, -ūs, F., hand; band, troop

many; see **multus**

Mārcellus, -ī, M., M. Marcell'us, a relation of C. Clau'dius Marcell'us, consul; both followers of Pompey

Mārcus, -ī, M., Mar'cus/Mark

mare, maris (-ium), N., sea

maritimus, -a, -um, of the sea, maritime, on the sea; **ōra maritima,** seashore; **rēs maritimae,** naval operations

marry (of bridegroom), **in mātrimōnium dūcō** 3; (of bride), **nūbō** 3

Mārs, Mārtis, M., Mars, god of war

Massilia, -ae, F., Massil'ia, a seaport town in Gaul, now Marseilles

Massiliēnsēs, -ium, M. pl., Massil'ians, the people of Massil'ia

māter, mātris, F., mother; **mātrēs familiae,** matrons

māteria, -ae (acc. **-am**); **māteriēs, -ēī** (acc. **-em**), F., material; timber

māternus, -a, -um, maternal

mātrimōnium, -ī, N., marriage; **in mātrimōnium dare,** give in marriage; **in mātrimōnium dūcere,** marry (said of bridegroom)

mātrōna, -ae, F., wife, matron, lady

Matrona, -ae, M., the Mat'rona, a river in Gaul, now the Marne

mātūrē (adv.), early, speedily, soon

mātūrō, -āre, -āvī, -ātum, ripen, mature; hurry

mātūrus, -a, -um, ripe, grown, of proper age; mature; early, speedy

mātūtīnus, -a, -um, early in the morning, (pertaining to the) morning

Maurētānia, -ae, F., Mau'rita'nia, country in Af'rica, now Morocc'o

maximē, very greatly, most (of all), mostly, chiefly, especially; **quam maximē,** as much as possible

maximus, -a, -um (superl. of **magnus**), greatest, largest, very great

mē (acc./abl. of **ego**), me

medicus, -a, -um, medical; (as noun) M., physician, surgeon

mediocris, -e, moderate, ordinary

mediocritās, -ātis, F., moderation; moderate size; mediocrity

mediterrāneus, -a, -um, inland, mediterranean; **Mare Mediterrāneum,** the Med'iterra'nean Sea

medius, -a, -um, middle (of), mid, midst of; (as noun) N., the middle

meī (gen. of **ego**)

melior, melius (compar. of **bonus**), better

melius (compar. of **bene**), better

membrum, -ī, N., limb, member

memor, gen., **-oris,** remembering, mindful (of)

memoria, -ae, F., memory, recollection; faculty of remembering; **(in) memoriā habēre/tenēre,** remember; **in memoriam,** in memory (of)

Menapiī, -ōrum, M. pl., the Mena'pii, a tribe of Bel'gic Gaul

mendīcus, -ī, M., beggar

mēns, mentis (-ium), F., mind, understanding; purpose; feeling

mēnsa, -ae, F., table

mēnsis, -is (-ium/-um), M., month

mentiō, -ōnis, F., mention

mercātor, -ōris, M., trader, merchant

Mercurius, -ī, M., Mer'cury, messenger of the gods

merīdiēs, -ēī, M., midday, noon; south

meritus, -a, -um, meriting; merited, deserved, just

Messāla, -ae, M., Mar'cus Vale'rius Messa'la, consul in 61 B.C.

Messāna, -ae, F., Messa'na, a town in Sicily, now Messi'na

mētior, -īrī, mēnsus sum, measure; distribute

metus, -ūs, M., fear

meus, -a, -um, my, mine, my own, of mine; (voc. sing.) **mī**

mihi (dat. of **ego**), (to) me

mīles, mīlitis, M., soldier

mīlitāris, -e, of a soldier, military; **rēs mīlitāris,** warfare, art of war

militia, -ae, F., warfare

mīlle (indecl. adj.), a thousand; (as noun) N. pl., **mīlia, mīlium,** thousands; **mīlle passūs/passuum,** a thousand paces, a mile; pl., **mīlia passuum,** miles

minae, -ārum, F. pl., threats

Minerva, -ae, F., Miner'va, goddess of wisdom

minimē (superl. of **parum**), least, not at all, by no means; no; **minimē saepe,** very seldom

minimus, -a, -um (superl. of **parvus**), smallest, least, very small

minor, minus (compar. of **parvus**), smaller, less, of less importance

Minucius, -ī, M., Mar'cus Minu'cius Ru'fus, named aide to Q. Fa'bius Max'imus by the people (217 B.C.)

Minucius pōns, Minucii pontis, M., Minu'cian Bridge (over the Tiber)

minuō, -ere, minuī, minūtum, lessen, diminish, decrease; settle

minus; see **minor**

minus (compar. of **parum**), less; not; **minus facile,** less easily, not so easily; **nihilō minus,** none the less, nevertheless; **sī . . . minus,** if not

mīror, -ārī, -ātus sum, wonder (at)

mīrus, -a, -um, wonderful, strange

misceō, -ēre, miscuī, mixtum, mix (up); mingle, unite; confuse, disturb

miser, misera, miserum, poor, wretched; unfortunate, unhappy

missiō, -ōnis, F., discharge; cessation

mittō, -ere, mīsī, missum, send; dismiss, release, let go; throw, hurl

modo (adv.), only; even; just now; **nōn modo . . . sed etiam,** not only . . . but also; **modo . . . modo,** now . . . now, sometimes . . . sometimes, at one time . . . at another (time)

modus, -ī, M., measure, size; amount; way, mode, manner, kind; **ejus modī,** of such a sort; **quem ad modum,** in what way, how; as; **tālī modō,** of such a kind, in such a way

moenia, -ium, N. pl., city walls, fortifications

molestia, -ae, F., annoyance

mollis, -e, smooth, soft

mōmentum, -ī, N., movement, action; influence; weight, importance; **mōmentō temporis,** in a short space of time, in a moment

moneō, -ēre, monuī, monitum, remind, advise, warn, admonish

mōns, montis (-ium), M., mountain; range of mountains; hill

mōnstrō, -āre, -āvī, -ātum, show; point out

montānus, -a, -um, of a mountain; (as noun) M., mountaineer

mora, -ae, F., delay; hindrance

morbus, -ī, M., disease, sickness

Morinī, -ōrum, M. pl., the Mor'ini, a tribe of Bel'gic Gaul

morior, morī, mortuus sum, die

moror, -ārī, -ātus sum, delay, linger

mors, mortis (-ium), F., death; **Mors, Mortis,** Death (personified)

mortālis, -e, mortal, fatal, deadly

mortuus, -a, -um, dead; (as noun) M., dead person; pl., the dead

397

mōs, mōris, M., custom; **mōs est,** it is usual/customary

mōtus, -ūs, M., movement, motion

moveō, -ēre, mōvī, mōtum, move; **castra/signa movēre,** break camp

mox (adv.), soon, presently, afterwards

mulier, -eris, F., woman, female; wife

multiplicō, -āre, -āvī, -ātum, multiply

multitūdō, -inis, F., multitude, crowd; the common people, population

multō (abl. as adv.), by much, much, by far, far

multum (adv.), much, very much, greatly, quite

multus, -a, -um, much; many (a); **multō diē,** late in the day; (as noun) M. pl., many, many persons; N. sing., much; N. pl., many things

mundus, -ī, M., universe, world

mūniceps, -cipis, M./F., citizen of a **mūnicipium;** fellow citizen

mūnicipium, -ī, N., (municipal) town

mūniō, -īre, -īvī, -ītum, wall in, fortify, defend; build, construct

mūnītiō, -ōnis, F., fortification

mūnus, -eris, N., service, office; gift

murmurō, -āre, -āvī, -ātum, murmur, make a noise, roar; rumble

mūrus, -ī, M., wall, city wall

mūsica, -ae, F., music

must **dēbeō** 2; also see pages 107-108

mūtō, -āre, -āvī, -ātum, change

mūtus, -a, -um, dumb, mute, silent

N

nam (conj.), for, inasmuch as

name (noun), **nōmen, -inis,** N.; (verb), **nōminō** 1

namque (conj.), for, for in fact

nancīscor, nancīscī, nactus sum, find; get (possession of), obtain

Narbō, -ōnis, M., Nar'bo, town in southern Gaul, now Narbonne'

nārrātor, -ōris, M., storyteller

nārrō, -āre, -āvī, -ātum, report, relate, tell

nāscor, nāscī, nātus sum, be born/produced; arise; (perf. part.—often with numeral), at the age of, old

nātiō, -ōnis, F., nation, tribe, people

nātū, (abl. as adv.), by birth; **major nātū,** older

nātūra, -ae, F., nature, character

nātūrālis, -e, natural, by nature

nātus, -ī, M., son, child

nauta, -ae, M., sailor

nāvicula, -ae, F., small boat

nāvigātiō, -ōnis, F., voyage, sailing

nāvigō, -āre, -āvi, -ātum, (set) sail

nāvis, -is (-ium), F., ship, vessel, boat; **nāvis longa,** warship, galley; **nāvis onerāria,** transport, freight ship; **nāvem cōnscendere,** embark, go aboard ship; **(ē) nāve ēgredī,** disembark; **nāvem/nāvēs solvere,** set sail, weigh anchor

-ne indicates direct question that may be answered "yes"/"no"; (conj. introducing indirect question), whether

nē (adv.), not; **nē . . . quidem,** not even, not . . . either; (conj.), that . . . not, in order that . . . not, in order not to; (after verbs of fearing) that, lest; **nē quis,** so that no one

nec; see **neque**

necessāriō (abl. as adv.), of necessity

necessārius, -a, -um, necessary, critical; (as noun) M. pl., friends, relatives

necesse (indecl. adj.), necessary

necessitās, -ātis, F., necessity, need

necō, -āre, -āvī, -ātum, kill

neglegō, -ere, neglēxī, neglēctum, disregard, neglect

negō, -āre, -āvī, -ātum, say no, say . . . not; deny; refuse

negōtiātiō, -ōnis, F., business deal

negōtium, -ī, N., business; task; trouble; **negōtium dare,** employ, commission, direct; **negōtium gerere,** do business

nēmō (nom.); **nēminī** (dat.); **nēminem** (acc.); (no gen./abl.); M./F., no one, nobody; not a single one

neque/nec (conj.), and not, not; nor; **neque . . . neque/nec . . . nec,** neither . . . nor; **neque sōlum . . . sed etiam,** not only . . . but also

Nerviī, -ōrum, M. pl., the Ner'vii, a tribe of Bel'gic Gaul

nesciō, -īre, -īvī, not know (how); be ignorant; **nesciō quis,** someone or other, somebody; **nesciō quid,** something or other; something; **nesciō cūr,** for some reason or other

neuter, -tra, -trum, neither; (as pron.) M. pl., neither side/party

nēve/neu (conj.), and not, nor; **nēve . . . nēve,** neither . . . nor

nex, necis, F., death, murder

niger, -gra, -grum, black

nihil/nīl (indecl.), N., nothing; (with gen.) no, none (of); (as adv.), not at all; **nōn nihil,** something; (as adv.), somewhat, to some extent

nihilum, -ī, N., nothing at all, not a bit, nothing; (abl. with compar.) **nihilō minus,** nevertheless

nisi/nī (conj.), if not, unless; (after a negative/interrog.), except, but

nōbilis, -e, noble; distinguished; (as noun) M. pl., nobles, men of high rank

nōbilitās, -ātis, F., fame; high rank; nobility; men of high rank

noceō, -ēre, -uī, -itum, harm, injure

noctū (adv.), by night, at night

nocturnus, -a, -um, of/by night, nightly, nocturnal, at night

nōlō, nōlle, nōluī, not wish, be unwilling; refuse; (imperative **nōlī/ nōlīte** with infin.), do not, don't . . .

nōmen, -inis, N., name; reputation, fame; (abl. **nōmine** with gen.), as

nōminātim (adv.), by name; in detail

nōminō, -āre, -āvī, -ātum, name, call

nōn (adv.), not; no; **nōn jam,** no longer; **nōn nihil,** something; **nōn numquam,** sometimes, a few times; **nōn modo/sōlum . . . sed (etiam),** not only . . . but also; **nōn sōlum . . . sed prope/paene,** not only . . . but almost.

nōnāgintā (indecl. adj.), ninety

nōndum (adv.), not yet

nōnne introduces a question with expected answer "yes"

nōnnūllus (nōn nūllus), -a, -um, (adj./pron.), some, several

nōnus, -a, -um, ninth

Nōreia, -ae, F., Nore'ia, a town in Nor'icum, now Neumarkt

Nōricus, -a, -um, of Nor'icum, Nor'ican, belonging to a German'ic tribe living between the Dan'ube and the Alps

nōs (1st pers. pron.), pl., we, us

nōscō, -ere, nōvī, nōtum, become acquainted with, recognize, learn; (perf.) know; (past perf.), knew

noster, -tra, -trum, our, ours, our own; (as noun) M. pl., our men

not, **nōn** (adv.)

nōta, -ae, F., mark, sign, token

nōtus, -a, -um, known, familiar, well-known, noted, famous

novem (indecl. adj.), nine

novissimus, -a, -um (superl. of **novus),** last, rear; (as noun) M. pl., those at the rear, rear ranks/line; **novissimum agmen,** the rear

novus, -a, -um, new; strange, unusual; **rēs novae,** revolution

nox, noctis (-ium), F., night; **ad multam noctem,** till late at night; **media nox,** midnight; **nocte,** at night, in the night; **prīmā nocte,** at nightfall; **proxima nox,** tomorrow night; **sub noctem,** at nightfall

nūbēs, nūbis (-ium), F., cloud

nūbō, -ere, nūpsī, nūptum (with dat.), marry (said of the bride)

nūdō, -āre, -āvī, -ātum, uncover, make/lay bare; deprive of

nūdus, -a, -um, naked, unprotected

nūllus, -a, -um, no, not any, none; (as noun) M. pl., none; sing., no one

num (interrog. particle introducing direct question with negative answer expected); (in indirect questions), whether

numerābilis, -e, that can be counted

numerus, -ī, M., number; amount, quantity; account, importance; **in numerō** (with gen.), among, as

Numidae, -ārum, M. pl., the Numid'-ians, a people of northern Africa

nummus, -ī, M., coin

numquam (adv.), never, not at all; **nōn numquam,** sometimes

nunc (adv.), now, at present

nūntiō, -āre, -āvī, -ātum, announce, report, carry a report; tell, order

nūntius, -ī, M., messenger; message

nūper (adv.), lately, recently

nympha, -ae, F., nymph

O

Ō, ō, (interjection), oh! O!

ob (with acc.), toward, against; on account of, by reason of, because of; **ob eam rem,** for this reason, therefore; **quam ob causam,** for this reason, why; **quam ob rem,** therefore; why; why?

obdormiō, -īre, -īvī, -ītum, go to sleep

obscūrus, -a, -um, dark, obscure

observō, -āre, -āvī, -ātum, observe, keep

obses, obsidis, M./F., hostage

obsideō, -ēre, -sēdī, -sessum, hem in, blockade, besiege, obstruct

obsidiō, -ōnis, F., siege, blockade

obstinātē (adv.), firmly, resolutely

obstruō, -ere, -strūxī, -strūctum, stop up, barricade

obtemperō, -āre, -āvī, -ātum, obey

obtineō, -ēre, -tinuī, -tentum, hold, occupy, have; possess; obtain

occāsiō, -ōnis, F., occasion, opportunity

occāsus, -ūs, M., a falling, setting; **sōlis occāsus,** sunset; the west

occidō, -ere, -cidī, -cāsum, fall (down); die; be killed; set (the sun)

occīdō, -ere, -cīdī, -cīsum, cut down, kill

occīsiō, -ōnis, F., a killing, slaughter

occultē (adv.), secretly, obscurely

occultō, -āre, -āvī, -ātum, conceal

occultus, -a, -um, hidden; (as noun) N., secret; **in occultō,** in secret

occupātiō, -ōnis, F., business, occupation

occupātus, -a, -um, occupied, engaged, busy

occupō, -āre, -āvī, -ātum, take possession of, occupy, seize; engage

occurrō, -ere, -currī, -cursum, run against, (run to) meet; oppose, resist

Ōceanus, -ī, M., the Ocean, the Atlantic Ocean

Ocelum, -ī, N., Oc'elum , a city of Cisal'pine Gaul

octāvus, -a, -um, eighth

octingentī, -ae, -a, eight hundred

octō (indecl. adj.), eight

octōgintā (indecl. adj.), eighty

oculus, -ī, M., eye

ōdī, ōdisse, ōsūrus (defective verb), hate, detest; see p. 454

odium, -ī, N., hatred

offendō, -ere, -fendī, -fēnsum, harm; **animum offendere,** offend

offēnsiō, -ōnis, F., offense, displeasure

offerō, -ferre, obtulī, oblātum, bring before, offer; expose; **sē offerre,** expose oneself to

officīna, -ae, F., workshop

officium, -ī, N., service, kindness; duty, official duty; allegiance

oleum, -ī, N., oil, olive oil

ōlim (adv.), once, formerly; some day

Olympus, -ī, M., Olym'pus, mountain in Thess'aly, thought by the ancients to be the home of the gods

ōmen, ōminis, N., omen, sign

omittō, -ere, -mīsī, -missum, let go, lose; disregard, neglect

omnīnō, (adv.), altogether, entirely, in all, only; in general, by all means; (after negative) at all

omnis, -e (adj.), all, every, whole; (as noun) N. pl., everything

on, **in** (with abl.)

one, **ūnus, -a, -um;** one of . . ., **ūnus ex . . .**

onerārius, -a, -um, fitted/suitable for freight; **(nāvis) onerāria,** transport, freighter, cargo vessel

onus, oneris, N., load, burden, weight; cargo; pack; responsibility

opera, -ae, F., work, service, care, effort, toil; attention; help; **operam dare,** give attention; take pains

opīniō, -ōnis, F., opinion, belief, expectation; impression; **contrā opīniōnem omnium,** contrary to popular opinion

oportet, -ēre, oportuit (impers.), it is necessary/right; (one) must/ought

oppidānus, -a, -um, of/pertaining to a town; (as noun) M. pl., townspeople, inhabitants of a town

oppidum, -ī, N., town, stronghold

opportūnē (adv.), opportunely, at the right time, conveniently

opportūnitās, -ātis, F., convenience, opportunity, advantage

opportūnus, -a, -um, favorable, advantageous

opprimō, -ere, -pressī, -pressum, oppress, crush, overpower; **somnō oppressus,** overcome by sleep

oppugnātiō, -ōnis, F., assault, siege

oppugnō, -āre, -āvī, -ātum, attack, assault, try to storm, besiege

(ops), opis (no nom./dat. sing.), F., aid; power; pl., power, resources

401

optimē (superl. of **bene**), best, very
well

optimus, -a, -um (superl. of **bonus**),
best, excellent, very good

opulentus, -a, -um, rich, wealthy

opus, operis, N., work; deed; fortification; want, necessity; **opus est,**
there is need, it is necessary; **magnō
opere,** greatly, very much; **quantō
opere,** how much? how greatly?

ōra, -ae, F., margin, shore, coast;
ōra maritima, coast, seashore

ōrāculum, -ī, N., oracle; prophecy

ōrātiō, -ōnis, F., oration, speech, discourse; argument; **habēre ōrātiōnem,** deliver/make a speech

ōrātor, -ōris, M., orator, speaker;
ambassador, spokesman

orbis, -is (-ium), M., circle; ring;
orbis terrārum, the earth/world

Orcus, -ī, M., Or'cus, the lower world

ōrdinō, -āre, -āvī, -ātum, set in
order, arrange; appoint; govern

ōrdō, -inis, M., row, rank, line; order

Orgetorīx, -igis, M., Orget'orix, a
Helve'tian chieftain

orior, orīrī, ortus sum, arise, rise;
appear, begin; **oriēns sōl,** sunrise;
the east; **ortā lūce,** at daybreak

ōrnāmentum, -ī, N., ornament, decoration, mark of honor

ornātus, -a, -um, ornate, beautiful

ōrō, -āre, -āvī, -ātum, speak; pray
(to), plead, ask for, beg

ortus, -ūs, M., rising; **ortus sōlis,**
sunrise

ōs, ōris, N., mouth; face

ostendō, -ere, ostendī, ostentum,
display, show, point out; make
known; **sē ostendere,** appear

ostentum, -ī, N., portent, sign

Ōstia, -ae, F., Os'tia, ancient seaport
near Rome at mouth of the Tiber

ōstium, -ī, N., door; mouth, entrance

ōtium, -ī, N., leisure, idleness, ease;
peace, quiet, tranquillity

ought, **dēbeō** 2

ovis, -is (-ium), F., a sheep

ōvum, -ī, N., egg; one of seven
egg-shaped balls by which laps in
circus races were counted

P

P. (abbr. for **Pūblius, -ī**)

pābulor, -ārī, -ātus sum, forage,
collect food

pābulum, -ī, N., food; forage

pācātus, -a, -um, peaceful

pācō, -āre, -āvī, -ātum, make peaceful, pacify, subdue; clear, rid

pactiō, -ōnis, F., a bargain, contract,
covenant, agreement, treaty

Padus, -ī, M., the Pa'dus, the largest
river in northern Italy, now the Po

paene (adv.), nearly, almost

pāgus, -ī, M., district, canton

palam (adv.), openly, in public

Palātinus, -a, -um, Pal'atine', pertaining to the Pal'atine' Hill, one of
the Seven Hills of Rome

palla, -ae, F., palla, robe, mantle;
curtain, tapestry

palūs, -ūdis, F., swamp, marsh

pānis, -is (-ium/-um), M., bread;
pl., loaves of bread

pār, gen., **paris,** equal, like; suitable;
a match (for); M. pl., equals, peers

parātus, -a, -um, prepared, ready

parcō, -ere, pepercī, parsūrus,
spare, show mercy to

parēns, gen., **-entis,** M./F., parent, father, mother; relative

pāreō, -ēre, -uī, obey, listen to

pariō, -ere, peperī, partum, obtain, win, procure

parō, -āre, -āvī, -ātum, prepare, furnish; get, acquire, procure

pars, partis, F., part, share, division; direction, quarter; **in omnēs partēs,** into every direction; **omnibus in partibus,** in all directions, on all sides; **ūnā ex parte,** on one side; **magnā ex parte,** to a great extent

partim (adv.), partly, in part

partior, -īrī, -ītus sum, share, divide

partly, **partim** (adv.)

parum (adv.), (too) little, not enough

parvus, -a, -um, small, little; humble

pāscor, pāscī, pāstus sum, be fed, pasture

passim (adv.), in every direction, everywhere, here and there

passus, -ūs, M., step; **mīlle passūs/ passuum,** a thousand paces, mile; **mīlia passuum,** miles

pāstor, -ōris, M., shepherd

patefaciō, -ere, -fēcī, -factum, open, throw/lay open; make accessible; disclose, reveal, bring to light

pateō, -ēre, -uī, lie or be open, stretch out, extend

pater, patris, M., father; pl., forefathers; senators; **pater familiae,** father/head of a family

patientia, -ae, F., endurance; resignation

patior, patī, passus sum, suffer; allow, permit

patria, -ae, F., native country/land

paucī, -ae, -a, few, (only) a few; (as noun) M. pl., a few (people); N. pl., a few things/words; **paucīs ante annīs,** a few years before

paucitās, -ātis, F., small number

paulātim (adv.), little by little, gradually

paulisper (adv.), for a little while

paulō (adv.), (by) a little

paulum (adv.), a little, somewhat

Paulus, -ī, M., Lu'cius Aemil'ius Paul'us, consul with C. Teren'tius Varr'o in 216 B.C. and commander (with Varr'o) of Roman army at Cann'ae

pauper, gen., **-eris,** poor, not wealthy

pavīmentum, -ī, N., pavement (of tiles/brick/stone)

pāx, pācis, F., peace; **bellō ac pāce,** in war and in peace

pecūnia, -ae, F., wealth, money

pecus, -oris, N., cattle; herd, flock

pedes, -itis, M., foot soldier, infantryman; pl., infantry

pedester, -tris, -tre, on foot; pedestrian, of a foot soldier; on/by land; **pedestrēs cōpiae,** infantry forces, infantry

peditātus, -ūs, M., infantry

pejor, pejus (compar. of **malus**), worse

pejus (compar. of **male**), worse

pellis, -is (-ium), F., skin, pelt, hide

pellō, -ere, pepulī, pulsum, beat; drive out/away; rout, defeat

pendeō, -ēre, pependī, hang (down)

pendō, -ere, pependī, pēnsum, weigh; pay; **poenās pendere,** pay, suffer the penalty

Penelope, **Pēnelopa, -ae,** F.

penetrālia, -ium, N. pl., inner chambers, interior rooms, the interior

403

per (with acc.), through, among, by, throughout; on account of; over; during; **per annum,** by the year, annually; **per sē,** of oneself

percipiō, -ere, -cēpī, -ceptum, seize, receive; learn; feel

percurrō, -ere, -currī/-cucurrī, -cursum, run through; hasten through

percutiō, -ere, -cussī, -cussum, thrust/pierce through; strike

perdūcō, -ere, -dūxī, -ductum, lead/bring through, conduct, bring, lead; construct; induce

pereō, -īre, -iī, -itūrus, go through; be lost; perish, die

perexiguus, -a, -um, very little

perfacilis, -e, very easy

perferō, -ferre, -tulī, -lātum, convey; endure, submit to; report, relate

perficiō, -ere, -fēcī, -fectum, accomplish, carry out, complete; cause

perfidia, -ae, F., treachery, perfidy

perfringō, -ere, -frēgī, -frāctum, break up/through

perfuga, -ae, M., deserter, fugitive

perfugiō, -ere, -fūgī, flee for refuge, desert

periculum, -ī, N., danger, risk; trial

peritus, -a, -um, experienced, skilled

permaneō, -ēre, -mānsī, -mānsum, continue, remain

permisceō, -ēre, -miscuī, -mixtum, mix together, mingle thoroughly

permittō, -ere, -mīsī, -missum, let go; leave, entrust; permit, allow

permōtus, -a, -um, disturbed, agitated

permoveō, -ēre, -mōvī, -mōtum, move strongly; alarm; influence

perniciēs, -ēī, F., destruction, ruin

perniciōsus, -a, -um, destructive

perpaucī, -ae, -a, pl., very few; (as noun), a very few

perpetuus, -a, -um, continuous, perpetual, lasting; the whole of; **in perpetuum,** forever, for all time

perrumpō, -ere, -rūpī, -ruptum, break through, force a passage

perscribō, -ere, -scripsī, -scriptum, write in full; record; report

persequor, -sequī, -secūtus sum, follow up, pursue

perspiciō, -ere, -spexī, -spectum, perceive, view; observe; explore

persuādeō, -ēre, -suāsī, -suāsum (with dat.), persuade, convince

perterreō, -ēre, -uī, -itum, frighten thoroughly, terrify

perterritus, -a, -um, terrified, thoroughly frightened

pertineō, -ēre, -tinuī, -tentum, extend; tend; lead; pertain

perturbātiō, -ōnis, F., disturbance, alarm

perturbātus, -a, -um, disturbed

perturbō, -āre, -āvī, -ātum, disturb (greatly), throw into confusion; dismay; alarm

perveniō, -īre, -vēnī, -ventum, come to through, arrive, reach, come; (of property) fall, revert

pēs, pedis, M., foot; (as a measure) a foot; **pedem referre,** retreat

pessimē (superl. of **male**), worst; most unkindly

pessimus, -a, -um (superl. of **malus**), worst; most wicked; very bad

petō, -ere, -īvī, -itum, pursue, seek, look for; attack, go to; ask (for); beg; **fugā salūtem petere,** flee, run away, run to a safe place

Petreius, -ī, M., Mar′cus Petre′ius, one of Pompey's three generals in Spain during the Civil War

phalanx, -angis, F., phalanx, close military formation

Pherae, -ārum, F. pl., Pher′ae, a city in Thess′aly, a region in northern Greece

philosophus, -ī, M., philosopher

Pīcēnum, -ī, N., Pice′num, a district in eastern Italy on the Adriat′ic Sea

Pīcēnus, -a, -um, of/relating to Pice′num

piger, -gra, -grum, lazy, sluggish, slow; unwilling

pīlum, -ī, N., pike, spear, javelin

pīrāta, -ae, M., pirate

Pisaurum, -ī, N., Pisaur′um, a town in Um′bria, in central Italy

Pīsō, -ōnis, M., Mar′cus Pi′so, consul in 61 B.C.; **L. Pīsō,** Lu′cius Pi′so, a Roman commander, grandfather of Lu′cius Pi′so, consul in 58 B.C.

placeō, -ēre, -uī, -itum, please, be pleasing; (impers.) **placet,** it is resolved/decided

plācō, -āre, -āvī, -ātum, soothe, appease, placate

plānitiēs, -ēī, F., level ground, plain

plānus, -a, -um, even, level, flat

plaustrum, -ī, N., wagon

plēbs, plēbis (plēbēs, -eī/-ī), F., the common people; plebs, plebeians

plēnē (adv.), fully, completely, wholly

plēnus, -a, -um, full; whole

plērique, -aeque, -aque, pl., very many, the most of; (as noun), a great many

plērumque (adv.), for the most/greater part, very often, generally

plūrimum (superl. of **multum**), most, very, generally, mostly; **plūrimum posse,** be most powerful

plūrimus, -a, -um (superl. of **multus**), most; pl.; very many; (as noun) N., very much, very many

plūs, plūris, N., more; (as adj.) pl., a number of, several; (as noun) M. pl., more

plūs, (compar. of **multum**), more; **plūs valēre,** be stronger

poena, -ae, F., punishment, penalty; **poenam/poenās dare,** pay the penalty

Poenus, -a, -um, Pu′nic, Car′thagin′-ian; (as noun) M., a Car′thagin′ian

poēta, -ae, M., poet

polliceor, -ērī, -itus sum, promise

Pompēiānus, -a, -um, of/relating to Pompe′ii; (as noun) M. pl., inhabitants of Pompe′ii

Pompēiānus, -a, -um, of/relating to Cn. Pom′pey; (as noun) M. pl., soldiers/men of Cn. Pom′pey

Pompēiī, -ōrum, M., Pompe′ii, a town in southern Campan′ia

Pompēius, -ī, M., Gnae′us Pom′pey, Roman general and statesman

Pompōnius, -ī, M., Mar′cus Pompo′nius, praetor at time of Roman defeat at Lake Tra′sumenn′us (now Tra′sime′no) in 217 B.C.

pondus, -eris, N., weight

pōnō, -ere, posuī, positum, put, place, lay; **arma pōnere,** lay down one's arms, surrender; **castra pōnere,** pitch camp, encamp

pōns, pontis (-ium), M., bridge; **pōns Minu′cius/Ful′vius,** bridges across the Tiber

populor, -ārī, -ātus sum, devastate, lay waste, ravage

populus, -ī, M., a group of people, nation; the people, the citizens

porta, -ae, F., gate; door, portal

portō, -āre, -āvī, -ātum, convey, carry, bring

portus, -ūs, M., harbor, port

poscō, -ere, poposcī, demand

possessiō, -ōnis, F., possession, property; occupation

possideō, -ēre, -sēdī, -sessum, have possession of, possess, occupy

possum, posse, potuī, be able, can; have influence; **plūrimum posse,** be most powerful; **minimum posse,** have little/no power

post (adv.), behind, in the rear; after, afterwards, later; (prep. with acc.), behind, back of; after

posteā (adv.), afterwards, later

posteāquam; see **postquam**

posteritās, -ātis, F., future generations, posterity; offspring

posterus, -a, -um, following, next; **posterō diē,** on the next day

posthāc (adv.), hereafter, in the future, afterward

postpōnō, -ere, -posuī, -positum, disregard, lay aside, put after

postquam/posteāquam (conj.), after, as soon as, when; also appears as **post . . . quam**

postrēmō (adv.), at last, finally

postrēmus, -a, -um (superl. of **posterus**), last

postrīdiē (adv.), next day, the following day; **postrīdiē ejus diēī,** the next/following/very next day

postulātum, -ī, N., demand

postulō, -āre, -āvī, -ātum, demand, require, ask for, insist

potēns, gen., **-entis,** powerful, influential; M. pl., the powerful

potentia, -ae, F., power, political influence; authority

potestās, -ātis, F., power, authority; opportunity; control; **potestātem facere,** grant opportunity/permission, give a chance

potior, -īrī, -ītus sum, become master of, get control of; possess

potius (adv.), rather

prae (with abl.), before, in front of, ahead of; in comparison with

praebeō, -ēre, -buī, -bitum, hold forth, give, present; display, show

praecēdō, -ere, -cessī, -cessum, go before/ahead; surpass, excel

praeceps, gen., **-cipitis,** headlong, headfirst; (of motion) quick, hasty; (of places) steep, precipitous

praeceptum, -ī, N., a command, rule, injunction, instruction, order, precept

praecipiō, -ere, -cēpī, -ceptum, enjoin upon, direct, give directions to, advise, order; teach, instruct

praecipuē (adv.), especially

praeclārus, -a, -um, famous, distinguished, remarkable, admirable; very bright, clear

praeclūdō, -ere, -clūsī, -clūsum, shut/close (in front)

praeda, -ae, F., booty, plunder

praedicō, -āre, -āvī, -ātum, proclaim, assert, claim, declare, boast

praedīcō, -ere, -dīxī, -dictum, foretell, predict; advise, warn

praedūcō, -ere, -dūxī, -ductum, construct in front

406

praefectus, -ī, M., overseer, superintendent; officer, prefect

praeficiō, -ere, -fēcī, -fectum, place over/in charge or command of

praemittō, -ere, -mīsī, -missum, send (forward/ahead)

praemium, -ī, N., reward, prize

Praeneste, -is, N., Praenes'te, a town in La'tium, now Pal'estri'na

praeparō, -āre, -āvī, -ātum, make ready, prepare

praepōnō, -ere, -posuī, -positum, place in charge/command of

praescrībō, -ere, -scrīpsī, -scrīptum, direct; dictate to

praesēns, gen., **-entis,** at hand, present; immediate, for the moment

praesentia, -ae, F., presence; **in praesentiā,** for the present

praesentiō, -īre, -sēnsī, -sēnsum, feel/perceive beforehand, foresee

praesertim (adv.), especially

praesidium, -ī, N., defense, protection, safeguard; garrison, guard; bodyguard; safety; relief, help

praestāns, gen., **-stantis,** outstanding

praestō, -stāre, -stitī, -stitum, stand before; excel, surpass; show; (impers.) **praestat,** it is better

praesum, -esse, -fuī, -futūrus, be ahead; be in command/charge of, command, preside over

praeter (with acc.), past, by; besides, in addition to; except; beyond

praetereā (adv.), in addition, besides (this), beyond this, moreover; else

praetereō, -īre, -iī/-īvī, -itum, go/pass by

praeteritus, -a, -um, past; (as noun) N. pl., the past

praetor, -ōris, M., praetor (a Roman magistrate who could serve as a judge, command an army, or govern a province)

praetōrius, -a, -um, praetorian; **praetōria cohors,** guard of honor

precēs, -ium, F. pl., prayers, entreaties

prehendō, -ere, -hendī, -hēnsum, grasp, seize

premō, -ere, pressī, pressum, press (hard); oppress

prepare, **parō** 1

pretiōsus, -a, -um, valuable, precious

pretium, -ī, N., price

prīdem (adv.), long ago; **jam prīdem,** this long time; long ago

prīdiē (adv.), (on) the day before

prīmō (adv.), at first, first

prīmum (adv.), (at) first; **quam prīmum,** as soon as possible

prīmus, -a, -um, first, foremost; (as noun) M. pl., the leading men; **in prīmīs/imprīmīs,** especially; **prīmā lūce/nocte,** at daybreak/nightfall

prīnceps, gen., **-cipis,** first, foremost, chief; (as noun) M., leader, chief

prīncipālis, -e, main, principal

prīncipātus, -ūs, M., first place, chief position; leadership, authority, supremacy

prior, prius, former, first

prīstinus, -a, -um, former; early

prius (adv.), before, previously, first, sooner

priusquam/prius . . . quam (conj.), before, sooner than; until

prīvātim (adv.), privately, as a private individual, in private life; at home

prīvātus, -a, -um, private, personal; (as noun) M., private citizen

prō (with abl.), before, in front of; in behalf of, in defense of, for; in place of/return for, instead of; in the character of, as; in accordance with, in consideration/view of

probō, -āre, -āvī, -ātum, test; show; prove; approve

prōcēdō, -ere, -cessī, -cessum, go forward, advance, proceed, come out

prōcōnsul, -sulis, M., proconsul, one who serves as consul (especially after having been consul)

procul (adv.), at a distance, afar

prōcumbō, -ere, -cubuī, fall/lie down

prōcurrō, -ere, -currī/-cucurrī, -cursum, run forward; charge

prōdeō, -īre, -iī, -itum, come out/forward, advance

prōdō, -ere, -didī, -ditum, hand down; reveal; give up, betray

prōdūcō, -ere, -dūxī, -ductum, lead/bring forth; draw up (troops); prolong

proelium, -ī, N., battle, engagement; **proelium committere,** begin battle; **proelium facere,** engage in battle

profectiō, -ōnis, F., a setting out, departure

prōferō, -ferre, -tulī, -lātum, bring out/forth/forward; **signa prōferre,** advance, march

prōficiō, -ere, -fēcī, -fectum, carry out; accomplish; make progress

prōficīscor, -ficīscī, profectus sum, set out/forth, start, go forward, march; migrate; depart

prōfugiō, -ere, -fūgī, flee from/before, escape

prōgredior, -gredī, -gressus sum, go on/forward, proceed, advance

prohibeō, -ēre, -hibuī, -hibitum, restrain, prohibit; keep (out/away from); prevent, hinder from, protect

proinde (adv.), therefore, accordingly

prōiciō, -ere, -jēcī, -jectum, hurl forward/down; **sē prōicere,** jump down; cast oneself

prōmittō, -ere, -mīsī, -missum, promise; **datā fidē prōmittere,** promise in good faith

prōmontōrium, -ī, N., promontory; headland

prōnūntiō, -āre, -āvī, -ātum, announce; order

prope (prep. with acc.), near, nearby, near to; (adv.), near(ly), almost

prōpellō, -ere, -pulī, -pulsum, drive forward/forth; repel, rout

properē (adv.), quickly, rapidly, hastily

properō, -āre, -āvī, -ātum, hasten

propinquitās, -ātis, F., nearness, vicinity

propinquus, -a, -um, near, neighboring; (as noun) M./F., relative

propior, -ius (adj.), nearer

propius (adv.), nearer, more nearly; (prep. with acc.), nearer (to)

prōpōnō, -ere, -posuī, -positum, display; point out, tell, explain; report; offer, propose

proprius, -a, -um, one's own, private, appropriate, characteristic

propter (with acc.), near; because of, on account of

propterea (adv.), for this/that reason, on account of this, therefore; **proptereā quod** (conj.), for the reason that, because, inasmuch as

prōsequor, -sequī, -secūtus sum, follow after, pursue

prōspiciō, -ere, -spexī, -spectum, look forward/out; look out for, provide, procure; see; watch

prōsum, prōdesse, -fuī, -futūrus, be of service; help, profit

prōtegō, -ere, -tēxī, -tēctum, cover over/in front; cover, protect

prōtendō, -ere, -tendī, -tentum, stretch

prōtinus (adv.), continuously; immediately

prōturbō, -āre, -āvī, -ātum, drive in confusion; dislodge

prōveniō, -īre, -vēnī, -ventum, come forth

prōvideō, -ēre, -vīdī, -vīsum, foresee; provide, care for

province, **prōvincia, -ae,** F.

prōvincia, -ae, F., province; **Prō-vincia, -ae,** F., the Province, (now Provence'); Nar'bonese' Gaul, the Roman province governed by Caesar

prōvocō, -āre, -āvī, -ātum, call forth, challenge, provoke

proximē (superl. of **prope**), nearest; last, most recently, lately

proximus, -a, -um, nearest, next; recent, last; **proximō diē,** on the next day, tomorrow; **proxima nox,** tomorrow night, the following night

prūdēns, gen., **-entis,** foreseeing; discreet, wise, intelligent

prūdenter (adv.), prudently, discreetly

prūdentia, -ae, F., foresight, prudence, wisdom

pūblicē (adv.), in the name of the people/the state; officially; for/on behalf of the state; at public expense

pūblicus, -a, -um, belonging to the people/the state, public; (as noun) N., public; **rēs pūblica, reī pūb-licae,** F., the state, government; public interests/affairs

Pūblius, -ī, M., Pub'lius, a given name

pudor, -ōris, M., shame, sense of shame

puella, -ae, F., girl, maiden

puer, puerī, M., boy, child; slave

puerīlis, -e, boyish, puerile, childish

puerulus, -ī, M., little boy; young slave

pugna, -ae, F., battle, fight

pugnō, -āre, -āvī, -ātum, fight, engage in battle

pulcher, -chra, -chrum, beautiful

pulsō, -āre, -āvī, -ātum, beat (on), knock

Pūnicus, -a, -um, Pu'nic, Car'thagin'ian

pūniō, -īre, -īvī, -ītum, punish

punish, **pūniō** 4

pupil, **discipulus, -ī,** M.

putō, -āre, -āvī, -ātum, consider, think, believe, suppose

Pȳrēnaeus, -a, -um, Pyr'ene'an; **Pȳrēnaeī Montēs,** Pyr'enees' Mountains

Q

Q. (abbr. of **Quīntus**)

quā (adv.), where, by which/what way/road

quadrāgintā (indecl. adj.), forty

quadringentī, -ae, -a, four hundred

quaerō, -ere, quaesīvī, quaesītum, seek, look for; ask, inquire; choose; ask for, desire

quaestiō, -ōnis, F., inquiry, investigation

quaestor, -ōris, M., quaestor (a Roman magistrate handling state finances)

qualis, -e (interrog. adj.), of what sort/kind/nature?

quam (adv.), to what degree, how; how greatly; how?; (conj. with compar.) than; (with superl.) as . . . as possible; **quam prīmum,** as soon as possible; **tam . . . quam,** so much . . . as, both . . . and; (with verbs implying comparison, such as **mālle**), than/to

quamquam (conj.), although, though

quandō (adv.), at any time, ever; (conj.), when; since

quandōquidem (conj.), since

quantum (rel. adv.), as much as, as far as, as long as, as; (interrog.), how much? how far?; **tantum . . . quantum,** as much . . . as

quantus, -a, -um (interrog. adj.), how great/much?; **quantō opere,** how much? how greatly?; (rel.) as great; **tantus . . . quantus,** as/so great/large/much as; (as noun) N., how much?, as much/so far (as)

quārē (rel. adv.), for which reason, therefore, why; (interrog.), why?

quārtus, -a, -um, fourth

quasi (adv./conj.), as if, as though, almost

quattuor (indecl. adj.), four

-que (attached to a word), and

queror, querī, questus sum, complain (of); lament

quī/quis, quae/qua, quod (indef. adj.—often after **sī**), some, any; see p. 433

quī, quae, quod (indef. pron.), anyone, anything, any, some

quī, quae, quod (rel. pron.), who, which, what; this, that; (rel. adj.), which, what, whatever; see p. 432

quī/quis, quae, quod (interrog. adj.), what? which?; see p. 433

quia (conj.), because

quicquam; see **quisquam**

quicquid; see **quisquis**

quīcumque, quaecumque, quod-cumque (indef. rel. pron.), whoever, whatever, whichever; everyone who, everything that

quīdam, quaedam, quoddam (indef. adj.), a certain, some, a kind of;

quīdam, quaedam, quiddam (indef. pron.), a certain one; somebody, someone, something; pl., some; see p. 433

quidem (adv.), indeed; at least, even; **nē . . . quidem,** not even, not . . . either

quiēs, quiētis, F., quiet, repose, rest

quiēscō, -ere, quiēvī, quiētum, rest, repose; rest from work; lie down; sleep; be free from

quiētē (adv.), quietly

quiētus, -a, -um, quiet, still

quīn (conj.), so that not, but that; (after words of doubt) that, that not; (after words of hindering) from; (adv.), indeed, moreover

quīndecim (indecl. adj.), fifteen

quīngentī, -ae, -a, five hundred

quīnquāgintā (indecl. adj.), fifty

quīnque (indecl. adj.), five

quīntāna, -ae (via), F., road in a Roman camp; see p. 273

Quīntus, -ī, M., Quin'tus, a given name

quīntus, -a, -um, fifth; **quīntus (-a, -um) decimus (-a, -um),** fifteenth

quis, quid (indef. pron.), anyone, anything; **nē quis,** so that no one; **sī quis,** if anyone, whoever; see p. 432

quis/quī, quae, quod (interrog. adj.), what? which? what kind/sort of?

quis, quid (interrog. pron.), who? which? what?; **nesciō quis,** someone or other, somebody; **nesciō quid,** something or other

quisquam, quicquam/quidquam (indef. pron.), anyone/anything (at all); (as adj.), any; see p. 432

quisque, quaeque, quodque (indef. adj.), each, every (one); see p. 433

quisque, quidque (indef. pron.), each (one), every (one); see p. 432

quisquis, quaequae, quidquid/ quicquid (indef. rel. pron./adj.), whoever, whichever, whatever

quō (interrog. adv.), where? to/in what place? in what direction?; (rel.) to which place/point, because

quō (conj.), whereby, in order that, so that (with compar.); **quō minus/ quōminus,** so that ... not, from, lest

quod (conj.), because; as to the fact that, whereas; **proptereā quod,** for the reason that, because; inasmuch as; **quod sī,** but/now/and if

quōmodo (adv.), in what manner? how?

quoniam (conj.), since, because

quoque (conj.), also, too

quot (indecl. interrog. adj.), how many?; (rel.), as many (as); see **tot**

quotannīs (adv.), every year, yearly

quotiēns (rel. adv.), as often as; (interrog.), how often?

quotiēnscumque (adv.), however often, as often as

R

radius, -ī, M., staff, stake; spoke; ray

rādīx, -īcis, F., root (of a plant); pl., foot (of a mountain)

raeda, -ae, F., traveling carriage

raedārius, -ī, M., driver of a **raeda**

rāmus, -ī, M., branch, bough

raptim (adv.), violently, hurriedly

rārō (adv.), seldom, rarely

ratiō, -ōnis, F., account, record; way, manner, plan; strategy, conduct; system; reason; judgment, consideration; **quā ratiōne,** on what terms

ratis, -is (-ium), F., raft

Rauracī, -ōrum, M. pl., Rau'raci, a Gall'ic tribe

Ravenna, -ae, F., Ravenn'a, a town in northern Italy, near the A'driat'ic

rebelliō, -ōnis, F., revolt, rebellion; renewal of war

Rebilus, -ī, M., Ga'ius Canin'ius Reb'ilus, one of Caesar's generals

recēdō, -ere, -cessī, -cessum, go/ draw back, recede, retreat, withdraw

recēns, gen., **-entis,** new, fresh, recent

recipiō, -ere, -cēpī, -ceptum, take/ get/bring back; receive; undertake; **sē récipere,** withdraw, retreat

recitō, -āre, -āvī, -ātum, read aloud

recognize, **recognōscō** 3

recognōscō, -ere, -cognōvī, -cognitum, recognize

rēctē (adv.), in a straight line; rightly

rēctus, -a, -um, straight, direct, right; (as noun) N., right, virtue

recuperō/reciperō, -āre, -āvī, -ātum, win/get back, recover

recūsō, -āre, -āvī, -ātum, refuse, decline

reddō, -dere, -didī, -ditum, give back, restore; give up; make; **jūs reddere,** administer justice

redeō, -īre, -iī, -itum, go back, return; **ad sē redīre,** recover consciousness

redigō, -ere, -ēgī, -āctum, drive back, bring under, reduce

redimō, -ere, -ēmī, -ēmptum, buy back, ransom; purchase

redintegrō, -āre, -āvī, -ātum, restore

reditus, -ūs, M., return

redūcō, -ere, -dūxī, -ductum, lead/bring back; extend back; construct

referō, -ferre, rettulī, relātum, carry/bring (back); repay; reply; mention, report; refer, lay before; **pedem/sē referre,** withdraw, retreat

reficiō, -ere, -fēcī, -fectum, make over; renew, repair

refugiō, -ere, -fūgī, flee (back), retreat; escape

refugium, -ī, N., recourse, taking refuge; refuge

rēgia, -ae, F., palace

rēgina, -ae, F., queen

Rēginus, -ī, M., Ga'ius Antis'tius Regi'nus, one of Caesar's generals

regiō, -ōnis, F., region, territory

Rēgium, -ī, N., Re'gium, a town on the strait of Messi'na, now Reg'gio di Cala'bria

rēgius, -a, -um, royal, regal

rēgnō, -āre, -āvī, -ātum, reign, rule

rēgnum, -ī, N., royal authority/power; sovereignty; rule; kingdom

regō, -ere, rēxī, rēctum, guide, direct, control; rule

regredior, -gredī, -gressus sum, march/go back; retire, retreat

rejiciō, -ere, -jēcī, -jectum, throw/hurl back, repel, drive back

religiō, -ōnis, F., religion; religious scruple; pl., religious matters

relinquō, -ere, -līquī, -lictum, leave (behind), abandon

reliquus, -a, -um, left, remaining, rest/remainder of; (as noun) the other(s), the rest; **in reliquum tempus,** in/for the future

remain, **maneō** 2; **remaneō** 2; **supersum, -esse, -fuī, -futūrus**

remaneō, -ēre, -mānsī, -mānsum, remain

remedium, -ī, N., remedy

remigrō, -āre, -āvī, -ātum, return

remissior, -ius, less severe, milder

remissus, -a, -um, mild

remittō, -ere, -mīsī, -missum, send back; give up, relax; remit

removeō, -ēre, -mōvī, -mōtum, move back/away; remove, withdraw

remūneror, -ārī, -ātus sum, repay

Rēmus, -a, -um, of the Re'mi; (as noun) M., one of the Re'mi; pl., the Re'mi, a tribe of Bel'gic Gaul

rēmus, -ī, M., oar

renovō, -āre, -āvī, -ātum, renew

renūntiō, -āre, -āvī, -ātum, bring back word; report

reor, rērī, ratus sum, reckon, think

repellō, -ere, reppulī, repulsum, drive back, repel; disappoint

repentīnō (adv.), suddenly

repentīnus, -a, -um, sudden, unexpected; new, fresh, recent

reperiō, -īre, repperī, repertum, find, discover, find out; develop

reportō, -āre, -āvī, -ātum, carry back, bring back; convey

reputō, -āre, -āvī, -ātum, reckon back, count, compute; think over

requiēscō, -ere, -quiēvī, -quiētum, have a rest, repose

rēs, reī, F., thing (exact meaning determined by context); matter, fact, affair, event; act, deed, exploit; circumstance, condition; action; reason; possession; **ad eās rēs cōnficiendās,** to accomplish this; **ob eam rem,** therefore; **quam ob rem/quās ob rēs,** therefore; why; why?; **rē vērā,** in fact; **rēs dīvīna,** religious matter; **rēs familiāris,** private property, estate; **rēs frūmentāria,** grain supply, provisions; **rēs gesta,** deed, act; **rēs mīlitāris,** warfare, art of war; military science; **rēs novae,** revolution; **rēs pūblica,** the state, government, public interests/affairs

rescrībō, -ere, -scrīpsī, -scrīptum, enroll; write again; transfer

reservō, -āre, -āvī, -ātum, keep back, save up, reserve

resistō, -ere, -stitī, stand still, remain behind; resist

respiciō, -ere, -spexī, -spectum, look back (at), regard, consider

respondeō, -ēre, -spondī, -spōnsum, answer, reply, respond

respōnsum, -ī, N., reply, answer

rēs pūblica; see **rēs**

restituō, -ere, -stituī, -stitūtum, put/place back, restore, rebuild, renew

retineō, -ēre, -tinuī, -tentum, hold/keep back, maintain, preserve; hold fast, keep, retain

retrahō, -ere, -trāxī, -tractum, bring/drag back; hold back; withdraw

reveniō, -īre, -vēnī, -ventum, come back

revertō, -ere, -vertī (active regularly in perf. tenses only), turn/come back, return

revertor, -vertī, -versus sum, turn back, return

revocō, -āre, -āvī, -ātum, recall

rēx, rēgis, M., king, ruler

Rhēnus, -ī, M., the Rhine, river between Gaul and Germany

Rhodanus, -ī, M., the Rhod'anus, a river in Gaul, now the Rhone

rīdeō, -ēre, rīsī, rīsum, laugh (at)

rīma, -ae, F., crack, cleft, fissure

rīpa, ae, F., bank (of a river), shore river, **flūmen, -inis,** N.; **fluvius, -ī,** M.

rōbustus, -a, -um, strong

rogō, -āre, -āvī, -ātum, ask; request

Rōma, -ae, F., Rome

Rōmānus, -a, -um, of Rome, Roman; (as noun) M., a Roman

Rōmulus, -ī, M., Rom'ulus, the legendary founder of Rome

Rōscius, -ī, M., Lu'cius Ros'cius, one of Caesar's generals

rōstrum, -ī, N., beak, snout, bill; beak (of a ship); pl., **rōstra,** the Ros'tra (platform for speakers in the Forum, adorned with beaks of captured ships)

Rubicō, -ōnis, M., the Ru'bicon', river in northern Italy, boundary between the Roman Republic and its provinces

Rūfus (-ī), M. Minucius (-ī), M., Mar'cus Minu'cius Ru'fus; see **Minucius**

Rūfus, -ī, M., Pub'lius Sulpic'ius Ru'fus, one of Caesar's generals

ruīna, -ae, F., downfall, ruin, destruction, calamity; pl., ruins

rūmor, -ōris, M., rumor, report

Runnimede, Run'nymede', a meadow on the south bank of the Thames, west of London, where the Magna Charta is said to have been signed

rūpēs, rūpis (-ium), F., rock, cliff

rūrsus/rūrsum (adv.), again

rūsticus, -a, -um, of the country, rural; (as noun) M., country person, rustic

Rutēnī, -ōrum, M. pl., the Rute'ni, a tribe of southwestern Gaul

S

Sabīnus, -ī, M., Quin'tus Titu'rius Sabi'nus, one of Caesar's generals

Sabīnus, -a, -um, Sa'bine; (as noun) M. pl., the Sa'bines, a people of ancient Italy; **ager Sabīnus,** Sabine territory

sacer, -cra, -crum, sacred, holy

sacerdōs, -dōtis, M./F., priest/priestess

sack, **saccus, -ī,** M.

sacrificium, -ī, N., sacrifice

sacrificō, -āre, -āvī, -ātum, sacrifice

saepe (adv.), often, frequently; **minimē saepe,** very rarely; **saepissimē,** very often; **saepius,** more often

saepenumerō (adv.), time and again

safe, **tūtus, -a, -um; incolumis, -e; salvus, -a, -um,** (adjs.)

sagitta, -ae, F., arrow

sagittārius, -ī, M., bowman, archer

saltus, -ūs, M., (mountain) pass, ravine

salūs, -ūtis, F., health, safety

salūtō, -āre, -āvī, -ātum, greet, hail

salveō, -ēre, be well/in good health; **salvē/salvēte** Good morning!/day!

salvus, -a, -um, safe

sānctus, -a, -um, sacred, inviolable

sānitās, -ātis, F., soundness; sanity

Santonī, -ōrum/Santonēs, -um, M. pl., the San'toni/San'tones, a people of Aq'uita'nia

sapiēns, gen., **-entis,** wise

sapienter (adv.), wisely, discreetly

sapientia, -ae, F., wisdom

sarcina, -ae, F., bundle, pack, portable luggage; pl., baggage, packs

satis (indecl. adj.), enough, sufficient; (as noun) enough; (adv.) enough, sufficiently, well, quite; **satis commodē,** to much advantage

satisfaciō, -ere, -fēcī, -factum, do enough; give satisfaction, make reparation, apologize

satum; see **serō**

Sāturnus, -ī, M., Sat'urn, a mythical king of La'tium honored as god of agriculture and civilization

saxum, -ī, N., rock, stone

say, **dīcō** 3

scelerātus, -a, -um, wicked, accursed; (as noun) M., scoundrel, rascal

scelus, -eris, N., evil deed, crime

schola, -ae, F., school

school, **schola, -ae,** F.

scientia, -ae, F., knowledge

scindō, -ere, scidī, scissum, tear down, destroy; split

sciō, -īre, -īvī, -ītum, know

Scipiō (-ōnis), Pūblius (-ī), M., Pub'lius Cornel'ius Scip'io Af'rica'nus Ma'jor, the conqueror of Hann'ibal

Scipiō, -ōnis, M., Quin'tus Caecil'ius Metell'us Pi'us Scip'io, to whose daughter (Cornel'ia) Pom'pey was married for political reasons

scout, **explōrātor, -ōris,** M.

scrībō, -ere, scrīpsī, scrīptum, write

scūtum, -ī, N., shield

sē/sēsē (acc./abl. of 3rd pers. reflex. pron.); see **suī**

seashore, **ōra (-ae) maritima (-ae),** F.

sēcessiō, -ōnis, F., withdrawal; secession

sēcrētō (adv.), secretly, stealthily

secundus, -a, -um, following, next, second; favorable, successful

sēcūrus, -a, -um, safe, secure

sed (conj.), but, on the contrary

sēdecim (indecl. adj.), sixteen

sedeō, -ēre, sēdī, sessum, sit; settle

sēdēs, sēdis (-ium/-um), F., seat; home

sēditiōsus, -a, -um, mutinous

Sedulius, -ī, M., Sedu'lius, a chief of the Lem'ovi'ces

see, **videō** 2

Segusiāvī, -ōrum, M. pl., the Seg'usia'vi, a tribe of southern Gaul

sēmita, -ae, F., footpath

semper (adv.), always, ever

Semprōnius (-ī), Tiberius (-ī), M., Tiber'ius Sempro'nius, consul with P. Cornel'ius Scip'io, and one of the generals in the battle of the Treb'ia (now Treb'bia) River, in 217 B.C.

senātor, -ōris, M., senator, one of a council of elders

senātus, -ūs, M., senate, council of elders; **ex senātūs cōnsultō,** according to/by a decree of the senate

senex, gen., **senis,** old, aged; (as noun) M., old man, elder

sentential, -ae, F., thought, feeling, opinion, judgment; **meā sententiā,** in my opinion; **mūtātā sententiā,** having changed one's mind

sentiō, -īre, sēnsī, sēnsum, perceive, feel, realize, know, sense

sēparātim (adv.), separately, privately

sēparō, -āre, āvī, -ātum, separate

sepeliō, -īre, -īvī/-iī ,sepultum, bury, destroy

septem (indecl. adj.), seven

septentriōnēs, -um, M. pl., stars of the Big Dipper; the north

septimus, -a, -um, seventh; **septimus (-a, -um) decimus (-a, -um),** seventeenth

septuāgintā (indecl. adj.), seventy

sepulchrum, -ī, N., tomb, grave

sepultūra, -ae, F., burial; **in sepultūram dare,** bury

Sēquana, -ae, M., the Seq'uana, a river of Gaul, now the Seine

Sēquanus, -a, -um, of the Seq'uani, Sequan'ian; (as noun) M. pl., the Seq'uani, Sequan'ians, a tribe of Cel'tic Gaul

sequor, sequī, secūtus sum, follow, pursue; maintain; accompany

serēnitās, -ātis, F., clear/fair weather; clearness

serēnus, -a, -um, clear, bright, fair

sermō, -ōnis, M., talk, conversation, discourse, speech; interview

serō, -ere, sēvī, satum, sow

serpēns, -entis, M./F., snake, serpent

serva, -ae, F., slave girl, servant girl

servilis, -e, of/pertaining to slaves

servitūs, -ūtis, F., slavery, servitude

servō, -āre, -āvī, -ātum, observe, guard, keep; save

servus, -ī, M., slave, servant

sēsē/sē; see **suī**

seu . . . seu; see **sīve . . . sīve**

sevērus, -a, -um, stern, cruel, severe

sēvocō, -āre, -āvī, -ātum, call aside

sex (indecl. adj.), six

sexāgintā (indecl. adj.), sixty

Sextus, -ī, M., Sex'tus, a given name

sextus, (-a, -um) et/ac trīcēsimus, (-a, -um) thirty-sixth

sī (conj.), if, in case, in the event that; **quod sī,** but if, now if, even if; **sī minus,** if not; **sī quis,** if any/ anyone, whoever

sibi; see **suī**

sīc (adv.), thus, so, in this way/manner; so, to such an extent/degree; **ut . . . sīc,** as . . . so, while . . . yet

Sicilia, -ae, F., Sic'ily, a large Med'-iterra'nean island

Sicoris, -is, M., the Sic'oris River (now the Se'gre), a tributary of the Hiber'us (now E'bro) in Spain

sīcut/sīcutī (adv./conj.), just as/as if

signifer, signiferī, M., standardbearer

signum, -ī, N., sign; signal; (military) standard, banner; **signa cōnsistere,** halt; **signa ferre,** advance (the standards); **signa īnferre/prōferre** advance (to the attack), charge; **signa movēre,** break camp

silēns, gen., **-entis,** silent

silentium, -ī, N., silence; **silentiō** (abl. as adv.), silently, in silence

silva, -ae, F., forest, wood, woods

similis, -e, like, similar, alike

simul (adv.), at the same time, to-gether; immediately; **simul atque/ ac,** as soon as; **simul . . . simul,** not only . . . but also; partly . . . partly

simulātiō, -ōnis, F., pretense, deceit

simulō, -āre, -āvī, -ātum, pretend

since, **cum** (conj. with subjunctive)

sine (with abl.), without

sing, **cantō** 1

singulāris, -e, single, alone; singular

singulī, -ae, -a, pl., one at a time, single; one each on a side; every

sinister, -tra, -trum, left

sinistra, -ae, F., the left hand; **ā sinis-trā,** on the left

Sinuessa, -ae, F., Sinuess'a, a town in La'tium

sīs (= sī vīs), if you please, please; pl., **sultis (= sī vultis);** see **volō**

situs, -ūs, M., site, situation

sīve/seu (conj.), or, or if; whether; **sīve . . . sīve,** whether . . . or

societās, -ātis, F., alliance; fellowship

socius, -ī, M., associate, partner, ally; comrade, companion

Sōcratēs, -is, M., Soc'rates, famous Athe'nian philosopher, sentenced to die by drinking hemlock in 399 B.C.

sōl, sōlis, M., sun; **oriēns sōl,** east; **sōlis occāsus,** sunset, west; **ortū sōlis,** at/from sunrise; **Sōl, Sōlis,** M., Sol, the sun god

soleō, -ēre, solitus sum (semidepo-nent), be accustomed

sōlitūdō, -inis, F., wilderness

solitus, -a, -um, customary, usual

sollicitō, -āre, -āvī, -ātum, agitate, incite, stir up, appeal to, tempt

sollicitus, -a, -um, agitated; thor-oughly/violently moved

solum, -ī, N., earth, ground; bottom

sōlum (adv.), only, merely, alone; **nōn sōlum . . . sed etiam,** not only . . . but also

sōlus, -a, -um, only, alone; lonely

solvō, -ere, solvī, solūtum, loosen, release; pay; (with/without **nāvem/ nāvēs**) set sail, weigh anchor

somnus, -ī, M., sleep; **ē somnō excitātus,** aroused from sleep

son, **filius, -ī,** M.

sonus, -ī, M., sound, noise

soror, -ōris, F., sister

sors, sortis (-ium), F., lot, prophecy, fate, destiny

sound retreat, **receptuī canō** 3

spargō, -ere, sparsī, sparsum, sow, sprinkle, scatter

spatium, -ī, N., space, extent; interval, distance; period/length of time

speciēs, -ēī, F., sight, view, look; appearance; semblance, pretext

spectāculum, -ī, N., show, display, spectacle, sight

spectātor, -ōris, M., spectator, viewer

spectō, -āre, -āvī, -ātum, watch, see; consider; face, be situated; look at

speculātor, -ōris, M., scout, spy

speculum, -ī, N., mirror

spēlunca, -ae, F., cave, cavern

spernō, -ere, sprēvī, sprētum, despise, spurn, scorn

spērō, -āre, -āvī, -ātum, hope (for)

spēs, speī, F., hope, expectation

spīritus, -ūs, M., breathing, breath (of life); high spirit, pride

splendidus, -a, -um, shining, bright

spoliō, -āre, -āvī, -ātum, despoil, plunder, strip

sponte (only abl., with **suā, meā,** etc.), of one's own accord, voluntarily

stabulum, -ī, N., stable, stall

stagnum, -ī, N., standing water, pool

starve to death, **famē morior** 3

statim (adv.), at once, immediately

statiō, -ōnis, F., standing, station, military post; sentry, picket

statuō, -ere, statuī, statūtum, stand, set up, make a stand; halt; station; determine, decide; pass sentence

statūra, -ae, F., height, stature, size

stella, -ae, F., star

Stellātis (campus/ager), the Stell'ate plain , a fruitful region in Campa'nia

stilus, -ī, M., style/mode of writing

stimulō, -āre, -āvī, -ātum, spur on, stimulate, rouse

stīpendium, -ī, N., tax, tribute; soldier's pay

stō, stāre, stetī, statūrus, stand; abide by (with abl.)

studeō, -ēre, studuī, desire, be eager (at/for), be anxious (for); be devoted (to), give/pay attention to, study, attach importance to

studium, -ī, N., enthusiasm, eagerness; loyalty; pursuit, study, interest

Styx, Stygis, F., the Styx, a river in the lower world

suādeō, -ēre, suāsī, suāsum (with dat.), urge, recommend, persuade, advise

sub (with abl.), under at; (place) at the foot of; (time) in, within

sub (with acc.), under, toward; (place) beneath, into; up to, close to; (time) just before, during

subdūcō, -ere, dūxī, -ductum, haul/ draw up, beach (ships); withdraw

subeō, -īre, -iī, -itum, go/come up (from below), come up (to), approach, advance; go under, take up; undergo, endure

subitō (adv.), suddenly

subjiciō, -ere, -jēcī, -jectum, throw under; place below/under; hurl from beneath; subject, expose; suggest; add

sublevō, -āre, -āvī, -ātum, lift/hold up; assist, aid

417

subluō, -ere, ____ , -lūtum, wash, flow around/along

subministrō, -āre, -āvī, -ātum, furnish, supply

submittō, -ere, -mīsī, -missum, lower, drop; send up/under/as aid, send

submoveō; see **summoveō**

subsequor, -sequī, -secūtus sum, follow up/after, follow (closely)

subsidium, -ī, N., (reserve) aid, assistance, help, relief; pl., reinforcements

subsistō, -ere, -stitī, make a stand (against), withstand; stop, halt; stay

subsum, -esse, be near/at hand

subtrahō, -ere, -trāxī, -tractum, withdraw; take away, subtract

succēdō, -ere, -cessī, -cessum, go under; come up to, advance; succeed

succīdō, -ere, -cīdī, -cīsum, cut (down/from under)

Suēbus, -a, -um, Sue'bian, of the Sue'bi; (as noun) M. pl., the Sue'bi/Sue'vi, a German tribe

Suessa, -ae, F., Suess'a, a town in Italy

sufficiently, **satis** (adv.)

suffrāgium, -ī, N., vote

suī, sibi, sē/sēsē, sē/sēsē (3rd pers. sing./pl., reflex. pron.), himself, herself, itself, themselves; (acc. as subject of infinitive), him, her, it, them; each other, one another; see **inter**

suitor, **procus, -ī,** M.

Sulla, -ae, M., Lu'cius Cornel'ius Sull'a, rival of Mar'ius, dictator in 81 B.C.

Sulla, -ae, M., Faus'tus Lu'cius Cornel'ius Sull'a, son of the dictator

Sulpicius, -ī, M., Pub'lius Sulpic'ius Ru'fus, one of Caesar's generals

sum, esse, fuī, futūrus, be, exist

summa, -ae, F., (sum) total; command; **summa imperī,** chief command

summoveō, -ēre, -mōvī, -mōtum, send away; drive away, remove

summus, -a, -um, highest, top of, chief, greatest, supreme; **summum imperium,** supreme command

sūmō, -ere, sūmpsī, sūmptum, take; assume; lay hold of; **supplicium sūmere,** inflict punishment (on)

sūmptuōsus, -a, -um, expensive

super (adv.), above, on top; (prep. with acc.), above, over, on top of

superior, -ius, upper, higher; superior; (time) earlier, former, previous

superō, -āre, -āvī, -ātum, rise above; overcome, conquer, defeat; be superior to; **vītā superāre,** survive

supersum, -esse, -fuī, -futūrus, be left/over; survive, remain

superus, -a, -um, upper; above

suppetō, -ere, -īvī, -ītum, be near/at hand; hold out

supplicātiō, -ōnis, F., public prayer, supplication; thanksgiving

supplicium, -ī, N., punishment

supplicō, -āre, -āvī, -ātum, kneel, beseech, entreat, implore

suprā (adv.), above; before, earlier; (prep. with acc.), above, on, over

suprēmus, -a, -um, highest, greatest, last, final

suscipiō, -cipere, -cēpī, -ceptum, take (up/on); undertake; begin

suspīciō, -ōnis, F., suspicion, distrust

suspicor, -ārī, -ātus sum, suspect

sustineō, -ēre, -tinuī, -tentum, uphold, support, sustain; withstand, resist, endure; hold out; **sē sustinēre,** hold oneself up, stand up

suus, -a, -um, (reflex. adj.), his/her/ its/their own; his, her, hers, its, theirs; one's (own); (as noun) M. pl., one's/his/their own men/troops/ friends/people/party; (as noun) N. pl., one's/his/her/their own possessions; his/her/their possessions

swim, **natō** 1

T

tabernāculum, -ī, N., tent

tabula, -ae, F., list; (writing) tablet; record; table

taceō, -ēre, -uī, -itum, be/keep silent

tacitus, -a, -um, silent; concealed, secret; tacit

taeda, -ae, F., torch

tālis, -e, such, of such a kind

tam (adv.), thus, so, so much, to such an extent; **tam . . . quam,** so much as, so . . . as; both . . . and

tamen (adv.), nevertheless, still, yet

tandem (adv.), at last, at length, finally

tantulus, -a, -um, so small, so little

tantum (adv.), so much, so greatly, to such an extent, so far; this much, only; **tantum . . . quantum,** as much . . . as

tantus, -a, -um, so great, so large, of such an extent; **tantus . . . quantus,** as/so great . . . as, as large . . . as, as much . . . as; (as noun) N., so much

tardē (adv.), slowly

tardius, (adv.), more/too slowly, less vigorously

tardō, -āre, -āvī, -ātum, make slow, retard, hinder, check

tardus, -a, -um, tardy, late, slow

taurus, -ī, M., bull

tē (acc./abl. of **tū**), you (sing.); **tēcum = cum tē**

teacher, **magister, -trī,** M.; **magistra, -ae,** F.

tēctum, -ī, N., roof; shelter, house

tegō, -ere, tēxī, tēctum, cover, protect; conceal

Tēlemachus, -ī, M., Telem'achus, son of Ulyss'es and Penel'ope

tell (say), **dīcō** 3; (relate), **nārrō** 1

tēlum, -ī, N., missile, weapon, javelin, dart, spear

temerārius, -a, -um, imprudent, rash

temere (adv.), rashly, indiscreetly

temeritās, -ātis, F., rashness

temperantia, -ae, F., prudence, selfcontrol, temperance

temperātus, -a, -um, mild, temperate

tempestās, -ātis, F., time, season; weather; storm, tempest

templum, -ī, N., temple, shrine

temptō, -āre, -āvī, -ātum, test, try; venture, attempt; tempt

tempus, temporis, N., time; a time, period, season; opportunity; **ex tempore,** without preparation, offhand

tendō, -ere, tetendī, tentum, stretch, aim, direct; make one's way; extend

teneō, -ēre, -uī, hold, possess, occupy; keep; **cursum tenēre,** keep a course; **(in) memoriā tenēre,** remember; **sē tenēre,** stay

tergum, -ī, N., back, rear; **ā tergō/ post tergum,** in the rear, behind; **tergum/terga vertere,** flee

terra, -ae, F., earth, land; region; **orbis terrārum,** the earth, the world

terrēnus, -a, -um, earthen, of earth

terreō, -ēre, -uī, -itum, frighten, alarm

terribilis, -e, dreadful, terrible

territus, -a, -um, frightened; terrified

terror, -ōris, M., panic, fear, fright

tertius, -a, -um, third; **tertius (-a, -um) decimus (-a, -um),** thirteenth

testāmentum, -ī, N., will, testament

testimōnium, -ī, N., proof, testimony

testis, -is (-ium), M./F., witness

Teutonī, -ōrum/Teutonēs, -um, M. pl., the Teu'toni/Teu'tones/Teu'tons, a German people/tribe

that (demonstrative adj./pron.), **ille, illa, illud; is, ea, id;** see p. 431

that/so that/in order that (conj.), **ut; nē** (with verbs of fearing); **quīn** (with negative expressions of doubt)

theātrum, -ī, N., theater (place for plays/games)

their/their own (when reflexive), **suus, -a, -um;** (when not reflexive), **eōrum, eārum, eōrum** (pers. pron.)

these, **hī, hae, haec; eī, eae, ea;** see p. 431

Thessalia, -ae, F., Thess'aly, a section of Greece

think, **putō** 1; (judge) **cēnseō** 2; **exīstimō** 1; **arbitror** 1; (believe) **crēdō** 3

Thrācia, -ae, F., Thrace, a region north of Greece

Tiberis, -is; (acc.) **Tiberim,** M., the Ti'ber River

tibi (dat. of **tū**), (to/for) you (sing.)

Tibur, Tiburis, N., Ti'bur (now Tiv'oli), a town in La'tium on the An'io River

Tigurīnus, -a, -um, of the Tig'uri'ni; (as noun) M. pl., the Tig'uri'ni, a tribe of the Helve'tians

timeō, ēre, -uī, fear, be afraid (of)/ fearful

timor, -ōris, M., fear, alarm; timidity

Titūrius, -ī, M., Quin'tus Titu'rius Sabi'nus, one of Caesar's generals

to, **ad, in** (preps. with acc.)

today, **hodiē** (adv.)

tolerō, -āre, -āvī, -ātum, endure, tolerate; (with **famem**) alleviate

tollō, -ere, sustulī, sublātum, lift, raise; take on board; exalt; remove, take away: do away with, abolish

Tolōsātēs, -ium, M. pl., the Tol'osa'tes, the people of Tolo'sa, modern Toulouse'

tormentum, -ī, N., torture, torment; military machine (for hurling missiles); pl., artillery

tot (indecl. adj.), so many; **tot . . . quot,** as many . . . as

totiēns (adv.), so often, so many times

tōtus, -a, -um, whole, the whole (of)

trādō, -ere, trādidī, trāditum, give/ hand over, deliver up, surrender; hand down, tell; teach; transmit

trādūcō, -ere, -dūxī, -ductum, bring/ lead across/over/through; transfer

trāgula, -ae, F., javelin, dart (light Gall'ic javelin thrown by strap)

trahō, -ere, trāxī, tractum, draw along/away, drag, draw, pull

trājectus, -ūs, M., crossing, passage

tranquillitās, -ātis, F., calm, calmness; tranquillity

trāns (with acc.), across, beyond, on the other side of, to the other side of

trānscendō, -ere, -scendī, -scēnsum, climb/scale/step over, pass over

trānsdūcō; see **trādūcō**

trānseō, -īre, -iī, -itum, cross, go over/across/through; **initium trānseundī facere,** be the first to cross

trānsferō, -ferre, -tulī, -lātum, carry/ bring over; transfer; **sē trānsferre,** devote oneself

trānsfigō, -ere, -fīxī, -fīxum, transfix, pierce through

trānsgredior, -gredī, -gressus sum, go across/through, pass over, cross

trānsitus, -ūs, M., a crossing/passing over; passage

trānsmarīnus, -a, -um, from beyond the sea, foreign, transmarine

trānsmittō, -ere, -mīsī, -missum, send across; bring over, transmit

trānsportō, -āre, -āvī, -ātum, carry/ take across; transport, convey

trānsvehō, -ere, -vexī, -vectum, carry across; convey; transport

Trebia, -ae, M., the Tre'bia (now Treb'bia), a river in Cisal'pine Gaul, where Hann'ibal conquered the Romans in 218 B.C.

Trebōnius, C., -ī, M., Ga'ius Trebo'- nius, one of Caesar's generals

trecentī, -ae, -a, three hundred

tremō, -ere, -uī, tremble, quake

tremor, -ōris, M., trembling, quake

trepidātiō, -ōnis, F., confusion, anxiety, alarm, agitation

trēs, tria, gen., **trium,** three; see p. 456

Trēverī, -ōrum, M. pl., the Trev'eri, a people of Bel'gic Gaul, whose ancient capital is now Trier (or Treves)

tribūnus, -ī, M., tribune, a Roman official; **tribūnus mīlitum,** military tribune

tribuō, -ere, tribuī, tribūtum, allot, assign, grant; pay; attribute

tribūtum, -ī, N., tribute, tax

trīcēsimus, -a, -um, thirtieth

trīduum, -ī, N., (period of) three days

trīgintā (indecl. adj.), thirty

triplex, gen., **-icis,** threefold, triple; in three divisions/lines

trīstis, -e, sad, grim, glum

trīstitia, -ae, F., sadness

triumphō, -āre, -āvī, -ātum, triumph, have a triumph

triumphus, -ī, M., triumph

Trōja, -ae, F., Troy, a city in A'sia Mi'nor

Trōjānus, -ī, M., a Tro'jan, an inhabitant of Troy

Troucillus; see **Valerius**

Troy, **Trōja, -ae,** F.

tū (2nd pers. pron.), you/yourself (sing.); pl., **vōs,** you/yourselves

tuba, -ae, F., trumpet

tueor, -ērī, tūtus sum, look/gaze at; see; watch, guard, protect

tuī (gen. of **tū**)

Tulingī, -ōrum, M. pl., the Tulin'gi, a German tribe

tum (adv.), then, at that time; thereupon, next; moreover; **cum . . . tum,** both . . . and, not only . . . but also

tumultus, -ūs, M., uproar, confusion, tumult, commotion; rebellion

tumulus, -ī, M., mound, small hill

tunc (adv.), then, at that time

Tūnēs, -ētis, M., Tu'nis, seaport of North Africa

tunica, -ae, F., tunic, robe

turba, -ae, F., crowd; tumult

turbātē (adv.), in confusion

turbō, -āre, -āvī, -ātum, confuse

Turonī, -ōrum, M. pl., the Tu'roni, a Gall'ic tribe

turpis, -e, ugly, shameful, dishonorable

turpitūdō, -inis, F., disgrace

turris, -is (-ium), F., tower

Tusculum, -ī, N., Tus'culum, an ancient town in La'tium

tūtē (adv.), safely

Tūtia, -ae, M., the Tu'tia, a river near Rome

tūtus, -a, -um (adj.), protected, safe; **in tūtō,** safe, in a safe place; (perf. part. of **tueor, -ērī,** behold, look at), having seen/looked at

tuus, -a, -um, your, yours (referring to one person)

U

ubi (rel. adv.), where, in which place; (interrog.), where?; (conj.) when, whenever; **ubi prīmum,** as soon as

ubīque (adv.), everywhere

ulcīscor, ulcīscī, ultus sum, take vengeance on, avenge, punish

Ulixēs, Ulixis, M., Ulys'es, king of Ith'aca, hero of Homer's Od'yssey

ūllus, -a, -um, any; (as noun) M., anyone, anybody

ulterior, -ius, farther, beyond

ultimus, -a, -um, farthest, last; end of; (as noun) M. pl., those in the rear

ultrā (adv.), beyond, farther; (prep. with acc.), on the other side of, beyond; **nē plūs ultrā,** nothing beyond; the height of excellence

ultrō (adv.), beyond; voluntarily; without any reason/cause/provocation; **ultrō citrōque,** back and forth

Ulysses, **Ulixēs, Ulixis,** M.

umerus, -ī, M., shoulder

umquam (adv.), at any time, ever

ūnā (adv.), at the same time, together; **ūnā cum,** along/together with

unda, -ae, F., wave

unde (rel. adv.), from which place, from where; from which (cause); (interrog.), from where? from what place/direction? from what cause?

ūndecim (indecl. adj.), eleven

under, **sub** (with acc./abl.)

ūndēvigintī (indecl. adj.), nineteen

undique (adv.), from all sides/directions, on all sides, everywhere

ūniversus, -a, -um, all together, all

ūnus, -a, -um, one, single; only, alone; the same, common; **ad ūnum,** to a man; **ūnā ex parte,** on one side; **ūnā vōce,** unanimously

urbānus, -a, -um, of the city, city

urbs, urbis (-ium), F., city; the City (Rome)

urgeō, -ēre, ursī, drive, hem in, oppress; overwhelm

ūrō, -ere, ussī, ustum, burn

ursa, -ae, F., bear

usque (adv.), all the way, even to, even, as far as; all the time; **usque ad,** up to, till

ūsus, -ūs, M., use, advantage; practice, experience, skill, need; **ūsuī/ ex ūsū esse,** be of advantage/ expedient; **ūsus est,** it is necessary

ut/utī (adv./conj.), as, when, since, as soon as, just as; inasmuch as, seeing that; though, although, as if; (introducing indirect question), how; **ut . . . ita/sic,** just as . . . so, while . . . yet, though . . . still; (conj. with clause of purpose), that, in order that, so that, in order to; (with clause of result), that, so that; (after verb of fearing), that . . . not

uter, utra, utrum, (interrog. pron.), which (of the two)?; (indef. pron.), whichever (of the two)

uterque, utraque, utrumque (adj./ pron.), each/either (of two), both; pl., both (sides/parties)

ūtor, ūtī, ūsus sum, use, employ, enjoy; take advantage of, adopt

utrimque (adv.), on/from both sides

utrum (conj.), whether; (used mainly in alternate questions), **utrum . . . an,** whether . . . or

ūva, -ae, F., grape; bunch of grapes

uxor, -ōris, F., wife

V

vacō, -āre, -āvī, -ātum, be empty/unoccupied

vādō, -ere, go, walk; hasten

vadum, -ī, N., shallow, shoal; ford

vae (interjection), alas! woe!

vagor, -ārī, -ātus sum, range, roam, wander; maneuver

valeō, -ēre, -uī, valitūrus, be strong/well; **valē/valēte,** goodby

Valerius, -ī, M., Ga'ius Vale'rius Dom'notau'rus, son of Cabu'rus

Valerius, -ī, M., Ga'ius Vale'rius Troucill'us, a Gall'ic interpreter and confidential friend of Caesar

valētūdō, -inis, F., (poor) health

validus, -a, -um, well, strong

vallēs, vallis (-ium), F., valley

vāllum, -ī, N., entrenchment, rampart

valor, -ōris, M., valor, strength

variētās, -ātis, F., difference, diversity

varius, -a, -um, various; changing

Varrō, -ōnis, M., Ga'ius Teren'tius Varr'o, in command of the Roman army with Aemil'ius Paul'us at the battle of Cann'ae in 216 B.C.

Varus, -ī, M., the Var, a river between the Province and Liguria

vāstō, -āre, -āvī, -ātum, lay waste, ravage, destroy

vāstus, -a, -um, vast, enormous

-ve = vel

vehementer (adv.), violently; severely, strongly; very much, greatly

vehiculum, -ī, N., vehicle

vehō, -ere, vexī, vectum, carry, convey, transport; (pass.) sail, ride

Veiī, -ōrum, M. pl., Ve'ii, an Etruscan city about 12 miles from Rome

vel (conj.), or; **vel . . . vel,** either . . . or

vellus, velleris, N., fleece

vēlō, -āre, -āvī, -ātum, cover, veil

vēlum, -ī, N., covering, veil; sail; **vēla dare/facere,** set sail

velut (adv.), as, just as, as it were

vēnātiō, -ōnis, F., hunting, hunt

vēndō, -dere, vēndidī, vēnditum, offer for sale, sell, vend

venēnum, -ī, N., poison, venom

Veneticus, -a, -um, Ven'etan, of the Ven'eti, a tribe of Cel'tic Gaul

veniō, -ire, vēnī, ventum, come; **in dēditiōnem venīre,** surrender

ventus, -ī, M. wind

Venusia, -ae, F., Venu'sia, an old town in Italy, now Veno'sa

Verbigenus, -ī, M., Verbig'enus, a canton of the Helve'tians

verbum, -ī, N., word, saying; pl., conversation; **verba facere,** speak

Vercassivellaunus, -ī, M., Vercass'-ivellau'nus, a Gall'ic leader

Vercingetorix, -īgis, M., Ver'cinget'-orix, a leader of the Arver'ni; commander in chief of the Gall'ic forces in the uprising of 52 B.C.

vērē (adv.), truly

vereor, -ērī, veritus sum, fear, dread

vergō, -ere, face; be situated

vēritās, -ātis, F., truth, honesty

vērō (adv.), in fact, indeed; but

versō, -āre, -āvī, -ātum, turn (often)

versor, -ārī, -ātus sum, be (engaged) in; be situated; remain, be

Verticō, -ōnis, M., Ver'tico, a Nervian

vertō, -ere, vertī, versum, turn, change; **tergum/terga vertere,** flee, take to flight; (pass. as reflex.) turn (oneself), turn one's attention

vērus, -a, -um, true, real; fair, just; (as noun) N., truth; **rē vērā,** in fact

Vesontiō, -ōnis, M., Veson'tio, chief town of the Seq'uani, now Besançon'

vesper, -erī/-eris, M., evening star, evening; **sub vesperum,** toward evening; **vesperī,** in the evening

vester, -tra, -trum, your, yours (of more than one person)

vestibulum, -ī, N., entrance, vestibule

vēstīgium, -ī, N., footstep, trace

vestis, -is (-ium), F., covering, clothing; pl., clothes, garments

vestrī (gen. of **vōs**)

Vesuvius, -ī, M., Vesu'vius, volcano in Italy, near ancient Her'cula'neum and Pompe'ii

veterānus, -a, -um, old, veteran

vetō, -āre, vetuī, vetitum, forbid

vetus, gen., -eris, old, longstanding, former; veteran

vetustās, -ātis, F., (great) age; (passage of) time

vexō, -āre, -āvī, -ātum, plunder, overrun; vex, annoy

via, -ae, F., way, road, street

Via (-ae) Appia (-ae), F., the App'ian Way, road from Rome to Cap'ua, later extended to Brundis'ium

Via (-ae) Flāminia (-ae), F., the Flamin'ian Way, road leading north from Rome to Arim'inum

Via (-ae) Latīna (-ae), F., the Latin Way, road leading from Rome to Casili'num (near Cap'ua), where it joined the App'ian Way

Via (-ae) Sacra (-ae), F., Vi'a Sa'cra (Sacred Way), a street in Rome, leading from the Forum to the Cap'itol

viātor, -ōris, M., traveler; courier

vicīnus, -a, -um, neighboring, near; (as noun), M., neighbor

victima, -ae, F., victim; animal for sacrifice

victor, -ōris, M., conqueror, victor; (as adj.), victorious

victōria, -ae, F., victory

victus, -a, -um, defeated; (as noun), M. pl., the vanquished

victus, -ūs, M., food; (way of) life

vīcus, -ī, M., street, quarter; village

videō, -ēre, vīdī, vīsum, see

videor, -ērī, vīsus sum, seem, appear; seem good/right/best/proper

vigilia, -ae, F., being awake; watching; guard, night watch; a watch (fourth part of the night); **dē quārtā vigiliā,** about the fourth watch

vigilō, -āre, -āvī, -ātum, watch, stand guard; be awake/vigilant

vīgintī (indecl. adj.), twenty

vīlicus, -ī, M., foreman, farm manager

villa, -ae, F., country house; estate

vincō, -ere, vīcī, victum, conquer, defeat, subdue; be victorious, win

vinculum, -ī, N., a fastening; chain

vīnea, -ae, F., vineyard; shed

vīnum, -ī, N., wine

violenter (adv.), violently

violō, -āre, -āvī, -ātum, violate, harm, injure, dishonor

vir, virī, M., man; husband

Viridomārus, -ī, M., Vir'idoma'rus, a chief of the Haed'ui

Virrius (-ī), Vibius (-ī), M., Vib'ius Virr'ius, a Cap'uan senator

virtūs, -ūtis, F., manliness, courage, valor; virtue; pl., good qualities

vīs (nom.); **vim** (acc.); **vī** (abl.), F., force, violence, strength, power; pl., **vīrēs, -ium,** strength; **vim facere,** use force; **omnī vī,** with all one's strength; see p. 456

vīsitō, -āre, -āvī, -ātum, see often

vīta, -ae, F., life; **ē vītā excēdere/discēdere,** die; **vītam agere,** live

vītō, -āre, -āvī, -ātum, avoid, escape

vīvō, -ere, vīxī, vīctum, live

vīvus, -a, -um, alive, living

vix (adv.), hardly, with difficulty

vōbīs (dat./abl. of **vōs**), (to/for) you

vocō, -āre, -āvī, -ātum, call, summon, invite; name

Vocontiī, -ōrum, M. pl., the Vocon'tii, a Gall'ic tribe

Volcae (-ārum) Arecomicī (-ōrum), M. pl., the Vol'cae Ar'ecom'icī, a tribe of southern Gaul

volō, -āre, -āvī, -ātum, fly, fly about

volō, velle, voluī, will, wish, be willing, want, desire; intend, mean

voluntās, -ātis, F., will, wish; consent

voluptās, -ātis, F., pleasure, delight

Volusēnus, -ī, C., M., Ga'ius Vol'use'nus Quadra'tus, a military tribune in Caesar's army

volvō, -ere, volvī, volūtum, roll, turn about/around

vōs (2nd pers. pron.), pl., you/yourselves

voveō, -ēre, vōvī, vōtum, vow; wish

vōx, vōcis, F., voice, sound; word; **magnā vōce,** in a loud voice

Vulcānus, -ī, M., Vul'can, god of fire

vulgus, -ī, N., the common people, the crowd, the public

vulnerō, -āre, -āvī, -ātum, wound

vulnus, vulneris, N., wound, injury; **vulnera (vulnus) facere/inferre,** inflict wounds (a wound)

W

wage (carry on), **gerō** 3

want, **cupiō** 3; **dēsīderō** 1; **volō, velle, voluī;** didn't/did not want, **nōlō, nōlle, nōluī**

warn, **moneō** 2

we, **nōs** (1st pers. pron.); see page 430

wear, **gerō** 3

what/which (interrog. pron.), **quis, quid;** (interrog. adj.), **quī/quis, quae, quod;** see pages 432, 433

when, **cum** (conj. with indicative, referring to pres./fut. time; with subjunctive, referring to past time)

which/who (rel. pron.), **quī, quae, quod;** (interrog. pron.), **quis, quid;** (interrog. adj.), **quī, quae, quod**

while, **dum** (conj. with pres. indic.)

who/whom/whose; see which

with, **cum** (prep. with abl.)

without, **sine** (prep. with abl.)

word, **verbum, -ī,** N.

wound (verb), **vulnerō** 1; (noun), **vulnus, vulneris,** N.

Y

you, **tū** (nom. sing.); pl. **vōs;** see p. 430

SUMMARY OF GRAMMAR

NOUNS AND ADJECTIVES

Declensions I and II

nouns

	Singular	Singular	Singular	Singular	Singular	Singular
Nom.	casa (F.)	sonus (M.)	puer (M.)	ager (M.)	vir (M.)	dōnum (N.)
Gen.	casae	sonī	puerī	agrī	virī	dōnī
Dat.	casae	sonō	puerō	agrō	virō	dōnō
Acc.	casam	sonum	puerum	agrum	virum	dōnum
Abl.	casā	sonō	puerō	agrō	virō	dōnō
	Plural	Plural	Plural	Plural	Plural	Plural
Nom.	casae	sonī	puerī	agrī	virī	dōna
Gen.	casārum	sonōrum	puerōrum	agrōrum	virōrum	dōnōrum
Dat.	casīs	sonīs	puerīs	agrīs	virīs	dōnīs
Acc.	casās	sonōs	puerōs	agrōs	virōs	dōna
Abl.	casīs	sonīs	puerīs	agrīs	virīs	dōnīs

adjectives

	Singular M.	Singular F.	Singular N.	Plural M.	Plural F.	Plural N.
Nom.	bonus	bona	bonum	bonī	bonae	bona
Gen.	bonī	bonae	bonī	bonōrum	bonārum	bonōrum
Dat.	bonō	bonae	bonō	bonīs	bonīs	bonīs
Acc.	bonum	bonam	bonum	bonōs	bonās	bona
Abl.	bonō	bonā	bonō	bonīs	bonīs	bonīs
Nom.	liber	libera	liberum	liberī	liberae	libera
Gen.	liberī	liberae	liberī	liberōrum	liberārum	liberōrum
Dat.	liberō	liberae	liberō	liberīs	liberīs	liberīs
Acc.	liberum	liberam	liberum	liberōs	liberās	libera
Abl.	liberō	liberā	liberō	liberīs	liberīs	liberīs
Nom.	sacer	sacra	sacrum	sacrī	sacrae	sacra
Gen.	sacrī	sacrae	sacrī	sacrōrum	sacrārum	sacrōrum
Dat.	sacrō	sacrae	sacrō	sacrīs	sacrīs	sacrīs
Acc.	sacrum	sacram	sacrum	sacrōs	sacrās	sacra
Abl.	sacrō	sacrā	sacrō	sacrīs	sacrīs	sacrīs

Declension III

masculine/feminine nouns

	Singular	Singular	Singular	Singular	Singular	Singular
Nom.	lēx (F.)	miles (M.)	frāter (M.)	collis (M.)	nūbēs (F.)	nox (F.)
Gen.	lēgis	militis	frātris	collis	nūbis	noctis
Dat.	lēgī	militī	frātrī	collī	nūbī	noctī
Acc.	lēgem	militem	frātrem	collem	nūbem	noctem
Abl.	lēge	milite	frātre	colle	nūbe	nocte
	Plural	Plural	Plural	Plural	Plural	Plural
Nom.	lēgēs	militēs	frātrēs	collēs	nūbēs	noctēs
Gen.	lēgum	militum	frātrum	collium	nūbium	noctium
Dat.	lēgibus	militibus	frātribus	collibus	nūbibus	noctibus
Acc.	lēgēs	militēs	frātrēs	collēs	nūbēs	noctēs
Abl.	lēgibus	militibus	frātribus	collibus	nūbibus	noctibus

neuter nouns

	Singular	Singular	Singular	Singular	Singular	Singular
Nom.	ōmen	caput	opus	iter	mare	animal
Gen.	ōminis	capitis	operis	itineris	maris	animālis
Dat.	ōminī	capitī	operī	itinerī	marī	animālī
Acc.	ōmen	caput	opus	iter	mare	animal
Abl.	ōmine	capite	opere	itinere	marī	animālī
	Plural	Plural	Plural	Plural	Plural	Plural
Nom.	ōmina	capita	opera	itinera	maria	animālia
Gen.	ōminum	capitum	operum	itinerum	marium	animālium
Dat.	ōminibus	capitibus	operibus	itineribus	maribus	animālibus
Acc.	ōmina	capita	opera	itinera	maria	animālia
Abl.	ōminibus	capitibus	operibus	itineribus	maribus	animālibus

Declension IV

m./f. nouns

	Singular	Plural
Nom.	exercitus (M.)	exercitūs
Gen.	exercitūs	exercituum
Dat.	exercituī	exercitibus
Acc.	exercitum	exercitūs
Abl.	exercitū	exercitibus

neuter nouns

	Singular	Plural
Nom.	cornū	cornua
Gen.	cornūs	cornuum
Dat.	cornū	cornibus
Acc.	cornū	cornua
Abl.	cornū	cornibus

Declension V

m./f. nouns

	Singular	Plural
Nom.	rēs (F.)	rēs
Gen.	reī	rērum
Dat.	reī	rēbus
Acc.	rem	rēs
Abl.	rē	rēbus

427

Declension III (continued)

adjectives

3-ending

	Singular (M.)	Singular (F.)	Singular (N.)
Nom.	ācer	ācris	ācre
Gen.	ācris	ācris	ācris
Dat.	ācrī	ācrī	ācrī
Acc.	ācrem	ācrem	ācre
Abl.	ācrī	ācrī	ācrī

	Plural (M./F.)	Plural (N.)
Nom.	ācrēs	ācria
Gen.	ācrium	ācrium
Dat.	ācribus	ācribus
Acc.	ācrēs	ācria
Abl.	ācribus	ācribus

2-ending

	Singular (M/F.)	Singular (N.)
Nom.	facilis	facile
Gen.	facilis	facilis
Dat.	facilī	facilī
Acc.	facilem	facile
Abl.	facilī	facilī

	Plural (M./F.)	Plural (N.)
Nom.	facilēs	facilia
Gen.	facilium	facilium
Dat.	facilibus	facilibus
Acc.	facilēs	facilia
Abl.	facilibus	facilibus

1-ending

	Singular (M./F.)	Singular (N.)
Nom.	fēlix	fēlix
Gen.	fēlīcis	fēlīcis
Dat.	fēlīcī	fēlīcī
Acc.	fēlīcem	fēlix
Abl.	fēlīcī	fēlīcī

	Plural (M./F.)	Plural (N.)
Nom.	fēlīcēs	fēlīcia
Gen.	fēlīcium	fēlīcium
Dat.	fēlīcibus	fēlīcibus
Acc.	fēlīcēs	fēlīcia
Abl.	fēlīcibus	fēlīcibus

Present Participle

	Singular (M./F.)	Singular (N.)
Nom.	portāns	portāns
Gen.	portantis	portantis
Dat.	portantī	portantī
Acc.	portantem	portāns
Abl.	portante/tī	portante/tī

	Plural (M./F.)	Plural (N.)
Nom.	portantēs	portantia
Gen.	portantium	portantium
Dat.	portantibus	portantibus
Acc.	portantēs	portantia
Abl.	portantibus	portantibus

IRREGULAR ADJECTIVES[1]

	Singular (M.)	Singular (F.)	Singular (N.)	Singular (M.)	Singular (F.)	Singular (N.)
Nom.	sōlus	sōla	sōlum	alter	altera	alterum
Gen.	sōlīus	sōlīus	sōlīus	alterīus	alterīus	alterīus
Dat.	sōlī	sōlī	sōlī	alterī	alterī	alterī
Acc.	sōlum	sōlam	sōlum	alterum	alteram	alterum
Abl.	sōlō	sōlā	sōlō	alterō	alterā	alterō

[1]alius, sōlus, ūllus, ūnus, tōtus, nūllus; alter, neuter, uter

COMPARISON

Regular Adjectives/Adverbs

	positive		superlative	
Adjectives	Adverbs		Adjectives	Adverbs
lātus, -a, -um	lātē		lātissimus, -a, -um	lātissimē
fortis, forte	fortiter		fortissimus, -a, -um	fortissimē
ācer, ācris, ācre	ācriter		ācerrimus, -a, -um	ācerrimē
facilis, facile	facile		facillimus, -a, -um	facillimē
fēlix, gen., -īcis	fēlīciter		fēlīcissimus, -a, -um	fēlīcissimē

Irregular Adjectives/Adverbs

	positive		superlative	
Adjectives	Adverbs		Adjectives	Adverbs
bonus, -a, -um	bene		optimus, -a, -um	optimē
malus, -a, -um	male		pessimus, -a, -um	pessimē
magnus, -a, -um	magnopere		maximus, -a, -um	maximē
parvus, -a, -um	parum		minimus, -a, -um	minimē
multus, -a, -um	multum		plūrimus, -a, -um	plūrimē

Comparatives of Adjectives/Adverbs

	regular			irregular	
Adjectives (M./F.)	Adjectives (N.)	Adverbs	Adjectives (M./F.)	Adjectives (N.)	Adverbs
lātior	lātius	lātius	melior	melius	melius
fortior	fortius	fortius	pejor	pejus	pejus
ācrior	ācrius	ācrius	major	majus	magis
facilior	facilius	facilius	minor	minus	minus
fēlīcior	fēlīcius	fēlīcius	—	[1]plūs	plūs

Declension of Comparative Adjectives

	Singular (M./F.)	Singular (N.)	Plural (M./F.)	Plural (N.)
Nom.	lātior	lātius	lātiōrēs	lātiōra
Gen.	lātiōris	lātiōris	lātiōrum	lātiōrum
Dat.	lātiōrī	lātiōrī	lātiōribus	lātiōribus
Acc.	lātiōrem	lātius	lātiōrēs	lātiōra
Abl.	lātiōre	lātiōre	lātiōribus	lātiōribus

[1]Used in singular as noun only.

PRONOUNS

First Person

| | personal | reflexive |
	Singular	Singular
Nom.	**ego**	—
Gen.	**mei**	**mei**
Dat.	**mihi**	**mihi**
Acc.	**mē**	**mē**
Abl.	**mē**	**mē**
	Plural	Plural
Nom.	**nōs**	—
Gen.	**nostrī**	**nostrī**
Dat.	**nōbīs**	**nōbīs**
Acc.	**nōs**	**nōs**
Abl.	**nōbīs**	**nōbīs**

Second Person

| | personal | reflexive |
	Singular	Singular
Nom.	**tū**	—
Gen.	**tuī**	**tuī**
Dat.	**tibi**	**tibi**
Acc.	**tē**	**tē**
Abl.	**tē**	**tē**
	Plural	Plural
Nom.	**vōs**	—
Gen.	**vestrī**	**vestrī**
Dat.	**vōbīs**	**vōbīs**
Acc.	**vōs**	**vōs**
Abl.	**vōbīs**	**vōbīs**

Third Person

not reflexive

(Forms of a demonstrative—usually **is, ea, id**—are used as third-person pronouns)

Third Person

reflexive

	Nom.	Gen.	Dat.	Acc.	Abl.
Sing.		**suī**	**sibi**	**sē**	**sē**
Plur.					

POSSESSIVE MODIFIERS

Referring to Singular Antecedent

1st person	**meus, -a, -um**
2nd person	**tuus, -a, -um** (of one person)
3rd person	**suus, -a, -um** (reflexive)

For declension, see **bonus,** p. 426

ejus (not reflexive) gen. sing. of **is, ea, id**

Referring to Plural Antecedent

1st person	**noster, -tra, -trum**
2nd person	**vester, -tra, -trum** (of more than one)
3rd person	**suus, -a, -um** (reflexive)

For declension, see **sacer, bonus,** p. 426

eōrum, eārum, eōrum (not reflexive) gen. pl. of **is, ea, id**

DEMONSTRATIVES

	Singular (M.)	Singular (F.)	Singular (N.)	Plural (M.)	Plural (F.)	Plural (N.)
Nom.	is	ea	id	eī	eae	ea
Gen.	ejus	ejus	ejus	eōrum	eārum	eōrum
Dat.	eī	eī	eī	eīs	eīs	eīs
Acc.	eum	eam	id	eōs	eās	ea
Abl.	eō	eā	eō	eīs	eīs	eīs

	Singular (M.)	Singular (F.)	Singular (N.)	Plural (M.)	Plural (F.)	Plural (N.)
Nom.	hic	haec	hoc	hī	hae	haec
Gen.	hujus	hujus	hujus	hōrum	hārum	hōrum
Dat.	huic	huic	huic	hīs	hīs	hīs
Acc.	hunc	hanc	hoc	hōs	hās	haec
Abl.	hōc	hāc	hōc	hīs	hīs	hīs

	Singular (M.)	Singular (F.)	Singular (N.)	Plural (M.)	Plural (F.)	Plural (N.)
Nom.	ille	illa	illud	illī	illae	illa
Gen.	illīus	illīus	illīus	illōrum	illārum	illōrum
Dat.	illī	illī	illī	illīs	illīs	illīs
Acc.	illum	illam	illud	illōs	illās	illa
Abl.	illō	illā	illō	illīs	illīs	illīs

IDENTIFYING PRONOUN

	Singular (M.)	Singular (F.)	Singular (N.)	Plural (M.)	Plural (F.)	Plural (N.)
Nom.	īdem	eadem	idem	eīdem	eaedem	eadem
Gen.	ejusdem	ejusdem	ejusdem	eōrundem	eārundem	eōrundem
Dat.	eīdem	eīdem	eīdem	eīsdem	eīsdem	eīsdem
Acc.	eundem	eandem	idem	eōsdem	eāsdem	eadem
Abl.	eōdem	eādem	eōdem	eīsdem	eīsdem	eīsdem

INTENSIVE PRONOUN

	Singular (M.)	Singular (F.)	Singular (N.)	Plural (M.)	Plural (F.)	Plural (N.)
Nom.	ipse	ipsa	ipsum	ipsī	ipsae	ipsa
Gen.	ipsīus	ipsīus	ipsīus	ipsōrum	ipsārum	ipsōrum
Dat.	ipsī	ipsī	ipsī	ipsīs	ipsīs	ipsīs
Acc.	ipsum	ipsam	ipsum	ipsōs	ipsās	ipsa
Abl.	ipsō	ipsā	ipsō	ipsīs	ipsīs	ipsīs

RELATIVE PRONOUNS

	Singular (M.)	Singular (F.)	Singular (N.)	Plural (M.)	Plural (F.)	Plural (N.)
Nom.	quī	quae	quod	quī	quae	quae
Gen.	cujus	cujus	cujus	quōrum	quārum	quōrum
Dat.	cui	cui	cui	quibus	quibus	quibus
Acc.	quem	quam	quod	quōs	quās	quae
Abl.	quō	quā	quō	quibus	quibus	quibus

INTERROGATIVE PRONOUNS

Who or what

	Singular (M./F.)	Singular (N.)	Plural (M.)	Plural (F.)	Plural (N.)
Nom.	quis[1]	quid	quī	quae	quae
Gen.	cujus	cujus	quōrum	quārum	quōrum
Dat.	cui	cui	quibus	quibus	quibus
Acc.	quem	quid	quōs	quās	quae
Abl.	quō	quō	quibus	quibus	quibus

INDEFINITE PRONOUNS

	Singular (M./F.)	Singular (N.)
Nom.	quisquam	quicquam/quidquam
Gen.	cujusquam	cujusquam
Dat.	cuiquam	cuiquam
Acc.	quemquam	quicquam/quidquam
Abl.	quōquam	quōquam

Quisquam is not found in the plural, and its forms are rarely used as adjectives.

	Singular (M./F.)	Singular (N.)	Plural (M.)	Plural (F.)	Plural (N.)
Nom.	quisque	quidque	quīque	quaeque	quaeque
Gen.	cujusque	cujusque	quōrumque	quārumque	quōrumque
Dat.	cuique	cuique	quibusque	quibusque	quibusque
Acc.	quemque	quidque	quōsque	quāsque	quaeque
Abl.	quōque	quōque	quibusque	quibusque	quibusque

	Singular (M./F.)	Singular (N.)	Plural (M.)	Plural (F.)	Plural (N.)
Nom.	aliquis	aliquid	aliquī	aliquae	aliqua
Gen.	alicujus	alicujus	aliquōrum	aliquārum	aliquōrum
Dat.	alicui	alicui	aliquibus	aliquibus	aliquibus
Acc.	aliquem	aliquid	aliquōs	aliquās	aliqua
Abl.	aliquō	aliquō	aliquibus	aliquibus	aliquibus

[1]All forms of **quis/quid** are used for the indefinite pronoun also.

432

INDEFINITE PRONOUNS (continued)

	Singular (M.)	Singular (F.)	Singular (N.)	Plural (M.)	Plural (F.)	Plural (N.)
Nom.	quīdam	quaedam	quiddam[1]	quīdam	quaedam	quaedam
Gen.	cujusdam	cujusdam	cujusdam	quōrundam	quārundam	quōrundam
Dat.	cuīdam	cuidam	cuidam	quibusdam	quibusdam	quibusdam
Acc.	quendam	quandam	quiddam[1]	quōsdam	quāsdam	quaedam
Abl.	quōdam	quādam	quōdam	quibusdam	quibusdam	quibusdam

INTERROGATIVE ADJECTIVES

	Singular (M.)	Singular (F.)	Singular (N.)	Plural (M.)	Plural (F.)	Plural (N.)
Nom.	quī/quis	quae	quod	quī	quae	quae
Gen.	cujus	cujus	cujus	quōrum	quārum	quōrum
Dat.	cui	cui	cui	quibus	quibus	quibus
Acc.	quem	quam	quod	quōs	quās	quae
Abl.	quō	quā	quō	quibus	quibus	quibus

INDEFINITE ADJECTIVES

	Singular (M.)	Singular (F.)	Singular (N.)	Plural (M.)	Plural (F.)	Plural (N.)
Nom.	quī/quis	qua/quae	quod	quī	quae	qua/quae
Gen.	cujus	cujus	cujus	quōrum	quārum	quōrum
Dat.	cui	cui	cui	quibus	quibus	quibus
Acc.	quem	quam	quod	quōs	quās	qua/quae
Abl.	quō	quā	quō	quibus	quibus	quibus

	Singular (M.)	Singular (F.)	Singular (N.)	Plural (M.)	Plural (F.)	Plural (N.)
Nom.	quisque	quaeque	quodque	quīque	quaeque	quaeque
Gen.	cujusque	cujusque	cujusque	quōrumque	quārumque	quōrumque
Dat.	cuique	cuique	cuique	quibusque	quibusque	quibusque
Acc.	quemque	quamque	quodque	quōsque	quāsque	quaeque
Abl.	quōque	quāque	quōque	quibusque	quibusque	quibusque

	Singular (M.)	Singular (F.)	Singular (N.)	Plural (M.)	Plural (F.)	Plural (N.)
Nom.	aliquī	aliqua	aliquod	aliquī	aliquae	aliqua
Gen.	alicujus	alicujus	alicujus	aliquōrum	aliquārum	aliquōrum
Dat.	alicui	alicui	alicui	aliquibus	aliquibus	aliquibus
Acc.	aliquem	aliquam	aliquod	aliquōs	aliquās	aliqua
Abl.	aliquō	aliquā	aliquō	aliquibus	aliquibus	aliquibus

[1]Corresponding adjective differs only in these forms (quoddam for quiddam).

VERBS

Conjugations I, II, III, III-iō, IV

principal parts

I	portō	portāre	portāvī	portātum
II	moneō	monēre	monuī	monitum
III	dūcō	dūcere	dūxī	ductum
III-iō	capiō	capere	cēpī	captum
IV	audiō	audīre	audīvī	audītum

indicative active (present system)

Present

Singular	Singular	Singular	Singular	Singular
portō	moneō	dūcō	capiō	audiō
portās	monēs	dūcis	capis	audīs
portat	monet	dūcit	capit	audit
Plural	Plural	Plural	Plural	Plural
portāmus	monēmus	dūcimus	capimus	audīmus
portātis	monētis	dūcitis	capitis	audītis
portant	monent	dūcunt	capiunt	audiunt

Imperfect

Singular	Singular	Singular	Singular	Singular
portābam	monēbam	dūcēbam	capiēbam	audiēbam
portābās	monēbās	dūcēbās	capiēbās	audiēbās
portābat	monēbat	dūcēbat	capiēbat	audiēbat
Plural	Plural	Plural	Plural	Plural
portābāmus	monēbāmus	dūcēbāmus	capiēbāmus	audiēbāmus
portābātis	monēbātis	dūcēbātis	capiēbātis	audiēbātis
portābant	monēbant	dūcēbant	capiēbant	audiēbant

Future

Singular	Singular	Singular	Singular	Singular
portābō	monēbō	dūcam	capiam	audiam
portābis	monēbis	dūcēs	capiēs	audiēs
portābit	monēbit	dūcet	capiet	audiet
Plural	Plural	Plural	Plural	Plural
portābimus	monēbimus	dūcēmus	capiēmus	audiēmus
portābitis	monēbitis	dūcētis	capiētis	audiētis
portābunt	monēbunt	dūcent	capient	audient

imperatives (active) [1]

Present		Future	
Singular	Plural	Singular	Plural
portā	portāte	portātō	portātōte
monē	monēte	monētō	monētōte
dūc[2]	dūcite	dūcitō	dūcitōte
cape	capite	capitō	capitōte
audī	audīte	audītō	audītōte

[1]For passive imperatives, gerundives, gerunds, and supines, see p. 443.

[2]Other irregular imperatives: **dīc, fac, fer** (sing.); **ferte** (pl.)

indicative passive (present system)

Present

Singular	Singular	Singular	Singular	Singular
portor	moneor	dūcor	capior	audior
portāris/-re	monēris/-re	dūceris/-re	caperis/-re	audīris/-re
portātur	monētur	dūcitur	capitur	audītur
Plural	**Plural**	**Plural**	**Plural**	**Plural**
portāmur	monēmur	dūcimur	capimur	audīmur
portāminī	monēminī	dūciminī	capiminī	audīminī
portantur	monentur	dūcuntur	capiuntur	audiuntur

Imperfect

Singular	Singular	Singular	Singular	Singular
portābar	monēbar	dūcēbar	capiēbar	audiēbar
portābāris/-re	monēbāris/-re	dūcēbāris/-re	capiēbāris/-re	audiēbāris/-re
portābātur	monēbātur	dūcēbātur	capiēbātur	audiēbātur
Plural	**Plural**	**Plural**	**Plural**	**Plural**
portābāmur	monēbāmur	dūcēbāmur	capiēbāmur	audiēbāmur
portābāminī	monēbāminī	dūcēbāminī	capiēbāminī	audiēbāminī
portābantur	monēbantur	dūcēbantur	capiēbantur	audiēbantur

Future

Singular	Singular	Singular	Singular	Singular
portābor	monēbor	dūcar	capiar	audiar
portāberis/-re	monēberis/-re	dūcēris/-re	capiēris/-re	audiēris/-re
portābitur	monēbitur	dūcētur	capiētur	audiētur
Plural	**Plural**	**Plural**	**Plural**	**Plural**
portābimur	monēbimur	dūcēmur	capiēmur	audiēmur
portābiminī	monēbiminī	dūcēminī	capiēminī	audiēminī
portābuntur	monēbuntur	dūcentur	capientur	audientur

Conjugations I, II, III, III-iō, IV

infinitives (active)

Present	Perfect	Future
portāre	portāvisse	portātūrum esse
monēre	monuisse	monitūrum esse
dūcere	dūxisse	ductūrum esse
capere	cēpisse	captūrum esse
audīre	audīvisse	audītūrum esse

participles (active)

Present (See p. 428)	Future
portāns	portātūrus, -a, -um
monēns	monitūrus, -a, -um
dūcēns	ductūrus, -a, -um
capiēns	captūrus, -a, -um
audiēns	audītūrus, -a, -um

indicative active (perfect system)

Perfect

Singular	Singular	Singular	Singular	Singular
portāvī	monuī	dūxī	cēpī	audīvī
portāvistī	monuistī	dūxistī	cēpistī	audīvistī
portāvit	monuit	dūxit	cēpit	audīvit

Plural	Plural	Plural	Plural	Plural
portāvimus	monuimus	dūximus	cēpimus	audīvimus
portāvistis	monuistis	dūxistis	cēpistis	audīvistis
portāvērunt	monuērunt	dūxērunt	cēpērunt	audīvērunt

Past Perfect

Singular	Singular	Singular	Singular	Singular
portāveram	monueram	dūxeram	cēperam	audīveram
portāverās	monuerās	dūxerās	cēperās	audīverās
portāverat	monuerat	dūxerat	cēperat	audīverat

Plural	Plural	Plural	Plural	Plural
portāverāmus	monuerāmus	dūxerāmus	cēperāmus	audīverāmus
portāverātis	monuerātis	dūxerātis	cēperātis	audīverātis
portāverant	monuerant	dūxerant	cēperant	audīverant

Future Perfect

Singular	Singular	Singular	Singular	Singular
portāverō	monuerō	dūxerō	cēperō	audīverō
portāveris	monueris	dūxeris	cēperis	audīveris
portāverit	monuerit	dūxerit	cēperit	audīverit

Plural	Plural	Plural	Plural	Plural
portāverimus	monuerimus	dūxerimus	cēperimus	audīverimus
portāveritis	monueritis	dūxeritis	cēperitis	audīveritis
portāverint	monuerint	dūxerint	cēperint	audīverint

Conjugations I, II, III, III-iō, IV

infinitives (passive)　　　　　　participles (passive)

Present	Perfect	Future		Perfect		Future
portārī	portātum esse	portātum īrī		portātus, -a, -um	portandus, -a, -um
monērī	monitum esse	monitum īrī		monitus, -a, -um	monendus, -a, -um
dūcī	ductum esse	ductum īrī		ductus, -a, -um	dūcendus, -a, -um
capī	captum esse	captum īrī		captus, -a, -um	capiendus, -a, -um
audīrī	audītum esse	audītum īrī		audītus, -a, -um	audiendus, -a, -um

indicative passive (perfect system)

Perfect

Singular	Singular	Singuiar	Singular	Singular
portātus sum	monitus sum	ductus sum	captus sum	audītus sum
portātus es	monitus es	ductus es	captus es	audītus es
portātus est	monitus est	ductus est	captus est	audītus est

Plural	Plural	Plural	Plural	Plural
portātī sumus	monitī sumus	ductī sumus	captī sumus	audītī sumus
portātī estis	monitī estis	ductī estis	captī estis	audītī estis
portātī sunt	monitī sunt	ductī sunt	captī sunt	audītī sunt

Past Perfect

Singular	Singular	Singular	Singular	Singular
portātus eram	monitus eram	ductus eram	captus eram	audītus eram
portātus erās	monitus erās	ductus erās	captus erās	audītus erās
portātus erat	monitus erat	ductus erat	captus erat	audītus erat

Plural	Plural	Plural	Plural	Plural
portātī erāmus	monitī erāmus	ductī erāmus	captī erāmus	audītī erāmus
portātī erātis	monitī erātis	ductī erātis	captī erātis	audītī erātis
portātī erant	monitī erant	ductī erant	captī erant	audītī erant

Future Perfect

Singular	Singular	Singular	Singular	Singular
portātus erō	monitus erō	ductus erō	captus erō	audītus erō
portātus eris	monitus eris	ductus eris	captus eris	audītus eris
portātus erit	monitus erit	ductus erit	captus erit	audītus erit

Plural	Plural	Plural	Plural	Plural
portātī erimus	monitī erimus	ductī erimus	captī erimus	audītī erimus
portātī eritis	monitī eritis	ductī eritis	captī eritis	audītī eritis
portātī erunt	monitī erunt	ductī erunt	captī erunt	audītī erunt

Conjugations I, II, III, III-iō, IV

subjunctive (active)

Present

Singular	Singular	Singular	Singular	Singular
portem	**moneam**	**dūcam**	**capiam**	**audiam**
portēs	**moneās**	**dūcās**	**capiās**	**audiās**
portet	**moneat**	**dūcat**	**capiat**	**audiat**

Plural	Plural	Plural	Plural	Plural
portēmus	**moneāmus**	**dūcāmus**	**capiāmus**	**audiāmus**
portētis	**moneātis**	**dūcātis**	**capiātis**	**audiātis**
portent	**moneant**	**dūcant**	**capiant**	**audiant**

Imperfect

Singular	Singular	Singular	Singular	Singular
portārem	**monērem**	**dūcerem**	**caperem**	**audirem**
portārēs	**monērēs**	**dūcerēs**	**caperēs**	**audirēs**
portāret	**monēret**	**dūceret**	**caperet**	**audiret**

Plural	Plural	Plural	Plural	Plural
portārēmus	**monērēmus**	**dūcerēmus**	**caperēmus**	**audirēmus**
portārētis	**monērētis**	**dūcerētis**	**caperētis**	**audirētis**
portārent	**monērent**	**dūcerent**	**caperent**	**audirent**

Perfect

Singular	Singular	Singular	Singular	Singular
portāverim	**monuerim**	**dūxerim**	**cēperim**	**audiverim**
portāveris	**monueris**	**dūxeris**	**cēperis**	**audiveris**
portāverit	**monuerit**	**dūxerit**	**cēperit**	**audiverit**

Plural	Plural	Plural	Plural	Plural
portāverimus	**monuerimus**	**dūxerimus**	**cēperimus**	**audiverimus**
portāveritis	**monueritis**	**dūxeritis**	**cēperitis**	**audiveritis**
portāverint	**monuerint**	**dūxerint**	**cēperint**	**audiverint**

Past Perfect

Singular	Singular	Singular	Singular	Singular
portāvissem	**monuissem**	**dūxissem**	**cēpissem**	**audivissem**
portāvissēs	**monuissēs**	**dūxissēs**	**cēpissēs**	**audivissēs**
portāvisset	**monuisset**	**dūxisset**	**cēpisset**	**audivisset**

Plural	Plural	Plural	Plural	Plural
portāvissēmus	**monuissēmus**	**dūxissēmus**	**cēpissēmus**	**audivissēmus**
portāvissētis	**monuissētis**	**dūxissētis**	**cēpissētis**	**audivissētis**
portāvissent	**monuissent**	**dūxissent**	**cēpissent**	**audivissent**

Conjugations I, II, III, III-iō, IV (continued)

subjunctive passive

Present

Singular	Singular	Singular	Singular	Singular
porter	**monear**	**dūcar**	**capiar**	**audiar**
portēris/-re	**moneāris/-re**	**dūcāris/-re**	**capiāris/-re**	**audiāris/-re**
portētur	**moneātur**	**dūcātur**	**capiātur**	**audiātur**
Plural	Plural	Plural	Plural	Plural
portēmur	**moneāmur**	**dūcāmur**	**capiāmur**	**audiāmur**
portēminī	**moneāminī**	**dūcāminī**	**capiāminī**	**audiāminī**
portentur	**moneantur**	**dūcantur**	**capiantur**	**audiantur**

Imperfect

Singular	Singular	Singular	Singular	Singular
portārer	**monērer**	**dūcerer**	**caperer**	**audīrer**
portārēris/-re	**monērēris/-re**	**dūcerēris/-re**	**caperēris/-re**	**audīrēris/-re**
portārētur	**monērētur**	**dūcerētur**	**caperētur**	**audīrētur**
Plural	Plural	Plural	Plural	Plural
portārēmur	**monērēmur**	**dūcerēmur**	**caperēmur**	**audīrēmur**
portārēminī	**monērēminī**	**dūcerēminī**	**caperēminī**	**audīrēminī**
portārentur	**monērentur**	**dūcerentur**	**caperentur**	**audīrentur**

Perfect

Singular	Singular	Singular	Singular	Singular
portātus sim	**monitus sim**	**ductus sim**	**captus sim**	**audītus sim**
portātus sīs	**monitus sīs**	**ductus sīs**	**captus sīs**	**audītus sīs**
portātus sit	**monitus sit**	**ductus sit**	**captus sit**	**audītus sit**
Plural	Plural	Plural	Plural	Plural
portātī sīmus	**monitī sīmus**	**ductī sīmus**	**captī sīmus**	**audītī sīmus**
portātī sītis	**monitī sītis**	**ductī sītis**	**captī sītis**	**audītī sītis**
portātī sint	**monitī sint**	**ductī sint**	**captī sint**	**audītī sint**

Past Perfect

Singular	Singular	Singular	Singular	Singular
portātus essem	**monitus essem**	**ductus essem**	**captus essem**	**audītus essem**
portātus essēs	**monitus essēs**	**ductus essēs**	**captus essēs**	**audītus essēs**
portātus esset	**monitus esset**	**ductus esset**	**captus esset**	**audītus esset**
Plural	Plural	Plural	Plural	Plural
portātī essēmus	**monitī essēmus**	**ductī essēmus**	**captī essēmus**	**audītī essēmus**
portātī essētis	**monitī essētis**	**ductī essētis**	**captī essētis**	**audītī essētis**
portātī essent	**monitī essent**	**ductī essent**	**captī essent**	**audītī essent**

Deponent Verbs (Conjugations I, II, III, III-iō, IV)

principal parts

I	cōnor	cōnārī	cōnātus sum
II	vereor	verērī	veritus sum
III	ūtor	ūtī	ūsus sum
III-iō	patior	patī	passus sum
IV	partior	partīrī	partītus sum

indicative (present system)

Present

Singular	Singular	Singular	Singular	Singular
cōnor	vereor	ūtor	patior	partior
cōnāris [1]	verēris [1]	ūteris [1]	pateris [1]	partīris [1]
cōnātur	verētur	ūtitur	patitur	partītur
Plural	Plural	Plural	Plural	Plural
cōnāmur	verēmur	ūtimur	patimur	partīmur
cōnāminī	verēminī	ūtiminī	patiminī	partīminī
cōnantur	verentur	ūtuntur	patiuntur	partiuntur

Imperfect

Singular	Singular	Singular	Singular	Singular
cōnābar	verēbar	ūtēbar	patiēbar	partiēbar
cōnābāris [1]	verēbāris [1]	ūtēbāris [1]	patiēbāris [1]	partiēbāris [1]
cōnābātur	verēbātur	ūtēbātur	patiēbātur	partiēbātur
Plural	Plural	Plural	Plural	Plural
cōnābāmur	verēbāmur	ūtēbāmur	patiēbāmur	partiēbāmur
cōnābāminī	verēbāminī	ūtēbāminī	patiēbāminī	partiēbāminī
cōnābantur	verēbantur	ūtēbantur	patiēbantur	partiēbantur

Future

Singular	Singular	Singular	Singular	Singular
cōnābor	verēbor	ūtar	patiar	partiar
cōnāberis [1]	verēberis [1]	ūtēris [1]	patiēris [1]	partiēris [1]
cōnābitur	verēbitur	ūtētur	patiētur	partiētur
Plural	Plural	Plural	Plural	Plural
cōnābimur	verēbimur	ūtēmur	patiēmur	partiēmur
cōnābiminī	verēbiminī	ūtēminī	patiēminī	partiēminī
cōnābuntur	verēbuntur	ūtentur	patientur	partientur

[1]Alternate ending is -re (cōnāre, cōnābāre, cōnābere, etc.).

infinitives

Present	Perfect	Future
cōnārī	cōnātum esse	cōnātūrum esse
verērī	veritum esse	veritūrum esse
ūtī	ūsum esse	ūsūrum esse
patī	passum esse	passūrum esse
partīrī	partitum esse	partitūrum esse

participles

Present[1]	Perfect[1]	Future[1]
cōnāns	cōnātus	cōnātūrus
verēns	veritus	veritūrus
ūtēns	ūsus	ūsūrus
patiēns	passus	passūrus
partiēns	partitus	partitūrus

indicative (perfect system)

Perfect

Singular	Singular	Singular	Singular	Singular
cōnātus sum	veritus sum	ūsus sum	passus sum	partitus sum
cōnātus es	veritus es	ūsus es	passus es	partitus es
cōnātus est	veritus est	ūsus est	passus est	partitus est

Plural	Plural	Plural	Plural	Plural
cōnātī sumus	veritī sumus	ūsī sumus	passī sumus	partitī sumus
cōnātī estis	veritī estis	ūsī estis	passī estis	partitī estis
cōnātī sunt	veritī sunt	ūsī sunt	passī sunt	partitī sunt

Past Perfect

Singular	Singular	Singular	Singular	Singular
cōnātus eram	veritus eram	ūsus eram	passus eram	partitus eram
cōnātus erās	veritus erās	ūsus erās	passus erās	partitus erās
cōnātus erat	veritus erat	ūsus erat	passus erat	partitus erat

Plural	Plural	Plural	Plural	Plural
cōnātī erāmus	veritī erāmus	ūsī erāmus	passī erāmus	partitī erāmus
cōnātī erātis	veritī erātis	ūsī erātis	passī erātis	partitī erātis
cōnātī erant	veritī erant	ūsī erant	passī erant	partitī erant

Future Perfect

Singular	Singular	Singular	Singular	Singular
cōnātus erō	veritus erō	ūsus erō	passus erō	partitus erō
cōnātus eris	veritus eris	ūsus eris	passus eris	partitus eris
cōnātus erit	veritus erit	ūsus erit	passus erit	partitus erit

Plural	Plural	Plural	Plural	Plural
cōnātī erimus	veritī erimus	ūsī erimus	passī erimus	partitī erimus
cōnātī eritis	veritī eritis	ūsī eritis	passī eritis	partitī eritis
cōnātī erunt	veritī erunt	ūsī erunt	passī erunt	partitī erunt

[1]For declension of participles see **portāns** (p. 428) and **bonus** (p. 426).

subjunctive

Present

Singular	Singular	Singular	Singular	Singular
cōner	**verear**	**ūtar**	**patiar**	**partiar**
cōnēris [1]	**vereāris** [1]	**ūtāris** [1]	**patiāris** [1]	**partiāris** [1]
cōnētur	**vereātur**	**ūtātur**	**patiātur**	**partiātur**
Plural	Plural	Plural	Plural	Plural
cōnēmur	**vereāmur**	**ūtāmur**	**patiāmur**	**partiāmur**
cōnēminī	**vereāminī**	**ūtāminī**	**patiāminī**	**partiāminī**
cōnentur	**vereantur**	**ūtantur**	**patiantur**	**partiantur**

Imperfect

Singular	Singular	Singular	Singular	Singular
cōnārer	**verērer**	**ūterer**	**paterer**	**partirer**
cōnārēris [1]	**verērēris** [1]	**ūterēris** [1]	**paterēris** [1]	**partirēris** [1]
cōnārētur	**verērētur**	**ūterētur**	**paterētur**	**partirētur**
Plural	Plural	Plural	Plural	Plural
cōnārēmur	**verērēmur**	**ūterēmur**	**paterēmur**	**partirēmur**
cōnārēminī	**verērēminī**	**ūterēminī**	**paterēminī**	**partirēminī**
cōnārentur	**verērentur**	**ūterentur**	**paterentur**	**partirentur**

Perfect

Singular	Singular	Singular	Singular	Singular
cōnātus sim	**veritus sim**	**ūsus sim**	**passus sim**	**partitus sim**
cōnātus sīs	**veritus sīs**	**ūsus sīs**	**passus sīs**	**partitus sīs**
cōnātus sit	**veritus sit**	**ūsus sit**	**passus sit**	**partitus sit**
Plural	Plural	Plural	Plural	Plural
cōnātī sīmus	**veritī sīmus**	**ūsī sīmus**	**passī sīmus**	**partitī sīmus**
cōnātī sītis	**veritī sītis**	**ūsī sītis**	**passī sītis**	**partitī sītis**
cōnātī sint	**veritī sint**	**ūsī sint**	**passī sint**	**partitī sint**

Past Perfect

Singular	Singular	Singular	Singular	Singular
cōnātus essem	**veritus essem**	**ūsus essem**	**passus essem**	**partitus essem**
cōnātus essēs	**veritus essēs**	**ūsus essēs**	**passus essēs**	**partitus essēs**
cōnātus esset	**veritus esset**	**ūsus esset**	**passus esset**	**partitus esset**
Plural	Plural	Plural	Plural	Plural
cōnātī essēmus	**veritī essēmus**	**ūsī essēmus**	**passī essēmus**	**partitī essēmus**
cōnātī essētis	**veritī essētis**	**ūsī essētis**	**passī essētis**	**partitī essētis**
cōnātī essent	**veritī essent**	**ūsī essent**	**passī essent**	**partitī essent**

[1]Alternate ending is **-re** (**cōnēre, cōnārēre; vereāre, verērēre;** etc).

imperatives (deponent verbs)

Present Singular	Plural	Future Singular[1]	Plural[1]
cōnāre	cōnāminī	cōnātor	cōnantor
verēre	verēminī	verētor	verentor
ūtere	ūtiminī	ūtitor	ūtuntor
patere	patiminī	patitor	patiuntor
partīre	partīminī	partītor	partiuntor

gerundives[2] | gerunds[2] | | | | supines[2] |

gerundives[2]	Gen.	Dat.	Acc.	Abl.	Acc.	Abl.
cōnandus, -a, -um	cōnandī	-ō	-um	-ō	cōnātum	cōnātū
verendus, -a, -um	verendī	-ō	-um	-ō	veritum	veritū
ūtendus, -a, -um	ūtendī	-ō	-um	-ō	ūsum	ūsū
patiendus, -a, -um	patiendī	-ō	-um	-ō	passum	passū
partiendus, -a, -um	partiendī	-ō	-um	-ō	partītum	partītū

imperatives (passive) of regular verbs

Present Singular	Plural	Future Singular[1]	Plural[1]
portāre	portāminī	portātor	portantor
monēre	monēminī	monētor	monentor
dūcere	dūciminī	dūcitor	dūcuntor
capere	capiminī	capitor	capiuntor
audīre	audīminī	audītor	audiuntor

gerundives | gerunds | | | | supines |

gerundives	Gen.	Dat.	Acc.	Abl.	Acc.	Abl.
portandus, -a, -um	portandī	-ō	-um	-ō	portātum	portātū
monendus, -a, -um	monendī	-ō	-um	-ō	monitum	monitū
dūcendus, -a, -um	dūcendī	-ō	-um	-ō	ductum	ductū
capiendus, -a, -um	capiendī	-ō	-um	-ō	captum	captū
audiendus, -a, -um	audiendī	-ō	-um	-ō	audītum	audītū

[1]Future imperatives in the singular are used for both 2nd and 3rd persons; in the plural they are used only for 3rd person.

[2]Gerundives, gerunds, and supines of deponent verbs are similar in both form and function to their counterparts in regular conjugations. Gerundives are passive in meaning; gerunds and supines are active.

Semideponent Verbs (Conjugations II, III)

principal parts

II	**audeō**	**audēre**	**ausus sum**[1]
II	**gaudeō**	**gaudēre**	**gāvīsus sum**[1]
II	**soleō**	**solēre**	**solitus sum**[1]
III	**fīdō**	**fīdere**	**fīsus sum**[1]

indicative

Present[1]		Perfect[1]	
Singular	Singular	Singular	Singular
audeō	**fīdō**	**ausus sum**	**fīsus sum**
audēs	**fīdis**	**ausus es**	**fīsus es**
audet	**fīdit**	**ausus est**	**fīsus est**
Plural	Plural	Plural	Plural
audēmus	**fīdimus**	**ausī sumus**	**fīsī sumus**
audētis	**fīditis**	**ausī estis**	**fīsī estis**
audent	**fīdunt**	**ausī sunt**	**fīsī sunt**
Imperfect		Past Perfect	
Singular	Singular	Singular	Singular
audēbam	**fīdēbam**	**ausus eram**	**fīsus eram**
audēbās	**fīdēbās**	**ausus erās**	**fīsus erās**
audēbat	**fīdēbat**	**ausus erat**	**fīsus erat**
Plural	Plural	Plural	Plural
audēbāmus	**fīdēbāmus**	**ausī erāmus**	**fīsī erāmus**
audēbātis	**fīdēbātis**	**ausī erātis**	**fīsī erātis**
audēbant	**fīdēbant**	**ausī erant**	**fīsī erant**
Future		Future Perfect	
Singular	Singular	Singular	Singular
audēbō	**fīdam**	**ausus erō**	**fīsus erō**
audēbis	**fīdēs**	**ausus eris**	**fīsus eris**
audēbit	**fīdet**	**ausus erit**	**fīsus erit**
Plural	Plural	Plural	Plural
audēbimus	**fīdēmus**	**ausī erimus**	**fīsī erimus**
audēbitis	**fīdētis**	**ausī eritis**	**fīsī eritis**
audēbunt	**fīdent**	**ausī erunt**	**fīsī erunt**

[1]The perfect system of a semideponent verb is passive in form, but active in meaning. The present system is active both in form and in meaning.

infinitives

Present	Perfect	Future	
Active	Passive	Active	
audēre	**ausum esse**	**ausūrum esse**	
fīdere	**fīsum esse**	**fīsūrum esse**	

participles

Present*	Perfect*	Future*
Active	Passive	Active
audēns	**ausus**	**ausūrus**
fīdēns	**fīsus**	**fīsūrus**

*For declension of participles see **portāns** (p. 428) and **bonus** (p. 426).

subjunctive

Present

Singular	Singular	Perfect Singular	Singular
audeam	**fīdam**	**ausus sim**	**fīsus sim**
audeās	**fīdās**	**ausus sīs**	**fīsus sīs**
audeat	**fīdat**	**ausus sit**	**fīsus sit**
Plural	Plural	Plural	Plural
audeāmus	**fīdāmus**	**ausī sīmus**	**fīsī sīmus**
audeātis	**fīdātis**	**ausī sītis**	**fīsī sītis**
audeant	**fīdant**	**ausī sint**	**fīsī sint**

Imperfect / Past Perfect

Singular	Singular	Singular	Singular
audērem	**fīderem**	**ausus essem**	**fīsus essem**
audērēs	**fīderēs**	**ausus essēs**	**fīsus essēs**
audēret	**fīderet**	**ausus esset**	**fīsus esset**
Plural	Plural	Plural	Plural
audērēmus	**fīderēmus**	**ausī essēmus**	**fīsī essēmus**
audērētis	**fīderētis**	**ausī essētis**	**fīsī essētis**
audērent	**fīderent**	**ausī essent**	**fīsī essent**

imperatives   gerunds   supines

Present Singular	Future[1] Singular	Gen.	Dat.	Acc.	Abl.	Acc.	Abl.
audē	**audētō**	**audendī**	**-ō**	**-um**	**-ō**	**ausum**	**ausū**
fīde	**fīditō**	**fīdendī**	**-ō**	**-um**	**-ō**	**fīsum**	**fīsū**

Plural	Plural	gerundives					
audēte	**audētōte**	**audendus, -a, -um**					
fīdite	**fīditōte**	**fīdendus, -a, -um**					

Gerunds and supines are active; gerundives are passive.

[1]Singular forms are used for 2nd and 3rd persons; plural for 3rd person only.

445

Irregular Verbs

principal parts

sum	**esse**	**fuī**	**futūrus**
possum	**posse**	**potuī**	——
eō	**īre**	[1]**iī**	**itum**
volō	**velle**	**voluī**	——
nōlō	**nōlle**	**nōluī**	——

indicative (present system)

Present

Singular	Singular	Singular	Singular	Singular
sum	**possum**	**eō**	**volō** *I want*	**nōlō** *I*
es	**potes**	**īs**	**vīs**	**nōn vīs**
est	**potest**	**it**	**vult**	**nōn vult**
Plural	Plural	Plural	Plural	Plural
sumus	**possumus**	**īmus**	**volumus**	**nōlumus**
estis	**potestis**	**ītis**	**vultis**	**nōn vultis**
sunt	**possunt**	**eunt**	**volunt**	**nōlunt**

Imperfect

Singular	Singular	Singular	Singular	Singular
eram	**poteram**	**ībam**	**volēbam**	**nōlēbam**
erās	**poterās**	**ībās**	**volēbās**	**nōlēbās**
erat	**poterat**	**ībat**	**volēbat**	**nōlēbat**
Plural	Plural	Plural	Plural	Plural
erāmus	**poterāmus**	**ībāmus**	**volēbāmus**	**nōlēbāmus**
erātis	**poterātis**	**ībātis**	**volēbātis**	**nōlēbātis**
erant	**poterant**	**ībant**	**volēbant**	**nōlēbant**

Future

Singular	Singular	Singular	Singular	Singular
erō	**poterō**	**ībō**	**volam**	**nōlam**
eris	**poteris**	**ībis**	**volēs**	**nōlēs**
erit	**poterit**	**ībit**	**volet**	**nōlet**
Plural	Plural	Plural	Plural	Plural
erimus	**poterimus**	**ībimus**	**volēmus**	**nōlēmus**
eritis	**poteritis**	**ībitis**	**volētis**	**nōlētis**
erunt	**poterunt**	**ībunt**	**volent**	**nōlent**

[1]Also **īvī**, with alternate perfect stem **īv-**

infinitives   participles

Present	Perfect	Future	Present	Future (active)	Future (passive)
esse	**fuisse**	**futūrum esse**	——	**futūrus, -a, -um**	——
posse	**potuisse**	——			
īre	**īsse/iisse**	**itūrum esse**	***iēns**	**itūrus, -a, -um**	****eundus, -a, -um**
velle	**voluisse**	——	**volēns**	——	
nōlle	**nōluisse**	——	**nōlēns**	——	

*Stem = **eunt-** (from gen., **euntis**).   **Gerund: **eundī, -ō, -um, -ō.**

indicative (perfect system)

Perfect

Singular	Singular	Singular	Singular	Singular
fuī	**potuī**	**iī**[1]	**voluī**	**nōluī**
fuistī	**potuistī**	**īstī/iistī**	**voluistī**	**nōluistī**
fuit	**potuit**	**iit**	**voluit**	**nōluit**

Plural	Plural	Plural	Plural	Plural
fuimus	**potuimus**	**iimus**	**voluimus**	**nōluimus**
fuistis	**potuistis**	**īstis/iistis**	**voluistis**	**nōluistis**
fuērunt	**potuērunt**	**iērunt**	**voluērunt**	**nōluērunt**

Past Perfect

Singular	Singular	Singular	Singular	Singular
fueram	**potueram**	**ieram**[1]	**volueram**	**nōlueram**
fuerās	**potuerās**	**ierās**	**voluerās**	**nōluerās**
fuerat	**potuerat**	**ierat**	**voluerat**	**nōluerat**

Plural	Plural	Plural	Plural	Plural
fuerāmus	**potuerāmus**	**ierāmus**	**voluerāmus**	**nōluerāmus**
fuerātis	**potuerātis**	**ierātis**	**voluerātis**	**nōluerātis**
fuerant	**potuerant**	**ierant**	**voluerant**	**nōluerant**

Future Perfect

Singular	Singular	Singular	Singular	Singular
fuerō	**potuerō**	**ierō**[1]	**voluerō**	**nōluerō**
fueris	**potueris**	**ieris**	**volueris**	**nōlueris**
fuerit	**potuerit**	**ierit**	**voluerit**	**nōluerit**

Plural	Plural	Plural	Plural	Plural
fuerimus	**potuerimus**	**ierimus**	**voluerimus**	**nōluerimus**
fueritis	**potueritis**	**ieritis**	**volueritis**	**nōlueritis**
fuerint	**potuerint**	**ierint**	**voluerint**	**nōluerint**

[1]With stem **īv-** these forms are **īvī**, etc., **īveram**, etc., **īverō**, etc.

subjunctive of irregular verbs

Present

Singular	Singular	Singular	Singular	Singular
sim	possim	eam	velim	nōlim
sis	possis	eās	velis	nōlis
sit	possit	eat	velit	nōlit
Plural	**Plural**	**Plural**	**Plural**	**Plural**
sīmus	possīmus	eāmus	velīmus	nōlīmus
sītis	possītis	eātis	velitis	nōlitis
sint	possint	eant	velint	nōlint

Imperfect

Singular	Singular	Singular	Singular	Singular
essem	possem	īrem	vellem	nōllem
essēs	possēs	īrēs	vellēs	nōllēs
esset	posset	īret	vellet	nōllet
Plural	**Plural**	**Plural**	**Plural**	**Plural**
essēmus	possēmus	īrēmus	vellēmus	nōllēmus
essētis	possētis	īrētis	vellētis	nōllētis
essent	possent	īrent	vellent	nōllent

Perfect

Singular	Singular	Singular	Singular	Singular
fuerim	potuerim	ierim [1]	voluerim	nōluerim
fueris	potueris	ieris	volueris	nōlueris
fuerit	potuerit	ierit	voluerit	nōluerit
Plural	**Plural**	**Plural**	**Plural**	**Plural**
fuerimus	potuerimus	ierimus	voluerimus	nōluerimus
fuerītis	potuerītis	ierītis	voluerītis	nōluerītis
fuerint	potuerint	ierint	voluerint	nōluerint

Past Perfect

Singular	Singular	Singular	Singular	Singular
fuissem	potuissem	īssem [1]	voluissem	nōluissem
fuissēs	potuissēs	īssēs	voluissēs	nōluissēs
fuisset	potuisset	īsset	voluisset	nōluisset
Plural	**Plural**	**Plural**	**Plural**	**Plural**
fuissēmus	potuissēmus	īssēmus	voluissēmus	nōluissēmus
fuissētis	potuissētis	īssētis	voluissētis	nōluissētis
fuissent	potuissent	īssent	voluissent	nōluissent

[1]With perfect stem **iv-** these forms are **iverim,** etc., and **ivissem,** etc.

imperatives of **sum/eō/nōlō**[1]

Singular	Plural	Future Singular[2]	Future 2nd Pers. Plural	3rd Pers. Plural
		Present	Future	Future
es	**este**	**estō**	**estōte**	**suntō**
ī	**īte**	**ītō**	**ītōte**	**euntō**
nōlī	**nōlite**	**nōlitō**	**nōlitōte**	**nōluntō**

Compounds of sum[3]

principal parts

absum[4]	**abesse**	**āfuī**	**āfutūrus**
adsum	**adesse**	**adfuī/affuī**	**adfutūrus**
dēsum	**dēesse**	**dēfuī**	**dēfutūrus**
praesum[4]	**praeesse**	**praefuī**	**praefutūrus**
prōsum	**prōdesse**[5]	**prōfuī**	**prōfutūrus**

indicative (present system)

Present

Singular	Plural
prōsum	**prōsumus**
prōdes	**prōdestis**
prōdest	**prōsunt**

Imperfect

Singular	Plural
prōderam	**prōderāmus**
prōderās	**prōderātis**
prōderat	**prōderant**

Future

Singular	Plural
prōderō	**prōderimus**
prōderis	**prōderitis**
prōderit	**prōderunt**

subjunctive (present system)

Present

Singular	Plural
prōsim	**prōsimus**
prōsīs	**prōsitis**
prōsit	**prōsint**

Imperfect

Singular	Plural
prōdessem	**prōdessēmus**
prōdessēs	**prōdessētis**
prōdesset	**prōdessent**

imperatives

Present

Singular	Plural
prōdes	**prōdeste**

[1]**Possum** and **volō** have no imperatives.

[2]Future imperatives in the singular are used for both 2nd and 3rd persons.

[3]The compounds of **sum** are conjugated in all forms like **sum** (see p. 446).

[4]Only two compounds of **sum** (**absum** and **praesum**) have a present participle: **absēns** (gen., **absentis**); **praesēns** (gen., **praesentis**).

[5]The prefix of **prōsum** changes to **prōd-** before a vowel.

Compounds of eō[1]

principal parts

abeō	abīre	abiī	abitum
adeō	adīre	adiī	aditum
exeō	exīre	exiī[3]	exitum
ineō	inīre	iniī	initum
praeeō	praeīre	praeiī[3]	praeitum
redeō[2]	redīre	rediī[3]	reditum
subeō	subīre	subiī[3]	subitum
trānseō	trānsīre	trānsiī	trānsitum

Compound of volō (magis + volō) = mālō

principal parts: **mālō   mālle   māluī**[4]

indicative		subjunctive	
Present		**Present**	
Singular	Plural	Singular	Plural
mālō *I prefer*	mālumus	mālim	mālīmus
māvīs	māvultis	mālīs	mālītis
māvult	mālunt	mālit	mālint
Imperfect		**Imperfect**	
Singular	Plural	Singular	Plural
mālēbam	mālēbāmus	māllem	māllēmus
mālēbās	mālēbātis	māllēs	māllētis
mālēbat	mālēbant	māllet	māllent
Future			
Singular	Plural		
mālam	mālēmus	Present Infinitive: **mālle**	
mālēs	mālētis	Perfect Infinitive: **māluisse**[4]	
mālet	mālent	**Mālō** has neither participles nor imperatives.	

[1]Compounds of **eō** are conjugated like **eō** throughout (see p. 446), and their infinitives, participles, imperatives, and gerunds are the same as those of **eō**, with the prefix added.

[2]The prefix **re-** becomes **red-** before a vowel.

[3]In these verbs (**exeō, praeeō, redeō, subeō**), as in **eō**, there is an alternate stem **-īv-** which may be used for the perfect system, both indicative and subjunctive.

[4]See the perfect system of **volō** (pp. 447-448). **Mālō** also has regular perfect endings: **māluī, māluistī, māluit**, etc.

450

Irregular Verb fiō[1]

principal parts: **fiō**   **fierī**   **factus sum**

infinitives   participles

Present	Perfect	Future	Present	Perfect	Future
fierī	**factum esse**	**factum īrī**	————	**factus, -a, -um**	**faciendus, -a, -um**

indicative   subjunctive

Present	Perfect	Present	Perfect
Singular	Singular	Singular	Singular
fiō	**factus sum**	**fiam**	**factus sim**
fis	**factus es**	**fiās**	**factus sīs**
fit	**factus est**	**fiat**	**factus sit**
Plural	Plural	Plural	Plural
fimus[2]	**factī sumus**	**fiāmus**	**factī sīmus**
fitis[2]	**factī estis**	**fiātis**	**factī sītis**
fiunt	**factī sunt**	**fiant**	**factī sint**
Imperfect	Past Perfect	Imperfect	Past Perfect
Singular	Singular	Singular	Singular
fiēbam	**factus eram**	**fierem**	**factus essem**
fiēbās	**factus erās**	**fierēs**	**factus essēs**
fiēbat	**factus erat**	**fieret**	**factus esset**
Plural	Plural	Plural	Plural
fiēbāmus	**factī erāmus**	**fierēmus**	**factī essēmus**
fiēbātis	**factī erātis**	**fierētis**	**factī essētis**
fiēbant	**factī erant**	**fierent**	**factī essent**
Future	Future Perfect		
Singular	Singular		

imperatives

Present

Future (Singular)	Future Perfect (Singular)	
fiam	**factus erō**	Present
fiēs	**factus eris**	Singular / Plural
fiet	**factus erit**	**fi** / **fite**
Plural	Plural	
fiēmus	**factī erimus**	
fiētis	**factī eritis**	
fient	**factī erunt**	

[1]The forms of **fiō** serve as the passive of **faciō,** including the present system, in which the endings are active.

[2]These forms do not occur in classical Latin.

Irregular Verb ferō   ferre   tulī   lātum

imperatives

Present Active	Present Passive	Future Active	Future Passive
Singular	Singular	Singular	Singular
fer	**ferre**	**fertō**[1]	**fertor**[1]
Plural	Plural	Plural	Plural
ferte	**feriminī**	**fertōte/feruntō**	—————/**feruntor**

indicative (active)

Present	Perfect
Singular	Singular
ferō	**tulī**
fers	**tulistī**
fert	**tulit**
Plural	Plural
ferimus	**tulimus**
fertis	**tulistis**
ferunt	**tulērunt**
Imperfect	Past Perfect
Singular	Singular
ferēbam	**tuleram**
ferēbās	**tulerās**
ferēbat	**tulerat**
Plural	Plural
ferēbāmus	**tulerāmus**
ferēbātis	**tulerātis**
ferēbant	**tulerant**
Future	Future Perfect
Singular	Singular
feram	**tulerō**
ferēs	**tuleris**
feret	**tulerit**
Plural	Plural
ferēmus	**tulerimus**
ferētis	**tuleritis**
ferent	**tulerint**

indicative (passive)

Present	Perfect
Singular	Singular
feror	**lātus sum**
ferris/-re	**lātus es**
fertur	**lātus est**
Plural	Plural
ferimur	**lātī sumus**
feriminī	**lātī estis**
feruntur	**lātī sunt**
Imperfect	Past Perfect
Singular	Singular
ferēbar	**lātus eram**
ferēbāris/-re	**lātus erās**
ferēbātur	**lātus erat**
Plural	Plural
ferēbāmur	**lātī erāmus**
ferēbāminī	**lātī erātis**
ferēbantur	**lātī erant**
Future	Future Perfect
Singular	Singular
ferar	**lātus erō**
ferēris/-re	**lātus eris**
ferētur	**lātus erit**
Plural	Plural
ferēmur	**lātī erimus**
ferēminī	**lātī eritis**
ferentur	**lātī erunt**

[1]These forms are used for both 2nd and 3rd person singular.

infinitives (active)   participles (active)

Present	Perfect	Future	Present (See p. 428)	Future
ferre	tulisse	lātūrum esse	ferēns	lātūrus, -a, -um

infinitives (passive)   participles (passive)

Present	Perfect	Future	Perfect	Future
ferrī	lātum esse	lātum īrī	lātus, -a, -um	ferendus, -a, -um

gerundives   gerunds   supines

		Gen. Dat.	Acc. Abl.	Acc.	Abl.
ferendus, -a, -um		ferendī -ō	-um -ō	lātum	lātū

subjunctive (active)   subjunctive (passive)

Present	Perfect	Present	Perfect
Singular	Singular	Singular	Singular
feram	tulerim	ferar	lātus sim
ferās	tulerīs	ferāris/-re	lātus sīs
ferat	tulerit	ferātur	lātus sit
Plural	Plural	Plural	Plural
ferāmus	tulerimus	ferāmur	lātī sīmus
ferātis	tulerītis	ferāminī	lātī sītis
ferant	tulerint	ferantur	lātī sint
Imperfect	Past Perfect	Imperfect	Past Perfect
Singular	Singular	Singular	Singular
ferrem	tulissem	ferrer	lātus essem
ferrēs	tulissēs	ferrēris/-re	lātus essēs
ferret	tulisset	ferrētur	lātus esset
Plural	Plural	Plural	Plural
ferrēmus	tulissēmus	ferrēmur	lātī essēmus
ferrētis	tulissētis	ferrēminī	lātī essētis
ferrent	tulissent	ferrentur	lātī essent

Compounds of fero[1]

afferō (ad)	cōnferō (con)	differō (dis)	inferō (in)	referō (re)
auferō (ab)	dēferō (dē)	efferō (ex)	offerō (ob)	trānsferō (trāns)

[1]See General Vocabulary for principal parts of these compounds, which (except for the prefix) have the same conjugation as **ferō**.

Defective Verbs ōdī and meminī

principal parts

ōdī[1]	ōdisse	ōsūrus
meminī[1]	meminisse	———

indicative		subjunctive	

Perfect

Singular	Singular	Singular	Singular
ōdī	meminī	ōderim	meminerim
ōdistī	meministī	ōderīs	meminerīs
ōdit	meminit	ōderit	meminerit

Plural	Plural	Plural	Plural
ōdimus	meminimus	ōderīmus	meminerīmus
ōdistis	meministis	ōderītis	meminerītis
ōdērunt	meminērunt	ōderint	meminerint

Past Perfect

Singular	Singular	Singular	Singular
ōderam	memineram	ōdissem	meminissem
ōderās	meminerās	ōdissēs	meminissēs
ōderat	meminerat	ōdisset	meminisset

Plural	Plural	Plural	Plural
ōderāmus	meminerāmus	ōdissēmus	meminissēmus
ōderātis	meminerātis	ōdissētis	meminissētis
ōderant	meminerant	ōdissent	meminissent

Future Perfect

Singular	Singular	infinitives	participles
ōderō	meminerō	Perfect	Perfect
ōderis	memineris	ōdisse	ōsus, -a, -um
ōderit	meminerit	meminisse	

Plural	Plural	Future	Future
ōderimus	meminerimus	ōsūrum esse	ōsūrus, -a, -um
ōderitis	memineritis		
ōderint	meminerint		

imperatives: **mementō** (Singular); **mementōte** (Plural)[2]

[1]**Ōdī** and **meminī** have no present system forms. In meaning, however, perfect forms = present; past perfect = imperfect; future perfect = future.

[2]**Ōdī** has no imperative forms.

Defective Verb coepī

principal parts: **coepī**[1]   **coepisse**   **coeptus**

indicative   subjunctive

Perfect   Perfect

Singular	Plural	Singular	Plural
coepī	**coepimus**	**coeperim**	**coeperīmus**
coepistī	**coepistis**	**coeperis**	**coeperītis**
coepit	**coepērunt**	**coeperit**	**coeperint**

Past Perfect   Past Perfect

Singular	Plural	Singular	Plural
coeperam	**coeperāmus**	**coepissem**	**coepissēmus**
coeperās	**coeperātis**	**coepissēs**	**coepissētis**
coeperat	**coeperant**	**coepisset**	**coepissent**

Future Perfect   infinitives   participles

Singular	Plural	Perfect	Perfect
coeperō	**coeperimus**	**coepisse**	**coeptus, -a, -um**
coeperis	**coeperitis**	Future	Future
coeperit	**coeperint**	**coeptūrum esse**	**coeptūrus, -a, -um**

Defective Verbs inquam/ajō

indicative   subjunctive

Present   Present   Present

Singular	Plural	Singular	Plural	Singular	Plural
inquam	**inquimus**	**ajō**	——	——	——
inquis	**inquitis**	**ais**	——	**ajās**	——
inquit[2]	**inquiunt**	**ait**[2]	**ajunt**	**ajat**	——

Imperfect   Future   Imperfect

Singular[3]	Singular[3]	Singular	Plural
——	——	**ajēbam**	**ajēbāmus**
——	**inquiēs**	**ajēbās**	**ajēbātis**
inquiēbat	**inquiet**	**ajēbat**	**ajēbant**

[1]Forms of **coepi** have the usual tense values of perfect, past perfect, and future perfect. The present system is supplied by **incipiō**. **Coepi** has no imperatives.

[2]**Inquit** and **ait** are also used for the perfect tense.

[3]**Inquam** has no plural forms in the imperfect and future tenses.

IRREGULAR NOUNS

	Singular	Plural	Singular	Plural	Singular	Plural
Nom.	domus (F.)*	domūs	bōs (M./F.)	bovēs	vīs (f.)	vīrēs
Gen.	domūs/ī	domuum/ōrum	bovis	boum/bovum	——	vīrium
Dat.	domuī/ō	domibus	bovī	būbus/bōbus	——	viribus
Acc.	domum	domūs/ōs	bovem	bovēs	vim	viris/ēs
Abl.	domū/ō	domibus	bove	būbus/bōbus	vī	viribus
Loc.	domī					

*Domus is declined according to Declension IV, but also has some forms of Declension II.

DECLINABLE NUMBERS

	M.	F.	N.	M.	F.	N.
Nom.	ūnus	ūna	ūnum	duo	duae	duo
Gen.	ūnīus	ūnīus	ūnīus	duōrum	duārum	duōrum
Dat.	ūnī	ūnī	ūnī	duōbus	duābus	duōbus
Acc.	ūnum	ūnam	ūnum	duōs	duās	duo
Abl.	ūnō	ūnā	ūnō	duōbus	duābus	duōbus

	M.	F.	N.		N. Pl.
Nom.	trēs	trēs	tria	mille (Sing.) is an in-	milia
Gen.	trium	trium	trium	declinable adjective;	milium
Dat.	tribus	tribus	tribus	milia (Pl.) is a neuter	milibus
Acc.	trēs	trēs	tria	noun.	milia
Abl.	tribus	tribus	tribus		milibus

DISTRIBUTIVE NUMBERS[1]

singulī	1	quīnī dēnī	15	octōgēnī	80
bīnī	2	sēnī dēnī	16	nōnāgēnī	90
ternī/trīnī	3	septēnī dēnī	17	centēnī	100
quaternī	4	duodēvīcēnī	18	centēnī singulī	101
quīnī	5	ūndēvīcēnī	19	ducēnī	200
sēnī	6	vīcēnī	20	trecēnī	300
septēnī	7	vīcēnī singulī	21	quadringēnī	400
octōnī	8	duodētrīcēnī	28	quingēnī	500
novēnī	9	ūndētrīcēnī	29	sescēnī	600
dēnī	10	trīcēnī	30	septingēnī	700
ūndēnī	11	quadrāgēnī	40	octingēnī	800
duodēnī	12	quīnquāgēnī	50	nōngēnī	900
ternī dēnī	13	sexāgēnī	60	singula milia	1000
quaternī dēnī	14	septuāgēnī	70	bīna milia	2000

[1]Distributive numbers answer the question, "How many at a time?" as one at a time,
singulī, -ae, -a; two by two, bīnī, -ae, -a, etc.

ROMAN NUMERALS

Cardinal		Numeral	Ordinal
[1]ūnus, -a, -um	I		[2]prīmus
duo, duae, duo	II		secundus
trēs, trēs, tria	III		tertius
quattuor	IV		quārtus
quīnque	V		quīntus
sex	VI		sextus
septem	VII		septimus
octō	VIII		octāvus
novem	IX		nōnus
decem	X		decimus
[1]ūndecim	XI		[2]ūndecimus
duodecim	XII		duodecimus
tredecim	XIII		tertius decimus
quattuordecim	XIV		quārtus decimus
quīndecim	XV		quīntus decimus
sēdecim	XVI		sextus decimus
septendecim	XVII		septimus decimus
duodēvīgintī	XVIII		duodēvīcēsimus
ūndēvīgintī	XIX		ūndēvīcēsimus
vīgintī	XX		vīcēsimus
vīgintī ūnus, -a, -um/ūnus et vīgintī	XXI		vīcēsimus prīmus
duodētrīgintā	XXVIII		duodētrīcēsimus
ūndētrīgintā	XXIX		ūndētrīcēsimus
trīgintā	XXX		trīcēsimus
quadrāgintā	XL		quadrāgēsimus
quīnquāgintā	L		quīnquāgēsimus
sexāgintā	LX		sexāgēsimus
septuāgintā	LXX		septuāgēsimus
octōgintā	LXXX		octōgēsimus
nōnāgintā	XC		nōnāgēsimus
centum	C		centēsimus
centum (et) ūnus	CI		centēsimus (et) prīmus
ducentī, -ae, -a	CC		ducentēsimus
trecentī, -ae, -a	CCC		trecentēsimus
quadringentī	CCCC		quadringentēsimus
quīngentī	D		quīngentēsimus
sescentī	DC		sescentēsimus
septingentī	DCC		septingentēsimus
octingentī	DCCC		octingentēsimus
nōngentī	DCCCC		nōngentēsimus
mille	M		millēsimus

[1]Cardinal numerals. (For declension of ūnus, duo, trēs, mīlia, see p. 432.)

[2]Ordinal numerals· prīmus, secundus, etc. (For declension, see bonus, p. 426.)

457

LATIN USAGE

ADJECTIVES

Declinable Adjectives

agreement

Agricola magnum leōnem vulnerāvit. Mīlitēs sunt fortēs.

An adjective agrees with its noun in gender, number, and case.

attributive/predicate relationship

a) **Agricola magnum leōnem vulnerāvit.** b) **Mīlitēs sunt fortēs.**

a) An attributive adjective is directly attached to a noun. b) An adjective connected with its noun by a form of **sum** is a predicate adjective.

comparative/superlative adjectives

altior/altissimus   celerior/celerrimus   facilior/facillimus   major/maximus

Translation of Latin comparative/superlative adjectives usually corresponds with English; e.g., **altior** (high<u>er</u>, tall<u>er</u>, deep<u>er</u> or <u>too/rather/quite</u> high, etc.); **altissimus** (high<u>est</u>, tall<u>est</u>, deep<u>est</u> or <u>very</u> high/tall/deep). Many Latin adjectives cannot be compared because of the nature of their meanings; e.g., **albus** (white), **Rōmānus** (Roman), **tōtus** (whole).

partitive adjectives

summus mōns   medius collis   īmō colle   fīnibus extrēmīs

Summus (top of), **medius** (middle of), **īmus** (bottom/foot of), and **extrēmus** (farthest part of) are all adjectives in Latin agreeing with their nouns. Caution: While "of" is required in translating each of these adjectives, the Latin genitive is not used.

substantive (noun) use of adjectives

Multī tē laudant.   Omnia parāta sunt.   Nostrī fortēs sunt.

Adjectives are sometimes used as nouns. In military expressions **nostrī** means <u>our men/soldiers</u>.

Indeclinable Adjectives

cardinal numbers

quattuor   septem   octō   decem   vīgintī   centum   mille

Most cardinal numbers, though often used as adjectives, have fixed forms and cannot be declined to show gender, number, and case (exceptions: **ūnus, duo, trēs**); nor do such adjectives change form to show degrees of comparison.

458

ADVERBS

Adverbs Admitting Comparison

adverbs from adjectives

bene (bonus)   **fortiter (fortis)**   **magis (major)**   **tardē (tardus)**

A great number of Latin adverbs are related to adjectives. Like the adjectives they can be compared (positive, comparative, superlative), some irregularly.

Adverbs Not Admitting Comparison

fixed forms

autem	dēnique	hodiē	intereā	jam	nunc
cotīdiē	etiam	hūc	interim	noctū	quoque
crās	hīc	ibi	ita	nōn	tamen
cūr	hinc	igitur	iterum	numquam	ubi

These adverbs and many others belong to a group of fixed forms in Latin; i.e., their forms never change, and they are not subject to comparison.

Use As Modifiers

position

Helvētii agrōs Haeduōrum lātē vāstābant. Cōnsul minimē saepe dīcēbat.

An adverb usually precedes the adjective, verb, or other adverb it modifies.

CONJUNCTIONS

Connectors

fixed forms

ac	atque	cum	enim	itaque	postquam	-que	sed	ubi
at	aut	dum	et	nam	quamquam	quod	sī	ut

Most connectors of words, phrases, clauses, and sentences have fixed forms; i.e., their forms do not change. (Exceptions: relative/interrogative pronouns)

with indicative mood

cum	postquam	quandō	quia	quoniam	ubi
dum (while)	quamquam	quasi	quod	sī	ut (as)

with subjunctive mood

cum (although, since, when)

dum/antequam/priusquam (until)

quīn (with negative expressions of doubt or hesitation)

sī (in clause expressing doubt of speaker or condition contrary to fact)

ut/nē (purpose); **ut/ut nōn** (result); **nē/ut** (fear)

459

Coördinators

ac/atque   et/-que   aut   vel/-ve   nec/neque   sīve   seu

Coördinating conjunctions join together words, phrases, clauses, or sentences of equal value or parallel structure.

N O U N S

Ablative Case

with prepositions

Accompaniment. **Cum sociīs fūgit. Cum Gallīs bellum gessērunt.**

A prepositional phrase (**cum** with ablative) may answer the question, "With whom?" In military expressions the preposition **cum** may be omitted if the modifier of the noun in the ablative is not a numeral; e.g., **Multīs mīlitibus flūmen trānsiit.**

Agent: **Explōrātor ā mīlitibus captus est. Ab amitā puella vocātur.**

With a passive verb a prepositional phrase (**ā/ab** with ablative) answers the question, "By whom?"

Manner: **Magnā cum cūrā omnia parāvimus. Rēx cum sapientiā regit.**

A prepositional phrase (**cum** with ablative) may answer the question, "In what manner?" The preposition **cum** is often omitted when a limiting adjective modifies the noun in the ablative; e.g., **Magnā cūrā omnia parāvimus.**

Place: **Prō ārā stābam. In montibus bēstiae reperiuntur. Sub terrā habitat.**

A prepositional phrase (**in, prō, sub** with ablative) may answer the question, "Where?" (See also "Locative Case," page 465.)

Place from Which: **Lēgātus ex oppidō profectus est.**

A prepositional phrase (**ā/ab, dē, ē/ex** with ablative) expresses "place from which" with verbs of motion, answering the question, "From where?" The preposition is omitted when the noun is **domus** or the name of a city, town, or small island; e.g., **Vīsne domō exīre? Lēgātus Genavā profectus est.**

Separation: **Ā Bibracte nōn amplius mīlibus passuum XVIII aberat.**

A prepositional phrase (**ā/ab, dē, ē/ex** with ablative) may express separation.

without prepositions

Ablative Absolute: **Caesare duce, mīlitēs laetī sunt. Tē duce, mīlitēs nōn timēbunt. Duce praesente, mīlitēs pugnant. Duce captō, hostēs fūgērunt.**

Additional information about a circumstance or event loosely connected with the rest of the sentence may be supplied by an ablative absolute consisting of two or more words in the ablative case. (For translation, see page 51.)

460

Cause: **Hostēs timōre fūgērunt. Dux cūris aeger erat.**

A noun in the ablative may express the cause of or reason for an action or condition. However, cause is often expressed by a prepositional phrase (**ā/ab, dē, ē/ex** with ablative or **ob/propter** with accusative); e.g., **Ex commūtātiōne rērum dolent. Hostēs propter timōrem fūgērunt.**

Comparison: **Puer est altior puellā.**

With the comparative form of an adjective or adverb, a noun in the ablative may express the person/thing with which comparison is made. Exception: If **quam** (than) is used, the word denoting the person/thing with which comparison is made is in the same case as the thing compared; e.g., **Puer est altior quam puella.**

Degree of Difference: **Arbor decem pedibus altior mūrō (quam mūrus) est.**

The degree to which one person/thing differs from another person/thing is often expressed by the ablative. The ablative of degree also occurs with certain adverbs **(ante, post);** e.g., **Paucīs ante diēbus hostēs oppidum dēlēverant.**

Description: **Labiēnus, homō magnā virtūte, Caesaris lēgātus erat.**

When modified by an adjective, a noun in the ablative case may describe a person/thing. (The genitive is also used for description; e.g., **Labiēnus, homō magnae virtūtis, Caesaris lēgātus erat.** However, in describing physical characteristics, the ablative is more commonly used. In expressing measure the genitive is always used.)

Means: **Gallī gladiīs pugnābant. Litterīs certior factus est. Magnō dolōre afficiēbantur. Breviōre itinere rediimus.**

The ablative of means answers the question, "How?" or "By what means?"

Respect: **Helvētiī reliquōs Gallōs virtūte praecēdunt.**

A noun in the ablative may indicate in what respect a statement is true.

Time: **Eō annō pater meus tēctum novum aedificāvit.**

A noun in the ablative may express the time at or within which an act takes place, answering the question, "When?"

complementary ablative

With Deponent Verbs: **Trōjānī et Latīnī eōdem jūre atque nōmine ūsī sunt.**

The deponent verbs **ūtor** (use), **fruor** (enjoy), **fungor** (perform), **potior** (gain possession of), and **vēscor** (feed upon) may be completed by a noun in the ablative. **Potior** is sometimes found with a genitive; e.g., **Urbis potīrī cupiunt.**

Separation: **Hōc cōnātū dēstitērunt. Suīs fīnibus eōs prohibent. Proeliō abstinēbat.**

Verbs of special meaning may be completed by a noun in the ablative to express separation, both literal and figurative.

With Adjectives/Participles: Certain adjectives and participles may also have their meaning completed by a noun in the ablative; e.g., **Ille omni metū liber esse vidētur. Helvētiī eā spē dējecti hōc cōnātū dēstitērunt.**

Accusative Case

direct object

Silvam vidēmus. Magister discipulōs laudat.

The direct object of a transitive verb is in the accusative case.

subject of infinitive

Explōrātor dīxit urbem incēnsam esse.

The subject of an infinitive in indirect statement is in the accusative case.

two accusatives

Illōs rēgēs tyrannōs appellāmus. Caesarem dictātōrem creāvērunt.

In addition to the direct object, a second (predicate) accusative occurs with such verbs as **appellō, nōminō, vocō,** and other verbs meaning name or call. It also occurs with **creō, dēligō, ēligō, legō,** and other verbs meaning appoint choose, or elect.

Two accusatives may also complete the verbs **doceō** (teach) and **rogō** (ask); e.g., **Pater filium multa docēbit. Puer patrem pecūniam rogāre nōluit.**

Compounds of **trāns** sometimes take two objects, one governed by **trāns,** the other by the simple verb; e.g., **Legiōnem flūmen trādūxit. Legiō flūmen trāducta est.** (With the passive of **trādūcō** and other compounds of **trāns,** the object governed by **trāns** may be retained.)

with adverbial significance

Prepositional Phrases: **Ante bellum amīcī sociīque fuerāmus. Is poēta inter barbarōs habitāvit.**

Objects of certain prepositions are in the accusative case. These prepositional phrases answer such questions as "When?" "Where?" "Where (to)?" "Why?"

| ad | apud | contrā | inter | ob | post | prope | super | trāns |
| ante | circum | extrā | intrā | per | praeter | propter | suprā | |

Objects of **in** and **sub** are in the accusative when motion is implied; otherwise, in the ablative.

Extent of Space/Time: **Puer quīnque milia passuum ambulāvit. Multās hōrās in insulā mānsī.**

An accusative without preposition may answer the questions, "How far?"/"How long?"

Place to Which: **Exercitus Rōmam redībit.   Eāmus domum!**

The accusative of **domus** and of names of cities, towns, and small islands (without a preposition) answers the question, "Where (to)?"

Dative Case

complementary dative

With Adjectives: **Filius tuus sorōribus benignus est.   Castra flūminī propinqua erant.**

The dative may be complementary to adjectives denoting friendly/unfriendly relationships, including the following:

Friendly Relationships		Unfriendly Relationships	
amīcus	friendly	**inimīcus**	unfriendly
benignus	kind	**infestus**	hostile
cārus	dear	**invīsus**	hated, hateful
grātus	pleasing	**ingrātus**	unpleasant
idōneus	fit, suitable	**aliēnus**	unsuitable
pār	equal	**dispār**	unequal
propinquus	near	. . . .*	
similis	like	**dissimilis**	unlike
ūtilis	useful	**inūtilis**	useless

With Compound Verbs: **Lēgātus legiōnī praeest.   Caesarī venientī occurrit.**

A noun in the dative case frequently depends upon a verb compounded with **ad, circum, com-, in, inter, post, prō,** or **super.**

With Transitive Compounds: **Labiēnum castrīs Caesar praefēcit.   Labiēnus castrīs praeficitur.**

A noun in the dative case and a noun in the accusative case may both occur with a compound verb when the simple verb from which the compound is formed is transitive.   (The dative is retained with passive forms of such compounds.)

With Special Verbs: **Liberī parentibus pārēre dēbent.   Rōmānī hostibus cēdere rēcūsāvērunt.**

A noun in the dative case may be complementary to certain verbs of special meaning, including those listed on the next page.

*Longinquus, the opposite of propinquus, is naturally used with a prepositional phrase or ablative of separation instead of the dative.

463

cēdō yield (to)	**pāreō** obey/be obedient
cōnfīdō trust/give trust	**placeō** please/be pleasing
crēdō trust/give trust	**resistō** resist/offer resistance
faveō favor/show favor	**studeō** desire/be favorable/be
imperō order/give orders	eager
noceō harm/do harm	**suādeō/persuādeō** persuade/make
parcō spare/show mercy	pleasing

specification

Agent: **Id Rōmānis faciendum est. Leō Herculi necandus est.**

With the future passive participle, a noun in the dative case usually designates the person(s) by whom something must be/ought to be done. When another dative depends on the future passive participle, the dative of agent is sometimes replaced by **ā/ab** with the ablative, to avoid confusion; e.g., **Principibus ā populō grātia referenda est.**

Indirect Object: **Fēmina puerō epistulam dedit. Pater liberis fābulam nārrat.**

With a verb meaning give, say, tell, or show, a noun in the dative case indicates the person to whom someone gives, says, tells, or shows something.

Possession: **Virō gladius erat. Magistrō multi libri sunt.**

A noun in the dative case may indicate the possessor when the word for the thing possessed is the subject of a form of **sum.**

Purpose: **Hunc librum dōnō misi. Qui novissimis praesidiō erant?**

A noun in the dative case sometimes expresses the purpose which something serves or is intended to serve.

Reference: **Qui novissimis praesidiō erant?**

In a sentence containing a dative of purpose, the person(s) with reference to whom an act is done or a situation exists is (are) often designated by a noun in the dative case.

Genitive Case

with certain adjectives

Complementary Genitive: **P. Cōnsidius rei militāris peritissimus habēbātur.**

Many adjectives in Latin have their meaning completed by a noun in the genitive case; e.g., **peritus** (skilled), **plēnus** (full), **studiōsus** (desirous).

with other nouns

Description/Measure: **Pater tuus erat homō magnae virtūtis. Fossam trium pedum fōdērunt.**

464

A noun in the genitive case with adjective/numeral modifier may specify a quality or measurement.

Material: **Exercitus virōrum fortium urbem dēfendēbat.**

A noun in the genitive case may indicate the persons/objects making up a collective noun or the material of which something is made.

Objective Genitive: **Quis spem salūtis habet? Is rēgnī cupiditāte inductus est.**

A noun in the genitive case may indicate the object of the action or feeling of another noun.

Partitive Genitive/Genitive of the Whole: **Trēs partēs cōpiārum iam trāductae erant.**

A noun in the genitive case may indicate the whole of which a part is mentioned.

Possession: **Casae agricolārum sunt parvae. Honōris causā opīniōnem ā cōn-sule petīvit.**

A noun that designates a possessor is in the genitive case.

Subjective Genitive: **Adventus Caesaris nūntiātus est.**

A noun in the genitive case may indicate the doer (subject) of the action denoted by another noun.

with special verbs

Magistrōrum interest. Hoc cīvitātis interest.

With the impersonal verb **interest** a complementary genitive designates the person(s) concerned.

Sceleris eum accūsāvērunt.

With a verb pertaining to judicial action, a complementary genitive may designate the charge of which a person is accused, condemned, convicted, or acquitted.

Locative Case

singular

Rōmae (at Rome) **domī** (at home) **Tarentī** (at Tarentum) **Bibracte** (at Bibracte)

With names of cities, towns, and islands, and also with **domus** (when it means "home"), "place where" is denoted by the locative case. In singular nouns of Declensions I and II the locative has the same form as genitive singular; in singular nouns of Declension III, the same form as ablative singular.

plural

Athēnīs (at Athens) **Veiīs** (at Veii)

In all plural nouns the locative has the same form as ablative plural.

465

Nominative Case

predicate noun

Frāter meus est agricola. Sumus nautae. Illī rēgēs tyrannī appellantur.

A predicate noun in the nominative case is often found with forms of **sum** and with the passive voice of **appellō, nōminō, vocō,** and other verbs meaning <u>name</u> or <u>call</u>. It also occurs with the passive voice of **creō, dēligō, ēligō, legō,** and other verbs meaning <u>appoint</u>, <u>choose</u>, or <u>elect</u>.

subject

Puella cum mātre ambulābit. Cūr urbs dēlētur? Quam fortēs sunt mīlitēs!

When the subject is a noun, the verb is always in third person. A subject agrees with its verb in number as well as in person.

Vocative Case

-**us** nouns of declension II

Ubi, Mārce, pater tuus est? Venī, amīce; ad scholam eāmus.

In -**us** nouns of Declension II the vocative singular ends in -**e.** (Exception: **deus,** which has no special vocative form) Nouns in -**ius** form the vocative singular in -**ī**; e.g., **fīlī (fīlius).** The vocative case of a noun is used in addressing a person or persons. (It usually is not the first word in the sentence.)

other nouns/all plurals

Ille liber novus est, magister. Vidēte, amīcī, templum.

Except in singular -**us** and -**ius** nouns of Declension II, the vocative has the same form as the nominative in all declensions.

PREPOSITIONS

Fixed Forms

position

In urbe mānsī. In urbem vēnī. Iter magnō cum perīculō fēcit.

A preposition usually precedes its object. However, when the object of a monosyllabic preposition is a noun modified by an adjective, the preposition sometimes stands between the adjective and noun. A preposition has only one form.

with ablative case

ā/ab   cum   dē   ē/ex   prae   prō   sine

Prepositions in this book which regularly occur with words in the ablative are listed above. Two others (**cōram** and **tenus**) also pattern with the ablative. When

466

cum occurs with certain pronouns it becomes enclitic (attached to the end of the pronoun); e.g., **mēcum, tēcum, nōbīscum, vōbīscum, quibuscum.**

with ablative/accusative case

a) **In urbe** mānsī.   b) **In urbem** vēnī.

Prepositions **in** and **sub** may be used with either ablative or accusative case: a) with ablative in expressions denoting existence or continuance in a place; b) with accusative in expressions denoting motion.

with accusative case

ad	apud	contrā	inter	ob	post	prope	super	trāns
ante	circum	extrā	intrā	per	praeter	propter	suprā	

Most prepositions found in this book (including those listed immediately above) occur regularly with the accusative case.

PRONOUNS

Declinable Pronouns

adjective use

Hic vir est altus. **Ille puer** bene labōrat. **Quōs librōs** puellae portābant?

All pronouns (except personal and reflexive) are also used as adjectives.

agreement

Homō quem vidēs amīcus est. **Quae urbēs** captae sunt? **Haec puella** est soror mea.

A pronoun agrees with its noun in gender and number. When used as an adjective a pronoun also agrees with its noun in case. (The case of a relative pronoun is determined by its use in the relative clause.)

declension

Ille adest. **Illam** vīdī. Quī scrīpsit **haec** verba? **Illud** dōnum tibi dabō.

All pronouns (except personal and reflexive) are declined as adjectives; i.e., they show gender contrasts, in addition to number and case.

demonstrative pronouns/adjectives

is, ea, id   unemphatic demonstrative often used as a personal pronoun (3rd person)
ille, illa, illud   stronger demonstrative than **is, ea, id;** often = "that" (over there)
hic, haec, hoc   demonstrative referring to this (of mine) or this (near me)
iste, ista, istud   demonstrative referring to this (of yours) or this (near you)

Forms of **hic** and **ille** may be used in the same sentence to contrast persons or things. In this use **ille** usually refers to "the former" and **hic** to "the latter."

467

identifying pronoun/adjective

Eadem audīre volunt. **Īdem** līberīs fābulās saepe nārrābat.

Īdem, eadem, idem identifies a person/thing with one that has just been mentioned or that is about to be mentioned.

indefinite pronouns/adjectives

Aliquis verba facit. Neque **quemquam** laudābō. **Nesciō quis** eum laudat.

Indefinite pronouns/adjectives present the idea of some person/thing without further explanation or description.

Aliquis, quisquam, quis, and **quī** are all indefinite, meaning "someone/anyone; something/anything." Their corresponding adjectives mean "some/any."

Nesciō quis/quī is often used in place of an indefinite pronoun.

Quīdam (a certain one/anyone) is less indefinite than **aliquis.**

Quisquam (anyone) occurs usually in negative or conditional sentences.

The most indefinite of the pronouns—**quis** (anyone/someone)—and its corresponding adjective are used after **sī, nisi, nē, num** as the least definite (vaguest) of indefinites.

intensifying pronoun/adjective

Ipse dīxit. **Ipsa** fēcī. **Ipsīs** sub **moenibus** pugnāvērunt.

Ipse, ipsa, ipsum emphasizes the word to which it refers. In English this emphasis is indicated by the use of pronouns ending in -<u>self</u>/-<u>selves</u>; e.g., He him<u>self</u> spoke. I made it my<u>self</u>. In the adjective use, "very" often translates the intensifying word; e.g., They fought under these <u>very</u> walls.

interrogative pronouns/adjectives

Quis es? Rogō **quis** sit. **Quem librum** legis? **Quid** facere vultis?

The interrogative pronoun **quis, quid** and its corresponding adjective are used to introduce a question, either direct or indirect. Following are the commonly used interrogative pronouns/adjectives:

quālis (of what kind?)	**quis, quid** (who, what?)
quantum (how much?)	**quisnam, quaenam, quidnam** (who, please?)
quantus (how great?)	**quot** (how many?)
quī, quae, quod (what sort of?)	**uter, utra, utrum** (which of the two?)

personal pronouns

Haec ego dīcō. Quid tū dīcis? Vīdimus tē; nōnne nōs vīdistī?

As the subject of a verb, a personal pronoun is rarely used except for emphasis or contrast.

Puerī vēnērunt; eōs vīdī. Eīs librōs meōs dedī. Ubi sunt librī eōrum?

The unemphatic demonstrative pronoun **is, ea, id** is commonly used as the personal pronoun of the third person.

reflexive pronouns

Vōs spectātis. Dōnum mihi dedī. Tē vulnerāvistī. Crēdimus nōbīs esse spem.

Genitive, dative, accusative, ablative cases of personal pronouns for first and second persons **(ego, nōs; tū, vōs)** may be used reflexively.

Narcissus sē spectat. Mīlitēs sē recēpērunt.

The reflexive pronoun of the third person singular/plural is **suī, sibi, sē/sēsē, sē/sēsē.**

relative pronouns/adjectives

Hostēs quī castra oppugnābant ā nostrīs captī sunt. Hostēs quōs nostrī cēpērunt fuerant fortēs.

A relative pronoun agrees in number and gender with the noun/pronoun it represents (the antecedent), but its case is determined by its use in the relative clause.

Is sum quī fēcī. Eī sunt quī domī manēbunt.

The relative pronoun **quī** may have the unemphatic demonstrative **is** for its antecedent.

Lēgātōs mīsit quī pācem peterent. He sent ambassadors to ask for peace.

The relative pronoun is used in a purpose clause with verb in the subjunctive. Here the relative is equivalent to **ut eī.**

Lēgātōs mīsit, quī pācem petiērunt. He sent ambassadors, who asked for peace.

A relative clause with verb in the indicative states a fact about a definite antecedent. (Here **quī = et eī.**)

Multī sunt quī dīcant. . . . There are many who say. . . .

A relative clause of description with verb in the subjunctive may describe a characteristic of an indefinite antecedent.

VERBS

Agreement

person endings

Puer labōrat. Puerī labōrant.

A verb agrees with its subject in person and number.

Mood

imperative

Dēsilite, commilitōnēs! **Dīc vērum!** **Manēte hīc!** **Ambulā** celeriter!

The imperative mood is used to express commands. With the second person, present tense, a vocative is either stated or implied. Although English has the imperative only in the present tense, Latin has a future imperative also, with third person forms as well as second person forms.

Nōlī hīc **manēre.** **Nē** hīc **mānseris.**

Negative commands (prohibitions) in the second person are commonly expressed by the imperative of **nōlō (nōlī/nōlite)** completed by an infinitive, or by **nē** with the perfect subjunctive.

indicative

Caesar Galliam vīcit. Diū et ācriter pugnātum est. Caesar dictātor creātus est.

A verb in the indicative mood states a fact.

Vīcitne Galliam Caesar? **Nōnne/Num** Caesar Galliam **vīcit?**

A verb in the indicative asking a direct question implies a statement of fact in the answer. The enclitic **-ne** asks for information; **nōnne** expects the answer "yes" or a repetition of the statement to indicate agreement; **num** expects a negative statement in reply. Interrogative words also often introduce direct questions with verbs in the indicative; e.g., **quis, quid, cūr, ubi, quālis, quantus, quot.**

Postquam id animadvertit, cōpiās suās Caesar in proximum collem subdūxit.

A verb appears in the indicative in a clause introduced by conjunctions **postquam, quamquam, quia, quod, quoniam, ubi,** and some others; also occasionally after **cum, sī,** and **ut** (as).

Proximī sunt Germānīs, quī trāns Rhēnum incolunt.

A descriptive clause introduced by a relative pronoun with a definite antecedent has its verb in the indicative.

infinitives

Omnēs redīre volunt. Dux iussit eōs castra movēre.

An infinitive may be used to complete the meaning of another verb. Some of the verbs which commonly pattern with an infinitive in this way are **cupiō, dēsīderō, iubeō, mālō, nōlō, possum, vetō, volō.**

Licet Helvētiīs ea iacere.

An infinitive often follows impersonal verbs/expressions such as **convenit, licet, mōs est, necesse est, oportet.**

470

Prōmīsit sē vellus trāditūrum esse sī Jāsōn labōrēs prius perfēcisset.

A verb becomes an infinitive in an indirect statement introduced by a verb of knowing, thinking, saying, hearing, observing, and the like. The subject of the infinitive within the indirect statement is in the accusative case. All subordinate clauses within an indirect statement have their verbs in the subjunctive. An accusative and infinitive construction in a direct statement is retained in indirect statement.

Sequence of tenses in indirect statement: a) If the time of the verb within the indirect statement is the same as that of the verb of "saying," the infinitive is present (active or passive). b) If the time of the verb within the indirect statement is earlier than the verb of "saying," the infinitive will be perfect (active or passive). c) If the time of the verb within the indirect statement is later than that of the verb of "saying," the infinitive will be future.

participles

pugnāns, -antis   pugnātus/pugnātūrus/pugnandus, -a, -um

A Latin verb has four participles: present active, perfect passive, future active, and future passive.

Milites fugientēs secūtī sumus.

The present active participle denotes an act taking place at the same time as the main verb.

Miles, vulnerātus sagittā, ambulāre nōn poterat.

The perfect passive participle denotes an act which took place before the time of the main verb.

Ad scholam ambulātūrus sum.

The future active participle is used chiefly with forms of **sum** to denote an act which someone intends to do or is about to do.

Hostēs nōbīs vincendī sunt.

The future passive participle is used chiefly with forms of **sum** to denote an act which ought to be done or must be done by someone.

subjunctive (independent)

Lūx fīat.   Nē mānserīs.

A verb in the subjunctive expresses a non-fact; i.e., a wish, a desire, a hope, a possibility, an exhortation, an alleged statement, a mild command. A subjunctive may also be used for a negative command (**nē** with perfect subjunctive).

subjunctive (in subordinate clauses)

Anticipatory: Urbs salva. erit, dum tū adveniās. The city will be safe until you come.

The subjunctive occurs after words meaning <u>until</u> or <u>before</u> (**dum, antequam, priusquam**) and after words meaning <u>provided</u>, <u>provided that</u>, <u>if only</u> (**dum, modo, dummodo**).

Conditional: Sī militēs flūmen trānseant, multī interficientur. If the soldiers should cross the river, many will be killed. **Sī Haeduī majōrēs cōpiās habērent, oppida dēfenderent.** If the Haedui had larger forces, they would defend the towns. **Sī Haeduī majōrēs cōpiās habuissent, oppida dēfendissent.** If the Haedui had had larger forces, they would have defended the towns.

The subjunctive is used in conditional clauses introduced by **sī** (if), when doubt is expressed or implied by the speaker or the condition is contrary to fact.

Cum Clauses: Herculēs, cum intellegeret periculum magnum esse, tamen negōtium suscēpit. Although Hercules knew the danger was great, he nevertheless undertook the task. **Cum bovēs in cavernam traherentur, putāvit Herculem hōs nōn inventūrum esse.** Since the cattle were being dragged into the cave, he thought Hercules would not find them. **Cum paulum sē ex timōre recēpisset, clāmāvit sē velle mōnstrum in Orcum reddere.** When he had recovered a little from fear, he shouted that he wanted to return the monster to the lower world.

Cum, meaning although, since, or when (if describing the situation in which the main act takes place), introduces a clause with a subjunctive verb.

Doubt/Hindrance Clauses: Nōn dubitō quin fortēs sint. I do not doubt that they are brave. **Hostēs impedīvimus nē trānsīrent.** We hindered the enemy from crossing.

Negative expressions of doubt are used with **quin** introducing a clause with verb in the subjunctive. Words indicating hindrance, check, prevention, and the like appear with **quin** (after a negative), **nē** (after affirmative), **quōminus** (after either negative or affirmative).

Fear Clauses: Timeō ut sē fortiter dēfendat. I am afraid that he may not defend himself bravely. **Periculum est nē cohors capiātur.** There is danger that the cohort may be captured. **Verēbantur nē exercitus noster in Galliā manēret.** They were afraid that our army would stay in Gaul.

With verbs meaning "fear" and other expressions denoting fear a subordinate clause with verb in subjunctive may occur, introduced by **nē** (that) or **ut** (that . . . not).

Indirect Questions/Statement: a) **Jāsōn dēmōnstrāvit quam ob causam vēnisset.** Jason explained why he had come. b) **Nūntius dīcit eās legiōnēs quae trāns flūmen sint in periculō esse.** The messenger says that those legions which are across the river are in danger.

472

a) An indirect question has its verb in the subjunctive. b) A subordinate clause in indirect statement has its verb in the subjunctive.

Noun Clauses of Desire: **Nūntius eī persuāsit ut rēgī auxilium ferret.** The messenger persuaded him to bring aid to the king. **Mīlitibus imperāvit nē saxa jacerent.** He commanded the soldiers not to throw rocks.

The subjunctive is used in noun clauses of desire, which occur after verbs signifying or implying desire or purpose. Such clauses are introduced by **ut** (that/to) or **nē** (that . . . not/not to).

Noun Clauses of Fact: **Itaque fīēbat ut bovēs minus lātē vagārentur.**

After verbs denoting accomplishment (**committō, faciō, efficiō, cōnficiō**) and after impersonal verbs/expressions such as **fit, accidit, mōs est** (it happens, etc.) there may be a noun clause of fact introduced by **ut** (that) or **ut nōn** (that not).

Purpose Clauses: **Vēnī ut tē vidērem.** I came to see you. **Mīlitēs missī sunt nē urbs caperētur.** The soldiers were sent so that the city might not be captured. **Puerum mittam quī tē adjuvet.** I will send a boy to help you. **Castella mūnit quō facilius eōs prohibēre possit nē trānseant.** He is building fortifications so that he can more easily prevent those men from crossing.

The subjunctive is used to express purpose in Latin. **Ut** (in order that) introduces the affirmative clause, and **nē** introduces a negative clause of purpose. Sometimes the relative pronoun **quī** (= **ut is/eī**) may be the connector. If a purpose clause contains a comparative form of an adjective/adverb, **quō** usually introduces the clause instead of **ut.**

Result Clauses: **Tempestātēs tantae erant ut ex portū proficiscī nōn audērēmus.** The storms were so great that we did not dare to set out from the harbor. **Columba tam celeriter volāvit ut incolumis ēvāderet.** The dove flew so fast that it escaped unharmed. (See also page 474, note 2.)

The subjunctive is used in subordinate clauses expressing result. The main clause will usually have **tam, ita, sīc, tantus,** or the like. **Ut** (affirmative) and **ut nōn** (negative) are the introductory words.

Tense

indicative

Time/Aspect: **Puer ad templum ambulābat.** The boy was walking to the temple.

In Latin the use of tense includes not only time, but also aspect; i.e., the kind of action which the verb reports.

Present: a) **Multōs librōs habēmus.** b) **Caesar multa bella gerit.**

a) The present tense in Latin, as in English, denotes present time. b) The present indicative is sometimes used in a narrative of past events to present a situation more vividly. This use is called the historical present.

Imperfect: **Virī saepe in forō ambulābant.** The men often strolled in the forum.

The imperfect tense represents a past act in progress or a past situation continuing. The imperfect indicative is sometimes used to denote a customary act or one of frequent occurrence in past time. It is often translated by the progressive past tense, but sometimes the simple English past is used as its equivalent.

Future: **Gallī Caesarem nōn capient.** The Gauls will not capture Caesar.

The future tense, as in English, denotes future time.

Perfect: **Milītēs suum mortuum ducem in castra portāvērunt.** The soldiers carried their dead leader into the camp.

The perfect tense is used most often to show a completed action in past time. It also may be equivalent to an English present perfect translated with the auxiliary verbs <u>have</u> or <u>has.</u>

Past Perfect: **Hostēs pontem trāns flūmen aedificāverant.** The enemy had built a bridge across the river.

The past perfect tense is used to represent an act as having occurred before some expressed or implied past time.

Future Perfect: **Cum pontem aedificāveris, exercitum trādūcēs.** When you (will) have built the bridge, you will lead the army across.

The future perfect tense is used to show that an act will occur before some expressed or implied future time. In Latin the future perfect is used more frequently than in English.

subjunctive

Four Tenses: Present, Perfect, Imperfect, Past Perfect

The subjunctive mood is more frequently used in Latin than in English. Because the subjunctive most often occurs in subordinate clauses, its tense relationship with the six tenses of the indicative as used in the main verb must be carefully observed.

Sequence of Tenses: a) If the main verb denotes present or future time, the subjunctive tense is regularly present or perfect.[1] b) If the main verb denotes past time, the subjunctive tense is regularly imperfect or past perfect.[2] (See pages 125-126, 167-168.)

[1] An imperfect subjunctive is sometimes used to express action which at some past time was thought of as future.

[2] In a result clause a perfect subjunctive sometimes occurs after a perfect indicative; e.g., **Columba tam celeriter volāvit ut incolumis ēvāserit.** The dove flew so fast that it escaped unharmed. (See page 473.)

Verbal Adjectives

gerundives

Obligation/Necessity: **Miles laudandus est. Carthāgō dēlenda est. Hostēs Caesarī vincendī erant.**

The gerundive is a verbal adjective, passive in meaning. In the nominative it is used to express obligation or necessity, in which case it is often combined with a form of **sum.** The word designating the person involved (agent) is in the dative case; see page 464.

Purpose: a) **Ad pācem petendam vēnimus.** b) **Cupidus urbis dēlendae Catō erat. Pācis petendae grātiā lēgātī adsunt.**

a) The accusative of the gerundive is often used with **ad** (seldom with other prepositions). **Ad** with the gerundive is used to express purpose.

b) The genitive of the gerundive is often used with nouns/adjectives and with **grātiā/causā. Grātiā/causā** with the gerundive are used to express purpose.

participles

Militēs fugientēs secūtī sumus. Miles, vulnerātus sagittā, ambulāre nōn poterat.

Participles are verbal adjectives. In their verbal aspect they express tense and voice, may have a noun/pronoun complement or a complementary infinitive. They may also be qualified by adverbs.

In their aspect as adjectives they are inflected and may agree with a noun/pronoun; some, like adjectives, may even be compared; e.g., **potēns, potentior, potentissimus.** Also like adjectives, some participles may stand for nouns; e.g., **adulēscēns.**

Verbal Nouns

gerunds

Ad bene vīvendum multa petīvit. Bene vīvendī causā multa petīvit.

The gerund is a verbal noun of neuter gender. It lacks a form for the nominative case and has no plural. In its verbal aspect, it is active in meaning. Because the gerund is verbal it may be qualified by an adverb. Grammatically, a gerund can be completed by a direct object, but this construction is generally avoided. A gerundive construction is used instead; see page 117.

The accusative of the gerund is often used with **ad** (seldom with other prepositions). **Ad** with the gerund is used to express purpose.

The genitive of the gerund is often used with nouns/adjectives and with **grātiā/causā. Grātiā/causā** with the gerund are used to express purpose.

475

infinitives

Labōrāre est ōrāre. Errāre hūmānum est.

The infinitive is an indeclinable verbal noun. It is often considered as the nominative replacement for the gerund. In its verbal aspect, the infinitive may have a subject and take a complement.

Voice

active/passive

Active: **Puer librum portat.**   **Quō mīlitem necāvit?**
Passive: **Liber ā puerō portātur.**   **Miles gladiō necātus est.**

In Latin the passive voice is used more frequently than in English. A noun or pronoun that indicates the person (or animal) by whom the act is done is in the ablative case with preposition **ā/ab** (by). A noun or pronoun that indicates the means or instrument by which an act is done is in the ablative case (without preposition).

ambulō   perventum est   faciō   sequor   audeō

Not all Latin verbs have both active and passive voice. In general, transitive verbs have passive voice; intransitive verbs usually do not, except when used as impersonal verbs; e.g., **perventum est.**

Some verbs have no passive because their meanings do not admit the use of such forms; e.g., **ambulō.** Others fail in the passive through lack of usage or because parts are missing; see defective verbs, pages 454-455.

The passive of **faciō** is supplied by another verb; see **fīō,** page 451.

A numerous group of verbs in all four conjugations, called deponents and semideponents, have passive forms with active meanings; see pages 440-443 and pages 444-445.

Deponent Verbs: **Rōmānī hostium equitēs secūtī sunt. Virī fugere cōnābantur. Eā urbe Rōmānī potītī sunt. Manū dextrā semper ūtitur.**

Deponents can be recognized by their principal parts, which are passive in form. (They do, however, have both active and passive participles.) Many deponents are completed by a direct object in the accusative case; a few have ablative complements; see page 461.

Semideponent Verbs: **Hostēs pugnāre nōn audent. Hostēs pugnāre nōn ausī sunt.**

The enemy do not dare (**audent**)/did not dare (**ausī sunt**) to fight.

Semideponents lack active forms in part, often in the perfect system. They can be recognized by their principal parts, which have some active and some passive forms; e.g., **audeō, -ēre, ausus sum.**

476

INDEX OF GRAMMAR

The following index contains a complete listing of the grammar taught in this book. It also includes references to the Summary of Grammar and Latin Usage sections, not only in connection with new grammar, but also for first-year forms and usage. All grammatical points needed by the second-year student may be found in a section called Latin Usage (pages 458-475), where the heads are arranged alphabetically. For example, to locate information about demonstrative pronouns, refer to this Index under Demonstratives or Pronouns; then turn to the pages indicated, where you will find demonstratives in alphabetical order.

ACKNOWLEDGMENTS

The courtesy of persons and institutions which permits reproduction of the pictures on the pages listed is acknowledged with thanks. Alinari and Art Reference Bureau, Inc. 10, 25, 65 bottom, 111, 213 (2), 232, 234, 251 bottom, 269, 275 top, 286 top, 288, 292, 343, 355; D. Anderson and Art Reference Bureau, Inc. 23, 31, 66, 210 top, 216; Art Color Slides, Inc. 21, 65 top, 83, 178, 210 center;—and The Metropolitan Museum of Art, French manuscripts: Limbourg—The Belles Heures of Jean, Duke of Berry—St. Charlemagne, The Cloisters Collection, Purchase, 1954, 180, and French sculpture: Saint Francis of Assisi, The Cloisters Collection, Rogers Fund, 1934, 184; Art Reference Bureau, Inc. 24; Associated Press Photo, Wide World Photos 95; Staatliche Museen zu Berlin 253 top; Biblioteca Vaticana 175; Bibliothèque Nationale 93, 315; Trustees of the British Museum 34, 253 center, 289, 307, 308, 309; The British Travel Association 283; Cl. Trincano, Collection Arthaud, Grenoble 27; The Colchester and Essex Museum, Colchester, England 301 bottom; Commissariat Général au Tourisme 229;—Photo Aérienne Greff, Pilote et Opérateur R. Henrard 313 bottom; Crown Copyright, R. A. F. Official Photo 126; William Egli 18;—and Stadtmuseum, Brugg 304;—and Musée de Saint-Germain-en-Laye 220, 237 (2), 248, 320 (3);—and Swiss National Museum 222, 262;—and Museo della Civiltà Romana, Rome 250 top right and bottom, 251 top, 252 top and right margin, 274 top left and right, 278, 280, 286 margin, 303 left, 318 top and bottom left; Enit 2, 16, 62; E. P. T., Naples 19; French Government Tourist Office 89, 90, 106, 223, 313 bottom;—and Photo Luder, 108; Giraudon 69, 99, 119, 134, 164, 186; Guildhall Museum, London 296, 310; Holiday and Don Almquist 209; C. M. Hutchinson 128, 149, 158, 212, 273 bottom center, 314, 349, 353; King's College, University of Durham, Newcastle upon Tyne 301 center; Rheinisches Bildarchiv, Kölnisches Stadtmuseum 270; The Metropolitan Museum of Art, Rogers Fund, 1918, 45, Rogers Fund, 1903, 253 bottom; Office du Tourisme, Montreux 226; Musée Archéologique de Dijon 218; Musée de Langres 221, 247; Musée de Saint-Germain-en-Laye 312 top; Museo Archeologico, Aquileia 40; Museo Capitolino 38, 123; Muséum Calvet, Avignon 7, 191, 195, 240; National Gallery of Art, Washington, D.C., Samuel H. Kress Collection 64 bottom; National Museum of Antiquities, Scotland 252 bottom right; The Art Museum, Princeton University 68 right; Régine Roberts 215; Royal Greek Embassy 68 left; Raymond V. Schoder, S. J. 26, 28, 29, 32, 147, 161, 203, 210 bottom, 211 (2);—and Soprintendenza alle Antichità della Campania 14; Israel Shenker 236; Soprintendenza alle Antichità della Campania, Napoli 115; Soprintendenza alle Antichità delle Province di Salerno e Potenza 112, 250 top left, 252 left margin; Soprintendenza Monumenti e Scavi in Libia, Archivio Fotografico della Libia Occidentale 43; Swiss National Tourist Office and B. Fransioli, Montreux 219; Rheinisches Landesmuseum, Trier 273 bottom left and right; UPI Photo 301 top; Union Valaisanne du Tourisme and Darbellay, Martigny 96, 102; U. S. Bureau of Public Roads, Department of Commerce 11; Archivio Fotografico Gallerie e Musei Vaticani 13, 274 bottom, 298.

The gracious consent of The White House for use of President Kennedy's letter on page 187 and special assistance by Louis Foucher of the Museum at Sousse and by Mme. Elfi von Saar are also gratefully acknowledged.